PROJECT FINANCING

PROJECT FINANCING

Editor

Rudra P. Pradhan

BLOOMSBURY

London • New Delhi • New York • Sydney

First published, 2013
First reprint, 2013

BLOOMSBURY PUBLISHING INDIA PVT. LTD.
London New Delhi New York Sydney

ISBN: 978-81-924302-2-5

Published by Bloomsbury Publishing India Pvt. Ltd.
VISHRUT Building, DDA Complex, Building No. 3, Pocket C-6 & 7
Vasant Kunj, New Delhi 110 070

Laser Typeset by DEEPA JUYAL
C2/01, Sector 17, Rohini, New Delhi 110 089

Printed at Anvi Composers
1 DDA Market, Block A-1B, Pachim Vihar, New Delhi 110 063

Preface

High economic growth is the principal objective of the developing world. The major precondition for attaining this goal is the availability of infrastructure in an economy, both in quantity and quality. Infrastructure is considered as the key, if not the engine of development. The lack of infrastructure not only affects economic growth but also creates other socio-economic problems like employment and quality of life. Augmentation of the necessary infrastructure requires huge amounts of finance, both domestic and international. There are many ways infrastructure can be financed – the important areas are budgetary and non-budgetary provisions, like accessing capital markets and institutional reforms. The objective of this book is to discuss the efficiency of infrastructure and its impact on economic growth, depending on the depth and diversity of the infrastructure sector in particular, and overall socio-economic development in general.

This book presents selected articles (38 out of 336) that were presented at the *International Conference on Frontiers of Infrastructure Finance (ICFIF 2011)*, organized jointly by the Vinod Gupta School of Management & RCG School of Infrastructure Design and Management, Indian Institute of Technology Kharagpur during December 28-30, 2012. The opinions expressed in the articles belong solely to the authors. The total number of articles included in this volume are 38 and they have been arranged in alphabetical order. The major themes in this book include infrastructure issues and challenges, particularly in the context of international finance.

We are very thankful to all the institutes/organizations for their support in organizing the conference. We are also grateful to the faculty, staff and students of the Indian Institute of Technology Kharagpur, India for their valuable support, kind cooperation and varied assistance rendered in producing this book.

Rudra P. Pradhan
Professor, IIT Kharagpur

Acknowledgements

The book has been prepared with grants from the Planning Commission, Government of India and the Council of Scientific and Industrial Research, India. We are grateful to these sponsors for their financial support and cooperation towards the preparation of this book. We are also very grateful for the support provided by two departments – Vinod Gupta School of Management and Ranbir and Chitra Gupta School of Infrastructure Design & Management, Indian Institute of Technology Kharagpur, India.

Contents

A Novel Strategic Way to Enhance the Effectiveness and Technicalities of Railway Safety and Security Measures

Pritam Dey and Sourav Chakraborty
Institute of Engineering & Management, Kolkata
E-mail: pritam_4uevr@yahoo.in

ABSTRACT

Railway safety is now progressing gradually and there has never been a better time to stop, reflect & re-think safety policies, as well as what governments, companies & individuals could be doing to improve safety. By railway safety acts everyone has the right to expect systematic & continuous improvement in safety. In this paper we have discussed a new strategic and technical planning for effective delivery of rail safety and security.

The main object is to detect missing railway tracks and prevent head-on-collisions of trains travelling in opposite directions. Derived from auto-focusing feature in digital cameras (where a high-intensity infrared beam is made to strike an object. Reflection of the beam on striking the object, determines the distance between the object and the camera. Hence depending upon which the focusing is adjusted automatically).

Keywords: Auto Focus, Infrared Beam, Head-on-Collision

CONCEPT

We need to introduce small size Frequency Reflector Antennas along the outer sides of the two railway tracks at distances (350 m) apart. These devices will operate using the power from a THIRD RAIL or a separate power source (Solar cells can also be utilized in order to ensure less power consumption from the Main supply. The solar cells should also have a separate storage facility to store part of the solar intensity in order to ensure power supply to the reflectors even at the night time. Hence this will reduce cost and improve the availability). These reflectors will also be connected to the adjacent tracks, in order to ensure safe stopping of the train, when the tracks are removed or missing (shown in Fig. 1). This can be achieved by using a switching system in which one switch will operate between the power source and the reflector, and the other between the track and the reflector. If either of the two switches is in the 'OFF' mode, the reflector will not operate. Each reflector along a certain journey should be tuned electronically (or by using GPS system) to a specific operating frequency, which it will reflect back. This may ensure Auto-piloting of the train, as the reflectors themselves will guide the train along its journey (directions to the reflectors being specified by GPS, according to which they will tune itself to the operating frequency of the journey).

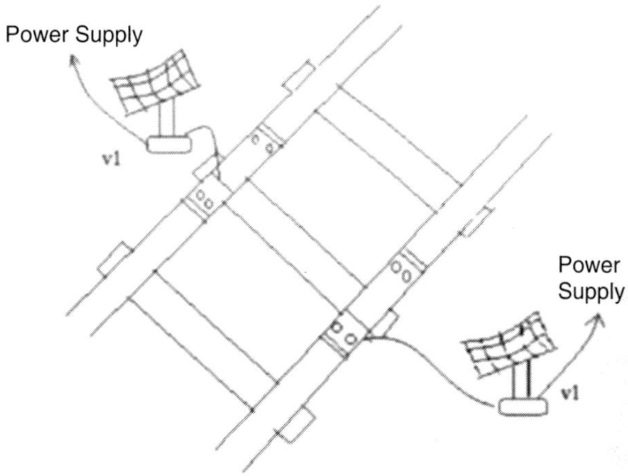

Fig. 1

Each journey should be allocated a certain frequency (to-and-fro; and restricted only between the source and destination stations of that journey) for the reflectors to operate on (Here the operating frequency is v1); Just like in air traffic, specific altitudes are designated to different aircrafts operating between different ports. This system will prevent a collision from taking place, as it will not allow another train traveling from the opposite direction and deviating from its own route, to enter the track meant for another journey (having a different operating frequency; so the reflectors won't be able to operate, and the deviated train will come to a safe stop. Shown in Fig. 2 and Fig. 3).

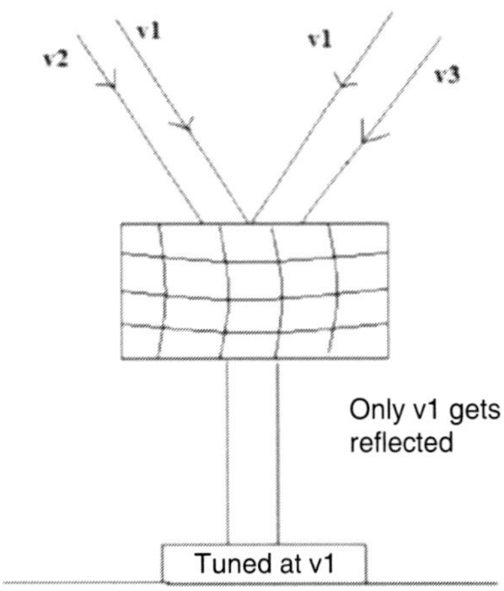

Fig. 2

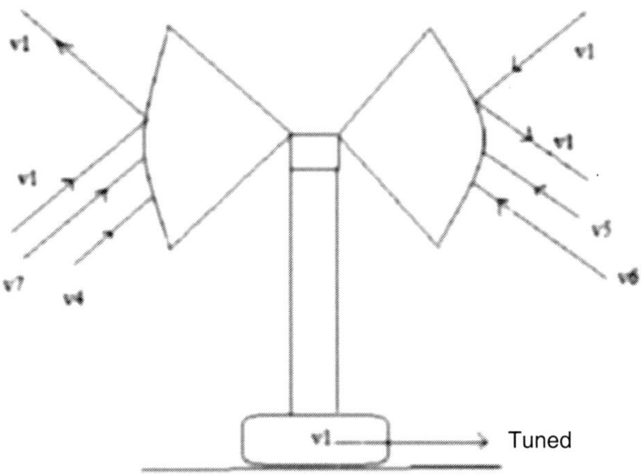

Fig. 3

Two high-intensity sources (S1 and S2) of infrared radiations and a Receiving antenna (Rcv.) are to be introduced on the Engine bogey as shown in Figure 4.

Fig. 4

Continuity System: For further safety and security precautions, the train's control system should check and the continuity of the reflected beams at the receiver Rcv. (at distances equal to that between two reflectors = 350 m). If the continuity is not obeyed, the train will come to an automatic stop (This can be ensured in two ways:

1. Through continuous graphical plotting (used in antenna aided communications) of the incoming reflected beams. Any unwanted gaps in the graph scale will cause the auto-braking of the engine.
2. Constructing a time-controlled closed switching circuit. The time is controlled w.r.t. the speed of the train at that instant and the distance between reflectors. If there is a delay in receiving the reflected beam, the switch will turn 'OFF' which in turn will activate the Automatic Braking System.)

MODE OF OPERATION

The high intensity infrared beams from S1 and S2 are made incident on the frequency reflector antennas on the outer sides of the tracks (the beam from S1 is focused on the right track reflector and that of S2 on the left track reflector). As infrared radiations are a form of Electromagnetic wave, they can be focused on the reflectors at large distances (5 to 7 km ahead). Each such beam is connected to an oscillator circuit, which oscillates the beam 2 to 3 degrees (left and right from the mean position) in S.H.M. Since Electromagnetic waves travel in straight lines, the S.H.M. oscillations allow the Source to find the Reflectors when taking turns, as the angle of travel changes.

The receiver Rcv. present on the train's system receives the reflected signals (green signal is provided) and allows the train to travel. When a signal is not received due to absence of an Operating reflector or deviation of the train from its own path (red signal is provided), the Automatic Braking System gets activated and hence brings the train to a safe stop.

(This is taken into consideration that by the time Rcv. gets the reflected beam, the position of the train has already changed. However this can be neglected as the train travels at a maximum speed of 90 km/hr = 25 m/s, whereas the infrared beam will travel at the speed of light. Hence there will hardly be any relative change to the position of the train by the time the reflected beam is received. Moreover, the beam is focussed at distances of 5-7 km away from the actual position of the train, thereby allowing the train to come to a safe stop if a red signal is provided.)

The continuity system should ensure that the reflected signals are received at continuous intervals (= 350 m). If this is violated, then again the Automatic Braking System will be activated and the train will be brought to a safe halt.

CONCLUSION

How well our policy and strategy are being implemented?

The soul vision of our idea is to ensure a safe trip & prevent human casualties. Implementation of our logic working on this purpose is yet to be done by any country. Our strategy is solely to prevent accidents in countries where we don't have fast electric trains running throughout the country.

How can we ensure security of the power supply?

The basic power supply needed to implement this project can be obtained from the sources which is driving the train. But we may also use alternative energy resources (solar panel) which can be securely drilled beside the railway tracks.

Technological innovations Vs Human factors?

A problem of safety can be due to different causes such as technical failures or human behavior. In order to secure the solar cells human factors comes in for maintenance and security. Increase in employment and increase in expenditure can compensate many lives of people using railways every day.

But here comes the logical thoughts between security and safety. The safety has been the core job of the railways since they exist and nobody will contest it. The security is a new request, a new need faced with attacks against people, goods or fittings. Here we have developed a complete security strategy which has to be implemented by the national authorities. The safety cause will be second to none and the security cause will be external to the railways. Because the best service in the railway industry is to transport passengers safely to their destination and people would not fear of their bound journey.

REFERENCES

[1] 17th International Railway Safety Conference, India.

[2] Railway Safety and Security Asia 2011.

[3] www.intlrailsafety.com

[4] Emerging Dimensions of Railway Safety (IRSC-2007).

[5] Safety vs Service in Railway Business (IRSC-2009).

A Study of the Public Transportation System in a Capital Complex, Arunachal Pradesh (With Special Reference to JnNURM)

Shibabrata Choudhury and Praveen Katiyar

North Eastern Regional Institute of Science and Technology, Arunachal Pradesh
E-mail: shibabrata.choudhury@gmail.com

ABSTRACT

The Jawaharlal Nehru National Urban Renewal Mission (JnNURM) at Arunachal Pradesh is amongst the nation's first phase pilot study of National Urban Transport Policy (NUTP). Objective of this project was to enhance the transportation facility for the urban poor. Arunachal Pradesh economic growth is often constrained due to inadequate transportation infrastructure and services. Frequent landslides due to heavy rain often create problems in transportation in Arunachal Pradesh. The rising population of the state with rising urban poverty and growing demands affect transportation service delivery. There is a need to revitalize this sector in the interest of 200 passengers daily using this system in the capital complex of Arunachal Pradesh. This paper outlines preference reasons for public transportation mode of communication in general and JnNURM in specific in capital complex of the state. This paper also analyzes the performance of JnNURM on a sustainable track in the years to come.

Keywords: JnNURM, Public Transportation System, Arunachal Pradesh

INTRODUCTION

The concentration of economic growth and socio-economic overheads in urban areas has been responsible for the rapid urbanization and growth of cities. The centralization of social services like education, health, as well as employment opportunities is a major cause of migration from rural Arunachal Pradesh to its capital complex. Road transport, the only transportation facility (excluding the unsafe Pawanhans helicopter services) in this locality play a vital role in speeding up the process of socio-economic growth of the areas. So road transportation helps in transporting both necessary productive resources for marketing, and human resources.

The Jawaharlal Nehru National Urban Renewal Mission operates 20 numbers of buses in about 20km radius of the capital complex in Arunachal Pradesh, providing transportation facility to more than 2000 peoples on daily basis. It is amongst the nation's first phase pilot study of National Urban Transport Policy (NUTP).

The objective of the study was to find out the preference reasons for public transportation mode of communication in capital complex, Arunachal Pradesh. The study also focuses the motivating factors to travel in public transportation in general and JnNURM in specific.

REVIEW LITERATURE

Rapid economic development exerts pressure on all infrastructure services vital for economic efficiency and social sustainability, particularly transport infrastructure (Justus (1998). There has been rapid growth in both vehicle production and registration worldwide. While 246 million motor vehicles were registered worldwide in 1970, that number had grown to 709 million in 1997 (Powers and Nicastri 2000). Vehicular emissions account for 40–80 percent of air quality problems in the megacities in developing countries (Ghose 2002).

In India, sustaining this increase in economic productivity is contingent on meeting the mobility demand that such economic growth creates, and hence on optimally utilizing existing infrastructure (Gowda, 1999). The efficiency, quality, and scope of urban transport facilities are affected by the financial position and financial challenges by city public transport undertakings (Kamble, 2010). According to Padam, S. and Singh, S.K. (2001) the financial problems stemming from India's low per-capita income are probably the most important challenges facing Indian urban public transport, but there are many others as well: inefficiency, roadway congestion, traffic accidents, lack of planning, overcrowding, noise, and total lack of coordination of any kind.

Dargay and Hanly (1999) passenger kilometers as the measure of demand for their aggregate area specific analysis of travel demand. However, using only the number of trips or passengers as a measure of travel demand ignores an important characteristic of demand, the length of each trip.

RESEARCH METHODOLOGY

Formal study type was being adopted to find out the answers for the research questions. The required data during the study was obtained from the following two sources: Secondary data was taken from various sources such as published research papers, official broacher and website of Ministry of Urban Transportation, Ministry of Urban Development, National Urban Transport Policy. The secondary data also collected from office of Arunachal Pradesh State Transport (APST) office, District Commissioner office at Papumpare, reference material from website and government websites, etc. Primary Data was collected from the passengers of public transport at Papumpare based on the questionnaire designed appropriate to reflect significantly to research study. For the study purpose, selective random sampling method was considered. The sample size was 75. The primary data were also collected through interview with the various stakeholders such as APST official personnel, people operating auto, and private buses. Personally travelled in various modes of transport systems of capital complex of Arunachal Pradesh for the observation studies that can strengthen this study was also adopted.

Collected data was analyzed by using various statistical methods. These are frequencies, percentages; means, weight-age average, and correlation were use for analyzing the collected data.

PUBLIC TRANSPORTATION AND JnNURM

The Jawaharlal Nehru National Urban Renewal Mission (JnNURM) was launched in December 2005 by the Central Government to provide financial assistance to cities for various urban development projects including urban transport and to improve the quality of life in Indian cities. It is a reform based mission. NUTP started up as a stimulus package of Rs. 1,20536 cores for 63 cities of the country. Buses contribute as the most important mode of Public transport across all cities in India. Under the Second Stimulus Package, purchase of buses for public transport was permitted under JnNURM during 2009 as a one-time measure. As per Press Information Bureau Government of India so far, a total of 15260 buses have been approved for 61 Mission cities.

Itanager, the capital complex of Arunachal Pradesh comes under the category C with less than one million populations and annual support Rs. 892.9 crore. In January 2010, 20 number of JnNURM buses launched in Arunachal Pradesh. In the month of February it was started operation in Arunachal Pradesh. The state seems to be committed to make its presence in national economic map. These days the state economy is characterized by its growth rates, expanding trade and markets, industrial development that started attracting foreign investments. The state economic growth is often constrained due to inadequate transportation infrastructure and services. The rising population of the state with rising urban poverty and growing demands affect transportation service delivery in towns and cities.

PREFERENCE REASONS OF PUBLIC TRANSPORTATION IN THE CAPITAL COMPLEX, ARUNACHAL PRADESH

A questionnaire survey was conducted to measure the mode of transportation used by the peoples for communication at the Capital complex of Arunachal Pradesh. In the

Table 1, 22 of them rely on two-wheelers, 11 rely on four–wheelers for transportation as well as using the public transportation and all are using the public transportation from total samples (75). This table says that the entire respondent uses the public transportation for communication at the Capital Complex, Arunachal Pradesh.

Table 1: Mode of Transportation Used by the Peoples of the Capital Complex, Arunachal Pradesh

Frequency	2-Wheeler	4-Wheeler	Public Transportation
Often	10	1	36
Very Often	8	6	30
Rarely	4	4	9

In itanagar, public transport is supplied mainly by private auto rickshaw, tempo, private buses, multi utility vehicles (Tata sumo, Bolero, etc.), and APST bus services for the population of 34,970. The government backed APST covers the whole Arunachal Pradesh. It is the largest state in the north east India that covers an area of 83,743 sq km, with evergreen forest covering more than 82 percent of the state. The state has the thinnest population density in the country with only 13 persons per sq km. In order to serve the whole state it is a difficult task to cater a qualitative service to every corner of the state. As a result the people over capital complex face very low bus service frequency. They depend mainly with the over-crowded 50 odds private services for transportation.

The majority of the people are dependent on the services in schools, colleges, university, hospitals, and other basic need based government services. The private businesses have also grown up based on to fulfill the demands of these people. Due to financial condition the personal vehicle seems not to be an affordable option for majority in the locality. Below table shows the vehicle registration in the whole papumpare district (the capital complex is situated in this district) in the last three years.

Table 2: Vehicles Registered under District Papumpare, Arunachal Pradesh

Vehicles	2008	2009	2010	2011 (up to March)
Two-wheeler	1370	3495	2774	417
LMV (private)	1768	3176	2941	645
Auto, tempo	70	144	51	15
LMV (passenger)	98	215	68	0

Source: District Transport Office, Naharlagun, Arunachal Pradesh.

Apart from the economic condition of the people the unfavorable geographic condition is also another cause for Public transportation. As the place is located in the hilly area, the narrow, curvy routes seems to be very much accident prone. The region's average rainfall of above 3000 mm per year and climatic variation from the sub-tropical in the south to Alpine in the north. Rainfall is not only restricted to the rainy season, it is perennial in this locality (Annexure-I). Heavy rain fall causes poor condition of road; moreover the landslides caused due to severe continuous rain stop the regular road communication. There are no planned parking places for the vehicles in many places of the city. Due to maintenance cost of vehicles, discomfort in travel, and parking of vehicles, it is often a convenient option to travel by the public transporter instead of personal vehicles.

MOTIVATING FACTORS TO TRAVEL IN JnNURM

As per the questionnaire survey based on two parameters cost and convenience amongst public transporters,the ranking was done on 1-10 ranking scale (with 1 as the minimum and 10 as maximum). It was calculated on the weighted average method.

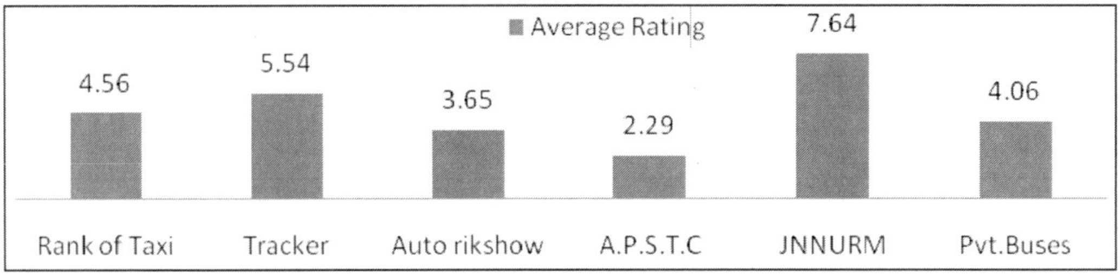

Fig. 1: Ranking of Public Transport Vehicles

As per the study it was found that JnNURM ranks the highest with 7.64 followed by tracker 5.54, taxi with 4.56. In this survey government led APST ranks the lowest with 2.29.

JnNURM offers the qualitative services at a cheaper rate as compared to its counter parts in the public transportation. The Table 3 shows various motivating factors and the respective score of JnNURM.

Table 3: Motivating Factors of JnNURM

Parameters	Score (Total 100)
Brand association	65
Wide area coverage	55
Group reservation	35
Value added services	29

PERFORMANCE OF JnNURM IN CAPITAL COMPLEX, ARUNACHAL PRADESH

The Table 4 shows the Correlation co-efficient between numbers of buses working, total working days by all running buses, distance covered by all buses, earning and expenses/month (Annexure II). The peculiarities of the geographic, road, frequent strikes have not allowed to maintain linear relationship with all variables.

Table 4: Correlation Co-efficient Matrix for JnNURM Buses

	Running Buses	Working Days	Distance Covered	Earning	Expenses
Running buses	1.00				
Working days	0.31	1.00			
Distance covered	0.35	0.46	1.00		
Earning	-0.10	0.41	0.41	1.00	
Expenses	0.03	0.53	0.66	0.65	1.00

The Figure 2 depicts a linear growth for the initial four months (i.e. from May to August).The fluctuation of 30 percentages down is observed in the month of September (Annexure-III & IV). However it recovered the trend in the following two months. Less number of passengers due to bad weather has made the income all time low in the month of January. Again due to bad road condition there was a road conversion taken place. Buses used to travel via Doimukh to Banderdewa, for which it has to cover an extra distance of 5 km. on each trip, so it could not make usual trips. It can be clearly observed this was the month when it has also witnessed the lowest expenses in the 11 months study.

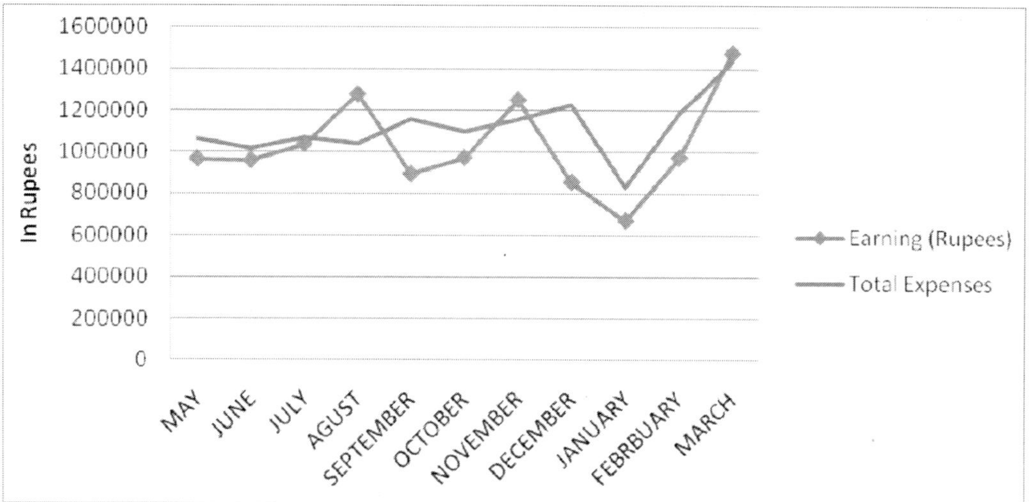

Fig. 2: Revenue and Expenses by JnNURM Buses from 2010 May till 2011 March

The authority has decided to double the ticket price due to compensate the extra lengthy route. The bus again came to its original trend along with the repairing of roads in a very fast pattern.

Ticket price was raised from March 2011. The previous price from Banderdewa to Itanagar was Rs. 20/- was modified as Rs. 30/-. In the initial phase there was a promotional motive due to which it has kept the price at Rs. 20/-, which was even lower than other transportation alternatives such as auto, ASTC bus. From the month of March the pricing is at par with the others. But As per JnNURM guideline it is Rs. 1.23 per kilometer, which comes around Rs. 42/- for the distance of Banderdewa to Itanagar. The higher pricing may not have any impact on maintaining JNURM leading position.

CONCLUSION

JnNURM buses are providing better facility to the urban people at the lower price. JnNURM buses helps to peoples of this locality by providing best way of communication mode of transportation at lower price and helps the socio-economic development of this locality. Having huge demand for various value added services for future use by the public, need to make better plan for more no. passenger can get the more benefit. However the state government should develop the infrastructure for main bus stoppage at the Capital complex. More no. of buses should be used for city services rather than staff and student services. For financial stability of JnNURM the authority must allow more no of buses for city services rather than for staff and student services, surprise ticket checking can compensate certain generic constraints at this place, as it has to prepare for tough challenges for its sustainability in long run.

REFERENCES

[1] Dargay, J. and M. Hanly (1999). Bus Fare Elasticities. Report to the UK Department of the Environment, Transport and the Regions. London, ESRC Transport Studies Unit, University College London: 132.

[2] Ghose, M.K. (2002). "Controlling of Motor Vehicle Emissions for a Sustainable City." *TERI Information Digest on Energy and Environment* 1(2): 273–88.

[3] Gowda, J.M. (1999). "Implications of Concessional Travel Facility on the Commercial Viability of SRTCs in India." *Indian Journal of Transport Management*, 149-157

[4] Kamble (2010). Financial Challenges Before the Urban Transport Undertakings: A Study of Kolhapur Municipal Transport (KMT), Transportation System and Studies edited by S. Sriraman, Himalaya Publishing.

[5] Powers, W.F. and P.R. Nicastri (2000). "Automotive Vehicle Control Challenges in the 21st Century." *Control Engineering Practice* 8(6): 605–18.

[6] Padam, S. and Singh, S.K. (2001). Urbanization and Urban Transport in India: The Sketch for a Policy. Pune, India: Transport Asia Project Workshop.

[7] Ward's Automotive Group (2008). Ward's Automotive Yearbook 2008. Southfield, MI: Penton Media. West, S.E., and IIIR.C. Williams (2005). "The Cost of Reducing Gasoline Consumption." *The American Economic Review* 95(2): 294–9.

[8] ABA (American Bus Association) (2007). Comparison of Energy Use and CO_2 Emissions from Different Transportation Modes. Washington, DC: American Bus Association.

[9] Census Commission of India, Archived from the original on 2004-06-16, retrieved 2008-11- 01.

[10] Central Pollution Control Board. October 1996. *Urban Statistics*. New Delhi.

[11] Ministry of Urban Development.

[12] Ministry of Urban Development.

[13] National Urban Transport Policy.

[14] National Urban Transport Policy 2006.

[15] Press Information Bureau Government of India, http://www.pib.nic.in

An Empirical Study to Assess the Service Quality and Customer Satisfaction Levels in the Telecommunication Industry: Using the SERVQUAL Model

Jai Parkash[1] and Anuradha[2]

[1] Sri Aurobindo College of Commerce and Management, Ludhiana (Punjab)
[2] Shree Atam Vallabh Jain College, Ludhiana (Punjab)
E-mail: jaiparkash1983@gmail.com

ABSTRACT

In Today's globalize and borderless market; quality, productivity and satisfaction level of customers pose a challenge for the success and growth of all firms. Further innovation and aggressive services environment has created more competition and variety of products and services. Customer satisfaction is considered as a pre-requisite for customer retention, loyalty, convenience which ultimately helps in realizing the goals like productivity, market share, growth, return on investment, etc. The concept of customer satisfaction and service quality is interrelated with each other. Moreover satisfaction of customer depends upon service quality and service quality is increasingly offered as a strategy by marketers to position themselves more effectively in the market place. The present paper endeavors to study the level of service quality in the telecommunication industry through a well drafted questionnaire and to study customers' perception on it. The companies chosen for the study are Airtel, Reliance, BSNL, Tata, Idea and Vodafone. To evaluate the impact, SERVQUAL model has been taken in to consideration based on the five dimensions of tangibility, reliability, responsiveness, assurance and empathy. Descriptive and Factor analysis has been used to analyse the data and interpret the results. The reliability of the data has been checked through cronbach alpha, KMO test and Bartlett test of sphericity. The results of the study explained that telecom management needs to emphasize on service quality. Due to the fact that telecom firms do not provide tangible products, their service quality is usually assessed by the level of quality. Thus, telecom management should pay attention to the staff skills, accuracy in transaction, variety in tariff plans and must offer fast and efficient services to its customers.

Keywords: Service Quality, Customer Satisfaction, SERVQUAL Model, Company Image

INTRODUCTION

In today's globalize and borderless market, quality, productivity and satisfaction of customers pose a challenge for the survival and growth of all firms. These growth and survival demands are further deepened by the need to attract and retain loyal customers. Thus, the customer is the main focus for any successful business. Business success depends on a firm's understanding and meeting customers' needs and demands. In Ghana, service provision has always suffered a setback as service firms have always been criticized for providing poor quality of services. Due to poor service quality especially by most state-owned enterprises (SOEs), the government has had to privatize them in order to improve upon their service delivery. Others, both private and public have been made more competitive by introducing the appropriate strategies to enhance quality of service and customer satisfaction as well as developing quality control circles (Boohene, 2011).

One most important industry in our economy is telecommunication. All social, political, economical, cultural, business and economic activities are undertaken using telecommunication. Without communication, no decision making, organizing, planning, influencing and co-coordinating can be done. The telecommunication industry provides both product and service to customers, but service is particularly important for this industry. Customer satisfaction is considered as a pre-requisite for customer retention, loyalty, convenience which ultimately helps in realizing the goals like productivity, market share, growth, return on investment etc. The concept of customer satisfaction and service quality is interrelated with each other. Moreover satisfaction of customer depends upon service quality and service quality is increasingly offered as a strategy by marketers to position themselves more effectively in the market place.

LITERATURE REVIEW

Charoensuk (2008) highlighted the use of e-service in the tele-communication Industry. The objective of the study was to examine the model that forms intention to use e-service in the tele communication Industry for both mobile and landline customers in Thailand. The findings of the study showed that level of intention to use e-service is enhanced by better managing traditional service quality, customer satisfaction, customer value and service experience consequently. In the end the author suggested the relationship paths to develop strong intention to use e-service in tele-communication Industry.

Khan (2010) in the paper examined the total quality management practices in Pakistan based on deming management model in tele communication Industry. The findings of the study suggested that integrated approach through internal co-operation and team work is required to implement the total quality management practices. The author suggested that to increase the level of service quality in tele communication industry, there should be employees' caring culture, building quality related competence and team work approach.

Olu (2010) in the study investigated the relationship between service quality and customer satisfaction in the tele communication Industry with a focus on mobile tele communication network (MTN). The objective of the study was to evaluate the strategies utilized by an organisation to deliver exceptional service quality and customer satisfaction. The researchers recommended that MTN should listen the customers' problems and should encourage suggestions for improving customer satisfaction.

Boohene et al. (2011) in the study investigated the determinants of customer loyalty in Vodafone. The study adopted SERVQUAL model for analyzing service quality. The result of the study indicated that there is a positive relationship between service quality and customer loyalty. However the results show a negative relationship between customer satisfaction and customer loyalty. The results of the findings suggest that telecom management needs to emphasize service quality as this Industry is not based on tangible products and the service quality is usually assessed by measure of the service providers relationship with customers. Thus telecom service management should pay attention to staff skill possession and offering fast and efficient services.

The above review indicates that there is a positive relationship between service quality and customer satisfaction level. But there has not been any systematic and comprehensive analysis to study the level of service quality on the customer satisfaction level. So, this paper tries to fill this research gap to assess service quality and customer satisfaction level in Tele-communication Industry using SERVQUAL Model.

OBJECTIVES AND RESEARCH METHODOLOGY OF THE STUDY

The main objectives of the study are as follows:

- To study the various factors important to assess customer satisfaction level
- To study the level of service quality in tele-communication industry.
- To evaluate the impact of service quality on customer satisfaction.

To achieve the above said objectives, two null hypotheses have been framed:

- For the customer satisfaction, all factors are equally important.
- There is no correlation amongst the different factors to judge the customer satisfaction.

SERVQUAL INSTRUMENT

SERVQUAL model developed by *Parasuraman, Zeithamal and Berry* have been used to study level of customer satisfaction. The model fills a gap between what the customer expect by way of service quality and what he is actually getting. Service quality is presented as a multi dimensional construct and in the original formulation Parasuraman *et. al* (1985) identified five components of service quality and each dimension has further four-five dimensions. A brief description of these dimensions is presented:

- *Tangibles* include the physical evidence of the service.
- *Reliability involves* consistency of performance and dependability. It also means that the firm performs the service first time and honours its promises.
- *Responsiveness* concerns the willingness or readiness of employees to provide service. It involves timeliness of service.
- *Assurance* involves the knowledge and courtesy of employees and their ability to convey trust and confidence. This assurance includes competence, courtesy, credibility and security.
- *Empathy* involves the provision of caring, individualized attention to customers. This empathy includes access, communication and understanding the customer.

SAMPLING AND DATA ANALYSIS

The data was collected from the customers using different connections of mobile networking through a structured questionnaire. The questionnaire was designed on the basis of SERVQUAL dimensions and the prior studies on the service quality. Likert scale was rated from 1 to 5 with referring 1 to strongly disagree and 5 to strongly agree. The customers from different regions of Ludhiana. Stratified random sampling technique was used a sample of 100 respondents was chosen. The data collected through the questionnaire was analyzed by using factor analysis. The 22 service quality variables were analyzed. The variables with factor loadings of 0.40 were considered and other items have been excluded. To check the reliability of the data, KMO, Bartlett's test of Sphericity and Cronbach Alpha were used. Only variables with factor loadings of 0.40 (Hatcher, 1994) were considered and other items are excluded. KMO, Bartlett's test of Sphericity and Cronbach alpha were used to measure the reliability of the data. In the statistics we assume that we are extracting factors of eigen value 1 or more have specified to the computer package while doing factor analysis. The objective is to reduce the variables to a fewer number of factors by retaining only those factors with an eigen value of 1 or more (in other words, factor must explain at least as much of the variance if not more, than a single original variable (Nargundkar, R., 2002).

DATA PRESENTATION AND ANALYSIS

The analysis of data has been categorized in to two parts. Part-I is related to the demographic profile of the respondents, their preference regarding the mobile connection, technology in services, duration of association with the company, attributes related to choosing a mobile network and per month expenditure incurred on mobile. Part-II is related to the level of service quality in telecommunication Industry with the help of SERVQUAL model. Let us discuss in detail.

Part-I

Table 1: Gender Profile of Respondents

Gender Profile	Frequency	Percent
Male	59	59.0
Female	41	100.0
Total	**100**	

Table 1 explains the gender profile of respondents. Out of the total sample of 100, 59 are male and 41 are female. This shows that more of the respondents in sample size are male.

Table 2: Occupational Profile of Respondents

Occupational Profile	Frequency	Percent
Serviceman	20	20.0
Businessman	23	43.0
Professional	15	58.0
Any other	42	100.0
Total	**100**	

Table 2 describes the occupational profile of respondents. From the total sample size; 23 are businessman, 20 are serviceman, 15 are professional and in any other are 42. In the category of any other, most of the respondents are housewives and students.

Table 3: Income of the Respondents

Income	Frequency	Percent
Below 15000	21	21.0
Rs.15000-20000	22	43.0
20000-25000	15	58.0
25000-30000	6	64.0
Above 35000	15	79.0
Any Other	21	100.0
Total	**100**	

Table 3 mentions the income of the respondents. 22 respondents having income 15000-20000, 21 are having below than 15,000, 15 are having above than 35,000 and 21 comes under any other category, that mainly belongs to students.

Table 4: Connection Preferred by the Respondents

Connection Preference	**Frequency**	**Percent**
Prepaid	43	43
Postpaid	57	100
Total	**100**	

Table 4 describes the connection preferred by the respondents. 43 percent prefer prepaid whereas 57 percent postpaid connection.

Table 5: Services Presently Availed by the Respondents

Present Services Availed	**Frequency**	**Percent**
BSNL	4	4.0
Tata	9	13.0
Reliance	10	23.0
Vodafone	20	43.0
Airtel	42	85.0
Idea	15	100.0
Total	**100**	

Table 5 describes the services presently availed by the respondents. Maximum respondents prefer Airtel (42), followed by Vodafone (20), Idea (15), Reliance (10), Tata (9) and BSNL (4).

Table 6: Technology Preferred by the Respondents

Technology Preference	**Frequency**	**Percent**
CDMA	10	10.0
GSM	66	76.0
Both	24	100.0
Total	**100**	

Table 6 shows the technology preferred by respondents in which 10 are using CDMA and 66 are using GSM and 24 are using both the services.

Table 7 shows usage of connection, 54 respondents are using the connection from more than 3 years, 20 from 2-3 years and 11 from less than 3 months.

Table 7: Usage of the Connection

Usage	Frequency	Percent
Less than 3 months	11	11.0
3-6 Months	4	15.0
6-12 months	5	20.0
1-2 years	6	26.0
2-3 years	20	46.0
More than 3 years	54	100.0
Total	**100**	

Table 8: Attribute in Choosing Mobile Network

Dimensions	Rank 1	Rank 2	Rank 3	Rank 4	Rank 5	Rank 6	Total	WAS	Overall Ranking
Network Performance	43	24	20	6	5	2	488	4.88	1
Range of Services	19	16	21	35	7	2	399	3.99	2
Service Plan	25	14	20	14	13	14	382	3.82	3
Accuracy of Bill	2	18	12	13	32	23	276	2.76	5
Brand Image	7	11	7	15	15	45	245	2.45	6
Customer Service Quality	4	19	20	17	29	11	319	3.19	4

Table 8 reveals the attributes in choosing mobile network by the customers of a particular company. Overall ranking was calculated for different attributes. Firstly the network performance was main reason for choosing the connection of particular company (4.88). Secondly the range of services offered by the companies. The main reason of choosing airtel is the range of services it offers to the customers (3.99). Thirdly, it's the service plan (3.82) either in prepaid or postpaid that attracts the customers towards a company. Fourthly the customer service quality (3.19), fifthly the accuracy of bill (2.76) and sixthly the brand image (2.45) that plays a little role while choosing a network. This shows that the customers want the accuracy in services and good network performance rather than the company from where they are taking services.

Every customer while obtaining some service from the company has some expectation. Table 9 shows the expectation of respondents from their service provider. Rank was given on the weighted average score of different dimension in which network service is the main consideration while choosing a particular connection (4.09) followed by the good service (3.42). With the speediness of network customers also want voice clarity (2.63) in the connection. Customers gave the fourth rank to price (2.54) and fifth to various schemes (2.30) offered by the companies.

Table 9: Expectation of Respondents from Service Provider

Dimensions	Rank 1	Rank 2	Rank 3	Rank 4	Rank 5	Total	WAS	Overall Ranking
Good Service	23	26	30	12	9	342	3.42	2
Network	55	18	9	17	1	409	4.09	1
Voice	7	22	21	27	23	263	2.63	3
Scheme	8	14	14	28	36	230	2.30	5
Price	7	20	25	16	32	254	2.54	4

Part-II

In order to know about the various factors considered important for the customers, two tests were conducted under the factor analysis to judge the reliability of data i.e. Kaiser-Meyer-Olkin measure of sampling adequacy and Bartlett test of sphericity. The results so obtained were subjected to both these tests. The value of KMO statistics in all the factors is larger than >0.5. Hence, all the factors are not considered equally important for measuring the service quality of tele-communication industry. Therefore, null hypothesis is rejected. Bartlett's test of sphercity shows the value of Chi-square which is significant at 0.000 levels in all the dimensions of service quality. These two tests show that the data is fit for conducting the factor analysis.

RESULTS AND DISCUSSIONS

Principal Component Factor Analysis with Varimax Rotation, Percentage of Variance Explained and Factor Loadings

Factor 1: Tangibility

Sr. No.	Variable	Factor Loading
1	Company provides good physical facilities to the customers	0.658
2	Tools and equipments used to provide services are up-to-date	0.799
3	Customer service staff is well dressed	0.258
4	The appearance of physical facilities of the company is in keeping with the type of telecom services	0.160
	Cronbach alpha	0.588
	Eigen value	1.874
	Percentage of variance (sum of square loadings)	46.857

Factor 2: Reliability

Sr. No.	Variable	Factor Loading
1	Company is accurate in performing different activities related to quality of service	0.671
2	It performs the services at designated time	0.587
3	The company keeps its records accurately	0.756
4	The company shows sincere interest in solving an unpredictable problem	0.75
	Cronbach alpha	0.500
	Eigen value	1.650, 1.152
	Percentage of variance (sum of square loadings)	70.055

Rotated Component Matrix

	Component	
	1	2
Accuracy	0.016	**0.819**
Performance	0.103	**0.759**
Records	**0.859**	0.135
Interest	**0.888**	0.001

Factor 3: Responsiveness

Sr. No.	Variable	Factor Loading
1	The company sends the bills statement on time	0.678
2	The staff prevents long waiting line and tells exactly when service will be rendered	0.592
3	Customer service staff is always willing to help the customers	0.725
4	The service staff responds back the customer quickly	0.653
	Cronbach alpha	0.574
	Eighen value	1.762
	Percentage of variance (sum of square loadings)	44.038

Factor 4: Assurance

Sr. No.	Variable	Factor Loading
1	The customer feels safe while transacting with the company.	0.503
2	The company has a good reputation in the market.	0.663
3	The company assures the customer that a problem will be handled.	0.705
4	The knowledge and skill of operational personnel is excellent.	0.794
5	The charges paid and the services availed are almost equal.	0.712
	Cronbach alpha	0.718
	Eighen value	2.416
	Percentage of variance (sum of square loadings)	48.318

Factor 5: Empathy

Sr No	Variable	Factor Loading
1	It provides individualized attention while solving the complaints	0.395
2	Waiting time to receive service is not extensive	0.503
3	The company gives discount offers to old customers	0.506
4	The company offers the best services which are not offered by the competitors	0.829
5	The network of company is very fast.	0.762
	Cronbach alpha	0.531
	Eighen value	1.704, 1.292
	Percentage of variance (sum of square loadings)	59.917

Rotated Component Matrix

	Component	
	1	2
Attention	–0.52	0.627
Waiting Time	0.071	**0.706**
Discount	0.359	0.614
Best Service	**0.897**	0.156
Network	**0.873**	0.005

Five factors have been extracted with the help of different dimensions of service quality. The percentage of variance explained by the factors individually varies from 44.038 to 70.055 and the communalities vary from 0.160 to 0.829. All the factors have been given appropriate names on the basis of various variables present in each case. The structure of these five factors is discussed below.

Tangibility

Different dimensions of 'tangibility' under were studied and four factors have been loaded on this factor. The factor loadings of all the statements were calculated and it has been found that the loading of two statements are greater than 0.4, whereas two factors having loading less than 0.4. The eigen value and cronbach alpha for this factor are 1.874 and 0.588 respectively. The eigen value of the factor was greater than one and indicates that it fits well with the data from all of the respondents on all of the statements. The analysis shows that eigen value explains 46.857 percent of the variance from all the respondents and there is only one factor extracted having the factor loading closer to 1. This shows that customers do not agree that customer service staff is well dressed and the appearance of physical facilities of the company is in keeping with the type of telecom services. On the other hand customers agree that company provides good physical facilities to the customers with up to date equipment. Therefore it implies that all the companies in tele communication industry provides new facilities to the customers.

Reliability

The reliability factor consisted of four variables and each of these variables was analyzed using factor analysis. The factor loading of all the statement was calculated and it was found that the loading of all the statements were greater than 0.4 and thus all were accepted. In this factor two variables have eigen values greater than 1 and as such two factors will be extracted with rotated component matrix and Kaiser Normalization. These are:

Component 1: Records, Interest
Component 2: Accuracy, Performance

In the first extraction, the variables named 'records' and 'Interest' having high loading and closer to 1. It can be inferred that company keeps its records accurately and also show sincere interests in solving an unpredictable problem. Further in the next category the respondents perceive that companies perform their services at designated time whether it is prepaid or postpaid and accurate in performing different activities related to quality of service.

Responsiveness

Different dimensions of 'responsiveness' under were studied and four factors have been loaded on this factor. The factor loadings of all the statements were calculated and it has been found that the loading of all statements are greater than 0.4, hence all statements are acceptable. The eigen value and cronbach alpha for this factor are 1.762and 0.574 respectively. The eigen value of the factor was greater than one and indicates that it fits well with the data from all of the respondents on all of the statements. The analysis shows that eigen value explains 44.038 percent of the variance from all the respondents and there is only one factor extracted having the factor loading closer to 1. Out of the four statements, there is only one statement having factor loading 0.725 which reveals that customer service staff is always willing to help the customers. This shows that the staff in tele-communication industry is co-operative and helpful in solving the grievances of the respondents.

Assurance

The 'Assurance' factor consisted of five variables and each of these variables was analyzed using factor analysis. The analysis shows that the eigen value represents 48.318

percent of the variance of data. The eigen value and cronbach alpha for this factor are 2.416 and 0.718 respectively. There are three variables having value closer to 1 and above 0.7. The variables extracted are 'knowledge', 'problem handling', 'charges'. These three factors explained that company always gives assurance about the problem handling and this is due to knowledge and skill of the staff. Further the charges for all the services like message service, value added services; internet facilities are almost equal to the amount paid which in turn increases the level of satisfaction for the customers.

Empathy

The 'empathy' factor consisted of five variables. The factor loading of all the statements were calculated and it was found that the loading of all the statements were greater than 0.4 and thus all were accepted. The value of Cronbach Alpha and eigen value is 0.531 and 1.704, 1.292 respectively which suggests a good consistency of the data. The analysis shows that the eigen value represents 59.917 percent of the variance of data. In the two variables, eigen values are having value greater than 1 which shows that the factor extracted would be equivalent to two. Rotated component matrix with Kaiser Normalization helped in data reduction. The matrix explains that the factors extracted are the combination of how many variables. The principal component analysis under the rotation converged in to two iterations. The following two components have been extracted.

Component 1: Best Service, Network
Component 2: Waiting Time

The above factor represents the combination of variables under empathy dimension. In the first extraction of factor loading, 'Best service' and 'Network' is having high loading which shows that the company offers the best services which are not offered by the competitors and there is no network problem faced by the customers. In the second extraction there is only one factor having high loading i.e.0.703, which shows that customers need not to wait for long time to receive the services.

CONCLUSION AND IMPLICATIONS

The study focused on the various dimensions of service quality being applicable on the tele-communication industry. The factors taken in to consideration provide a wide platform to the tele-communication industry to consider the various factors important for the customer satisfaction and the further improvement. There is a lot of improvement in service quality. Five dimensions were developed having the various sub-dimensions to measure the service quality. These scales measured tangibility, reliability, responsiveness, assurance and empathy. These factors give a wide choice in selecting the various factors important for the service quality. In order to judge the level of satisfaction among customers regarding the tele-communication services, a list of 22 service variables compiled in to the five dimensions. The results showed that all the factors are not equally important for measuring the level of satisfaction. Different dimensions show different results. In tangibility dimension, results shows that all the companies in tele communication industry provides new facilities to the customers. In the reliability dimension companies kept all the records properly and also show interest in solving the problems of customers. In responsiveness dimension, the results show that the customer service staff is always willing to help the customers. So the conceptualization of SERVQUAL instrument provided immense help in determining the level of service quality and the expectation of customers from telecommunication the Industry. With the help of SERVQUAL model companies can be more focused in delivering the qualitative broadband and mobile services to the customers.

REFERENCES

[1] Boohene, R. and Agyapong, G. (2011), "Analysis of the Antecedents of Customer Loyalty of Tele-Communication Industry in Ghana: The Case of Vodafone (Ghana), International Business Research, Vol. 4, No. 1, pp. 229-238.

[2] Charoensok, S. (2008), "Understanding the Transformation of Current Service Quality Perception to Intention to Use E-Service in Telecommunication Industry," *ABAC Journal*, Vol. 28, No. 3, pp. 52-70.

[3] Duojo (2010), "Relationship between Service Quality and Customer Satisfaction in the Telecommunication Industry: Evidence from Nigeria" Broad Research in Accounting, Negotiation and Distribution, Vol. 1, Issue 1, 2010.

[4] Khan, M.A. (2010), "Evaluating the Deming Management Model of Total Quality in Tele-Communication Industry in Pakistan – An Empirical Study", *International Journal of Business and Management*, Vol. 5, No. 9, pp. 46-54.

[5] Parasuraman, A., V.A. Zeithamal and L.L. Berry (1985), "A Conceptual Model Service Quality and its Implication for Future Research", *Journal of Marketing*, Vol. 49, pp. 41-50.

[6] Parasuraman, A.V.A. Zeithamal and L.L Berry (1988), "SERVQUAL: A Multi Item Scale for Measuring Consumer Perception of Service Auality", *Journal of Retailing*, Spring, pp. 12-40.

[7] Parasuraman, A.V.A. Zeithamal and L.L Berry (1993), "More on Improving Service Quality Measurement", *Journal of Retailing*, Vol. 69, pp. 140-147.

An Overview of Micro Finance and SHGs: Some Major Pitfalls

Manish Kumar and Ravish Kumar Chourasiya
T.M.B.U., Bhagalpur, Bihar
E-mail: manishbeyond@gmail.com; rvsch2005@rediffmail.com

ABSTRACT

The Indian economy is one of the fastest growing but 42 percent of the population is living on less than Rs.56 a day (World Bank Report, 2005). Finding a solution (generally believed to the finance) to the root cause of poverty is indispensable. Finance is not the solution to all problems facing the poor. Finance may be considered as the "key factor" in any development initiative but it is also supplemented by other critical elements for development like expertise, knowledge and perseverance on the part of the individual. Moreover, support service from government and non-governmental Agencies is a must. Micro-Finance has a broad meaning and it covers all types of micro-products (financial and non-financial) and micro-service targeted at the poor. It refers to loans, savings, insurance, transfer services, marketing assistance, training, development, support service and other financial products targeted at low income clients (Khandelwal, 2007). Micro credit is more popularly used as an intervention strategy of poverty eradication, employment generation and small enterprises creation. Micro finance is "credit plus" where micro- credit". The basic objective of providing microfinance is setting-up of micro enterprises in order to mitigate poverty and empower the poor. Micro-enterprises contribute towards job stability, social security coverage, employment, technical assistance and stability, social security coverage employment, technical assistance and stabilizing behavior. This objective is being attempted through micro financing to/through SHG's. "SHG is a voluntary association of people that helps itself through its own initiation and enterprise to develop economically, socially and politically". Self-help groups are voluntary, small group structures for mutual aid and accomplishment of a special purpose, satisfying a common need, overcoming a common handicap or life-disrupting problems and bringing about desired social and/or personal change (www.selfhelpnetwork.wichita.edu). Microfinance intervention outcomes are positive in some studies and negative in some. It has empowered the poor, particularly women. It has improved the livelihood and socio-economic status of the clients.

Keywords: Micro Finance, SHGs

CONCEPT OF MICRO FINANCE

Micro Finance has now been widely accepted as an effective intervention strategy for poverty alleviation, which is easily accessible to the poor, reduces transaction cost and where repayments are designed to fit cash flow for the borrowers. It includes thrift, credit and other financial services and products of very small amount (sarma, 2007). There may be various medium of micro finance; however, the most prominent among them has been the medium of self-Help Groups.

Among micro-financial services, micro-credit has predominated, on the assumption that it will deliver higher incomes and increased assets to the poor through micro-enterprises. Micro credit is the extension of small loans to individuals who are too poor to qualify for traditional bank loans, as they have no assets to be offered as guarantee. The RBI in its Report (1999-2000) has defined Micro Credit "as provision of thrift, credit and other financial services and products of very small amount to the poor in rural, semi-urban and urban areas for enabling them to raise their income levels and improve living standards. Micro credit Institutions are those which provide these facilities". The Micro credit loans are enough for hardworking micro-entrepreneurs to start or expand small businesses, manufacturing and other service activities. Micro credit system works as an integral part of the SHG mechanism. In India, micro credit has worked largely through SHGs. Predominated by women, these are formed with simple rules-save, accumulate and give loans to each other.

The micro credit fund which is created out of micro savings is kept in a bank and is recycled by lending to group members. Members are engaged in micro enterprises to supplement the family income. Linkages are established with local banks and other financial agencies to facilitate credit. Micro credit to SHGs has been paving the way for opening up a large number of mini ventures (production and marketing) in rural areas, which has not only generated gainful occupation but also provided scope for transformation of rural society (Anbalagan et al., 2005).

SOME DEFINITIONS OF MICRO FINANCE

R.P. Christan (1997) defines micro finance as a means of providing varieties of financial services to the poor, based on market driven and commercial approaches. These services include saving, insurance, money-transfer and credit. MF movement till date has generally favoured micro credit to households not having access to FFIs.

RBI Task Force on Micro Finance defines micro finance as provision of thrift, credit and other financial services and products of very small amount to the poor to raise their income levels and improve living standards. The task force also designates these institutions that provide mF services as micro finance institution (mFIs).

CONCEPT OF SHGs

Self-help Groups (SHGs) are mostly informal groups (of 15 to 20 member) where members pool savings and re-lend in the groups on a rational basis. An SHG in general, consists of persons from a homogeneous class so that they can think together as to how basic problems can be solved. As the name itself indicates the number of an SHG are required to contribute small amount of savings to form a pooled fund out of which member can take loans with a very low interest rate. Such activities by the member help them to have first hand experiences of small scale financial managements including the knowledge of priority in offering financial assistance. In the process the members also realize the necessity of financial discipline and repayment of credits taken by members of such groups from their pooled resources. Taking into consideration the financial activities of such SHGs various financial institutions come forward and provide credits to such groups which are much more than their accumulated pooled fund. The bank loans are given without any collateral and at existing rates of interest. The concerned members having experienced the benefits of financial discipline by being able to save and borrow money as and when required, the members of the groups can decide the terms of loans to their own members without facing any delay in the execution.

Thus NABARD has started providing adequate credit to various SHGs from the year 1992 under the banner of SHG Bank Linkage Programme in the world for poverty alleviation.

SELF-HELP GROUPS (SHGs) AND BANK LINKAGE PROGRAMME

Rural credit during seventies focusing on individual households called for shift to a group based approach due to inadequacies. In 1991-92, NABARD launched the SHG-Bank linkage programme on a pilot basis to finance SHGs across the country through the formal banking system. High repayment rates by the SHGs encouraged the banks to finance SHGs.

Formulation of SHGs is, however, dependant on the intervening agency, who has so far been NGOs/MFIs, RRBs, banks and DRDAs. SHGs are being promoted primarily under the two separate schemes of NABARD/Ministry of finance and the Ministry of Rural Development. The total number of SHGs formed is reported to be approximately 2.3 million that covers nearly 30-35 million BPL households (more than 50 percent of all BPL households). However, there is one important difference between the two. While the SHGs promoted by Ministry of Rural Development enjoys credits linked subsidy, those promoted by NABARD do not have any such facility. Despite this, the credit disbursed to SHGs under the NABARD programme has been more than under SGSY.

The success of the concept of micro-credit through self help groups (SHGs) has encouraged the Government of India to establish a National Level Micro-Credit organization/Rashtriya Mahila Kosh (RMK) (National credit fund for women) under the ministry of women and child Development in 1993, with an initial corpus of Rs. 31 crore. The objective was to help women organize income generating activities to improve their socio economics status. RMK had disbursed cumulative loan of Rs. 151 crore up to July 2006, benefiting 5.50 lakh women and the recovery rate is above 91 percent. In 1996, Reserve Bank of India included financing of SHGs as main stream activities of banks under the priority sector lending programs. The SHG Bank linkage Programme covered over 24.3 million families by March 2005. Under the Bank-SHG Linkage programme, 2.24 million SHGs were linked, up to 31st March 2006, of which 90 percent were women's groups.

FORMS OF MFIS IN INDIA

In India, there are varieties of MFIS providing MF services to the poor families, called micro finance providers. In formal financial sector, there are CBs, RRBs and Co-operative Banks while NGOs, SHGs, and Non NBFCs in informal sector to act as MFIS. These mF service providers are broadly divided into these broad categories.

Non-profit MFIS

- Societies registered under Societies Registration Act, 1860 or similar state Acts.
- Public Trust registered under the Indian Trust Act, 1882
- Non-profit companies registered U/S 25 of Companies Act, 1956.

Mutual Benefit MFIS

- State Credit Co-operative.
- National credit Co-operatives.
- Mutually Aided Co-operative Societies.

For Profit MFIS

- NBFCs registered under the Companies Act, 1956.

It is to be noted that banks could be called MFIS as they provide small credit under Bank-SHG linkage programme. In the same footing NABARD, SIDBI, RMK could also be considered as MFIS.

Participating Agencies

The different agencies implementing mF may broadly be divided into following three categories.

Agencies Implementing mF Activities

- Agencies that directly lend to the borrowers and carry related activities comprising of recovery, monitoring, follow up, etc.
- Agencies that only promote and provide linkage to SHGs and not directly involve in micro lending.
- Agencies which are dealing with SHGs and plan to carry micro finance related activities.

Agencies Providing Supports

These include organizations that provide support to implementing agencies in the form of resources, training and development, counseling, net-working, etc. They operate at national or state level with or without mF activities.

FFIs-Banks

The formal financial institutions are active in formation of SHGs, providing financial support and related activities. CBs, RRBs, Co-operative, Development banks like NABARD, SIDBI and RMK fall under this category.

SHGs-BANK LINKAGE

With a view to bring the banking services to the reach of unbaked rural poor through micro credit mechanism, a pilot scheme was launched by national bank for Agriculture and Rural Development (NABARD) in 1991-92. Reserve bank of India directed the commercial bank for active participation in the linkage programme to ensure flow of adequate and timely easy credit to the rural sector (Table 1 and 2). Later the Scheme was extended to regional rural banks and co-operatives.

Since then, SHGs and their linkage with FFIs have proved to be very effective due to the following reasons:

- The system is more flexible which suits the peculiarities of rural sector.
- The association of persons in the groups is based on social commitment with mutual trust and confidence.
- It encourages the saving habits of the poor.
- The common fund meets the credit need of the poor.

Table 1: Bank-SHGs Linkages (Cumulative up to 2005-06) (Amount Rs. Crore)

Year Ending 31st March	No. of SHGs Linked	No. of SHGs Refinanced	Bank Loans	Refinanced by NABARD
2000-01	263825	213213	481	400
2001-02	461478	340131	1026	796
2002-03	717360	493634	2049	1419
2003-04	1079091	611043	3904	2124
2004-05	1618476	824888	6898	3086
2005-06	2238565	900000	11398	4157

Source: NABARD, Annual Report, Various Issues.

Table 2: Bank Loans Outstanding Against SHGs: As on March 31, 2007

Agency	No. of SHGs	% Share	Amount (Rs. crore)	% Share	Per SHG Outstanding Loan (Rs.)
1	2	3	4	5	6
Commercial Bank (Public Sector)	1,81,353	62.5	8,225	66.5	45,435
Commercial Bank (Private sector)	82,663	2.9	535	4.3	64,719
Subtotal (Commercial Bank)	1,893,016	65.4	8,760	70.8	46,277
Regional Rural Banks	729,255	25.2	2,802	22.7	38,419
Co-operative Banks	272,234	9.4	804	6.5	29,546
Total	2,894,505	100.0	12,366	100.0	42,724

- The system is cost effective.
- SHGs make the linkage of rural poor with the FFIs and their access to banking services.
- Interest on borrowers charged by the SHGs is comparatively low than charged by the village moneylenders.
- Minimum formalities and easy terms of the SHGs attract the poor people belonging to backward classes and the women.
- Recovery of advances rate is quite high due to social contract of the members and their active participation.
- SHGs help the rural poor to get ride from the clutches of the village money-lenders.

MICRO FINANCE AND THE GOVERNMENT

It was announced in the Union Budget for 2005-06 that the Government of India intends to promote micro-finance institutions (MFIs) in a big way. For this purpose, the Micro-Finance Development Fund (MFDF) was re-designated as Micro-Finance Development and Equity Fund (MFDEF) and the corpus of the fund was increased form was increased from Rs. 100 crore to Rs.200 crore. MFDEF is expected to play a vital role in capitalization the MFIs and thereby improving their access to commercial loans.

The Central Government is considering the need to identify and classify the MFIs and rate such institutions to empower them to intermediate between the lending banks and the clients. To facilitate the process of rating of MFIs, NABARD has decided to extend financial assistance to commercial banks and RRBs by way of grant to enable them to avail the services of credit rating agencies for rating of MFIs.

MAJOR PITFALLS OF MICRO FINANCE

Problem of Marketing

One of the greatest problems that the mFIs are facing is the lack of market for their products and services. Members of the mFIs lack minimum skill and knowledge of marketing functions. Also there is no institutional support for it. Many of the members of the mFIs have expressed their concerns for poor marketing of their products. Few of the SHGs of Jaipur block are engaged in making poly bags, cane products, processed food products etc. However, they find no scope for their products. The local meals (fairs) and festival occations are the only scope for the same. There is need for regular and all season market for the products of the SHGs.

Moreover, the women SHGs due to many family and social barriers, lack mobility, do not have marketing strategies and face competition and challenges from organized retail markets. Also, they mostly depend upon the male non-members and market middlemen for the same. It not only adds to the cost of marketing, but also kills the profit. Maa Biraja SHG of Tipara has viewed that they largely depends on male non-members of it community for marketing, that minimizes the profit margins.

Male Interventions

Since evolution of human civilization, women are dominated by their male counterparts within and outside the family and are deprived of equity, status, justice and all basic amenities of life. It is observed in the present study that male intervention also is a big challenge for SHGs as well. Many women members of the sample SHGs have honestly confessed the presence of male non-members in the meetings of the groups and major decision maker in many strategic issues. Yhe investigator realized this fact when he personally met many male counterparts of the women members while collecting of data.

It is found that the accounts of a majority of the SHGs are maintained and retained by the male non-members. This causes many problems including corruption, lack of transparency, and related issues. In many cases the true members do not have access to their group accounts. The case of Digvijay SHG of Govinpur is very realistic and worth nothing. Due to adequate education and minimum accounting skill the group had taken the help of one local youth. By using his ill intention and dominating stand, that youth demanded a lump sum amount from the group. When the group members denied this, he did not return the records for a long.

Lack of Monitoring

Another major concern for the mFIs is the absence of regular monitoring SHGs are informal association of poor persons who needs a strong monitoring mechanism and guidance. However, there is absence of any such mechanism. The NGOs, bank and government pay much importance in formation of groups and less for post-working of the groups. Also the officials do not get much of their surplus time to pay visit and attend the meetings of the groups for redressal of the grievances. Studies show that about 70 percent of the SHGs are not properly working for a longer period. No meeting is held in case of more than 76 percent cases two year after the formation of the group. Members of Maa Biraja SHG of Tipara have demanded for the regular and periodic visit of Government and NGO officials to their groups. They appealed the investigator to remain present in the coming meeting of the grievances redessal. Similarly, the bank to which the SHGs are linked are not paying importance for the projects causing failure of the SHG-Bank Linkage mission.

Diversion of Funds

Diversion of funds from economic activities towards consumption needs is a major challenge for the SHGs. It has been studies that a majority of 65 percent of the groups do not make the proper use of bank credit. Most of the members are more interested for the subsidy benefits than the credit for investment purpose. On getting the loans and subsidies, the amount is distributed among the members who mostly spend the amount for personal and consumption needs. This affects the very mission of micro credit and the repayment ability of the members as well.

Poor Social Infrastructure

Another key problem affecting the growth of mFIs and financial inclusion is the poor social infrastructure. Social infrastructure in general and education in particular have bearing on the growth of social infrastructure. Educated people are more aware and have access to financial institutions for credit and to the government officials. They make productive use of available resources and get benefits out of these. It has been seen in the present study that educated members of the group are the true beneficiaries of the micro finance. On the other hand, undereducated members make unproductive use of the funds and get nothing out of it.

Lack of Audit System

SHGs are informal groups of individuals based on mutual understanding and beliefs. There is no such uniform accounting procedures and practices to be followed by the SHGs in keeping accounting of the groups. This results in lack of transparency and accountability and leads to misappropriation and corruption. Also, no statutory audit system is applicable to the SHGs to check the books of accounts.

Other Key Issues

There are many key issues which affect the working and viability of the SHGs. These include apathy of bank personnel in serving the rural poor members of the mFIs, non-cooperation from the family members, absence of managerial, marketing and commercial skill among the members, low level of education and awareness, lower income, low disposal income, gender issues, legal issues, rate of interest, choice of poor activities, subsidy, capacity building among other. Most of the bank employees have expressed their inability in serving the SHGs. They do not find surplus time beyond their working hours to attend the meeting and participate in the decision making process of the groups. The officials of the Government and NGOs are of the similar view. They find little time to monitor the working of the groups giving feedbacks.

RECOMMENDATIONS

The following measures are required to upload the mF movement in the rural sector and bring the rural poor within the reach of organized financial market and services.

1. It is highly recommended to have an integrative approach between the SHGs, NGOs, Government mechanism and other promoting agencies in promoting mFIs.
2. Post information monitoring and feedback to the SHGs must be given in regural intervals.
3. Federation of the SHGs in Gram Panchayat level and higher levels should be formed to promote co-operation and mutual help between the SHGs in their functioning.
4. Pre-loan trainings to the members must be given to improve knowledge, skill and efficiency in all managerial aspects.

5. Government must provide adequate platforms for marketing of the products of the SHGs. A product procurement mechanism may be developed like that of crop procurement and export promotion council.
6. A suitable and standardized accounting practice must be developed and put into use in SHGs to maintain books of account. This is to bring Transparency in accounting practice. Also, it will be of great help in analysis and disclosure of financial statements.
7. Annual audit of the accounts of SHGS must be done including the financial and social audit.
8. Grievances redressal cells may be forms at micro as well as macro level to solve the disputes within the groups and outsides.
9. Specialized officials may be employed in the banks and government offices to deal the mFIs. This will be very much helpful in monitoring, serving mFIs. This will be very much helpful in monitoring, serving, mFIs and preventing non-member intervention in the affairs of the SHGs.

REFERENCES

[1] Economic Survey of India, 2007-08.

[2] File://f:/Reservebankofindia.htm.

[3] Agriculture & Rural Development Working Paper-9 on Innovative Financial Services for Rural India, the World Bank.

[4] Khan M.K., "Rural Poverty in Developing Countries: Implications for Public policy", IMF March 2001.

[5] Global hunger index 2007, International Food Policy Research Institute, Washington.

[6] Wages Report in Rural India, 2006, Labour Bureas, New Delhi.

[7] Rural Banking, Shri MAhila SEWA Sahakari Bank Ltd., Ahmedabad.

[8] Debt and Investment Survey, Government of India, 1992.

[9] Chirstan R.P., "Banking Services for the poor: Monitoring for Financial Services", Washington D.C.A CCSON International, 1992.

[10] File://F:/mf-6/Reserve bankofindia.htm.

[11] Ibid.

Analysis of the Competitiveness of the Three International Airports in Kerala Using the Fuzzy Linguistic Approach

Igy George and K.C. Sankaranarayanan

Cochin University of Science and Technology, Cochin, Kerala
E-mail: igythomas@gmail.com; kcskollara@gmail.com

ABSTRACT

This paper intends to study about the competitiveness of three international airports in Kerala by using fuzzy linguistic approach. The latest global trend in the aviation sector is towards the expansion of the existing airports and also construction of new airports to meet the growing air traffic demand. With the concept of global village taking root among the nations in the world, there is a strong linkage between the nations and the changes at the global level are reflected in the national and regional levels. Kerala, a small state in the southern part of India, is already having three international airports. With two more airports in the pipe line, it would be relevant to analyse the competitiveness of the existing three international airports at Calicut, Cochin and Trivandrum. The competitiveness is analysed based on six factors which are important from the point of view of an airport. These factors are geographic characters, accessibility to the airport, environmental effects of airport, airport area development and airport charges The fuzzy linguistic approach is used for finding the competitiveness.For this purpose, two fuzzy linguistic variables are defined: importance(X) and competitiveness(Y). The paper brings out the relative competitiveness of the three airports under study.The study shows that Cochin International Airport is the most competitive airport in Kerala. The results also highlight the relevance of Green field airports under the Indian context.

Keywords: Airports, Competitiveness, Fuzzy Linguistic, Heuristic Algorithm, Green Field Airports, Kerala

INTRODUCTION

Airports today drive global commerce, and it is predicted that the airports of the future will be a commerce hub. Next generation airports will be destination sites, providing not only multimodal transport networks for worldwide commerce, but also leisure outlets (Senguttavan P.S., 2006). There exist a vast potential for growth in the air transport sector. The term airport was first used by the American print media in the year 1919. According to the official definition adopted by the Convention on International Civil Aviation signed in Chicago in 1944; an airport is said to be an area of land or water used or intended to be used for landing and takeoff of aircrafts, including buildings and facilities (NBB working paper No. 158, Zantke (1976). As per the specification listed by the International Civil Aviation Organization (ICAO), the main part of the airport is the zone stretching from the takeoff and landing strip, along the taxiways and the parking areas for aircraft (ICAO 2006). Airports are operated differently but maintain some common features. Differences in operation are at the micro level. World air traffic as per the airbus Global Market Forecast (GMF) for the 20 year 2010-2029 is projected to grow at 4.8% per annum. ICAO data show that air traffic has doubled every 15 years and Airbus GMF 2010 projects the air traffic to double in the next 15 years.

History of civil aviation in India started from the year 1912. Till the year 1994, airports in India were owned by the Government of India as per the Airport Corporation Act of 1953. The liberalization and open sky policies of the Government acted as a catalyst for growth in the civil aviation sector. The Airport Corporation Act of 1994 ended the monopoly of government sector and allowed private operators to enter into this field. At present, private airlines account for around 75% of the domestic aviation market, thus making India the ninth largest aviation market in the world.

Civil aviation history of Kerala started in 1932 (then it was Travancore) when Col G.V. Raja started the Royal Flying club at Trivandrum. Kerala the southernmost tiny state which is leading the other states in infrastructure penetration is now having three operative international airports and two more airports in the pipeline. The factors which influence the growth of air traffic in Kerala and make it a fertile ground for aviation industry are the favorable climatic conditions, high density of population, increasing number of expatriates, boom in the service sector etc..Moreover the present generation is giving more importance to speed and competency. Time is the essence of all activities. As stated by Garry S Becker (1965) in his Theory of Allocation of Time, "time is the major constraint not the budget". The air traffic is showing remarkable progress over the past few years. More and more people are using air traffic and during the year 2010-11, the combined passenger movement of the three international airports in Kerala registered a growth of 10.5% over the previous year. With more and more people visiting the airports, the need to maintain the airports under the international standards is becoming mandatory. Though the international airports are operated differently, they are maintaining some common features. The main concerns of the international airports are understanding, maintaining and improving the quality of service at the airports. (Yeh & Kuo, 2003).

Chou (2009) stated that main concerns of international airports are evaluation and improvement of the quality of service provided to the passengers. With three airports in the proximity, a study about the competitiveness of the airports is expected to be of useful to the policy makers as well as the airline companies.

The concept of competitiveness is the result of a long history of thoughts which has helped to define various aspects of this modern and complex concept (IMD World Competitiveness Year Book 2011). Competitiveness is primarily understood as being better than others. In India there are very few studies which analaysed the competitiveness of airports. Senguttavan, P.S. (2011) attempted to analyse the competitiveness index of the airports. Gillen and Lall used the Data Envelopment Analysis method while Kim & Ye, (2003) used empirical statistics in their study of the competitiveness of airports. Yonghwa Park(1997) used the fuzzy linguistic approach in the 'competitiveness analysis of major airports in Asia'.

According to Senguttavan, P.S. (2006), five major factors that determine airport competitiveness are spatial factors, facility factors, demand factors, service factors and managerial factors. These were first analysed by Park (2003). Using these five factors he analysed the competitive status of major airports in the East Asia region. In an earlier study (Park, 1997) he used factors such as geographical characteristics, socio-economic factors and environmental effectsonly In 2003 Park used a multi-decision-criteria approach for analysing the competitiveness of cargo operations of airports. Deviating from Porter's (1980) Five Forces, Park examined five-core-factors consisting of spatial, facility, demand, service and managerial aspects.

In India, no study, to our knowledge, is seen concentrated on this aspect using fuzzy linguistic approach. So this paper intends to study about the competitiveness of three international airports in Kerala using fuzzy linguistic approach. The three airports under study are Calicut (Karipur), Cochin (Nedumbassery) and Trivandrum.

The paperis organized under six sections. The first section provides an introduction. Section 2 gives an overview of the three international airports in Kerala. Section 3 presents the methodology, section 4 analyses the competitiveness of the airports by using fuzzy linguistic approach. Section 5 presents the result and finally section 6 draws the conclusion.

OVERVIEW OF THREE INTERNATIONAL AIRPORTS IN KERALA

The three airports at Calicut, Cochin and Trivandrum are handling both international and domestic flights. Thiruvananthapuram and Kozhikode Airports are owned by the Government of India and the Kochi Airport is owned by the Cochin International Airport Ltd (CIAL), a company set up by Government of Kerala with Public Private Participation(PPP).

Calicut (Kozhikode) International Airport (IATA: CCJ, ICAO: VOCL), also known as Karipur Airport, is an International Airport serving the city of Kozhikode (Calicut), Kerala, India. It is the seventh busiest airport in the country in terms of international passenger traffic and the 12th busiest airport in India in terms of overall passenger traffic. Airports Authority of India has provided runway lead-in lighting system for the first time in India at Calicut airport. The airport which is called the 'Gateway to Malabar' is the third busiest airport in Kerala after Cochin International Airport and Trivandrum (Thruvananthapuram) International Airport. The following are the major achievements of Kozhikode International Air Port during 2009-10. Apron layout was revised to accommodate more wide bodied aircrafts. Common Use Terminal Equipment (CUTE) and three Aerobridges were commissioned. (Kerala Economic Review 2010). The infrastructure at present did not allow the airport to service more international flights and operate jumbo flights. More than 1,000 acres of land is needed for any expansion. But the State government struggled even to acquire 137 acres for improving infrastructure. Calicut airport, less than 30 km from the city, was unsuitable for future development as it had a tabletop runway. The scarcity of land in and around the airport offered limited scope for development. The airport is situated on 375 acres of land.

Cochin International Airport Limited (CIAL) also known as 'Nedumbassery Airport' was incorporated as a Public Limited Company on 30 March 1994. With equity participation from the Government of Kerala, Industrialists, NRIs, Financial Institutions, Airport Service Providers and the Public, the Cochin International Airport Limited (CIAL) has emerged as a model enterprise. This is the first International Airport in India outside the ambit of the Government of India and the first of its kind developed under the PPP model, in the history of civil aviation in India. CIAL has the fourth largest international passenger traffic in India with annual passenger movement over 4.34 million and 356 aircraft movements per week. The international and domestic terminals cover 478,000ft^2 and 100,000ft^2 respectively. The terminals feature fully computerised check-in counter displays, closed-circuit camera system, fire detection and control system and integrated flight information display system (FIDS) and public address system. The international terminal handles a peak capacity of 2,400 passengers an hour. It houses India's largest duty free shop called Cochin Duty Free.

The domestic terminal complex of CIAL has a peak hour passenger handling capacity of 800. It features a large shopping complex with 21 shops. The following developmental activities have been carried out during 2009-10 at Cochin International air port. CIAL has planned Golf Course with 18 holes and 9 holes of that has already been completed and is open for the players. The Airport also has a Museum constructed in an area of around 2 acre and is now opened for the public. CIAL also plans to develop a full-fledged airport city called Aerotropolis in 450 acres of land. The proposed project will include an aircraft maintenance, repair and overhaul facility, aviation academy, star/budget hotels, golf course, convention / exhibition centre, logistics centre, amusement park and cultural village.

CIAL Academy is offering a MBA and various Diploma courses. CIAL has opened a Tourism Website to help tourists traveling through CIAL. Many charter flight operations were there in 2009-10 from Frankfurt, Dusseldorf and Munich to promote tourism. CIAL has commissioned 3 bays of which 2 are designed to cater B – 737-800 type aircrafts and the other for B-747 type aircrafts. The bay designed for B-747 is planned to cater cargo operation with additional space for cargo handling. The airport has introduced recently on-line checking facility for international passengers.. (Economic Review 2010)

Trivandrum International Airport (IATA: TRV, ICAO: VOTV) is located in Thiruvananthapuram and is the first airport in the state of Kerala. It is the first International airport in a non-metro city in India. It is considered as an "all weather" airport in the country and is ISO 9001-2000 certified. It is the 8th busiest airport in the country in terms of international passenger traffic and 10th busiest in terms of overall passenger traffic. In addition to civil operations, Trivandrum Airport also caters to the IAF (Indian Air Force) and the Coast Guard for their strategic operations. IAF has an exclusive apron to handle all their operations. Billed as one of the most technologically and architecturally advanced terminals of the Airports Authority of India (AAI) in non-metro cities, the Rs.300-crore terminal, has all the potential to be developed as a multi-modal transport hub. On being integrated with other modes of transport such as rail, road and inland waterways, as mooted by the AAI, passengers will get seamless transport in their chosen mode.

Table 1: Data Related to the Three International Airports in Kerala for the Year 2010-11

		Calicut	Cochin	Thiruvanathapuram
Airport type		Public	PPP	Public
Operator		AAI	CIAL	AAI
Runway		2860 mt.	3400 mt.	3398
Area		375 acres	1300 acres	583 acres
International aircraft movement(nos.)		13806	18537	16656
Passenger movement per annum (nos. in millions)	International	1.83	2.36	1.84
	Domestic	0.23	1.98	0.68
Cargo (international) MT		21964	32198	37795
Total floor space of terminals		200000 sq.ft.	578000 sq.ft.	322000 sq.ft.
Peak hour passenger capacity international + domestic		1000	3200	1600

METHODOLOGY – FUZZY LINGUISTIC APPROACH.

In 1965 Lotfi A. Zadeh published his seminal work "Fuzzy Sets" which described the mathematics of fuzzy set theory, and by extension fuzzy logic. This theory proposed making the membership function (or the values False and True) operate over the range of real numbers [0.0, 1.0]. Since human judgments are often vague and cannot estimate an individual's preference with an exact numerical value, it is more realistic to use linguistic terms to describe the desired value and important weight of criteria. For example 'very low', 'low', 'fair', 'high', 'very high', etc. (Bellman & Zadeh, 1970; Zadeh, 1975). Because of this type of existing fuzziness in the process, fuzzy set theory is an appropriate method for dealing with uncertainty and the subjective evaluation data can be more adequately expressed in linguistic variables (Bellman & Zadeh, 1970*)*. A linguistic variable is defined as a variable, the values of which are words, phrases, or sentences in a given language where such a language can either be natural or artificial (Schmucker, 1983). Each linguistic variable may be assigned one or more linguistic values, which are in turn connected to a numeric value through the mechanism of membership functions.

Fuzzy numbers are a fuzzy sub-set of real numbers, and they present the expansion of the idea of a confidence interval. Fuzzy set theory was developed exactly based on the premise that the key elements in human thinking are not numbers, but linguistic terms or labels of fuzzy sets (Bellman & Zadeh, 1970; Zadeh, 1975). Fuzzy set theory has been applied to solve many decision-making problems. Fuzzy numbers are utilized to denote the approximate reasoning of linguistic (Zadeh, 1975). They are used to convey the subjective evaluation of decision-makers. Tsaur (2002) argued that it is difficult to describe and measure the quality of airline service due to its heterogeneity, intangibility and inseparability. In addition, human judgments are often vague and it is not easy to express the importance of evaluation criteria and the satisfaction of airport service using an exact numerical value. It is more realistic to use linguistic terms to describe the perceptive value and importance of evaluation criteria. Because of this type of existing fuzziness in the evaluation of the quality of airport service, fuzzy set theory is an appropriate method for dealing with uncertainty. The subjective evaluation data can be more adequately expressed in linguistic terms.

In applying a fuzzy linguistic variable approach to the measurement of competitiveness of the three airports in Kerala, this analysis has adopted the methodology of Karwowski & Mital (1986) and Wilhelm & Parsaei (1991). In order to analyse airport's competitiveness, two fuzzy linguistic variables are defined: importance (X) and competitiveness (Y). Where variable X is the importance associated with each of the competitive factors, and the other variable Y is the competitiveness of each airport to represent its potential market power in Kerala.

The general terms, competitiveness and importance, are still imprecise and can be further modified using a linguistic hedge or modifier, which is an operation that modifies the meaning of a term or, more generally, of a fuzzy set (Zimmerman,1991).The concept of linguistic hedges or modifiers is very important and useful for using linguistic variables in fuzzy logic. A hedge acts as a modifier in order to determine the meaning of an arbitrary term of the set using natural language statements such as very, fairly, highly, indeed, more or less, low etc.

The primary values of the two variable X and Y are defined on the universe of discourse [0,1] and the operators' form using a linguistic hedge , can be given new variable values. Suppose $R_{(x)}$ and $R_{(y)}$ are defined as a semantic rule for associating a meaning with each variable name and it is also a fuzzy subset on the universe of discourse for linguistic variable X and Y. Therefore we assume that the primary values of X = importance of variables and new variable values using hedges are as follows:

$R_1(x)$ = {most important (A_1)} = x^4
$R_2(x)$ = {more important (A_2)} = x^2
$R_3(x)$ = {important (A_3)} = x
$R_4(x)$ = {less important (A_4)} = $x^{.5}$
$R_5(x)$ = {unimportant (A_5)} = $1-x$
$R_6(x)$ = {least important (A_6)} = $1-x^2$

The new values of linguistic modified variables are defined such as

$R_1(y)$ = {indeed superior (B_1)} = y^6
$R_2(y)$ = {more superior (B_2)} = y^3
$R_3(y)$ = {superior (B_3)} = $y^{1.5}$
$R_4(y)$ = {average (B_4)} = y
$R_5(y)$ = {inferior (B_5)} = $1-y^{1.5}$
$R_6(y)$ = {more inferior (B_6)} = $1-y^3$
$R_7(y)$ = {most inferior (B_7)} = $1-y^6$

To solve the fuzzy relation of two linguistic variable X and Y, heuristic algorithm methodology is used. In this analysis, the methodology used by Sanchez (1976)for solving the basic linguistic equation is adopted.

$$x_i = r_{ij}\ y_j \qquad \{Eq.\ 1\}$$

where x_i is the value of importance of a competitive factor i,
y_j is the value of competitiveness of an airport j
r_{ij} is a fuzzy relation of factor i and airport j

Since $_{xi} = r_{ij}\ y_j$, we get

$$r_{ij} = x_i^T \oplus y_j \qquad \{Eq.2\}$$

where x_i^T is the transpose of x_i

$\oplus$ is a compositional operator

$$= \begin{Bmatrix} 1 & \text{if} & R_i(x) \leq R_j(y) \\ R_j(y) & \text{if} & R_i(x) > R_j(y) \end{Bmatrix} \qquad \{\text{Eq. } 3\}$$

The intersection of these fuzzy relation r_{ij} for j = 1, 2, 3 are obtained by fuzzy intersection as

$$R_j = \bigcap_i r_{ij} = \underset{i}{\text{Min}}\,(r_{ij}) \qquad \{\text{Eq. } 4\}$$

Hence the competitiveness of each airport $R_{j\,max}(y)$ can be described by a fuzzy relation as a rule of compositional inference. Competitiveness of each airport is then calculated using the fuzzy relation

$$R_{j\,max}(y) = \underset{y}{\text{Max}}\, R_j(y) \qquad \{\text{Eq. } 5\}$$

ANALYSIS

Analysis of Airport Competitiveness using Heuristic Algorithm

Information was collected by interviewing the experts associated with airports through personal interviews. Thirty persons were selected, ten each from three airports, based on their expertise in the area. A comprehensive literature review was conducted to select the factors influencing the airport competitiveness. Nine factors which are considered to be important in determining the competitiveness of the airports were initially selected for preliminary scrutiny. During the course of interviews with the experts, the factors which are relevant in determining the competitiveness of airports in the circumstances prevailing in Kerala were identified and six factors are selected. Out of these six factors, except one, all five factors are analysed using secondary data while the factor related to environmental effects is analysed using primary data which was collected using questionnaire from residents near the airports. The factors are explained below:

- *Airport facilities:* This included both aeronautical and non-aeronautical facilities. Aeronautical facilities include Land facilities, Navigational facility, Passenger facility, number of aircrafts, destination, connectivity to different area, apron service, Cargo, Hangarage, etc.
  Non-aeronautical facilities include commercial activities, gastronomy, leisure services, parking facilities, visitor's facilities, etc.
- *Geographical factors:* This included tropical conditions, terrain, location, catchment area, networks, etc.

- *Accessibility:* This included the availability of various modes of transports to reach the airport and the network to reach various landmarks from the airport.
- *Environment:* Environmental issues affecting the community near the airport, such as air, noise and water pollution are included in this factor.
- *Airport Regional Development:* Potential for banking, leisure and sports complexes, industrial zones, convention centers, etc., are include in the regional development factors.
- *Airport Charges:* Landing and Parking charges, X-ray baggage and rental charges, and passenger charges are included in this factor.

Through the survey, the importance of each of the influencing factors to the airport competitiveness was assessed linguistically by selecting values of the variable X= importance, which is shown in Table 2.

Table 2: Linguistic Assessment of the Importance of Each Factor

Criteria	Factors	Relative Degree of Importance
A_1 = [0.90, 1.00]	Airport Facilities (APF)	1.00
A_2 = [0.80, 0.89]	Airport Geographic Characteristics (AGC)	0.95
A_3 = [0.70, 0.79]	Airport Accessibility (ACS)	0.90
A_4 = [0.60, 0.69]	Environmental Effects (ENV)	0.74
A_5 = [0.50, 0.59]	Airport Regional Development (ARD)	0.65
A_6 = [0.00, 0.49]	Level of Airport Charges (LAC)	0.54

By personal interview with the airport experts, the relative degree of competitiveness of each airport was calculated and then the set of airport competitiveness is assessed by using values of the linguistic variable Y which is the competitiveness. The value related to the competitiveness of each airport is then divided into seven linguistic criteria which are:

B1 = [0.96, 1.00], B2 = [0.91, 0.95],
B3 = [0.86, 0.90], B4 = [0.81, 0.85],
B5 = [0.76, 0.80], B6 = [0.71, 0.75]
B7 = [0.00, 0.70]

where, U is the set of universe of discourse [0, 1]

$$= \{0.0, 0.1, 0.2, 0.3, 0.4, 0.5, 0.6, 0.7, 0.8, 0.9, \text{and } 1.0\}.$$

The linguistic assessment r_{ij} in equation (Eq.2) uses the compatibility functions of fuzzy linguistic variables of value X = importance and Y = competitiveness in respect of each airport and their influencing factor. The intersection R_j of the fuzzy relations associated

Table 3: Linguistic Assessment of the Competitiveness of Each Airport

Factor	Airports		
	Calicut	Cochin	Trivandrum
APF = A_1	B_4	B_1	B_2
AGC = A_1	B_5	B_2	B_3
ACS = A_1	B_4	B_2	B_2
ENV = A_3	B_2	B_3	B_3
ARD = A_4	B_5	B_1	B_4
LAC = A_5	B_2	B_1	B_2

with each airport are computed for the three selected airports on the six influencing factors. The maximum competitiveness of each airport can be calculated as:

Calicut: $R_{1(max)}(y)$ = [0.000 0.001 0.008 0.027 0.064 0.125 0.216 0.343 0.512 0.729 1.000]

Cochin: $R_{2max}(y)$ = [0.000 0.000 0.000 0.001 0.004 0.016 0.047 0.118 0.262 0.531 1.000]

Trivandrum: $R_{3max}(y)$ = [0.000 0.001 0.008 0.027 0.064 0.125 0.216 0.586 1.000 1.000 1.000]

RESULTS

The relative Euclidean distance defines *f(A)* in terms of a metric distance of A from any of the nearest crisp sets. The study adopted the procedure followed by Park, Y (1997) in analysing the competitiveness of Major Airports in Asia using Fuzzy theory. Each airport's competitiveness is measured by applying this distance and the airport having the shortest distance is the most competitive airport compared to the other two international airports in Kerala. The relative Euclidean distance (δ_j) can be defined as:

$$\delta_j = \frac{1}{n}\left[\sum_y \left[R^*(y) - R_{j\,max}(y)\right]^2\right] \quad \text{for } j = 1, 2, 3$$

where n is the number of elements in the universe of discourse

$R^*(y)$ is the ideal compatibility function in terms of the linguistic variable of *indeed superior* for an airport j

$R_{jmax}(y)$ is the maximum compatibility function for the competitiveness of the airport j

The competitiveness of the three international airports in Kerala can be represented in terms of a Euclidean distance, and airport having minimum relative distance from the ideal linguistic assessment of competitiveness is chosen as the most competitive airport.

Table 4: Relative Euclidean Distances for the Three Airports in Kerala

Ranking	Airport	Relative Distance
1	Cochin	0.00
2	Calicut	0.04
3	Trivandrum	0.092

Since the relative distance from the ideal linguistic assessment of competitiveness is minimum for the Cochin International Airport, it is the most competitive airport in Kerala.

CONCLUSIONS

The respondents who are experts in their area of operation assessed the importance of the factors influencing the competitiveness of the airports. The fuzzy linguistic approach employed in the study converted the influencing factors represented by linguistic variables in to competitiveness of finite scale. Basically heuristic algorithms solve really difficult problems reasonably well within a reasonable amount of time. The factor, airport facilities which included both aeronautical and non-aeronautical facilities, ranked first in the analysis of important influencing factor. Next came the geographical facilities closely followed by airport accessibility. Other factors in the order of preference are Environmental Effects, Airport Regional Development and Level of Airport Charges.

The competitiveness of each airport is calculated by the relative Euclidean distance and the most competitive airport in Kerala is found to be the Cochin International airport Limited (CIAL). Incidently, CIAL is the first Greenfield airport in the country under Public Private Participation (PPP) and the result of this study may be considered as a pointer towards the equity structure of future airports in India.

REFERENCES

[1] Airbus Industries, Global Market Forecast (2010-2029), Airbus Industries, Toulouse.

[2] Airport Authority of India Traffic Figures, 2009-2011.

[3] Airport Council International, *Quarterly Bulletin*, Q1 2011.

[4] Bellman, R.E. and Zadeh, L.A. (1970), Decision-making in a Fuzzy Environment, Management Service, 17, 141-164.

[5] Chou, C.C. (2009b), A Model for the Evaluation of Airport Service Quality, Transport 162, 207-213.

[6] Cochin International Airport Limited,(CIAL), Annual Reports.

[7] David Gillen, Ashish Lall (2003), Some Competitive Advantages for Low Cost

Carriers: Implications for Airports, *Journal of air Transport Management*, Vol. 10, No. 1, pp. 41-50.

[8] Garry S. Becker (1965), A Theory of the Allocation of Time – *The Economic Journal*, Vol. 75, No. 299, pp. 493-513, http://www.jstor.org

[9] http://www.aai.aero/misc/trivandrum_airport.pdf

[10] ICAO (2006b), Annexes to Convention on International Civil Aviation – Annex.14. Aerodromes, Montreal, Canada.

[11] IMD World Competitiveness Year Book 2011, App. III.

[12] Karwowski, Mital (1986), Potential Applications of Fuzzy Sets in Industrial Safety Engineering, Fuzzy Sets and Systems, Vol. 19, pp. 105-120.

[13] Kaufmann, A. (1975), Introduction to the Theory of Fuzzy Sets, Vol. 1, Academic Press, New York.

[14] Kerala Economic Review, Govt. of Kerala, 2010.

[15] Park, Y. (1997), Applications of a Fuzzy Linguistic Approach to Analyse Asian Airports Competitiveness, Transportation Planning and Technology, Vol. 20, pp. 291-309.

[16] Park, Y. (2003), An Analysis of Competitive Strength of Asian Major Airports, *Journal of Air Transport Management*, Vol. 9, pp. 353-360.

[17] Porter, M.E. (1980), "Competitive Strategy – Techniques for Analyzing Industries and Competitors", Free press, New York.

[18] Sanchez, E. (1976), Resolution of Composite Fuzzy Relation Equations, Information and Control, Vol. 30, pp. 38-48.

[19] Schmucker (1983), Fuzzy Sets, Natural Language Computations and Risk Analysis, Computer Science Press, Rockville, Maryland.

[20] Senguttavan, P.S. (2011), Indian Airport Competitiveness and its Efficiency, Key Strategy to Develop an Airport Hub, AIRNETH-IFFAD seminar.

[21] Senguttavan, P..S. (2006), Air Cargo: Engine for Economic Growth and Development – A Case Study of Asian Region, METRANS – 2006.

[22] Tsaur, S.H, Chang, T.Y and Yen, C.H. (2002), The Evaluation of Airline Service Quality by Fuzzy MCDM, Tourism Management, 23, 107-115.

[23] Yeh, C.H. and Kuo, Y.L. (2003), Evaluating Passenger Service of Asia-Pacific International Airports, Transportation Research Part E, 39, 35-48.

[24] Zadeh, L.H. (1965), Fuzzy Sets, Information and Control, Vol. 8, pp. 338-353.

[25] Zantke, S. (1976), "Flughafen", ABC des Luftverkehrs, Hamburg, Germany.

[26] Zimmerman, H.J. (1991), Fuzzy Set Theory and its Applications, 2nd Edition, Kluwer Academic, Bost.

Analyzing Consumers Perceptions about the Performance of the State Run Telecom Operator-BSNL by Identifying Parameters of Churn and Retention

Debabrata Datta[1], Susmita Chatterjee[2] and Soumalya Mukhopadhyay[3]

[1] Institute of Management Technology, Ghaziabad
[2] Narula Institute of Technology
[3] Indian Statistical Institute, Kolkata
E-mail: susmita.cb@gmail.com

ABSTRACT

Indian telecom sector has undergone rapid progress since the early 1990s, when the process of privatization began. Advent of mobile telephony brought about a sea change in this industry. However the state run Bharat Sanchar Nigam Limited, which is the corporatized form of the erstwhile Department of telecommunications, finds the going tough in the new competitive scenario. This paper looks at the perception of customers regarding the performance of BSNL in comparison to others and makes statistical and econometric analysis of the data of the survey. Subscriber retention is the utmost necessity for survival for any operator .The subscriber churn and in turn retention depends on various service attributes and also subscriber characteristics. The churn probability is positively related to quality of service and the transparency of the service provider. The link between service attributes and behavioral intentions such as defection and loyalty established through the binary outcome model. The cluster analysis of different service providers with respect to service attributes puts a clear picture of Indian oligopolistic telecom market. The empirical analysis employed for above two purposes.

Keywords: Consumer's Perception, BSNL

INTRODUCTION

The Indian Telecommunications network is the second largest in the world. The sector is growing at a rate of 46-50% during the recent years. This rapid growth is possible due to rapid technological strides and also various positive decisions of the Government. Presently, all the telecom services have been opened for private participation. The process of liberalization in the country began in the right earnest with the announcement of the New Economic Policy in July 1991.Government of India awarded licenses to private operators for providing cellular services in the four metro cities, and a duopoly model of competition was adopted for each service area. Telecom equipment manufacturing was delicensed in 1991 and value added services were declared open to the private sector in 1992, following which radio paging, cellular mobile and other value added services were opened gradually to the private sector. The first National Telecom Policy (NTP 1994) was announced in 1994.The formulation of NTP1994 was followed by the launch of mobile telephony in India in 1995.The prices however were very high both for handsets and services in the initial period. The introduction of NTP 1999 has heralded pro-consumer policies. In the year 1999 the government released the National Telecom Policy in 1999 (NTP 99) in order to help the transition and to encourage faster telecom development, essentially increasing the number of players in each service area.

Department of Telecommunications was corporatized On October 1st, 2000 by the formation of Bharat Sanchar Nigam Limited (BSNL) and transfer of the service providing functions of erstwhile DoT to BSNL. The state run operators BSNL and MTNL, controlled entirely by the government, remain at present the vestiges of public sector presence in the telecom industry in India. BSNL launched its cellular services from Kolkata and Bihar during January 2002. BSNL has played major role in spreading telephones to rural areas of the country at affordable rates.

However the trend of market share since the inception of BSNL shows that BSNL is continuously losing ground. The market share of BSNL and MTNL, the two PSUs, was more than 85 % at the time of formation of BSNL, but this has since declined to less than 37%. As per the latest report, BSNL has been relegated to the fourth position in terms of market share in India's telecom market. The share of BSNL alone has dropped from about 20% in March 2006 to 13.3% in December 2008. Moreover, BSNL has lower average revenue per user (ARPU) than the average subscriber of private sector operators. During the quarter October-December 2008 the blended ARPU of BSNL/ MTNL wireless subscribers was Rs 195 per month as against Rs 225 for private SPs. This figure further plummeted to Rs 131 in 2010-11. This difference is more striking for postpaid subscribers who have a higher ARPU than prepaid subscribers.

Performance of BSNL as a business entity clearly shows that there are disturbing trends in the pattern of business growth and profitability. The state owned telecom enterprise (SOTE) is in vulnerable position on account of the capacity extension, retention of existing customer base, financial statements, though all of these are particularly interrelated. Here, we are trying to examine the problem from demand side. It is needless to say that the customer attraction and retention is the necessary and sufficient for survival of a company.

Analysis of customer retention has received recent attention in both economics and marketing literatures. Rust and Zahorik (1993) and Zeithaml et al. (1996) examine the link between service attributes and behavioural intentions, such as defection and loyalty. Li (1995) and Bhattacharya (1998) empirically analyse this relationship by employing hazard rate models to relate customer characteristics to churn rates. Katz and Aspden (1998) also examine ISP subscriber turbulence in their study of Internet dropouts in the US. Their survey data from 1995 to 1996 have shown that dropouts are younger, poorer, and less well educated than retained users. Further, Cai et al. (1998) use multi-attribute choice experiments to focus on the relationship between customer churn behaviour and the service attributes of Californian electrical utilities. In their study, various levels of service are contrasted with a range of price discounts to test the threshold points at which a loyal customer is induced to switch to a competitor. Probability estimates of churn are calculated using a logit model. Gary Madden, Scott J. Savage, Grant Coble-Neal (1999) analyses the churn probability in Australian ISP market with different service providers. Following these previous works, this study develops a probability model (binary logit) for subscriber churn from the state owned telecom operator BSNL. The binary logit model relates the probability of subscriber churn to different service attributes enabling the churn probability to be calculated. Model estimation is on data obtained from the questionnaire based survey of BSNL service users. The paper is organised as follows. In Section 2 the clustering of different service providers of Indian oligopolistic mobile market is done according to different service attributes. Section 3 describes the state of BSNL. Section 4 outlines the survey method and mobile subscriber profile for respondents. Summary information of data is provided therein. A model of subscriber churn is developed in Section 5, whilst in Section 6, estimation results are reported and also a nonparametric test (sign test) is conducted to get answer about the question of privatisation of the company. Section 7 contains concluding remarks.

THE CLUSTERING OF INDIAN MOBILE SERVICE PROVIDERS

The cluster analysis is done to see how consumers are ranking private players and BSNL with respect to different service parameters. The result showed that the state run operator is far away from leading companies like Airtel and Vodafone and only close to Reliance Telecommunications in terms of efficiency. The diagrammatic representation of the clustering data clearly reveals that BSNL has to improve the network quality and also overall performance. The results are in the appendix.

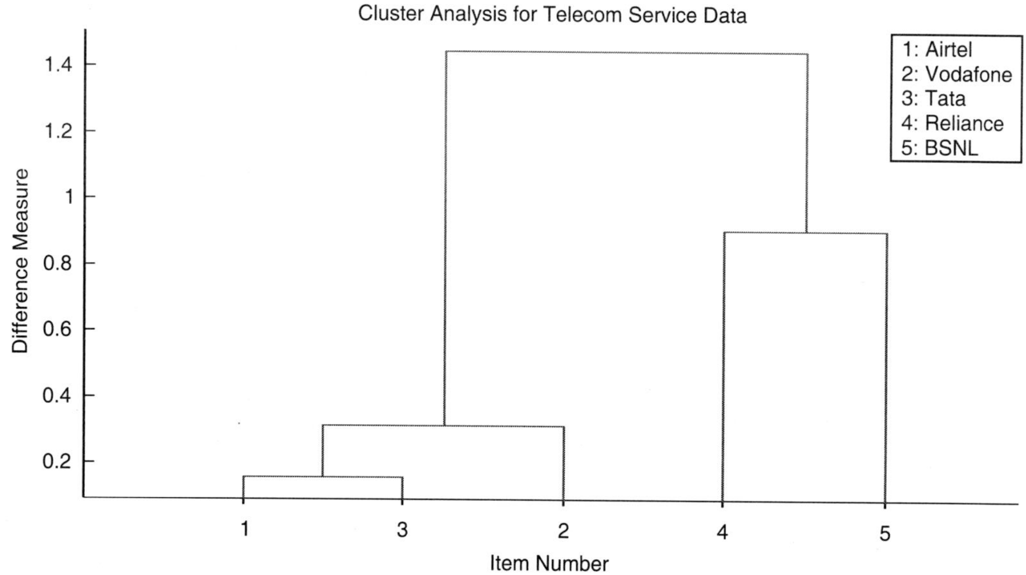

Fig. 1: The Clustering of Different Telecom Service Providers with Respect to Service Attributes

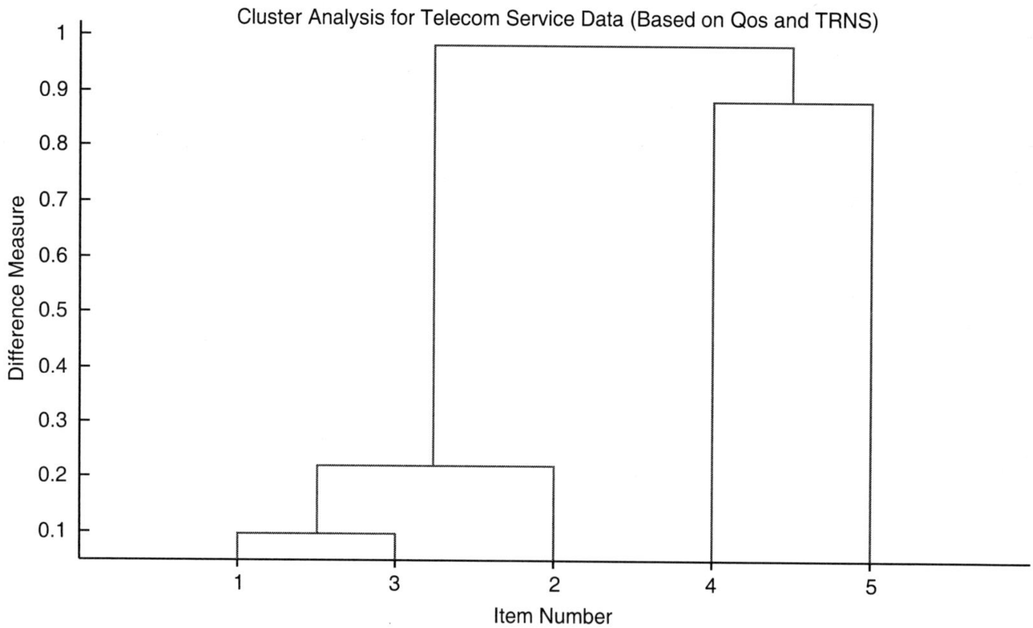

Fig. 2: Clustering of Telecom Service Providers with Respect to Quality of Service (QoS) and Transparency (TRNS)

THE STATE OF BSNL

An account of a comparative study of the market growth of various telecom competitors can exhibit how much the BSNL is lagging behind in terms of total subscribers (mobile +WLL+ Wireline, August 2010).The total telecom market has displayed a YoY growth of 59%. Market players like Airtel, Reliance, Vodafone, Idea and Tata Indicom have managed outstanding upward climb through the market ladder. BSNL, on the contrary, is struggling at a distant bottom. While Idea, Airtel, Reliance, Vodafone and Tata Indicom have achieved 57%, 51%, 48%, 47% and 45% growth rate of subscribers' number respectively, BSNL is limping with a growth rate of 11% only.

Financial State of BSNL

It is observed that the subscription to fixed line telephony of BSNL has actually fallen over the period. Data shows that BSNL's wire line subscribers have dropped from 37.51 million in March 2006 to 29.5 million in December 2008, a decline of about 21%. During the same period, BSNL's wirleline revenue has dropped from Rs 32,355 crore during 2005-06 to Rs 23,716 crore during 2007-08, a decline of about 30%. Although there has been increase in number of subscribers of mobile telephony, this growth in wireless revenue has not been enough to offset the decline in wire line revenue so that overall income from services has declined from Rs 36,139 crore during 2005-06 to Rs 32,360 crore in 2007-08.

BSNL had a leading position in internet and broadband. As of December 2008, BSNL accounted for approximately half of both the 12.85 million internet connections and 5.52 million broadband connections. There was an additional 101 million of wireless internet connections for which the break-up by operators is not available. During the year 2008 the number of internet connections increased by about 20%, the number of broadband connections by about 75%, and the number of wireless internet connections by about 100%. BSNL's income from broadband was about Rs 900 crore during 2008. But it is to be kept in mind that unless service quality and particularly complaint redressal system is streamlined, BSNL will be hard pressed to maintain its position in the internet and broadband as well.

The market share of the BSNL is in decreasing mode. The declining average revenue per user (ARPU) is also evident from the data source.

Customer Base Analysis

Year	ARPU
2008	175
2009	180
2010	131

Source: Telecom position paper (GoI), 2010.

The SOTE is getting the legacy operator advantage for spectrum allocation for third generation technology and wireless broad band services but cannot deploy the new technology which will give revenue spurt due to the lack of network equipment. BSNL has a demand for three crore connections which cannot be accomplished due to the capacity crunch. In this aspect private operators are way ahead. The telecom giant Airtel is providing 25 lakh connections per month with their existing infrastructure. In the south and southwest zone of the BSNL, circle there is huge capacity crunch.

Growth of the Telecom Market: Market Share in % Terms

	Total	Wireline	Wireless
TOTAL MARKET	59	5	94
Bharti Airtel	20.617	8.879	21.063
Reliance	16.496	3.357	17.197
Vodafone Essar	16.107		16.966
BSNL/MTNL	15.749	83.677	12.126
Tata	11.066	3.42	11.474
Idea	1.297		10.846
Aircel	6.357		6.696
Uninor	1.287		1.356
Sistema	.823	0.101	.920
Videocon	0.519		.547
Loopmobie	0.424		.443
Stel	0.215		.227
HFCL	0.160	.508	.141
Etisalat	.006		.007

Source: Telecom Live, October 2010.

Estimate of Financial Status (all figures in Rs. cr)

	FY 07	FY 09	FY14	CAGR(09-14)
Income from services	34616	29190	33856	3%
Other income	5099	5798	5883	0%
Total costs	31466	34432	39001	3%
EBITDA	18178 (46%)	10170 29%)	9747 (25%)	–1%
Profit from core business	3150	–5241	–5145	0%
PBT	8154	592	738	5%

Source: Annual Reports of BSNL, BCG analysis.

The core business of BSNL has nosedived since FY 07. The downward trend is still continuing and the business is all set to continue being unprofitable without top line growth. An analysis of BSNL's business report has shown that the CAGR of its income from several sources is almost negligible. The EBITDA is disappointing with a CAGR of –1% and that sums up the highly slippery and slipshod ground on which BSNL is tight walking.

The above analysis of the performance of BSNL shows that the matter needs serious study. First and foremost requirement right at this moment is to understand the standing of the BSNL in the eyes of the existing and prospective customers. Whatever corrective steps are undertaken, that should be based on sound market survey and research. In view of this growing problem of BSNL there is an urgent necessity of studying the perception of customers regarding BSNL. This argument needs no elaboration that unless people form a good image of BSNL as a quality service provider it is really difficult for BSNL to survive in the highly competitive telecom market. We therefore have undertaken a small survey of customers based in the city of Kolkata regarding their perception of BSNL and tried to obtain customer retention parameters.

SURVEY METHOD AND MOBILE SUBSCRIBER PROFILE

A profile of mobile subscribers of Kolkata mega polis was obtained from a primary survey conducted from February through May 2011. A questionnaire was administered for gaining the opinions of the customers of different service providers. The customers are from different socio economic background and they are getting the service from different service providers including the state owned operator BSNL and other private players –namely Vodafone, Airtel, Tata Tele Services, and Reliance. These consumers are taking various pricing plans. In this paper we are not taking any segmentation according to these plans nor are we making any segmentation on the basis of prepaid and postpaid service. Respondents were asked to supply information on their service provider BSNL regarding different service attributes. Another question asked respondents to indicate whether they intended to change their service provider in the near future and the reason for intended churn and are they in favour of privatisation.During the survey 200 mobile subscribers who are currently using BSNL service, have been interviewed for which 174 valid responses were obtained.

Approximately 40% of the respondents indicated their intention to churn within next few months if they got more lucrative offers from other existing private players and expecting new companies to come up with further more attractive price offerings. Table 1 lists the factors considered important by subscribers in choosing their service provider. Quality of service (QoS) is indicated by the drop rate and connect time, while Call time service (Cats) is measured by signaling and congestion. In office service (Ios) and Complaint handling(Comh) is the help desk support. Transparency (Trn) is the monetary transaction process (Billing service, call rates). Service features are deemed important in the decision of whether subscribers intend to remain with their current service provider. We have also taken Call charge (Chr) as an indicator variable.

Table 1: Factors of Service Features (%)

	Not Important	Reasonably Important	Very Important
Quality of service	0	5	95
Call time service	2	8	90
In office service	5	12	83
Complaint handling	4	20	76
Transparency	3	6	91

The respondents are allowed multiple responses.

Table 2: Ranking of BSNL for Different Attributes (%)

	Low Rank	High Rank	Medium Rank
Quality of service	7	33	60
Call time service	20	75	5
In office service	31	54	15
Complaint handling	20	51	31
Transparency	82	16	2

The respondents are allowed multiple responses.

Table 2 reports the ranking to know the position of BSNL in the consumers' perception and it is viewed that the company is ranked low (60% respondents ranked low) with respect to Quality of service. It is also evident that the company has goodwill enough for the monetary transaction which is reflected through high ranking (82% respondents ranked high) with respect to transparency attribute.

A MODEL OF MOBILE SUBSCRIBER CHURN

The likelihood that a mobile subscriber churns is examined here in the context of discrete choice.

The attributes, such as Qos, Cats, Ios, Comh, Trn, are playing crucial role when deciding on whether to churn or retention. The customers with similar demographic characteristics exhibit similar preferences; demographic profiles can be associated with the probability of making a decision to churn. But here we are taking the focus group with different demographic characteristics and we are concentrating on a particular service provider BSNL. The company's service attributes are related to utility derived and intern to churn probability.

A binomial logit model is used is used to relate the probability of a subscriber leaving BSNL with Network operation and Administrative and marketing variables. A dichotomous (0,1) variable is used to classify subscribers as to whether they intend to churn (CHURN = 0) or unlikely to churn (CHURN = 1) within the next few months. The model is of the form:

$$Y_i = u_{i+1} - u_i$$

$$Y_{i=1} = G(X_i/\beta)$$

Π if ith member does not intend to churn,

$$= 0, \text{ otherwise.}$$

$$p_i\,(Y_{i=1}/X_i) = \Pi_i$$

$$= G(X_i/\beta), \text{ cdf of logistic distribution.}$$

$$\Pi_i^{\wedge} = G(X_i/\beta^{\wedge})$$

Y_i is the binary response

u_i is the systematic part

p is the probability that the subscriber will not churn from BSNL,

X_i is a vector of attributes.

Variables included in the churn model can be grouped into two categories. Network operation variables include Quality of service and Call time service. Administrative and marketing variables encompass Inoffice service, Complaint handling and Transparency. All the catergrical variables are measured on a five point Likert scale, ranging from 'very good' to 'very poor'. The variable Chr is a dummy and binary in nature and described as follows:

Chr = 1, if the consumer (the respondent here) thinks call charge is low in BSNL
= 0, otherwise.

MODEL RESULTS

The binary logit model is used to deal with the issue of how likely an observation is to belong to each group that is churn and unlikely to churn. Thus the model resembles the regression by showing the causal relationship between independent and dependent variable by estimating the probability. The probability of churn from BSNL modelled using the binary logit model in SPSS 17.

Table 3: Maximum Likelihood Estimation Results

Variables in the Equation							
		B	**S.E.**	**Wald**	**df**	**Sig.**	**Exp (B)**
Step 1	Qos	1.203	.284	17.942	1	.000	3.330
	Comh	.306	.380	.649	1	.421	1.358
	Ios	.665	.363	3.351	1	.067	1.944
	Cats	.267	.301	.786	1	.375	1.306
	Trn	.450	.240	3.510	1	.061	1.568
	Chr	–.325	.464	.488	1	.485	.723
	Constant	–8.749	1.466	35.593	1	.000	.000

The parameter estimates reveal that the Network operation variable – Qos is significant at 1% level and transparency is significant at 10% level of significance. The price sensitivity is captured by the variable Call charge (Chr) but according to the econometric analysis it has found insignificant. The constant term is highly significant and the reason might be presence of omitted variables those are not considered in our analysis and this is the limitation of our study.

We have applied sign test to evaluate the mass opinion about the privatization of the telecom operator. An opinion poll taken during the survey asked 200 subscribers to give their opinion about the privatization policy of the government in terms of overall performance of the telecom service providers including BSNL. Results of the survey showed 109 respondents express their confirmation for privatization by rating high the performance of private players. 25 respondents indicated no differences. Now the answer the question arises that – does the survey indicate a significant difference between public and private operators in terms of public opinion about their overall performance?

The answer of the query comes from the use of sign test. We see that n = 200 – 25 = 175 individuals were able to indicate the preference for privatization. By applying the sign test formulae we find that the sampling distribution of the number of plus signs has the following properties:

$$\mu = .50n = .50(175) = 87.5$$
$$\sigma = \sqrt{.25n} = \sqrt{.25(175)} = 6.6$$

In addition with n=175 we can assume that the sampling distribution is approximately normal.

Since the distribution is approximately normal, we used the table of areas for the standard normal probability distribution to develop the rejection rule for the test. With $\alpha = .05$, the rejection rule for this two tailed test is as follows.

$$\text{Reject } H_0 \text{ if } z < -1.96 \text{ or if } z > +1.96$$

Using the number of times the no-privatization policy received the higher rating as the number of plus signs (x = 66), we have the following value of the test statistic.

$$z = x - \mu/\sigma = -3.26$$

So we reject the hypothesis that there is no difference in opinion for privatization at the .05 level of significance. This study suggests that the privatization is perceived to have more public support than state operation in telecommunications.

CONCLUDING REMARKS

As the acquisition of subscribers is expensive, it is important to telecom operator survival that the company should retain current subscriber base. The company must improve the network quality without reluctance and using proper infrastructure. Being public sector and having the benefit of transparency belief of consumers, the company should capitalise this by proper marketing in different segments in an environment of strong price competition. The empirical results provide some focus regarding BSNL subscribers' churn. There is a general industry belief that subscribers are highly price responsive and will churn to gain small discounts but in our analysis we found that quality sensitivity is significant rather than price sensitivity. But here we have considered only one price attribute which is through econometric analysis not at all significant. The results for non-price attributes are enlightening. The most important characteristic, other than prices, is quality of service.

ACKNOWLEDGEMENTS

The authors would like to gratefully acknowledge Prof. Sabyasachi Bhattacarya of Agriculture Research Unit of ISI, for his helpful comments. The authors are also thankful to Research fellows of the unit for their supports in several occasions. The authors are however solely responsible for the paper and the shortcomings, if any. The opinions, findings or conclusions expressed in this paper are those of the authors and do not reflect the views of the named institution or individuals.

REFERENCES

[1] Bhattacharya, C.B., 1998. When customers are members: customer retention in paid membership contexts. *Journal of the Academy of Marketing Science* 26, 31–44.

[2] Cai, Y., Deilami, I. and Train, K., 1998. Customer retention in a competitive power market: Analysis of a 'double-bounded plus follow-ups' questionnaire. *Energy Journal* 19, 191–215.

[3] Gary Madden, Scott J. Savage and Grant Coble-Neal (1999). Subscriber Churn in the Australian ISP market. Communications Economics Research Program, School of Economics and Finance, Curtin University of Technology, *Information Economics and Policy* 11 (1999) 195–207.

[4] Katz, E. and Aspden, P., 1998. Internet Dropouts in the USA. *Telecommunications Policy* 22, 327–339.

[5] Katz, E. and Aspden, P., 1997. Barriers to and Motivations for Using the Internet: Results of a National Opinion Survey. *Research Journal: Policy and Applications* 7, 170–188.

[6] Li, S., 1995. Survival Analysis. *Marketing Research* 7, 17–23.

[7] McFadden, D., 1981. Econometric Models of Probabilistic Choice. In: Manski, C., McFadden, D. (Eds.), *Structural Analysis of Discrete Choice with Econometric Applications*, The MIT Press, Cambridge, pp. 198–272.

[8] Zeithaml, V., Leonard, L. and Parasuraman, A., 1996. The Behavioural Consequences of Service Quality. *Journal of Marketing* 60, 31–46.

APPENDIX

Results of Cluster Analysis

% Mean Calculation %

```
a = mean (Airtel);        v = mean (Vodafone);        t = mean (Tata);
r = mean (Reliance);      b = mean (BSNL);
```

% Data Matrix %

```
data = [a; v; t; r; b]
```

% Result %

```
%X=pdist (data, 'euclidean');
%Y=linkage (X, 'average');
%dendrogram (Y)
%hold on
%xlabel ('Item number')
%ylabel ('Difference Measure')
%title ('Cluster analysis for telecom service data')
```

% Clustering Based on the 2 Most Significant Factors Based on Logistic

% Regression %

```
p4 = data (:, 1);
q4 = data (:, 5);
datanew4 = [p4 q4]
```

% Result %

```
%X4 = pdist (datanew4, 'euclidean');
%Y4 = linkage (X4, 'average');
%dendrogram (Y4)
%hold on
%xlabel('Item number')
%ylabel('Difference Measure')
%title('Cluster analysis for telecom service data (Based on Qos and TRNS')
```

Application of Public-Private Partnerships in Infrastructure Projects

Renuka Vilas Bhoge and Vikram Kumar
School of Planning and Architecture, New Delhi
E-mail: renukabhoge@gmail.com; ar.vikramkumar@gmail.com

ABSTRACT

The urbanization in India is witnessing a growth at an estimated pace of 27.8%. This phenomenal growth in the urban population due to economic activity, particularly in the vicinity of the urban areas is resulting into ever increasing migration from the rural areas. To be "the engine of economic growth" cities need infrastructure services and sustain the same for social and economic growth. All this development is of very ambitious scale and it comes with the price tag. The price tag attached to the infrastructure projects cannot be solely taken by the Indian Government. It is being increasingly recognized in India that lack of good quality infrastructure is a bottleneck that must be removed in order to maintain the growth rate shown by the country in the past two year. To achieve the targeted economic growth, there is an urgent need to increase the level of investments in infrastructure. The innovative solution to this is Public Private Partnership that has been adopted by many other countries also. The projected investment in the Infrastructure projects in the Eleventh Plan is more than twice the investment during the Tenth Plan. As a result, the role of private investment in funding infrastructure projects assumes greater significance in delivering the Eleventh Plan targets.

PPP projects typically involve transfer or lease of public assets, delegation of governmental authority for recovery of user charges, operation and/or control of public utilities/services in a monopolistic environment and sharing of risk and contingent liability by the Government. The terms of the project agreements as well as the bidding process for award of concessions are usually complex because of the nature of risks and involvement of many stakeholders such as project sponsors, lenders, government agencies, users and regulatory authorities.

Keywords: PPP, Infrastructure Projects, Economic Growth

INTRODUCTION

The Department of Economic Affairs (DEA) defines PPPs as:

PPP means an arrangement between a government or statutory entity or government owned entity on one side and a private sector entity on the other, for the provision of public assets and/or related services for public benefit, through investments being made by and/or management undertaken by the private sector entity for a specified time period, where there is a substantial risk sharing with the private sector and the private sector receives performance linked payments that conform (or are benchmarked) to specified, pre-determined and measurable performance standards.

The level of private sector participation in infrastructure can cover a spectrum from short-term service contracts at one end all the way through to full privatisation (disinvestment) at the other. Service contracts and disinvestments are generally not considered as PPPs in India. An infrastructure PPP in India is therefore more than just a short-term contract for services with the private sector but does not go so far as to include complete private sector ownership and control.

PPP MODAL VARIANTS

Public-private partnership's (PPPs) can take a range of types encompassing various roles, ownership arrangements, and allocations of risk between the private and public partners. These different types are called PPP modes. Common examples of different modes are management contracts, lease, build-own-operate (BOO) contracts, and build-operate-transfer (BOT) contracts. In the roads sector, BOT is a common PPP mode, with revenues for the private operator often being from tolls (BOT Tolls contract) or from a fixed annual/semi-annual payment (BOT Annuity contract).

Types of PPP Delivery Models

- Supply/service contracts
- Management contracts
  - *Maintenance management*
  - *Operational management*
- Turnkey projects
- Lease/Affermage
- Concessions types
  - *Franchise*
  - *BOT (Build - Operate - Transfer)*
  - *BTO / BTSM (Build - Transfer - Operate / Build - Transfer - Service - Maintain*
  - *DBO (Design - Build - Operate)*
  - *BOOT (Build - Own - Operate - Transfer)*
  - *BROT (Build - Rehabilitate - Operate - Transfer)*

  - *LROT (Lease - Renovate - Operate - Transfer)*
- Private ownership of assets
- Build-Own-Operate type of arrangement
  - *Private Finance Initiative (a more recent innovation)*
  - *DBFO (Design - Build - Finance - Operate)*
  - *DCMF (Design - Construct - Manage - Finance)*
  - *DBFOM (Design - Build - Finance - Operate - Maintain)*
- Divestiture by license or sale
- Joint Ventures

What is PPP in Infrastructure?

Physical infrastructure, such as roads, water and sanitation networks, and transportation systems, involve large investments that can put a strain on the public purse. This strain is especially great for countries, such as India, whose economies are undergoing rapid development and urbanisation and have a great need for expanded infrastructure.

Public-private partnerships (PPPs) are increasingly being used by governments and public sector authorities throughout the world as a way of increasing access to infrastructure services for their citizenry and economies at a reduced cost.

The Objectives of a PPP in Infrastructure are to:

- Increase the availability of infrastructure services
- To do so with greater efficiency (lower cost for the level of services provided) than could be achieved using the traditional public sector approach

PPPs Make this Possible because:

- PPPs allow access to the substantial financial resources of the private sector
- PPPs enable the public sector to benefit from private sector technical expertise, experience and efficiency
- PPPs enable the public sector to transfer project-related risks to the private sector

A PPP Typically has the following Characteristics:

- The private sector is responsible for carrying out or operating the project and takes on a substantial portion of the associated project risks
- During the operational life of the project the public sector's role is to monitor the performance of the private partner and enforce the terms of the contract
- The private sector's costs may be recovered in whole or in part from charges related to the use of the services provided by the project, and may be recovered through payments from the public sector

- Public sector payments are based on performance standards set out in the contract
- Often the private sector will contribute the majority of the project's capital costs, although this is not always the case

It will often be necessary to build or add to existing assets in order to meet the infrastructure needs of the economy and users. However, an important part of the infrastructure PPP concept is that:

- A PPP is focused on outputs, and
- The outputs of the PPP are infrastructure *services*, not infrastructure *assets*.

The reason for the focus on outputs and services rather than assets is to encourage efficient use of public resources and improved infrastructure quality.

A PPP brings the public and private sectors together as partners in a contractual agreement, for a pre-defined period (eg. 30 years) matched to the life of the infrastructure assets used to provide the services. The private partners (investors, contractors and operators) provide specified infrastructure services and, in return, the public sector either pays for those services or grants the private partner the right to generate revenue from the project. For example, the private partner may be allowed to charge user fees or receive revenue from other aspects of the project.

The best PPPs will have the public and private partners working together to build and sustain a long-term relationship that is of benefit to all.

PPP in Management of Infrastructure Services

Since, infrastructure services (especially; water supply, sewerage, sanitation, waste disposal, street lighting etc.) have interrelated interest in terms of energy demand and management of service delivery; it is desirable to consider these services under one organizational framework. Therefore proposed PPP model addresses energy, financial and managerial issues across the boundaries of individual infrastructure services as a system.

PPP in Sewerage System

Pollution caused by sewage discharged from cities and towns is the primary cause for degradation of our water resources. A solution to this problem not only requires bridging the ever widening gap between sewage generation and treatment capacity (generation being 29000 million litre per day against the existing treatment capacity of 6000 million litre per reduction by a factor of almost 5) but also calls for development of facilities to divert the treated sewage for use in irrigation to prevent nutrient pollution of water bodies, utilize the nutrient value of sewage in irrigation and bring down fresh water use in irrigation.

The State Governments have failed to recognize its importance during the last 30years. It is a matter of grave concern that due attention is not paid to operation and maintenance of existing sewage treatment facilities by State Governments and , as a result,45 of the 115 sewage treatment plants studied recently by Central Pollution Control Board failed to achieve the standards.

Sewerage in the Indian Perspective

Although the annual estimated precipitation, including snowfall, in India is 4000 billion cubic metres (bcm) but the total water resources available for utilization, including ground water, is only about 1122 bcm. With the increasing population as well as all round development in the country, the competing demand for water for irrigation, domestic use and power generation sectors are exerting enormous pressure on our water resources as utilization of water has also been consequently increasing at a fast pace.

Since 1951, the actual utilization of groundwater has increased from10% to 53.2 % (230 bcm), respectively, of the utilizable potential. The precarious balance between growing demands and supplies brings forth the importance of recycling and reuse of water so that same water can be used for multiple uses one after the other thereby reducing demand for fresh supplies.

Disposal of about 29000 MLD domestic sewage from cities and towns is the biggest source of pollution of water bodies in India. A large number of rivers stretches are severely polluted as a result of discharge of domestic sewage. Treatment of domestic sewage and subsequent utilization of treated sewage for irrigation can prevent pollution of water bodies, reduce the demand for fresh water in irrigation sector and result in huge savings in terms of nutritional value of sewage in irrigation.

Waste Water Reuse

The main opportunities for reuse of treated wastewater in and around the city are considered to be irrigation and horticulture. There is also some demand for use as cooling water in the power stations. Other options include groundwater recharge, return to the raw water source, and the treatment and reuse of sullage water, i.e. water that does not contain human excreta, for flushing toilets, etc.

Presently DJB supplies about 138 MGD of treated wastewater to the Irrigation Deptt. This is discharged directly to the irrigation channels from the sewage treatment plants.

A number of small effluent reuse projects are in the planning or implementation stages. They comprise horticultural, irrigation and industrial uses, and will use up to 46 MGD (210 MLD).

DDA is responsible for 4,451 hectare of open spaces, all of which are irrigated via tube wells. There is also irrigation of MCD open spaces, central government properties, private parks and properties, road verges, sports stadiums, etc.

CASE STUDY: ALANDUR SEWERAGE PROJECT

General

This case study describes an example of good governance by using alternative institutional arrangements to finance a Sewerage project. The location is Alandur, classified as an adjacent urban area by the Chennai Metropolitan Development Authority (CMDA). Alandur is the first municipality in the country where initiative has been taken to finance, develop and implement core urban infrastructure projects on a commercially viable basis by using the *public-private partnership* as a model.

The initiative will certainly improve the living conditions, as also the social and economic life of the residents of the town.

The Background

Tamil Nadu is one of the most urbanized states in the country as more than one-third of its population (roughly 34%) lives in the urban areas and provision of water supply and sewerage is the shared responsibility of the state utility and the local body.

About the Municipal Agencies of Tamil Nadu

Tamil Nadu Water Supply and Drainage Board (TWSADB) implements, whereas the local body maintains and collects water and sewerage tax/ charges. But In case of Chennai, Chennai Metropolitan Water Supply and Sewerage Board (CMWSSB)" is responsible for provision and Maintenance of water and sewerage services and also collects taxes and charges in the metropolitan area of Chennai including Alandur.

Interestingly only one- fifth ($1/5^{th}$) of the state's total urban population is being served by the sewerage system. Considering the acute problem of proper sanitation the Tamil Nadu Urban Infrastructure Financial Services Limited (TNUIFSL), the state asset management company was nominated as the principal agency to coordinate the investigation and detailed studies, and to structure the finance for the projects.

Location

Alandur municipality (AM) is a selection grade municipality, which falls under the geographical boundaries of Kanchipuram district of Tamil Nadu state. It is located adjacent to Chennai, which is at a distance of 14 km on the southern side and forms apart of the Chennai Metropolitan Area (CMDA).

Table 1: The Basic Information on Alandur

Sl. No.	Particulars	Details
1.	**Area:**	19.5 sq. km
2.	**Population:** 1991 Census 2000 Estimated 2027 Estimated	1,25,444 1,65,000 3,00,000
3.	Households	19800
4.	**Existing water supply:** Source Quantity supplied	 Palar River 4.5 millions liters per
5.	Per capita supply	33 liters per capita per day (lpcd)
6.	**Proposed water supply:** Source Quantity to be supplied Per capita	 Krishna River supplied 30 mlpd 100 lpcd
7.	**Sewerage at present**	No sewerage system at present. Waste disposal in open storm` drain 60 kms length
8.	**Length of roads**	135 km
9.	Revenue expenditure: approx.	Rs. 369 lakh

Source: Alandur Municipality.

Sewerage System before Implementation of Project

Alandur municipality initiated the Alandur Sewerage Project (ASP) that presents a unique case in the area of public private partnership in the urban sanitation sector and placed underground drainage system in Alandur municipality with a view to improve the living conditions of its residents. Currently, the towns either have septic tanks or holding tanks and the municipality collects the sewage periodically in the tankers and disposes

Table 2: Cost of the Work

Sl. No.	Work Component	Cost in Rs.(lakh)
1	Sewer lines	1860.79
2	Pumping station	244.90
3	Pumping main	594.31
4	House service connections	225.00
5	**Base cost**	**2925.00**
6	Physical contingency (5%)	146.25
7	Price contingency (10%)	304.12
8	**Capital cost**	**3375.37**

them in the low-lying areas outside the municipal limits. The sullage and sewage overflow from septic tanks from the households is presently let into the open storm water drains, which finally accumulate as stagnant water in the south-eastern corner of the town, creating a breeding ground for mosquitoes and diseases. This has increased the health risks in the town, and has also affected the ground watercourses. Thus for improving the prevailing sanitary conditions in the town.

Table 3: Sources of Finance

Sl. No.	Sources of Finance Amount in Rs Lakh	Amount	% to Total
1	**Loan** :TUFIDO TNUIFSL	1620.00 420.00	46.82 12.13
2	TUFIDO for supervision	100.00	2.89
3	GOT to bridge the gap	320.00	9.24
	Deposit collection from public	800.00	23.12
	Interest from deposits	200.00	5.78
	TOTAL	**3460**	**100**

Project Details

- GOT also agreed to pay a maximum amount of Rs 30 per month/sewer connection in order to balance the revenue account budget of sewerage.
- Area of the land = .5 hectares
- Cost of the land works out to be approximately Rs. 25 lakh at current price.
- Income from connections Rs. 1300 lakh.

MANAGEMENT OF PROJECT RISKS AND SECURITY MECHANISMS

Lenders

- In case of Alandur project, however, proper care has been taken for the risk of cost escalation, cost overrun and time delays
- Necessary clearance for the project works has been taken in advance from different agencies
- A security net was provided in the terms and conditions of loan agreement and the BOT contract.
- TUFIDCO and TNUDF had stipulated that the entire revenue receipts including grants from the state government and collections on account of taxes, duties and user charges should be escrowed in favour of them in order to ensure timely repayment of loans by separate ESCROW account.

SUMMARY

Integrated WTP, STP, and solid waste to power generation plant is an integrated project which will be on BOT basis of concession period calculated on the basis of cash flow statement illustrated in detail in financial analysis. This concession period is worked out around 20 years of period in which private consortium will be managing all the services water, solid waste, sewage and street lighting as per the terms and clauses of agreement.

After completion of this period the services and the complex will be transferred to concerned authority or the period will be extended as per the condition at that time. Integrated processing complex will handed over in similar situation as if now well operational condition. During this period any tariff related to these will be directly collected by concessnaire at the predefined rates.

PPP in Urban Transport

Public transport is the primary mode of transport in the bigger cities and metros. City bus transport is the most common and predominant form of public transport in cities with population greater than 1 million. Since the beginning of 2000, there has been a good rise in the implementation of the concept of PPPs among urban transport undertakings.

PPP in Bus Terminus

Bus terminal PPP's involve the development of real estate along with the construction of bus terminals. Typically, development of bus depots or terminals is based on Build-operate-Transfer (BOT) projects, which involve development of real estate at the site on a commercial basis. The private operator develops the commercial facility and leases out the premises to earn revenues. In addition, the private operator also operates and maintains the bus terminals, earning revenue from the bus terminal. It was observed that bus terminals primarily earn revenue from:

1. Income from "Adda" fees for the parking of private and inter-state buses.
2. Annual lease of parking spaces outside terminal.
3. Revenues from the lease of shops.
4. Advertisement rights.

Typically, bus depots, which host intra-city buses, will not earn revenues from adda fees and advertisement rights as a depot is used to maintain buses and park them during non-operational hours. The scope for earning revenue by the private operator is less in this case.

CASH FLOW FOR STP			Line Losses	0%	Per day	217.92													
			Per day	217.92	ML				Total Saleable Units		79,541	ML	1unit = 1KL						
				79540.8	ML per year				Inflation		3%								
			Rate	0.01	L				Levelised Tariff		0.01	Rs. /L							
			Revenue	795.408	MR				Analysis Period		20	Years							
		79540800	10	79.5408					Equity return										
(Rupees in Million)									Interest on LT		10%								
Particulars	**Var Price**	**Unit**	**Year 0**	**Year 1**	**Year 2**	**Year 3**	**Year 4**	**Year 5**	**Year 6**	**Year 7**	**Year 8**	**Year 9**	**Year 10**	**Year 11**	**Year 12**	**Year 13**	**Year 14**	**Year 15**	**Year 16**
pumping station			200.00																
sewer mains			1,000.00																
STP			800.00																
IDC			270.66																
Finance charges (.5% of the debt.)			11.77																
Collection			1,000.00																
X			0.00																
Contingencies (3%)			80.02																
Total Capital Cost		**3,362.45**	**3,362.45**	**0.00**	**0.00**	**0.00**	**0.00**	**0.00**	**0.00**	**0.00**	**0.00**	**0.00**	**0.00**	**0.00**	**0.00**	**0.00**	**0.00**	**0.00**	**0.00**
Equity	0.30	**1,008.74**	1,008.74	0.00	0.00	0.00	0.00	0.00	0.00	0.00	0.00	0.00	0.00	0.00	0.00	0.00	0.00	0.00	0.00
Debt	0.70	**2,353.72**	2,353.72	0.00	0.00	0.00	0.00	0.00	0.00	0.00	0.00	0.00	0.00	0.00	0.00	0.00	0.00	0.00	0.00
Particulars	**Var Price**	**Unit**	**Year 0**	**Year 1**	**Year 2**	**Year 3**	**Year 4**	**Year 5**	**Year 6**	**Year 7**	**Year 8**	**Year 9**	**Year 10**	**Year 11**	**Year 12**	**Year 13**	**Year 14**	**Year 15**	**Year 16**
Sales	0.01	79,540.80			795.41	795.41	795.41	795.41	795.41	795.41	795.41	795.41	795.41	795.41	795.41	795.41	795.41	795.41	795.41
STP Plant	in Crore																		
O&M cost	13.44	10,000,000.00			134.40	138.43	142.58	146.86	151.27	155.81	160.48	165.30	170.25	175.36	180.62	186.04	191.62	197.37	203.29
Electricity	9.60	10,000,000.00			96.00	98.88	101.85	104.90	108.05	111.29	114.63	118.07	121.61	125.26	129.02	132.89	136.87	140.98	145.21
lease rent	0.20				20.00	20.60	21.22	21.85	22.51	23.19	23.88	24.60	25.34	26.10	26.88	27.68	28.52	29.37	30.25
Total Variable Cost					**250.40**	**257.91**	**265.65**	**273.62**	**281.83**	**290.28**	**298.99**	**307.96**	**317.20**	**326.72**	**336.52**	**346.61**	**357.01**	**367.72**	**378.75**
Contribution					**545.01**	**537.50**	**529.76**	**521.79**	**513.58**	**505.13**	**496.42**	**487.45**	**478.21**	**468.69**	**458.89**	**448.80**	**438.40**	**427.69**	**416.66**
Annual Debt Service					284.80	284.80	284.80	284.80	284.80	284.80	284.80	284.80	284.80	284.80	0.00	0.00	0.00	0.00	0.00
Interest on Loan					270.56	242.08	213.60	185.12	156.64	128.16	99.68	71.20	42.72	14.24	0.00				
Interest on WK					17.12	17.63	18.16	18.70	19.27	19.84	20.44	21.05	21.68	22.33	23.00	23.69	24.40	25.14	25.89
Net Cashflow from the operation					**-27.47**	**-7.01**	**13.20**	**33.17**	**52.88**	**72.32**	**91.50**	**110.40**	**129.01**	**147.32**	**435.89**	**425.10**	**413.99**	**402.55**	**390.76**
Capital Employed			-1,008.74	0.00	0.00	0.00	0.00	0.00	0.00	0.00	0.00	0.00	0.00	0.00	0.00	0.00	0.00	0.00	0.00
NCF available for Equity			**-1,008.74**	**0.00**	**-27.47**	**-7.01**	**13.20**	**33.17**	**52.88**	**72.32**	**91.50**	**110.40**	**129.01**	**147.32**	**435.89**	**425.10**	**413.99**	**402.55**	**390.76**
Internal Rate of Return			**10.67%**																
NPV			-1,008.74	0.00	-27.47	-7.01	13.20	33.17	52.88	72.32	91.50	110.40	129.01	147.32	435.89	425.10	413.99	402.55	390.76

Year 17	Year 18	Year 19	Year 20	Year 21	Year 22	Year 23	Year 24	Year 25
0.00	**0.00**	**0.00**	**0.00**	**0.00**	**0.00**	**0.00**	**0.00**	**0.00**
0.00	0.00	0.00	0.00	0.00	0.00	0.00	0.00	0.00
0.00	0.00	0.00	0.00	0.00	0.00	0.00	0.00	0.00

Year 17	Year 18	Year 19	Year 20	Year 21	Year 22	Year 23	Year 24	Year 25
795.41	795.41	795.41	795.41	795.41	0.00	0.00	0.00	0.00
209.39	215.67	222.14	228.81	235.67	0.00	0.00	0.00	0.00
149.56	154.05	158.67	163.43	168.34	0.00	0.00	0.00	0.00
31.16	32.09	33.06	34.05	35.07				
390.12	**401.82**	**413.87**	**426.29**	**439.08**	**0.00**	**0.00**	**0.00**	**0.00**
405.29	**393.59**	**381.53**	**369.12**	**356.33**	**0.00**	**0.00**	**0.00**	**0.00**
0.00	0.00	0.00	0.00	0.00	0.00	0.00	0.00	
26.67	27.47	28.29	29.14	30.01	30.91	31.84		
378.63	**366.12**	**353.24**	**339.98**	**326.32**	**-30.91**	**-31.84**	**0.00**	**0.00**
0.00	0.00	0.00	0.00	0.00	0.00	0.00	0.00	0.00
378.63	**366.12**	**353.24**	**339.98**	**326.32**	**-30.91**	**-31.84**	**0.00**	**0.00**
378.63	366.12	353.24	339.98	326.32	-30.91	-31.84	0.00	

Thus, the development of bus depots on a PPP basis would involve construction and transfer of the bus depot from the private operator to the transport authority on a turnkey basis. The commercial facility would continue to be operated by the private operator to help him in recouping the capital expenditure he has incurred in the project.

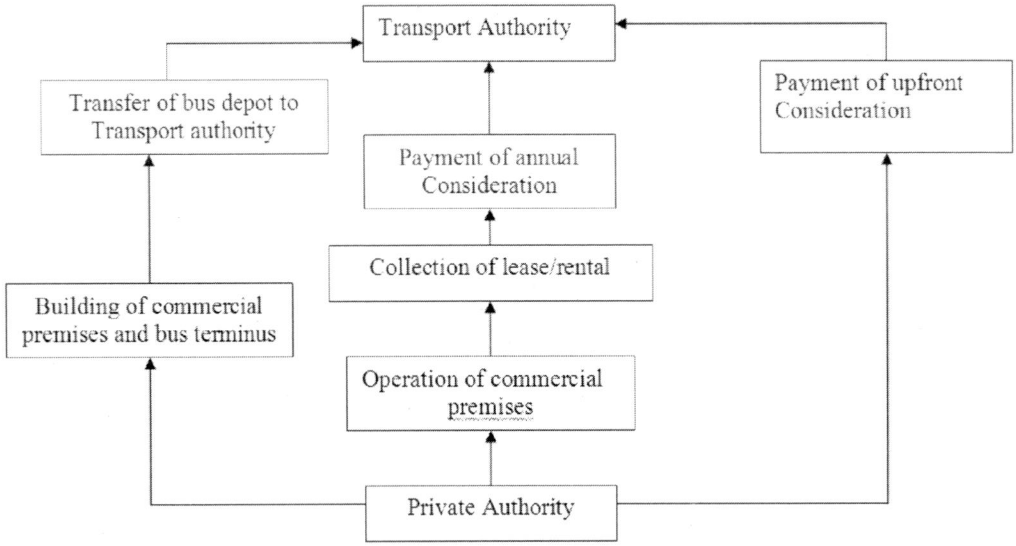

Fig. 1: PPP in Bus Terminus

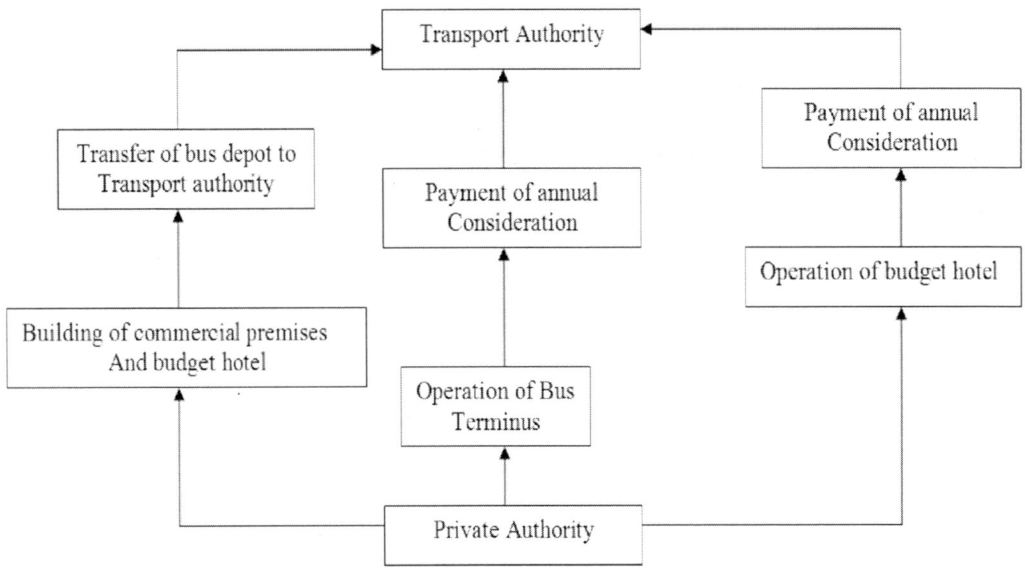

Fig. 2: PPP in Bus Terminus

As per the figure above, the private operator would construct the commercial and bus depot facility.

The private operator is chosen through bidding in the following ways:

1. Payment of the highest upfront payment for the land: In this case the upfront payment for the land will be fixed and the annuity payments on revenues will also be fixed.
2. Lowest duration of concession period: In this case the concession period and annuity payments based on revenues will also be fixed.

Transport Authority

- There will be a clear demarcation for the space for the commercial complex and the bus depot.
- It will also lay down specifications of the bus depot.
- It would transfer the development rights to the private operator once upfront payment is remitted and a performance guarantee is submitted.
- An independent engineer constituted and appointed by Transport authority would monitor the construction of the bus depot.

Private Operator

- The private operator would submit a detailed project report (DPR) to transport authority for approval, detailing his plans for development of the project.
- The private operator will develop the bus depot as per the specifications given by transport authority and hand over the bus depot to the transport authority.
- The private operator will construct, design, operate and maintain the commercial facility and collect the revenues that would accrue from the venture.
- The private operator would pay the transport authority either in terms of a share in revenues or fixed annuity.

Table 4: Responsibility Sharing between the Bus Transport Authority and the Private Entity

Activity	Govt. Body	Private Operator
Demarcation of bus terminus and commercial space	√	
Physical specification of the bus terminus	√	
Transfer of lease right to private operator	√	√
Preparation of detailed project report		√
Capital expenditure (construction of bus terminus and commercial facility)		
Operation and maintenance of bus terminus	√	
Operation and maintenance of commercial facility		√
Collection of revenue		√

- At the end of the concession period, the contractor would transfer back the commercial premises to transport authority as per the terms and conditions of the agreement.

Preparatory Work by Transport Authority

1. Provision of a clear demarcation of the commercial and bus terminus space.
2. Preparation of physical specifications of the bus depot along with related activities of the bus terminus like fuelling station, rest rooms, administrative offices and maintenance sheds.
3. Schedule for the implementation of the bus terminus.

Table 5: Key Risks of the Private Developer and Transport Authority

Activity	Private Operator	Transport Authority	Comments
Commissioning Risk			
Procurement of buses for the commencement of operations		Yes	The buses will have to be procured as per the bus delivery schedule by the bus transport authority or ULB
Demand (usage) Risk			
Demand for buses is not adequate	Yes		The private operator collects the revenues and hence the demand risk is transferred to the private operator.
Performance Risk			
Adherence to the service quality and performance parameters	Yes		The private operator is required to adhere to the service and performance quality standard failing which he would be required to pay fines/penalties.
Financial Risk			
Cost for procurement of buses	Yes	Yes	The bus transport authority or ULB will receive from the private operator the money it has contributed to procurement of buses and therefore the risk of cost of procurement of buses is shared.
Collection of fares	Yes		The private operator is responsible for the collection of fares through its mechanisms.
Force Majeure Risk			
Force Majeure Risk	Yes	Yes	Each party is to bear their individual cost pertaining to their respective assets.
Operating Risk			
Provision of operation and maintenance of the buses	Yes		The private operator operates and maintains the buses. The bus transport authority or ULB would periodically inspect buses and would levy fines if buses do not meet specifications.
Labour	Yes		The private operator will arrange for the driver of the bus and other personnel for O & M and administration of the system.

4. List of allowed commercial activities.
5. Preliminary demand assessment and financial feasibility of running of a commercial facility at the project site.

Asset Ownership

The ownership of both the bus depot and commercial facility resides with the transport authority at all times and the transport authority shall only enter into a lease agreement with the private operator for the development of the commercial facility and bus depot. Upon the termination of the contract, the commercial facility would be transferred to transport authority.

Amritsar Bus Terminus Complex

The Intercity Bus Terminal of Amritsar city was developed at the same location as the existing bus terminal. The project involved demolishing the existing terminal building and complex and development of a modern state-of-the-art Intercity Bus Terminal to cater to the growing demands of the city. The project is under operation by a private operator for a period of 11 years and 5 months, which includes the construction period. At the end of the concession period, the project will transfer back to the concessioning authority free of all encumbrances.

PPP Structure of the Project

Through a two stage bidding process, DoT, GoP awarded the contract to Rohan Rajdeep Infrastructure (a partnership between Rohan Builders (India) Pvt Ltd, Rajdeep Buildcon Pvt Ltd and Rajdeep Road Developers Pvt Ltd) to undertake the development and operation of a modern bus terminal at Amritsar on a BOT basis.

Subsequent to signing of the concession agreement, the private operator established a Special Purpose Vehicle (SPV) called the Rohan Rajdeep Infrastructure (India) Pvt Ltd. for executing the project. Under the concession agreement, the private operator was responsible for finance, building, operations and maintenance of the Amritsar Intercity Bus Terminal complex for a concession period of 11 years and 5 months. The private operator was required to pay a project development fee of 35 lakhs for the project site lease and a lease rental of 50,000 per month for use of the project site over the concession period.

Within the concession agreement, two potential revenue streams for the private operator were identified. The first revenue stream was through the operations of the bus terminal. The operator had the right to collect from bus operators what was termed as "adda fees" which was the charge payable by buses for use of the terminal facilities. The

AMRITSAR BUS TERMINUS COMPLEX	
land acquisition charges	Rs. 30 lakh
clearance charges	Rs. 35 lakh
cost of construction of bus terminus building	Rs. 1974 lakh
lease rental is to be given to the government @ Rs. 50000 per month	Rs. 6 lakh per year
debt part	Rs. 1200 lakh
equity part	Rs. 900 lakh
adda fees	at the rate of Rs. 100 per bus assuming 2000 buses per day
sub lease of parking area	at the rate of Rs. 50 per bus assuming 200 buses per day
annual lease of shops	at the rate of Rs. 2500 per shop for 50 shops in the premises
advertisement rights	at the rate of Rs. 800/sqm for 100 sqm of advertisement area
IRR	

CASH OUT																											
particulars		unit	year 0	year 0.5	year 1	year 1.5	year 2	year 2.5	year 3	year 3.5	year 4	year 4.5	year 5	year 5.5	year 6	year 6.5	year 7	year 7.5	year 8	year 8.5	year 9	year 9.5	year 10	year 10.5	year 11	year 11.5	TOTAL
land acquisition		lakh	30																								30
clearances		lakh	35																								35
construction of workshops		lakh	0																								0
construction of BUS TERMINUS		lakh	1,974																								1,974
lease rental @ 50000 per month				3	3	3	3	3	3	3	3	3	3	3	3	3	3	3	3	3	3	3	3	3	3	3	69
contingencies (3%)		lakh	61.17																								61.17
O&M				0.5	0.5	0.5	0.5	0.5	0.5	0.5	0.5	0.5	0.5	0.5	0.5	0.5	0.5	0.5	0.5	0.5	0.5	0.5	0.5	0.5	0.5	0.5	11.5
Total Capital Cost	2,100.17																										
Equity	900.17																										
Debt	1,200.00																										
Repayment of Loan		lakh		90.12	90.12	90.12	90.12	90.12	90.12	90.12	90.12	90.12	90.12	90.12	90.12	90.12	90.12	90.12	90.12	90.12	90.12	90.12	90.12	90.12	90.12	90.12	2072.76
TOTAL CASHOUT			2,100.17	93.62	93.62	93.62	93.62	93.62	93.62	93.62	93.62	93.62	93.62	93.62	93.62	93.62	93.62	93.62	93.62	93.62	93.62	93.62	93.62	93.62	93.62	93.62	
Present value of cash out	2,665.29																										4253.43
CASH IN																											
particulars		unit	year 0	year 0.5	year 1	year 1.5	year 2	year 2.5	year 3	year 3.5	year 4	year 4.5	year 5	year 5.5	year 6	year 6.5	year 7	year 7.5	year 8	year 8.5	year 9	year 9.5	year 10	year 10.5	year 11	year 11.5	TOTAL
revenue from bus terminus		lakh																									
adda fees		lakh		350	327	381.5	356.43	356.43	388.51	388.51	423.47	423.47	461.59	461.59	503.13	503.13	548.41	548.41	597.77	597.77	651.57	651.57	710.21	710.21	774.13	774.13	11888.9
sub-lease of parking areas		lakh		15	16.35	16.35	17.82	17.82	19.43	19.43	21.17	21.17	23.08	23.08	25.16	25.16	27.42	27.42	29.89	29.89	32.58	32.58	35.51	35.51	38.71	38.71	589.24
annual lease of shops		lakh		7.5	8.18	8.18	8.91	8.91	9.71	9.71	10.59	10.59	11.54	11.54	12.58	12.58	13.71	13.71	14.94	14.94	16.29	16.29	17.76	17.76	19.35	19.35	294.62
advertisement rights		lakh		5	5.45	5.45	5.94	5.94	6.48	6.48	7.06	7.06	7.69	7.69	8.39	8.39	9.14	9.14	9.96	9.96	10.86	10.86	11.84	11.84	12.9	12.9	196.42
TOTAL CASHIN				377.5	356.98	411.48	389.1	389.1	424.13	424.13	462.29	462.29	503.9	503.9	549.26	549.26	598.68	598.68	652.56	652.56	711.3	711.3	775.32	775.32	845.09	845.09	
present value of CASHIN	4,263.02																										
CASHIN-CASHOUT			-2,100.17	283.88	263.36	317.86	295.48	295.48	330.51	330.51	368.67	368.67	410.28	410.28	455.64	455.64	505.06	505.06	558.94	558.94	617.68	617.68	681.7	681.7	751.47	751.47	
CUMULATIVE CASH FLOW			-2,100.17	-1,816.29	-1,552.93	-1,235.07	-939.59	-644.11	-313.60	16.91	385.58	754.25	1,164.53	1,574.81	2,030.45	2,486.09	2,991.15	3,496.21	4,055.15	4,614.09	5,231.77	5,849.45	6,531.15	7,212.85	7,964.32	8,715.79	
TOTAL PROFIT IN PRESENT VALUE	1,597.74																										
NPV																											
																											12969.2
IRR		0.16																									

Fig. 3: Cash Flow for Amritsar Bus Terminus Complex

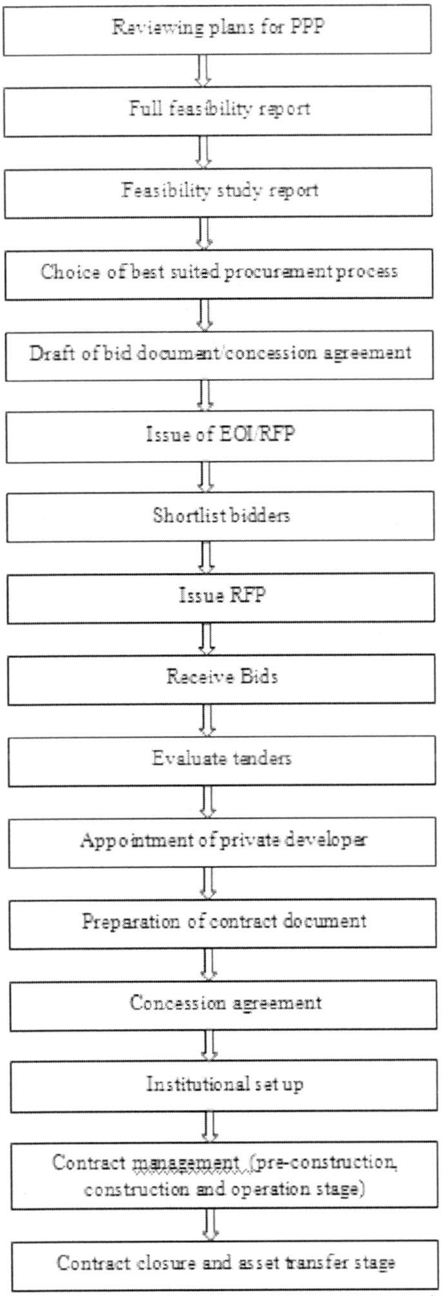

Fig. 4: PPP Procedure for Bus Terminus Project

second source of revenue was commercial rentals from shops located within the Intercity Bus Terminal complex. Other sources of revenue included the sale of advertising rights as well as parking fees.

Financing Information

The project cost for the Amritsar Intercity Bus Terminal was expected to be approximately 19 crores at the time of project conception. But on account of an escalation in input costs during the construction period and quality assurances maintained by the private operator, the project cost finally worked out to 21.34 crores. Of this amount, the debt component was 12 crores while the equity component was 9.34 crores.

PPP in Airport

To sustain the present and future requirements, the country requires additional funds to the tune of Rs. 40,000 crores (modernization + Greenfield + non metro airports) + Rs. 454 crores for airports in North East are required. The revenue surplus generated by AAI in 2005-06 was Rs. 812 crores. Clearly the deficit in funds can only be met through Public sector Participation.

Introduction

The civil aviation traffic has seen an unprecedented traffic in the past few years on account of booming Indian economy, growing tourism industry, entry of low cost carriers in the private sector, liberalization of international bi-lateral agreements and liberalization of civil aviation policy. In future also the civil aviation traffic is expected to grow at the same pace

Table 6: Infrastructure Requirements and Investment Proposal

Total number of projects	8
Country with highest number	India
Total investments	$4552 million
Country with highest investments	India
Most expensive project	BROT Concession for Indira Gandhi International Airport: New Delhi
Concession (ROT, RLT, BROT)	2
Divestiture	0
Greenfield project (BOT, BOO)	4
Management and lease contract	2

Table 7: Sources of Revenue in Airports

Particulars	Airport	Indicative Cost Rs. (In crores)
Restructuring / Modernization for world class airports	Delh & Mumbai	15,000
	Chennai & Kolkatta	5,000
Green Field Airports	Bangalore, Hyderabad, Goa, Pune, Navi Mumbai, Nagpur (Hub) and Greater Noida	10,000
Upgradation	25 selected airports	7,000
Modernization / Improvement	55 airports	3,000
Total investment by 2010		40,000

Dev. Of airports in North East Region (excluding Green Field Airports	Terminal Building / Car Parking / Cargo etc.	Air Side	ATS Facility	Total Rs. (In crores)
Total	225	167	62	454

despite current slowdown due to global recession. But airport infrastructure has not kept pace with the growth of the civil aviation traffic. This has resulted in congestion and inefficient services in major airports, limited landing slots, inadequate parking bays and congestion during peak hours for airlines. Development of quality infrastructure will have an impact on international competitiveness and economic growth.

This requires faster development of civil aviation infrastructure on public private

Table 8

Aeronautical Revenue	Non Aeronautical
Aircraft Landing Fees	Duty Free Shopping
Aircraft Parking Fees	Catering & Business
Passenger Service Fee	Car Parking & Car Rental
Air Traffic Control	Airline Terminal Rents
Ground Handling Charges	Commercial Rents
	Property Development
	Advertising
Source: Graham Anne, Managing Airports, An International Perspective.	

Table 9: Revenue and Expenses of an Airport

Revenue Structure	Expenses
1. Revenues from aeronautical activities ❑ **Revenues from air traffic operations** • Landing charges • Passenger service charges • Cargo charges • Parking and hangar charges • Security charges • Noise-related charges • Other charges on air traffic operations ❑ **Revenues from ground-handling charges** **2. Revenues from non-aeronautical activities** • Aviation fuel and oil concessions (including throughput charges). • Restaurants, bars, cafeterias and catering services • Duty-free shops • Automobile parking • Other concessions, and commercial activities operated by the airport • Rentals • Other revenues from non-aeronautical activities **3. Bank and cash management revenues (interests received from investments)** **4. Grants and subsidies**	**1. Development Stage** ❑ Land Cost ❑ Construction Cost • Terminal Building • Cargo Terminal • Runway • Taxiway • Apron • Hangers ❑ Miscellaneous **2. Operation and maintenance stage** ❑ Personnel costs ❑ Supplies ❑ Services contracted **3. Capital costs** ❑ Depreciation and/or amortization ❑ Interest ❑ Other capital costs **4. Administrative overhead** **5. Other non-capital costs**

partnership mode. In tune with the requirement many initiatives have already been started in the 10th five year plan and they are expected to continue in the 11th plan also.

The passenger traffic has grown tremendously during the last five years. It has grown from 5.92 crores in 2004-05 to 11.68 crores in 2007-08 showing an overall growth (CAGR) of 25%. The main factors contributing to this growth include the growth of the economy, falling fares, and increasing capacities of domestic private airlines. Notwithstanding the slowdown in the year 2008-09 and in the current year, the passenger traffic over the next 12 yrs is expected to grow from 11.97 crores in 2010-11 to reach 31.66 crores by 2022-23 with a growth (CAGR) rate of 8.44%.

(a) **Aeronautical or Airside Revenues** –Sources of income which arise from airport traffic activities related to the operation and landing of aircraft, passengers or freight.
(b) **Non Aeronautical or City side revenues** – Sources of income that are not directly related to the operation of aircraft, notably income from commercial activities within the terminal and rents for terminal space and airport land (Graham 2008).

Introduction to Amritsar Airport

Rajasansi International Airport located on the Amritsar-Ajnala Road, near the village of Rajasansi. As a government designated international airport, the airport currently handles

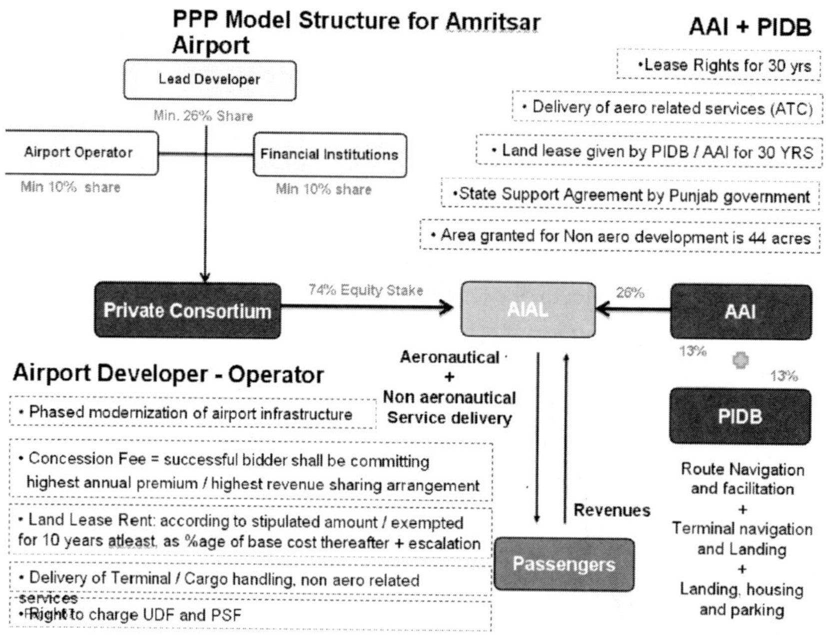

Fig. 5: PPP Model Structure for Amritsar Airport

Risk Category	Risk Identification (Description of Risk	Risk Assessment (Direct Consequences)	Risk Allocation		Risk Mitigation
			Public	Private	
Risks in Terms of Reference for privatization	• Unclear bid evaluation methodolgy in Terms of Refernce resulting in failed bidders soughting legal help (like the case of reliance) • Absence of detailed development plans provided by government in TOR resulting in form and scale of airport development been left to the bidders to determine	• Difficulty in assessing the bids as none of the developers provide similar outputs • Delay in time due to reviewing and re-reviewing bids to assess on common parameters	√	√	• The Government on its part should outline a clear TOR providing information on size and capacity of the infrastructure required so that all developers work on common grounds • This may be done by preparing concept designsfor passenger terminals and airside infrastructure under Government's own funding using consultants.
Land Acquisition Enchroachment	• Delays in the land acquisition and in providing unencumbered right of way to theAirport operator (Notice to proceed to the Contractor) can lead to delays in the start of construction resulting in escalation of project cost. Sometimes land may be enchroached upon by slum dwellers or certain airport dependent agencies (like in MIAL) • Additionally, the risk of the costs of acquisition not being contained within the estimates provided in the project cost estimates also increases.	• A delay in land acquisition will stall the airport project and result in a direct escalation in overall project cost. It also renders prospective non aero revenue from enchroached land useless • Land Acquisition delays all mandatory clearances and concerned approvals from the regulatory authority.	√	X	• Timely provision of land for construction of facilities and systems should be made a condition precedent to the Lease Concession Agreement. • For delay related to consents, approvals, clearances, the government should grant necessary permissions and the same should be executed within specified time • On delay, the concession period should be extended by an equal period be extended by an equal period
Delays in project development	During the development phase, the critical activities that may be associated with risks are: • Delay in Finalization of the project structure • Finalization of the contractual framework viz. the Concession Agreement, the Contract, and O&M Agreement • Availability of requisite approvals and clearances • Achievement of Financial Close • Delay in project commissioning • Resistance/ protests by interest groups (unions/ NGOs, etc.)	• Increased project cost due to premature resource mobilization and delay in their use. The storage costs of materials and equipments increases resulting in unnecessary expenditure. • Delay in commencement of construction activities, site mobilization, resulting in changes in project schedule and milestones	X	√	• Arranging finance during the project development phase to ensure availability of funds to meet development expenditure • Employing consultants with correct management skills • Sensitizing government to the number, type and timing of government approvals much in advance of the requirement for the approvals. • Incorporating the concerns of lenders and potential equity investors in project structure and legal documentation prior to approaching the market for funds.
Risks in designing Airport Development Proposals	• **Airside and Terminal Design:** Results from the actions of the bidders' professional designers, / intervention of the developer in over-ruling the advice of architects and engineers • **Capacity and Site Expandability:** Too much capacity in a bid proposal represents an excessive capital while insufficient capacity will possibly create congestion and delays	• Cost of modification, redesign costs, master planning and phased development redesign. • Delay in project schedule, time related delays	X	√	• Scope Management plan should be in place and care should be taken that deviations from scope should be kept minimum • Design should be freezed at an early stage after due consideration & discussions with all the concerned consultants
Environmental Risks	The risks that the project could have an adverse environmental impact which affects project costs not foreseen in the environmental impact assessment	Additional costs incurred to rectify any adverse environmental impact on the project plus time delays	√	√	• Environment Impact Assessment should be fairly detailed • Construction practices should be such that it does not encourage environmental contamination at any cost

Fig. 6: Risk Matrix

about 90 commercial flights a week, both international and domestic. The integrated terminal building at Amritsar have peak hour passenger handling capacity of 1200 passengers and annual handling capacity of 14.6 lakh passengers.

PPP in Health Care Facility

During the 7th India Health Summit 2010, the Government has mentioned that PPP can be a vital instrument to augment the public health care system. 2-3% of GDP is allocated to healthcare infrastructure in India. According to PwC, India will see a 140% increase in health spending between 2010 and 2020. With only 20% of healthcare delivery provided through public health units and the Government not intending to spend more on capital expenditure, more PPP initiatives are being proposed.

PPP in Healthcare

A health services PPP can be described as a long-term contract (typically15 to 30years) between a public-sector authority and one or more private sector companies operating as a legal entity. The government provides the strength of its purchasing power, outlines goals for an optimal health system, and empowers private enterprise to innovate, build,

Management Contract	The infrastructure is owned by public sector with private participation in operating and managing the facility typically for a fee typically to improve quality with the contract period defined and linked to quality of service
Leasing	Public sector infrastructure is on a short to medium term lease to private players who operate the facility with specific buy back arrangements from the government during the lease period in the form of a percentage of beds or other subsidies on capital expenditure[11]
Joint Venture	Generally formed as a legal entity or an SPV, with equity participation from both the government and the private players. Government contributions can vary from upfront capital infusion into the SPV, land lease, or financial concessions on capital infused by private player. Equity objectives can be achieved through specific arrangements like a buy-back by government on a certain % of beds
BOO/BOT	The public sector contracts with a private entity to design, build, and operate the capital asset. The public sector remains responsible for raising the required capital and retains ownership of the facility. This type of PPP is also called "Build Own and Operate" BOO The private sector is assigned all aspects of the project. The ownership of the new facility is transferred to the private sector – either indefinitely, or for a fixed period of time. This type of arrangement also falls within the domain of PPP. This arrangement is also referred to as Build Operate, Own, Transfer ("BOOT").
Concession	This works more like a long term lease where a private player takes over the management of a state owned enterprise including significant investment risks. The ownership and investment decisions during the lease period no longer remain with the state. Government regulation may stipulate a certain percentage of services on identified demand segments through schemes like prepaid vouchers.

Fig. 7: Models for PPP in Healthcare in India

	A	B	C	D	E	F	G
1	**COMPARATIVE ANALYSIS OF CASE STUDIES**						
2	**Parameters**	**Sports Injury Center**	**Greenfield Superspecialty Hospital**	**Multispecialty Hospital**	**Rajiv Gandhi Superspecialty Hospital**	**I.P. Apollo Hospital**	**Uttarakhand Medical College**
3	**Location**	Safdarjung Hospital, Delhi	Mohali	Nangal, East Punjab	Trans Yamuna, East Delhi	Mathura Road, Delhi	Uttarakhand
4	**Project Status**	Operations started from 26th September, 2010	Construction starts from August 2011	Under construction RFP invited on 28th February, 2011	Foundation stone - January 2000; Target date - March 2003	Operations started from late 1998 with 70 admissions month and 60% occupancy	NA
5	**Area**	945.62 sq.m. (lower basement) in a 35-bedded G+7-2 building of plot area 2618.32 sq.m	3.15 acres	1.82 acres	13.81 acres	15 acres	25 acres
6	**Healthcare Services**	On PPP - only diagnostics and Pathology Lab.	Upgradation of 70-bedded hospital to 200- bedded Cancer, Trauma and superspecialty	Minimum 50- bedded multispecialty hospital	650 - bedded tertiary care teaching hospital	600- bedded multispecialty hospital	Existing 200 bed hospital to be upgraded to 500 bed + a medical college
7	**Non - medical services**	NA	NA	NA	NA	NA	NA
8	**PPP Model**	BOT	DFBOT	DFBOT	Design - Build	BOT	BOT
9	**Proposed concession period**	5 years for path lab and 10 years for diagnostic	50 years	50 years	NA as operated by Govt.	30 years	30 years renewable for another 30 years
10	**Construction period**	30 months for whole building	18 months	12 months	36 months	24 months	NA
11	**Estimated project cost**	17 crores for PPP (70.72 crores whole project cost)	100 crores	NA	218.65 crores	NA	174 crores
12	**Contracting Authority**	HSCC India Ltd.	PIDB and PHSC	PIDB and PHSC	DDA	DDA	
13	**Ownership**		Govt. of Punjab	Govt. of Punjab	Ministry of Health, GoI	Govt. of Delhi	Govt. of Uttarakhand
14	**Private Partner**	Mahajan Imaging Center and P.Bhasin Path. Lab	Max Healthcare Pvt. Ltd.	Based on evaluation of bid	Sub contractors and non- clinical service providers	IMPL	NA
15	**Share holding Pattern**	Private partners 68.80%, Govt 14.72%, Miscellaneous 17.06%	NA as totally financed by private partner	NA as totally financed by private partner	NA	GoD 26%, AHEL (Contractor-Pharmacy) - 26%, Land + Miscellaneous 48%	GoU 7.00%, Private partner 58.00%; Land cost 16.33%, Miscellaneous 18.67%
16	**Revenue sharing Pattern**	Mahajan Imaging Center – 74% & Govt. body 26%; P.Bhasin Path. Lab. – 68.50% & Govt. body 31.5%	NA	NA	NA	NA	NA
17	**Annual concession fee**	26% by Mahajan and 31.5% by P.Bhasin to SIC	5% of gross revenue to GoP	to be increased after every 3 (three) years at the rate of 10%, over the preceding Annual Concession Fee	NA	NA	NA
18	**Upfront consideration**	NA	6.31 crores	Based on evaluation of bid	NA	NA	NA
19	**Project Development Advisor**	NA	IL&FS	Feedback Ventures Pvt. Ltd., Chandigarh	NA	NA	NA
20	**Private provider's responsibilities**	Provide brand new medical equipments on wet lease; provide medical services on CGHS rates	design, finance, construct and manage the hospital for the said concession period	Demolish existing constructed structure; plan, design, finance, construct, operate and maintain Multispecialty Hospital	develop detailed design, build and provide non- clinical services only (as per the regulations)	construct and manage the hospital for the said concession period	construct and manage the hospital and medical college for the said concession period

21	**Contracting authority's responsibilities**	Provide the private parties rent free furnished accomodation + electricity and water supplies + general security and common facilities	provide vacant possession of site on nominal lease,	Transferred the Project Site on leasehold basis,	a preliminary design developed by administration to be provided to the bidders in addition to project agreement, relevant schedules and other technical documentation	provide vacant possession of site on nominal lease	provide land for expansion and Govt support amount viz. 21 crores
22	**Incentives to private partner**	Only the provision of free furnished accomodation and facilities	Options to choose any multispecialty except mandatory 50- beds for trauma and 50- beds for cancer; to charge market rates from patients	Options to choose any multispecialty, to charge market rates from patients; no upper limit on the number of beds (subject to developmental controls)	NA	NA	Interest bearing soft loan Rs. 20.00 Crores repayable - optional; annual support equivalent to present value of rs. 81.00 crores over 30 years
23	**Benefit to Govt.**	Regular revenue earning without having any investment or responsibilities of the equipments and services	Saving of capital and recurring expense of Rs. 100 Cr. Over 50 years concession period; upgrading healthcare facilities	Saving of capital and recurring expense Over 50 years concession period	NA	NA	Saving of capital and recurring expense of Rs. 190 Cr. Over 30 years concession period; upgrading healthcare facilities to tertiary level
24	**Cost Breakup**	Developmental (construction) cost of diagnostic and imaging centre - 2.40 Cr.; cost of equipment & installation for imaging - 11 Cr. And for path. Lab. - 70 L.	NA	NA	Land: 6 crores; project capital: 87.65 crores; equipment: 60 crores; O&M: 65 crores	NA	Land: 49 crores, project cost: 174 crores; Net recurring expenses: 86 crores; Govt. support: 21 crores
25	**Benefits for poor**	All services on CGHS rates for all sections of society	NA	NA	NA	1/3rd beds free with medical (consulatations and nursing) and diagnostics; Out of pocket expenses - only drugs and consumables	50% seats for Govt quota at lower fess for poor students; creation of over 600 jobs for local population
26	**Occupancy**	40- 45 patients on each normal day (as the beginning of operations period, so due to lack of awareness)	NA	NA	NA	70 admissions per month - 60% occupancy	NA

maintain and/or manage delivery of agreed-upon services over the term of the contract. The private sector receives payment for its services and assumes substantial financial, technical and operational risk while benefiting from the upside potential of shared cost savings.

PPP IN HOUSING PROJECTS

PPP in Housing

Public Private Partnership (PPP) Project means a project based on a contract or concession agreement, between a Government or statutory entity on the one side and a private sector company on the other side for delivering an infrastructure service on payment of user charges. Three fundamentals of a successful PPP are

1. Government-planned project
2. Genuine risk allocation
3. Mutually valuable

Sustainable Housing

Sustainability in housing covers three broad themes: environmental issues, economic issues and social issues, and is a measure of the positive contribution a project makes in both local and global terms to the built environment. Sustainable housing reforms would generally look into: Social concerns, economic reforms, Environmental impacts, Water, Energy, Waste minimization, Health & safety.

West Bengal Housing Board

The first initiative to introduce a public private partnership in the housing sector, in India was taken by the West Bengal government with the formation of the Bengal Ambuja Housing Development United in 1993.

Key Learnings

- Government had equal share in equity and risk
- Private player was aided by the Government to overcome land acquisition & approval concerns
- The government was weak on project marketing as it lacked the resources, but private participation took care of this concern

Uttar Pradesh Housing and Urban Planning Department (Awaas Bandhu)

Awaas Bandhu is a committee formed under Housing and Urban Planning Department, Uttar Pradesh to ensure the planned development of urban areas and to create an enabling environment to provide affordable housing.

Key Learnings

- Stringent pricing and buying eligibility norms ensure units reach targeted end users
- Lack of basic infrastructure deters end users from taking possession
- Freezing design units, instead of the basic size and specifications results in value optimization.

Dharavi Slum Rehabilitation

The Slum Rehabilitation Authority of Maharashtra decided to redevelop dharavi as an integrated suburb with modem amenities. These facilities would include primary and secondary schools, technical institutes, dispensary, municipal hospital retail markets, sport complexes apart from residential development.

Key Learnings

- Interaction and consultation with various stakeholders such as beneficiaries, development authorities, developers, NGO's etc. is necessary for successful implementation of the project
- Quality infrastructure is essential in order to reduce the disparity between the slum dwellers and other individuals.
- Relaxing FSI norms is an excellent way to increase bidder interest

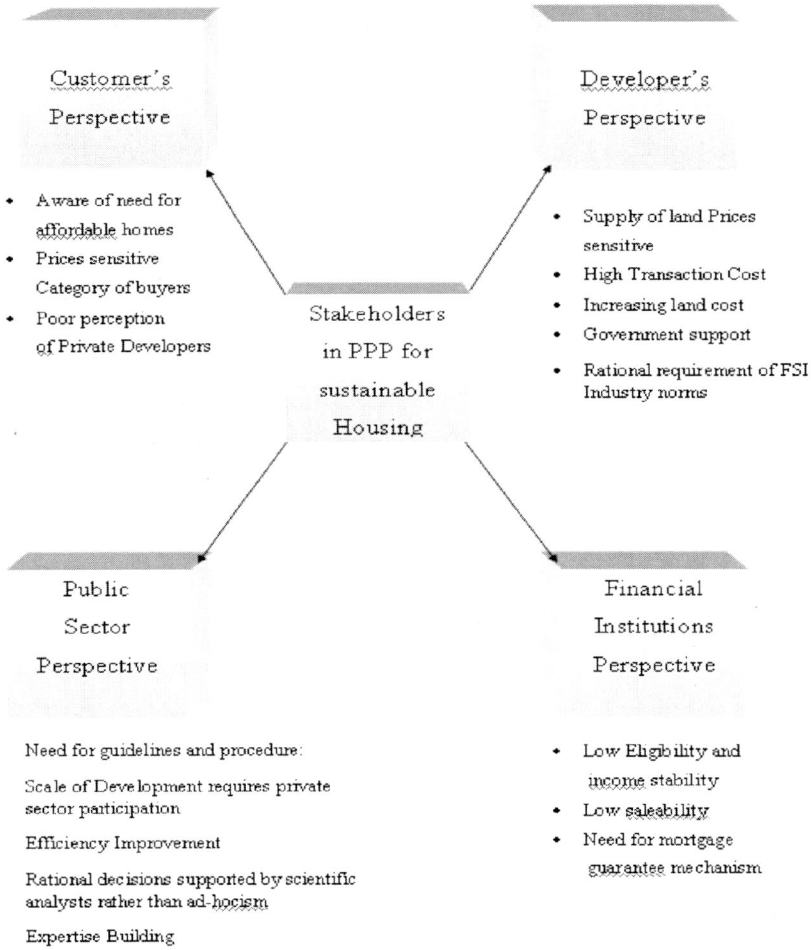

Fig. 8: PPP for Sustainable Housing

Pimpri-Chinchwad Municipal Corporation

Housing for Urban Poor under BSUP (JNNURM) mode. The project aims at providing housing for the economically weaker section of the society. PCMC has fortified and acquired sites across the city under EWS housing.

Key Learnings

- Issue of Land TDR (in phases) as a compensation for their land costs is a good way of making the project financially feasible. However it has to be ensured that these TDR's are not misused.
- Increase in FSI and government grants are effective means of generating developer's interest

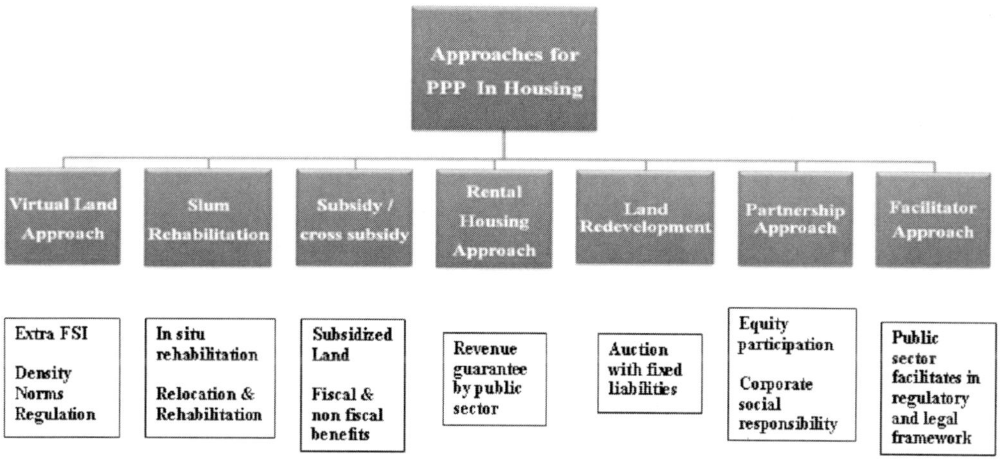

Fig. 9: Approaches for PPP in Housing

1. Virtual Land Approach

The virtual land approach increases the buildable space on a piece of land. This approach creates an opportunity for the developer to increase the scope of development. The developer benefits in the form of earning higher profits as the land earns him a premium, while the Government benefits on account of providing more affordable homes due to increase in density. This is done by:

1. Relaxation of FSI norms (i.e increasing FSI for the developer)
2. Relaxation of Development control regulations relating to density norms

Strengths

- Enables government to leverage the potential of the given land parcel.
- The project becomes more viable for the private player as scale goes up.

Examples

- Dharavi Redevelopment and Airport Slum Redevelopment (Mumbai)
- Mass housing projects in Uttar Pradesh

Graphical Representation

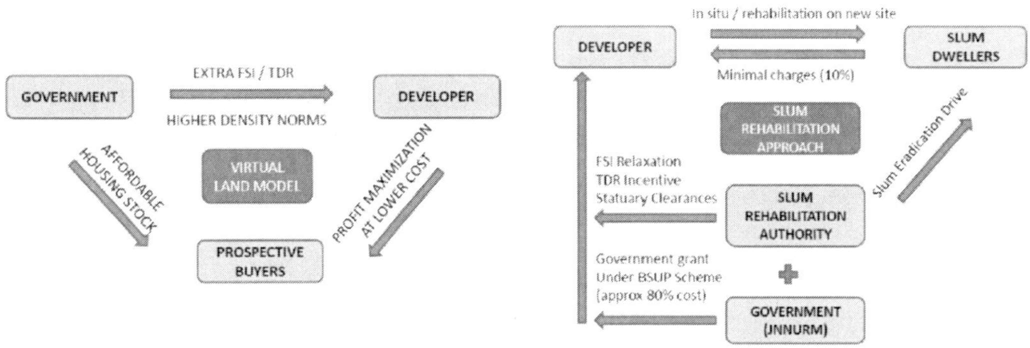

Fig. 10: Virtual Land and Slum Rehabilitation Approach

2. Slum Rehabilitation

In situ Development

Here the slums are to be rehabilitated on the same site. Accordingly, the developer has to make provisions for transit arrangements for the slum dwellers

Development Shifted to Other Site

Here a new location is identified for the slum dwellers. The developer undertakes the construction at the new identified location free from any existing developments. Once the Construction is completed, the slum dwellers" are relocated to the newly constructed units.

Strengths

- active facilitation by the public sector, for various statuary clearances and approvals
- Incentives like TDR and extra FSI

Examples

- Dharawi Redevelopment Project
- Delhi (DDA slum redevelopment Programme)
- Nagpur and Pimpri Chinchwad (Pune) slum redevelopment

3. Subsidy/Cross Subsidy

Under this approach the Government provides various forms of grants, exceptions, fiscal and non-fiscal benefits and aids to the private developer or the private user.

Direct Subsidy Approach

In a direct subsidy approach the government's responsibility as a stake holder is to facilitate the development activity by direct fiscal means, like Stamp Duty exception, City Development charges waiver, Tax concession in the form of Tax deferral, Tax credits, etc.

Cross Subsidy Approach

Under this approach the government provides land parcels to the developer at reasonable or subsidized rates, with all approvals and pre construction formalities in place. The developer has to carry out construction of residential dwellings, such that a certain fixed percentage of the total units are to be constructed towards lower and middle income groups.

Examples

- Awas Bandhu planned by Uttar Pradesh Housing and Urban Planning Department
- Alliance between West Bengal Housing Board & Kolkata Metropolitan Development Authority

Graphical Representation

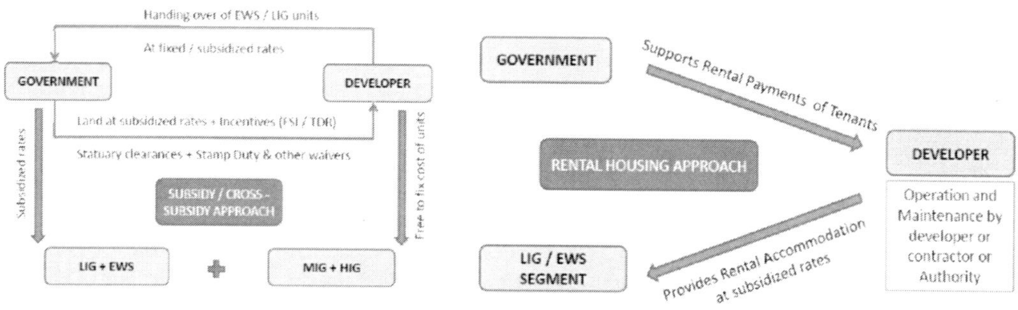

Fig. 11: Subsidy/Cross Subsidy and Rental Housing Approach

4. Rental Housing Approach

The joint venture approach to a rental housing solution involves a grant and a subsidy based approach. To meet the long term housing need, the public sector provides housing in private rented accommodation in receipt of rent supplement payments.

- Under the PPP arrangement, developers enter into long term agreements to make property available to local authorities for letting to rental housing.
- Responsibility for the management and maintenance of the properties over the contract period may be held by the developer or outsourced or even passed to the local authority.

Strengths

- For the tenant it brings greater choice and longer term security
- For the landlord it brings in certainty about future income.
- Pushes the private rented market to improve standards
- It also acts as an effective slum prevention model

Graphical Representation

5. Land Redevelopment

Land development via PPP approach is an efficient model wherein the public party provides land and invites private players for its commercial exploitation. Under majority of the arrangement the public/government body recovers the costs for the land and infrastructure outside the plan by fixing a reserve price. The type of land parcels used under this model are:

- Partly used Condition
- Dilapidated Condition
- Open land parcels

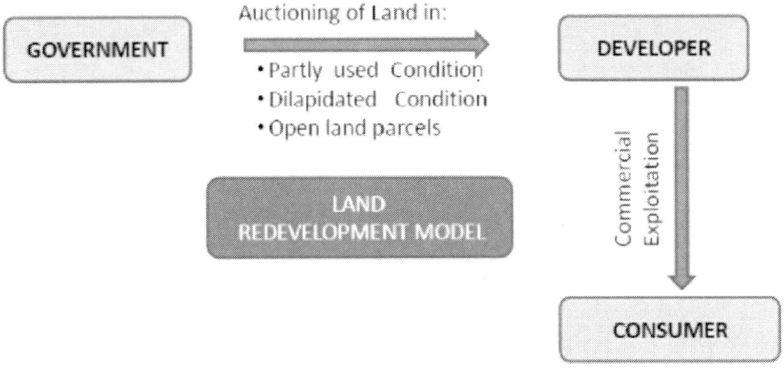

Fig. 12: Land Development Model

- Sensible risk-sharing among the public and the private sector partners. Financial rewards to the private party commensurate with the achievement of pre-specified outputs
- An auction approach or a bid methodology is followed in partner selection

Strengths

- Clarity of Objective
- Quality and Quantitative control
- Value Maximization

6. Partnership Approach

The objective of the partnership approach is to address the concern of housing shortage by pooling in public and private income.

Join Development Format

Under this format land is the contribution of the Government as part of the equity and the funds required for the construction and marketing activity is pooled by a private player or a pool of these private players

Joint Venture Format

Under this format the public body contributes equity in the form of cash, whereas the private player also pools in private resources. The pooled fund is then utilized by the Joint Venture formed for the land procurement and project development marketing.

Examples

West Bengal Housing Board (WBHB) and Gujarat Ambuja Cement Ltd.

Strengths

The consumer confidence for the project is high.

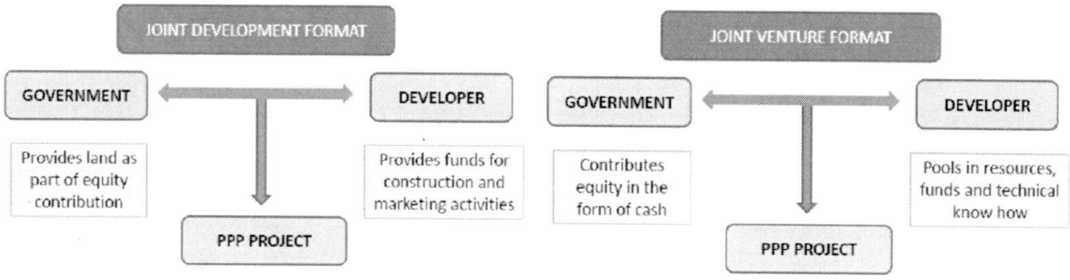

Fig. 13: Joint Development and Joint Venture

7. Facilitator

A prevalent PPP approach to housing involves public sector being a facilitator in the partnership. Essentially the government carries out the role of setting the regulatory and legal frameworks in place whereas the private sector offers financial, technical and managerial support for such infrastructure projects.

Public sector supports land acquisition at reasonable prices, single window clearance for project approvals and ensuring time bound responses from different agencies. This essentially creates an environment of core competence where the government ensures efficiency in providing regulatory assistance while the private player concentrates on its core competence in project delivery

Strengths

Consumer confidence: The governments association with the project, boosts the consumer confidence about project delivery with quality standards.

Easy project funding: The financial institutions show keenness in financing the projects which fall under the government recommended schemes as they attach lower risk weights to the project.

No cost on government balance sheets: Under this arrangement the government only plays the role of a facilitator in creating essential environment for development. Thus there is no cost involved from the government side which could affect its balance sheet.

CASE-STUDY

PCNTDA (Pimpri-Chinchwad New Town Development Authority) Development of Eco-Friendly and Affordable Township, Pune

Project Location and Site

The Pimpri-Chinchwad New Township Development Authority (PCNTDA) approves setting up of the first pilot project of eco-housing under the Jawaharlal Nehru National Urban Renewal Mission (JNNURM) scheme on public private partnership (PPP) basis in Sector 12, Bhosari Village, near Pune on 53 hectare (approx. 130 acres) land.

Site Statistics

- Area: 53 hectares
- Trapezoidal in shape with a frontage of about 800 meters on the Spine road
- Surrounded by a 20 meter arterial road . Well developed internal roads (6 meters)

PCNTDA'S Key Obligations

- Payment of Grant of Rs. 225 crores as per schedule linked to handover schedule
- Allow FSI of 2.5 as an incentive instead of 1.0
- Accept BSUP Facilities/ Affordable Housing stock (bidding parameter) on its completion
- Transfer of Lease Rights in phases linked to construction milestones
- Facilitate clearances of Govt. agencies on reasonable effort basis

Developer (Consortium of Mumbai-based D.B. Realty, Man Infrastructure and Ajwani Developers)

- Developer shall construct 5,040 housing units under (BSUP) scheme of JNNURM
- Master planning for the entire 53 hectares of land
- Development, construction and marketing of 7.951akh square meters of integrated real estate space.
- Developer shall construct affordable housing stock (l ,30,599 square meters) and handover to PCNTDA free of cost
- Developer shall undertake eco-friendly initiatives
- Upfront payment of Rs. 50 crores & submission of performance Security of Rs. 100 crores

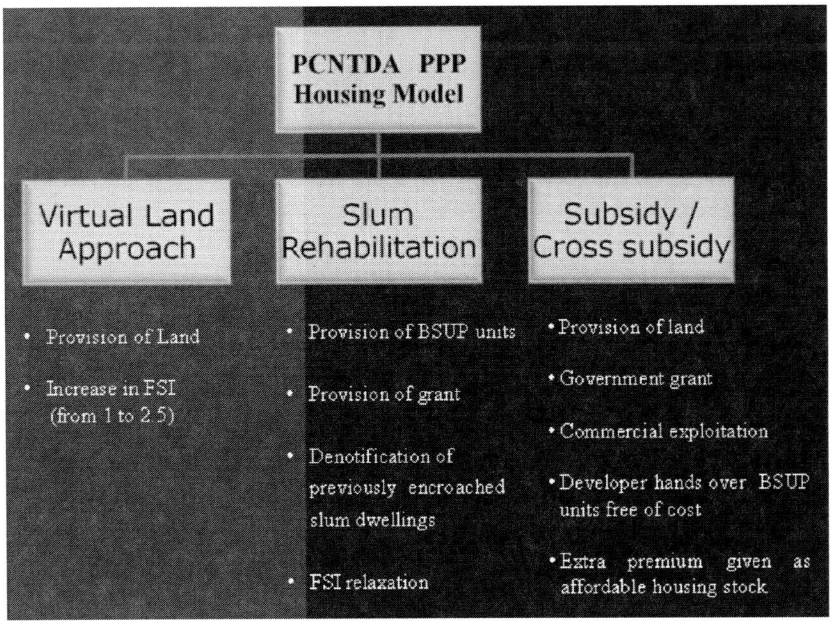

Fig. 14: PCNTDA PPP Housing Model

Project Outcome in Terms of Housing Stock

Net Plot Area – 3.89 lakh sq.mt
Maximum Allowable FSI – 9.72 lakh sq m (FSI = 2.5)
BSUP Area (5040 Units) – 1.76 lakh sq.mt

Total FSI for PPP = 7.96 lakh sq.mt (9.72 lakh sq.mt – 1.76 lakh sq.mt)

Table 10: Cash Outflow and Inflow

EXPENDITURE (Cash outflow)
Land Cost (nil in this case as it is provided by PCNTDA)
Cost of construction (for BSUP units + amenities) @ approx. 90 crores
Cost of construction (for Affordable Housing stock) @ approx. 209 crores
Cost of construction (for infrastructure) @ approx. 100 crores
Cost of construction for remaining 6.45 lakh FSI
Pre-Operative Cost (variable due to reduced cost of statutory clearances)
Financing Cost @ 1% on Deb
Upfront Payment on signing of agreement @ 50 crore
Performance Security @ 100 crore:
Repayment of Term Loan after construction perioc
Total Expenditure (Cash outflow) = sum of rows under cash outflov
RECEIPT OF CASH (Inflow)
Term Loan (Debt) = 70% of (cost of construction - Government Grant
Government Grant (225 crores for BSUP units
Revenue from sales of residential units built out of available FS
Revenue from sales of commercial space:
Total recipt or Cash Inflow = sum of all rows under cash inflov
Net cash flow for project = (Cash inflow - Cash outflow)

Table 11: Financial Analysis and Risk Matrix

Description	Amounts
Gap funding for BSUP by developer (5040 housing units + physical and social infrastructure amounting 100 crs)	Rs. 190 crs
Upfront payment at time of signing of agreement	Rs. 50 crs
Construction value of 1,30,599 sqm carpet area (Affordable Housing Stock offered) @ Rs. 16, 000 per sqm	Rs. 209 crs
Total value derived	Rs. 449 crs
FSI available for developer for exploitation (after netting out FSI for BSUP and affordable stock units)	6,45,391 sqm
Value offered per FSI	Rs. 6955/sqm Rs.646/sqft

Table 12: Risk Management

Type of Risks	Ris Allocation		Risk Mitigation
	Public	Private	
Project Development Stage			
Land Acquisition	√	X	Land alloted by PCNTDA
Delays in project development	√	X	Appointment of CRISIL as consultant
Design Risk	X	√	Well laid out scope
Environmental Risks	√	√	Environment Impact Assessment in place for Eco-friendly housing
Project Construction Stage			
Construction Risks (excluding costs overruns)	X	√	Performance Security of 100 crs. Grant & Lease rights linked with project milestones
Project Cost Risk / Cost Overruns	X	√	Fairly Detailes Estimates and Project cash flows
Performance Related Risks	X	√	Performance Security of 100 crs.
Commissioning risk	√	√	Timely Application & Strict monitoring
Post construction stage			
Termination Risk	X	√	Compensation Package in agreement
Commercial Risk	X	√	Feasibility Studies done by CRISIL
Financial Risks			
(a) Interest Rate Risk	X	√	Mix of fixed & floating interest rates
(b) Foreign Exchange Exposure/currency risk	X	√	Assistance from Government/PCNTDA
(c) Inflation Risks	√	X	Assistance from Government/PCNTDA
Throughout the project cycle			
Force Majeure	√	X	Insurance cover
Social and Political Risk			
(a) Political change Scenario	√	X	Covered in agreement
(b) Events of War	√	X	Covered in agreement
(c) Nationalization or Revocation	√	X	Covered in agreement
(d) Social Risk	√	√	Insurance cover

Bidding Parameter (Maximum Carpet Area of Affordable housing stock = 1.30 lakh sq.mt)

FSI remaining with developer to be used in Residential Housing and Commercial Land use

7.96 lakh sq.mt – 1.30 lakh sq.mt = approx. 6.66 lakh sq.mt

Table 13: Risks Faced by Different Stakeholders in a Sustainable PPP Housing Project

Government	Service delivery – road getting developed in time, quality of service – riding quality
Private developer	Adequate return on investment – Project development within cost, no time overruns, revenues as expected (materialization of traffic, willingness to pay)
Lenders	Return of interest and principal – Project getting adequate returns, no voluntary default by developer
Public / users	Cost effective service, desirable service levels, minimum access to non-tolled alternative routes
Public / project affected parties	Fair rehabilitation and resettlement assistance / compensation
Civic society	Environment risk – air/noise pollution, excessive falling of trees

CONCLUSION

Thus PPP has applications in various infrastructure related projects.

REFERENCES

[1] Position Paper on the Airports Sector in India, May 2009, Department of Economic Affairs, Ministry of Finance, Government of India.

[2] Government of India, Ministry of Finance, Department of Economic Affairs Approach Paper on Defining Public Private Partnerships, Discussion Note, February 2010.

[3] www.pppinindia.com

[4] Position Paper on the Solid Waste Management Sector in India, November 2009, Department of Economic Affairs, Ministry of Finance, Government of India.

[5] National Urban Housing and Habitat Policy 2007, Ministry of Housing and Urban Poverty Alleviation, New Delhi

[6] PPP Handbook.

[7] Eleventh Five Year Plan, Volume 3, Planning Commission, Government of India.

[8] Financing and Pricing of Urban Infrastructure: HSMI, New Delhi.

[9] India Infrastructure Report 2006, 2008, 2009, 2010: Source – HSMI.

[10] Prasad, B.V.S., Gowri Shankar K.; "Airport Infrastructure In India: Changing Landscape", ICFAI University Press, ISBN: 978-81-314-2465-0.

[11] Model Concession Agreement for Greenfield Airports, Planning Commission, Government of India.

Assessment of the Fundamental Value and Its Relationship with Market Price

Munmun Mohanty[1] and Shradhanjali Panda[2]

[1] Ravenshaw University, Cuttack
[2] United School of Business Management, Bhubaneswar
E-mail: munmunmohanty@rediffmail.com; shradha313@yahoo.co.in

ABSTRACT

In the broadest terms, fundamental analysis involves looking at any data, besides the trading patterns of the stock itself that can be expected to impact the price or perceived value of a stock. Fundamental, intrinsic or fair value as the name implies, it means getting down to basics of a share or the true worth of a share. Where as technical analysis focuses only on the trading and price history of a stock. As no financial market is purely efficient and does not behave rationally every time, fundamental value differs from market value. But, fundamental value has a close relationship with the market value. Fundamental or intrinsic value shows whether a share is overvalued or undervalued. It helps the investor for adopting proper buying and selling strategy in that particular share for making profit. It shows whether the market price is cheap or fair. This empirical study aims at assessing the fundamental value or intrinsic value of a share using Gordon and Shapiro model (1956) of general dividend discounted model. The model assumes a unique dividend growth rate as 'g'. Along with it the study analyses the deviation of the calculated intrinsic value with its market price. It focuses on Indian Pharmaceutical sector taking 'A' category shares into consideration as these shares are traded every day. The present study checks whether the share is overpriced or under priced by comparing the calculated fundamental value with that of the market value.

Keywords: Fundamental Value, Market Price, Valuation of Stock

INTRODUCTION

In today's scenario calculation of actual value of a stock is must before any investment in share market. Because rise and fall of a share price is because of fall in either earnings or valuation. Valuation of a share depends on many factors like market capitalization, managerial efficiency and transparency, earnings visibility, margin, sector, market sentiment, replacement cost etc. That is the reason even experienced investors also find it difficult to go for a proper valued stock for investment. Unfortunately in India 90% of stock market investors don't know about the basic and fundamental of share valuation and their risk profiles. This paper tried to assess the fundamental value of some Pharmaceutical companies traded under "A" category of shares in National Stock Exchange. In order to calculate their fundamental values the present study has used Constant growth rate model.

LITERATURE REVIEW

Economists believe that no valuation model gives accurate result in real life. Still the need is there to go for a valuation method by which it can be known whether the price is overvalued or undervalued and the market behaves rationally. Number of reaserch works has been done in this context and few are highlighted below.

A. Alford (1992) states that the price-earnings (P/E) valuation method measures a firm's stock price against its earnings capacity and the P/E multiple calculated from a range of comparable firms. The method's accuracy is tested in the selection of comparable firms based on industry type, risk, and earnings growth. Industry basis and a combination of risk and earnings growth best determine firm comparability. However, practice shows industry basis is used more often since companies in the same industry approximate similar risk and earnings growth and follow similar accounting methods. Large firms have greater use of the industry based selection than small firms. Valuation accuracy is positively related to firm size and negatively related to leverage differences adjustment.

S.N. Kaplan and R.S. Ruback (1995) compare the market value of highly leveraged transactions to the discounted value of their corresponding cash flow forecasts. For the authors' sample of 51 highly leveraged transactions completed between 1983 and 1989, the valuations of discounted cash flow forecasts are within 10 percent on average of the market values of the completed transactions. Their valuations perform at least as well as valuation methods using comparable companies and transactions. The authors also invert their analysis by estimating the risk premium implied by transaction values and forecast cash flows and relating those risk premiums to firm and industry betas, firm size, and firm book-to-market ratios.

Ohlson (1995) argued that dividends were paid out of book value and not current earnings and that they reduced market value on a dollar to dollar basis since dividends reduce book value on a dollar to dollar basis and do not affect the abnormal earnings sequence.Monchul Kim and Jay.R.Titter (1999) shows that valuing IPOs on the basis of the Price-to-Earnings, Price-to-Sales, Enterprise value-to-Sales and Enterprise value-to-Operating Cash flow ratios of comparable firms is of on limited use if historical numbers rather than forecasts are used. This is largely due to the wide variation of these ratios for young firms within an industry. P/E multiples using forecasted earnings result in much more accurate valuations than multiples using trailing earnings.

Berkman et al. (2000) compare estimates of value derived from conventional discounted cash flow and price earnings valuation methods to the market price. They suggest that the best discounted cash flow method and the best price earnings comparable method have similar accuracy. The median absolute pricing error is around 20% and the models explain around 70% of the cross sectional variation in market price scaled by the book value. Mark Kamstra (2003) argues that forecasted future cash flows can be unreliable in computation of fundamental value of the stocks and used a new valuation approach "Kamstra 2001" to check if market prices reflected gross over valuation of various stocks compared to the estimated fundamental values. This approach uses a statistical model of discounted dividend growth rates. It permits more flexible modeling of autocorrelation in growth rates. His study focuses in the context of efficient markets and highlights on the efficient markets implications of the deviations observed between market and fundamental prices. He suggests that algorithmic valuation techniques provide a rough starting point for firm valuation.

Ingolf Dittmann, Ernst. G. Moug and Johaness (2005) studied how the use of alternative valuation methodologies affects investment performance for a sample of 53 German venture capitalists. They measured the investment performance by the amount of investments they need to write off and by the number of companies they take public and find that a significant number of investment managers use discounted cash flow (DCF) techniques, but only a minority appears to use a discount rate related to the cost of capital. The majority applies DCF using subjective discount rates. They presented evidence that the use of DCF is correlated with superior investment performance only if applied in conjunction with an objectifiable discount rate. Also, funds that invest with a longer horizon perform better. The use of multiples is not significantly correlated with investment performance and a focus on fundamental values confers an advantage.

OBJECTIVE OF THE STUDY

Having discussed all the techniques and importance of valuation, the study aims at finding out the fundamental value of the shares of Pharmaceutical companies that are traded in "A" category of shares. The objective of the study is to calculate the intrinsic or fundamental value of the shares using Constant growth model and to compare it with their respective market prices and to study the deviation with its cause.

DATA AND SAMPLE SIZE

For the study companies are taken from "A" category of shares of National Stock

Exchange. As these shares are traded everyday, i.e. either bought or sold, these are taken for the study for finding out the correct fundamental value. Having picked the companies their corresponding Income Statement, Balance sheet, Debt equity ratio, EPS, DPS and β values for 10 years are collected from CMIE data base. The sample size of the study is 5 and the time period for the study is from 1st April, 2001 to 1st April, 2010. To calculate the market prices of the shares, average closing prices are taken from official website of National Stock Exchange, i.e. www.nseindia.com.

RESEARCH METHODOLOGY

In order to find out the fundamental or the actual value of the shares, the income statement, Balance sheets for ten years (i.e. from 2001 to 2010) are examined. The study uses the constant growth model, i.e. **V0 = D1/ (k – g)** for evaluation of intrinsic value. The argument before this model is, the fundamental value of a share is the discounted value of all its future cash flows. The rationale for the model lies in the present value rule, i.e. the value of any asset is the present value of expected future cash flows discounted at a rate appropriate to the riskiness of the cash flows. There are two components in this model, i.e. expected dividend and cost of equity (Ke). To obtain the expected dividend, the study calculated "g" or growth rate, DPS growth rate and EPS growth rate using the following formulae.

Calculation of Growth Rate "g"

$$g = ROE \times B$$

where ROE = Net Income / Shareholder's equity and
B or Retention Ratio = Retained Earnings / Net Income (1)

Calculation of EPS and DPS Growth Rate

There are two ways to calculate the EPS and DPS growth rate for the year 2011. First calculating the growth rate for each year (from 2001 to 2010) and then finding out the average of it. Second method is using the compounding technique of time value of money. For more robustness the second method is adopted in the present study i.e. applying the compounding technique of time value to the growth rate of the year 2001 to forecast the growth rate for the year 2011. (2)

Using these above calculated growth rates future dividend (for the year 2011) is calculated. Calculation of forecasted dividend for a future period using this constant growth rate may not hold true practically but for the theoretical implementation of the constant growth model this assumption is taken into consideration. (3)

Cost of Capital (Ke) is calculated using CAPM model. It believes that past is a better indicator for future and CAPM model is theoretically better grounded. For calculation of cost of equity the following formula is used.

$$Ke = Rf + \beta\ (Rm - Rf) \tag{4}$$

To compare the calculated fundamental values of the companies to that of the market price of the respective companies' shares, the average market price from 1st April, 2011 to 1st July, 2011 are taken into consideration. The closing prices are taken for the calculation of average market price from the official website of National Stock Exchange, i.e. www.nseindia.com. (5)

ANALYSIS AND INTERPRETATION OF RESULTS

To interpret the result, the study has used growth rate (g = ROE×B), DPS growth rate and EPS growth rate of each company. These calculated growth rates using compounding technique of time value are shown in the table below.

Table 1: Growth Rates

Name of the Company	Growth Rate (g = ROE * B)	DPS Growth Rate	EPS Growth Rate
GlaxoSmithKline	22%	52%	54%
Ranbaxy	23%	51.8%	54%
DrReddy	36%	60%	58%
Sun Pharmaceuticals	26%	44%	42%
Cipla	19%	36%	34.6%
Lupin	17%	34%	32.4%

Interpretation

Table 1 shows the 3 growth rates calculated using compounding technique of time value. In looking at earnings on a share basis, investors can understand the portion of a company's profit that can be assigned to each share of common stock. Because it accounts for the number of shares outstanding, EPS is seen as a critical variable in determining the real value of a share. There is a close relationship between Earning per Share and Dividend per Share. The DPS ratio is very similar to the EPS. EPS shows what shareholders earned by way of profit for a period whereas DPS shows how much the shareholders were actually paid by way of dividends. In the above table it is quite clear that both EPS and DPS growth rates are having comparatively smaller deviation with each other than that of growth rate "g". The EPS and DPS growth rates show somehow closer relationship between one another. But, in some cases the EPS and DPS growth rates are quite double of that of the growth rate "g".

Table 2 shows the calculated fundamental value of the company's shares using the above growth rates and the average market price of the respective companies. To calculate the average market price of the companies the closing prices of the share price from 1st April, 2011 to 1st July, 2011 are taken into consideration.

Table 2: Comparison of Calculated Fundamental Value and Market Price

Name of the Company	Market Value (average market price from 1st April, 2011 to 1st July, 2011)	Fundamental Value (using g = ROE × B)	Fundamental Value (using DPS growth rate)	Fundamental Value (using EPS growth rate)
Sun Pharmaceutical Ind. Ltd.	Rs 458	Rs 267. 241	Rs 440	Rs 508
Ranbaxy Drugs Ltd.	Rs 496.407	Rs 231	Rs 402	Rs 510
GlaxoSmithkline Pharmaceuticals Ltd.	Rs 2286.811	Rs 1744	Rs 1900	Rs 2480
Dr Reddy's Pharma Ltd.	Rs 1610.768	Rs 878	Rs 1200	Rs 1519
Cipla Ltd.	Rs 319.653	Rs 210	Rs 280	Rs 339
Lupin Pharmaceutical Ltd.	Rs 432.811	Rs 202	Rs 308	Rs 425

Interpretation

The above table compares the calculated intrinsic values to that of the market prices. It clearly shows valuation using growth rate "g" gives somehow a significant different value. But the models using EPS growth rate and DPS growth rate somehow gives a bit closer values to that of market price. For more accurate judgment the percentage differences are calculated and given below.

Table 3: Deviation between Fundamental Value (using three growth models) and Market Price

Name of the Companies	"g" Value Deviation (%)	DPS Growth Rate Deviation (%)	EPS Growth Rate Deviation (%)
GlaxoSmithKline	23.7	16.88	8.48
Ranbaxy	53.42	19	3
DrReddy	45.46	25.51	5.71
Sun Pharma	41.66	4	10
Cipla	34.48	12.4	6.2
Lupin	53.34	28.7	1.6

Interpretation

Table 3 shows the deviation between the fundamental values and that of the respective market price. The model using growth rate "g" gives significant deviated result in almost all cases. All the deviations are more than 20% and even in case of Ranbaxy company the deviation is the highest one, i.e. 53.42%. The reason behind this high margin of deviation can be the use of constant growth rate. A company may show high growth rate in one year and it may be low in following years. But, the assumption of the study treats it constant. As a result a high deviation occurs between the calculated value and the market price.

In case of DPS growth rate model the deviation is somehow moderate. The highest deviation is 28.7% in case of Lupin and the lowest one is 4% in case of Sun pharmaceutical. However both EPS and DPS growth rates are moving in same direction and the calculated intrinsic values are somewhat closer to each other than model using growth rate "g". It can be expected that DPS should be as good as EPS.

EPS growth rate model clearly gives more accurate result than the rest two models. Even in case of Lupin the deviation is only 1.6% which indicates its effectiveness in assessment of intrinsic value of a share. The highest deviation is 10% in Sun Pharmaceutical case, which is not a significant margin. The calculated values using this model in case of Sun Pharma, GlaxoSmithKline, Cipla and Ranbaxy shows that these are under-priced shares and Dr Reddy and Lupin are overpriced.

LIMITATION OF THE MODEL

Though Dividend Discount Model is philosophically correct approach for valuation, yet it has some real life limitations. These are as follows.

- The formula for constant growth model, $V0 = D1 / (r - g)$ is only true when growth rate is less than r, i.e. $g \leq r$.
- It assumes a constant growth rate that can only be used in the companies where the growth rate is constant for years and in real life it may be a difficult task.
- It also assumes a constant growth rate for net cash flows and a constant dividend payout ratio, which may not be true for all companies.
- This model completely ignores the changes in working capital.

CONCLUSION

Gordon Growth model is a widely used model in the area of share valuation. While implementing it in assessment of fundamental value of a share some pitfalls occur. First, forecasting the correct future dividend and growth rate. Second, use of CAPM model for finding out cost of capital which is theoretically sound but practically may give deviated result. Third, whether cost of capital or Weighted Average Cost of Capital (WACC) would be used for discounting the future cash flows. So, this method is extremely sensitive for small changes in growth rate and discount rate.The present study used the Constant Growth model to assess the intrinsic value of 6 Indian Pharmaceutical companies. For the implementation of the model 3 growth rates (growth rate 'g", DPS growth rate and EPS growth rate) were calculated and growth rate and dividend for the year 2011 is forecasted. The market price of the respective shares was calculated taking the average of the closing prices from 1st April, 2011 to 1st July, 2011. By comparing the market price with that of above discussed 3 constant growth models, the study found that EPS growth rate model gives more accurate result. By analyzing the deviation, it can be safely concluded that EPS growth model may be used for assessment of the intrinsic value of the shares. It can be more acceptable if manipulation of EPS values can be minimized by the companies. Though in theory this model works great but in practical cases some difficulties arrive. In real life company's growth rate will change, sometimes dramatically, from year to year. It is very rare that the growth rate will be constant for a longer period. Future research is required to overcome this problem and to obtain a proper growth model for valuation of shares.

REFERENCES

[1] Adams et al., August (2009), "A comparison of alternative approaches to equity valuation of privately held entrepreneurial firms", *Journal of Finance and Accountancy*, vol. 1, pp. 2-15.

[2] Alford, A. (1992), "The effect of the set of comparable firms on the accuracy of the price-earnings valuation method", *Journal of Accounting Research*, vol. 30, no. 1 (Spring), pp. 94-108.

[3] Dittman, I., Maug, E. and Kemper, J. (2004), "How fundamental are fundamental values: Valuation methods and their impact on the performance of German venture capitalists", *Social Science Research Network*, vol. 10, pp. 609-638.

[4] Hickman, Kent and Petry, H. Glen (1990), "A comparison of stock price predictions using court accepted formulas, dividend discount and p/e models", *Financial Management*, summer, vol. 19, no. 2, pp. 76-87.

[5] Kamstra Mark (2003), "Pricing firms on the basis of fundamentals", *Economic Review*, Federal Reserve Bank of Atlanta, 1st quarter, pp. 49-70.

[6] Kaplan, S.N., Ruback, R. (1995), "The valuation of cash flow forecasts: An emipirical analysis", *Journal of Finance*, vol. 50, no. 4 (September), pp. 1059-93.

[7] Kim, M., Ritter, R. Jay (1999), "Valuing IPOs", *Journal of Financial Economics*, vol. 53, no. 3 (September), pp. 409-437.

[8] Lang, M. (1991), "Time varying stock price response to earnings induced by uncertainty about the time series process of earnings", *Journal of Accounting Research*, vol. 29, pp. 229-257.

[9] Lie, E., Lie, J. Heidi, "Multiples used to estimate corporate value", *Financial Analysts Journal*, April 2002, vol. 58, pp. 44-55.

[10] Ohloson, J. (1995), "Earnings, book value and dividends in security valuation", *Contemporary Accounting Research*, Spring, vol. 11, pp 661-687.

[11] Pandey, A. (2009), "Studying earnings management in initial public offerings (IPOs) and its impact on IPO pricing in India", Working paper, no. 284, IIMB.

[12] Rojid, S. et al., "Learning models and stock valuation: Evidence from the stock exchange of mauritius", Working paper no. 332, Department of Finance and Accounting, Faculty Law and Management, University of Mauritius.

[13] Shiab-Al-Mohammad et al. (2006), "Common stock appraisal in relation to their P/E ratios using risk-adjusted measures: An emerging market prospective", *Jordan Journal of Business Administration*, vol. 2, no. 2, pp. 1-14.

[14] Teoh, S.H., Welch, I. and Wong T.J. (1998), "Earnings management and the long run market performance of IPOs", *Journal of Finance*, vol. 53, pp. 1935-1974.

[15] Teregrossa, J.S. (2005), "Discerning the the determinants of common stock valuation: An empirical analysis", Presented paper in the *International Conference on Policy Modelling*, Istanbul, May.

[16] Thomas, J., Nissim, D and Thomas, J., "Equity valuation using multiples", March 2001, *Journal of Accounting Research*, vol. 40, issue 1, pp. 135-172.

[17] Tulisan, P.C. , "Financial management: A self study textbook", 1st edition, S. Chand Publication, pp. 8.1-8.40.

[18] Zarwin, P. (1990), "What determines earnings-price ratios: revisited", *Journal of Accounting Auditing and Finance*, vol. 5, pp. 439-454.

Websites

[1] www.damodaran.com

[2] www.indianmba.com

[3] www.investopedia.org

[4] www.moneychimp.com

[5] www.nseindia.com

[6] www.wikipedia.org

Building Social Capital: The Importance of Entrepreneurial Social Infrastructure

Kalpana Sahoo[1], Ratikanta Biswal[2] and Nihar Ranjan Agasti[2]

[1] Sri Sri University, Bhubaneswer

[2] Asian School of Business Management, Bhubaneswar

E-mail: klpnsahoo@gmail.com; rimun143@gmail.com; niharagasti@gmail.com

ABSTRACT

21st century capitalism is shifting focus from making money to making meaning (ends vs. means, trailing indicators vs leading indicators). India is considered as the world's largest and most diverse democracy. The country has seen remarkable social, agricultural, and industrial progress within twenty years. Life expectancy has doubled and has opened new avenues of technologies such as specialized colleges, research institutions, the systems for financing and accrediting educational institutions. On the other hand, India has the world's worst poverty, the most widespread malnutrition, and the most extensive use of child labor. Government needs to follow a concerted effort to increase additional job opportunities for its people and create good infrastructure for technical and industrial training facilities. To improve the welfare of the organized and unorganized sector, the situation demands a good social infrastructure. Social infrastructure refers to those factors which render the human resources of a nation suitable for productive work. When considering a country to enter into globalization, it should evaluate whether the country has an adequate social infrastructure to foster economic growth. Social infrastructure refers to the facilities and mechanisms that ensure education, health care, community development, income distribution, employment and social welfare. The economy cannot be looked at in isolation without considering the basic needs of the people, and a significant level of social infrastructure is needed in this sector. Furthermore, the nature of the effect of economic and social infrastructure both depends on social capital which is a key for understanding, stimulating and enabling a conducive environment for such growth. Social capital, which is based on trust, reciprocity, networks and collective action, takes time to develop and needs a concrete attention. Improvements in the social sector pave the way for equity and in turn for economic development. In fact, effective human development and economic development itself depend on the development of social infrastructure. Thus, this paper tries to highlight the importance of social infrastructure which needs to build a social capital for its success.

Keywords: India and Its Social Infrastructure, Entrepreneurial Social Infrastructure, Concept of Social Capital

INTRODUCTION

The infrastructure development of any country includes both economic infrastructure development and also the social infrastructures. Development of economic infrastructure cannot usher in overall development at the desired level if the social infrastructure is not simultaneously developed. The capacities and technical refinement of the economic infrastructure like roads, sewers, electricity, open spaces, gardens and the evolving requirements of social infrastructures like shopping complexes, restaurants, medial facility zones, schools etc, are clearly delineated. Education, health, social security, water supply, shelter and sanitation etc, has to be developed to ensure proper social infrastructure. Social infrastructure is defined as building strong communities through the continuing development and delivery of activities, resources and support to strengthen the skills and confidence of people and community groups to enable them to take effective action and leading roles (Strong Communities Report Summary). Social infrastructure refers to the facilities and mechanisms that ensure education, health care, community development, income distribution, employment and social welfare. The economy cannot be looked at in isolation without considering the basic needs of the people, and a significant level of investment is needed in this sector. In this sense both economic and social infrastructure are interconnected and interdependent and in these terms and perspectives both economic and social infrastructures are crucial element for development of an economy and even growth is linked to infrastructure as infrastructure is linked to growth. So, the development of India is incomplete without social development and that would require focus on the infrastructure strategy for social research in India. Human development and improvement in the quality of life is the ultimate objective of all planning programmes leading to higher economic and social development. There exists a very strong linkage between attaining economic prosperity and enriching the quality of life, which is reflected in the social indicators of health, longevity, literacy and environmental sustainability. These indicators serve as valuable inputs for developing suitable policy initiatives.

There is a positive relationship between infrastructure investment and economic development. This relationship suggests that infrastructure has a high potential payoff in terms of economic growth. The importance of infrastructure has been generally taken as self-evident. It has been repeatedly emphasized that provision of adequate quality infrastructure is a pre-requisite for accelerated economic development. It has been seen that the link between infrastructure and economic development become more prominent when public investment on infrastructure construction and maintenance become a valuable policy tool to provide economic stimulus during recessions. It can also be an instrument for employment and intensive economic growth if non-negotiate quality and cost effectiveness is maintained with labour based approaches to infrastructure development. Wisely deployed investments helps in overcoming fiscal constraints and cut back in infrastructure developed. Further, the least cost approach to improve the supply of infrastructure should be followed by inter regional integration of infrastructure networks, so that efficient policies can be well drafted.

The effectiveness of infrastructure investment, i.e. whether it provides the kind of services valued by user varies according to its quality, quantity, and reliability, supplying to the demanded mask is essential along with efficiency, it is one of the ingredients to realize the potential returns. As the World Development Report 1994, states that the demand for infrastructure services is itself sensitive to economic growth, which is notoriously difficult to predict.

INDIA AND ITS SOCIAL INFRASTRUCTURE

Social infrastructure refers to those factors which render the human resources of a nation suitable for productive work. India is drastically different in terms of how its labor laws are regulated, how its citizens are educated, and how their health is handled. When considering a country to enter into globalization, things should evaluate whether the country has an adequate social infrastructure to foster economic growth. India is reportedly the world's largest and most diverse democracy. The country has seen remarkable social, agricultural, and industrial progress. Life expectancy has doubled and the specter of famine no longer stalks the sub-continent. On the other hand, India (and the south Asian region as a whole) has the world's worst poverty, the most widespread malnutrition, and the most extensive use of child labour.

The Economic way of thinking discusses the importance of social cooperation. It states that we depend on processes of coordination for far more than we usually think of as economic goods. It further goes on to explain that economic way of thinking has a lot to do with the notion that everything depends on what people believe to be benefits and costs and the relative value they place on those benefits and costs. The social infrastructure of India will directly impact how thing is able to operate in India. The Indian government has expressed a strong commitment towards education for all of its citizens. Education is highly valued in India and considered a great asset among its people. India has one of the lowest female literacy rates in Asia. The low level of literacy has a negative impact on women's lives, as well as on their families' lives and on their country's economic development. Numerous studies show that illiterate women have high levels of fertility and mortality, poor nutritional status, low earning potential, and little autonomy within the household.

Literacy in India has improved steadily over the years. Many states have started 'total literacy campaigns to eliminate illiteracy among the disadvantaged populations. The literacy rate varies from state to state. For example, the rate in Tripura is quite high and the state has a good network of educational institutions, including technical institutions. The largest barrier to literacy in the country is intense poverty. It becomes possible due to social infrastructure.

ENTREPRENEURIAL SOCIAL INFRASTRUCTURE (E.S.I.)

Flora and Flora (1993) developed the Entrepreneurial Social Infrastructure (E.S.I.) as a framework of components, structure, and process indicators that encourage collective action to achieve tangible goals in which social capital is a necessary, but not a complete prerequisite. Communities that engage in collective action to better the community are "entrepreneurial" (Flora et al., 1998). Flora et al., 1998 discusses the relationship between collective action within the community and the social infrastructure. Wilkinson (1991) differentiates between different types of collective action through the "social field" (development in the community) and "community field" (development of the community) which demonstrate that collective action of the social fields does not necessarily lead to the development of the community field. Flora et al. (1998), suggests keeping collective action separate from E.S.I. in order to assess which types of community development are necessary and able to be maintained .Flora et al, (1997a) found that communities with high amounts of social capital, such as "strong social networks, strong norms based on a dominant religion, intergenerational continuity of leadership and high level of trust," the greatest density of organizational interlocks, and projects implemented in the last five years which promoted collective action within the community field led to the development of the strongest community field. Recent research has shown the importance of social capital as indicated by entrepreneurial infrastructure, for economic development,

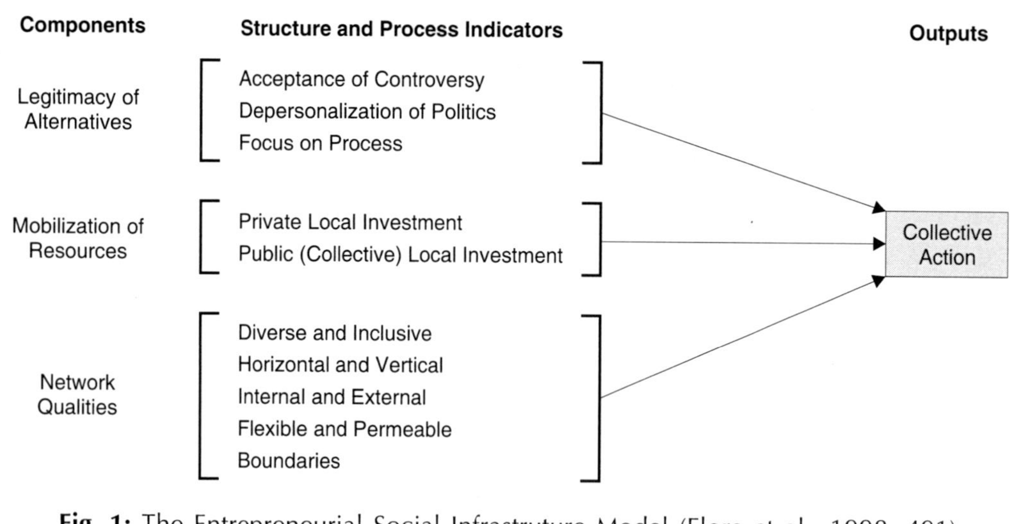

Fig. 1: The Entrepreneurial Social Infrastruture Model (Flora et al., 1998: 491)

particularly self-development, where a larger proportion of the value-added by an enterprise within a community remains in that community.

Flora et al. (1993) had found that those communities with a recent locally generated economic development project were more likely to possess the presence of the E.S.I. main components (Figure 1). The following components encompass the E.S.I. framework: legitimacy of alternatives (there is access to the involvement of diverse range of residents and a diversity of information), the mobilization of diverse resources, (donors will invest in community projects and local residents will support local taxes to contribute to the overall bettering of the community), and the presence of network qualities (social networks, both internal and external to the community, that are discussing, planning, and contributing to community projects are essential to the establishment of a strong social infrastructure) (Flora et al., 1998).

- A newspaper that initiated the flow of information about local issues. This provided a way that controversial issues could be exposed and discussed by the community in an unbiased fashion in which the diversity of opinions of the community could be included. **(Legitimacy of Alternatives)**
- Financial institutions which play a financial role to community projects by providing commercial loans at a low-interest; Grants, donations, foundations or other contributions of service on a financial committee **(Resource Mobilization)**
- Larger number of horizontal/vertical linkages within and outside the community **(Network Qualities)**

According to Flora et al. (1998), the presence of E.S.I. indicators are first dependent upon the presence of social capital, the broadness of community participation in local projects, and the ability to create and participate in local community economic development projects. These factors will significantly enhance the likelihood of a greater amount of Entreprenuerial Social Infrastructure (E.S.I.). First, it indicates the demographics, location, economic base, and governance structures of the community. Then it leads to the operationalization of the components of E.S.I.

THE CONCEPT OF SOCIAL CAPITAL

Social capital is a sociological concept, which refers to connections within and between networks. This new interest in social capital provides an opportunity for the policy makers to advance social agendas, but at the same time challenges them because it requires a better understanding on how health, income inequalities and social capital interact. Social capital is a key concept in the recognition of interconnections between social and economic outcomes. Social capital, according to Lane and Dorfman (1997), is a measurement of the levels of social trust and active relationships in the social networks of a community.

Woolcock (1998) defines social capital as 'encompassing the norms and networks facilitating collective action for mutual benefit'. Thus, a social capital is viewed as a community resource of networks, norms and trust that can be drawn on to build the community's capacity to develop and respond effectively to change. Social Capital theory provides a theoretical framework/ perspective from which to draw knowledge and ideas for engaging people within communities. Understanding the importance of trust and the strong correlation with community involvement and reciprocal behaviour, should influence the design of engagement strategies and help us to understand why one community engagement model or strategy will not suit all communities. L.J. Hanifan's (1916) indicates that "social capital" in reference to social cohesion and personal investment in the community. In defining the concept, Hanifan contrasts social capital with material goods by defining it as: the term 'Social sector' refers to the factors, which contribute to human capital formation and human development. Social development is recognized not only as a means to development, but also an end in itself, in terms of expanded individual opportunities, capabilities and freedom.

SOCIAL CAPITAL ACTS AS A TOOL FOR ENTREPRENEURIAL SOCIAL INFRASTRUCTURE

Social capital is an important community asset. Communities historically have very different levels of social capital. For example, in Robert Putnam's (1993) study of development in Italy, he found that social capital was the determinant of both governmental efficiency and economic development. He found that social capital sprang from ancient roots. In particular, he found a good predictor of social capital in the 1990s was the level of social capital in the middle Ages, as indicated by the presence of choral societies, male singing groups associated with towns. The three influential 'schools of thought' related to social capital were respectively led by Putnam, Bourdieu and Coleman. Robert Putnam (1995) conceived social capital as a community level resource and defined it as "features of social organization such as networks, norms and social trust that facilitate co-ordination and co-operation for mutual benefit". The French sociologist, Pierre Bourdieu,(1986) put an emphasis on social capital as the sum of resources, actual or virtual, that accrue individuals as a result of their membership of networks. Coleman (1988), eventually, mainly wrote on the link between social capital and the education process, and thus the role of the family. There is no general agreement on the definition of social capital, but there are three main issues which might be relevant to health and education which are the indicators of social infrastructure. The first is the distinction between an individual or a collective level of definition of social capital i.e. social capital is a resource which facilitates ends for individual or for a social group. However, collective social capital cannot be simply the sum of individual social capital. If social capital is a resource available through social networks, the resources that some individuals claim come at the expense of others. Secondly, these definitions do not really differentiate what social capital is from what social capital does, or what are the sources and the consequences of social capital. To confuse the sources of social capital with the benefits derived from them leads to circular reasoning because the presence of social capital is often inferred from the assets that an individual or group acquires. Thirdly, social capital is almost always understood as a concept, which can only have positive effects without considering its possible negative implications.

Entrepreneurial social infrastructure suggests ways of increasing social capital. Entrepreneurial social infrastructure consists of legitimization of alternatives, diverse networks and resource mobilization as we have mentioned earlier in Figure1. Mahyar Arefi (2003) identifies consensus building as a direct positive indicator of social capital. Consensus implies "shared interest" and agreement among various actors and stakeholders to induce collective action. Collective action is thus an indicator of increased social capital. Social capital and human capital operate at multiple levels of analysis (Oh et al., 2004; Van Deth, 2004).

Legitimization of Alternatives

Some communities seek the answer, while other communities consider many ways to getting things done. It is legitimate to look at alternatives. In such communities, there are shared goals with an understanding that there are alternative ways of meeting those goals. Like continuous improvement in industry, solutions are not sought, but countermeasures are implemented as progress towards goals is constantly monitored and alternative ways of getting there assessed. Where there is a high level of legitimization of alternatives, different points of view within the community are both accepted and valued by others in the community. This leads to acceptance to controversy, which is different than conflict. Where there is conflict, lines are drawn in the sand and one is labelled according to one's stance on a particular issue. When everything appears smooth and everyone agrees on everything, no discussion occurs. New issues are not brought forward, visions of the future are not shared, and alternative ways of getting there are not developed. In this situation, conflict often lies right beneath the surface.

There is awareness that the public sector is important in bringing about change at the local level, and there is higher participation in both civic and governmental organizations as a result. The success of one person is viewed as occurring at the expense of another. These are communities where controversy does not occur, because people do not politically express different points of view.

Diverse Networks

The social capital of a team can complement human capital "by affecting the conditions necessary for exchange and combination to occur" (Nahapiet & Ghoshal, 1998), as well as by increasing the amount of information and resources that are flowing through it.

Networks in communities with high social capital are diverse and inclusive. While there is room for subgroups with high levels of social capital (communities of interest within communities), communities of place require diversity. If a community development project is on-going with the desire to create more jobs, local people who will take those jobs need to be part of the process so there can be a better link between human capital and the manufactured capital offering employment opportunities.

Resource Mobilization

Resource mobilization is the last critical area where social capital is built. First, resources in the community must be seen as available to all. This applies to private resources, such as access to credit, as well as public resources, such as quality schooling, recreation and other opportunities. This does not mean there cannot be criteria for access, but the criteria should be well-known and there should be opportunities for people to increase their chance for access.

When mobilizing private resources, it is important for financial institutions to figure out how to give loans in the appropriate amount, with the appropriate terms, to all levels of entrepreneurs and citizens. In such a community, private citizens of all levels contribute whatever money they can when there is a need, and opportunities are available for individuals to contribute their time and goods to good causes. The ability to mobilize private resources is a critical part of creating social capital, giving everyone a chance to give.

Creating social capital takes conscientious effort. It means that each individual citizen must be included, not just to meet their needs, but for the assets which they can offer the community. It is equally important to mix the human capital and social capital in a proportional way. Without human capital, social capital can be acquired. Studies of human capital have often emphasized not just individual skill and experience, but also factors that contribute to social capital, such as the sharing and exchange of information associated with skill development and application (Pil & Leana, 2000; Inkpen & Tsang, 2005; Wright et al., 2001). At the same time, building and leveraging human capital is subject to complex social processes as individuals share experiences, tell stories, and engage in other forms of knowledge exchange (Nahapiet & Ghoshal, 1998; Orr, 1996). In order to understand the social capital in implementing E.S.I, we need to understand the relationship between human capital and social capital.

RELATIONSHIPS BETWEEN HUMAN AND SOCIAL CAPITAL: A FRAMEWORK

How might we go about thinking about the relationships between human and social capital? Figure 2 provides a framework for considering these.

	Human Capital	**Social Capital**
Focus	Individual agent	Relationships
Measures	Duration of schooling	Attitudes/values
	Qualifications	Membership/participation
		Trust levels
Outcomes	Direct: income, productivity	Social cohesion
	Indirect: health, civic activity	Economic achievement
		More social capital
Model	Linear	Interactive/circular

Fig. 2

Focus

The key distinction between human and social capital is that the former focuses on individual agents, and the latter on relationships between them and the networks they form. In an economic context, the inclusion of social capital draws attention to the obvious, but often under regarded fact, that individuals and their human capital are not discrete entities that exist separately from the rest of the organization, or from other social units. The acquisition, deployment and effectiveness of skills depend crucially on the values and behaviour patterns of the contexts within which these skills are expected to operate. Focusing on relationships rather than agents is a gestalt switch. On the other hand, it is not an alternative, but a complement, at least in a partial sense.

Input/Measure

Human capital is measured primarily by levels of qualification achieved. The inadequacy of this is often acknowledged (Behrman, 1997), but the availability of large data sets allowing easy measurement ensures that it continues to dominate. Social capital is far more diffuse. It is measured broadly, and often simplistically, in terms of attitudes or values, or by levels of active participation in civic life or in other networks. The relevance of this to economic growth can be seen in a number of ways. It gives greater prominence, for example, to informal modes of learning, and the skills acquired through learning-by-doing. Network membership provides access to important information and ideas, often in a relatively unstructured way. The overlap between different spheres of activity comes into the equation. One example is the interaction between learning related to economic production and that which goes on in the domestic sphere. Another is the question of how far organizations actively encourage their staff to play a part in the life of the surrounding community – in the course of which they may well acquire skills which impact significantly on their economic performance.

Outcomes

The output of human capital is generally measured in terms of enhanced income or productivity. Social capital can been linked directly to economic performance at very different levels – at the level of nation states (e.g. Fukuyama, 1996), at the regional level (e.g. Maskell et al., 1998) or between and within communities or organizations (Grootaert, 1998). It also has wider outcomes – including the generation of further social capital. Some of these – for example the maintenance of social cohesion – in turn contribute indirectly to enhanced economic performance. Looked at from a social capital perspective, the direct impact of training may be as much in the strengthening of networks and information flows as in the acquisition of individual competencies or improving productivity.

Models

Human capital suggests a direct linear model: investment is made, in time or money, and economic returns follow. This has considerable appeal, both for its methodological manageability, and in terms of political acceptability. That is, it enables analysts to deploy existing tools to estimate the returns to investment, and politicians to justify expenditure on human capital formation. Social capital has a much less linear approach, and its returns are less easily definable. On the one hand, this incurs the charge of circularity, and it makes it harder to specify what kinds of return might be expected, by when.

CONCLUSION

Social entrepreneurial infrastructure does not seek its own limited resources keep them from pursuing their visions. They use scarce resources efficiently, and they leverage their limited resources by drawing in partners and collaborating with others. They explore all resource options, from pure philanthropy to the commercial methods of the business sector. They develop resource strategies that are likely to support and reinforce their social missions. They take calculated risks and manage the downside, so as to reduce the harm that will result from failure. They need to understand the expectations and values of communities. They seek to create real social entrepreneurial infrastructure for the benefits of their communities and need to understand the relationship between social capital and human capital. Social capital appears to be positively related to organizational effectiveness and to play a central role in reducing organizational transaction costs (Fukuyama, 1995). It also facilitates coordinated action to achieve desired goals (Leana and Buren, 1999), justifies organizational commitment (Watson & Papamarcos, 2002), and results in a significant positive impact on product innovation (Nahapiet & Ghoshal, 1998).

Without some foundation of trust, social capital cannot develop – the essential connections will not form. So trust is a precondition of healthy social capital for the building of better social infrastructure . On the other hand, the trust-based connections that characterize social capital lead to the development of increased trust as people work with one another over time. Besides, individuals are not placed in a fixed social setting and a sustained belief in the ability of systems, rather than personal trust, is required to maintain the conditions of expanded choices and opportunities. As Luhmann argues that modern societies are characterized by the increasing importance of system trust, which is built upon the life that others also trust, not simply rest on bonds between people (Luhmann, 1988). In the final analysis so far, we have focused on relationship of the social infrastructure and economic development. So we simply reach the conclusion that social infrastructure is an enormously important for economic development and it works directly and indirectly on a number of determinants of social development which is directly linked with the economic prosperity. It can be achieved by implementing social capital in the communities.

REFERENCES

[1] Arefi, M. (2003). Revisiting the Los Angeles Neighborhood Initiative (LANI): Lessons for Planners. *Journal of Planning Education and Research*, vol. 22 iss. 4, p. 384.

[2] Behrman, J. (1997). "Conceptual and Measurement Issues" in eds. Jere Behrman and Nevzer Stacey *The Social Benefits of Education* (Ann Arbor: University of Michigan Press): 17-67.

[3] Bourdieu, P. (1986). "The Forms of Capital". In J. Richardson (Ed.), *Handbook of Theory and Research for Sociology of Education (pp. 241-58).* New York: Greenwood Press.

[4] Coleman, J.S. (1988). Social Capital in the Creation of Human Capital. *The American Journal of Sociology,* 94 (Supplement): S95-S120.

[5] Flora, C.B. & Flora, J.L. (1993). "Entreprenuerial Social Infrastructure: A Necessary Ingredient." *The Annals of the American Academy of Political and Social Science* 529: 48-58.

[6] Flora, J.L., Hales, B., Petrzelka, P., Trca-Black, S. and Jeff Zacharakis-Jutz (1997a). "Social Reconnaissance: Field Research by a Student Team to Inform a Participatory Community Development Project." Paper presented at the Annual Meeting of the Community Development Society, Athens, GA, July 27-30.

[7] Flora, J.L., Hales, B., Petrzelka, P., Trca-Black, S. and Jeff Zacharakis-Jutz (1998). "Social Capital and Communities of Place." *Rural Sociology* 63(4) 481-506.

[8] Fukuyama, F. (1996). *Trust: The Social Virtues and the Creation of Prosperity* (Harmondsworth: Penguin Books).

[9] Grootaert, C. (1998). *Social Capital: The Missing Link?* Working Paper No. 3. (Washington, D.C.: World Bank Social Capital Initiative).

[10] Hanifan, L.J. (1916). "The Rural School Community Center", *Annals of the American Academy of Political and Social Science* 67: 130-138.

[11] Inkpen, A.C. and Tsang, E. (2005). Social Capital, Networks, and Knowledge Transfer. *Academy of Management Review,* 30: 146–165.

[12] Lane, B. and Dorfman, D. (1997). *Strengthening Community Networks: The Basis for Sustainable Community Renewal*, Northwest Regional Educational Laboratory, Portland.

[13] Leana, C. and Buren, H. (1999). Organizational Social Capital and Employment Practices. *The Academy of Management Review,* 24(3): 538-556.

[14] Luhmann, N. (1988). Familiarity, Confidence, Trust: Problems and Alternative. In Gambetta, D.(Ed). *Trust: Making and Breaking Cooperative Relations.* Oxford, Blackwell.

[15] Maskell, P., H. Eskelinen, I. Hannibalsson, A. Malmberg and E. Vatne (1998). *Competitiveness, Localised Learning and Regional Development: Specialization and Prosperity in Small Business Economies* (London: Routledge).

[16] Nahapiet, J. and Ghoshal, S. (1998). Social Capital, Intellectual Capital, and the Organizational Advantage. *Academy of Management Review,* 23: 242–266.

[17] Oh, H., Chung, M. and Labianca, G. (2004). Group Social Capital and Group Effectiveness: The Role of Informal Socializing Ties. *Academy of Management Journal,* 47: 860–875.

[18] Orr, J. (1996). *Talking about Machines: An Ethnography of a Modern Job.* Ithaca, NY: Cornell University Press.

[19] Pil, F.K. and Leana, C.R. (2000). Free-Agency Versus High Involvement Approaches to Skill Development. In C.R. Leana and D.M. Rousseau (Eds.), *Relational Wealth:* 116–129. New York: Oxford University Press.

[20] Putnam, R. (1993). *Making Democracy Work: Civic Tradition in Modern Italy.* Princeton: Princeton University Press.

[21] Putnam, R. (1995). Tuning In, Tuning Out: The Strange Disappearance of Social Capital in America. *Political Science and Politics,* 28(4): 664-683.

[22] Van Deth, J. (2003). Measuring Social Capital: Orthodoxies and Continuing Controversies. *International Journal of Social Research Methodology,* 6(1): 79–92.

[23] Warren, R. (1975). Context and Isolation: The Teaching.

[24] Watson, G. and Papamarcos, S. (2002). Social Capital and Organizational Commitment. *Journal of Business and Psychology,* 16(4): 537-552.

[25] Wilkinson, K. (1991). *The Community in Rural America.* New York: Greenwood Press.

[25] Woolcock, M. (1998). 'Social Capital and Economic Development: Toward a Theoretical Synthesis and Policy Framework', *Theory and Society*, 27, pp. 151–208.

Web Sources

[1] http://www.thehindubusinessline.com/features/eworld/article2021368.ece?homepage =true assessed on 12th May, 2011.

[2] http://economictimes.indiatimes.com/news/news-by-company/corporate-trends/ sustainability-interwoven-with-interests-of-country-and-corporate/articleshow/ 8742341.cms assesssed on 13th May, 2011.

Building Social Capital through Agriculture Finance: A Case Study of the Prathama Bank

Jeet Singh[1] and Preeti Yadav[2]

[1] Moradabad Institute of Technology, Moradabad
[2] Institute of Rural Management, Jaipur
E-mail: jsy2626@rediffmail.com; py1717@rediffmail.com

ABSTRACT

The concept of social capital is gaining more and more importance in social science research for various reasons. The positive connection between effectiveness of various development programmes and social capital existing in the participants is one of them. Thus various issues such as what is social capital, how can it be generated, how it can be used more effectively for mutual benefit, how can it be measured, etc. become vital for policy makers as well as for practitioners and researchers. Banks and microfinance institutions for instance very frequently bank on creation of social capital to bring out desirable change at macro level. In fact it is the basic fundamental principle of regional rural banks as well as microfinance to replace physical capital or collateral required for acquiring loan with social capital or peer pressure and monitoring. The present paper attempts to understand the role of social capital in the context of development programmes and more specifically agriculture finance and microfinance programmes. Social capital refers to those stocks of social trust, norms and networks that people can draw upon to solve common problems. Networks of civic engagement, such as neighborhood associations, sports clubs, and cooperatives, are an essential form of social capital, and the denser these networks. The more likely those members of a community will cooperate for mutual benefit. This is so, even in the face of persistent problems of collective action (tragedy of the commons, prisoner's dilemma, etc.), because networks of civic engagement: (i) make possible coordination and communication, and thus create channels through which information about the trustworthiness of other individuals and groups can flow, and be tested and verified; (ii) promote powerful norms of generalized reciprocity by creating expectations that favour given now will be returned later; Formation and use of social capital is considered to be one of the emerging tools of development programmes. It is valued as one of the crucial link to replace physical capital with social intermediation in agriculture finance. The paper analyses the meaning and role of social capital with specific reference to agriculture finance provided by Prathama Bank in Moradabad district (first regional rural bank in India) and tries to measure its impact on social empowerment of farmers with the help of empirical findings. The paper is based on primary data collected of 200 farmers by using judgemental sampling. A Likert scale is used to find the perceptions of farmers about the changes which agriculture finance programme has brought out in their lives with respect to various parameters related to awareness building, capacity building and active and collective participation in social and political life to bring out desirable changes. The paper concludes that agriculture finance programme implemented by the bank has created a social capital which has an empowering effect on farmers. The paper suggests that creation of social capital is not an automatic outcome and the banks have to create and nurture it deliberately by implementing specific policies such as capacity building programmes, developing decision making abilities, etc.

Keywords: Agriculture Finance, Collective Action, Social Capital, Social Empowerment

INTRODUCTION

Social capital refers to those stocks of social trust, norms and networks that people can draw upon to solve common problems. Networks of civic engagement, such as neighborhood associations, sports clubs, and cooperatives, are an essential form of social capital, and the denser these networks, the more likely the members of a community will cooperate for mutual benefit. It's a set of informal norms in the society. The informal norms that constitute it lead to greater trust and cooperation in society. These informal norms are related to traditional virtues like honesty, honouring commitments, sincere discharge of duties, reciprocity etc. Maybe this is what makes Social Capital an elusive and ignored subject in public debates. A high social capital has not only social benefits but also economic benefits. Studies by World Bank have shown that social cohesion is critical for societies to prosper economically and for development to be sustainable. A perfect example would be Japan, who shattered in Second World War rose back due to its high social capital. For a modern stable democracy, social capital is sine qua non.

In a world where isolation, loneliness and individualistic tendencies have increased, social capital is a neglected but vital component of society. As the name suggests, social capital is a form of collective wealth. But social capital is not measured in dollars or material possessions. Its wealth lies in the strength of a society's social networks, and the inclinations that arise from these networks for people to do things for each other. Social capital resides in many resources, institutions, and even practices of communities, but a dominant theme is that social capital is strengthened when people create and interact through their networks. These networks may have their bases in service clubs, social organizations, or economic activity, as in the case of members of a co-operative.

Social capital is defined as "the advantage created by a person's location in a structure of relationships. It explains how some people gain more success in a particular setting through their superior connections to other people". Social capital is productive, since two farmers exchanging tools can get more work done with less physical capital; rotating credit associations can generate pools of financial capital for increased entrepreneurial activity; and job searches can be more efficient if information is embedded in social networks. Social capital also tends to cumulate when it is used, and be depleted when not, thus creating the possibility of both virtuous and vicious cycles that manifest themselves in highly civic and uncivil communities. A high incidence of social capital in a community is often accompanied by lower crime rates, higher productivity, stable workforces, higher inclination to innovation, longer life spans, less dependence on social services; etc. It's a set of informal norms in the society. The informal norms that constitute it lead to greater trust and cooperation in society. These informal norms are related to traditional virtues like honesty, honouring commitments, sincere discharge of duties, reciprocity, etc. May be this is what makes Social Capital an elusive and ignored subject in public debates. A high social capital has not only social benefits but also economic benefits. Studies by World Bank have shown that social cohesion is critical for societies to prosper economically and for development to be sustainable. A perfect example would be Japan, who shattered in Second World War rose back due to its high social capital. For a modern stable democracy, social capital is sine qua non.

REVIEW OF THE LITERATURE

Social capital is a sociological concept which has been applied to a variety of issues in recent times. Bard, 1985 defined the concept as the aggregate or the actual or potential resources which are linked to possession of a durable network of more or less institutionalized relationships of mutual acquaintance or recognition. As the concept experienced considerable theoretical and empirical analysis various other definitions have emerged over the years. Baker (1990) defined the concept as a .resource that actors derive from specific social structures and then use to pursue their interests; it is created by changes in the relationship among actors. And according to Putnam (1995), social capital refers to features of social organization such as networks, norms and social trust that facilitates coordination and cooperation for mutual benefits. Some of the attempts to evolve empirical measures of social capital include the recent works of scholars based on experiences in Tanzania, Indonesia, South Africa and other developing countries. For instance, in their consideration of the various mechanisms by which local social capital affects outcomes Narayan and Pritchett (1999) defined social capital as the quantity and quality of associational life and the related social norms. The authors examined the effects of social capital on household income in rural Tanzania. In defining social capital for their empirical analysis the respondents were asked questions about group membership and characteristics of each group in which individuals reported membership. Such characteristics were kin heterogeneity of membership, income heterogeneity of membership, group functioning, group decision making and voluntary membership. They assumed that being a member of each group made a greater contribution to social capital if the group was more heterogeneous across kinship groups, more inclusive and horizontal and better functioning. Hence the contribution of each group to social capital was made an equally weighted sub-index of these three characteristics. Other studies which have used characteristics of group membership as proxy for social capital include Grooataert (1999) and Maluccio et al. (2000). The main characteristics considered were gender composition, group performance, income heterogeneity and measures of meeting attendance by group members. Both studies found positive and significant impact of social capital on household welfare.

Number of studies focus on positive and negative impact of social capital while judging the performance of development programmes. Blair and Carroll (2008) give a precise explanation of how social capital can be used as a tool for community development. They state that social capital can be used for bonding or uniting individuals within a group or network as well as bridging or overcoming vertical barriers with unequal social status or power to work together. It helps local communities in different ways such as reducing cost of negotiations and monitoring due to increased trust established within the society, improving efficiency of transactions and mitigating negative economic effects on non-market transactions such as damage to environment, etc. as individuals who are part of same network also share trust, same values and reciprocity. Social capital also acts as a catalyst for encouraging innovations due to increased trust, improving quality of life, taking local competitive advantages in global competition, mitigating economic development conflicts due to availability of common platform to discuss issues and development of social economies. Coffe and Geys (2005) study the impact of social capital on financial performance of local governments such as 300 Flemish municipalities assuming that social capital is likely to increase public monitoring abilities, effectively resolve social problems and lead officials to better performance. The authors selected three indicators to judge the level of social capital in the municipalities such as the density of voluntary organizations, rate of political participation and crime rate per capita in municipal areas. The empirical results showed that not only social capital had significant positive impact on budgetary surplus in Flemish municipalities; it also showed that one standard deviation improves the municipality budget surplus with 2 to 2.25 percent of total revenues. Pronyk et al (2008) study the impact of social capital in health intervention programmes in providing HIV training and reducing women's vulnerability in it in South African villages. The experiment was conducted in few villages where group microfinance showing the evidence of social capital and comparison villages with no evidence of social capital. The study found out that the impact of social capital was significantly high in bringing out desirable change.

OBJECTIVE OF THE STUDY

The present study aims at the following objectives:

1. To understand the role of social capital in the context of development programmes and more specifically agriculture finance and microfinance programmes;
2. To analyze the meaning and role of social capital with specific reference to agriculture finance provided by Prathama Bank in Moradabad district (first regional rural bank in India); and
3. To measure the impact of social capital on social empowerment of farmers with the help of empirical findings.

RESEARCH METHODOLOGY

Research Type	:	Empirical
Type of Sampling	:	Judgemental Sampling
Sampling Unit	:	Farmers and members of self help groups
Sampling Universe	:	Village Asmoli in District Moradabad, Uttar Pradesh
Sample size	:	200
Data Type	:	Primary as well as Secondary Data
Data Source	:	Survey through questionnaire and review of literature.

FEATURES OF SOCIAL CAPITAL

1. "Relationships among actors (individuals, groups, and/or organisations) that create a capacity to act for mutual benefit or a common purpose";
2. It can be accumulated over time and then drawn on in the future for use in achieving certain goals;
3. Is a collective resource rather than accruing to an individual;
4. Circumstances may result in having access to greater or lesser stocks of a community's social capital.

Importance of Social Capital

1. It allows communities to advance smoothly;
2. It allows people to resolve collective problems more easily;
3. It widens our awareness of the many ways we are linked;
4. The networks filled with social capital assist in the achievement of our goals.

Positive Social Capital Looks Like

1. People feel that they are part of the community;

2. Citizens feel useful and help in a variety of community activities and ventures;
3. Citizens actively participate in community networks such as public meetings, organizations, etc.;
4. Individuals help strangers and involve them;
5. Neighbors keep an eye on each other's home.

Five Mechanisms for How Social Capital Affects Outcomes

The five mechanisms for how social capital affects outcomes are:

1. Improve society's ability to monitor the performance of government, either because government officials are more embedded in the social network or because monitoring the public provision of services is a public good;
2. Increase informal insurance (or informal safety nets) between households, thereby allowing households to pursue higher returns, but more risky, activities and production techniques;
3. Facilitate the diffusion of innovations by increasing inter-linkages among individuals;
4. Reduce information imperfections and expand the range of enforcement mechanisms, thereby increasing transactions in output, credit, land and labour markets;
5. Increase possibilities for co-operative action in solving problems with a local common property element.

Five Aspects of Social Capital

The five aspects of social capital are mentioned in Table 1 below:

Table 1

Sl. No.	Aspects
1.	**Civic Engagement: How civically engaged are people in your community?**
	(a) Have you attended a community parade or celebration in the past 12 months? (b) Have you helped plan or lead a meeting or activity? (c) Have you volunteered your time in the past 12 months?
2.	**Trust: Do people trust or feel safe in your community?**
	(a) Do you feel safe walking down the street at night in your community? (b) Overall, can you trust your local government to do what is right?
3.	**Civic Responsibility: Do citizens feel a sense of civic duty**
	(a) You lost your wallet with Rs. 5000 in it. How many people in your community would return it? (b) A terrible storm hit your community and left people homeless. How many people would help out in any way?

4.	**Networks and Connections** "Bonding" – connecting with those people who are similar "Bridging" – connecting with those are engaged in different networks "Linking" – connections with organizations that have resources within and outside the community
	(a) Have you been involved in any sports, garden, recreational, investment or hobby group in the last 12 months? (b) Have you been involved in a youth or parents' organization in the past 12 months?
5.	**Collective Community Vitality: Each individual is important to the community's vitality!**
	(a) How often do young people move away from your community to find better opportunities? (b) How often do people of different races, ethnicities, and religions get along with one another?

CONCEPTION OF SOCIAL CAPITAL

In conceptualizing social capital a distinction can be made between formal and informal social capital.

1. **Formal social capital:** It refers to formally defined patterns of behaviour, norms of exchange, networks and institutions. The measures of this kind of social capital can be found: e.g. the extent of civil society (measured by the number/membership of NGOs in economy).
2. **Informal social capital:** It refers to those networks which operate outside of this formal system; it refers to things such and kinship, informal networks between

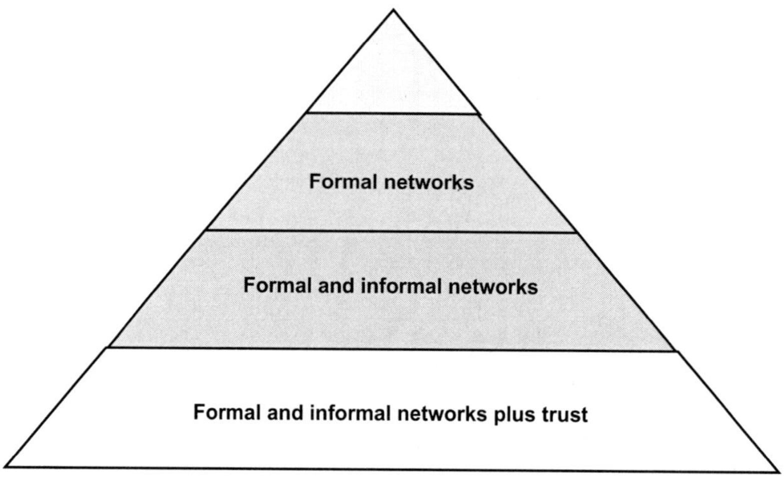

Fig. 1: Pyramid of Social Capital Concepts

individuals, families and groups. This is more problematic, requiring surveys of household to be carried out. The collection of such data is expensive, and in the absence of this data, presents problems for the study in hand.

3. **Formal and informal networks plus trust:** A distinction can be drawn between the extent of social networks and the quality of social networks. It is into the latter that the concept of trust is important. Virtually every commercial transaction has within itself an element of trust, certainly any transaction conducted over a period of time. It can be plausibly argued that much of economic backwardness in the world can be explained by the lack of mutual confidence. It can be seen that trust is closely related to economic performance.

The Figure 1 shows narrow and broad conceptions of social capital.

MEASUREMENT OF SOCIAL CAPITAL

There are a number of different aspects to social capital and measuring the level of social capital in communities can be complex. In many surveys respondents are asked a range of questions that cover a variety of issues. They commonly focus on:

1. Levels of trust – for example, whether individuals trust their neighbours and whether they consider their neighbourhood a place where people help each other.
2. Membership – for example, to how many clubs, societies or social groups individuals belong.
3. Networks and how much social contact individuals have in their lives – for example, how often individuals see family and friends.

NETWORKS

Formal and informal networks are central to the concept of social capital. They are defined as the personal relationships which are accumulated when people interact with each other in families, workplaces, neighbourhoods, local associations and a range of informal and formal meeting places.

Different types of social capital can be described in terms of different types of networks:

1. **Bonding social capital**: Describes closer connections between people and is characterised by strong bonds e.g. among family members or among members of the same ethnic group; it is good for 'getting by' in life.
2. **Bridging social capital:** Describes more distant connections between people and is characterised by weaker, but more cross-cutting ties e.g. with business associates, acquaintances, friends from different ethnic groups, friends of friends, etc, it is good for 'getting ahead' in life.

3. **Linking social capital**: Describes connections with people in positions of power and is characterised by relations between those within a hierarchy where there are differing levels of power; it is good for accessing support from formal institutions. It is different from bonding and bridging in that it is concerned with relations between people who are not on an equal footing. An example would be a social service agency dealing with an individual, e.g. job searching at the Benefits Agency.

EMPIRICAL STUDY OF MEASURING THE EFFECTIVENESS OF SOCIAL CAPITAL

Measuring social capital is complex yet very important task for researchers. World Bank has identified number of innovative quantitative as well as qualitative tools to assess different dimensions of social capital such as groups and network, trust, collective action, social inclusion and information and communication. They include community profiling, asset mapping, community and household questionnaires, attitudinal surveys, polling methods, experiments, etc. Devine and Robert (2001) comment that surveys and polling methods along with other quantitative tools though helpful in establishing correlation between variables have a major limitation in understanding social relations as they cannot provide an account of internal and underlying social processes that relate things together. A multi layered and a multi method research technique such as combination of quantitative and qualitative tools like assessing voluntary activism, citizen's auditing, etc., is a better way to assess social capital. Karlan (2005) tries to assess as well as predict the trustworthiness which is a very critical factor for successful implementation of micro finance programme by making experiments such as 'Trust games' between the members of micro finance organization. The trust game experiment was also used by Cassar, Crouley and Wydick (2007) to find out the relevance of social capital on the performance of group lending of few microfinance programmes in South Africa. Almost all the studies conducted previously state on using a combination of various research tools such as survey, personal interviews and focused group discussions.

Creation of social capital plays a very vital role in creating collective consciousness amongst disempowered villagers especially women. The idea of power is at the root of the concept of empowerment. Economic empowerment focuses more on 'power to' which means that higher access to credit and savings and other economic resources such as business training, etc lead to better economic position of villagers especially women leading further to better bargaining position at home and in community. Self empowerment focuses on 'power within' i.e. development of self esteem, confidence and leadership qualities. Social and political empowerment which concentrate on 'power with' and 'power over' means that social capital created through network helps them to bring out social mobilization, build alliances and act as a collective force to bring out changes in gender based social structure. It is assumed that social capital plays a very crucial role in social empowerment of villagers especially women which can be viewed in terms of higher level of consentization of women in enhancing awareness and knowledge, higher level of interactive activities leading to higher mobility, higher collective action and better decision making abilities and better social position in the family and neighbourhood.

METHODOLOGY

To find out the relationship between creation of social capital and the social empowerment, a judgemental sample of 200 farmers as well as members of Self Help Groups (SHGs) are selected for conducting survey to assess the impact of social capital on their social empowerment. These members are from fifteen self help groups which were formed under the programme of finance by Prathama Bank branch at village Asmoli in district Moradabad (Uttar Pradesh). Moradabad (also known as Brass City) as a city is one of the most urbanized and fast developing cities in India. In its high appetite for industrial growth, number of small surrounding villages is getting converted into industrial zones and thus semi urban areas. Transition of these villages into semi urban areas comes with a mixed outcome for local citizens. On one hand it gives the local citizens better job opportunities and better infrastructure, and on other hand it demolishes agriculture and local jobs and increases the social pressures within the community. It is very essential at this juncture that these local communities are brought in to trust, helped to take advantages of modern development and brought into mainstream development process. Prathama Bank (the first regional rural bank of India) promoted by Syndicate Bank, Government of India and UP Government using agriculture finance, microfinance programme as a tool to empower local communities through development of capacity building of local villagers and creation of social capital.

Brief Profile of the Respondents

The brief profile of the respondents is given in Table 2.

The socio-economic profile states that members belong to lower or lower middle income group. Majority come from lower caste and does not have adequate literacy to get jobs in an organized sector. Though the percentage of literate respondents is 87, but majority of the respondents have not passed even 10th class. The number of years of association varies from 1 year to 7 or 10 years.

Sources of creation and sustenance of social capital

In order to create and sustain new social capital it is very necessary that potential members are made aware about the agriculture finance and microfinance programmes

Table 2

Sl. No.	Particulars	
1.	Percentage of male respondents	71.0
2.	Average age of respondents	37.43 (8.423)
3.	Percentage of married respondents	88.5
4.	Average no. of family members	4.79 (1.045)
5.	Average no. of earners in the family	1.56 (0.720)
6.	Percentage of literate respondents	87
7.	Average monthly family income (Rs.)	6758 (3225)
8.	Average no. of years of association with Prathama Bank and self-help group	4.285 (1.77)

Note: Figures in bracket denote Standard Deviation.

and are introduced in the groups as well as at individual level. At the same time it is also essential that group meetings are held at the regular frequencies to increase the level of interactivity.

Table 3 gives the details of the creation and sustenance of the social capital.

The data in Table 3 shows that most of the farmers or SHG members have been introduced to any kind of social organization for the first time (88.5%). Most of them have been introduced by existing borrowers or existing members of SHG. This shows that the formal creation of social capital of formation of SHG is backed by informal trust and solidarity between existing borrowers or existing members. The high frequency of meeting per month with bank officials or within SHG and higher opportunities to

Table 3

Sl. No.	Particulars	
1.	Percentage of farmers or members informed about the finance programme by other existing or SHG members	84.5
2.	Percentage of farmers or members informed about the finance programme by friends or relatives	14.0
3.	Percentage of farmers or members joined any social organization or associated with bank for the first time	88.5
4.	Average number of meeting held per month within the SHG or with bank officials	1.76
5.	Percentage of members enjoyed leadership positions in SHGs	27.5

members to work at responsible positions such as chairman, secretary or treasurer of SHG by rotation method has helped in sustaining the social capital.

Measuring Effectiveness of Social Capital

It is assumed that social capital created with the help of formal and informal sources (NGO and group members) will help farmers or SHG members in enhancing their awareness and knowledge about various issues related to health, sanitation, education of their children, etc; enhance their decision making ability, enhance their social status at home and in neighbourhood and lead them to collective action for their better livelihood. As most of these issues are related to the perception of the participants, the farmers and SHG members were asked about the change perceived by them before and after joining SHG or before or after taking a agriculture loan from the bank. These changes were ranked in Likert scale such as:

5 = Very Good than before 4 = Better than before 3 = No change
2 = Worse than before 1 = Worst than before

Thus any score above 3 shows the positive perception about that parameter by the farmer or member of SHG. In all 13 variables were selected for measuring change in perceptions. The details of factor analysis and the reliability test of the selected 13 variables are given in Table 4.

Table 4

Sl. No.	Parameter of Measuring Social Capital	Variables	Cronbach's Alpha Value
1.	Access for awareness and capacity building	Access to Education and Training	0.83
		Access to Financial Help	
		Awareness about Children's Education	
		Access to & Awareness about Sanitation	
		Access to & Aware about Family Planning	
		Access to & Aware about Health Care	
2.	Improvement in decision making ability	Improvement in decision making abilities in family decisions	0.81
		Improvement in decision making abilities in family expenses	
3.	Improvement in social status and mobility	Satisfied with improvement in social status and mobility	0.78
		Satisfied with improvement in the social status within Family	
		Satisfied with improvement in the social status within neighbourhood	
4.	Collective action	Higher participation in collective process for social issues	0.71
		Higher participation in electoral process	

In order to see the effectiveness of social capital on overall social empowerment of farmers who have taken agriculture loan from the Prathama Bank and SHG members, the farmers and the SHG members were divided into 3 categories as per their years of association with the Bank and SHG respectively, such as new members (having associated with Bank or SHG for less than or up to 1 year), 1 to 3 years and more than 3 years.

Hypotheses

Higher years of association with the Bank or SHG should lead to higher social capital and would lead to higher social empowerment in terms of higher level of awareness, decision making abilities and collective action.

Table 5 shows the perceptions of the farmers and the SHG members related to the changes before and after association with the bank or joining SHG.

Table 5

Sl. No.	Particulars	Association Up to 1 Year	Association from 1 to 3 Years	Association Above 3 Years	Combined
1	Access to education and training	3.5556 (0.615)	3.7778 (0.950)	3.8686 (0.829)	3.82 (0.843)
2	Access to financial help	3.3889 (0.916)	3.5111 (0.548)	3.8978 (0.909)	3.77 (0.862)
3	Awareness about children's education	3.0556 (0.639)	3.5556 (0.942)	3.6934 (0.781)	3.61 (0.826)
4	Access to and awareness about sanitation	3.2778 (0.669)	3.4000 (1.031)	3.5182 (1.043)	3.47 (1.102)
5	Access to and aware about family planning	2.8883 (0.785)	3.2000 (1.099)	3.4526 (1.063)	3.34 (1.063)
6	Access to and aware about health care	3.0556 (0.639)	3.3556 (0.980)	3.4015 (0.981)	3.36 (0.957)
7	Improvement in decision making abilities in family decisions	3.3889 (0.607)	3.5778 (0.722)	3.7445 (0.569)	3.68 (0.617)
8	Improvement in decision making abilities in family expenses	3.5556 (0.511)	3.6000 (0.617)	4.1095 (0.564)	3.95 (0.620)
9	Satisfied with improvement in social status and mobility	3.8333 (0.618)	4.000 (0.768)	4.1460 (0.600)	4.09 (0.648)
10	Satisfied with improvement in the social status within family	3.3333 (0.685)	3.5556 (0.840)	3.7810 (0.905)	3.69 (0.882)

Sl. No.	Particulars	Association Up to 1 Year	Association from 1 to 3 Years	Association Above 3 Years	Combined
11	Satisfied with improvement in the social status within neighbourhood	3.3333 (0.685)	3.6667 (0.738)	3.7080 (0.729)	3.66 (0.732)
12	Higher participation in collective process for social issues	3.1667 (0.618)	3.4444 (0.586)	3.7445 (0.514)	3.63 (0.571)
13	Higher participation in electoral process	3.1667 (0.785)	3.2444 (0.733)	3.7591 (0.600)	3.59 (0.703)

Note: Figures in brackets denote standard deviation.

Table 5 depicts the difference about the perception between three categories of borrowers and SHG members classified as per their years of association with bank and with SHG respectively. The social empowerment is measured on 13 parameters which collectively measure the changes in the level of knowledge and awareness, decision making abilities, changes in social status and willingness for collective action. The overall impact on social empowerment is found by getting a mean of all the 13 variables. It has been found to be positive in all the three categories and growing with more years of association. The change is found out to be significantly higher in some parameters like decision making ability, access to education and training, awareness about healthcare, social status in family and neighbourhood and participation in electoral process and other social issues.

FINDINGS AND SUGGESTIONS

After going through the above study the researchers present the following findings and suggestions:

1. Agriculture finance programme implemented by the bank has created a social capital which has an empowering effect on farmers. The creation of social capital is not an automatic outcome and the banks have to create and nurture it deliberately by implementing specific policies such as capacity building programmes, developing decision making abilities, etc.
2. An important determinant of the role of social ties that emerges from the literature is the existence and durability of credit systems characterized by the closeness of the borrowers to the source of funds (and, in a related fashion, the endogeneity of the lending methodology). When the credit provider is closely related to the borrower (and, presumably, the arrangement between them is of their own design), the role of interpersonal ties is a central element in ensuring repayment.

3. There are various ways to evaluate the impact of social capital. Taking perceptions of the participants related to the change which they perceived after association with Prathama Bank is only one of the ways of evaluation which is used in the present study.
4. The overall impact on social empowerment is found by getting a mean of all the 13 variables. It has been found to be positive in all the three categories and growing with more years of association. Respondents associated for many years with SHG are more socially empowered than respondents who joined recently or within one year.
5. The regular events or activities conducted to run agriculture finance or microfinance programmes such as organizing conferences and seminars, conducting monthly or bi-monthly meetings, peer monitoring on individual member's financial transactions, using social network, creating a platform for collective action create social capital. This can be further enhanced by providing access to capacity building, creating awareness, building decision making abilities and enhancing social mobility.
6. Loan officers and borrowers develop special relationships in the field has been reported. We found during this study that Prathama Bank Officers often fulfilled the roles of village counsellors, money managers, and conflict mediators at the same time (Ito1999). The positive aspects of the social relationships that evolve between bank staff and borrowers are also now called social capital.
7. Literature on the subject supports the argument that organizations can deliberately enhance social capital. Banks as well as microfinance organizations play a imperative role in creating social capital by implementing well designed social capital strategy which emphasizes on strong commitment of field level staff of banks to the organization's goals, continuous relations between staff and the borrowers, implementation of credit plus policies such as training on human rights, skill up-gradation, collective actions, etc.
8. Development financial programmes like agriculture finance or microfinance can build social capital to improve the effectiveness of desired outcome such as social empowerment of villagers especially women. The present study shows that there is a positive relationship between the years of association with Prathama Bank or SHG and the social empowerment which is created with the help of social capital.
9. Public policy can help in bringing more flexibility in regulations, facilitating competition and helping existing financial institutions to change their strategies for poverty alleviation. Regional Rural Banks like Prathama Bank and Micro finance organizations can capitalize on internationally acclaimed cases such as Grameen Bank and attract more funds from various sectors and adopt good practices from them. The trust formed between lender and borrower plays a very important role to make agriculture finance and microfinance programmes viable.

10. Social interactivity also plays an important role in enhancing social capital. For this two resources are required: (a) 'knowledge resources' or in other ways we can say the common understanding of community, group members, collective information, skill sets, etc., and (b) 'identity resources' or in other words building up a sense of belongingness and encourage participation for bringing out change. Quantitative interactivities such as frequencies and intensities as well as qualitative interactions such as knowledge, community resources and information available and the degree to which community members build each other's self confidence and encourage community members for positive identity are important for creation of positive social capital.
11. The use of existing social ties improves the access of the poor to credit, but that they do so through various channels whose relative importance is subject to significant debate. This is especially true in view of the large variations in geographical, economic, social and political settings in which these lending programs operate.
12. Social capital can be intentionally enhanced by building credit discipline, well documented inter borrower relations, etc. Banks can do by forming horizontal and vertical networks, establishing new norms or fostering a new level of social trust for collective action such as creation of social collateral, group liability, compulsory attendance for meetings, strict adherence to the essential principles, rotating leadership, empowering women, etc.

CONCLUSION

Social capital has a profound impact in many different areas of human life and development: it affects the provision of services in both urban and rural areas; transforms the prospects for agricultural development; influences the expansion of private enterprises; improves the management of common resources; helps improve education; can prevent conflict; and can compensate for a deficient state. More generally, it helps alleviate poverty for individuals and for countries as a whole. Lest this sound excessively simplistic or overly generalized, we note that the extent to which social capital matters varies tremendously across settings, as do the aspects of social capital that are effective.

To conclude we can say that the existing literature and present study show that there is a positive and strong relationship in social capital and social empowerment. It is also seen that in most cases regional rural banks and microfinance has helped creating and sustaining positive social capital where villagers and especially women have benefitted by enhancing their level of consciousness, awareness, decision making abilities and improvement in wellbeing through collective action. It is expected that the focal point of agriculture finance and microfinance has to be more on leveraging social capital for to catalyze social change rather than for financial sustainability.

REFERENCES

[1] Baker, W.E. (1990). Market Networks and Corporate Behaviour, *Am. J. Sociol.*, 96: 589-625.

[2] Blair, J. and Carrol, M. (2008). *Social Capital, Economic Development Journal,* Summer, 7, 3, 42 – 49.

[3] Cassar, A., Crowley, L. and Wydick, B. (2007). The Effect of Social Capital on Group Loan Repayment: Evidence from Field Experiments. *The Economic Journal.*

[4] Coffe, H. and Geys, B. (2005). Institutional Performance and Social Capital; An Application to the Local Government Level. *Journal of Urban Affairs*, 27, 5, 485-501.

[5] Devine, F. and Robert, J. (2003). Alternative Approaches to Researching Social Capital: A Comment on van Deth's Measuring Social Capital. *International Journal of Social Research Methodology*, 6, 1, 93-100.

[6] Grootaert, C. (1999). Social Capital, Household Welfare, and Poverty in Indonesia, Local Level Institutions, Working Paper No. 6, Washington D.C.: The World Bank.

[7] Maluccio, J., L. Haddad and Julian (May 2000). Social Capital and Household Welfare in South Africa, 1993-1998, *Journal of Development Studies.*

[8] Narayan, D. and Lant Pritchett (1999). Cents and Sociability: Household Income and Social Capital in Rural Tanzania, *Economic Development and Cultural Change*, 47(4): 871-897.

[9] Narayan and Pritchett (1997). Cents and Sociability: Household Income and Social Capital in Rural Tanzania, *World Bank*, Washington DC, USA.

[10] Pronyk, P., Harpham, T., Busza, J., Phetlag, G., Morison, L., Hargreaves, J., Kim, J., Watts, L. and Peter, J. (2008). Can Social Capital be intentionally generated? A Randomized Trial from Rural South Africa. *Social Science & Medicine*, November, 67, Issue 10, 1559-1570.

[11] Putnam, R. (1995). Bowling Alone: America's Declining Social Capital, *Journal of Democracy*, 6(1): 65-78.

[12] Putnam, R (2000). Bowling Alone: The Collapse and Revival of American Community, New York: Simon and Schuster: 288-290.

[13] Karlan, D. (2005). Using Experimental Economics to Measure Social Capital and Predict Financial Decisions. *The American Economic Review,* 95, 5, 1688-1966.

[14] Evaluation Study Series: Orissa RO: No. 10: Evaluation Study of SHG Bank Linkage Programme in KBK Region in Orissa, NABARD, Orissa Regional Office Bhubaneswar, 2004-05.

The Degree of Global Competition in the Steel Industry

Paroma Mitra (Mukherjee)[1] **and Dilip Roy**[2]

[1] Durgapur Institute of Management and Science, Durgapur
[2] Burdwan University, Burdwan
E-mail: paromamitra@rediffmail.com; dr.diliproy@gmail.com

ABSTRACT

To examine the present status and future prospects of an industry one needs to examine the degree of competition either globally or locally. Present work is an attempt to measure the extent of global competition in steel sector, a basic ingredient for developing economic infrastructure for a nation. Based on the global competition, time series analysis has been carried out to indicate the past trend and future direction. The position of India has also been indicated along with those of a few leading nations. In that context, importance of labour cost, availability of raw materials, cost of energy consumed has been highlighted to gain competitive advantage.

Keywords: Global Competition, Crude steel Production, Market Share

INTRODUCTION

Globalization and trade liberalization coupled with easy flow of information and advancement in communications technology have resulted in an unprecedented intensification of market competition worldwide. With this backdrop, Porter (1998) stressed upon the urgency of strengthening competence of nations, countries and firms to handle the resultant threats. He has commented that competitiveness has become a "central preoccupation of both developed and developing countries in an increasingly open and integrated world economy". However, meaning, implication, adaptation and achievement of competitiveness may vary from firm to firm, industry to industry and nation to nation across the world (Haider, 2007). According to *Global Competition Report 2007-08*, USA is the leading country and is followed by Switzerland, Denmark, Sweden, Germany, Finland and Singapore in the stated order. Chile is the highest rank country in

Latin America followed by Mexico and Costa Rica. China and India continue to be the two leaders among the large number of developing countries. India's rank is 48th according to the Global Competitive Index (GCI). GCI is constructed based on 12 sub measures of competitiveness. It provides with a comprehensive portray of the competitiveness landscape for countries around the world at all stages of development. The sub measures are institution, infrastructure, macroeconomic stability, health and primary education, higher education and training, goods market efficiency, labour market efficiency, financial market sophistication, technological readiness, market size, business sophistication and innovation.

It is well known that steel (the carbon alloy of Iron) is crucial for the development of any economy and is considered to be the backbone of human civilization. To measure the socio-economic development and standard of living in any country, the level of per capita consumption of steel is treated as one of the important indices. It is a product which has large and technologically complex industry having strong forward and backward linkages in terms of material flows and income generation. It has been the key material with which the world is continuously developing. It is also essential for a low-carbon world in transport, construction, housing and power generation.

At present Steel industry is a booming industry in whole world. After adoption of the liberalization policies all over the world, the steel industry is growing rapidly. The increasing demand for it was mainly generated by the adoption of various projects.

According to International iron and Steel Institute (IISI), the most significant growth of steel production in the world was observed during the period 1960 to 1974. It was due to doubling of steel consumption around the whole world. Between these years, the world steel industry grew, at a rate of 5.5%. But a phase of decline could be noticed from the year 1975 to 1982 due to various reasons like mismatch between capacity, demand and production of steel and consequent drop in prices of steel. At that time, many companies sold their products below cost of production only to survive in global market. Other reason for the downward trend was collapse of Soviet Union and severe financial crisis in most of the South East Asian countries as well as in Korea and Japan.

World steel production has been growing since 1994. Only in 1998 the production was slightly less than trend. But it again steered up its acceleration from very next year. In 2004, production crossed the threshold of 1 billion metric tons for first time. The International Iron and Steel Institute has announced that world crude steel output touched 1,351.3 million metric tons (mmt) in the year 2007 with an increment of 9.02% over 2006. It represents the highest level of crude steel output. That year is the fifth consecutive year as world crude steel production grew by more than 7%. In 2008 world steel production has been reported to be 1,326.5 mmt.

In the 20th Century, steel industry was developed in Western Europe for the first time. Next development was in USA followed by the Soviet Union, Eastern Europe and Japan. But "Olympic 2008" tilted the balance in favour of developing countries such as China, South Korea, India and Brazil. In fact, towards the end of the last century, growth of steel production was carried forward by these countries. Production and consumption of steel grew steadily in China from 2002. It accelerated its momentum during the closing years i.e. from 2006 onwards.

This paper deals with the relevance and appropriateness of these happenings by measuring the degree of global competition among the steel producing countries.

THE OBJECTIVE OF THE STUDY

The global scenario of steel industry can help us to know the position of Indian companies with respect to its global competitors. The objective of our study is therefore to measure the global competition among the steel producing countries. This measure is to be further studied over years to identify the secular trend, if any. In case the trend is a linear one it will be possible to portray the performance of India in terms of increasing or decreasing behavior of the trend line. If the degree of competition increases, then it may become a threat for India, if the market share is not maintained or improved. On the other hand, if it decreases and even if the market share of India is static, it can be an opportunity for India.

LITERATURE REVIEW

Porter (1990, 1998) said that in the nations have their own competitive advantages in the modern competitive marketplace. A nation's competitiveness depends on the capacity of its industry to innovate and upgrade. Companies gain edge over the world's best competitors only under pressure and challenge. They also gain advantage from having strong domestic rivals, aggressive home-based suppliers, and demanding local customers. As the basis for global competition has shifted more and more to the creation and assimilation of knowledge, the role of the nation has came in the front position. Competitive advantage can be created and maintained through a highly localized process. Differences in national values, culture, economic structures, institutions, and histories all contribute to competitive success. Ultimately, a nation succeeds in a particular industry only if its home environment is the most forward-looking, dynamic, and challenging. According to (Abdel- Latif, 1993; and Sachwald, 1994) "product quality, innovativeness, design, distribution network, after sales service, transaction costs, institutional factor relating to the bureaucracy of export procedures and other non price factors are factors for measuring the competitiveness of a manufacturing firm or an industry". According to Lall (2001) developing countries' policy makers worry about national competitiveness and closely watch indices ranking international competitive performance. According to some researchers, one may examine labour costs, unit cost, exchange rate, interest rate, prices of inputs and other quantitative factors for measuring the competitiveness of a firm or an industry (Edwards and Schoer, 2002, Edwards and Golub, 2004, Fukunishi, 2004). Porter and Toming (2006) stated that competitiveness can be defined as a country's share in world market for its products which makes it a zero-sum game because one country's gain comes at the cost of other countries. Prahalad and Ramaswamy (2004), explored why, despite unbounded opportunities for innovation, companies still can not satisfy customers and sustain profitable growth. They believed that, India will become a leader of the world in future. As Easterly (2005) points out, there are strong indications that differences in institutions greatly explain the differential in growth between countries. Institution effects go beyond the effect of getting inflation right or correcting other macroeconomic weaknesses. Nayak (2007) in his paper presented a comprehensive overview of the results in the world Economic Forum's new Global Competitiveness Index.

Chandler (1990) elaborated that the historical development of commodity chains, began as a nation-state commodity chain within organizational boundaries. This allowed the development of vertically integrated corporations in the U.S. steel industry that left a segmented production process which could be disaggregated through the winds of 'global capitalism' (Gereffi, 1994). According to (Gereffi, 1994), the growth of economic globalization showed by the steel industry is one of the fundamental market transitions from industrial to post-industrial capitalism. Gereffi & Korzeniewicz (1994) describes that Crude steel production, is a basic backward linkage in commodity chains, especially the motor vehicle commodity chain. Chatterjee, and Mukherjee (1995), in their article observed that the globalization of the Indian economy has brought challenges for steel companies e.g. Tata Steel. The Indian firm is highly prepared to deal with the changes that have surfaced from economic globalization and to succeed in this international arena. This enthusiasm for success can be clearly observed from the fact that it has been introducing major modernization plans since 1980 to upgrade and adopt new technology to sustain its leadership in the competitive market. Tata Steel has also embraced new business strategies such as cost control, improved customer orientation and focus on steel-making areas. It can also boast of a workforce having healthy relationship with management, as may be seen from the absence of strikes or labor disputes since 1940. (Bacon and Blyton, 1996) in their paper presented an overview of the international and U.S. steel industry as steel industry is noted to have an extreme cyclical (boom and bust) nature, with great crises in overproduction and under demand. They have also argued that, there are no significant multinational steel companies, as national steel companies still feed home market demand for steel production. In the last half of the 20th century, economic globalization has led to the development of global commodity chains (GCC), through two major transitions – one is investment-based globalization – or investment by transnational corporations and another is trade-based globalization or growth in international trade (Gereffi 2001). Maasoumia, Prowseb, and Slottjec (May 2002), in their paper described a mode of economic analysis that can be used to measure market power in the context of antitrust litigation in the steel plate industry. Wolf J. (2007) in his study focused on Global Commodity Chain (GCC) and studied the globalization process of production in one of the core component to national modernization. He had attempted to present a case study approach to the globalization of an industry and development of a GCC. Steel being a crucial commodity in the industrialization of nations, is also dependent on raw materials and a notoriously intense production process that is being transformed by the development of recycling as a major link in the production process.

METHODOLOGY OF THE STUDY

The detailed methodology adopted for carrying out the present study is outlined below. The methodology discusses elaborately period of study, scope of study, and techniques used for in-depth analysis.

PERIOD OF STUDY

The study covers a period of seven years from 2002 to 2008. Depending on the availability of secondary data, information has been obtained from website of International Iron and Steel Institute (IISI), World Steel Association.

SCOPE OF STUDY

This study will be of help to researchers, economists, and company planners to measure the degree of global competitiveness in their respective studies.

TECHNIQUES USED FOR IN-DEPTH ANALYSIS

For analysis we have made two parts – the first part deals with descriptive analysis and second part deals with statistical analysis. The statistical analysis is to find out the trend in degree of competition among the global competing countries in steel industries, and consider null hypothesis H_0 that there is no increase in the global competition in the steel industry against the alternative hypothesis H_a that there is increase or decrease in the same.

Test Procedure for Examining Degree of Competition Among the Global Nations

In order to find out the degree of competition, we shall collect the market shares of nations competing in global steel production. Following Roy (2006) the formula for degree of competition will be: $\left(1-\sqrt{\Sigma m_i^2}\right)$, where m_i is the market share of each individual nation in global steel production, i ranging from 1 to k. For each year we can calculate one such measure, generating there by a time series data. One can next carryout trend analysis.

Test Statistic

The under lying statistic for regression coefficient is t-statistic. The t-statistic is used to test hypothesis about an unknown population mean where the value of standard deviation is unknown. The formula for the t-statistic is

$$t = \frac{\hat{\beta}}{\left[\hat{\sigma}\sqrt{\left\{\frac{1}{\Sigma(x_i - x)^2}\right\}}\right]}, \text{ where } \hat{\sigma} = \sqrt{\left\{\frac{\Sigma(y_i - \hat{\alpha} - \hat{\beta}x_i)^2}{(n-2)}\right\}}.$$

Here, y_i is the ith observation on the α dependent variable.
x_i is the ith observation on the independent variable.
$\hat{\alpha}$ is the estimated intercept
$\hat{\beta}$ is the estimated regression coefficient or slope.
n is the number of observation.

For a study y represents the degree of competition and x represents the time.

Sequence of the Analysis

While trying to measure the degree and nature of global competition among the steel producing countries, we first started with taking the major steel producing countries with their production figures in tonnage. We have collected time series data of production of major steel producing countries from IISI for 2004 and 2006. As it is not possible to include all the countries in our study, and presented only the data of production of top ten major steel producing countries in the world. The countries which have been selected for this study are China, Japan, United States, Russia, South Korea, Germany, India, Ukraine, Italy and Brazil. We have included the rest of the countries under the group "other". Then we have first calculated their market share for seven years, viz., 2002 to

2008. We have next calculated squares of these individual market shares for a particular year and then added those squares to get Σm_i^2 for that year. The entire process can be repeated for obtaining Σm_i^2 for all the years. Next, we have calculated the value of $(1 - \sqrt{\Sigma m_i^2})$ to obtain the degree of competition for all the years. All those $(1 - \sqrt{\Sigma m_i^2})$ values calculated for the period under study have given rise to a time series data on the degree of competition. We have next plotted these values against time to get an idea about the trend equation to find out if the competition is stagnant, increasing or decreasing.

DESCRIPTIVE STUDY OF GLOBAL COMPETITION

From Table 1 it is observed that, the market share of China for steel production consistently increased from 2002 to 2008. It had maintained a steady rise in the market share as 20%, 23%, 26%, 31%, 34%, 37%, and 38% during the period 2002 to 2008. It can be opined that China has increased its market share at the cost of South Korea, Japan, USA, Russia, and others. Japan has shown a declining state from 12% to 9% from 2002 to 2008. The market share of US has decreased from 10% to 7% from 2002 to 2008. Russia's market share has declined slightly from 7% to 5% during the said period. South Korea had shown a steady market share, with a slightly negative trend from 5% to 4% in the period. Germany also lost its market share by 5% during 2002 to 2003, then 4% during 2004 to 2007 and by 3% in 2008. *India has passed through a slow but steady progress with a market share of only 3% during 2002 to 2006. It followed by 1% increment during 2007 to 2008.* The market share of Ukraine has fall from 4% to 3 % from 2002 to 2008. Italy has shown inconsistent performance regarding market share. Its share was 3% during 2002 to 2005, and then fell to 1% in 2006 again rises to 2% during 2007 to 2008. The market share of Brazil was retained as 3% during the period with an exception of 1% in 2006. It is very much clear from Table 2 that for "others" country market share of steel production is also declining from 26% in 2002 to 22% in 2008. Only in year 2003 its share increased by 2%, i.e. 28%.

From Table 1 it can be noted that China was the market leader in global steel production from 2002 to 2008. Japan, United States, and Russia follow China with second, third and fourth position during this period. Indian steel industry steadily improved from 9th position in 2002 to 8th position in 2003. In 2004 the industry again gets back to 9th position. That year was a turning point. Continuous improvement helped to achieve India 5th position for the two consecutive years 2007 and 2008. To achieve that position India had to compete mainly with South Korea, Germany, Ukraine and Brazil.

Table 1: Rank-wise Global Steel Production of Top Ten Producing Countries from 2002 to 2007 (in tonnage)

Country	2008		2007		2006		2005		2004		2003		2002	
	Rank	Tonnage	Rank	Tonnage	Rank	Tonnage	Rank	Tonnage	Rank	Tonnage	Rank	Tonnage	Rank	Tonnage
China	1	501	1	495	1	423	1	349	1	281	1	220	1	182
Japan	2	119	2	120	2	116	2	113	2	113	2	111	2	108
United States	3	92	3	98	3	99	3	95	3	100	3	90	3	92
Russia	4	69	4	72	4	71	4	66	4	66	4	63	4	60
South Korea	6	54	6	52	5	49	5	48	5	48	5	46	5	45
Germany	7	46	7	49	6	47	6	45	6	46	6	45	6	45
India	**5**	**55**	**5**	**53**	**7**	**44**	**8**	**38**	**9**	**33**	**8**	**32**	**8**	**29**
Ukraine	8	37	8	43	8	41	7	39	7	39	7	37	7	34
Italy	10	31	10	32	9	32	10	29	10	29	10	27	10	26
Brazil	9	34	9	34	10	31	9	32	8	33	9	31	9	30
Others		297		303		283		281		284		267		231
World		1327		1,351		1,244.18		1,132		1,067.		965		904

Source: Rank-wise major steel producing countries, IISI, 2004 and 2006.

Table 2: The Market Share of Top Ten Producing Countries of Global Steel production (m_i) and the Rest of the World

Country	2002	2003	2004	2005	2006	2007	2008
China	.20	.23	0.26	0.31	0.34	0.37	0.38
Japan	.12	.12	0.11	0.10	0.09	0.09	0.09
United States	.10	.09	0.09	0.08	0.08	0.07	0.07
Russia	.07	.07	0.06	0.06	0.06	0.05	0.05
South Korea	.05	.05	0.04	0.04	0.04	0.04	0.04
Germany	.05	.05	0.04	0.04	0.04	0.04	0.03
India	**.03**	**.03**	**0.03**	**0.03**	**0.03**	**0.04**	**0.04**
Ukraine	.04	.04	0.04	0.03	0.03	0.03	0.03
Italy	.03	.03	0.03	0.03	0.01	0.02	0.02
Brazil	.03	.03	0.03	0.03	0.01	0.03	0.03
Others	.26	.28	0.27	0.25	0.23	0.22	0.22
Total	**1**	**1**	**1**	**1**	**1**	**1**	**1**

Source: Derived from Table 1.

TREND ANALYSIS OF DEGREE OF COMPETITION

We shall proceed with the original time series data set on global steel production from 2002 to 2008. The formula to be used for measuring the degree of competition is $(1 - \sqrt{\Sigma m_i^2})$, where m_i is the market share of the ith country. We shall represent this with the help of Table 2, and Table 3 respectively.

To examine the trend of competition over the years for detecting any change in the

Table 3: The Degree of Global Competition $(1 - \sqrt{\Sigma m_i^2})$ in Global Steel Industry Plotted Against Time Over the Years

Year	Σm_i^2	$\sqrt{\Sigma m_i^2}$	$1-\sqrt{\Sigma m_i^2}$
2002	0.1497	0.387	**0.613**
2003	0.1707	0.413	**0.587**
2004	0.1737	0.417	**0.583**
2005	0.1866	0.432	**0.568**
2006	0.194	0.44	**0.56**
2007	0.2142	0.463	**0.537**
2008	0.2131	0.462	**0.538**

Source: Derived from Table 2.

degree of competition in global steel production, we would like to plot the values of $(1 - \sqrt{\Sigma m_i^2})$ over the years, which can be observed in Table 3.

In view of Figure 1, we propose to go for linear regression analysis. We shall consider null hypothesis H_o that there is no change in the degree of global competition in steel production over the years against alternative hypothesis H_a that there is an increase or decrease in the same over the years.

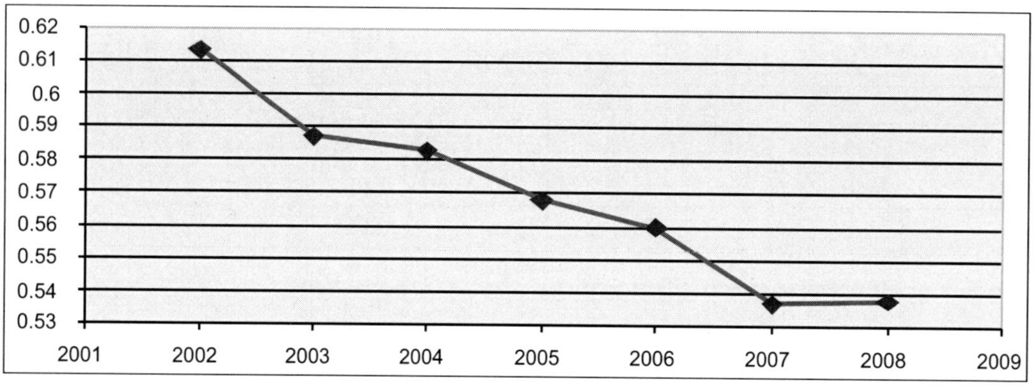

Fig. 1: Graph for the Degree of Global Competition

Let the linear trend equation of *global competitiveness of steel producing countries* be represented by

$$GC_t = a + b\,t + \varepsilon_t \qquad (1)$$

where GC_t is the global competitiveness during the period t, a and b are the regression parameters, t is the time variable, and ε_t is the error term. Using the least square method one can estimate a and b using time series data from Table 3. The estimated value of a and b are $\hat{a}$ and $\hat{b}$. Here $\hat{\alpha}$ is .5125 and $\hat{\beta}$ is .032.

To examine the significance of b value, the regression coefficient of this linear regression curve, we like to test the null hypothesis, H_0: b = 0 against the alternative hypothesis that b is greater or lesser than zero, i.e. H_a: b > 0 or H_a: b < 0. The test statistic is

$$t = \hat{b} / \left[\hat{\sigma}\sqrt{\{1/\Sigma(x_i - x^-)^2\}}\right] \quad \text{where } \hat{\sigma} = \sqrt{\{\Sigma y_i - \hat{a} - \hat{b}x_i)^2/(n-2)\}}$$

The observed value of t is –10.49, with a tail probability of .0001, which is less than .05. Hence rejecting the null hypothesis at 5% level of significance, i.e. the global competitiveness of world steel production is "significantly decreasing over time" as the coefficient of time is negative. The multiple correlation, i.e. R value, is 0.98 which is also on the higher side. The corresponding analysis of variance table provides with F ratio as 110.01 for which the upper tail probability is 0.0001, which is less than 5% level of significance. So, we conclude that, *the linearly decreasing trend equation is a good fit for the said problem.* We can see the trend line in the graph for the degree of competition, presented under Figure 2.

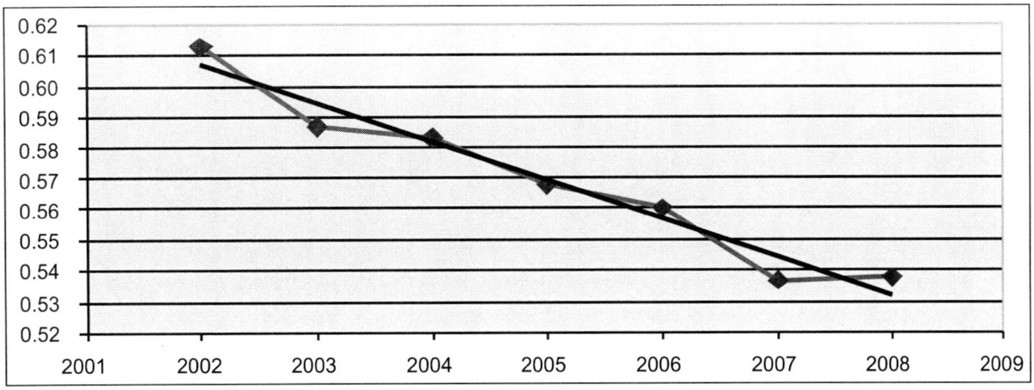

Fig. 2: Trend Line in the Graph for the Degree of Global Competition

MANAGERIAL IMPLICATIONS AND SUGGESTIONS

We have noticed from the output table for degree of competitiveness among the global steel production countries that the global competition in crude steel production is decreasing over the years. So, decreasing global competition coupled with increasing market share of India indicates a positive sign for Indian companies.

To remain afloat in the global market, **Porter's (1980)** generic strategy of overall cost leadership may be the ideal choice. Reduction of manufacturing cost can ensure the competitive edge in the global market and can also accelerate the rate of growth within the country, largely with the cost of labour and energy. Russia, India, Ukraine, Brazil are able to produce steel at the lowest cost because of a combination of cheap energy and labor. The US's cost of steel production is moderate in nature. Unlike many other commodities, China is not the lowest-cost steel producer though Chinese labor is cheap, but energy in China is still costly. As a result, China produces steel at a cost 20% below that of US, but energy cost in China is higher than that of Russia, India, Ukraine, and Brazil. If we observe the average labour cost from 2002 to 2005 of different countries, we can note that the average cost of labour of China was 0.95 US $/hour, same for India was 0.8 US $/hour, Ukraine was 0.7 US $/hour and Brazil was 2.9 US $/hour. These were on the lower side in comparison to countries like United States (22.7 US $/hour), Japan (20.6 US $/hour), South Korea (11.1 US $/hour), Italy (18.8 US $/hour) and Germany (30.1 US $/hour).

In China and India the energy costs are comparatively high. For that they have resorted to the same measures taken by United States and Germany. According to Wikipedia, USA is having 7th position in per capita Green House Gas emission in 2005. Where as Russia's rank is 18th. Rank of Germany is 25th. South Korea's rank is 31st. Italy is in 45th rank. China's rank is 72nd. Rank of Brazil is 74th. The rank of India is 120th. Steelmaking equipment and technologies are available around the world. The most recent plants, regardless of their location, can make use of state-of-the-art processes. In developed countries, steel's energy intensity and fierce global competition have driven inefficient producers from the marketplace. In the past we have notice that there was a reduction in energy intensity of the steel sector in USA [33% from 1990-2007]. This clearly shows the lowest emitting production path must be sought to survive naturally in the steel sector. This may be one of the important reasons for decrease in the market share of United States, Japan, Russia, South Korea and Germany.

For availability of raw material for steel production Ukraine is the country which is completely self sufficient in iron ore, coke, manganese and various supplementary materials. Kryvy Rih basin is the source of most iron ore (about 90%) in the world, which is in Ukraine. The total iron ore deposits in Ukraine (categories A, B, and C) amount to 27 billion tons. But there is concentration of the ownership of most raw materials in the hands of a few major steel groups, which is challenging the survival of the second tier steelmakers in the Ukraine. Dubious privatization process has also resulted in conflicts over access to raw material in Russian steel plants. China mainly depends on imported iron ore and dependency has increased by 30% in the last 10 years. As a result the cost of iron ore for China rose up to 9.5% in 2007. As demand increase, the prices of iron ore raised by 65% in 2008 from 2000, inducing thereby steel production costs by more than 20%. On the whole, while the Chinese steel industry is thriving, the industry is generally undergoing restructuring, and mergers and consolidations, as pricing and market mechanisms are addressed.

Regarding investment in steel industry, Brazil lacks strong infrastructure, because it never took the time to invest in it. According to a report by the World Steel Dynamics (WSD), the Indian steel industry has entered a period of massive growth not only in steel demand but also in steel making capacities. A host of steel companies have lined up with major investment proposals. Furthermore, with 13 billion tons of iron ore deposits, which is 5th largest in the world, and an expanding consumer market, the Indian steel industry is likely to receive huge domestic and foreign investments. Arcelor Mittal and Posco have assured a combined investment of US$ 32 billion. Also, China's largest investment in India – more than US$ 1.999 billion over 5-10 years – is slated to come up in Karnataka with the setting up of Xindia Steels. Going by the ball park estimate of US$ 1.01 billion investment per MT of additional capacity, the Indian steel industry is likely to attract an investment of US$ 69.97 billion by 2011-12 and US$ 220.02 billion by 2019-20.

However, there are some threats which are still affecting the overall performance of the Indian steel sector. The cheap import and antidumping duty imposed by USA badly affected the steel industry in the recent past. Further, in the domestic front, the per capita consumption is only 26.7 Kg against a global average of 121.0 kg. To ensure competitive advantage, there should be a general consensus that the steel industry has to concentrate on the following aspects: reduction in operating cost, better management of working capital, and product inventory, improvement in techno-economic parameters, and substitution of raw materials by their cheaper versions. Differentiated sourcing and effective supply chain management can also help this process of cost reduction.

CONCLUSION

Thus, we finally conclude that the global competition for steel production is decreasing over the years. Whereas, the market share of India is increasing. This indicates an opportunity for Indian steel companies.

Among the top ten producing countries of global steel production the market shares of China and India are increasing. For Japan, United States, Russia, South Korea, Germany, Ukraine, and Italy these are decreasing. Rest for Brazil the market share remains constant over years.

Thus, India except china is in a best position compare to other countries in terms of market share and also in terms of labour cost, an availability of raw material and growth rate of investment.

If it can reduce the cost of energy consumption it may come out in the global market.

REFERENCES

[1] Abdel-Latif and Abla M. (1993), "The non price determinants of export success or failure: the Egyptian ready-made garment industry, 1975–1989", *World Development*, Vol. 21, No. 10, pp. 1677-1684. International Iron and Steel Institute, 2004 and 2006.

[2] Bacon, N. and Blyton, P. (1996), "Re-casting the Politics of Steel in Europe: The Impact On Trade Unions", *West European Politics* 19: 770-786.

[3] Chandler J.A. (1990), "Scale and Scope: The Dynamics of Industrial Capitalism", Cambridge: Belknap Press.

[4] Chatterjee, A. and Mukherjee, T. (1995), "Staying Ahead of Global Competition:

The Tata Steel Strategy", Braybrooke Press Ltd., *Journal of General Management*, 1995.

[5] Easterly, W. (2005), "National Policies and Economic Growth: A Reappraisal", *Handbook of Economic Growth*, ed. by Philippe Aghion and Steven Durlauf Elsevier.

[6] Edwards, L. and Volker, S. (2002), "Measures of Competitiveness: A Dynamic Approach to South Africa's Trade Performance in the 1990's", *The South African Journal of Economics*, Vol. 70, No. 6, pp. 1008-1045.

[7] Edwards, L. and Stephen, S.G. (2004), "South Africa's International Cost Competitiveness and Exports in Manufacturing", *World Development*, Vol. 32, No. 8, pp. 1323-1339.

[8] Fukunishi, T. (2004), "International Competitiveness of Manufacturing Firms in Sub- Saharan Africa", Institute of Developing Economies Discussion Paper No. 2, Chiba, Japan, Institute of Developing Economies.

[9] Gerrefi, G. and Miguel K. (eds). (1994), "Commodity Chains and Global Capitalism", Westport, CT: Praeger Publishing.

[10] Gereffi, G. (2001), "Shifting Governance Structures in Global Commodity Chains, With Special Reference to the Internet", *American Behavioral Scientist* 44: 1616-1637.

[11] Haider, M. Z. (2007), "Competitiveness of the Bangladesh Readymade Garment Industry in Major International Market", *Asia pacific Trade and Investment Review*, Vol. 3, No. 1.

[12] Lall, S. (2001), "Competitiveness Indices and Developing Countries: An Economic Evaluation of the Global Competitiveness Report", Queen Elizabeth House, Oxford, UK.

[13] Maasoumi, E., Prowse, S.D. and Slottje, D.J. (2002), "Measuring Market Power in the Steel Industry", JEL Classification Numbers: L41, L12, L61.

[14] Nayak, K.M. (2007), "Measuring Global Competitiveness through Index", *Conference Proceedings of Conference on Global Competition & Competitiveness of Indian Corporate*, 19 May, 2007, pp. 101 – 113. DSpace at Indian Institute of Management Kozhikode. Retrieved from http://dspace.iimk.ac.in/bitstream/2259/446/1/101-114++.pdf

[15] Porter, M. (1990, 1998, 2003), "Competitive Strategy", Free press, New York, 1980, republished in 1990, 1998, 2003.

[16] Porter, M. (1990, 1998), "The Competitive Advantage of Nations", New York: The Free Press, 1990, republished in 1998.

[17] Prahalad, C.K. and Ramaswamy, V. (2004), "The Future of Competition", Penguin Books India.

[18] Roy D. (2006), "Discourse on Strategic Management", Asian Books Private Ltd., Chapter 13.

[19] Wolf, J. (2007), "Globalization in the Steel Industry: The Market and Commodity Chain Transitions from Industrial to Post-Industrial Capitalism", http://www.allacademic.com /meta/p_mla_apa_research_citation/0/2/0/0/7/p20079_index.html.

Deploying Internet Services Over a Broadcast Satellite Network and Communication: Challenges and Opportunities in the Global Information Infrastructure

Nimesh I. Modi

H. North Gujarat University, Patan
E-mail: nim_placement@indiatimes.com

ABSTRACT

The purpose of this paper is to discuss broadband technology and its use in satellite communication and also use of direct broadcast communication satellite and law profile, portable receive antennas is an effective means to provide communication to military force in the field, enabling access to a wide range of information sources. Global Broadcast service (GBS) will provide. In today's economy, enterprises and their IT organizations need to do more with less. It is the responsibility of IT to optimize limited resources and garner the greatest return on corporate budgets. The purpose of this paper to discuss Broad band Technology and its use in satellite communication, trends and future growth will be presented based on current industry predications by independent Research Companies. Learn how your organization can better protect and communication managing solutions. Terrestrial based broadband options (i.e. Cable modem and Digital subscriber Line (DSL)) will be use of satellite for future broadband communication. This paper presents the evolving architecture of the GBS Internet and experience with the implementing the access, routing, transport and middle ware protocols use in the GBS internet. GBS will provide broadcast video, voice and data from stateside and other information sources to users in theater operations.

Keywords: Internet Services, Broadcast Satellite Network

INTRODUCTION

Power full currents in communications and networking have recently mingled together. The integration of direct broadcast Ground Stations, Satellite and Set Top Boxes and internet software routing protocols, end to end transport, and a large installed base of inexpensive network-centric applications makes a great deal of good sense for field commanders and troops, who stand to have powerful application supported by the delivery of information from remote sources. The integration of direct broadcast and internet technologies, Require the careful solution of Technical Problems and Reports on our efforts to solve them. According to Recent Study, the satellite segment of the broadband communications market will increase. We need to aim for the heavens and create a GAN (Global Area Network).Satellite communications is the next step in providing global broadband communications every corner of the globe. Economic Play a Significance Role in the lack of terrestrial infrastructure, but is not the only Reason. Economics aside, there are areas of the world that even if the money was there the terrain just will not allow fiber or any other terrestrial network. These areas either remotely placed in the middle of the ocean or are located in mountainous regions where running cable is not feasible. In this Situation, only satellites can provide access to the internet.

Broadband satellite communication has much to offer the globe community and there are numerous companies competing for their share of the market. This paper will focus on the future of satellite communications and its place in the global information infrastructure and it will discuss networks proposed by the aforementioned companies above (ICO-Teledesic, Sky Bridge and Astrolink). There will also be a comparison of satellite communications and terrestrial communications to include cable modem and Digital Subscriber Loop (DSL). Who knows that the future might bring? Knowledge liberates the masses, and maybe, someday, the world will become a single global community allowing us to overcome both social and cultural barriers to work together and make this world a better place to live.

We review early influence on the GBS network Architecture and protocols, including work done for joint warrior interoperability Demonstration (JWID95) and Commercial direct broad-cast Communications systems. We then discuss the design of the BADD GBS network Architecture, Which is intended to use open internet Technology that permits inter operation with Exiting and future systems. At the same time, the GBS internet Architecture exploits special capabilities of GBS, Such as native multicast. We discuss also the technical challenges overcome, such as how to utilize effectively links that are unidirectional, how to implement connectionless internet service over connections oriented Asynchronous Transfer Mode (ATM) links, how to achieve high through put with "long fat pipe "(high-latency, high speed) links, and how to implement desirable services [such as World Wide Web (WWW) browsing and periodically "pushed" data distribution] effectively.

BACKGROUND

Motivated by the success of commercial direct broadcast satellite systems, such as

DirecTV and Prime star the Air Force space and Missile systems center (SMC) is engaged in the acquisition of a GBS System, which will provide in-theater communications over satellite. The GBS Satellite is expected to be geosynchronous orbiting communications platform that receives an uplink stream, reamplifies it, and transmits the stream over an earth coverage or spot-beam downlink antenna. Numerous receiving able to pick up the satellite's Transmissions by pointing at the satellite a small dish antenna of about 18 inches' diameter and selecting the proper frequency.

The Data rate of the GBS is nominally 20 Mega symbols per seconds using Quadrature phase shift keying (QPSK) yielding 2 bits per symbol or 40 megabits per seconds. The Receiver has only a Receive capability and must there for use an alternate channel for sending traffic. Indeed, this unidirectional characteristic of the GBS presents a challenge to system designers and implementers, to whom a bidirectional channel would permit a more-familiar milieu for deploying internet protocols. Broadband technology can use a single medium (wire) to carry several channels at once. In contrast baseband transmission allows only one signal at a time (Webopedia, 2001). Broadband communication is becoming more and more of a necessity in order to keep up with the need for speed and the internet.

Streamlining of information includes TV shows, news clips, concerts, large software applications and much more. Streaming media requires 20 to 30 times more bandwidth than static web pages (Baugh, 2001). Broadband technology can provide this bandwidth using digital subscribers Loops (DSL) Cable modem and satellite links. Broadband technology affords consumers the following benefits:

- Faster Internet Access
- An Always on connection so one does not have to wait to log on the internet
- Interactive video and data content, including streaming video and electronic Magazines
- Large file downloads to include Graphics, Databases and Games
- Better Video and Graphics
- 3D Product Visualization
- Content on Demand, pay-per-view services

Broadband technology, used in conjunction with satellite networks, will help alleviate the congestion of terrestrial backbone networks and provide information to the edge of the internet faster and with fewer chances for information loss. A terrestrial broadcast of streaming media to multiple users connected to the internet, a standard broadcast over the internet from a centralized content provider must be transmitted over numerous router hops before arriving at the internet service provider (ISP). The internet is a point to point information provider. If a million users request the same streaming media from a content provider, it will be processed and transmitted as a million different transmission, then efficiency would increase dramatically and there would be fewer chances for information loss and transmission degradation. Broadband Satellite will work in conjunction with terrestrial networks to provide the most efficient means to get from the content source to the user. Satellite will also make available the internet and all of its information to areas of the world that currently do not have the infrastructure to gain access to it through terrestrial means. Broadband satellite communication will help integrate the population of the world into a single community.

TELEDESIC'S TECHNOLOGY

Teledesic was the first corporation to coin the phrase "Internet-in-the-security". This Phase represents the vision of telecommunications pioneer Craig McCaw who founded Teledesic in 1990. To strengthen the satellite telecommunications industry, ICO-Teledesic collaborating with Ellipso to form joint venture, the Teledisc network is able to support millions of users simultaneously using "standard" equipment. Teledesic's satellites will transmit signals using a portion of the high frequency ka band. Most users have two way communications. GEO Satellites experience that annoying half second delay that you experience when making some long distance phone calls. Since LEOs are 25 times closer to the Earth than GEOs, they can operate in tandem with small, low-power terminals and antennas. These compact terminals can be mounted on top of your house and connect inside to either a computer network or a PC. Their original network scheme included 840 satellites each.

This network of satellite will offer areas of the world access to the internet that currently do not have the terrestrial infrastructure to gain access or access is extremely limited. This could be due to their remote locations and the high cost of terrestrial based communications or the terrain in which they live in. with the activation of Teledesic's "Internet-in-the-Sky" ™, even the most remote and underdeveloped regions of the earth will have easy access to the internet. Teledesic's space segment uses Asynchronous Transfer Mode (ATM) or fast-packet switching. These packets are fixed in length and are comprised of a header that is always 5 bytes in length and then a payload section that carriers 48 bytes of digital user information like Voice, data, video etc. The teledesic network combines the use of destination based packet addressing and an adaptive packet routing algorithm to achieve both low delay low delay variability across the entire network. Each packet contains its destination address and each node within the network determines the least delay path for each packet. This means that packets that belong to the same session may travel completely different paths in order to arrive at the same destination. When they arrive at the destination, they will be recorded into their proper sequence to eliminate the effect of timing variations through the network. Teledesic uses fiber optics as the standard for service quality that its system must emulate. They place stringent on the system design, including low error rate, high availability, flexibility, capacity and low latency-in other words, it must have fiber like characteristics. The network consists of a ground segment and a space segment. Ground terminals are placed at the edge of the Teledesics network and perform as the interface between the satellite network, Terrestrial network and end users. These ground terminal act as isolation translator to keep the internal Teledesic network protocol used in the satellite communication separate from the standard terrestrial protocols. The terminal supports a wide range of data rates and interface with multiple protocols to include IP, ISDN, ATM and others.

ICO OVERVIEW

ICO is a next-generation satellite Communications Company. ICO designed and developed a constellation of medium earth orbit (MEO) satellites to provide worldwide voice and data services utilizing the S-band of radio frequency. ICO's F2 satellite was launched in June 2001. ICO F2 operates globally in compliance with regulations promulgated by the United Kingdom and the International Telecommunications Union (ITU).

The remaining ten MEO satellites are in advanced stages of near-completion. Construction of these satellites was stopped in 2004 due to a dispute and resulting lawsuit between ICO and its prime contractor, The Boeing Company. In October 2008, ICO received a jury award in the amount of $603 million in compensatory and punitive damages against The Boeing Company, and its subsidiary, BSSI. The case is currently under appeal. In the United States, ICO's subsidiary, DBSD North America, is a mobile satellite services (MSS) operator. DBSD is working to meet the demand for 'all things mobile' by building a hybrid system to offer satellite and terrestrial wireless services throughout the United States. DBSD's network is being designed to provide wireless voice, data, video, and/or Internet service throughout the United States on mobile and portable devices. DBSD is authorized by the Federal Communications Commission (FCC) to offer MSS services in the United States using a geostationary (GEO) satellite, and DBSD received authorization from the FCC to integrate an ancillary terrestrial component (ATC) into its MSS system to provide integrated satellite and terrestrial services. DBSD's first GEO satellite, ICO G1, successfully launched from Cape

Canaveral on April 14, 2008 DBSD North America sought protection in the United States Bankruptcy Court under Chapter 11 in May, 2009, and the company is currently completing a transfer of ownership process, pending final approval from the FCC and the US Bankruptcy Court. ICO Global will be a minority shareholder in DBSD following the conclusion of the bankruptcy process

GEO PROCESS

DBSD North America's G1 satellite was developed with Space Systems/Loral Inc. (Loral), a world leader in satellite design and manufacturing. Loral built the G1 satellite as well as certain ground-based systems related to its operation.G1 successfully launched from Cape Canaveral on April 14, 2008. The design is based on a Loral 1300 standard satellite platform that has been optimized for GEO MSS/ATC communications requirements. It features an expected 15-year service life and a 12-meter reflector (antenna) that focuses the 2 GHz signals on North America. A major feature of this next-generation mobile satellite is the size of the reflector, which is a key to providing quality services to a full range of portable devices The G1 satellite is designed to enable DBSD to provide continuous service coverage in all 50 states, as well as Puerto Rico and the U.S. Virgin Islands. If appropriate regulatory approval is granted by other countries, the GEO satellite is capable of providing service beyond the United States, including Canada. Multimedia application over GEO Broadband services, Like Video Telephony, Video Conferencing, Broad casting, Audio, Electronic Commerce, Tele commuting, Distance learning, Telemedicine, corporate networking and Collaborative working.

DIGITAL SATELLITE

For those households receiving digital satellite broadcasts, a satellite dish is also required. This could be a fixed dish pointing to the appropriate satellite transmitting the digital broadcasts they want to receive. Alternatively, it could be a steer able dish – however, some satellite broadcasters claim that if the dish is not permanently pointing to their satellite, software upgrades to the set-top box may not be possible. The satellite towards which the dish needs to point varies from country to country. For example in Italy the two commercial digital satellite broadcasters Stream and Telepiù plus the public service operator RAI all use Eutelsat's Hot Bird II satellite. As a contrast, in the United Kingdom Sky Digital and the BBC use one of the Astra satellites.

DIGITAL TERRESTRIAL

It is only possible to receive terrestrial digital signals to the home in the United Kingdom and Sweden at present – although other countries in Europe, notably Denmark and Spain, will soon start transmitting signals. These systems use an existing aerial, which has to be connected to the set-top box. The set-top box may be also connected to a telephone line to provide a return channel for interactive services. In the USA the transition from analogue to digital TV is linked with the move from Standard Definition TV (SDTV) to High Definition TV (HDTV). This started in late 1998, with SDTV and HDTV being broadcast simultaneously. It is planned that all major cities will have terrestrial digital broadcasting by 2000 and by 2006 all stations are scheduled to be running all-digital services.

CONCLUSION

Now in Today's Environment Broadband communications will become a necessity for business and private citizen to perform the functions and also wish to functions in near future. With satellite communications networks will link all the unit of the business and remote employee with seamless

High-speed access point from any where in the world and not to worry about infrastructure communication in the world. And also Reliable multicast are used to support Reliable flow controlled data exchange, the letter allowing for data to be delivered Simultaneously to a number of Receivers. Other Services such as web access are supported by caching schemes that place frequently requested information at sites in the theater of operations to promote low response times and reduced connection on the satellite links. The system operational and in use by military commends. Extensions to the core system, enhanced security, and support for quality of service, are currently being designed, implemented and evaluated. Today many urban area problems of connections by cable or any other sources painfully and slow. Satellite communication share and transmission of information at high speed , with communication comes comes knowledge and understanding and with knowledge and understanding ,the world will continue to shrink and become global community.

REFERENCES

[1] Communication Satellite Antennas: System Architecture, Technology, and Evaluation by Robert 2009.

[2] Satellite Communications Systems: Systems, Techniques and Technology by Gerard Maral (2010), fifth edition.

[3] Satellite Communications Systems Engineering: Atmospheric Effects, Satellite Link Design and System Performance (Wireless Communications and Mobile Computing) by Dr. Louis J. Ippolito (2008).

[4] Introduction to Satellite Communication (Artech House Space Applications) by Bruce R. Elbert (2008).

[5] Satellite Communications by Timothy Pratt (2002).

[6] Satellites and the Internet: Challenges and Solutions by D.C. Palter (2004)

[7] Introduction to Satellite Systems, Technology Basics, Market Growth, Systems, and Services by Ben Levitan and Lawrence Harte (2003).

[8] http://en.wikipedia.org/wiki/Direct-broadcast_satellite

[9] http://www.satellites.co.uk/forums/meeting-place/70593-how-broadcast-satellite-channel.html

[10] http://searchmobilecomputing.techtarget.com/definition/direct-broadcast-satellite

[11] http://www.satellites.co.uk/forums/meeting-place/70593-how-broadcast-satellite-channel.html

[12] http://ieeexplore.ieee.org/xpl/freeabs_all.jsp?arnumber=718562

[13] http://spacejournal.ohio.edu/issue17/main.html

[14] Online Journal of Space Communication An International Electronic Journal

[15] J.E. Drummond, Comparison of Low Earth Orbit and Geosynchronous Earth Orbit, Power Conversion Technology, Inc., 1980.

[16] Mark M. Hopkins, The Satellite Power Station and Non-cost Uncertainty Aspects of Risk. The Rand Corporation, 1980.

[17] Allan Kotin, Satellite Power System (SPS) State and Local Regulations as Applied to Satellite Power System Microwave Receiving Antenna Facilities, DOE/NASA, October 1978.

[18] Geoffrey A. Landis, Reinventing the Solar Power Satellite, National Aeronautics and Space Administration, Glenn Research Center, Cleveland, Ohio, 2004.

[19] John C. Mankins, A Fresh Look at Space Solar Power: New Architectures, Concepts and Technologies, IAF-97-R.2.03, 38th International Astronautically Federation, Advanced Projects Office National Aeronautics and Space Administration, 1997.

Economic Analysis of the Procurement and Utilization of Storage in Warehouses of India under the Public Distribution System of Rice

Basistha Chatterjee

Asian School of Business Management (ASBM), Bhubaneswar, Orissa
E-mail: basisthachatterjee@yahoo.com

ABSTRACT

The PDS as well as TPDS shown a poor impact while considering the state wise success throughout India. the study was focused at finding the relationship between procurement and capacity of the warehouses of PDS. Furthermore, the study attempted in finding the relationship between procurement and capacity of the warehouses of PDS. Another magnitude of the study was to observe the extent of utilization of those warehouses. The specific objectives undertaken in the study are: to analyze the procurement amount of different food grains under TPDS and future estimation as well as stock of food grains and to estimate future stock position; to examine the relationship among different procurement agencies under TPDS; to examine the warehouse utilization level by finding relationship between total capacity and actual procurement; to examine the relationship between allocation of food grain under different Government schemes. Secondary data regarding procurement amount of various food grains for PDS purpose during 2005 to 2010 were collected from different Annual Reports of Ministry of Consumers' Affairs, Government Of India. Moreover, secondary data regarding the procurement of rice by major agencies, i.e. Food Corporation of India (FCI) and State Agencies for central pool, total storage capacity of FCI in million tones, year-wise minimum support price of wheat, common paddy and grade A Paddy, allocation and off-take of food grains under Targeted Public Distribution System (TPDS), allocation and off-take under BPL and AAY Schemes and utilization level of warehousing capacity during 2002 to 2009 were also collected. Mainly tabular method was adopted in analyzing and presenting the data. Regarding statistical techniques apart from mathematical tools like per cent distribution regression technique, correlation technique and T-test were conducted. Forecasting wherever needed were conducted using linear regression method to analyze the trend of procurement, distribution and minimum support price of various food grains, especially of paddy. To find out the relationship between the variables like the rice procurement between FCI and state agencies, stock and capacity Karl Pearson's coefficient (or correlation) was used. To test the hypothesis about coefficient of correlation T test was used (both one-tailed and two-tailed according to heteroscedasticity). The study found that rice procurement between FCI and state agencies it was found to be inversely correlated although they are linearly related. As per implication, policy makers may have a serious clue in this issue to revitalize the existing system. Stock and capacity were found to be highly correlated but are not linearly related. This growth is needed to be sustained. It was also found that, even if growth of per cent utilization of hired warehouses also declined in the year 2007-08, utilization of owned warehousing was also observed to be increased. Especially, in recent years, the per cent utilization of owned warehouse was found to be remarkable. The study has also observed an inverse relationship between the total TPDS allocation and total TPDS off-take which is a worrying factor and necessary measure should be taken by the Central Government to empower the State Governments.

Keywords: TPDS, Procurement, Warehouse, Off-take

INTRODUCTION

The poor impact of the Public Distribution System (PDS) scheme already observed especially in poor states such as Bihar, Uttar Pradesh, Madhya Pradesh, Orissa and Rajasthan which forced us to realize that there is a need for strengthening of PDS in these states. It was also felt that had the scheme been not universal, but properly targeted, greater impact would have been there. The PDS had its ultimate objectives of improving distribution of basic goods, controlling prices of essential commodities, meeting consumption needs of masses, maintaining quality at low cost, bringing stability in prices and to weave the production and marketing system into a unified whole. PDS was initiated soon after the Bengal famine in 1943. It was replaced by Targeted PDS (TPDS) in which targeting was shifted to the poor households instead of poor regions. The families belonging to below poverty line were provided huge amount of subsidy and 10 kg of food grain per family per month was provided. The non-poor got no subsidy and were served by fair shops for proper distribution of food grains by competing with private shops. Hence, the need of the hour is to encourage proper targeting to have better results and to pursue PDS by finding answer to the automatically raised issue- whether the PDS proved to be a flash in the pan or a nine days' wonder. This study attempted to find answer to the question by throwing light to other aspects in this regard and not being confined into finding impact of PDS and poverty. Rather, the study was important in finding the relationship between procurement and capacity of the warehouses of PDS. Another importance of the study was to observe the extent of utilization of those warehouses. After realizing the importance of the study, following objectives are set out.

OBJECTIVES

1. To analyze the procurement amount of different food grains under TPDS and future estimation..
2. To analyze stock of food grains and estimate future stock position.
3. To examine the relationship among different procurement agencies under TPDS.
4. To examine the warehouse utilization level by finding relationship between total capacity and actual procurement.
5. To examine the relationship between allocation of food grain under different Government schemes.

REVIEW OF LITERATURE

Radhakrishna, R. et al. (1997) opined that taking India as a whole, the impact of poverty was moderate; subsidies were estimated to have reduced poverty by 1.6 per cent in rural areas and 1.7 per cent in urban areas. About 12 million persons may have moved out of poverty in 1986-87 due to income transfers from PDS. Still this number was small considering the absolute number of poor in India 274 million during that period of time.

Heckman et al. (1997, 1998) shown that failing to control for matching on the common support of the control propensity score distribution with that of the treated is the single most important source of bias. Potentially more important than bias due to selection on unobservable. Planning Commission, Ninth Five Year Plan (1997-2002) mentioned that, "coarse grains that are inexpensive can provide substantially higher calories for the same cost. If made available through PDS at subsidized rates, these will be self targeting and improve calorie intake and reduce hunger among the poorest segments of population.

Planning Commission, Tenth Five Year Plan (2002-2007) opined that, there has been a continuous increase in PDS expenditure, which rose from Rs 12,120 crores in 2000-01 and further to a record level of Rs 25,800 crores in 2003-04. But responding to a popular pressure to continue the scheme as welfare measure along with a price stabilization instrument, food subsidies went up sharply to 5.2 per cent in 2003-04.

METHODOLOGY

In order to fulfill the above objectives secondary data regarding procurement amount of various food grains for PDS purpose during 2005 to 2010 were collected from different Annual Reports of Ministry of Consumers' Affairs, Government of India. Moreover, secondary data regarding the procurement of rice by major agencies, i.e. Food Corporation of India (FCI) and State Agencies for central pool, total storage capacity of FCI in million tones, year-wise minimum support price of wheat, common paddy and grade A Paddy, allocation and off-take of food grains under Targeted Public Distribution System (TPDS), allocation and off-take under BPL and AAY Schemes and utilization level of warehousing capacity during 2002 to 2009 were also collected from the Annual Reports of Ministry of Consumers' Affairs, Government Of India. Mainly tabular method was adopted in analyzing and presenting the data. Regarding statistical techniques apart from mathematical tools like per cent distribution regression technique, correlation technique and T-test were conducted. Forecasting wherever needed were conducted using linear regression method to analyze the trend of procurement, distribution and minimum support price of various food grains, especially of paddy. To find out the relationship between the variables like the rice procurement between FCI and state agencies, stock and capacity Karl Pearson's coefficient (or correlation) was used and calculated in MS EXCEL. To test the hypothesis about coefficient of correlation T test was used using MS EXCEL both one-tailed and two-tailed according to heteroscedasticity.

RESULTS AND DISCUSSION

Table 1: Year-wise Procurement of Rice, Wheat and Coarse Grains during 2005 to 2010

(Figures in lakh tonnes)

Year	Rice	Wheat	Coarse grain	Total
2005-06	276.56	147.85	11.54	435.95
2006-07	251.07	92.26	0.002	343.33
2007-08	284.91	111.27	2.03	398.21
2008-09	336.83	226.82	13.75	577.40
2009-10	260.00	253.82	3.20	493.89
2015-16 (Forecasted)	323.99	189.52	10.21	523.72

Source: Annual Report, 2005-06 and 2009-10, Ministry of Consumers' Affairs, GOI.

Table 1 delineated the year-wise procurement amount of rice ,wheat and coarse grains for the time duration of 2005 to 2010. Procurement of rice was observed to be highest in the year 2008-09 and lowest in the year 2006-07. According to forecasting for the year 2015-16 the procurement of rice will reach about 324 lakh metric tonnes. In case of procurement of wheat huge year wise fluctuation during first five years was noticed. The maximum amount of procurement was observed in 2009-10 and minimum was observed in the year 2006-07. According to forecast for the year 2015-16 the procurement amount of wheat will reach about 190 lakh metric tonnes. In case of the coarse grains (like oil seed, sugar, etc.) the maximum procurement was seen in the year 2008-09. The minimum coarse grain procurement year was 2006-07. The forecast reflected that it may reach upto 10.21 lakh metric tonnes in the year 2015-16. So, from the table it can be said that the procurement was least in the year 2006-07 irrespective of the type of grains. The regression equation for rice was found as: $Y_r = 266.082+5.264X_r$. For wheat the regression equation was $Y_w = 157.734+2.89X_w$. For the other coarse grains the regression equation was $Y_{ocg} = 6.984–0.2932X_{ocg}$. Where Y_r, Y_w and Y_{ocg} are amount of food grain procured as rice, wheat and other coarse grains in the respective years respectively. X_r, X_w and X_{ocg} are the years of procurement of rice, wheat and other coarse grains respectively.

Table 2: Year-wise Stock of Food Grains in Central Pool during 2000 to 2009

(Figures in lakh tonnes)

Year	Stock	Year	Stock
2000	318.89	2006	192.60
2001	457.68	2007	174.92
2002	581.12	2008	191.87
2003	482.05	2009	361.89
2004	250.16	2015 (Forecasted)	31.86
2005	216.97	2020 (Forecasted)	(–) 106.69

Source: Annual Report, 2005-06, Ministry of Consumers' Affairs, GOI, page 18; Annual Report, 2008-09, Ministry of Consumers' Affairs, GOI, page 37.

It is of utmost need to stock adequate food grains for the success of the PDS system. Table 2 reflected that during last ten years maximum amount of stock of food grain in the central pool was in the year 2002 followed by 2003. The forecast indicated that with the proceedings of time stock of the central pool might be reduced significantly to 32 lakh tonnes and even less than that after 10 years from now. This may be due to the country's self sufficiency of production in the future capable of meeting the need of people for the future years. The consequent effect of less dependency of PDS support was also hereby visualized from the table. The regression equation revealed as $Y_{cp} = 475.22 – 27.71 X_{cp}$ whereas Y_{cp} is the amount of procurement in the central pool and X_{cp} refers to the year of procurement of the central pool for the stock of food grains.

Rice is the staple food of most of the states in India. People of lower income heavily depends on the PDS of rice. Table 3 depicted the year-wise procurement of rice by major agencies i.e. Food Corporation of India (FCI) and State Agencies for central pool during 2001 to 2009. Table showed that apart from the year 2008-09 FCI and the state agencies procured significant amount of rice. From the year 2008-09 the delegation of more procurement was given on the state agencies. The year wise total procurement of rice

Table 3: Year-wise Procurement of Rice by Major Agencies for Central Pool during 2001 to 2009

(Figures in lakh tonnes)

Year	Procurement by FCI	Procurement by State Agencies	Total Procurement
2001-02	118.72	94.04	212.76
2002-03	72.96	91.14	164.10
2003-04	109.73	118.55	228.28
2004-05	116.31	130.52	246.83
2005-06	109.77	166.80	276.56
2006-07	168.85	81.90	250.75
2007-08	124.28	160.65	284.93
2008-09	27.63	309.22	336.85

Source: Annual Report, 2005-06 and 2009-10, Ministry of Consumers' Affairs, GOI.

shown a little fluctuation over the time period during 2001 to 2009 which was observed to reach its peak in the year 2008-09. While finding if there was a correlation between the rice procurement between FCI and state agencies it was found to be inversely correlated as suggested by the the negative value of the correlation co-efficient, i.e. r = –0.7348. To test the hypothesis (Ho = FCI procurement and State Agencies procurement are linearly related) and as the respective means are unequal, both one and two tailed T-test (heteroscedastic) were conducted. In both the tests the calculated T were observed to be less than the tabulated T at both 5% and 10% level of significance with 7 degrees of freedom, the null hypothesis was accepted at 5% and 10% level of significance with 7 degrees of freedom, i.e. they are linearly related.

Table 4: Year-wise Total Storage Capacity with FCI during 2000 to 2009

(Figures in million tonnes)

Year	Capacity	Year	Capacity
2000	25.40	2006	22.83
2001	31.44	2007	22.28
2002	35.84	2008	21.66
2003	31.73	2009	23.09
2004	27.24	2015 (Forecasted)	14.062
2005	23.37	2020 (Forecasted)	8.147

Source: Annual Report, 2005-06, 2008-09 and 2009-10, Ministry of Consumers' Affairs, GOI.

Table 4 delineated the year wise total storage capacity of FCI in million tonnes. The maximum storage capacity was observed in the year 2002 followed by the year 2003 and

2001 respectively. In the year 2008 it was at its lowest capacity. The regression equation found in this regard is: Yf= 32.99–1.183 Xf. whereas is the amount of storage capacity of FCI in million tonnes and is the respective year of storage by FCI. The forecast revealed that FCI storage capacity might be reduced to 14.062 by the year 2015 and further reduced to 8.147 by the year 2020 respectively.

While observing the relationship between table number 2 and table number 4 it was observed that the stock and capacity were highly correlated as denoted by r= 0.91685. Both the one and two tailed heteroscedastic T-test revealed that the calculated value of T greater than tabulated value of T at both 5% and 10% level of significance at 9 degrees of freedom. Hence the null hypothesis, i.e. rejected (stock and capacity are linearly correlated) and the alternative hypothesis was accepted which told that the stock and capacity are not linearly related.

Table 5: Year-wise Minimum Support Price of Wheat, Common Paddy and Grade-A Paddy

(Figures in Rs per quintal)

Year	Wheat	Common Paddy	Grade-A Paddy
2001-02	610	530	560
2002-03	620	530	560
2003-04	620	550	580
2004-05	630	560	590
2005-06	640	570	600
2006-07	650	580	610
2007-08	750	645	675
2008-09	1000	850	880
2009-10	1080	950	980
2015-16 (Forecasted)	5943.84	1140.36	1170.56

Source: Annual Report, 2005-06, 2008-09 and 2009-10, Ministry of Consumers' Affairs, GOI.

Table 5 depicted the year-wise minimum support price of wheat, common paddy and grade A Paddy. In all cases the minimum support price was found to be increasing year wise. The regression equation for the minimum support price of wheat as found by statistical analysis is that: Y_{msp}=521.05X_{msp} – 1871.91. In case of common paddy the equation was: Y_{cp}=390.66+49.98 X_{cp}. In case of grade A paddy the regression equation was: Y_{Ap}= 420.56+50X_{Ap}. Here Y_{msp}, Y_{cp} and Y_{Ap} denote the minimum support price of wheat, common paddy and grade-A paddy respectively. X_{msp}, X_{cp} and X_{Ap} refers to the year of wheat, common paddy and grade-A paddy respectively. It was also found that during 2009-10 the minimum support price of wheat, common rice and grade A rice reached their respective peaks. Similarly during 2001-02 lowest minimum support price was observed. The forecast told that during 2015-16 the minimum support price of wheat, common paddy and rice will certainly increase substantially and they might touch Rs 5943.84 per quintal, Rs 1140.36 per quintal and Rs 1170.56 per quintal respectively.

Table 6: Year-wise Allocation and Off-take of Food Grains under TPDS

(Figures in lakh tonnes)

Year	Total TPDS Allocation	Total TPDS Off-take	% of Off-take
2000-01	274.59	117.89	42.93
2001-02	300.08	135.67	45.21
2002-03	743.28	200.66	26.99
2003-04	712.32	239.30	33.58
2004-05	716.99	293.55	40.94
2005-06	716.22	307.95	43.11
2008-09	395.01	221.87	56.17

Source: Annual Report, 2005-06 & 2008-09, Ministry of Consumers' Affairs, GOI.

Table 6 illustrated the year wise allocation and off-take of food grains under Targeted Public Distribution System (TPDS). The total allocation was observed to be highest in the year 2004-05 followed by 395.01. The total TPDS off-take was observed to be highest in 2005-06. But in case of % off-take is concerned 2008-09 was observed to be the highest (56.17%) followed by 2001-02 (45.21%). In 2001-02 the lowest % off-take was observed. The negative correlation co-efficient value, i.e. –0.4681 indicated that there was an inverse relationship between the total TPDS allocation and total TPDS off-take.

Table 7 illustrated the year-wise allocation and off-take under BPL and AAY Schemes. The maximum BPL allocation was observed during 2002-2003 where as the highest off-take of BPL was observed to be during 2003-04. A steady increase of % of-take (BPL) was observed from 2001-02 to 2004-05. Highest allocation as well as off-take for AAY was observed during 2005-06. Interestingly, in this year the % off-take (AAY) was at its maximum. The range of % off-take by AAY was very high during 2001-02 to 2005-06 ranging from 85.61% to 91.75%. However, the % of total off-take shown a steady increase during 2000-01 to 2005-06.

Table 8 clearly depicts that during 2004-05 to 2009-10 the owned warehousing capacity was gradually increased. Apart from the year 2007-08 the utilization of owned warehousing was also observed to be increased. In recent years the % of owned warehouse utilization is significant (87%). A little fluctuation in the capacity of hired warehouses are also noticed. Apart from year In the year 2007-08 and 2008-09 the capacity of hired warehouses were noted to be declined. The growth of % of utilization of hired warehouses

Table 7: Year-wise Allocation and Off-take under BPL and AAY Schemes

(Figures in lakh tonnes)

Year	BPL Allocation	BPL Off-take	% of BPL Off-take	AAY Allocation	AAY Off-take	% of AAY Off-take	Total Allocation BPL + AAY	Total Off-Take BPL + AAY	% Off-take
2000-01	159.71	96.53	60.43	55.87	0.24	0.43	215.58	96.77	44.89
2001-02	178.66	100.52	56.26	19.60	16.78	85.61	198.26	117.30	59.16
2002-03	227.71	135.13	59.34	41.28	35.39	85.73	268.99	170.52	63.39
2003-04	225.49	158.04	70.09	45.56	41.65	91.42	271.05	199.69	73.67
2004-05	212.77	173.81	81.69	60.54	54.63	90.24	273.31	228.44	83.58
2005-06	191.99	155.03	80.75	80.69	74.03	91.75	272.68	229.06	84.00
2008-09	Data un-available	100.31	–	Data un-available	63.26	–	395.01	221.87	56.17

Source: Annual Report, 2000-01 and 2008-09, Ministry of Consumers' Affairs, GOI.

Table 8: Year-wise Utilization Level of Warehousing Capacity

(Figures in lakh million tonnes)

Year	Owned			Hired			Total		
	Capacity	Utilized	% Utilized	Capacity	Utilized	% Utilized	Capacity	Utilized	% Utilized
2004-05	66.20	40.71	60	31.86	20.87	66	98.06	61.58	63
2005-06	66.83	44.83	67	35.28	26.76	76	102.11	71.59	70
2006-07	66.88	49.74	74	35.82	29.75	83	102.70	79.49	77
2007-08	67.27	48.30	72	32.02	24.42	76	99.29	72.72	73
2008-09	67.47	55.15	82	31.93	26.21	82	99.40	81.36	82
2009-10	67.73	58.90	87	39.89	33.93	85	107.62	92.83	86

Source: Annual Report, 2009-10, Ministry of Consumers' Affairs, GOI.

also declined in the year 2007-08. However, the per cent utilization of the total warehousing capacity was found to be increasing during the total span i.e., 2004-05 to 2009-10.

CONCLUSIONS

The initial letdown of PDS as the study implied, was due to the fact that procurement was least in the year 2006-07 irrespective of the type of grains. The forecast indicated that with the proceedings of time stock of the central pool might be reduced significantly to 32 lakh tonnes and even less than that after 10 years from now. This may be due to the country's self sufficiency of production in the future capable of meeting the need of people for the future years. Moreover, the rice procurement between FCI and state agencies it was found to be inversely correlated although they are linearly related. The policy makers may have a serious clue in this issue to revitalize the existing system. Stock and capacity were found to be highly correlated but are not linearly related. This growth should be sustained. It was also found that, even if growth of per cent utilization of hired warehouses also declined in the year 2007-08, utilization of owned warehousing was also observed to be increased. Especially, in recent years, the per cent utilization of owned warehouse was found to be remarkable. The study has also observed an inverse relationship between the total TPDS allocation and total TPDS off-take which is a worrying factor and necessary measure should be taken by the Central Government to empower the State Governments.

REFERENCES

[1] Annual Report, 2005-06, Ministry of Consumers' Affairs, GOI, p. 18.

[2] Annual Report, 2008-09, Ministry of Consumers' Affairs, GOI, p. 37.

[3] Heckman, J., H. Ichimura and P. Todd, 1997, Matching as an Econometric Evaluation Estimator I: Evidence from Evaluating a Job training Program, *Review of Economic Studies*, 64, pp. 605-654.

[4] Planning Commission (1997-2002), Ninth Five Year Plan, Vol. 2, p. 555.

[5] Planning Commission (2002-2006), Tenth Five Year Plan, Vol. 2, p. 368.

[6] Radhakrishna R., Subbarao K., Indrakant S. and Ravi K. (1997), Public Distribution: A National and International Perspectives, World Bank Discussion (380), pp. 44-45.

Economic Regulation of Indian Airports

Sumana Chaudhuri
National Institute of Industrial Engineering (NITIE), Mumbai
E-mail: sumanachaudhuri@yahoo.co.in

ABSTRACT

In the context of regulatory objectives & principles for airport regulatory process, regulatory approach on a number of important aspects would need to be considered. The regulatory approach could have reference to international examples and the context of Indian airports and air navigation services. Across sectors and regulatory jurisdictions, certain forms of regulation like Price Cap Regulation, Rate of Return Regulation and Sliding Scale Regulation are generally adopted. The article discusses the different types of regulatory mechanisms in the light of public private partnership airports in India and attempts to suggest the best possible ones in accordance to the learning from International experience. For successful implementation of any regulation it should be light handed or light touch to optimize a fair rate of return for the investors and adequate price monitoring and realistic long-term commitment for all stakeholders.

Keywords: Airport Regulation, Airport Economic Regulatory Authority (AERA), Price Cap Regulation, Rate of Return Regulation, Sliding Scale Regulation

INTRODUCTION

The Report on "Approach to Regulation of Infrastructure" presented by the Planning Commission, Government of India on 15 September 2008 to the Indian Parliament is a comprehensive document analyzing the current state of regulatory law and the associated institutional framework in India applicable to some of the key infrastructure sectors including airports (CoI, Regulation Law and Policy, September 2008). As outlined in the Report, infrastructure development in India is expected to follow a very different path in the years ahead compared to the past, with a much larger role for private investment in one form or other of public-private partnership.

The Eleventh Five Year Plan has set an ambitious target of increasing total investment in infrastructure from around 5% of GDP in the base year of the Plan 2006-07 to 9% by the terminal year 2011-2012. Around 30% of the required investment of around

Rs. 2,056,150 crores (US$ 514 billion) will have to come from private capital. The ability to mobilize private resources on this scale depends critically upon the creation of a supportive investor-friendly environment and the regulatory system is a critical component of that environment.

The relevant statute that govern the airport and airport infrastructure in India are the Aircraft Act 1934, Airports Authority of India Act 1994 and Air Corporation (Transfer of Undertaking and Repeal Act) 1994. In all cases Airports Authority of India is the operator as well as the regulator. Director General of Civil Aviation (DGCA) and the Bureau of Civil Aviation Security (BCAS) regulates the safety and technical aspects.

Airports are an essential part of the India's growing air transport network. Consequently, the trend for privatizing airports is of importance to all stakeholders in the industry which has already been discussed.

The key factor is that an airport can efficiently deliver the cost and service levels that airlines require and customers warrant. A strong focus should be made for management of airports. Good Airport Governance is important to achieve efficiency improvement.

This article reviews the experiences of other countries in their approach to regulation of airports and airport infrastructure. In order to eliminate the potential of airports to exercise monopoly and protect the public interest, it has become increasingly necessary to set a common regulatory framework. The existing regulatory approaches regarding airports in India and their economic implications are also analyzed.

REGULATION

Meaning of Regulation

Regulation is "controlling human or societal behaviour by rules or restrictions." (Bert-Jaap Koops et al., 2006) Regulation can take many forms: legal restrictions promulgated by a government authority, self-regulation by an industry such as through a trade association, social regulation (e.g. norms), co-regulation and market regulation.

Common examples of regulation include controls on market entries, prices, wages, development approvals, pollution effects, employment for certain people in certain industries, standards of production for certain goods, the military forces and services.

Reasons for Regulation

(a) **The presence of monopoly power:** In utility industry, where there is a strong possibility of existence of a natural monopoly, firms often tend to restrict the production of goods and services or set prices to such high levels that does not create a level playing field for other operators in the economy (Baumol and Bradford,

1970). While regulation is necessary to keep a tab on prices and ensure a competitive market, it does not guarantee that it creates efficiency in the system.

(b) **To account for spillover costs**: Regulation is also important where the prices charged by the operator do not reflect all the costs, including social costs, involved in the production process. Airlines taking off and touching down at airports create a lot of sound pollution by planes flying at sub sonar speeds. Regulation in such cases aims to protect the surrounding environment by making it mandatory for airport operators to construct sound abatement walls around the periphery of the airport to minimize sound pollution.

(c) **To compensate for inadequate information**: Regulation is often necessary to lower the cost of obtaining information. Operators and suppliers often make profit by providing less than adequate information or camouflaging facts that make claims deceptive. Till recently, most airlines in India showed a low basic fare in advertisements under "Fare" category and fuel surcharge and miscellaneous charges under "Taxes" thus giving the consumer a wrong impression that government is responsible for all that huge tax component. The fact is, that apart from the nominal Passenger Service Fee, no other taxes are received by the Government. The Ministry of Civil Aviation has regulated that henceforth all airlines must correctly advertise the fares under various heads and not misrepresent fares.

(d) **Other reasons for Regulation**: Sometime, regulation is warranted to create entry barriers so that the firms do not enter into price cutting, with a large number of firms entering the fray to create a hyper competitive market (MacAvoy and Robinson, 1985, Brock, 1981). Also, regulation protects weak firms if their bargaining power with the suppliers is low or customers if they are treated unjust.

Regulation of Infrastructure Services

The regulation of infrastructure services arises from the necessity of correcting market failures that take place when there is no competitive environment, such as the case of the natural monopoly, or when there is competition without fulfilling the required conditions (Williamson 1976). According to Goldberg (1976), regulation may be viewed as a "transaction cost saving device for controlling the behavior of natural monopolies in cases where transaction specific investments lead to incontestability of monopoly markets while at the same time locks the sellers' investment into that transaction." Empirical evidence shows that utilities privatization brings greater benefits when it is accompanied by an effective regulatory regime (Wallsten, 2001; Zhang *et al.*, 2003; Pargal, 2003).

Regulation of Airports

Air passengers and airliners must be guarded against any monopoly pricing by the developers of airport infrastructure at the same time the latter must be ensured return on investment and security of their expectations. Therefore, regulation as a governance structure has to protect both parties' reasonable interests; otherwise inefficient outcomes will occur (Hartmut Wolf, 2002).

Airport authority and the regulator are bound to each other by bilateral relationship and needs to be protected against each others' opportunistic motives. While considering the governance of airports, it has been observed that indivisibilities in airport infrastructure investment prevent self-enforcement of regulatory contracts if no institutional safeguards against opportunism exist (Hartmut Wolf, 2002).

Independent and transparent economic regulation can reduce uncertainty on both the users and the regulated companies, helping to reduce investor risks and financing costs. The stability provided by an effective regulatory framework can also attract longer-term investment finance into the industry, avoiding the potential volatility in infrastructure asset prices driven by short-term speculative finance.

Regulation may be broadly understood as an effort by the state to address social risk, market failure or equity concerns through rule-based direction of social and individual action. Economic regulation is seen to be that part of regulation which seeks to achieve the effective functioning of competitive markets and where such markets are absent, to mimic competitive market outcomes to the extent possible. The purview of economic regulation includes the two core regulatory tasks which are the setting of maximum tariffs and enforcing of minimum service standards. The other functions of economic regulation are also to identify and address subsidies and cross-subsidies in the pricing of infrastructure services. States generally use economic regulation in a broader context to achieve a range of non-market objectives which include ensuring universal and equitable access, consumer protection and maintaining safety and health standards.

Airport regulation means that the task of controlling the behaviour of the airport company is not performed by the users of that airport, but by a regulator, who simultaneously acts as a principal for the regulated airport and as an agent for the airport users (Hartmut Wolf, 2002).

Types of Airport Regulation

Airport regulation can be categorized into three types (Wolf, 2002).

1. **Internal Regulation**: The state acts as owner of the airport company and exercises ownership rights to control its activities by means of internal command. A pre-condition for internal regulation is only partial divestiture of airport companies by public owners. Internal regulation eliminates the risk of regulation to a considerable extent. However, it might lead to inefficient outcomes for socio-political reasons.
2. **Ex-Ante Regulation**: they are bound by specific regulations enforceable in a court of

law, leaving the regulator little room for discretion. Ex-Ante rules are usually effective in protecting the airport company's quasi-rents and therefore facilitates the complete privatization process. It may be noted that such inflexible rules can lead the airport company to behave opportunistically, as in situation where they earn a fixed return on capital employed irrespective of the cost (Averch and Johnson, 1962). This makes ex-ante regulation heavy handed.

3. **Ex-Post Regulation**: This form of regulation allows for discretion by the regulator, as the flexibility to lower airport charges ex-post, thus making regulation a repeated game between Airport Company and the regulator. This makes regulation more light handed by virtue of design of a relational regulatory contract that is self-enforceable.

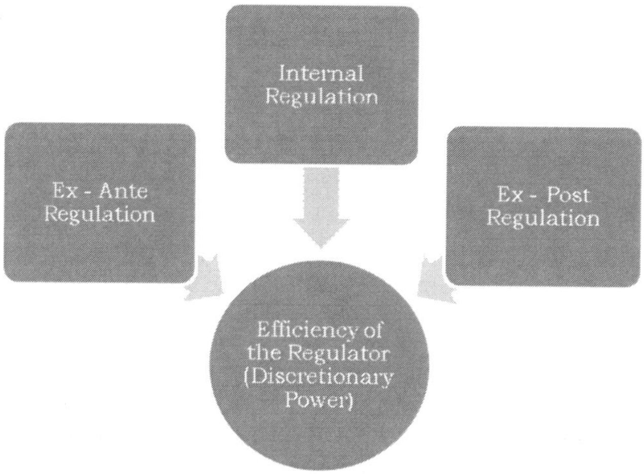

Fig. 1: Types of Airport Regulation (adapted from Wolf, 2002)

A critical analysis of the types of airport regulation leads to the following observations:

Firstly, there exist complementarities between the form of airport privatization and the framework in which the airports will operate. As a thumb rule, if the airports' quasi-rents are protected then it makes sense for full privatization, otherwise, partial divestiture can be a possible solution.

Secondly, the inflexible ex-ante rules can be avoided by effective and light handed ex-post regulation, which calls for a strong institutional mechanism. In this context, it may be referred that examination of the results of empirical studies about the relative performance of public and private companies' reveal that private companies that are heavily regulated do not perform better than public ones (Vickers, 1988).

Thirdly, the implementation of ex-post control mechanisms is best achieved in countries which had already privatized or actively pursuing the process of airport privatization of not only a few, but a large number of airports.

REGULATORY ENVIRONMENT: EXPERIENCE WITH DEVELOPED AND DEVELOPING COUNTRIES

Developed Countries

Cost of service regulation or Rate of Return Regulation (RoR) was first introduced in USA in the public utility industries in the early 1900s (Crew and Kleindorfer, 1996, 2002). Countries such as Netherlands, Spain and Portugal also followed *RoR regulation.* There was however quite a few drawbacks associated with RoR regulation. To overcome these difficulties, *Price-cap regulation* was introduced in the 1980s by UK Treasury economist Stephen Littlechild (Beesley and Littlechild, 1983), which has been applied to all of the privatized British network utilities. This form of regulation is also known as *Consumer Price Index* (CPI – X) Regulation or Retail Price Index (RPI – X) Regulation. Most of the European Union countries, including Australia and New Zealand also followed Price-cap regulation. RoR and Price Cap Regulation are the two main types of globally adopted regulatory mechanism. They however have their own merits and demerits. To keep the efficiency by balancing risk and incentives, different countries have taken flexible and light handed regulation. It has many variants like Sliding Scale Regulation (Austria), Earnings Sharing (USA) and Price Monitoring (Australia).

Developing Countries

Airport regulation around the world is much talked about and its economic impact has been researched. Recognizing this strategic importance of regulation, many developing nations have tried to incorporate the successful regulatory framework of the developed nations in governance of their airports. Guasch (2001), while conducting a study for World Bank, observed that price cap regulation is the well established and preferred form of Economic Regulation in Latin American countries. Iossa & Stroffolini, 2002, while observing the PCR in developing countries found that higher profits could be earned through *increase in efficiency*, which in turn is a *welfare enhancing measure*. Welfare is enhanced through gain in both *productive and allocative efficiencies* (at periodic reviews of the regulatory regime). To hold on to the allocative efficiency, firms try to reduce the cost, thus leading to underinvestment. This in turn leads to reduction in service quality and deterioration of capital stock over time with consequential damaging effect in the long run. Calzolari, 2001 also highlights the information asymmetry associated with PCR, especially in case of MNCs, with multi country operations, with differing levels of profit in each country, thus hindering the ability of the regulator to regulate effectively. Working in the same direction, Kirkpatrick, Parker and Zhang (2004), on a large sample size of 36 developing countries, found that in 24 countries the Price Cap method is used, while 16 counties have implemented rate of return regulation. The earlier two works focuses on the popularity of Price Cap Regulation in developing countries. However, in a different perspective put by Newberry, 1999, Price Cap Regulation seems to be less preferred choice for the private investors, rather Rate of Return Regulation, where revenue model is based on the cost, may be less prone to regulatory opportunism. In this regard, Alexander et al., 2001 observed that cost of capital will be higher under a Price Cap than Rate of Return Regulation. In similar lines, a World Bank research project on price caps and infrastructure contracts in Latin America conducted by Estache et al. (2003), has been identified that "the adoption of price caps, implied higher costs of capital and hence, tariffs and brought down levels of investment." This finding suggests that in uncertain environment as in the case of developing economies, rate of return seems to be a better choice for the investors. There is also an inherent problem to operate PCR successfully in developing countries. PCR usually allows for "Cost Pass Through" for any upward revision of prices. This however works best in those developed economies like UK where inflation is low. In developing economies where there is a large fluctuation in inflation, PCR is not at all effective. All other things being the same, RoR more or less guarantees a steady profit which at least equates the cost of capital. The other advantage of RoR Regulation is that firms are financed to meet agreed output targets. In the survey conducted by Kirkpatrick, Parker and Zhang (2004), regulators operating price caps are more concerned with the issues of information asymmetries (96% of the countries) as compared with 59% of the countries operating Rate of Return Regulation. The same survey also points out that Price Caps are associated with employment distortions and under investment, which is undesirable in developing economies, where infrastructure development is the key criterion. Price Caps are also prone to political pressures to lower the caps in the event of a firm started earning above average profits by lowering costs. Thus, in brevity, Rate of Return Regulation is easier to comprehend and more transparent than Price Caps, where calculation of the X factor and "Cost Pass Throughs" are debatable, especially in the absence of a standardized global benchmarking. In this context it is apt to put forward the observation made by Jamison (2005), that in the case of Rate of Return Regulation in developing countries the Averch Johnson effect (which is often observed in developed countries) would not hold good, except so if the investment is warranted for greater social and economic wellbeing, rather than simply politically motivated "gold plating" efforts by the private investors. As there is no price fluctuation in RoR regulation, as compared to a PCR regime, the environment is stable and secure for investors.

Some of the inefficiencies associated with Rate of Return Regulation in a developing economy may be less of a problem in an economy's context that is trying to make additional investment into industries and expand services to underserved population. Incentive to over expand the asset base is less in developing countries, where there is usually a desperate need for more investment to improve the quality and scope of service provision. The major role of Rate of Return Regulation is to create incentives for rapid investment in key infrastructure schemes at a time when cost minimization is less of a priority.

However a purely adapted model often is devoid of the flexibilities required to function in the more complex interplay of societal considerations, government control, political interference, resource capacities, implementation capabilities and other stakeholders' interests as observed in a developing economy. They are possibly more expensive to run in relation to GDP than in developed economies (Domah *et al.*, 2003).

Therefore the regulatory mechanism tends to be less effective (Parker, 2002) and calls for re-appraisal to check its suitability in a developing economy's context.

The research relating to competition among airports mostly relates to developed countries. In the context of developing countries, there has been little occurrence of competition among airports, as there are fewer airports or a single airports in the major cities (Grimsey and Lewis, 2007).

The environment of business in a developing economy is volatile in nature, with high degree of perturbation in the inflation; cost and revenue could not be reasonably represented well in advance and high regulatory uncertainty.

Under this circumstance, economic thought would dictate a government to opt for a regulation that optimizes the benefits of price cap and rate of return regulation. Rate of return regulation could be a possible choice for airport regulation, which is easy to implement and monitor and conducive to a developing economy as it provides a stable and secure environment by minimizing price fluctuations.

REGULATION OF AIRPORTS

There is a strong ground for analyzing the *economic regulation of airports.*

Air passengers and airliners must be guarded against any monopoly pricing by the developers of airport infrastructure at the same time the latter must be ensured return on investment and security of their expectations. *Therefore, regulation as a governance structure has to protect both parties' reasonable interests; otherwise inefficient outcomes will occur* (Wolf, 2002).

Airport authority and the regulator are bound to each other by bilateral relationship and needs to be protected against each others' opportunistic motives. While considering the governance of airports, it has been observed that *indivisibilities in airport infrastructure investment prevent self-enforcement of regulatory contracts if no institutional safeguards against opportunism exist* (op cit, 2002).

Airport regulation signifies that a regulator simultaneously acts as a principal for the regulated airport and as an agent for the airport users (op cit, 2002).

Around the world there has been extensive reform of airports. Airports have been either corporatized or privatized. Ownership status has changed for the airport operators. Economic regulation as a discipline emerged to incentivize airport developers to produce and price efficiently. In 1970, on the perspective of US network industries like US Aviation (which is mainly public utilities), Kahn (1970) observed that because of the *natural monopoly* characteristics (possibility of exploitation of market power), competition cannot exist. These justify economic regulation, which can also be expressed as price or profit regulation. Kahn (1970) suggested *marginal cost as the basis of efficient pricing*. But the problem with *marginal cost pricing* was later identified by Kahn (1989) in a revised version of his earlier work and he recommended charging price according to *willingness to pay* (WTP).

It is important for us to discuss the objectives of these institutional and regulatory reforms. The overriding objective is to promote *economic efficiency*. This involves production at minimum cost, provision of services at a quality level which users are willing to pay for, efficient levels of investment, price structures that reflect cost or ration capacity efficiently where it is in short supply, or which enable *cost recovery at minimum dead weight loss*. It also involves provision of adequate services to facilitate airline competition, and the development of non-aeronautical services which are complementary to the main business. The institutional and regulatory framework should create incentives for the pursuit of efficiency, although it must be recognized that a balance between objectives will normally have to be sought, and that a "first best" is rarely attainable (Forsyth et al, 2008).

In this regard it is worthwhile to mention that in recent years Australia has migrated from Price Cap Regulation to *Price Monitoring* (in 2002), which is efficient and flexible regulation. The rationale for moving to Price Monitoring is that in the earlier regime of direct regulation, the allocative efficiency gains from keeping prices close to costs were likely to be outweighed by productive efficiency losses from regulation. Price Monitoring is advantageous to both the regulator and the regulated firm as it allows more suppleness to the regulator to review the performance and at the same time offer greater pricing freedom for the airport operator. Price Monitoring also combine strong incentives for efficiency with flexibility to allow for external factors that impact on the airports' performance, thereby lowering the risks of profit volatility and firm failure. To achieve this objective, it is necessary to establish clear criteria for performance, which are consistent with incentives of the firm to be efficient (Forsyth, 2008).

There exist *strong interdependencies between airport regulation and competition*. Recent reviews establish the linkages that exist between competition policy and airport regulatory mechanisms (Guiomard, 2008). This highlights that high degree of co-operation between the authorities in charge of competition law and regulation law enforcement is necessary. *Combining regulatory and competition policy competencies concerning the airports might be the best institutional design* (Duijm, 2008).

It is the responsibility of the Government to make better use of evidence-based policy-making for effective regulatory governance of airports. This means making better use of research and analysis in both policy-making and policy implementation. Regulation should be an evidence based approach that allows for the systematic consideration of the benefits and costs of a regulatory proposal to the economy and society.

AIRPORT REGULATION IN INDIA

According to Observations on White Paper No. 01/2009-10 issued by Airports Economic Regulatory Authority (AERA) of India on 22 December 2009, Airports Council International (ACI) submitted their views on 5 January 2010 (ACI, 2010), which clearly favor an *incentive based regulatory model.* The major reason to opt for incentive based regulation is that it gives the regulated firm to keep costs at a minimum, while maintaining productive efficiency. Incentive based regulation also promotes and remunerates investment, increases service quality, results in diversification of airport revenues and allows for flexibility between aircraft related and passenger related charges. ACI also recommends a *Dual Till Approach* in the context of Indian Airports.

Airports in India are making a bet on the future shifting from a system where supply lagged demand, to be 'ahead of the game' in terms of capacity and innovation. This is an important and costly transition. The private sector has shown considerable confidence in the Indian market and has been reliant on concession agreements concluded with the Government of India. These agreements already include major commitments in terms of concession payments and obligations on capital investment and service standards putting pressure on profitability. The regulatory approach should therefore take a long term view and honor the significant ambitions and challenges during the transition period to reassure investors of the viability of the airport business in India.

The form of economic oversight selected can ultimately protect stakeholders from risk and uncertainty, but this result is more likely to be the case in a mature and stable system. In a developing phase however it requires a certain degree of flexibility to respond to the extraordinary challenges. Similar to the market, a regulatory regime needs to grow and mature over time to become robust, reliable and effective to achieve its objectives and earn trust with the stakeholders.

CONCLUSION

To summarize, following issues are critical to establish a successful economic regulatory regime for airports and air navigation services in India:

(a) Form of regulation – whether Price Cap, Rate of Return or Sliding Scale;

(b) Till – Treatment of non-aeronautical revenues and adoption of Single, Dual or Hybrid (Shared) till;
(c) Form of Price Control and Tariff Structure – Should the regulator set individual tariffs or the operator should have flexibility within the 'aggregate' determined by the regulator;
(d) Service Quality Monitoring – Setting and monitoring of standards, and ensuring compliance

It is the responsibility of the Government to make better use of evidence-based policy-making for effective regulatory governance of airports. This means making better use of research and analysis in both policy-making and policy implementation. Regulation should be an evidence based approach that allows for the systematic consideration of the benefits and costs of a regulatory proposal to the economy and society.

Good performance of Airports results from good governance, and ultimately from a good regulation. In order to drive performance in air service provision, greater attention should be focused on governance. In view of recent thrust toward public private partnership in development of Indian airports, a comprehensive regulatory strategy needs to be prepared to capture the best investment opportunities. Transparency in the operations and in the revenue and risk sharing is the best path toward good governance.

REFERENCES

[1] Averch, H., and L.L. Johnson (1962), "Behaviour of the Firm under Regulatory Constraint," *American Economic Review*, Vol. 52 (5), pp. 1052–1069.

[2] Baumol, W.J. and Bradford, D.F. (1970), "Optimal Departures from Marginal Cost Pricing," *American Economic Review*, Vol. 60 (3), pp. 265–283.

[3] Beesley, M. and Littlechild, S.C. (1983), "The Regulation of Privatized Monopolies in the United Kingdom", *RAND Journal of Economics*, Vol. 20, No. 3, pp. 454–472.

[4] Burns, P., Turvey, R., Weyman-Jones, T. (1995), "General Properties of Sliding Scale Regulation", Centre for the Study of Regulated Industries, London, Technical Paper, No. 3.

[5] Burns, P., Turvey, R., Weyman-Jones, T. (1998), "The Behaviour of the Firm under Alternative Regulatory Constraints", *Scottish Journal of Political Economy*, Vol. 45 No. 2, pp. 133–157.

[6] Crew, M.A. and Kleindorfer, P.R. (1996), 'Incentive Regulation in the United Kingdom and the United States: Some Lessons', *Journal of Regulatory Economics*, Vol. 9, pp. 211–225.

[7] Crew, M.A. and Kleindorfer, P.R. (2002) 'Regulatory Economics: Twenty Years of Progress?' *Journal of Regulatory Economics*, Vol. 21, No. 1, pp. 5–22.

[8] Currier, Kevin (2008), "Price Cap Regulation of Airports: A New Approach." *Economics Bulletin,* Vol. 12, No. 8, pp. 1 – 7

[9] Domah, P., Pollitt, M.G., Stern, J. (2003), "Modelling the Costs of Electricity Regulation: Evidence of Human Resource Constraints in Developing Countries", *Risk Regulation, Accountability and Development Workshop*, University of Manchester, Manchester, 26/27 June.

[10] Goldberg, V.P. (1976), "Regulation and Administered Contracts", *Bell Journal of Economics*, Vol. 7(2), pp. 426–452.

[11] Hartmut Wolf (2002), "Airport Privatisation and Regulation—Getting the Institutions Right", Second German Aviation Seminar, 8-9 November 2002, Bremen, accessed from Institut für Weltwirtschaft, http://www.ifw-kiel.de

[12] John Braithwaite, Cary Coglianese, David Levi-Faur (2007), "Can Regulation and Governance Make a Difference?" *Regulation & Governance*, Wiley Interscience, Vol. 1(1), pp. 1–7.

[13] Julia Black (2002), "Critical Reflections on Regulation," *Australian Journal of Legal Philosophy*, Vol. 27, pp. 1–36.

[14] Lyon, T.P. (1996), "A Model of Sliding-Scale Regulation", *Journal of Regulatory Economics*, Vol. 9, pp. 227–247.

[15] MacAvoy, P. W. and Robinson, K. (1985), "Losing by Judicial Policy Making: The First Year of the AT&T Divestiture," *Yale Journal on Regulation*, Vol. 2(2), pp. 225–262.

[16] Mark Smyth (2006), "Airport Regulation and Credit Ratings," IATA Economic Briefing, May 2006, pp. 1-2, accessed from http://www.iata.org/economics on 2 May 2009.

[17] Marques R. (2006), "A Yard Stick Competition Model for Portuguese Water and Sewerage Services Regulation", *Utilities Policy*, Vol. 14(3), pp. 175–184.

[18] Pargal, S. (2003), "Regulation and Private Sector Investment in Infrastructure: Evidence from Latin America", *Policy Research Working Paper*, World Bank, Washington, DC, No. 3037.

[19] Parker, D. (1999), 'Regulating Public Utilities: What Other Countries can Learn from the UK Experience', *Public Management*, Vol. 1, No. 1, pp. 93–120.

[20] Parker, D. (2002), 'Economic Regulation: A Review of Issues', *Annals of Public and Cooperative Economics*, Vol. 73, No. 4, pp. 493–519.

[21] Rui Cunha Marques, Ana Oliveira – Brochado, (2007), "Comparing Airport Regulation in Europe: Is There Need for a European Regulator?" FEP Working Paper Series, No. 259, pp. 1–21, accessed from http://www.fep.up.pt

[22] Sappington, D. (2002), "Price regulation", in Cave, M., Majumdar, S., Vogelsang, I. (Eds), *The Handbook of Telecommunications Economics, Volume 1: Structure, Regulation and Competition*, Elsevier, Amsterdam.

[23] Stephen Breyer and Paul W. MacAvoy (1994), "Regulation and Deregulation", in John Eatwell, Murray Milgate and Peter Newman ed. *The New Palgrave Dictionary of Economics*, The Macmillan Press, London, pp. 128–133.

[24] Vickers, J., and G. Yarrow (1988), "Privatisation: An Economic Analysis." Cambridge, Mass.

[25] Victor Prins and Paul Lombard (1995), "Regulation of Commercialized State-Owned Enterprises: Case Study of South African Airports and Air Traffic and Navigation Services", *Journal of Air Transport Management,* Vol. 2, No. 314, pp. 163–171.

[26] Wallsten, S.J. (2001), "An Econometric Analysis of Telecom Competition, Privatization and Regulation in Africa and Latin America", *Journal of Economic Behaviour & Organisation*, Vol. 42, pp. 43–74.

[27] Williamson, O.E. (1976), "Franchise Bidding for Natural Monopoly in General and with Respect to CATV", *The Bell Journal of Economics*, Vol. 7(1), pp. 73–104.

[28] Zhang, Y.F., Parker, D. and Kirkpatrick, C. (2003), "Electricity Sector Reform in Developing Countries: An Econometric Assessment of the Effects of Privatisation, Competition and Regulation", Working Paper No. 31, Centre on Regulation and Competition, Institute for Development Policy and Management, University of Manchester, Manchester.

Books

[1] Baldwin, Robert and Martin Cave (1999), "Understanding Regulation: Theory, Strategy and Practice", Oxford: Oxford University Press, Chapter 17.

[2] Bös, D. (1994), "Pricing and Price Regulation: An Economic Theory for Public Enterprises and/Public Utilities", Amsterdam: North Holland/Elsevier Newbery.

[3] Brock, G.W. (1981), "The Telecommunications Industry: The Dynamics of Market Structure", Cambridge, Mass: Harvard University Press.

[4] D.M. (1999), "Privatization, Restructuring and Regulation of Network Industries", Cambridge, Mass.: MIT Press.

[5] Doganis, R. (2002), "Airport Business", Routledge.

[6] Graham Anne (2003), "Managing Airports: An International Perspective," Elsevier Sciences.

[7] Graham, A. (2004), Managing Airports: An International Perspective, 2nd ed., Elsevier.

[8] Laffont, J.-J. and Tirole, J. (1993), "A Theory of Incentives in Regulation and Procurement," Cambridge Mass: MIT Press.

[9] Levinson, David, Garcia, Reinaldo and Carlson, Kathy (2006) "A Framework for Assessing Public Private Partnerships, in Institutions and Regulatory Reform in Transportation" (ed. Piet Rietveld and Roger Stough), Edward Elgar Publishers.

[10] Littlechild, S.C. (1983), "Regulation of British Telecommunications," London: HMSO.

[11] Mark A. Jamison (2008), "Regulation: Price Cap and Revenue Cap", Encyclopedia of Energy Engineering and Technology, ed. Barney L. Capehart, Francis and Taylor, p. 1245.

[12] Peter Forsyth (2008), "The Economic Regulation of Airports," German Aviation Research Society, Ashgate Publishing.

[13] Richard De Neufville, Amedeo R. Odoni (2009), "Airport systems", McGraw Hill.

Notes

[1] Anonymous (2000), Telecommunications Regulation Handbook (2000), The World Bank, Information for Development (InfoDev), accessed from http://www.infodev.org/en on 6 May 2009.

[2] Betancor, Ofelia and Roberto Rendeiro, (1999), "Regulating Privatized Infrastructures and Airport Services", University of Las Palmas.

[3] Bert-Jaap Koops et al. (2006), Starting Points for ICT Regulations, Deconstructing Prevalent Policy One-liners, Cambridge University Press, Cambridge, p. 81.

[4] David Gillen and Hans-Martin Niemeier (2007), "Comparative Political Economy of Airport Infrastructure in the European Union: Evolution of Privatization, Regulation and Slot Reform", Research Papers and Publications in Transportation and Logistics (TLOG), Sauder School of Business, accessed from http://www.sauder.ubc.ca on 16 May 2009.

[5] Hodges, A. and D. Grayson (2001), 'Everybody's Business', London, UK: International Business Leaders Forum.

[6] Mike Tretheway (2001), "Airport Ownership, Management and Price Regulation", Report prepared for the Canada Transportation Act Review Panel, InterVISTAS Consulting Inc., accessed from http://www.InterVISTAS.com on 8 May 2009.

[7] PC inquiry into Airport Pricing-2006-IATA Submission, pp. 1–14, accessed from http://www.iata.org

[8] Sanjay K. Sinha (2005), "Mobilizing Private Investment in Airport Development in India", India Infrastructure Summit, March 29, 2005, accessed from http://www.crisil.com on 16 May 2009.

[9] The Committee on Infrastructure (CoI), Government of India, Report on Regulation and Policy 2008, accessed from http://infrastructure.gov.in on 12 April 2009.

[10] Anonymous (2009), "Patel Hints at Allowing Foreign Carriers Invest in Indian Ones", *Economic Times*, 28 May 2009, accessed from http://economictimes.indiatimes.com on 30 May 2009.

[11] Anonymous (2009), "DGCA May Make Flight Delays Public", *Times of India*, Mumbai edition, 28 May 2009.

Reports

[1] Subir Gokarn (2002), "Civil Aviation in India: Deregulation and Constraints to Growth and Efficiency," in *India Infrastructure Report 2002: Governance Issues for Commercialization*, 3i Network, Oxford University Press, pp. 296–300.

[2] *Scheme and Guidelines for India Infrastructure Project Development Fund*, Department of Economic Affairs, Ministry of Finance, Government of India, 2007.

Web

[1] Airport International, http://www.airport-int.com

[2] Airports Authority of India, http://www.aai.aero

[3] Arab News, http://www.arabnews.com

[4] Bay Area Rapid Transit District (BART), http://www.bart.gov

[5] Bechtel Corporation, http://www.bechtel.com

[6] Bengaluru International Airport Limited (BIAL), http://www.bengaluruairport.com

[7] Booz Allen Hamilton, http://www.boozallen.com

[8] Bureau of Civil Aviation Security (BCAS), http://www.bcasindia.nic.in

[9] Confederation of Indian Industry, http://www.ciionline.org

[10] Directorate General of Civil Aviation [DGCA], India, http://www.dgca.nic.in

[11] Federal Aviation Administration, http://www.faa.gov

[12] FKI Logistex, http://www.fkilogistex.com

[13] Flughafen Stuttgart GmbH (FSG), http://www.flughafen-stuttgart.de

[14] International Air Transport Association, http://www.iata.org

[15] International Civil Aviation Organization, http://www.icao.int

[16] InterVISTAS, http://www.intervistas.com

[17] KPMG, http://www.kpmg.com

[18] Ministry of Civil Aviation, http://civilaviation.nic.in

[19] Skytanking Holding GmbH, http://www.skytanking.com

[20] The Airports Authority of India (AAI), http://www.airportsindia.org.in

[21] The Canadian Council for Public-Private Partnerships, http://www.pppcouncil.ca

[22] The Hindu, http://www.thehindubusinessline.com

[23] European Commission, http://ec.europa.eu/governance/docs/doc5_fr.pdf

[24] World Bank, http://www-wds.worldbank.org/external/default/WDSContentServer/WDSP/IB/2006/03/07/000090341_20060307104630/Rendered/PDF/34899.pdf)

Effectiveness of Knowledge Management and Human Resource Management in the Microfinance Sector to Increase Sustainability and Investment Opportunities

Mahuchhanda Karmakar[1] and Sharmistha Banerjee[2]

[1] Army Institute of Management, Kolkata
[2] University of Calcutta, Kolkata
E-mail: mkarmakar4@gmail.com

ABSTRACT

Micro finance plays an important role in the inclusive growth and in sustaining the efforts of the poverty alleviation tool in developing country like India. Despite its long history, the sector has not witnessed the existence of sustainable institutions. In the context of liberalized financial systems, microfinance allows millions of households, usually excluded from classical financial services, to begin or reinforce their own activities and become microentrepreneurs .The implications of macroeconomic stability for sustainable microfinance are not much different from those for the rest of the financial sector. The microfinance industry has been changing. The changes in the microfinance industry may be observed in concepts, vision, practice and opportunities. Although the industry has expanded in different dimensions, it continues to face many challenges. In the present economy, organizations are experiencing radical change of fast changing consumer behavior pattern, emerging new markets due to globalization, short product life cycle ,growing new networks due to advent in information and technology, emergence of new competitors, diversity in work force, makes it essential for the organizations to be more responsive and adaptive in order to survive. Traditional linear model of OD intervention must change to develop a more holistic approach. The approach should be to identify the key leverage points within the work place, and guide the organization to bring in the necessary changes to improve personal and overall organizational effectiveness. Yet inspite of MFIs tremendous growth potential and an important poverty alleviation tool.One problem that continues to challenge the optimal performance of the MFIs is its unsustainability. MFIs have their unique features due to its client base size and nature of transaction and special interventions are required to address those challenges adequately. The recent growth in information technology has led to an economy where application of knowledge becomes a key element to derive sustained competitive advantage. It has become imperative to generate new knowledge and find innovative ways to respond effectively to these challenges and problems. Knowledge Management (KM) caters to the critical issues of organizational adaption, and survival in face of increasingly discontinuous environmental change. It embodies organizational processes that seek synergistic combination of data and information processing capacity of information technologies, and the creative and innovative capacity of individuals working in the organization.

There is no doubt that some of these problems have significant correlation to issues of human resource management. This book proposes to explore as to how knowledge management and human resource management can help in the understanding of the inherent pattern in the seemingly unpredictable, chaotic world of business and would help in facilitating the understanding of the sustained development of microfinance institution. The paper seeks to explain some human resource concerns that derive from the responsibilities provided for key stakeholders in congruence with the Knowledge managemnt initiatives. Adopted is largely a critical analysis of the existing relevant literature, published papers & case studies of MFIs. There are other state level publications and commissioned papers from which data are sourced. Yet inspite of MFIs tremendous growth potential and an important poverty alleviation tool, one problem that continues to challenge the optimal performance of the MFIs, is its unsustainability. MFIs have their unique features due to its client base size and nature of transaction and special interventions are required to address those challenges adequately. The paper discovers that some of the factors that have affected the sustainability of micro finance institutions in India and the effective knowledge management and human resource intervention in addressing them. The proposed article will help to fundamental interdisciplinary work between knowledge management and human resource management and its real time application in the field of business management of micro finance institutions in the present times.These recommended actions may be collaborated by the key stakeholders whose roles were analyzed. The paper concludes with a discussion of the necessary roles of the state to promote MFI. The role of the state encompasses insuring a minimum banking structure in the rural areas, subsidizing microfinance start-up capital and innovations, and investing in complementary services such as infrastructure, health, and education. MFIs in recent years had grown with too much rapaciousness and with too little regulation.The level and the quality of the products and services offered by the microfinance institution can grow with proper systematic interventions especially in the quality of life of the clients served, growth insocial capital, improvents in the environmemt. This paper tried to analyse the role of Knowledge management and Human resource management in addressing these challenges adequately. This could be a further refined for any research work in future in this sector. The concept of application of knowledge management and human resource management in contemporary business has gained much importance in the present times.However few studies have been undertaken to use the concept of knowledge management and human resource management in forming a theoretical framework for analyzing its role in sustained capacity building of the microfinance institutions in India. This paper is an attempt in that direction.

Keywords: Microfinance Institutes, Human Resource Management (HRM), Knowledge Management (KM), Human Development Index (HDI)

INTRODUCTION

In a developing country like India where a significant level of population is in the rural areas, with little or no access to mainstream financing options, micro finance has a huge role to play to bring about poverty alleviation. Micro finance brings the rural populace closer to living a better lifestyle by helping them with small credit amounts that they acquire with minimum or no collateral. Micro finance institutions (MFI) are important developmental tools that can be used to take care of the credit needs of the economically poor citizens, so that they can avail financial services at a substantially affordable cost[14]. This special class of citizen constitutes a significant percentage of the Indian population. In India 37.2% of the national population and 41.8% of the rural population lives below the poverty line [20]. The persistent poverty level of a significant portion of the population can dampen the prospects for economic growth of the country.

Study has shown that if the credit is utilized properly for the purpose for it was sanctioned, its impact that is, the flow of benefits to the beneficiaries will help in improving the economic status of the economically poor people [10]. Commercial banking had this strong belief that collateral is essential for borrowing. Technology of the conventional commercial banking system made it inappropriate to provide financial services where the size of the transaction is small. Thus people, particularly, those living on low incomes, could not access mainstream financial products such as bank accounts, credit, remittances and payment services, financial advisory services, insurance facilities, etc.

Micro finance institutions (MFIs) on the other hand receive low-income client's deposits (savings), which it turns into loans to individual for economic projects. The concept of collateral has been further broadened by the inclusion of personal reputation peer support, group based savings mobilization as successfully shown by Grameen Bank [24]. MFIs have proved that banking with the poor can be profitable if the risks are managed, costs are contained if the clients are treated as active partners in the business[2].

India needs growth to address the problem of poverty as well as interstate and interpersonal income distribution disparities. Access to finance by the poor and vulnerable groups is a prerequisite for poverty reduction. Dependency ratio is an age-population ratio of those typically not in the labor (the dependent part) and those typically in the labor force (the productive part). It is used to measure the pressure on productive population [11].

It is seen from the graph (Fig. 1) that if dependency rate is reduced, the gross domestic savings increases. That means if total number of earning members in the household increases, then there would be more disposable domestic income, which in turn would help in generating more gross domestic savings. Increased domestic savings would result in greater GDP. MFIs by providing access to organized finance to the vulnerable groups,

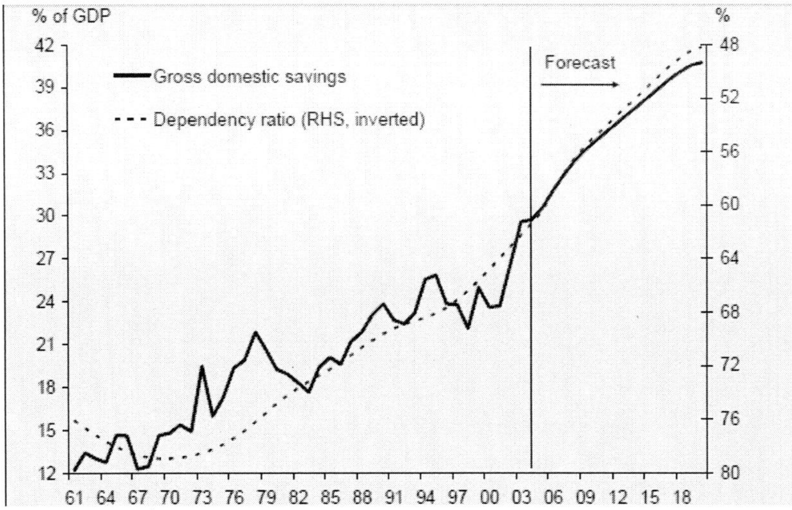

Fig. 1

Source: World Development Indicators, UN, Goldman Sachs Economic Research Global Economic Paper No. 152.

at an affordable cost can help in achieving this. MFIs could play a significant role in facilitating financial inclusion, as they are uniquely positioned in reaching out to the rural poor. Having greater acceptability amongst the rural poor as for understanding the issues related to the poor, and having flexibility in operations MFIs provides a level of comfort to their clientele.

Yet in spite of MFIs tremendous growth potential and an important poverty alleviation tool, one problem that continues to challenge the optimal performance of the MFIs, is its unsustainability. MFIs have their unique features due to its client base size and nature of transaction hence special interventions are required to address those challenges adequately. Poor people have smaller, irregular, and often more unreliable incomes, the great bulk of which may be spent as soon as it is received way. MFI can help them by providing them the access to their past income stored in savings by the micro savings schemes. MFIs by providing micro credit against their future income can facilitate them to take advantage of economic opportunities to increase their level of output, hence move out of poverty. Credit facilitates the poor to help overcome their liquidity constraints and undertake some income generating activities and be a part of the productive workforce of the country by decreasing the dependency ratio (fig 1). Furthermore, credit helps poor to smoothen their consumption patterns in times of lean periods of the year [4].

Studies have shown that micro credit will help to maintain the productive capacity of rural poor households [6; 7; 16; 23]. The success of Grameen Bank with community-based credit programs, in which the poor were subjected to peer accountability showed that providing financial services to the economically poor should that MFIs could be viable as well as profitable [24].

MICROFINANCE IN INDIA AND ITS CHALLENGES

Since independence the emphasis of the policy makers were to improve the lives of the economically poor citizens of India to bring about inclusive growth. This was also reflected in the first five-year plans, which were directed at "social justice " along with " growth with equity"[25]. However it did not trickle down into the rural sector as expected. This realization led to the restructuring of banking institutions. Immediately after the independence, much emphasis was given to the India banking industry to the development of the Indian economy. The nationalization of banks in 1969 was a step to make the government more control of credit delivery so that the need for rural credit could be taken care off. However as these expansions took place, systematic capacity enhancement was not adequate to increase the flow of funds to the rural sector of the country. Absence of collateral among the poor geographically dispersed rural belt (resulting in geographically customers), inadequate training of the rural co-operative banks discouraged the flow of funds to the rural sector.

Informal and formal sources of credit often are too costly for, or unavailable to, the rural poor [9]. The poor want credit that is available on acceptable terms and when they need it. Micro-finance refers to small savings; credit and insurance services extended to socially and economically disadvantaged segments of society. In recent times MFIs are increasingly attracting private investments as the social responsible investments (SRI). SRI ranks high on an investor's agenda as SRI strives to consider both the social and the commercial dimensions of investments [13]. Community investment strategies like micro finance has strong potential growth rate. Reason being, that micro finance sectors which traditionally dealt with providing working capital loans to the economically weak citizens are now exploring new avenues like consumer's loan, micro savings, micro insurance, micro leasing, micro transfers. Hence, even though the policy makers tried means to provide financial support to the credit deficient areas of the country, the efforts made were not able to achieve the success that they envisaged as more and more emphasis is being focused on achieving certain quantitative targets. In India MFIs have maximum outreach in the southern states [22]. Efforts were continuously made by the government to increase the outreach of the MFIs. Micro Finance Development Fund (MFDEF) set up by (National Bank for Agriculture and Rural Development (NABARD) was specifically designed to meet the equity needs of the MFIs. However in its effort to increase the client base of the MFIs, inadequate attention was paid to the qualitative aspects of lending leading to loan defaults and erosion of repayment ethics by all categories of borrowers.

This resulted in a disturbing growth in overdue, which not only hampered the recycling of scarce resources by banks, but also affected profitability and viability of financial institutions, which in turn affected the development of rural finance. Although out the focus of the Indian MFIs was primarily to increase its outreach, however there is a growing realization to analyze as to how to help it develop sustainability [13].

Fundamental questions remain about MFIs long-term viability as a model for the supply of micro credit to low income families. The lack of technically equipped human resources, operational systems and infrastructure, are the primary constraints that continue to plague the MFIs. Like any retail financial system, MFIs requires a number of services and support functions to remain viable over the long term.

The challenge the micro finance industry continues to face in sustaining its growth is developing its human resource capacity. The MFIs is a human capital-intensive industry especially in the critical area of credit operation. For the sustained growth in MFIs it is essential to have a highly skilled workforce.

KNOWLEDGE MANAGEMENT, HUMAN RESOURCE MANAGEMENT AND ITS IMPLICATIONS FOR MICROFINANCE INSTITUTIONS

The concept of human resource management for sustainable development of the MFIs will be discussed in this paper. Decenzo & Robbins(1998) defined HRM as being "people oriented" approach in management, this approach has to do with their recruitment & selection, training & developing their skills, motivating them to their higher levels of performance and ensuring that they continue to maintain their level of commitment to the organization. The primary aspect of HRM that this article would be using for the theoretical framework for analysis for the sustainable development of the MFIs is education, skill acquisition, human resource development in all ramifications and provisions for social welfare. HRM at the macro level can be understood to be the process of determining the policies and programmes that will develop, allocate and utilize human resources with a view to develop the nation's overall HDI (human development index).

Some key concepts of HRM would be used in this paper to develop the micro finance clients to maximize their capacity building so as to empower them to utilize the services provided to them by the MFIs. Also if effectively used, HRM can help to attract, motivate and retain the MFI's employees so as to develop a high performance workforce who would be equipped to deliver the required output.

The recent developments in information technology have transformed ways in how banking institutions operate, like automated teller machines (ATM), credit/debit cards, internet banking, online money transfers etc. However only certain privilege section of the society have access to such technology.

The rapid growth of information technology has led to an economy where application of knowledge becomes a key element to derive competitive advantage [5]. In this sense knowledge management (KM) is a collection of different techniques used by organization to acquire, organize and to share knowledge within the organization. The traditional focus on managing people has undergone a paradigm shift to managing organizational capacities, managing relationships and managing learning and development [22]. The dramatic changes in the global economy opened up challenges for all the financial and non-financial organizations. It has become imperative to obtain and generate new knowledge in order to respond effectively to these pressures and constraints.

Knowledge management (KM) is the creation, dissemination and utilization of knowledge is about transforming information into usable knowledge and ensuring that it reaches the right people at the right time. When knowledge management enables agencies to learn from their own and others' experience, it greatly contributes to effectiveness. By emphasizing knowledge management as an organizational objective, MFI.s can succeeded in creating a culture of intellectual exchange and shared responsibility. Important inputs for a successful implementation of knowledge management system (KMS) are technology, infrastructure, and trained human resources as facilitators, having appropriate information knowledge about their unique clients.

KM promotes an integrated approach to identify, capture, retrieve, share and evaluate an organization's information assets (knowledge). This knowledge could be databases, documents, policies; explicit knowledge or expertise and experiences embedded within an individual; tacit knowledge [17]. Knowledge creation is important for innovation, which in turn helps an organization to become more dynamic and fluid allowing individuals and groups to work together. Innovation can be in terms of product designs, channel configuration and technology usage. The MFIs clientele requires products, which are customized, taking into consideration their varied needs. MFIs could be given the freedom to develop their own products, suited to local requirements and needs of the poor. The approach should be kept simple which should guarantee the beneficiaries a credit limit, subject to adherence to simple terms and conditions. Given the lower level of awareness of this market, capturing customer information and using this appropriately and proactively is of immense importance. ITC's rural initiative like e-choupal and more recently FINO by ICICI are live examples of such strategies. The success of Grameen Bank showed that there is no intrinsic contradiction between commercial viability and fair access for the poor.

Hence it can be said that widening and deepening the outreach of the poor through MFIs has both social and commercial dimensions. Since the sustainability of MFIs and their clients complement each other, it follows that building up the capacities of the MFIs and their primary stakeholders are pre-conditions for the successful delivery of flexible, client responsive and innovative micro finance services to the poor. Here, innovations are important for strategic linkages and for new approaches centered on the issues surrounding the poor, and the reengineering of the financial products to be offered to them. As knowledge creation is the core competence for any organization to gain competitive advantage [5]. This knowledge may relate to new channels of distribution of funds to the credit deficient areas, creating databases for the credit history of the clients and information sharing among the MFIs clients for their background checking to decide on their pay back capacities. MFIs had grown over the years with little regulations that has fastened a breakdown in lending discipline with multiple loans to overextended borrows and allowed some unscrupulous players to thrive.

Knowledge management system (KMS) can help in development of business information tools to provide the right kind of customer's background information such as how a person has handled past debt obligations. KM caters to this critical issue of information acquisition, data retrieval and data sharing. It embodies organization's processes that seek synergistic combination of data and information processing capacity of information technologies. Here KM can be utilized to collect relevant information from various domains and create databases supported by organization's intranets. KMS software tools like data warehousing is a step in that direction. From credit history and personal background, honesty and reliability of the borrower to repay credit debt can be determined. The use of KMS can also help to assist with performance monitoring and made available weekly checks of portfolios at risk and pinpointed the centers that seek greater attention.

KM also helps in the standardization of processes of the MFIs with the necessary mechanisms to enforce performance standards. Local entities are usually better off when they can offer standardized products that have been developed by using the MIS, rules, and risk mitigation strategies. KMS tools like data warehousing; data mining can be used for refining the financial product being offered and bridging the information gap. It could also help in analyzing the capacity of the borrowers as to how much debt a borrower can comfortably handle.

The issue of geographically dispersed clients (rural India) and their geographical inaccessibility coupled with low literacy rate makes it imperative to enforce the KMS tools can help in information updates about the business transactions to ensure regulatory compliance. From a technological viewpoint, use of biometric devices for authentication to identify customers can also be helpful especially where the literacy level is low and the clients are geographically dispersed. In view of the increasing importance of coordination and continuous interactions among the branches to enhance the understanding of issues and to maintain the flow of information through relevant feedback, it becomes essential for the MFIs to have a robust KMS at its end. The rural poor people may face many different problems as they not a homogeneous group. Therefore, a sustained effort must be made to gather information.

The strong link between the human resources and knowledge results in the concept of knowledge as a strategic asset that is generated and utilized through human resources. The work of HRM is to implement systems and tools so as to maximize the potentials of the human resource available within the organization. The role of HRM within the MFIs is to support each individual with strategies, systems and tools so as to develop a high performance work system (HPWS). Here KMS tools like K-mapping can be helpful. K map is all about keeping a record of information about knowledge in the organization. K map, shows details of every bit of knowledge that exists within the organization including the location, quality, accessibility of the knowledge. It helps an organization to appreciate as to about the ways to manage the loss of intellectual capital. It allows an organization to fully leverage the existing expertise resident within the organization. Much of the administrative work of the HR department can be automated through the use of KM tools. Data warehousing would particularly help in developing the HRIS. MFIs can use the KMS tools for systematic databases for each employee. This is particular helpful in the process of recruitment & selection. To support the process of employee acquisition for MFIs, KMS tools like data mining could be utilized. Data mining is the process of extracting patterns from data. It is fast becoming an important tool to transform data into information. It could be used by the HRM department to find critical important quickly, to improve decision making and problem solving by providing applicable information. KMS supported by management information system (MIS) could be useful in monitoring compliance with the lending terms.

India is one of the fastest growing emerging economies in the world with an expanding and liberalized financial system. Thus it becomes imperative for the MFIs in India to recognize the critical significance of ensuring quality human resources to be able to discharge all the responsibilities effectively and efficiently. For that it is important to have a standardized HR policy in place. The HR policy encompassing the recruitment and selection strategy, compensation policy, training need analysis programme, an annual training plan, periodic review of the competencies necessary for the MF industry to grow for MFIs to remain competitive in the market.

One of the key ingredients in a sustainable MFI is the training of the managers, staff and field workers for their capability building for existing talent to ensure they are equipped to drive growth. Empowering the existing staff with adequate training in leading universities and research organizations is another important task of human resources management. Investments in human development are important. The MFIs should constantly strive to enhance the professional skills of the staff through appropriate training as well as providing scope for learning in every important area relevant to the MFIs, for the staff at all levels. Personnel handling micro finance projects should have a baseline of knowledge.

Studies have shown that training enhances the productive skills of an worker managers can train their clientele so that could handle their money in better ways by increasing their financial capability [4; 12]. This would also help in inculcating a sense of credit discipline in them. Any employment generating skills requires training; the MFIs could play an important part in training their clients in skill development and individual level capacity enhancement. MFIs can also train individuals or group of people in the area of different innovate ways to market their products. Majority of the MFI's clients are from economically poor background with no or little knowledge about handling small enterprises. Hence systematic intervention required by the MFIs to provide them guidance for skill and capacity development for income generating activities, identifying entrepreneurial and suitable employment opportunities. This is possible if the MFIs themselves have a dedicated HR department investing in training and development.

Micro finance industry is not well organized in terms of its compensation structure [18]. The level of hierarchy and its accompanying compensation packages are not well defined in this sector. Hence becomes difficult to find the balance between employee's expectation and employer's affordability without losing the staff to competition. Thus it would be beneficial if a comprehensive compensation structure should be formulated which would be at par with other institutions of the same field, so that a greater pool of talent could be attracted at the recruitment stage for the MFIs. Special incentive could be introduced for customer retention and real time loan repayment for the MFI's personnel,

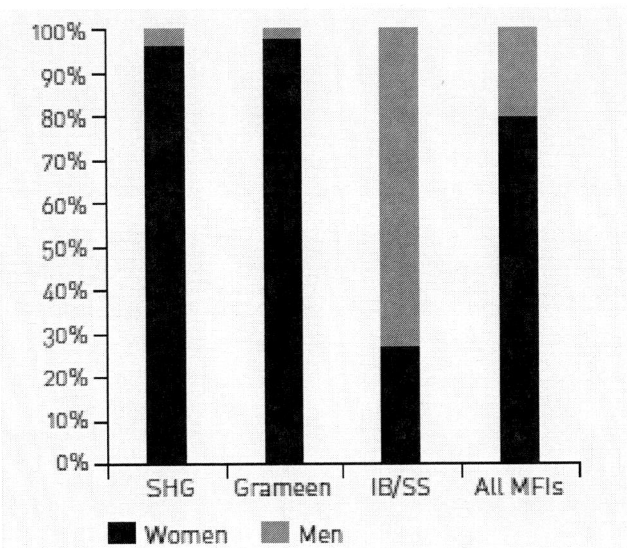

Fig. 2

Source: SIDBI assessment report of the MFIs 2007.

so that quality of service can be enhanced. Incentives could also be given by the MFI's management for special efforts rendered by an individual staff, to achieve desired levels of financial inclusion, by bringing in more economically poor people under its gambit of operation. Thereby by newer customer acquisition, the outreach of the MFIs could be significantly expanded. To motivate staff handling microfinance investments, to develop core competence, special reward fro competence building can be introduced. "Hand in Hand" a MFI based in Chennai, India, has a special competency development programme for its staff members. Where by they are encouraged to undergo a diploma course in micro finance, from Indian Institute of Banking and Finance, Mumbai whereby their course fee is sponsored by the organization [18].

Change should also be in the quality of people hired. The industry needs to find mangers who can raise resources and manage assets and liabilities as also liquidity. Appropriate remuneration packages must be offered to attract greater pool of talent in this sector. Also it has been studied [19] that majority, of the total clientele of the MFIs are women, hence if greater emphasis is provided in recruiting more female employees by the MFIs , then it could better facilitate the dealing with the client base.

CONCLUSION

Microfinance has ushered in a new understanding of the poor and the potential for the financial services to enable the poor to escape from poverty. MFIs can be used as an essential developmental tool to bring about inclusive growth. There is a tremendous growth potential for the MFIs. In order to sustain the growth there is a need for professionally managed MFIs serving the poor. Access to micro finance can help poor people in their struggle to climb out of poverty, giving them economic freedom, dignity, and the ability to contribute to the wealth of their community thereby decreasing the dependency ratio and increasing the gross domestic savings.

The range of complex issues and challenges that is unique for the MFIs, clearly highlights the importance of the quality of human resources available. Management skills, management information systems, compensation strategies, training policies, standardization of policies and procedures are some of the human resource challenges that are need to be addressed appropriately. So that the improvement in the quality and viability of financial services offered by the MFIs could be taken care of. This article aimed to assist the MFIs so as to stimulate rural-based poverty reduction, in a developing country like India, by addressing the KMS initiatives and the human resource management issues. This article tried to explain some human resource concerns that derive from the responsibilities provided for key stakeholders in congruence with the Knowledge management initiatives.

REFERENCES

[1] Binswanger and Khandker (1995), The Impact of Formal Finance on the Rural Economy of India, *Journal of Development Studies*, 32 (2): 234-65.

[2] Burgess and Pande (2002), "Do Rural Banks Matter? Evidence from the Indian Social Banking Experiment.

[3] DeCenzo, D.A. and Robbins, S.P. (1998), Personnel/Human Resource Management, Prentice-Hall, India.

[4] Friedlander, Greenberg and Robins (1997), "Evaluating Government Training Programs for the Economically Disadvantaged", *Journal of Economic Literature* Vol. 35, No. 4 (Dec. 1997), pp. 1809-1855.

[5] Grant, R.M. (1991a);" The Resource Based Theory of Competitive Advantage: Implications for Strategy Formulation", *California Management Review,* 33, pp. 114-135.

[6] Heidhues, F. (1995), Rural Finance Markets – An Important Tool to Fight Against Poverty. *Quarterly Journal of International Agriculture*, 34 (2): 105-8.

[7] Hulme, David and Paul, Mosley (1996), Finance Against Poverty. Vols 1-2, London and New York: Routledge.

[8] Hulme David (2000), Impact Assessment Methodologies for Microfinance: Theory, Experience and Better Practices, *World Development*, 28 (1): 79-98.

[9] Khan and Hasan, M (2003), "Rural Poverty in Developing Countries Implications for Public Policy", Economic Issue No 26, International Monetory Fund.

[10] Kumar and Singh (2007), "Impact of Cooperative Credit on the Agriculture Sector of Himachal Pradesh: A Study of the Mid-Hill Zone", *Social Change*, June 2007, Vol. 37: 53-68.

[11] Kogel, T. (2005), "Youth Dependency and Total Factor Productivity", *Journal of Development Economics* 76, 147–173.

[12] LaLonde (1995), "The Promise of Public Sector-Sponsored Training Programs", *The Journal of Economic Perspectives* Vol. 9, No. 2 (Spring, 1995), pp. 149-168.

[13] Microfinance: An Emerging Investment Opportunity, Deutsche Bank Research, December 19, 2007.

[14] Morduch (1999), "The Microfinance Promise", *Journal of Economic Literature*, Vol. 37, No. 4 (Dec., 1999), pp. 1569-1614.

[15] Mosely, Paul and David Hulme (1998), Microenterprise finance: Is there a conflictbetween growth and poverty alleviation? World Development 26: 783-90.

[16] Navajas, Sergio; Mark, Schreiner; Richard, L. Mayer; Claudio, Gonzalez-vega and Jorge, Rodriguez-Meza (2000), Microcredit and the Poorest of the Poor: Theory and Evidence from Bolivia, World Development, 28 (2): 333-46.

[17] Nonaka, I. and Takeuchi, H. (1995), *The knowledge-creating company.* New York: Oxford University Press.

[18] Srinivasan, N. (2009), "Micro finance in India. Sector wise report" *Sage publications India Ltd.* ISBN: 978-81-321-0298-4.

[19] SIDBI assessment report of the MFIs 2007.

[20] UNDP Global Developmental Report 2010.

[21] Dr. Vinod Kumar (2009), " Micro Finance" University Science Press .

[22] Ulrich, D. (1997), *Human Resource Champions: the next agenda for adding value and delivering results.* Harvard Business School Press, Boston

[23] Westover J. (2008), The Record of Microfinance: The Effectiveness/Ineffectiveness of Microfinance Programs as a Means of Alleviating Poverty. Electronic Journal of Sociology, ISSN: 1198 3655.

[24] http://www.grameen-info.org/

[25] http://planningcommission.gov.in/

Financial Development and Economic Growth in Select Asian Countries

Rudra P. Pradhan and Aadra Gunashekar
Indian Institute of Technology Kharagpur
E-mail: rudrap@vgsom.iitkgp.ernet.in; aadrag24@gmail.com

ABSTRACT

The paper investigates the causal nexus between financial development and economic growth for Bangladesh, Bhutan, India, Pakistan, Sri Lanka, China, Hong Kong, Japan, South Korea, Indonesia, Malaysia, Philippines, Singapore, Thailand and Vietnam for the period 1961-2011. Using cointegration tests and vector error correction model, the results suggest that in the case of Bangladesh, Sri Lanka and South Korea financial development causes economic growth, whereas in the case of Bhutan, India, Malaysia, Philippines and Singapore economic growth causes financial development. The results further suggest that in the case of China, Hong Kong, Japan, Indonesia and Vietnam we get two-way causality between financial development and economic growth, while in the context of Thailand we do not find any causal link between the two. At the panel setting, the results find the unidirectional causality from economic growth to financial development in South Asia and South East Asia, while no sign of causality between financial development and economic growth in East Asia.

Keywords: Financial Development, Economic Growth, Asia

INTRODUCTION

Financial development is a primal to economic development (Graff, 2003; Levine, 1997). The relationship between economic growth and financial development has been the focus of an immense theoretical and empirical research work since the seminal work of Schumpeter (1911). However, there are two schools of thought: first, finance is a constituent to economic growth (Jalil et al., 2010; Christopoulos and Tsionas, 2004; Calderon and Liu, 2003; Levine, 2003; Beck et al., 2000; Xu, 2000; Levine et al., 2002; Luintel and Khan, 1999; Neusser and Kugler, 1998; Levine, 1997; Greenwood and Bruce, 1997; Berthelemy and Varoudakis, 1996; King and Levine, 1993); second, finance is an inconsequential to economic growth (Stern, 1989; Lucas, 1988; Robinson, 1952). For more details, see Robinson (1952), Lucas (1988), Stern (1989), Eng and Habibullah (2011), Mukhopadhyay et al. (2011), Tekin (2012); Demetriades and Luintel (1996), Blackburn and Hung (1998), Luintel and Khan (1999), Levine (1999), Caleron and Liu (2003), Ang (2008), Wolde-Rufael (2009), Pradhan (2011), Bangake and Eggoh (2011) and Hassan et al. (2011), Abu-Bader and Abu-Qarn (2008), Tekin (2012), Gries et al. (2009), Liang and Teng (2006), Odhiambo (2009), Demetriades and Hussein (1996), Arestis and Demetriades (1997), Christopoulos and Tsionas (2004), Eller et al. (2006), Jalil and Ma (2008), Abu-Bader and Abu-Qarn (2008), Enisan and Olufisayo (2009) and Hassan et al. (2011). The present paper focuses the first view, indicating the direction of causality between finance and growth.

Schumpeter (1911) argues that well executing financial system can contribute economic growth by technological constructs which may occur due to efficient allocation of financial streams, while Robinson (1952) states that financial development is a consequence of betterments in economic growth. So, there are two hypotheses on the finance-growth nexus. First, supply-leading hypothesis, indicating finance is an instrument to economic growth (Rousseau and Wachtel, 2000; King and Levine, 1993). Supply-leading view works in two different ways: first, by transferring resources from customary low growth sector to modern high growth sectors and second, by motivating the enterprises response to the modern sectors. Second, demand-following view: this holds that finance actually responses to change that happen in the real sector or 'where enterprise extends, finance follows' (Robinson, 1952). The demand-following approach actually involves the measurement of growth in demand of financial services which exclusively rely on economic growth and the process of commercializing and advancement of agriculture, industry and other sectors. The study aims in making a contribution to the existing discussion by exhibiting empirical evidence from selected Asian countries during the period 1961-2010. The residual of the paper is organized into three sections including earlier introduction. Section first discusses the methods of study. Next section presents the empirical results. Last section provides conclusion and policy implications.

METHODS OF STUDY

The paper makes an attempt to examine the nexus between financial development and economic growth in Asia. Financial development, in general, represents an increase in volume of financial services of banks and other financial intermediaries as well as of financial transactions of capital markets (Graff, 2003). It includes both financial widening and financial deepening. Financial widening refers to the expansion of financial services and growth of financial institutions, while financial deepening refers to either an increase in per capita amount of financial services and institutions or an increase in the ratio of financial assets to income (Ahmed and Ansari, 1998). It can be noted that financial development, by widening and diversifying the financial markets, leads to superior allocation of resources and is considered as direct inter-mediate input in the production process. It raises the productivity of other factors of production (like social indicators) and profitability of producing units and thereby, permits higher levels of output, income and employment.

Financial development is a multidimensional concept, which involves number of items. The study uses seven major items under the financial development, depending upon the availability of data and as per the relevance of economic growth in the Asian countries. The items in the study are given as follows: Broad money (BRM); Claims on private sectors of the economy (CLP); Domestic credit (DOC); Private sector credit (PSC); Total reserves (TOR); Liquid liabilities (LIL); and Market capitalization (MAC).

The econometric tools used in this study are Principal Component Analysis (PCA) and Granger causality analysis. PCA is used to construct the composite index of financial development, which can signal the overall position of financial development in Asia. On the other hand, Granger Causality (GC) test is used to know the casual-nexus between financial development and economic growth. The detail discussion of these two techniques is given below.

Principal Component Analysis

The method of Principal Component Analysis is a special case of the more general method of factor analysis. PCA transforms the original set of variables into smaller set of linear combinations that account for most of the variance of the original set. The aim of the method of principal component is to construct out of a set of variables, X_j's (j = 1, 2, ..., k) new variables (P_i) called 'Principal Components', which are linear combinations of the X's.

The first principal component (P_1) is determined as the linear combination of X_1, X_{-2}, ..., X_m provided that the variance contribution is maximum. The second principal component (P_2), independent from the first principal component, is determined as to provide a maximum contribution to total variance left after the variance explained by the first principal component, then the third and the other principal components are determined as to provide the maximum contribution to the remaining variance and independent from each other. The aim here is to determine a_{ij} coefficients providing the linear combinations of variables based on the specified conditions. The following formula is used to have financial development index:

$$FSDI = \sum_{i=1}^{7} a_i \frac{X_{ij}}{Sd(X_i)} \quad (1)$$

where *FSDI* = Composite index of financial sector development; *Sd* = Standard Deviation; X_{ij} = i^{th} items in j^{th} year; a_i = Factor loadings as derived by PCA.

The composite index of financial development is the sum total of broad money, claims on private sectors, domestic credit, private sector credit, total financial reserves, liquid liabilities and market capitalization. That means FSDI provides the overall status of financial development in Asia. It provides the overall status of financial development in 15 selected Asian countries, namely Bangladesh, Bhutan, India, Pakistan, Sri Lanka, China, Hong Kong, Japan, South Korea, Indonesia, Malaysia, Philippines, Singapore, Thailand and Vietnam.

Granger Causality Test

The Granger causality (GC) test is usually applied to know the direction of causality between two (or more) time series variables. This study uses GC for individual country analysis and at the panel setting. The traditional GC (Granger, 1981) is used for the individual country analysis, while panel VAR (Holtz-Eakin et al., 1988) is used at the panel setting. For traditional GC, the following two models (Model 1 and Model 2) can be used for detecting the causal nexus between financial development and economic growth.

Model 1

If the two variables are individually integrated of order one [I (1)] and not cointegrated, then the test of causality requires the estimation of following:

$$PGDP_t = \eta + \sum_{i=1}^{p} \alpha_i PGDP_{t-i} + \sum_{j=1}^{q} \beta_j FSDI_{t-j} + \varepsilon_t$$

$$FSDI_t = \mu + \sum_{i=1}^{r} \gamma_i FSDI_{t-i} + \sum_{j=1}^{s} \lambda_j PGDP_{t-j} + \xi_t$$

where, *PGDP* is per capita economic growth and *FSDI* is finance sector development index.

Model 2

If the two variables are individually I (1) and cointegrated, then the test of causality requires the estimation of following:

$$\Delta PGDP_t = \eta + \sum_{i=1}^{p} \alpha_i \Delta PGDP_{t-i} + \sum_{j=1}^{q} \beta_j \Delta FSDI_{t-j} + \delta EC_{t-1} + \varepsilon_t$$

$$\Delta FSDI_t = \mu + \sum_{i=1}^{r} \gamma_i \Delta FSDI_{t-i} + \sum_{j=1}^{s} \lambda_j \Delta PGDP_{t-j} + \delta EC_{t-1} + \eta_t$$

where, EC stands for error correction term and other notations are defined earlier.

However, for panel setting, we use the following two models (Model 3 and Model 4) for causal nexus between financial development and economic growth:

Model 3

If time series variables are 1 (1) and not cointegrated, then the test of causality requires the estimation of following:

$$\Delta GDP_{it} = \eta_j + \sum_{k=1}^{p} \alpha_{ik} \Delta PGDP_{it-k} + \sum_{k=1}^{s} \lambda_{ik} FSDI_{it-k} + \Delta\varepsilon_{it}$$

$$\Delta FSDI_{it} = \eta_j + \sum_{k=1}^{p} \alpha_{ik} \Delta PGDP_{it-k} + \sum_{k=1}^{s} \lambda_{ik} FSDI_{it-k} + \Delta\varepsilon_{it}$$

Model 4

If time series variables 1 (1) and cointegrated, then direction of causality is tested by using error correction model. The process requires the estimation of following:

$$\Delta PGDP_{it} = \eta_j + \sum_{k=1}^{p} \alpha_{ik} \Delta PGDP_{it-k} + \sum_{k=1}^{s} \lambda_{ik} FSDI_{it-k} + \eta_i EC_{1it-k} + \Delta\varepsilon_{1it}$$

$$\Delta FSDI_{it} = \eta_j + \sum_{k=1}^{p} \alpha_{ik} \Delta PGDP_{it-k} + \sum_{k=1}^{s} \lambda_{ik} FSDI_{it-k} + \eta_i EC_{1it-k} + \Delta\varepsilon_{1it}$$

Over and above, we use the above four models for studying the casual nexus between financial development and economic growth in selected Asian countries, both at individual country level and panel setting. But the choice of a particular model depends upon the order of integration and the cointegrating relationship (yes/ no). For knowing the order of integration, we deploy traditional Augmented Dickey Fuller (Dickey and Fuller 1981) unit root for individual country analysis and LLC (Levin et al., 2002) and IPS (Im et al., 2003) unit root tests for panel of 15 Asian countries. For knowing the cointegration relationship, Johansen (Johansen, 1988) test is deployed for individual country analysis, while Pedroni (2004) test is used for the panel of 15 countries. Moreover, Fisher (1932) derives a combined test that uses the results of the individual independent tests, while Maddala and Wu (1999) use Fisher's result to propose an alternative approach to testing for cointegration in the panel data by combining tests from individual cross-sections to obtain at test statistic for the full panel. The details of these two tests (unit root and cointegration) are not discussed here due to space constraints and can be incorporated, if there is any need of the requirement.

The study covers 15 Asian countries namely Bangladesh, Bhutan, India, Pakistan, Sri Lanka, China, Hong Kong, Japan, South Korea, Indonesia, Malaysia, Philippines, Singapore, Thailand and Vietnam. These are broadly grouped into three different regions such as South Asia, East Asia and South East Asia. The countries, under different regions, have been selected on the basis of purchasing power parity classification of the World Bank. The data are annual time series over the period 1961-2011. It has been collected from International Financial Statistics, International Monetary Fund, Washington, World Development Indicators, World Bank, Washington and CIA World Fact Book.

EMPIRICAL RESULTS AND DISCUSSION

As discussed above, financial development plays an active role in accelerating the

Table 1: Unit Root Test Results

Country	Individual Country Unit Root Test (ADF)					
	FSDI		Conclusion	PGDP		Conclusion
	LD	FD		LD	FD	
Bangladesh	–0.07	–6.60*	I [1]	–0.01	–9.60*	I [1]
Bhutan	0.89	–6.50*	I [1]	–1.52	–4.50*	I [1]
India	–0.51	–6.60*	I [1]	–2.00	–4.60*	I [1]
Pakistan	–1.73	–6.60*	I [1]	–0.15	–5.20*	I [1]
Sri Lanka	–1.74	–7.40*	I [1]	–0.82	–6.90*	I [1]
China	–0.95	–6.40*	I [1]	–2.23	–4.00*	I [1]
Hong Kong	–0.84	–4.50*	I [1]	–1.32	–4.00*	I [1]
Japan	–1.89	–8.40*	I [1]	–1.59	–4.10*	I [1]
South Korea	0.48	–5.10*	I [1]	–2.50	–4.80*	I [1]
Indonesia	–2.20	–3.50*	I [1]	–0.30	–5.30*	I [1]
Malaysia	–2.31	–5.80*	I [1]	–1.95	–5.00*	I [1]
Philippines	–1.21	–4.50*	I [1]	–1.59	–4.00*	I [1]
Singapore	–0.86	–6.00*	I [1]	–2.05	–3.50*	I [1]
Thailand	–1.05	–3.80*	I [1]	–1.52	–3.80*	I [1]
Vietnam	–0.87	–3.80*	I [1]	–1.59	–3.80*	I [1]
	Panel Unit Root Test (at first difference level)					
South Asia	1.44	–3.50*	I[1]	2.47	–3.20*	I[1]
East Asia	–1.34	–5.80*	I[1]	–0.09	–6.60*	I[1]
South East Asia	–1.99	–4.30*	I[1]	–1.37	–5.70*	I[1]
Total Asia	–0.82	–4.80*	I[1]	4.16	–10.0*	I[1]

Note: FSDI: Financial Sector Development Index; BGDP: Per Capita Gross Domestic Product; ADF: Augmented Dickey Fuller Test; LLC: LLC statistics; IPS: IPS statistics; PP: PP statistics; I (1): Integrated of order one; and *: Indicates statistically significant at 5% level.

Table 2: Cointegration Test

Countries	Hypothesized Cointegrating	Number of Relationships	Hypothesized Cointegrating	Number of Relationships	Conclusion
	H_0	H_A	H_0	H_A	
	r = 0	r > 0	r ≤ 1	r > 1	
	λ–Max	λ–Tra	λ–Max	λ–Tra	
Bangladesh	18.9*	19.2*	0.17	0.18	(1)
Bhutan	17.2*	17.5*	0.33	0.33	(1)
India	5.11	8.73	3.63	3.64	(0)
Pakistan	16.7*	16.8*	0.04	0.04	(1)
Sri Lanka	18.2*	24.1*	5.92*	5.92*	(2)
China	18.7*	23.4*	4.68*	4.68*	(2)
Hong Kong	18.4*	20.9*	2.57	2.57	(1)
Japan	12.8*	13.0*	0.16	0.16	(1)
South Korea	20.1*	20.7*	0.16	0.61	(1)
Indonesia	7.10	7.11	0.11	0.01	(0)
Malaysia	19.3*	22.0*	2.78	2.78	(1)
Philippines	7.22	8.85	1.64	1.64	(0)
Singapore	16.7*	16.9*	0.15	0.15	(1)
Thailand	20.8*	22.9*	2.12	2.12	(1)
Vietnam	8.12	8.25	0.13	0.13	(0)
	Panel Cointegration				
South Asia	29.5*	35.6*	19.9*	19.9*	(2)
East Asia	25.0*	20.4*	21.0*	21.0*	(2)
South East Asi	29.7*	33.8*	20.5*	20.5*	(2)
Total Asia	66.3*	69.1*	60.6*	60.6*	(2)

Note: r indicates the number of cointegrating relationships; *: Indicates statistically significant at 5% level; and parentheses indicate the number of cointegrating vectors.

pace of economic growth. However, the common question is whether financial development causes economic growth or vice versa. To answer this question, we deploy the Granger causality test. However, the precondition to this test is to know the order of integration of time series variables (financial development and economic growth) and their cointegrating relationship. So the discussion of this section follows with unit root test, cointegration test and causality test. Our estimating results are based on individual country analysis and at the panel setting.

Coming to stationarity issue, we find time series variables are non-stationary at the level data but found stationary at the first difference (see Table 1). This indicates that the variables are integrated of order one [i.e. I (I)]. This is exclusively true for all the countries

Table 3: Results of Panel Cointegration Test

Test Statistics	Calculated Value	Probability	Conclusion
South Asia [5]			(1)
Panel v-statistic	3.970	[0.00]	
Panel ρ-statistic	–1.346	[0.09]	
Panel PP-statistic	–1.718	[0.04]	
Panel ADF-statistic	–0.950	[0.17]	
Group ρ-statistic	0.153	[0.56]	
Group PP-statistic	–1.346	[0.09]	
Group ADF-statistic	–1.040	[0.15]	
East Asia [4]			(1)
Panel v-statistic	1.629	[0.05]	
Panel ρ-statistic	–1.713	[0.04]	
Panel PP-statistic	–1.837	[0.03]	
Panel ADF-statistic	–0.625	[0.27]	
Group ρ-statistic	–2.656	[0.00]	
Group PP-statistic	–2.326	[0.01]	
Group ADF-statistic	–2.610	[0.00]	
South East Asia [6]			(1)
Panel v-statistic	0.554	[0.29]	
Panel ρ-statistic	–0.957	[0.17]	
Panel PP-statistic	–1.630	[0.05]	
Panel ADF-statistic	–0.994	[0.17]	
Group ρ-statistic	–0.502	[0.30]	
Group PP-statistic	–1.650	[0.05]	
Group ADF-statistic	–1.830	[0.03]	
Total Asia [15]			(1)
Panel v-statistic	2.010	[0.02]	
Panel ρ-statistic	–1.320	[0.09]	
Panel PP-statistic	–1.220	[0.11]	
Panel ADF-statistic	0.550	[0.52]	
Group ρ-statistic	–1.298	[0.09]	
Group PP-statistic	–1.994	[0.02]	
Group ADF-statistic	–2.911	[0.00]	

Note: [ ]: The parentheses indicate the probability of significance; ( ): parentheses indicate number of cointegrating vectors; and other notations are defined earlier.

Table 4: Granger Causality Test

Country	DV →	ΔFSDI	ΔPGDP	EC	Major Findings	Conclusion
Model 1: Individual Country Causality						
Bangladesh	ΔFSDI	–	2.81*	–2.21	FSDI => PGDP	
	ΔPGDP	1.55	–	1.05	PGDP ≠> FSDI	UDC (→)
Bhutan	ΔFSDI	–	0.70	–0.79	FSDI ≠> PGDP	
	ΔPGDP	4.76*	–	–2.58*	PGDP => FSDI	UDC (←)
India	ΔFSDI	–	0.58	–	FSDI ≠> PGDP	
	ΔPGDP	15.9*	–	–	PGDP => FSDI	UDC (←)
Pakistan	ΔFSDI	–	1.23	–1.19	FSDI ≠> PGDP	
	ΔPGDP	3.83*	–	–4.15*	PGDP => FSDI	UDC (←)
Sri Lanka	ΔFSDI	–	2.31*	1.46	FSDI => PGDP	
	ΔPGDP	1.17	–	–2.80*	PGDP ≠> FSDI	UDC (→)
China	ΔFSDI	–	5.70*	–2.12	FSDI => PGDP	
	ΔPGDP	11.8*	–	1.10	PGDP => FSDI	BDC (↔)
Hong Kong	ΔFSDI	–	3.07*	1.64	FSDI => PGDP	
	ΔPGDP	10.2*	–	–2.55*	PGDP => FSDI	UDC (↔)
Japan	ΔFSDI	–	2.25*	–0.27	FSDI => PGDP	
	ΔPGDP	3.84*	–	–3.37*	PGDP => FSDI	BDC (↔)
South Korea	ΔFSDI	–	2.35*	2.92	FSDI => PGDP	
	ΔPGDP	1.28	–	–2.68*	PGDP ≠> FSDI	UDC (→)
Indonesia	ΔFSDI	–	2.66*	–	FSDI => PGDP	
	ΔPGDP	5.75*	–	–	PGDP => FSDI	BDC (↔)
Malaysia	ΔFSDI	–	2.53*	–3.52*	FSDI => PGDP	
	ΔPGDP	1.29	–	–2.76*	PGDP ≠> FSDI	UDC (←)
Philippines	ΔFSDI	–	0.07	–	FSDI ≠> PGDP	
	ΔPGDP	13.0*	–	–	PGDP => FSDI	UDC (←)
Singapore	ΔFSDI	–	0.22	0.30	FSDI ≠> PGDP	
	ΔPGDP	10.2*	–	–2.65*	PGDP => FSDI	UDC (←)
Thailand	ΔFSDI	–	0.28	0.41	FSDI ≠> PGDP	
	ΔPGDP	1.55	–	–3.20*	PGDP ≠> FSDI	NOC (≠)
Vietnam	ΔFSDI	–	6.05*	–	FSDI => PGDP	
	ΔPGDP	2.39*	–	–	PGDP => FSDI	BDC (↔)
Model 2: Panel Causality						
South Asia	ΔFSDI	–	0.28	0.45	FSDI ≠> PGDP	
	ΔPGDP	3.50*	–	-3.50*	PGDP => FSDI	UDC (←)
East Asia	ΔFSDI	–	0.31	0.05	FSDI ≠> PGDP	
	ΔPGDP	1.27	–	-3.00*	PGDP ≠> FSDI	NOC (≠)
South East Asia	ΔFSDI	–	0.87	-2.46	FSDI ≠> PGDP	
	ΔPGDP	6.78*	–	-3.89*	PGDP => FSDI	UDC (←)
Total Asia	ΔFSDI	–	0.36	2.33*	FSDI ≠> PGDP	
	ΔPGDP	9.91*	–	4.42*	PGDP => FSDI	UDC (←)

Note: *: Indicates statistically significant at 5% level; =>: Unidirectional causality; ≠>: No Causality; UDC (←): Unidirectional causality from economic growth to finance development; BDC (↔): Bidirectional causality between economic growth and finance development; UDC (→): Unidirectional causality from finance development to economic growth; NOC (≠): No causality between economic growth and finance development; EC: Error correction term; and other notations are defined earlier.

under the present study, both individually and collectively (i.e. at the panel setting). The following results give an indication of cointegartion relationship among the time series variables (financial development and economic growth). The Johansen Maximum Likelihood test (λ_{Tra} & λ_{Max}) is used to ascertain whether or not the variables are cointegrated at individual country analysis, while Pedroni and Fisher's panel cointegration is used for panel setting. The results of both the statistics are reported in Tables 2 and 3. The results indicate that the variables under study are cointegrated (both at individual level and panel), indicating the existence of long run association between financial development and economic growth. Having confirmation about the cointegration among financial development and economic growth, the next step is to check their direction of causality. The Granger causality, based on vector autoregressive (VAR)/vector error correction model (VECM), is deployed for the same. VAR model is used for absence of cointegration, while VECM is used for the presence of cointegration. Table 4 provides the empirical results of VECM.

The estimated results suggest that for Bangladesh, Sri Lanka and South Korea there is a unidirectional causality from financial development to economic growth, whereas for Bhutan, India, Malaysia, Philippines and Singapore economic growth causes financial development. For China, Hong Kong, Japan, Indonesia and Vietnam we get two-way causality between financial development and economic growth, while in the context of Thailand we do not find any causal link between the two. At the panel level, the results find the unidirectional causality from economic growth to financial development in South Asia and South East Asia, while no sign of causality between financial development and economic growth in East Asia. But for total Asia, the results suggest one-way causality from economic growth to financial development. That means economic growth is very instrumental in Asia to boost the financial development in the region.

CONCLUSION AND POLICY IMPLICATIONS

This study has yielded mixed evidence on the finance-growth relationship in the context of 15 Asian countries. The findings suggest that in the case of Bangladesh, Sri Lanka and South Korea, financial development leads to economic growth, lending support to the supply leading hypothesis. This is similar to the lines of several earlier studies (see, for instance,). In the case of Bhutan, India, Malaysia, Philippines and Singapore, economic growth leads to financial development, bringing support to the demand following hypothesis. This is similar in lines of. In case of China, Hong Kong, Japan, Indonesia and Vietnam, economic growth and financial development cause each other, imparting to the support of both 'demand following' and 'supply leading' hypothesis. This is similar lines of the findings by In the case of Thailand, financial development does not cause economic growth.

It can be noted that financial development may not be salutary for economic growth for various reasons. First, underlying volatility and arbitrariness of stock market pricing process under developing countries conditions make it a mediocre guide to efficient investment allocation. Second, integration between the stock markets and currency markets in the wake of unfavourable economic shocks may worsen macroeconomic instability and can reduce the long-run economic growth. Third, stock market development is probably undermining the existing group-banking systems in the developing countries, which, even though their many difficulties, have not been without merit in several countries, not least in the extremely successful East Asian economies.

Indubitably, it could be that below a level of financial development there is no effect on economic growth or a lower effect and a larger effects as financial development cross a particular threshold limit (see, for instance, Chrisopoulos and Tsionas, 2004). The lack of same not only affects the finance-growth nexus (McKinnon, 1973) but also overall socio-economic development in the country (see, for instance, Greenwood and Jovanovic, 1990). Hence, government has to take the initiative with greater caution.

The policy implication of these findings is that if policymakers want to promote economic growth, the attention should be on long run policies on financial development. This requires well-developed financial systems, particularly with sound financial intermediation and liberalized financial indicators like interest rate, all of which are important for the efficient allocation of financial resources, which in turn help to maintain sustainable economic growth.

REFERENCES

[1] Abu-Bader, S. and Abu-Qarn, A.S. (2008). Financial Development and Economic Growth: The Egyptian Experience. *Journal of Policy Modelling*, 30(5): 887-898.

[2] Ahmed, S.M. and Ansari, M.I. (1998). Financial Sector Development and Economic Growth: The South-Asian Experience, *Journal of Asian Economics*, 9(3): 503-517.

[3] Ang, J.B. (2008). What are the Mechanisms Linking Financial Development and Economic Growth in Malaysia? *Economic Modelling*, 25(1): 38-53.

[4] Arestis, P. and Demetriades P. (1997). Financial Development and Economic Growth: Assessing the Evidence. *The Economic Journal*, 107(5): 783-799.

[5] Bangake, C. and Eggoh, J.C. (2011). Further Evidence on Finance-Growth Causality: A Panel Data Analysis. *Economic Systems*, 35(2): 176-188.

[6] Beck, T., Levine, R. and Loayza, N. (2000). Finance and Source of Growth. *Journal of Financial Economics*, 58(1-2): 261-300.

[7] Berthelemy, J.C. and Varoudakis, A. (1996). Economic Growth, Convergence Clubs, and the Role of Financial Development. *Oxford Economic Papers*, 48(2): 300-328.

[8] Blackburn K. and Hung V.T.Y. (1998). A Theory of Growth, Financial Development and Trade. *Economica,* 65(257): 107-124.

[9] Calderon, C. and Liu, L. (2003). The Direction of Causality between Financial Development and Economic Growth. *Journal of Development Economics,* 72(1): 321-334.

[10] Christopoulos, D.K. and Tsionas, E.G. (2004). Financial Development and Economic Growth: Evidence from Panel Unit Root and Cointegration Tests. *Journal of Development Economics,* 73(4): 55-74.

[11] Demetriades P. and Luintel (1996). Financial Development, Economic Growth and Banking Sector Controls: Evidence from India. *The Economic Journal,* 106(435): 359-374.

[12] Demetriades, P. and Hussein, K. (1996). Financial Development and Economic Growth: Cointegration and Causality Tests for 16 Countries. *Journal of Development Economics*, 51(2): 387-411.

[13] Dickey, D.A. and Fuller, W.A. (1981). Likelihood Ratio Statistics for Autoregressive Time Series with a Unit Root. *Econometrica*, 49(4): 1057-1072.

[14] Eller, M. Haiss, P. and Steiner K. (2006). Foreign Direct Investment in the Financial Sector and Economic Growth in Central and Eastern Europe: the Crucial Role of the Efficiency Channel. *Emerging Markets Review,* 7: 300-319.

[15] Eng, Y. and Habibullah, M.S. (2011). Financial Development and Economic Growth Nexus: Another Look at the Panel Evidence from Different Geographical Regions. *Bank and Bank Systems,* 6(1): 62-71.

[16] Enisan, A.A. and Olufisayo, A.O. (2009). Stock Market Development and Economic Growth: Evidence from Seven Sub-Sahara African Countries. *Journal of Economics and Business,* 61: 162-171.

[17] Fisher, R.A. (1932). Statistical Methods for Research Workers, Forth Edition, Edinburgh, Oliver and Boyd.

[18] Graff, M. (2003). Finance Development and Economic Growth in Corporatist and Liberal Market Economies. *Emerging Market Finance & Trade*, 39(2): 47-69.

[19] Granger, C.W.J. (1981). Some Properties of Time Series Data and their Use in Econometric Model Specification. *Journal of Econometrics*, 16(1): 121-130.

[20] Greenwood, J. and Bruce, S. (1997). Financial Markets in Development, and the Development of Financial Markets. *Journal of Economic Dynamics and Control,* 21(2): 145-181.

[21] Greenwood, J. and Jovanovic, B. (1990). Finance Development and Economic Development. *Economic Development and Cultural Change*, 15(3): 257-268.

[22] Hassan, K.M., Sanchez, B. and Yu, J.K. (2011). Financial Development and Economic Growth: New Evidence from Panel Data. *The Quarterly Review of Economics and Finance,* 51: 88-104.

[23] Holtz-Eakin, D., Newey, W. and Rosen, H.S. (1988). Estimating Vector Auto Regressions with Panel Data. *Econometrica,* 56(6): 1371-1395.

[24] Im, K.S., Pesaran, M.H. and Shin, Y. (2003). Testing for Unit Roots in Heterogeneous Panels. *Journal of Econometrics,* 115(1): 53-74.

[25] Jalil A. and Ma, Y. (2008). Financial Development and Economic Growth; Time Series Evidence from China and Pakistan. *Journal of Economic Cooperation,* 29(2): 29-68.

[26] Jalil, A., Feridun, M. and Ma, Y. (2010). Finance-Growth Nexus in China Revisited: New Evidence from Principal Components and ARDL Bounds Tests. *International Review of Economics and Finance,* 19(4): 189-195.

[27] Johansen, S. (1988). Statistical Analysis of Cointegration Vectors. *Journal of Economic Dynamics and Control,* 12(2-3): 231-54.

[28] King, R. and Levine, R. (1993). Finance and Growth: Schumpeter Might be Right. *The Quarterly Journal of Economics,* 108(3): 717-737.

[29] King, R.G. and Levine, R. (1993). Finance and Growth: Schumpeter Might be Right? *Quarterly Journal of Economics,* 108(3): 717-737.

[30] Levine, A., Lin, C.F. and Chu, C.S. (2002). Unit Root Tests in Panel Data: Asymptotic and Finite Sample Properties. *Journal of Econometrics,* 108(1): 1-24.

[31] Levine, R. (1997). Financial Development and Economic Growth: Views and Agenda. *Journal of Economic Literature,* 35(2): 688-726.

[32] Levine, R. (1999). Law, Finance and Economic Growth. *Journal of Financial Intermediation,* 8: 8-35.

[33] Levine, R. (2003). More on Finance and Growth: More Finance, More Growth? *Federal Reserve Bank of St. Louis Review,* 85(4): 31-46.

[34] Levine, R., Loayza, N. and Beck, T. (2000). Financial Intermediation and Growth: Causality Analysis and Causes. *Journal of Monetary Economics,* 46(1): 31-77.

[35] Liang, Q. and Teng, J. (2006). Financial Development and Economic Growth: Evidence form China. *China Economic Review,* 17: 395-411.

[36] Lucas, R. (1988). On the Mechanics of Economic Development. *Journal of Monetary Economics,* 22(1): 3-42.

[37] Luintel, K. and Khan, M. (1999). A Quantitative Reassessment of the Finance-Growth Nexus: Evidence from a Multivariate VAR. *Journal of Development Economics,* 60(2): 381-405.

[38] Maddala, G.S. and Wu, S. (1999). A Comparative Study of Unit Root Tests with Panel Data and a New Simple Test. *Oxford Bulletin of Economics and Statistics*, 61: 631-652.

[39] McKinnon, R. (1973). Money and Capital in Economic Development. The Brooking Institution, Washington DC.

[40] Mukhopadhyay, B., Pradhan, R.P. and Feridun, M. (2011). Finance-Growth Nexus Revisited for Some Asian countries. *Applied Economics Letters,* 18(16): 1527-1530.

[41] Neusser, K. and Kugler, M. (1998). Manufacturing Growth and Financial Development: Evidence from OECD Countries. *Review of Economics and Statistics,* 80(4): 638-646.

[42] Odhiambo, N.M. (2009). Finance-Growth-Poverty Nexus in South Africa: A Dynamic Causality Linkage. *The Journal of Socio-Economics,* 38: 320-325.

[43] Pedroni, P. (2004). Panel Cointegration: Asymptotic and Finite Sample Properties of Pooled Time Series Tests with an Application to the PPP Hypothesis: New Results. *Econometric Theory*, 20(3): 597-627.

[44] Pradhan, R.P. (2011). Financial Development, Growth and Stock Market Development: The Trilateral Analysis in India. *Journal of Quantitative Economics,* 9(1): 134-145.

[45] Robinson, J. (1952). The Generalization of the General Theory. In *The Rate of Interest and Other Essays*, London: Macmillan.

[46] Rousseau, P. and Wachtel, P. (2000). Equity Markets and Growth: Cross Country Evidence on Timing and Outcomes, 1980-1995. *Journal of Banking and Finance,* 24(12): 1933-1957.

[47] Schumpeter, J.A. (1911). The Theory of Economic Development. Harvard University Press, Cambridge, MA.

[48] Stern, N.H. (1989). The Economics of Development: A Survey. *Economic Journal,* 99(397): 597-685.

[49] Tekin, R.B. (2012). Economic Growth, Exports and Foreign Direct Investment in Least Developed Countries: A Panel Granger Causality Analysis. *Journal of Economic Modelling,* 29(3): 868-878.

[50] Wolde-Rufael, Y. (2009) Re-examining the Financial Development and Economic Growth Nexus in Kenya. *Economic Modelling,* 26: 1140-1146.

[51] Xu, Z. (2000). Financial Development, Investment and Economic Growth. *Economic Inquiry,* 38(2): 311-344.

Entropic Order Quantity (EnOQ) Repair and Waste Disposal Discounted Model with Pre- and Post-Deterioration

Monalisha Pattnaik
Utkal University, Bhubaneswar
E-mail: monalisha1977@gmail.com

ABSTRACT

The issues of entropic order quantity repair and waste disposal discount in inventory management have become a matter of great interest. I present and analyse an entropic order quantity inventory model under pre- and post deterioration discount with two component demand caused by investment strategy subject to a discount level constraint over a finite planning time. To handle this multiplicity of objectives in a sensible approach, entropic order quantity model with pre- and post deterioration of perishable items to optimize its payoff is proposed. A numerical example is given to demonstrate the flow of the optimal decision for retailer and it is also given to evaluate the difference between crisp entropic order quantity (EnOQ) and economic order quantity (EOQ) models separately. Two models are developed for the problem by employing different modelling approaches over finite planning horizon. One of the repercussions of this convergence is that if the entropy cost could be reduced effectively, then the total profit per unit time could be automatically improved. This nonlinear programming problem with constraints can be regarded as a model of decision problems where human estimation is influential.

Keywords: EnOQ, EOQ

INTRODUCTION

Entropy is normally defined as the amount of disorder of the system. Inventory management has been changing rapidly in recent years in response to international competition and new technology. The classical economic order quantity (EOQ) chooses a batch size that minimises the total cost calculated as the sum of two conflicting cost functions, the ordering cost and the inventory holding costs. The entropic order quantity

(EnOQ) is derived by determining a batch size that minimizes the sum of the above two costs and entropic cost. This paper deals with an entropic order quantity model with cash discounts under pre and post deterioration of the perishable products. The predominant criterion in traditional inventory models is minimization of long run average cost per unit time. The costs considered are usually fixed and variable ordering cost and holding cost. Costs associated with disorder in a system tied up in inventory are accounted for by including an entropy cost in the total costs. Jaber, Bonney, Rosen and Moualek [1] proposed an analogy between the behaviour of production system and the behaviour of physical system. Pattnaik [2] introduced the use of entropy cost in the context of EOQ model. This paper suggested the concept of entropy cost to account for hidden cost such as the additional managerial cost that is needed to control the improvement process.

To derive the entropic model for deteriorating items the paper first defines a system. Analogously, a production system could be described by its characteristics. Reducing the price of a commodity below the market price may increase customer demand and produce a commodity flow (sales) from the system to its surroundings which include the market and the supply system, resembles a physical system. The commodity sales to the market that are converted to revenue and deterioration of some of the items held in inventory that become waste. It is assumed that no returns will occur. Hence with commodities the lower their prices the more commodities will sell and this is the repairing procedure of the production system. Analogously, the lower price in a market system, the higher the sales. The concept of commodity deterioration also applies to heat, in that temperature will normally decay over time, due to several physical factors. Waste of thermal energy is to be anticipated and avoided where possible. Similarly commodity deterioration is best planned for and, where possible, avoided.

Every organisation dealing with inventory faces a number of fundamental problems. Pricing decision is one of them. Therefore, price can be considered as an important tool to influence demand. This led many researchers to investigate pricing strategy on inventory models in details. But in real world, it exists and is quite flexible in nature. On the other hand, in order to motivate customers to order more quantities, usually suppliers offer discount on selling prices both pre and post deterioration rate. Dave, Fitzapatrick and Baker [3] developed an inventory model under continuous discount pricing. Khouja [4] studied an inventory problem under the condition that multiple discounts can be used to sell excess inventory. Shah and Shah [5] mentioned that discount is considered temporarily for exponentially decaying inventory model. However, most of the studies except few, do not attempt to unify the two research streams: temporary price reductions and deterioration. As a result, the effect of discount for deteriorating items on revenue has been ignored and the models deal with cost minimization rather than with profit maximization objective function. Generally no one has tried to introduce a temporary discount on selling price before the start of deterioration as well as a discount on selling price as the deterioration starts to enhance the demand in order to boost the inventory depletion rate. This paper represents the issue in details.

Recently a number of research articles appeared which deal with the EOQ problem under constant demand. In last two decades the variability of inventory level dependent demand rate on the analysis of inventory system was described by researchers like Pal, Goswami and Choudhury [6] and Goswami and Choudhury [7]. They described the demand rate as the power function of on hand inventory. There is a vast literature on stock development inventory and its outline can be found in the review article by Urban [8] where he unified two types of inventory level dependent demand by considering a periodic review model. Researchers such as Chung, Tsu and Liang [9], Goyal and Giri [10], Raafat [11] and Skouri, Konstantaras, Papachristos and Ganas [12] discussed the EOQ model assuming time value of money, demand rate, deterioration rate, shortages and so on a constant or probabilistic number or an exponential function. This paper considers two component demand function which is initially depending on inventory up to deterioration and then becoming a constant function till stock is zero level at the end of the cycle.

Product perishability is an important aspect of inventory control. Deterioration in general, may be considered as the result of various effects on stock, some of which are

Table 1: Major Characteristics of Inventory Models on Selected Researches

Author(s) and published Year	Structure of the Model	Deterioration	Inventory Model	Discount Allowed	Demand	Back-Logging Allowed
Panda et al. (2009)	Crisp	Yes (heaviside)	EOQ	Yes	Stock dependent	No
Jaber et al. (2008)	Crisp	Yes (on hand inventory)	EnOQ	No	Unit selling price	No
Chung et al. (2007)	Crisp	Yes (exponential)	EOQ	No	Selling price	Yes (partial)
Skouri et al. (2007)	Crisp	Yes (weibull)	EOQ	No	Ramp	Yes (partial)
Pattnaik (2010)	Crisp	Yes (constant)	EnOQ	Yes, instant deterioration	Constant	No
Pattnaik (2011)	Crisp	Yes (heaviside)	EnOQ	Yes, post deterioration	Stock dependent	No
Present paper (2011)	Crisp	Yes (heaviside)	EnOQ	Yes, pre and post deterioration	Stock dependent	No

damage, decay, decreasing usefulness and many more. While kept in store fruits, vegetables, food stuffs, etc., suffer from depletion by decent spoilage. Decaying products are of two types. Product which deteriorate from the very beginning and the products which start to deteriorate after a certain time. Lot of articles are available in inventory literature considering deterioration. Interested readers may consult the survey paper of Weatherford and Bodily [13] and Panda, Saha and Basu [14].

The purpose of this paper is to investigate the effect of the approximation made by using the average payoff when determining the optimal values of the policy variables. In this paper it is focused exclusively on the cost of entropy. A policy iteration algorithm is designed with the help of Deb [15] and optimum solution is obtained through LINGO software. In order to make the comparisons equitable a particular evaluation function based on discount is suggested. Numerical experiments are carried out to analyse the magnitude of the approximation error. The remainder of this paper is organised as follows. In first section assumptions and notations are provided for the development of the model. Next section describes the model formulation. An illustrative numerical experiment is given to illustrate the procedure of solving the model is discussed in the next section. Finally, last section summarizes the concluding remarks and provides some suggestions for future research.

NOTATIONS AND ASSUMPTIONS

Notations

C_0 : set up cost

c : per unit purchase cost of the product

s : constant selling price of the product per unit *(s > c)*

h : holding cost per unit per unit time

r_1 : discount offer per unit before deterioration.

r_2 : discount offer per unit after deterioration.

$\acute{a}_1$: the effect of pre-deterioration discount on demand.

$\acute{a}_2$: the effect of post deterioration discount on demand.

R : demand function.

S : entropy generation rate.

$(EC)_{WD}$: entropy cost with deterioration in the cycle.

$(EC)_{WOD}$: entropy cost without deterioration in the cycle.

Q_1 : order level for pre- and post-deterioration discount on selling price.

T_1 : cycle length of the inventory model.

Assumptions

1. Replenishment rate is infinite.

2. The deterioration rate $\tilde{\theta} = \theta H(t - \tau)$, $(0 < \theta \leq 1)$ constant where t is the time measured from the instant arrivals of a fresh replenishment indicating that the deterioration of the items begins after a time τ from the instant of the arrival in stock.

   $H(t - \tau)$ is the well known Heaviside's function. $H(t-\tau) = \begin{cases} 1, t \geq \tau \\ 0, \text{otherwise} \end{cases}$
3. Demand depends on the on hand inventory up to time τ from time of fresh replenishment beyond which it is constant and defined as follows.

   $$R(I(t)) = \begin{cases} a + bI(t), & t < \tau \\ a, t \geq \tau \end{cases}$$

   where $a > 0$ is the initial demand rate independent of stock level and condition of inventory and $b > 0$ is the stock sensitive demand parameter $I(t)$ is the instantaneous inventory level at time t.
4. r_1, $(0 \leq r_1 \leq 1)$ is the percentage pre- deterioration discount offer on unit selling price. $\alpha_1 = (1 - r_1)^{n_1}$, ($n_1$, the set of real numbers), is the effect of pre-deterioration discount on demand. r_2, $(0 \leq r_2 \leq 1)$ is the percentage discount offer on unit selling price during deterioration. $\alpha_2 = (1 - r_2)^{n_2}$, ($n_2$, the set of real numbers), is the effect of discounted selling price on demand during deterioration. α_2 is determined from priori knowledge of the seller such that the demand rate is influenced with the reduction rate of selling price.
5. Entropy generation rate must satisfy $S = \dfrac{d\sigma(t)}{dt}$ where, $\sigma(t)$ is the total entropy generated by time t and S is the rate at which entropy is generated. The entropy cost is computed by dividing the total commodity flow in a cycle of duration T_i. The total entropy generated over time T_i as $\sigma(T_i) = \int_0^{T_i} S dt$, $S = \dfrac{R(I\ (t))}{s}$.

   Entropy cost per cycle is

   $$EC(T_i) = (EC)_{WOD} + (EC)_{WD} = \frac{D(\tau)}{\sigma(\tau)} + \frac{Q_{i\ WD}}{\sigma(T_i)} \quad (i = 1)$$

   EC is measured in an appropriate price unit with no deterioration and with deterioration respectively.

MATHEMATICAL MODEL

At the beginning of the replenishment cycle the inventory level raises to Q_I. As time progresses it decreases due to instantaneous stock dependent demand up to the time τ.

After τ deterioration starts and the inventory level decreases for deterioration and constant demand. Ultimately inventory reaches zero level at T_1. It is assumed that before the start of deterioration from time t_1, r_1% discount on unit selling price of the product is given in order to boost the demand of fresh items. Clearly, this discount is continued for the period of time $(\tau - t_1)$. As deterioration starts from τ, r_2% discount on unit selling price is provided to enhance the demand of decreased quality items. This discount is continued for the rest of the replenishment cycle. Then the behaviour of inventory level is governed by the following system of linear differential equations and it is depicted in Figure 1.

$$d(I(t))/dt = -a - b\,I(t) \qquad 0 \le t \le t_1 \tag{1}$$

$$= -\alpha_1\left(a + b\ I(t)\right) \qquad t_1 \le t \le \tau \tag{2}$$

$$= -\left[\alpha_2\, a + \theta\, I(t)\right] \qquad \tau \le t \le T_1 \tag{3}$$

With the initial boundary condition

$I(0) = Q_1,\ 0 \le t \le t_1$

$I(T_1) = 0,\ \ \tau \le t \le T_1$

Solving the equations,

$$I(t) = \frac{a}{b}\left[e^{-bt} - 1\right] + Q_1 e^{-bt}, 0 \le t \le t_1 \tag{4}$$

$$I(t) = \frac{a}{b}\left[e^{-\alpha_1 b\ (t-t_1)-bt_1} - 1\right] + Q_1\ e^{\alpha_1 b\ (t_1-t)-bt_1} t_1 \le t \le \tau \tag{5}$$

$$I(t) = \frac{a\alpha_2}{\theta}\ \left[e^{\theta(T_1-t)} - 1\right],\quad \tau \le t \le T_1 \tag{6}$$

Now, at the point $t = \tau$, we have from equations (5) and (6)

$$Q_1 = \left[\frac{a\alpha_2}{\theta}\left(e^{\theta(T_1-\tau)} - 1\right) + \frac{a}{b}\right] \times e^{\alpha_1 b\ (\tau-t_1)+b\ t_1} - \frac{a}{b} \tag{7}$$

By using equations (4), (5) and (6) for different $I(t)$ in the respective intervals the holding cost of inventories in the cycle is,

$$HC = h\int_0^{t_1} I(t)dt + h\int_{t_1}^{\tau} I(t)dt + h\int_{\tau}^{T_1} I(t)dt$$

$$= h\int_0^{t_1}\left[\frac{a}{b}\left[e^{-bt} - 1\right] + Q_1 e^{-bt}\right]dt + h\int_{t_1}^{\tau}\left[\frac{a}{b}\left[e^{-\alpha_1 b\ (t-t_1)-bt_1} - 1\right]\right.$$

$$\left. + Q_1\ e^{\alpha_1 b\ (t_1-t)-bt_1}\right]dt + h\int_{\tau}^{T_1}\left[\frac{a\alpha_2}{\theta}\ \left[e^{\theta(T_1-t)} - 1\right]\right]dt$$

Purchase cost in the cycle is given by $PC = cQ_1$.

Entropy cost in the cycle is $EC = (EC)_{WOD} + (EC)_{WD}$

$$= \frac{D(\tau)}{\sigma(\tau)} + \frac{Q_{i\ WD}}{\sigma(T_1)}$$

where $$D(\tau) = \int_0^{t_1} R(I(t))\,dt + \int_{t_1}^{\tau} R(I(t))\,dt$$

$$Q_{i\ WD} = Q_1$$

$$\sigma(\tau) = \int_0^{\tau} S dt = \int_0^{t_1} \frac{R(I(t))}{s} dt + \int_{t_1}^{\tau} \frac{R(I(t))}{s} dt = \frac{1}{s} D(\tau)$$

$$\sigma(T_1) = \int_{\tau}^{T_1} \frac{R(I(t))}{s} dt = \int_{\tau}^{T_1} \frac{a}{s} dt = \frac{a}{s}(T_1 - \tau)$$

$$EC = s + \frac{sQ_1}{a(T_1 - \tau)}$$

Total sales revenue in the order cycle can be found as

$$SR = s\left[\int_0^{t_1} (a + bI(t))\,dt + \alpha_1(1 - r_1)\int_{t_1}^{\tau}[a + bI(t)]\,dt + \alpha_2(1 - r_2)\int_{\tau}^{T_1} a\,dt\right]$$

Thus total profit per unit time of the system is $\pi_1(r_1, r_2, t_1, T_1) = \dfrac{TP_1}{T_1}$

$$= \frac{1}{T_1}[SR - PC - HC - EC - OC]$$

On integration and simplification of the relevant costs, the total profit per unit time becomes

$$\pi_1 = \frac{1}{T_1}\Bigg[sat_1 + s\alpha_2(1 - r_2)a(T_1 - \tau) + (sb - h)\left(-\frac{at_1}{b} + \left(Q_1 + \frac{a}{b}\right)\frac{1 - e^{-bt_1}}{b}\right)$$

$$+\left[s\alpha_1 b(1 - r_1) - h\right]\left[\frac{a(t_1 - \tau)}{b} + \left(\frac{a}{b} + Q_1\right)e^{-bt_1}\left(\frac{1 - e^{\alpha_1 b(t_1 - \tau)}}{b\alpha_1}\right)\right] + s\alpha_1(1 - r_1)a(\tau - t_1)$$

$$-h\frac{a\alpha_2}{\theta}\left[\frac{e^{\theta(T_1 - \tau)} - 1}{\theta} - (T_1 - \tau)\right] - s - \frac{sQ_1}{a(T_1 - \tau)} - cQ_1 - C_0\Bigg] \tag{8}$$

The pre deterioration discount on selling price is to be given in such a way that the discounted selling price is not less that the unit cost of the product, i.e. $s(1 - r_1) - c > 0$ similarly, $s(1 - r_2) - c > 0$. Applying these constraints on unit total profit function, the maximization problem is

Maximize $\pi_1 (r_1, r_2, t_1, T_1)$

$$\text{Subject to } \{r_1, r_2\} < 1 - \frac{c}{s} \quad \forall \quad r_1, r_2, t_1, T_1 \geq 0. \tag{9}$$

The objective here is to determine the optimal values of r_1, r_2, t_1 and T_1 to maximize the unit profit function. It is very difficult to derive the results analytically. Thus some numerical methods must be applied to derive the optimal values of r_1, r_2, t_1 and T_1, hence the unit profit function. There are several methods to cope with constraint optimization problem numerically. But here LINGO software is applied to derive the optimal values of the decision variables.

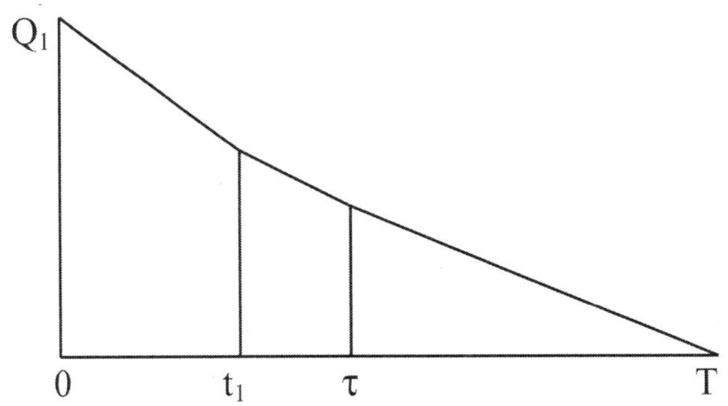

Fig. 1: Inventory Model of Both Pre- and Post-Deterioration Discount

NUMERICAL EXAMPLE

Let the parameter values are a = 80, b = 0.3, h = 0.6, s = 10.0, C_0 = 100.0, c = 4.0, θ = 0.03, τ =1.2, n_1 = 2.0 and n_2 = 2.0. With the help of LINGO software the optimum values of the decision variables are listed in Table 2.

For the entropic order quality model with both pre and post deterioration discounts, the pre-deterioration discount on unit selling price is 37.09% and discount starts at time 0.1770513 and continued to τ =1.2, then the product starts to deteriorate. During this time in order to enhance inventory depletion rate, 50.09% discount is provided for remaining time of replenishment cycle. Hence the profit per unit time is 692.7293 with the optimal order quantity, 1595.249 and the cycle length, 2.858826 respectively. The unit profit and order quantity for the case of crisp EOQ model are 749.6949 and 1652.540 less by 8.2233565% and 3.5913516% respectively from CEnOQ model. The cycle length

Table 2: Optimal Values of the Decision Variables, Order Quantity and Profit Per Unit Time of CEnOQ and CEOQ Models

Nature of Discount	Decision Variables	CEnOQ	CEOQ	% Change
With pre and post deterioration discounts	r_1	0.3709945	0.3898235	–5.0752774
	r_2	0.5009602	0.5668512	–13.152911
	t_1	0.1770513	0.1709742	3.432395
	T_1	2.858826	2.418452	15.40402
	Q_1	1595.249	1652.540	–3.5913516
	SR	9614.512	9479.388	1.40541714
	PC	6380.996	6610.160	–3.5913515
	HC	1022.914	956.1273	6.5290630
	EC	130.2092	–	–
	OC	100.000	100.000	0
	π_1	692.7293	749.6949	–8.2233565

Table 3: Relative Error of Pre and Post-Deterioration Discounted CEnOQ Model with Other Models

Model	r_1	r_2	t_1	T_1	Q_1	EC	π_1
CEnOQ	0.37099	0.50096	0.1770513	2.858826	1595.249	130.2092	692.7293
CEnOQ (Pattnaik, 2010)	–	0.04635	–	1.917616	173.6135	21.3170	362.0803
% Change	–	90.7478	–	32.92296	89.11684	83.6287	47.73134
CEOQ (Pattnaik, 2010)	–	–	–	2.000859	164.9528	20.30512	361.2894
% Change	–	–	–	30.01117	89.65975	84.40577	47.8455
CEnOQ (Pattnaik, 2011)	–	0.41379	1.2	2.831899	673.5408	61.59181	582.2379
% Change	–	17.4006	–85.24573	.9418901	57.77833	52.69780	15.51709
CEOQ (Pattnaik, 2011)	–	0.45417	1.2	2.572020	654.5585	–	606.3850
% Change	–	9.34007	–577.76966	10.03230	58.96826	–	12.46436
CEOQ (Panda et al., 2009)	0.38982	–	0.1709739	1.20	376.47	–	573.2467
% Change	–5.07561	–	3.43256446	58.02473	76.40055	–	17.24809

is 2.418452 and 15.40462% more than that for CEnOQ model with both types of discounts.

The relative difference in Table 2 is marked larger than the ones found in the previous experiments when the ordering policy is optimal. This indicates that there exists case in which the relative difference is non-negligible.

Comparative Evaluation

From the Table 3 for pre and post deterioration discounted CEnOQ model 37.09% and 50.09% discounts are provided on unit selling price to earn more profit than that with other models. It also indicates that the repair and waste disposal discounted model is provided to earn [12.46%, 47.85%] more profits from every other compared models. This paper investigates a computing schema for the EOQ in introducing the entropy cost. The results are approximate, i.e. it permits better use of CEnOQ with pre and post deterioration discounts as compare to other models. It indicates the consistency of the both aforesaid models. Though higher amount of percentage discounts are offered on unit selling price in the form of pre and post deterioration discounts for larger periods of time in lower unit sales revenue, still it is more profitable. Because the inventory depletion rate is much higher for discount enhanced demand resulting lower amount of inventory holding cost and deteriorated items. Therefore it is always profitable to apply both forms of discounts on unit selling price to earn more profit.

CONCLUSION

This paper deals with the emerging research of developing entropic order quantity model for perishable items. Conventional wisdom suggests that the concept of entropy and two component stock dependent demand, are promising mechanisms for achieving an optimization profit. Finally, in numerical experiments the solution from the discounted model evaluated and compared to the solutions of EOQ policies.

However, it is observed that the performance differences among a set of different inventory policies in the existing literature. Although there are minor variations that do not appear significant in practical terms, at least when solving the single level, incapacitated version of the lot sizing problem. From the analysis it is demonstrated that the retailer's profit is highly influenced by offering pre and post discount on selling price. The results of this study give managerial insights to decision maker developing an optimal replenishment decision for deteriorating product. Compensation mechanism should also be included to induce collaboration between retailer and dealer in a meaningful supply chain.

In general, for normal parameter values the relative payoff differences seem to be fairly small. Conventional wisdom suggests that workflow collaboration in an entropic model in a varying deteriorating product in market place are promising mechanism and achieving a cost effective replenishment policy.

As with most management science applications; the models developed were purely theoretical. In this study, the retailer's ultimate demand was treated as a certainty and was assumed to be stock dependent. This theory postulates that the approach proposed in the paper based on EnOQ model seems to be a pragmatic way to approximate the optimum payoff of the unknown group of parameters in inventory management problems. The assumptions underlying the approach are not strong and the information obtained seems worthwhile. Its use may restrict the model's applicability in the real world. Incorporation of cash discounts structure and entropy cost into the analysis can be really challenging but they are more realistic and therefore can justifiably be used in actual situations. Given the inherent complexities of the real world, simple models lend themselves to the search for solutions, which are relatively robust over a wide range of situations rather than optimal for a narrow set of circumstances. So, this paper sets the stage to incorporate entropy cost into the analysis. The results of this waste disposal and repair model suggest that a firm which is unable to estimate its cost parameters properly may find ordering in larger lots an appropriate policy to counter entropy effects. Further investigation of the model reveals that accounting for entropy cost may be more relevant for low demand and expensive items, than for high demand and low-priced items. The proposed model can be extended in several ways. It is believed, however, that the present models provide a good starting point in this research stream. The use of other replenishment policies such as partial backlogging model and the use of other demand-side revenue boosting variables such as promotional efforts are potential areas for future research.

REFERENCES

[1] Chung, Y.D., Tsu, P.H. and Liang, Y., Determining optimal selling price and lot size with a varying rate of deterioration and exponential partial backlogging. *European Journal of Operational Research,* 2007; 181: 668-678.

[2] Dave, D.S., Fitzapatrick, K.E., and Baker, J.R., An advertising inclusive production lot size model under continuous discount pricing. *Computational Industrial Engineering,* 1995; 30: 147-159.

[3] Deb, K., *Optimization for Engineering Design.* Prentice-Hall of India: New Delhi, 2000.

[4] Goswami, A., and Choudhury, K.S., An EOQ model for deteriorating items with linear time dependent demand rate and shortages under inflation and time discounting. *Journal of Operational Research Society,* 1995; 46(6): 771.

[5] Goyal, S.K., and Giri, B.C., Recent trends in modelling of deteriorating inventory. *European Journal of Operational Research,* 2001; 134: 1-16.

[6] Jaber, M.Y., Bonney, M., Rosen, M.A., and Moualek, I., Entropic order quantity (EnOQ) model for deteriorating items. *Applied Mathematical Modeling,* 2009; 33(1): 564-578.

[7] Khouja, M., Optimal ordering, discounting and pricing in the single period problem. *International Journal of Production Economics,* 2000; 65: 201-216.

[8] Pal, S., Goswami, K., and Chaudhuri, K.S., A deterministic inventory model for deteriorating items with stock dependent demand rate. *Journal of Production Economics,* 1993; 32:291-299.

[9] Panda, S., Saha, S. and Basu, M., An EOQ model for perishable products with discounted selling price and stock dependent demand. *CEJOR,* 2009; 17:31-53.

[10] Pattnaik, M., An entropic order quantity (EnOQ) model with post deterioration cash discounts. *International Journal of Contemporary Mathematical Sciences*, 2011; 6(19): 931-939.

[11] Pattnaik, M., An Entropic Order Quantity model (EnOQ) under instant deterioration of perishable itpems with price discounts. *International Mathematical Forum*, 2010; 5(49):49-52.

[12] Raafat, E., Survey of literature on continuously deteriorating inventory model. *Journal of Operational Research Society,* 1991; 42: 27-37.

[13] Shah, N.H., and Shah, Y.K., An EOQ model for exponentially decaying inventory under temporary price discounts. *Cahiers du CERO,* 1993; 35: 227-232.

[14] Skouri, K., Konstantaras, I., Papachristos, S. and Ganas, I., Inventory models with ramp type demand rate, partial backlogging and weibull deterioration rate. *European journal of Operational Research,* 2007.

[15] Urban, T.L., Inventory model with inventory level dependent demand a comprehensive review and unifying theory. *European Journal of Operational Research,* 2005; 162:792-804.

[16] Weatherford, L.R. and Bodily, S.E., A taxonomy and research overview of perishable asset revenue management: yield management, overbooking, and pricing. *Operations Research,* 1992; 40: 831-844.

Environmental Impact of Thermal Power Stations (With Particular Reference to India)

Meera Lal
BITS-Pilani, Hyderabad Campus, Hyderabad
E-mail: lalmeera@yahoo.com

ABSTRACT

An enabling environment needs to be created to channel more domestic and foreign capital into Indian infrastructure. The growing momentum of public private partnerships has to be supported and the huge capital outlays required for the infrastructure sector to fulfill national plans and objectives have to be provided for. The future economic development route for India is likely to result in rapid and accelerated growth in Industrial energy demand, with shortages and problems. Due to the predominance of fossil fuels in the generation mix, there are large negative environmental externalities caused by electricity generation. This however is subject to controversy as many believe renewable energy resources are expensive and fossil fuels on the other hand are more cost-effective. But one cannot deny the deteriorating and hazardous environmental impact of fossils and hence cannot be ignored. What is required perhaps is focused mitigation of the harmful emissions and to find alternative cost effective energy solutions. Recent development and promotion of solar energy in the transport sector in Japan can be exemplary example to emulate. The power sector alone in India has a 40 percent contribution to the total carbon emissions. There are opportunities for renewable energy technologies under the new climate change regime as they meet the two basic conditions to be eligible for assistance under UNFCCC mechanisms: they contribute to global sustainability through GHG mitigation; and, they conform to national priorities by leading to the development of local capacities and infrastructure. This paper discusses the renewable and carbon market linkages and assesses mitigation potential of power sector renewable energy technologies under global environmental intervention scenarios for GHG emissions reduction. An overall energy system framework is used for assessing the future role of renewable energy under baseline and different mitigation scenarios over a time frame of 35 to 40 years. The methodology uses an integrated bottom-up modeling framework. Looking into past performance trends and likely future developments, analysis results are compared with officially set targets for renewable energy. Our Government is seriously seized of implementation problems and logjams in delivery of critical infrastructure projects at the same time seriously considering the environmental impact.

Keywords: Infrastructure, Thermal, Environment, Public-Private Partnership, Fossil Fuels, GHG Mitigation

ENERGY DEMAND OUTLOOK

Energy is the most important and central element in the process of development. Realising this aspect, energy development has attracted large public spending in the planned growth of the economy. Efforts to increase efficiency and production of thermal power along with promotion of fossil fuels and new and renewable sources of energy in an efficient fashion have ensured a minimum supply of energy in the country. The decade of 90s has also witnessed gradual entry of the private sector companies and restructure of the public sector.

The world's primary energy demand is projected to increase by more than 53% from current levels to 2030, an average annual growth of about 1.7%. It is assumed that in 2030, the total energy demand will be 17 billion tons of oil equivalents (btoe). This scenario, prepared by the International Energy Agency (IEA) and referred to as the Reference Scenario, suggests that more than two-thirds of the increase in world energy use will come from developing countries where economic and population rates will continue to be significant.

Table 1: World Primary Energy Demand in the Reference Scenario (mtoe)

Sector	1980	2004	2010	2015	2030	2030	2004-2030
Coal	1785	2773	3354	3666	4441	25.9%	1.8%
Oil	3107	3940	4366	4750	5575	32.6%	1.3%
Gas	1287	2302	2686	3017	3869	22.6%	2.9%
Nuclear	186	714	775	810	861	5.0%	0.7%
Hydro	148	242	280	317	408	2.9%	2.0%
Biomass and waste	765	1176	1283	1375	1645	9.6%	1.3%
Other renewables	33	57	99	136	296	1.9%	6.6%
Total	7,261	11,204	12,389	14,402	**17,095**	100%	1.6%

Source: International Energy Agency, World Energy Outlook, 2006.

Fossil fuels will account for more than 83% of the projected increase in primary energy demand of which oil will continue to remain the major component of the primary energy mix. Natural gas demand will grow mainly due to increased preference for gas-based electricity generation. However, coal will still continue to be the predominant source for electricity generation. Shares of nuclear power and hydropower will remain generally constant at 6% and 3% respectively. The share of biomass-based energy consumption is expected to actually reduce due to increased use of modern fuels in rural regions of developing countries. The share of other renewable sources, excluding large hydro and biomass, will be about 6.6% of the global primary energy demand in 2030.

The energy demand in Asia is increasing rapidly due to the unprecedented economic growth in the region. According to the International Energy Agency, primary energy demand in the developing Asia will grow from 2.9 billion tons of oil equivalent (btoe) in 2004 to 5.8 btoe in 2030. *This huge growth is definitely not sustainable if most of this energy will have to be met by fossils fuels. Increased fossil fuel consumption will significantly increase greenhouse gas (CHG) emissions and result in dangerous levels of global warming as has been emphasized in the Copenhagen summit.*

Apart from this another important consequences is the volatility of international oil prices which has placed an extra and disproportionate burden on developing countries and has promoted use of indigenous sources of energy, in particular fossil fuels. A comprehensive and co-ordinated approach is necessary. This will hence encompass policy decisions, legal and regulatory framework, energy conservation, reduction in fossil fuel use, increase in renewable sources of energy and market orientation towards sustainable development.

Advanced coal power technologies are needed along with Bio-mass and Wind-Based power generation. There is urgent need for Technology transfer and Indigenous R&D. Total Deregulation invariably leads to greater privatization without state or public oversight with oligopolistic control of assets by a few big firms. Hence, everybody now acknowledges that the sector needs stricter, transparent and effective regulation. Electricity is too precious for our lives to be left to the markets alone. Developing countries (esp. Asia) can lead the way through leap-jumping.

My paper has tried to evaluate the existing scenario in the power sector in India in particular Thermal power and its future, reliance on coal imports, the hazards of oil spill and environmental repercussions and ultimately promoting renewable energy resources as alternatives for the future. The existing Energy Policy has also been discussed and some action points recommended.

'POWER ON DEMAND BY 2012'

Power is a critical infrastructure for economic development and for improving the quality of life. The achievement of increasing our installed power capacity from 1362 MW to over 1, 00,000 MW and electrification of more than 500,000 villages is highly impressive in absolute terms. However, it is a matter of concern that the annual per capita consumption of India, at about 350 kWh is among the lowest in the world.

There is no doubt however, that Indian energy has undergone a distinct change during the last three decades as a result of the planning process. While the development of the industrial and transport sectors has been based mainly on commercial energy, the agricultural sector has been shifting gradually to the use of oil and gas as a consequence of modernization of agricultural practices. *However, the industrial preference for commercial forms of energy has resulted in the rapid demand for them and the growth rate of commercial energy consumption has been outpacing the overall growth of the economy. Imports of coal and oil to meet the requirements have put severe pressure on India's foreign exchange reserves as well as time constraints and availability of these imports.* Hence, the problems have aggravated in recent years and it appears they have not been addressed satisfactorily. Investments in infrastructure have intrinsically long gestation coupled with relatively low returns which have rendered projects commercially unprofitable. However, with a new thrust on Infrastructure development in the coming Plans, Banks and Large Corporate Houses have ventured into power sector and have obtained licenses for Ultra Mega Power projects. Power is a key driver for GDP growth. The aggregate installed capacity is about 1, 36, 000 MW. Projected addition at the end of 11th Plan has been estimated to be over 68,000 MW Further addition of about 86,500 MW whose benefit might spill over to the 12th Plan period. These initiatives include certain *Ultra Mega Power Projects (UMPP) of 4,000 MW each in Thermal Power.* A recent development is the entry of Reliance Industries Limited into thermal Power. With the government envisaging to award 15 ultra-mega power projects, of which three—Sasan, Krishnapatnam and Tilaiya—have already gone to ADAG (Anil Dhirubhai Ambani Group) and the fourth one Mundra has been allocated to the Tata's. RIL are thus seen entering into Thermal power projects. The table below shows the maximum extent of dependency on Thermal power.

Table 2: Sector-wise/Type-wise Capacity Addition Programme during Ninth Plan (Figures in MW)

Sector	Hydro	Thermal	Nuclear	Total
Central	3455.0	7,574.0	880.0	11,909.0
State	5814.7	4,933.0	–	10,747.7
Private	550.0	17,038.5	–	17,588.5
Total	9819.7	29,545.5	880.0	40,245.2

Source: CEA.

INDUSTRIAL DEMAND FOR POWER

India is a major producer of several energy intensive commodities. It ranks among the top five producers worldwide of aluminum, cement, steel, fertilizers, textiles, sugar, and paper. The demand for these products is growing faster than that worldwide because of the steady and relatively faster economic growth, and increased materialization of the Indian economy. The construction sector, which constitutes a major demand for products such as steel, cement, aluminum, etc., has grown faster than the rest of the Indian economy and as infrastructure expansion is targeted by the Indian government; demand for these products is likely to increase in future. The quality of the technology being used to produce these products varies across sectors, but a few common features are worth observing in this context. *Nitrogenous fertilizers*, i.e. *ammonia and urea fertilizers*, are highly energy intensive employing natural gas, associated gas, naphtha, fuel oil, and *coal* as their major feed-stocks. Gas-based ammonia plants represent the most energy-efficient technology in India, which compares well with that in other countries in the world. Salient international comparisons are shown in Table.

Table 3: Average Energy Consumption for Ammonia Plants

Country	MKCal/t	Country	MKCal/t
UK	7.4	*India*	*9.4*
Indonesia	8.2	USA	10.2
Malaysia	9.2	UAE	12.1

Source: CEA.

Coal is also the major fuel used for heat production in the cement industry. The dry process uses between 750-800 kcal/kg of cement clinker compared to the more energy-intensive wet process, which uses between 1350-1500 kcal/kg of clinker. The electricity consumption of cement plants averages around 120 kWh per ton of cement produced. Conversion of all 61 kilns (8.5 mt) operating on wet process in India to the dry process could save 1.2 million tons of coal, which in turn could be used to manufacture 7.8 mt of cement. About 25% of the wet process capacity is amenable to conversion.

Integrated primary steel plants in India usually employ the blast furnace-basic oxygen/open hearth furnace process route for iron and steel production *using mostly coal technology*. Nearly 30% of the total steel production is through the open-hearth process, an obsolete technology by world standards. Secondary steel production takes place in mostly privately owned small steel plants employing the electric arc furnace process or the induction furnace process. New plants using the COREX process are now being built that will definitely be much more energy efficient.

COAL RESERVES

The large coal reserves in the country provide a ready and economic resource, which ensures energy security. Hence, coal would continue to be the mainstay fuel for power generation till 2012. Emphasis has been laid on setting up large pit head stations to avoid high costs associated with transportation of high ash bearing Indian coal and overstraining the already stretched rail network. To reduce the environmental impact and increase efficiency, the strategies adopted by the Ministry include introduction of large sized units (660 MW) employing the state-of-the-art super critical technology. Further, in view of their shorter gestation period, higher thermal efficiency and environmental benefits, few combined cycle power projects have been identified. Coastal locations have been given preference for such plants in order to minimize cost.

Coal is the most important resource for power generation in India, taking care of half of the primary energy needs and a third of total energy needs. Coal reserves in India are substantial high but low in quality. Because of economic and security reasons, coal would play a vital role as a raw material for power generation. Most of the coal based power plants use conventional sub critical pulverized coal technologies and below par in converting coal to electricity. The reasons for the bad performance of the coal based power plants are due to:

- Challenges in the coal supply industry.
- Not having clear-cut performance standards.
- Negligible incentive for continual performance improvement due to negligible competition.
- Insufficient investments in R&D.
- Substandard operational and management practices.
- Not having sufficient facts and accountability.

Controls to check the negative impact on the eco-system due to the usage of coal is not sufficient. There is not much initiative to upgrade current technology and to come up with new technology for generating power based on coal.

JSW Energy Ltd. (JSWEL) is a power project development company, which is developing and maintaining power projects in India. *The company has two thermal power projects* under operation, with a combined installed capacity of 860 MW. JSWEL is a part of the JSW Group, a leading business group in India. JSW Group has a presence in high growth sector like Steel, Energy, Aluminium, Cement, Infrastructure and Logistics.

ENVIRONMENTAL IMPACT OF THERMAL POWER

Air Pollution

Initially, perceptions of objectionable effects of air pollutants were limited to those easily detected through odour, soiling of surfaces and smoke stacks. However, today it has become clear that the concern is more over long term/chronic effects. These have been found in sulphur di-oxide (SO_2), Carbon Mono-oxide (CO), Nitrogen oxide (NO_2), Ozone (O_3), suspended particulates and non-methane hydrocarbons (NMHC) now referred to as volatile organic compounds (VOC). There is substantial evidence linking them to health effects at high concentrations. Three of them namely O_3, SO_2 and NO_2 are also known phytotoxicants (toxic to vegetation). Later Lead (Pb) was added to this list.

Ash Content

Thermal Power Stations in India, where poor quality of coal is used, add to environmental degradation problems through gaseous emissions, fly ash and bottom ash. Growth of manufacturing industries has further aggravated the situation. The fly ash generated in thermal power station causes many hazardous diseases like Asthma, Tuberculosis, etc.

Harmful Emissions and Other Pollutants

Nitrogen Oxide (NO_2)

Most of the NO_2 is emitted as NO which is oxidized to NO_2 in the atmosphere. All combustion processes are sources of NO_2 at the high temperature generated in the combustion process. Formation of NOX is due to thermal NO_2 which is the result of oxidation of nitrogen in the air due to fuel NO_2. Some of NO_2 are converted to NO_3 in the presence of O_2. Some of NO_2 is oxidized to NO_3, an essential ingredient of acid precipitation and fog. In addition, NO_2 absorbs visible light and in very high concentrations they can contribute to a brownish discoloring of the atmosphere.

Sulphur Oxide

The combustion of sulphur contained in fossil fuels, particularly coal is the primary source of SO_2, which is harmful. About 97 to 99% of SO_2 emitted from combustion sources is in the form of Sulphur Di-oxide which is a pollutant; the remainder is mostly SO_3, which in the presence of atmospheric water is transformed into Sulphuric Acid at higher concentrations. These produce deleterious effects on the respiratory system often leading to terminal diseases.

Low Quality imports of Coal

Large amount of imports are mostly from China which is of low quality leading to greater environmental hazards.

Water Pollution

In thermal power stations the source of water is river, lake, pond or sea from where water is usually used. There is possibility of water being contaminated from the source itself. Further contamination or pollution can increase by the pollutants of thermal power plant waste such as inorganic or organic compounds.

Land Degradation

The thermal power stations are generally located on the non-forest land and do not involve much Resettlement and Rehabilitation problems. However, the effects due to stack emission, etc., on flora and fauna, wild life sanctuaries and human life etc. need to be carefully evaluated for any adverse effects. One of the serious effects of thermal power is the dumping ground for ash disposal and hazardous elements that percolate to ground water through ash disposal in ash ponds. Due to enormous quantity of ash content in the Indian coal, it has been calculated that approximately 1 Acre per MW of installed thermal capacity is required for such ash disposal. International consultants have estimated that if this trend continues, by the year 2014-2015, nearly 1000 sq. km of land will be required for this extent of ash disposal only.

Noise Pollution

Noise pollution at Thermal Plants has become prominent these days since expansion of residential complexes have led to these being constructed near the plants themselves. Moreover, the workers inside the plant are all the time exposed to such hazardous noise pollution many a times making hearing impaired. Some areas inside the plant have noisy equipments such as crushers, belt conveyors, fans, pumps, milling plant, compressors, boiler, turbine, etc.

GO GREEN POLICY

It is recognized that industrialized countries are largely responsible for the historic build up of greenhouse gases in the atmosphere, and that developing countries need to expand their economies in order to meet social and development objectives. Therefore, China, India and other developing countries do not have quantified, binding emission reduction commitments for the period from 2008-2012. However, it was agreed that they still share a *'common but differentiated responsibility'* to reduce emissions.

The overall objective of the international climate regime is to achieve *"stabilization of greenhouse gas concentrations in the atmosphere at a level that would prevent dangerous anthropogenic (human) interference with the climate system"*. National emissions reduction obligations under the Kyoto Protocol (2005) range from 8% for the European Union to 7% for the United States, 6% for Japan, 0% for Russia and permitted increases of 8% for Australia and 10% for Iceland.

By July 2009, 186 countries ratified the protocol. Of these, 38 industrialized countries (plus the EU as a party in its own right) are required to reduce their emissions to the levels specified for each of them in the treaty. 145 developing countries have ratified the protocol, including Brazil, China and India, but have no reduction obligation.

In 2009 United Nations Climate Change Conference, was held commonly known as **the Copenhagen** Summit. The Copenhagen Accord was drafted by the US, China, India, Brazil and South Africa and judged a "meaningful agreement" by the United States government. It was "taken note of", but not "adopted", in a debate of all the participating countries and hence was not passed unanimously. At present, there is no formal, common mechanism for collecting and compiling coal-fired plant efficiencies and specific CO_2 emissions from the different regions of the world. There is hence need to define an all-inclusive methodology for the rationalization of reported plant efficiency values from different plants in different regions.

ENERGY POLICY OF INDIA

The **Energy Policy of India** is characterized by tradeoffs between four major drivers:

- Rapidly growing economy, with a need for dependable and reliable supply of electricity, gas and petroleum products;
- Increasing household incomes, with a need for affordable and adequate supply of electricity, and clean cooking fuels;
- Limited domestic reserves of fossil fuels, and the need to import a vast fraction of the gas, crude oil, and petroleum product requirements, and recently the need to import coal as well; and
- Indoor, urban and regional environmental impacts, necessitating the need for the adoption of cleaner fuels and cleaner technologies.

These trade-offs are often difficult to achieve. For example, the supply of adequate, yet affordable electricity generated and used cleanly is a continuing challenge because expansion of supply and adoption of cleaner technologies, especially renewable energy, often means that this electricity is too expensive for many Indians, particularly in rural areas.

In recent years, these challenges have led to a major set of continuing reforms and restructuring. The challenges in addressing energy security are numerous (managing market volatility; maintaining reserve stock, etc.) Along with this as seen above there is the continuing and glaring problem of the *hazardous effects of thermal power stations on the environment which requires immediate considerations.* Hence there is a need for an appropriate macro-economic policy framework that focuses on comprehensive plans to mitigate energy supply risks as well as environmental hazards.

ALTERNATIVE ENERGY REVOLUTION

Clean Coal Technologies

Clean coal technologies offer the potential for significant reduction in the environmental emissions when used for power generation. These technologies may be utilized in new as well as existing plants and are therefore, an effective way of reducing emissions in the coal fired generating units. Several of these systems are not only very effective in reducing SO_2 and NO_2 emissions but, because of their higher efficiencies they also emit lower amount of CO_2 per unit of power produced.

Blending of various grades of raw coal along with beneficiation will ensure consistency in quality of coal to the utility boilers. This approach assumes greater relevance in case of multiple grades of coals available in different parts of the country and also coals of different qualities being imported by IPPs. Ministry of Environment and Forests, June 1998 has stipulated the use of raw or blended or beneficiated coal with ash content of not more than 34% on an annual average basis. This has been imposed w.e.f. 1st June 2001.

Ministry of Coal, Ministry of Power, CEA and World Bank have constituted a Steering Committee to carry out cost benefit analysis of using clean coal technologies and assess and prioritize technically feasible and economically viable measures to improve coal quality.

Refurbishment of Existing Thermal Power Stations

Continuous deterioration in performance of thermal power stations has been observed since early 1980's. Therefore, Renovation and Modernization Schemes (R&M Schemes) were drawn and executed for improving the performance of existing thermal power stations. This being a capital-intensive activity, pollution control in these power stations has accounted for a large portion-around 40% of Rs. 12 Billion kept for R&M schemes under phase-I. During phase-I, 163 units of 34 thermal power stations have been covered. As a result of R&M schemes the thermal stations these have achieved 10,000 million units of additional generation per annum against the target of 7000 million units. Encouraged by the results achieved, R&M phase-II programme has been introduced.

Solar Thermal Technology

A number of solar thermal applications have been developed in India as a viable alternative, which include water/air heating, cooking, drying of agricultural and food products, water purification, detoxification of wastes, cooling and refrigeration, heat for industrial processes, and electric power generation. Most of the solar thermal devices and systems are manufactured in India. Evacuated tube collectors (ETC) are being used in one of the configurations of solar water heating systems which are being imported and marketed in the country by the solar thermal industry.

Other major renewable energy initiatives include:

1. installation of 1 million household solar water heating systems,
2. electrification by renewable mini-grids of 24,000 villages without electricity,
3. deployment of 5 million solar lanterns and 2 million solar home lighting systems,
4. establishment of an additional 3 million small biogas plants.

Solar heating systems to dry food and other crops can improve the quality of the product while reducing waste. Solar driers outclass traditional open-air drying and have lower operating costs than mechanized fuel-based driers. The three types of solar driers are natural convection, forced convection, and tent driers. A photovoltaic panel is being used to generate electricity for the fan. Tent driers combine the drying chamber and collector and allow for a lower initial cost. Drying times are not much lower than for open-air drying, but the main purpose is to provide protection from dust, dirt, rain, wind, and predators; tent driers are usually used for fruit, fish, coffee, or other products for which wastage is otherwise very high.

Geothermal Power

Indian geothermal power is another active renewable resources of energy in India that have the capacity to produce 10,600 MW of power – a figure which is five time greater than the combined power being produced from non-conventional energy sources such as wind, solar and biomass. With escalating environmental problems with coal based projects, India has to depend on clean, cheap, rural based and eco-friendly geothermal power for the future.

Geothermal power directly exploits the natural flow of heat from the ground. The accessible energy from natural decay of radioactive elements in the earth's crust, and mantle is roughly equal to that of incoming solar energy, particularly during the day. Oils from plants and seeds are often used as a replacement for non-renewable diesel. Methane is also considered as a renewable source of energy used in some Indian factories.

Geothermal is a domestic energy resource with cost, reliability and environmental advantages over other conventional energy sources. For generation of electricity, hot water is brought from the underground reservoir to the surface through production wells, and is flashed to steam in special vessels by release of pressure. The steam is separated from the liquid and fed to a turbine engine, which turns a generator. As a result of today's geothermal production, consumption of exhaustible fossil fuels is offset and has declined considerably, This has further reduced the release of acid-rain and greenhouse gases that are caused by fossil-fuel use. Systems for use of geothermal energy have proven to be extremely reliable and flexible.

The scope is immense but requires both public and private sector support. With increasing oil prices, the Gulf –Oil spill creating havoc both in ocean and on land, CO_2

emissions, threats to the climate and energy security, Energy Efficiency (EE) assumes a larger role and should have a higher priority than other energy sources. *EE contributes to reduced fossil fuel consumption, improved public health, induces commercial savings, and contributes to achievement of MDGs.* EE thus needs to be developed in a comprehensive manner, addressing both supply and demand side efficiencies. Concerted efforts from all concerned and policy support is required.

In its pursuance of sustainable energy development, the Government of India *needs to identify, define and separate economic, social and environmental policy objectives. There is a crucial need to reduce subsidies by central and state governments to the electricity sector.*

RENEWABLE VS. CONVENTIONAL FOSSIL FUELS

A Controversy

Some experts are of the opinion that Renewable energy technologies are still primitive compared to fossil fuels:

- While fossil fuel plants deliver hundreds of megawatts from a single site, renewable energy sources are still struggling in the realm of kilowatts.
- Renewable energy sources are not perennial as mistakenly perceived; wind and solar energy are intermittent while bio-mass and small hydro supplies are finite.
- While fossil fuel based electric power plants deliver capacity utilization ranging from seventy to ninety percent, the best that renewable energy sources can deliver is thirty percent. Only combustion plants (with their emission problems) can deliver sixty to seventy percent.
- Captive power plants using renewable energy sources do not save on costs. They are an additional financial burden for industries and would not come into being if power supply was regular and there was no load shedding.

Some critics believing in *'Trade-offs'* have even come to the conclusion that fossil fuel is the only alternative to normal electricity generation. It would be cheaper, in the long run, to provide electricity to rural communities through the conventional fossil fuel route than through renewable energy sources. Given the fact that India is exempt from the norms of the Kyoto Protocol when it comes to green house emissions, it would be foolhardy to initiate steps to move away from coal fired thermal plants – at least in the medium term. At a time when serious efforts are being made to reform the electric power sector letting market signals have a greater say, creating subsidy and grants driven islands of renewable energy would go against the grain.

These experts are of the opinion that "A single large combined-cycle gas plant can produce more electricity than all the wind and solar facilities in the United States combined…the 1875MW Teesside plant in England produces more electricity each year than the world's millions of solar panels and 30,000 wind turbines combined.... *In India the 2,100 MW coal fired plant of National Thermal Power Corporation at Korba in the new state of Chhattisgarh generates more electricity than all the capacities installed under wind, solar and bio-mass energy.* Quite simply, renewable energy sources are no match for fossil fuels when it comes to average installed capacity of a single plant".

However, the truth still remains and one cannot wish away the fact that in spite of all concerted efforts to completely do away the ill-effects emanating from Thermal power stations, the hazardous impact is still prevailing and affecting the environment adversely. Though, we have observed various contradictory views regarding renewable energy resources and fossil fuels, one has nevertheless to arrive at some compromise with *a judicious mix of both conventional and non-conventional energy sources for an emerging economy like India. A balance mix is required in the energy sector. Along with the traditional resources- thermal, hydro- electricity, the new areas of renewable energy resources are required to be exploited to get the best results and continuous availability of power supply.* In this the International experiences, particularly in the Wind and Solar power can become guiding force for our development. Further R & D in Bio-mass is required to make it commercially viable. In this again the emphasis on Public-Private partnership cannot be undermined. In this one can emulate international experiences, in particular the wind power and solar energies being exploited in Australia and other Western countries.

It can thus be concluded that both conventional and non-conventional renewable sources have their own standing in the development and generation of the power sector. However, since emerging countries like India would be requiring increased demand for power in the near future exploiting renewable resources in particular for domestic consumption can ease the strain on electricity demand.

REFERENCES

[1] Arun, T. and F. Nixson (2000). "The Reform of the Power Sector in India: 1991-1997." *Journal of Energy*, New Delhi.

[2] Balaji Reddy (2007). "Crude Oil and Natural Gas Reserves Divided between Two Superpower Blocks – Third World War Over Underwater Reserves?", *Economic Times.*

[3] Datta, M. (1961). "Electricity Supply in India and an Analysis of Power". *Census of India.*

[4] David, ed. (2005). "Global Experience with Electricity Reform", *Economic and Political Weekly*, December Issue.

[5] "Energy Infrastructure." (Winter 1998), *The Journal of Developing Areas* 32, 199-220.

[6] Govil, Keshavendra (2001). "Electricity Generation – Policy, Technology and Economy", New Delhi.

[7] Hans, Asha (1986). "The Power Sector in India", Sterling Publishers Private Limited, New Delhi.

[8] "Initiatives in India." *Energy Policy* (1996), 821-5.

[9] Karwa, D.V., J. Sathaye, A. Gadgil, M. Mukhopadhyay (1998). 'Energy Efficiency and Liberalisation and International Competition in India.' London: Sage Publications, 2001.

[10] Meyers, S.P. (1998). "Improving Energy Efficiency: Strategies for Supporting Sustained Energy". New Delhi.

[11] Ministry of Power (2004). "Widening Scope for Private Participation", Government of India. India's Electricity Sector.

[12] Pachauri, R.K. (2004). "Living with Coals: India's Energy Policy in the 21st Century." *Journal of Energy*. New Delhi.

[13] Parikh, Kirit (1998). "The Enron Story and its Lessons", *The Journal of International Trade & Economic Development & Participation.*

[14] "Shaping India's Power Industry. Emerging Policy" (1995). PHD *Chamber of Commerce and Industry*, pp. 981-90.

[15] Power Finance Corporation, *New Delhi – Annual Reports, 2008, 2009, 2010.*

[16] Prakash, Gyan (1999). "Another Reason. Science and the Imagination of Modern India". Princeton. Princeton University Press.

[17] Ranganathan, V. (1961). "Electricity Privatization Revisited: A Commentary on the Case for New Cases", *Registrar General, India and Ministry of Home Affairs*, New Delhi.

[18] Rugman, Jonathan (2000). "Power Failure". *Channel 4 News, Special Reports.*

[19] Santanu Guru (2002). "Renewable Energy Sources in India – Is It Viable?" *Working papers Series, Julius Simon Centre for Policy Research*, New Delhi.

[20] Shah, Maya (1951-77). *Growth, Productivity and Technical Progress in Electricity in India*, New Delhi.

[21] Smith, Thomas. "India's Electric Power Crisis: Why Do the Lights Go Out?" *Asian Survey* 33.

[22] Vivek Karandikar, Ashish Rana, Ravikumar Prekki, Prasanna Dani (2005). "Modeling Electricity Sector in India with Sub-regional Details Energy Research Group", Reliance Industries Ltd., Mumbai, India. Presentation at *International Energy Workshop 2005 Pa-lu-lu Plaza Kyoto,* Kyoto, Japan 5-7 July.

[23] *World Bank Operations Evaluation Department. OED Précis.* "Reforming India's Energy Sector", 2001.

Financial Systems and Their Role in the Development of Infrastructure Projects in India

Nilesh Rambabu Singh, Narinder Puri and Anil Kumar Sharma
Indian Institute of Technology, Roorkee
E-mail: nil23dce@iitr.ernet.in; krbmnpuri@yahoo.co.in; anilfdm@iitr.ernet.in

ABSTRACT

In India, infrastructure is the critical necessity to meet the growth requirement and development of every sector in economy. In this view financial system plays a very pivotal role in assisting the development process. It helps in proper channelization of funds crucial to the overall development of economy. The objective of this paper is to explore the Indian Financial System, to study the effectiveness of financial system in infrastructure development and finally to find out different avenues, policies, reforms and services beneficial to infrastructure development and construction industry in particular. The research addresses role of financial institution with respect to infrastructure development, though the results will be broadly relevant to all of architecture, engineering, construction and finance industry respectively.

Keywords: Financial Systems, Financial Institution, Financial Markets, Infrastructure

INTRODUCTION

'Infrastructures are usually considered to be necessary for industrialization, economic growth and overall development of the country' (Algarni, Arditi and Polat 2007, p. 729). 'In general, implementing infrastructure projects require a large capital investment and involves long payback period' (Shen and Wu 2005 study, cited in Algarni, Arditi and Polat 2007, p. 728). 'The roots of many construction problems could be better understood if they are examined within a broader institutional framework that includes not only the construction and property industries, but also the cluster of its related and supporting industries including banking and institutional investment sectors' (Chiang, and Tang 2003, cited in Chiang and Chang 2009, p. 834). In an earlier study, Ganesan et al. 1996, cited in Chiang and Chang 2009, p. 834 also examined the issue of how the productivity and performance of the construction industry were linked to its related and supporting sectors. In this view, *financial system* plays a very pivotal role in assisting the economic development process.

"Financial System" consists of institutional units and markets that interact, typically in a complex manner, for the purpose of mobilizing funds for investment, and providing facilities, including payment systems, for the financing of commercial activity (Financial System 2011a). Financial System broadly includes *endogenous and exogenous constituents,* where endogenous constituents are at the national level and exogenous constituents are at the international level. In general, "Financial Systems" can be considered as a group of interacting, interrelated and interdependent constituents forming a complex whole. It comprises of a set of complex and closely interconnected *financial institutions, financial markets, financial instruments, financial practices, financial services, financial transactions, auditing, tax system and finally the financial regulatory and legal bodies* (Financial System 2011b). 'Financial system plays a very important role in the overall development of a country. Through financial system, entire finances are channelized in such a way so that each sector of economy like industry, agriculture, and services can be well-developed' (Chugh 2005, p.4).

In India, physical infrastructure has emerged as the single biggest constraint to the country's attempts to achieve 9% – plus economic growth (Sikarwar 2011, p. 1). 'The *Confederation of Indian Industry (CII)* report 2007 on Infrastructure has identified the development of adequate infrastructure as the most critical prerequisite for sustaining the current growth momentum of the economy and to ensure inclusiveness of the economic growth process'. Generally, almost any sector of economy is dependent on the infrastructure facilities, which can be proactively developed and supported by the financial system. With infrastructures development in mind, this paper presents a brief overview of the '*Indian Financial System*' and its role in the infrastructure development. The results will be broadly relevant to the architecture, engineering, construction and finance industry as well.

LITERATURE REVIEW

Financial systems are one of the important supporting sectors to infrastructure development process and construction industry in particular. In this respect the following section presents a brief review of literature available on '*Indian Financial System*'. Shah and Patnaik 2011 presents a brief review of the current financial system, the difficulties involved, economic consequences of the financial policies, changes in financial system in recent decades and finally issues and policies. The workshop on Current development in India's financial System 2009 presents a report on (1) Global financial crisis: Indian and International perspectives, (2) Legal and regulatory framework for India's financial system and (3) Recent development in the Indian banking sector and Capital market. Merton and Bodie 2004 proposes a functional approach for designing and managing the financial systems of countries, regions, firms, households, and other entities. It is synthesis of the neoclassical, neo-institutional, behavioral perspectives. Merton provides a functional perspective on the dynamics of institutional and uses a series of examples to illustrate the breadth and depth of institutional change that is likely to occur. Rousseau and Sylla 2001 bring together two strands of the economic literature, i.e. on the finance-growth nexus and that on capital market integration and explore each strand through both institutional/country and formal quantitative analysis. Caballero and Krishnamurthy 2005 present a model of flight to quality episodes that emphasizes financial system risk and the Knightian uncertainty surrounding these episodes. Greenwood, Sanchez, and Wang, 2010 tries to answer the question, "how important is financial development for economic development'? A costly state verification model of financial intermediation is presented to address this question. Levine 2002 discusses the relative merits of banks based verses market-based financial system. The results indicate that although overall financial development is robustly linked with economic growth, there is no support for either the bank-based or market based view. Also recent researches argues that classifying countries as bank based or market is not a fruitful way to distinguish financial system. Giavazzi, and Giovannini 2010 reviews the factors that makes a financial system fragile and discuss the interaction between financial fragility and monetary policy. Ju and Wei 2008 try to answer the question "Does finance follows the real economy, or the other way around?" by developing a general equilibrium theory to unify the two competing school of thoughts. Hanson and Khathuria 1999 discuss the importance of incentives and legal, regulatory and supervisory issues in reform. Further, it briefly describes the history of India from financial repression to financial liberalization. Finally it summarizes the seven interrelated challenges India faces in its financial sector reforms. Cho 2001 discusses Indian Capital Market on recent development and policy issues. Morrisson and Pyle 1978 discusses the potential risk faced by financial institution such as, 1] credit risk, defaults or delays in repayments, 2] fraud, embezzlement or insider abuse, 3] liquidity risk or high cost of obtaining needed cash, 4] interest-rate risk, differential changes in the value of assets and liabilities as interest rates shift. The report concludes with a discussion of the regulatory implication of the study.

OBJECTIVE OF THE STUDY

Since the present study is related to *infrastructure development* and *financial system* it has the following key objectives:

1. To explore the '*Indian Financial System*' and it's various constituents.

2. To study the *effectiveness* of the Indian Financial System in the infrastructure development.
3. To find out different *avenues, initiatives, policies, reforms and services* beneficial to infrastructure development and construction industry in particular.

OVERVIEW OF INDIAN FINANCIAL SYSTEM

The main governing body of Indian Financial System is the *Ministry of Finance* which is an important ministry within the Government of India. It is concerned with *financial legislation, financial institutions, capital markets, center and state finances, union budget and taxation*. The following section presents a brief overview of the present 'Indian Financial System' which can be classified into different constituents.

Indian Financial Institutions

"Indian Financial Institution" consists of *banking institution, non-banking intuitions, development financial institutions, mutual funds, insurance companies' pension system and other public and/or private sector financial institution.* These financial institutions may be further referred to as public finance institutions, private financial institution or semi-governmental finance institutions. "Indian Banking Sector" consists of *Reserve Bank of India* (RBI) as the central bank of the country. It further includes *public (nationalized) and/or private sector banks, commercial bank, cooperative banks (scheduled and non-scheduled banks) development banks, investment banks, regional rural banks, merchant banks and foreign banks, etc.* Finally worth to mention is the *indigenous bankers,* which include individual bankers like Shroffs, Seths, Sahukars, Mahajans, etc. "Indian Non-banking Companies" have come into being in public sector as well as private sectors. Numerically most of them are in private sector. 'Nonbanking companies engage in various *funds based* as well as *non-fund based* activities' (Chandra 2006, p.35). "Indian Development Financial Institutions" consist of *All India institutions and State level institutions.* "Indian Mutual Funds Companies" consist of *public sector mutual funds and private sector mutual funds.* "Indian Insurance Companies" primarily consist of *public sector insurance companies and private sector insurance companies.* Public sector companies include Life insurance Company of India (LIC), General Insurance Company of India (GIC), etc. "Indian Pension System" comprises of three main components such as *Civil servant pension,* the mandatory program run by *Employee's provident fund organization of India* and the *unorganized pension sectors.* Finally, the other public and/or private sector financial institution includes variety of institutions such as *Finance associations, Finance advisories, Finance research institutes, Financial consultancies, Post office saving banks, Financial information services, Chamber of Commerce, Non-profit Organizations and Financial Societies, etc.*

Indian Financial Markets

The Indian Stock Exchanges which is also popularly known as the the '*Indian Share Market*' or '*Indian Stock Market*' consist of 23 stock exchange recognised by government under the *Securities Contract Regulation Act 1956*' (Chandra 2006, p. 215). The principle stock exchanges accounting for the bulk of the trading on the Indian Stock Market are *Bombay Stock Exchanges (BSE)* , *National stock Exchanges (NSE)*. In addition to this, there are *Regional Stock Exchanges* and *Commodity Exchange Markets.*

"Indian Financial Markets" can be broadly categorized into different sub-types such as *capital market, money market, commodity market, derivative market, future market, forward market, insurance market, foreign exchange market, spot market or cash market, and over-the counter market.* 'Indian Capital Market' usually provide long term financing and investment. "Indian Capital Markets" consist of '*Indian Stock Market*' (Indian Equity Market) and '*Indian Bond Market*' (Indian Debt Market). The Indian Stock market consist of *primary* and *secondary market,* new securities (IPO) are issued in the primary market and outstanding securities are traded in the secondary market. 'Indian Bond Market' consist of *wholesale debt market* and *retail debt market.* "Indian Money Market" provide short term financing and investment with original maturities of one year or shorter in time. 'Indian Derivatives Market' provides instruments for the management of financial risk. "Indian Futures Market" provides standardized forward contracts for trading products at some future date. 'Indian Forward Market' is the over-the-counter financial market in contracts for future delivery, so called forward contracts. 'Indian Commodity Market' facilitates the trading of commodities. It consists of both *retail and the wholesale market* in the country. 'Indian Commodity Market' facilitates multi-commodity exchange within and out the country based on requirement. 'Indian Spot Market' or "Cash market" is a public financial market, in which financial instruments or commodities are traded for immediate delivery. 'Over-the-Counter Market (OTC)' or "Off-Exchange Trading" is to trade various financial instruments directly between two parties. 'Indian Foreign Exchange Market', also known as the Forex or FX market facilitate the trading of foreign exchange. Finally the 'Indian Insurance Market' facilitates the redistribution of various risks.

Indian Financial Instruments

Financial Instruments can be basically categorized depending on the type of financial market it is being issued and traded. Further, categorization can be done on the basis of time, i.e. short, medium and long term. The 'Capital Market Instruments' take care of the borrower's long term needs. The varied types of Indian Capital Market Instruments are *equity, debt and hybrid securities.* The different equity instruments are *equity share, preference share, depository receipts such as GDRs/ADRs and warrants, etc.* The different debt instruments are *bonds, debenture and term loans, etc.* The hybrid instruments have both the features of equity and debt such as the *warrants, convertible debentures, etc.* The 'Money Market Instruments' take care of the borrower short-term needs and render liquidity to the lenders. The varied type of Indian Money Market instruments are *treasury bills (T-Bills), repurchase agreements, commercial papers (CP), certificate of deposit (CD), inter-bank term money, inter-corporate deposits (ICD), call/notice money and banker's acceptance, etc.*

The 'Indian Commodity Market instruments' include commodity trading such as *spot trading, forward contract, future contracts, commodity stocks, commodities index funds, physical commodities, hedging and delivery and condition trading, etc.* The 'Indian Derivative Market Instruments' include *common derivatives such as futures, options, forwards and swaps.* The other type of derivative instruments *are equity based derivative, debt based derivative, credit derivative, currency based derivatives, derivatives as insurance and derivative as speculative opportunities.* 'The most commonly traded derivative in Indian Market is *trade index futures, stock index future, stock futures, single stock futures, index options, stock index option, and stock options*' (Hull 2009, p. 313). The 'Foreign Exchange Instruments' is a standardized contract or security that has foreign exchange as the underlying asset. These Foreign exchange instruments are the *major spots, minor and exotic spots and options, etc.* Foreign exchange instruments includes traditional *forex instruments* such as FX swaps, spot, forward, *derivative instruments* such as currency swaps, options futures, *equity and debt instruments* such as ADR, GDR, Euro Bond, Foreign Bonds, etc. 'Insurance Markets Instruments' include *insurances plans, pension plans, insurance policy, insurance certificates, etc.* Finally 'Over-the Counter Market Instruments' generally include *interest rates forward and swap products, etc.*

Indian Financial Practices

'Financial Practices' are the standards, fundamentals, concepts, conventions, principles, norms, assumption, methods, classification, theoretical base and technology used in the financial context. The most common are *accounting practices, finance practices, banking practices, market practices, corporate practices, public finance practices, etc.* Accounting practices includes the *accounting principles which consist of accounting concepts and accounting conventions, accounting standards (AS-1 to AS-32), accounting period, book-keeping entry system such as single entry system and double entry-system, fair value accounting, FIFO and LIFO methods, Generally Accepted Accounting Principles GAAP, International Financial Reporting System IFRS and classification of accounts.* Generally, output of the accounting is input to Finance Management such as the *Trial Balance, Profit and Loss Account or Income statement, Statement of Owners Equity or Equity Statement, Balance sheet or Statement of financial Position, Cash flow Statements, etc.* The 'Finance Practices' are primarily concerned with the *Financial Analysis and Planning, Fundamental Valuations Concept, Capital Budgeting, Financing such as short term, medium term and long term financing, Capital Structure and Dividend Policies, Debt and Hybrid financing, Working Capital Management, Corporate Valuation, Restructuring and Value Creation Financial Risk Management and finally International Financial Management.*

'Banking Practices' includes the *general obligations* such as compliance with law, retention of rights, training and competency, etc., *disclosure* such as terms and conditions, operation of accounts, cost of credit and account suitability, etc., *principle of conduct* such as pre-contractual conduct, changes to terms and conditions, privacy and confidentiality, guarantees, etc., *the Resolution of disputes, monitoring and sanctions* such as internal dispute resolution, external dispute resolution, etc. (Code of Bank Practice 2003).

Indian Financial Services

'Financial Services' are the product and services offered by financial institutions like banks of various kinds for the facilitation of various financial transactions and other related activities like loans, insurance, investment opportunities and money management as well as providing information on the stock market and other issues like market trends' (Financial Services 2011). 'Financial service providers are banking and non-banking institutions, financial institutions, credit unions, credit cards companies, stock brokerage, financing companies, investment funds, insurance companies, leasing and factoring, mutual funds companies and some government sponsored enterprises agencies either carry out particular services and or several services' (Pandian 2009, p. 5). 'Indian Financial services' include *baking services, financing services, investment services, credit services, insurances services, foreign exchange services, auditing services and other financial services.* Banking services includes *money deposits, providing personal loans, commercial loans, mortgage loans, line of credit, payment system, retail banking, wholesale banking, investment banking, issuance of credit cards and debit cards, providing ATMs, providing transfer of funds, providing overdrafts guarantees and notary services* for financial and other documents. While non-banking financial services are fund based services as well as non-fund based services. The principle fund-based services are *leasing, hire purchase, microfinance and bill discounting,* the main non-fund based activities are *issue management, corporate advisory services, loan syndication, and forex advisory services* (Chandra 2006, p.35). Financing services include *personnel finance, consumer finance, project finance, corporate finance, etc.* Investment Services includes *asset management, hedge fund management and custody services, etc.* Insurance services include *insurance brokerage, insurance underwriting and reinsurance, etc.* Foreign Exchange Services includes *currency exchange, foreign currency banking, wire transfer and offshore banking, etc.* Auditing Services include services such as audit of *banks, financial institutions,*

PSUs, and public and private companies, management audit, tax audit, process/system audit internal and external audit, etc. The other financial services include *intermediations or advisory services, privately equity, venture capital, conglomerate and debt resolution, leasing, factoring, bill discounting, securitizations, venture capital, credit rating, mutual funds, merchant banking, Wealth management and Risk Management and Compliance,* etc.

Indian Financial Transactions

'Financial transaction' is transfer or exchange of money, funds, commodity or services between individuals, banks, financial institutions, financial markets corporates and businesses. Financial transactions can be inter-transaction or intra-transactions. The main factors of transactions are time, cost, mode, medium, speed and efficiency. The mediums of exchange are currencies such as banknotes, funds, cheques, drafts, bill of exchange, commercial papers, commodity money, electronic-money, etc. The most common type of transactions includes *purchase, loan, mortgage, bank account, credit-card, debit card, bill payment, net banking, insta-Alerts, phone banking and electronic fund transfers.*

INDIAN AUDIT PROCESS

Audit is the evaluation of a person, organization, system, process, enterprise, project or product. It is carried out for the verification of the financial statements of a legal entity, with a view to express an audit opinion. The audit opinion is a reasonable assurance that the accounting and financial statements are presented fairly, in all material respects, or give a true and fair view in accordance with the financial reporting framework. The organizations subject to auditing are Union and State Government departments including the Indian Railways, Defense, Posts and Telecommunications, Public commercial enterprises controlled by the Union and State governments, i.e. government companies and corporations, non-commercial autonomous bodies and authorities owned or controlled by the Union or the States bodies and authorities substantially financed from Union or State finances, notable among these are some of the local bodies and Panchayati Raj Institutions, and finally the banks, financial institutions, corporates, PSUs, and public and private companies, etc. In India, Comptroller and Auditor General of India (CAG) is the supreme audit intuition which includes The Indian Audit and Accounts Department (IA&AD) discharging duties mandated to it.

INDIAN TAX SYSTEM

'India has a well-developed taxation structure. The tax system in India is mainly a three tier system which is based between the Central Government, State Governments and the Local Government organizations. In most cases, these local bodies include the local councils and the municipalities' (Tax System in India 2011). The taxes are classified as *direct taxes* and *indirect taxes.* 'The Central Government levies direct taxes such as *personal income tax, capital gain tax and corporate tax*, and indirect taxes like *custom duties, excise duties, service tax and central sales tax, etc.* The states are empowered to levy state taxes such as *sales tax/VAT, etc.* In addition, there are some other state and local taxes applicable such as *octroi/ entry tax, stamp duty on asset transfer, property/building taxes, agriculture income tax, etc.* (Indolink 2011).

INDIAN FINANCIAL REGULATORY AND LEGAL BODIES

Finally, Regulatory bodies is the another important constituent of the financial system. The primary function of *regulatory authority is registering, regulating, providing guideline, issuing directions, promoting, prohibiting, calling for information and levying fees and other charges* (Machiraju, H., 2010, p. 229). It primarily includes Ministry of Finance (Government of India), Reserve Bank of India (RBI), Securities and Exchange Board Of India (SEBI), Insurance Regulatory and Development Authority (IRDA), Financial Services Appellate Tribunal (FSAT), National Stock Exchange (NSE), Bombay Stock Exchange (BSE), Foreign Investment Promotion Board (FIPB), Pension Fund Development Regulatory and Development Council (PFRDA), Financial Stability and Development Council (FSDC) and National Treasury and Management Agency (NTMA). There are also other government bodies which perform quasi-regulatory functions, including NABARD, NHB and DICGC. At the same time, voluntary association such as Foreign Exchange Dealers Association (FEDA) also assists in the regulatory functions.

There are also legal acts governing the Indian financial system such as the Reserve Bank of India Act 1938, Banking Regulation Act 1949, Securities Contracts (Regulation) Act 1956, Securities and Exchange Board of India Act 1992, Preference Shares (Regulation and Dividend) Act 2011, Financial Sector Law Reforms Commission 2011, Foreign Exchange Management Act 1999, Securitization and Reconstruction of Financial Assets and Enforcement of Security Interest Act 2002 and The Micro Finance Institutions (Development and Regulation) Bill, 2011.

INFRASTRUCTURE DEVELOPMENT IN INDIA

'Infrastructure projects in India are conceptualized and enacted at two distinct levels (1) at the *National Level* by the *Union Government* or its affiliated agencies, and (2) at the *State Level* by the respective *State Governments* or their associated nodal agencies' (Mahalingam 2010, p. 419). The apex body in the union government includes the Prime Minister's Office (PMO), Cabinet Secretariat, and Planning Commission, etc. *Prime Minister's Office (PMO)* consists of Advisor to the Prime Minister on Public Information

Infrastructure and Innovations, National Advisory Council (NAC), National Innovation Council (NIC). *Cabinet Secretariat* consists of various Cabinet Minister, Minister of State, Cabinet Committees, etc. Cabinet Committees consists of important committees such as the Cabinet Committee on Infrastructure (CCI), Public–Private Partnership Appraisal Committee (PPPAC), Cabinet Committee on Economic affairs (CCEA), etc. *Planning Commission* consists of Secretariat for Infrastructure, Economic Advisor Council to the Prime Minister. The different ministries in the union government which are directly or indirectly associated with the infrastructure development process includes various *departments, directorates, attached offices, subordinate offices, autonomous bodies, societies, academics/institution, companies, boards/ undertaking, bureaus, commission, committees, mission, council, regional offices, field offices, secretariat, statutory bodies, constitutional bodies, independent department, regulatory authorities, advisory bodies, arbitration bodies, projects, programmes, affiliated organizations, PSU's/joint ventures, division, unit, wings, and banks and financial institutions, etc.*

The apex body in the state government includes the Chief Minister's Office (CMO) and in union territories includes the Administrator. The different ministries in the state government which are directly or indirectly associated with the infrastructure development process includes various *departments, directorates, attached offices, subordinate offices, autonomous bodies, societies, academics/institutions, companies, boards/undertakings, bureaus, commissions/ committees/missions, administrative units, councils, regional /field offices, districts, revenue divisions, tallukas, panchayat unions, revenue villages, municipalities/council/boards, town panchayats, secretariats, statutory/constitutional bodies, projects/programmes, affiliated organizations, PSUs/joint ventures, divisions/unit/wings, zilla/talluka/village, panchayat, municipal corporations, banks and financial institutions and other various bodies, etc.* Besides the union and state government bodies there are standing committees, advisory committees, Ad-Hoc committees and cells in the respective parliamentary houses like Lokshaha (house of people) and Rajyashaba (council of state) Apart from the Government organization there private *companies, associations, institutes, and organizations* at national and international level such as the construction, design, architecture, engineering, real estate, contractors, consultancies, equipment, machinery, cement, steel and other material, labour, suppliers and various other construction related entities *(for a more comprehensive and detailed information refer* to the sites http://goidirectory. nic.in/union_index.php & http://www.fundoodata.com/).

EFFECTIVENESS OF FINANCIAL SYSTEMS IN INFRASTRUCTURE DEVELOPMENT

Financial System plays an important role in supporting the emergence and development of infrastructure projects. The *effectiveness* of the financial system is the ability to produce a decided, decisive or desired effect towards achieving the growth and economic development. The main feature of the financial system includes the required institutional framework for the proper functioning of its various constituents. In infrastructure development context effectiveness of financial system can be termed as the proper channelization of funds across the different sectors. Further effectiveness can be termed as the provision of various institutional setups and needed facilities. The key variables in measuring the effectiveness of financial system are the indicator, integration, inclusion, outreach, harmonization, flexibility, liquidity, coherence, accessibility, sustainability, stability, resilience, clarity, efficiency, channelization, regulation, enablers, mechanism, visibility, technology, visibility, network, information system, awareness, etc.

Indicator is any group of statistical values that is taken together to give the health of the financial system. *Integration* is the extent of functioning of the various constituents of the financial system as a unified whole. *Inclusion* is the delivery of financial services at an affordable cost to every section of society, business and economy. *Outreach* is to reach out to every section of society, business and economy. *Harmonization* is to bring in consonance or accord to form a congruent or consistent arrangement of the different constituents of financial system. It also includes creating common standards across the whole system. *Flexibility* is the capability of the financial system to adapt to new, different or changing requirement or to respond to potential internal and external changes affecting its value delivery in a timely and cost-effective manner. *Liquidity* is the ability of the financial system to convert it covert into cash. *Coherence* of the financial system is the systematic or logical connection or consistency of the different constituents. *Accessibility* of the financial system is the capability to be reached or easy to communicate or deal with. *Sustainability* is the capability of the financial system to provide services and standards according to the long term plan without the need to increase rates or reduce services. *Stability* of the financial system is described as the condition where the financial intermediation process functions smoothly and there is confidence in the operation of key financial institutions and market within the economy. *Resilience* is the ability of the Financial System to regain or recover from or adjust easily to adverse situation such as the recession. *Clarity* in financial system enables its customer to simplify their operation with an integrated, modular solution to optimize and automate core operational processes to manage network build and movements, develop and sell next generation products, and deliver and assure the quality of customer services. *Efficiency* of the financial system is the capability of interacting, transacting and transferring of funds between different interrelated and interdependent constituents in a smooth and speedy way. *Channelization* of the financial system is the ability of the financial system to transfer funds from surplus to deficit units. *Regulation* is the mechanism of the financial system to adjust to different adverse condition. *Enablers* in the financial system are the means knowledge or opportunity to make possible, practical or easy to deal with. *Mechanism* is the fundamental processes involved in or responsible for action, reaction and other natural phenomenon. *Visibility* in the financial system is the ability to see various opportunities and threat. *Network* is the interconnection between the different constituents and parts of the system with latest technology, equipment's and facilities, etc. *Information system* is the instrument that combines interrelated interacting constituents to work as a coherent entity. *Technology* is the making, usage and knowledge of tools, techniques, systems or methods of organization in order to solve a problem or serve some purpose. *Awareness* in the financial system is the knowledge of different constituents and their functions.

AVENUES, INITIATIVES, POLICIES, SERVICES AND REFORMS BENEFICIAL TO INFRASTRUCTURE DEVELOPMENT

Infrastructure projects in India are classified based on the size of investment as *Mega, Major and Medium project* (Narayan, 2005). The infrastructure sector can be classified according to the various sectors such as the *power and energy, railways, ports, civil aviation, road, telecommunication, communication & information technology, environment and forest, water resources oil and gas pipelines and other sectors, etc.*, at the Center and the State level. The center is classified on the basis of different zones such as the north, east, west, south, north-eastern, north-western, south-eastern, south-western, etc. The state is classified into division which includes several districts, city, town, *talluka and village.* Further classification is done on the basic of region such as *border, coastal, urban or rural, etc.*

The different avenues available for infrastructure development include the banks, financial institution, investment, development and finance corporations at the Center, State, Urban and Rural level. Among the different institutions includes the India Infrastructure Finance Company Limited (IIFC), Industrial Development Bank of India (IDBI), Industrial Finance Corporation of India (IFCI), Industrial Investment Bank of India (IIBI), Shipping Credit and Investment Company of India Ltd. (SCICI), Housing and Urban Development Corporation Ltd. (HUDCO), Indian Renewable Energy Development Agency Ltd. (IREDA), Insustrial Credit and Investment Corporation of India (ICICI), Power Finance Corporation Ltd (PFC), Rural Electrification Corporation Ltd (REC), Indian Railways Finance Corporation Ltd (IRFC), Infrastructure Development Finance Co. Ltd (IDFC), Infrastructure Leasing and Finance Company (IL&FS), Housing Development Finance Corporation (HDFC), Non-Lapsable Centre Pool of Resources (NLCPR), National Bank for Agriculture and Rural Development (NABARD), Rural Development Bank (RDB), National Housing Bank (NHB), Small Industries Development Bank of India (SIDBI), The Export Import Bank of India (Exim Bank), Unit Trust of India (UTI), Life Insurance Corporation of India (LIC), General Insurance Corporation of India (GIC), Risk Capital and Technology Finance Corporation Ltd.

(RCTC), Securities Trading Corporation of India Ltd. (STCI), Discount and Finance House of India Ltd. (DFHI), Technology Innovation Management and Entrepreneurship Information Service (TIME IS), Tourism Finance Corporation of India Ltd. (TFCI), North-East Region Development Financial Corporation (NEDFi), State Financial Corporations (SFCS), State Industrial Investment/Development Corporations (SIDCS), Urban and Rural Development Financial Corpoations, Asset leasing, Assets Based Securitisation, Hedge funds, Pension Funds and Mutual Funds Compnies, etc. There are also International financial institutions most prominent among them are the International Bank of Reconstruction and Development (IBRD), International Development Association (IDA), International Monetary Fund (IMF), Asian Development Bank (ADB), International Bank of Reconstruction and Development (IBRD), International Development Association (IDA), International Finance Corporation (IFC), International Monetary Funds (IMF), Organization for Economic Corporation (OECD), United Nations Development Programme (UNDP) and United Nations Industrial Development Organisation (UNIDO) and the World Bank Group, etc. The other avenues include the banks, financial institutions and stock markets around the world.

There are several *infrastructure development initiatives* such as the India Infrastructure Project Development Fund (IIPDF), India Development Fund (IDF), Infrastructure Development Fund (IDF), Infrastructure Debt Funds (IDF), Rail Development Fund (RDF), Central Road Fund (CRF). Power Development Funds (PDF), Regional Infrastructure Development Funds (RDF), Urban Development Fund (UDF) and Rural Infrastructure Development Fund (RIDF), etc. The other funds include the Institutional Development Funds (IDF) initiated by the World Bank. The different type of Infrastructure financing techniques includes Public Private Partnership (PPP), Viability Gap Funding (VGF), Special Purpose Vehicle (SPV), Build Operate Transfer (BOT) and its variants such as the BOT, BOO, BLT, BOOM, BOOT, BOOTT, BTO, DBFO, DBO, DBOM, DOB, ROO, ROT, etc. Some center based enforcement agencies include Central Integrated Action Plan (IAP), Technical Advisory group of Unique Projects (TAGUP). Some center based programmes includes Accelerated Irrigation Benefit Programme, Accelerated Urban Water Supply Programme, Accelerated Rural Water Supply Programme.. There are scheme's such as Ten Year tax Holiday for core sector namely road, highways, waterways, water supply, sanitation and solid waste management system. The five year tax holiday telecom sector namely the telecommunication, internet service providers and broadband networks. Tax incentives for the investors providing long-term finance or investing in the equity capital of the enterprises engaged in infrastructure facility (Kapila, 2004, pp. 547-591).

There are several policies which are beneficial to Infrastructure development process are Company Policy, Industrial policy, Economic Development Vision Policy, Industrial Infrastructure Development Policy, Communication and Information Policy, Energy Policy of India, Environment Policy, Foreign Trade Policy, Exim Policy, Housing Policy, Economic Policy, Regulatory Policy, Information Policy, Monetary Policy, Transportation Policy, Urban Policy, Rural Policy and Water Policy, etc. There are other sectors-wise policies in infrastructure sector for highway, Railways, Ports, Airports, Telecom and Power, etc. (for a more detailed information refer to http://infrastructure.gov.in/).

The various services for the infrastructure development includes visioning, documemntation, finance, magemenment, consultancy, technology, project management, project development, project implementation, project finance, investment banking, private equity, trust & fiduciary, auto infrastrucure, execution, depository, custodian & proffessional clearing sevices and other financial assistance required during the projet cycle.

The various reforms in the Infrastructure Sector include the Regulatory Framework for the Infrastructure Sector in India, Power sector reforms such as the Central Electricity Regulatory Commission, State Electricity Regulatory Commission, Civil Aviation sector reforms such as the Airport Economic Regulatory Authority (AERA) and the Draft Regulatory Reform Bill 2009 for infrastructure sector. The key provision for the draft bill includes the institutional framework for regulatory commissions, their role and functions. Water resources sector reforms such as State Water Resources Regulatory Authorities, Port sector reforms such as Port Regulatory Authority Bill 2011 are proposed before parliament.

DISCUSSION AND CONCLUSION

The role of financial system within an economy is primarily proper channelization of funds from surplus to deficit units, to intermediate between those that provide funds and those that need funds, and finally to transform, manage and mitigate risk. Financial system provides a medium within which financial claims can be traded under established rules of conduct which facilitate the management and transformation of financial risk. Further financial system can be described as an example of system evolved through a *spontaneous order.* More specifically it can be regarded as a complex system composed of interconnected parts that as a whole exhibit one or more properties. Much of the events in the financial system are supervenient event. A systems complexity may be of one or two form disorganized complexity or organized complexity. In essence disorganized complexity is a matter of a very large number of parts, and organized complexity is a matter of the subject system exhibiting emergent properties. Where emergence is the way the financial system has arisen out of a multiplicity of relative lively simple interaction. Here, Emergence is central to the understanding of the financial system from the perspectives of theories of *integrative levels* and *complex system.* While the financial system has evolved out of spontaneous order, there are patterns of systematic planning such as evolution of Banking System started by the direct intervention of the government in 1930 which led to the establishment of Reserve Bank of India (RBI) in 1934. The nationalization of banks during 1969 and 1980, Liberalization and introduction of internationally accepted banking practices in 1992, development of appropriate regulatory framework in 1998 for the derivative trading and second generation financial sector reforms of 2008, etc.

The financial markets are overwhelmed by the information asymmetries and resulting coordination problems and a strong regulatory structure to maintain the health of the system is inevitable. 'India has witnessed a considerable development in the credit and capital markets both from regulatory and legal perspective. It has deepened and more integrated globally' (Current development in India's financial market 2009, p.4). The phenomenal success story of the capital market can be attributed to the cautious regulation and reforms such as establishing the Securities and Exchange Board of India (SEBI) in 1992, the alternative National Stock Exchange (NSE) and number of reforms such as dematerialization, screen based trading and so on. Indian equity market has come to have a dominant role in Indian finance. The financing of firm has shifted away from debt to equity (Current Development in India's Financial System 2009, p.18). For a long time, government funding is the main source of financing for large infrastructure projects. Apart from government funding raising funds from capital or money market has become an alternative source of financing. Bond is one of the most popular debt finance instrument in developed countries such as US and UK. Nevertheless it is a challenging task as far as the Asian arena is concerned since the bond markets are not as mature (Lam, Chiang and Chan 2011). Rangarajan 2011 asserts the importance of an appropriate financing mechanism for infrastructure projects which includes developing a vibrant corporate debt market.

Governments has put in public domain a Draft Regulatory Reform Bill 2009 for infrastructure sector which aims at setting up commissions to oversee the regulations in infrastructure sectors and are expected to result in a faster decision making regime. Initiative like Central Integrated Action Plan, India Infrastructure Project Development Fund (IIPDF), Infrastructure Debt Funds (IDF) and Infrastructure Development Fund (IDF) are definitely positive steps toward infrastructure development. Further"Reforms in infrastructure sectors would not only imply regulatory reforms, but would require developing market structure for introduction of competition, allowing more players other than public-owned entities, and undertaking financial sector reforms (Sarkar and Srivastava 2002).

While there are different set of financial institutions available still there is requirement of more sophisticated institutions. Gopinath 2011 asserts the need of more financial institutions with financial inclusion and competition as important criteria in the policy.

Further, for proper circulation of finances there is a need to develop a systematic *Recovery Mechanism*, which will facilitate the individual, companies, project and programs for repayment of their financial obligations. With respect to this, in-depth study is required 1] between the interfaces of the different constituents of the financial system, 2] between the interfaces of the different sector of the economy, 3] between the interfaces of the different constituents of financial system and different sectors of the economy 4] study for measurement of effectiveness of financial system and 5] restructuring of the financial system into a well-defined constituents, functions and responsibilities. These studies would facilitate the planning process and growth momentum in the country.

REFERENCES

[1] Algarni, A.M., Arditi, D. and Polat, G., 2007, 'Build-Operate-Transfer in Infrastructure Projects in the United States', *Journal of Construction Engineering and Management,* vol. 133, no. 10, pp. 728-735.

[2] Caballero, R. and Krishnamurthy, A., 2005, 'Financial System Risk and Flight to Quality', *National Bureau of Economic Research,* Massachusetts Avenue, Cambridge, Working Paper 11834.

[3] Chandra, P., 2006, 'Financial Management, Theory and Practice', Sixth Edition, Tata McGraw-Hill Publishing Company Limited, New Delhi.

[4] Chiang, Y.H. and Cheng, E.W.L., 2009, 'Perception of Financial Institutions Towards Financing PFI Projects in Hong Kong', *Journal of Construction Engineering and Management,* vol. 135, no. 9, pp. 833-840.

[5] Cho, Y.J., 2000, 'Indian Capital Markets, Policy and Issues', *Graduate of School of International Studies,* Sogang University, Seoul, Korea.

[6] Chugh, P., 2005, 'Indian Banking Today, Impact of Reforms', Kanishka Publishers, Distributors, New Delhi.

[7] Code of Bank Practice 2003, Australian Bankers Associations', <www. bankers.asn.au>.

[8] Current Developments in India's Financial System 2009,'Workshop on Current Developments in India's Financial System', Inwent Capacity Building International Germany, Federal Ministry for Economic Cooperation and Development, viewed on 26 May 2011, < http://www.icrier.org/pdf/ICRIERapr il09inet.pdf >.

[9] Financial System 2011a, 'Glossary of Statistical Terms OECD', viewed on 25 May 2011, <http://stats. oecd.org /glossary/detail.asp?ID=6189>.

[10] Financial System 2011b, *Wikipedia*, viewed on 26 May 2011, < http:// en.wikipedia.org/wiki/Financial_ system>.

[11] Giavazzi, F. and Giovannini, 2010, 'Central Banks and the Financial System', *National Bureau of Economic Research,* Massachusetts Avenue, Cambridge, Working Paper 16228,

[12] Greenwood, J., Sanchez, J. and Wang, C., 2010, 'Quantifying the Impact of Financial Development on Economic Development', *National bureau of Economic Research,* Massachusetts Avenue, Cambridge, Working Paper 15893.

[13] Gopinath, S., 2011, 'One Can't Work on a Template at RBI', ET Exclusive Q&A, *Economics Times*, 21 June, p. 14.

[14] Hanson, J. and Khathuria, S., 1999, 'Indian Financial System: The Challenges of Reform', Oxford University Press, New Delhi, India.

[15] Hull, J., 2009, 'Options, Futures and Other Derivatives', Seventh Edition, Pearson Prentice Hall, New Delhi.

[16] Indolink 2011, 'Indian Tax System 2011', viewed on 18 June 2011, <http://www.indolink.com/Consulate/i ebo /tax.htm>.

[17] Ju, J. and Wei, S., 2008, 'When is Quality of Financial System a Source of Comparative Advantage?', *National Bureau of Economic Research,* Massachusetts Avenue, Cambridge, Working Paper 13984.

[18] Kapila, U., 2004, 'Indian Economy Since Independence', New and Revised Fifteen Edition, Academic Foundation, New Delhi.

[19] Lam, P.T.I., Chiang, Y.H. and Chan, S.H., 2011, 'Critical Success Factors for Bond Financing of Construction Projects in Asia', *Journal of Management in Engineering,* Article in press.

[20] Levine, R., 2002, 'Bank Based or Market Based Financial System: Which is Better?', *National Bureau of Economic Research,* Massachusetts Avenue, Cambridge, Working Paper 9138.

[21] Machiraju, H., 2010, 'Indian Financial System', Fourth Edition, Vikas Publishing House Pvt Ltd., New Delhi.

[22] Mahalingam, A., 2010, 'PPP Experiences in Indian Cities: Barriers, Enablers, and the Way Forward', *Journal of Construction Engineering and Management,* vol. 136, no. 4, pp. 419-429.

[23] Merton, R., 1995, 'Financial Innovation and the Management and Regulation of Financial Institutions', *National Bureau of Economic Research,* Massachusetts Avenue, Cambridge, Working Paper 5096.

[24] Merton, R. and Bodie, Z., 2004, 'The Design of Financial System: Towards a Synthesis of Function and Structure', *National Bureau of Economic Research,* Massachusetts Avenue, Cambridge, Working Paper 10620.

[25] Morrisson, J. and Pyle, D., 1978, 'Interest Rate Risk and the Regulation of Financial Institutions', *National Bureau of Economic Research,* Massachusetts Avenue, Cambridge, Working Paper 266.

[26] Murgude, G. and Topkar, V., 2006, 'Model For Design Of Capital Structure and Concession Period of BOT Project', M-Tech Civil Dissertation, Veermata Jijabai Technological Institute, Mumbai 19, Autonomous Institute Affiliated to University of Mumbai.

[27] Narayan, J., 2005, 'Contract Management is the Key to Project Management', *Vision to Reality, V2R–The Project Management Way,* 19th IPMA World Congress 2005, New Delhi India.

[28] Pandian, P., 2009, 'Financial Services and Markets', Vikas Publishing House Pvt Ltd, New Delhi.

[29] Rangarajan, C., 2011, 'Give Banks License to Non-Corporates First', *Economics Times,* 11 July, p. 1.

[30] Rousseau, P. and Sylla, R., 2001, 'Financial System, Economic Growth and Globalization', *National Bureau of Economic Research,* Massachusetts Avenue, Cambridge, Working Paper 8323.

[31] Sarkar, S. and Srivastava, L. 2002, 'Reforms in the Infrastructure Sectors: Next Steps', *Proceedings of the National Conference* held from 28 to 29 November 2001 in New Delhi, Tata Energy Research Institute, New Delhi, India.

[32] Shah, A. and Patnaik, I., 2011, 'Reforming the Indian Financial System', *National Institute of Public Finance and Policy,* New Delhi, viewed on 26 May, <http://www.nipfp.org.in>.

[33] Sikarwar, D., 2011, 'Infrastructure Debt Funds to Roll Out Soon', *Economics Times,* 3 January, p. 1.

[34] Tax System in India 2011, 'India Business Directory, *Business Maps of India*', viewed on 15 June 2011, <http://business.map sofindia.com/india-market/ com modity.html>.

Globalization: Is the Labour Market Falling Behind the Global Consumer Market?

Sankha Dip Datta and Sayantan Banerjee
Institute of Management Technology, Nagpur
E-mail: sankha2399@gmail.com; sayantanbnrj@gmail.com

SECTION 1: SOCIOECONOMIC POLICIES

HUMAN RESOURCE MANAGEMENT

- Refers to the activities an organization carries out to use its human resources effectively
- Four major tasks of HRM
  - Staffing policy
  - Management training and development
  - Performance appraisal
  - Compensation policy

International Human Resource Management

- Strategic role: HRM policies should be congruent with the firm's strategy and it's formal and informal structure and controls
- Right People, Right Place, Right Time
- Task complicated by profound differences between countries in labor markets, culture, legal and economic systems

Basic Steps in International HRM

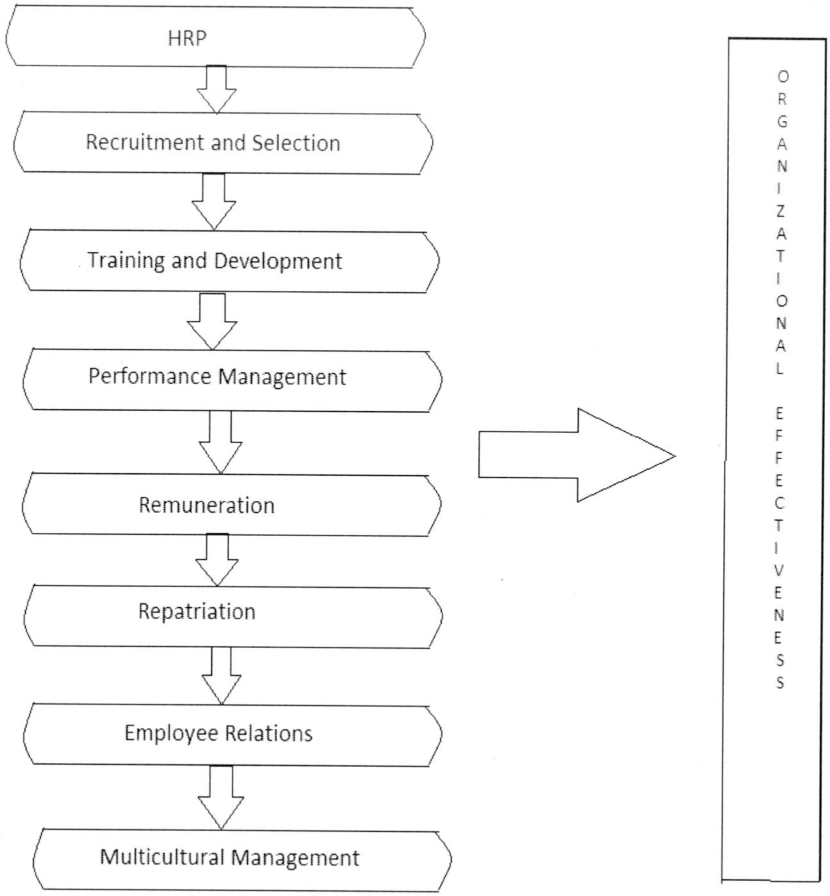

International Businesses have Choices of Hiring Three Categories of Employees

- PCNs – Parent Country Nationals
  The employees working in the country of the company belonging to some other countries.
- HCNs – Host Country Nationals
  Employees of same country where the company belongs to.
- TCNs – Third Country Nationals
  Employees working in a country other than their home country with the headquarters of the company in some third country.

Strategy, Structure and Control Systems

Structure and Controls	International Strategy			
	Multidomestic	**International**	**Global**	**Transnational**
Centralization of operating decisions	Decentralized	Core competency centralized Rest decentralized	Some centralized	Mixed centralized and decentralized Informal matrix
Horizontal differentiation	Worldwide area structure	Worldwide product division	Worldwide product division	Informal matrix
Need for coordination	Low	Moderate	High	Very high
Integrating mechanisms	None	Few	Many	Very many
Performance ambiguity	Low	Moderate	High	Very high
Need for cultural controls	Low	Moderate	High	Very high

STAFFING POLICY

- Staffing policy
  - Selecting individuals with requisite skills to do a particular job
  - Tool for developing and promoting corporate culture
  - View People as Resource ($in profit out)
- Types of Staffing Policy
  - Ethnocentric
  - Polycentric
  - Geocentric

Ethnocentric Policy

- Key management positions filled by parent-country nationals
- Advantages:
  - Overcomes lack of qualified managers in host nation
  - Unified culture
  - Helps transfer core competencies (and skills back)
- Disadvantages:
  - Produces resentment in host country
  - Can lead to cultural myopia

Polycentric Policy

- Host-country nationals manage subsidiaries
- Parent company nationals hold key headquarter positions

- Best suited to multi-domestic businesses
- Advantages:
  - Alleviates cultural myopia
  - Inexpensive to implement
  - Helps transfer core competencies
- Disadvantages:
  - Limits opportunity to gain experience of host-country nationals outside their own country.
  - Can create gap between home-and host-country operations.

Geocentric Policy

- Seek best people, regardless of nationality
  - not always possible
- Best suited to Global and trans-national businesses
- Advantages:
  - Enables the firm to make best use of its human resources
  - Equips executives to work in a number of cultures
  - Helps build strong unifying culture and informal management network
- Disadvantages:
  - National immigration policies may limit implementation
  - Expensive to implement due to training and relocation
  - Compensation structure can be a problem.

Comparison of Staffing Approaches

Staffing Approach	Strategic Appropriateness	Advantages	Disadvantages
Ethnocentric	International	Overcomes lack of qualified managers in host nation Unified culture Helps transfer core competencies	Produces resentment in host country Can lead to cultural myopia
Polycentric	Multidomestic	Alleviates cultural myopia Inexpensive to implement	Limits career mobility Isolates headquarters from foreign subsidiaries
Geocentric	Global and transnational	Uses human resources efficiently Helps build strong culture and informal management network	National immigration policies may limit implementation Expensive

THE EXPATRIATE PROBLEM

- Expatriate: citizens of one country working in another
  - Expatriate failure: premature return of the expatriate manager to his/her home country
  - Cost of failure is high: estimate = 3X the expatriate's annual salary plus the cost of relocation (impacted by currency exchange rates and assignment location)
- Inpatriates: expatriates who are citizens of a foreign country working in the home country of their multinational employer

Expatriate Failure Rates

Recall Rate Percent	Percent of Companies
U.S. multinationals	
20–40%	7%
10–20	69
<10	24
European multinationals	
11–15%	3%
6–10	38
<5	59
Japanese multinationals	
11–19%	14%
6–10	10
<5	76

Reasons for Expatriate Failure

- **US multinationals**
  - Inability of spouse to adjust
  - Manager's inability to adjust
  - Other family problems
  - Manager's personal or emotional immaturity
  - Inability to cope with larger overseas responsibilities
- **European multinationals**
- Inability of spouse to adjust
- **Japanese Firms**
  - Inability to cope with larger overseas responsibilities
  - Difficulties with the new environment
  - Personal or emotional problems
  - Lack of technical competence
  - Inability of spouse to adjust.

Expatriate Selection

- Reduce expatriate failure rates by improving selection procedures

- An executive's domestic performance does not (necessarily) equate his/her overseas performance potential
- Employees need to be selected not solely on technical expertise but also on cross-cultural fluency.

Four Attributes that Predict Success

- Self-Orientation
  - Possessing high self-esteem, self-confidence and mental well-being
- Others-Orientation
  - Ability to develop relationships with host-country nationals
  - Willingness to communicate
- Perceptual Ability
  - The ability to understand why people of other countries behave the way they do
  - Being nonjudgmental and being flexible in management style
- Cultural Toughness
  - Relationship between country of assignment and the expatriate's adjustment to it.

TRAINING AND MANAGEMENT DEVELOPMENT

- Training: Obtaining skills for a particular foreign posting
  - Cultural training : Seeks to foster an appreciation of the host-country's culture
  - Language training : Can improve expatriate's effectiveness, aids in relating more easily to foreign culture and fosters a better firm image
  - Practical training: Ease into day-to-day life of the host country.
- Development: Broader concept involving developing manager's skills over his or her career with the firm
  - Several foreign postings over a number of years
  - Attend management education programs at regular intervals

Repatriation of Expatriates

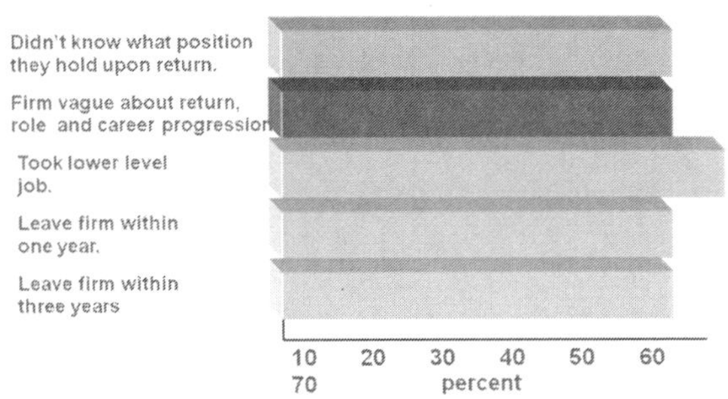

Management Development and Strategy

- Development programs designed to increase the overall skill levels of managers through:
  - On going management education.
  - Rotation of managers through a number of jobs within the firm to give broad range of experiences.
- Used as a strategic tool to build a strong unifying culture and informal management network.

  Above techniques support transnational and global strategies.

PERFORMANCE APPRAISAL

- Problems: Unintentional bias
  - Host-nation biased by cultural frame of reference
  - Home-country biased by distance and lack of experience working abroad.
- Expatriate managers believe that headquarters unfairly evaluates and under appreciates them.
- In a survey of personnel managers in U.S. multinationals, 56% stated foreign assignment either detrimental or immaterial to one's career.

Guidelines for Performance Appraisal

- More weight should be given to onsite manager's evaluation as they are able to recognize the soft variables
- Expatriate who worked in same location should assist home-office manager with evaluation
- If foreign on-site managers prepare an evaluation, home-office manager should be consulted before completion of formal the terminal evaluation.

COMPENSATION

- Two issues:
  - Pay executives in different countries according to the standards in each country? or Equalize pay on a global basis?
  - Method of payment

Compensation for 4 Positions in 26 Countries

	CEO	HR Director	Accountant	Mfg. Employee
Argentina	$860,704	$326,874	$63,948	$17,884
Australia	646,316	235,316	57,129	29,703
Belgium	655,390	286,222	63,883	34,336
Brazil	597,454	287,683	44,605	10,480
Canada	742,228	188,070	44,866	36,289
China (Shanghai)	93,393	58,278	14,552	3,021
France	540,260	224,112	69,554	34,741
Germany	421,622	189,785	61,375	36,934
Hong Kong SAR	635,186	211,321	56,711	16,691
Italy	567,685	254,138	59,388	29,469
Japan	545,233	235,536	59,107	51,997
Malaysia	350,558	130,771	24,522	7,453
Mexico	648,695	239,028	41,582	14,302
Netherlands	621,153	217,142	48,838	27,892
New Zealand	258,114	111,803	38,382	15,931
Singapore	621,871	239,376	51,733	16,912
South Africa	406,263	179,268	43,234	7,974
South Korea	194,421	109,637	41,365	17,904
Spain	399,423	196,305	56,332	22,746
Sweden	440,265	166,312	43,438	32,564
Switzerland	448,422	175,008	66,121	41,104
Taiwan	179,486	102,491	30,652	11,924
Thailand	145,173	98,120	19,175	6,293
United Kingdom	719,665	268,302	107,839	28,874
United States	1,403,899	306,181	66,377	44,680
Venezuela	609,097	272,212	41,192	11,221

National Differences in Corporate-Compensation

	CEO	HR Director	Accountant	Mfg. Employee
Argentina	$860.704	$326.874	$63. 948	$17. 884
Canada	742.228	188. 070	44.866	36.289
Germany	421.622	189.785	61.375	36.934
Taiwan	179.486	102.491	30,652	11.924
United Kingdom	719.665	268.302	107.839	28.874
United States	1.403.899	306.181	66.377	44.680

National Differences in CEO Pay for Midsized Companies

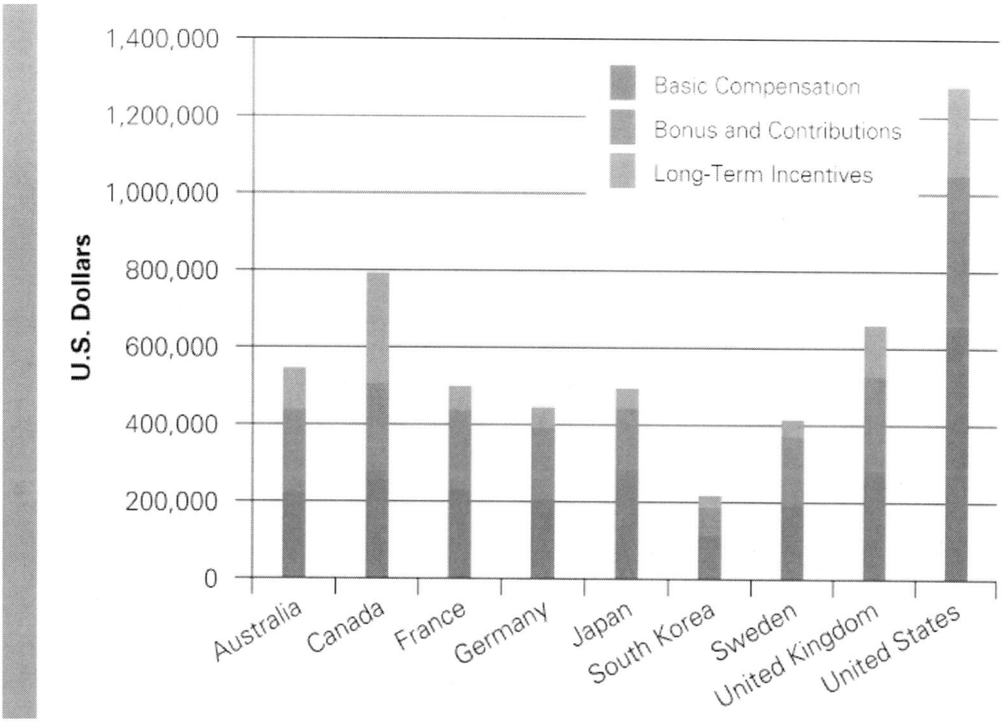

Compensation Issues

Type of Company	Payment
Ethnocentric	**How much home-country expatriates should be paid.**
Polycentric	**Pay can and should be country-specific.**
Geocentric/Transnational	**May have to pay its international cadre of managers the same.**

Expatriate Pay

- Typically use balance sheet approach
  - Equalizes purchasing power to maintain same standard of living across countries
  - Provides financial incentives to offset qualitative differences between assignment locations.
- Pay for Schools, health care, etc.

Components of Expatriate Pay

- Base Salary: Same range as a similar position in the home country.
- Foreign service premium: Extra pay for work outside country of origin.
- Allowances: Hardship, housing, cost-of-living and education allowances.
- Taxation: Firm pays expatriate's income tax in the host country.
- Benefits: Level of medical and pension benefits identical overseas.

The Balance Sheet

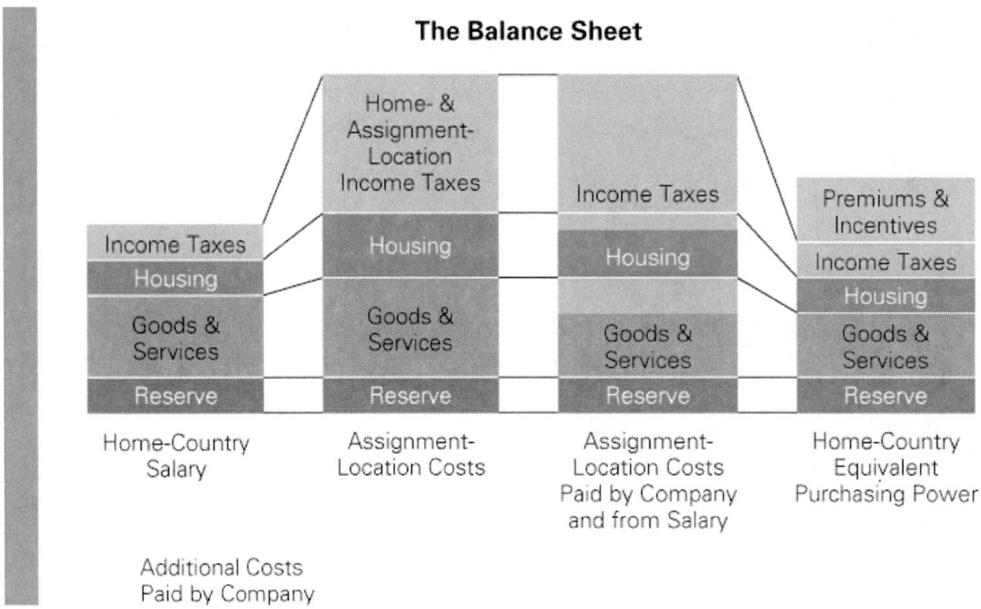

INTERNATIONAL LABOUR RELATIONS

- Key issue: Degree to which organized labor can limit the choices of an international business.
- Aims to foster harmony and minimize conflicts between firms and organized labor.

CASE STUDY: *COCA COLA*

Coca Cola is a multinational company with operations in 200 countries and 80% of operating income from businesses outside U.S. The philosophy which is the essence of Coca Cola's cross border management mentality is 'think globally, act locally'.

The corporate HRM binds its various divisions and groups by propagating a common HR philosophy and developing a group of internationally minded mid-level managers for senior management.It has a common salary philosophy – total compensation package competitive with best of companies of local market.HRM orientation session provide a medium of communication and learning for HRM professionals.

Coca Cola staffs its operations with local personnel because they are better equipped but expatriates are needed for 2 reasons: to improve employee skill base and senior managers having international exposure. It has a global service program where they add value by expertise they bring to each assignment and enhance contribution to the company by international experience. The ultimate goal is to build a cadre of high level managers from which future senior mangers will be drawn.

Concerns of Organized Labor

- Multinational can counter union bargaining power with threats to move production to another country
- Multinational will keep highly skilled tasks in its home country and farm out only low-skilled tasks to foreign plants
  - Easy to switch locations if economic conditions warrant
  - Bargaining power of organized labor is reduced
- Attempts to import employment practices and contractual agreements from multinationals home country

Strategy of Organized Labor

- Attempts to establish international labor organizations
- Lobby for national legislation to restrict multinationals
- Attempts to achieve international regulations on multinationals through such organizations as the United Nations

SOME THEORIES OF THE LABOUR MARKET

- **The Cost of Labour varies inversely to the Unemployment Rate and directly to the Quality of Labour.**

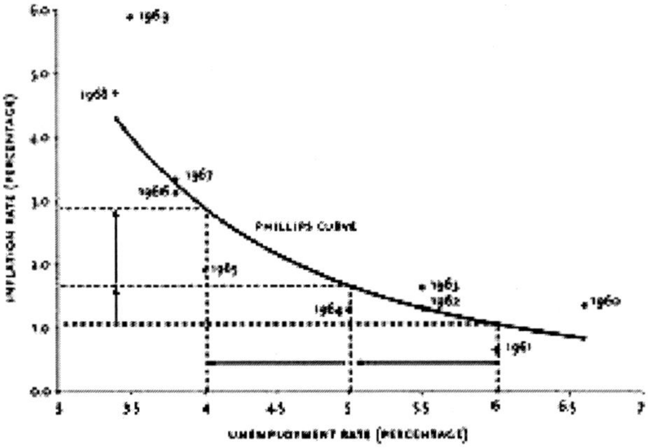

- The Supply of Labour goes down and the Cost of Labour goes up as the global economy transforms from an Industry Driven to a Knowledge Driven Economy.

Data on Hourly Wages in USA

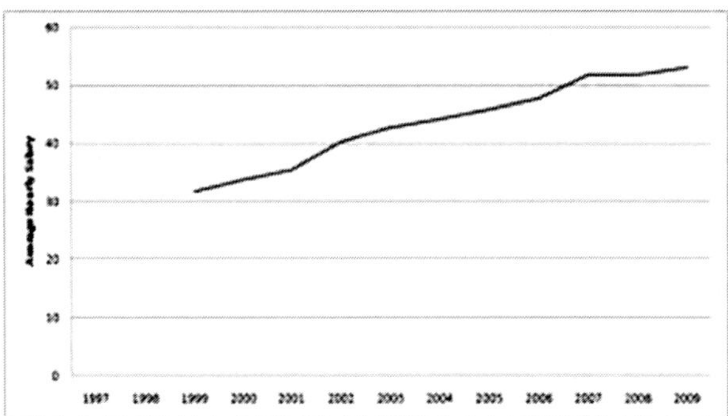

Data on Hourly Wages in Europe

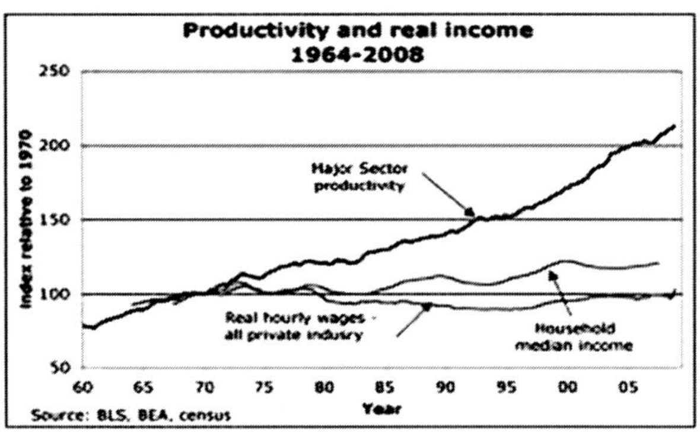

Data on hourly wages in Japan

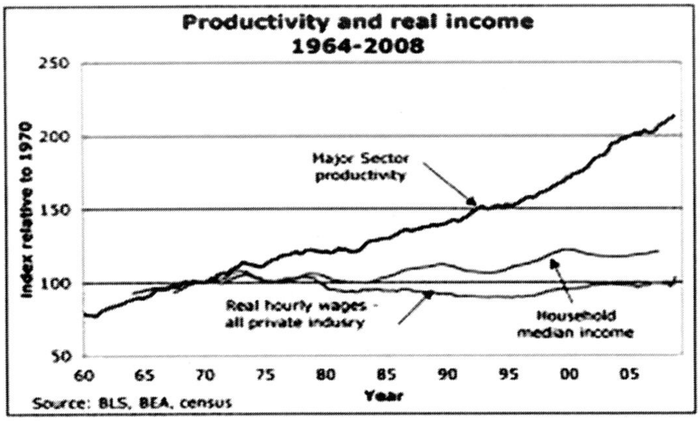

A PARADOX

- The Cost of Labour has gone up as the Demand for Labour has fallen. WHY?

SECTION 2 : INDUSTRIAL AND BUSINESS POLICIES

INTRODUCTION

Industrial Relations (IR) is concerned with the relationship between management & workers and the role of regulatory mechanism in resolving any industrial dispute through:

- Collective Bargaining
- Role of Management, unions and government
- Machinery for resolution of industrial disputes
- Individual grievance and disciplinary policy and practice
- Labor legislation
- Industrial relations training

IMPORTANCE OF IR

- Key for increased productivity in industrial establishments
- Protect workers' interests & to improve their economic conditions
- Protects rights of managers

KEY APPROACHES TO INDUSTRIAL RELATIONS

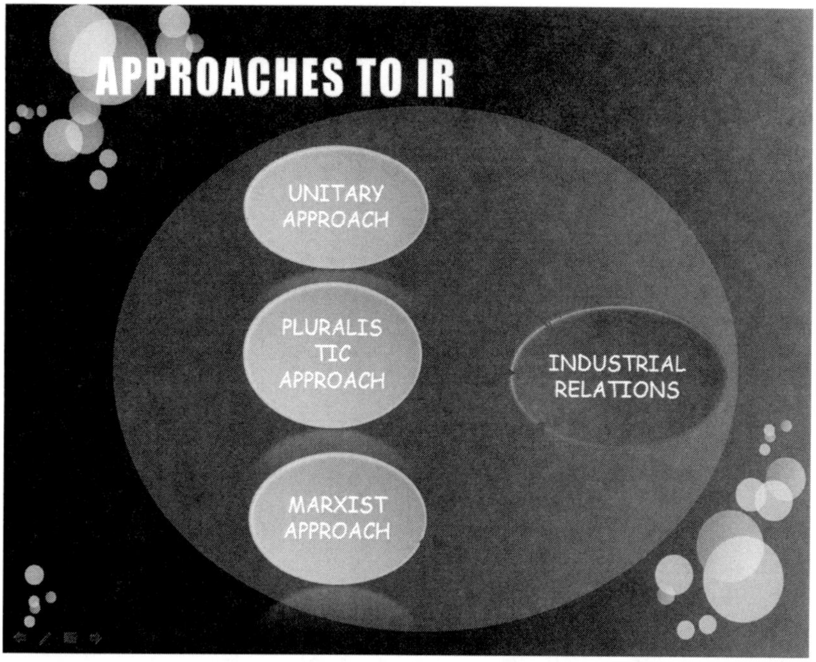

UNITARY APPROACH

- Mutual co-operation, individual treatment, team work and shared goals
- No we-they feelings
- Assumption – everyone benefits when focus is on common interest and promotion of harmony
- Advocates- reactive IR strategy & Critics- seducing away from

PLURALISTIC APPROACH

- Organizations are coalitions of common interests, where Management's role is to mediate amongst different interest groups
- Trade Unions are legitimate representatives of employee interests
- Stability in IR is due to compromises between Management & Union

MARXIST APPROACH

- Conflict arises due to division in society between owners of resources and labourers
- Industrial conflict related with political and social unrest
- Consider pluralistic as supporting Capitalism & unitary as detestable

3 Major Parties to Industrial Relation

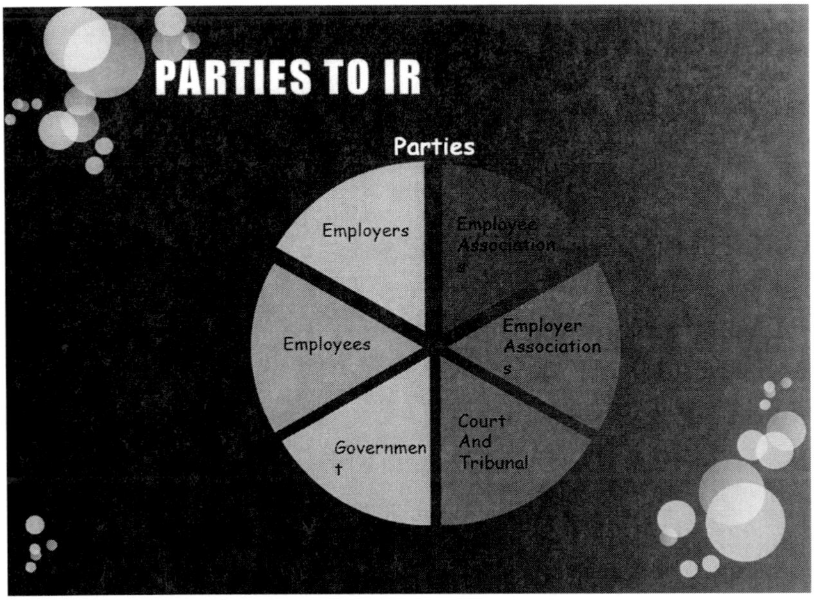

Workers and their Associations

The personal characteristics of workers, their culture, educational attainments, qualifications, skills, attitude towards work, etc. play an important role in industrial relations. It is also called Trade Union

Employers and their Associations

The employers are a very important variable in industrial relations. They provide employment to workers and try to regulate their behavior for getting high productivity from them. In order to increase their bargaining power, employers in several industries have organized employers' associations. These associations put pressure on the trade unions and the Government.

Government

The Government or State exerts an important influence on industrial relations through such measures as providing employment, intervening in working relationships. and regulating wages, bonus and working conditions through various laws relating to labor. The Government keeps an eye on. Both the trade unions and employers' organizations to regulate their behaviors in the interest of the nation.

IR STRATEGY

It is necessary to have an unambiguous strategy for IR .Generally employer- employee relations are usually presumed to be satisfactory until they get out of hand, managers, rarely, feel the need to act before the trouble breaks out. But it has not continued for a long time because of growing competition, difficult economic environment ,rising labor cost and so many reasons due to which conflict arises .

Internal Factors

- Attitudes between management ,employee and unions.
- using absolute authority management enforce decisions to the employee and unions.
- Difference in opinion between management and union.
- Present and future strength of the unions.
- Technological changes, expanding and running down also affect the employment and opportunities.

External Factors

- Authority and Effectiveness of the employers association.
- To carried out bargaining at national, local or plant level.
- Employment and pay situation –Nationally and locally.
- Legal frame work with in which IR exists.

ROLE OF HRM

- To keep the workforce motivated, competent and trouble-free.
- Ensure better recruitment and hiring, induction, training and development, safety and health, remuneration, welfare, etc.
- Contribute to the quality of work life (QWL) of the employees.
- Better QWL leads to motivation and satisfaction.

TRADE UNION

- In India as per Trade Unions Act, 1926, Trade Unions are voluntary organisations of workers or employers formed to promote and protect their interests through collective action.
- Must be a combination of workers or employers, either permanent or temporary
- Could include federation of two or more unions.
- To regulate among workmen, between workmen and employers or among employers themselves.

Strategic Choices Before Managers

- Decide whether the organisation should remain union-free or allow unionisation.
- If union-free is chosen, managers must take steps to keep unions away from the organisation.
- If unionisation is allowed, managers have to decide what type of union-management relationship they want.
- Choose the type of tactic to use while negotiating a new wage settlement.

Reasons for Joining Unions

- DISSATISFACTION
  - Unsatisfied personalities, interests and preferences.
  - Unrealistic job previews given creating expectations
  - Poor day-to-day management and supervisory practices
- LACK OF POWER
  - Instrument to influence the management
- UNION INSTRUMENTALITY
  - Instrument of removing dissatisfaction

Strategic Choices Before Unions

- Bread and Butter vs Political Objectives : Economic issues and Political participation
- Adversarial vs Co-operative Role : Challenge Management or Co-operate with management
- Traditional Issues vs New Services : Stick to old issues or accommodate changes in social attitude.

Union Tactics

- Strike
  - Temporary suspension of funtions
- Political Patronage
  - Making recognition and patronage to a political party for direction and influencing government
- Blackmail
  - Threat of discontinuing operations and non-cooperation with the management.

Trade Union Movement in India

- Enactment of Trade Union Act ,1926

- 1930's not favorable for Trade union movement
- Three Central labor organizations formed post independence
- Presently there are more than 66000 registered unions.

Trends in Trade Union Movement

- Change in attitude of union towards management, industry, and government
- Depoliticisation of unions taking place
- Formation of union on basis of religion and caste
- Associations are highly fragmented thus multiplicity of unions
- Phenomenon of outside leadership
- Clout of central trade unions has started fading.
- Unity in Trade unions taking place to fight for survival
- Professionalism in trade union getting intense

Union Free Companies

Features

- Increased cost because of high remuneration
- Loss of control over operations
- Loss of freedom to reward superior performance
- Lack of ability to adapt to changing demands.

Benefits

- Cooperation with the management is more
- Improved communication and enforcement of norms and discipline
- Volunteering to pay cuts, cost saving can be done easily
- Demonstrating an attitude of pro-industrial democracy and openness

Tactics Used

1. Effective supervision
2. Open communication
3. Effective personal research
4. Healthy and Safe work environment
5. Effective employer-employee relationship
6. Effective remuneration
7. Effective training and development programmes
8. Effective personal planning, recruitment and selection

PERSONNEL RESEARCH

Range of research areas include:

- **Wage surveys**: They reveal the level of employee satisfaction among other factors.
- **Effectiveness** of various recruitment sources
- **Test validation**: In a dynamic labor market, tests tend to get outdated frequently, so validating is imperative before applying any test.
- **Effectiveness of training efforts**: Essential for ensuring efficiency in employee performmance
- **Supervisor's effectiveness survey**: Another key factor in deciding employee satisfaction.
- **Job analysis**: Specific approaches such as result oriented, contextual or potential based approach need to be adopted as per the specific work environment.
- **Performance appraisal validation**: Most critical aspect of any modern Performance Management System
- **Turnover analysis**: Reveals the success or failure of the Industrial relation policy.

HR PRACTICES AND IRRELEVANCE OF UNIONS

HR practices threaten the very relevance of trade union

- Individualization of employment contract
- Demise of union representations

Union Legislation

- Bread and Butter vs Political Objectives
- Adversarial vs Co-operative Role
- Traditional Issues vs New Services

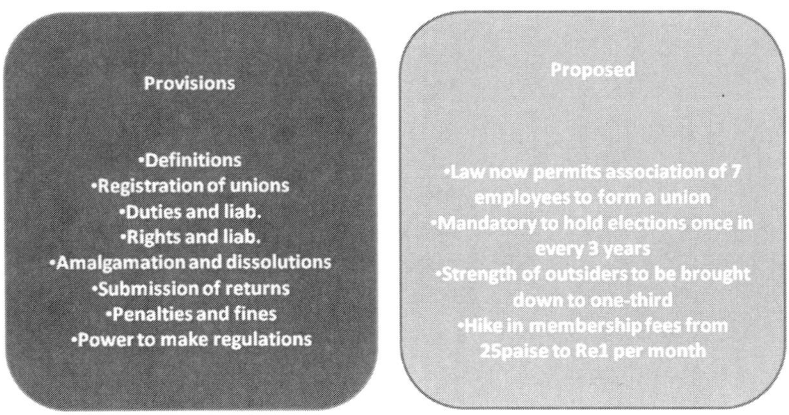

Inter-temporal Transition of Districts between 1991 and 2001: Prospects for 2011

Buddhadeb Ghosh[1] and Swagata Gupta[2]

[1] International Statistical Education Centre, Indian Statistical Institute, Kolkata
[2] Population Studies Unit, Indian Statistical Institute, Kolkata
E-mail: buddhadeb_ghosh@yahoo.com

There is wide consensus among social scientist and policy makers alike that the states in India have been diverting apart in economic levels over the last few decades except some selected social development indicators. Applied empirical studies on state level divergence abound in India most of which base their arguments on economic logic. But nobody does know for sure what is happening across the districts over time, though in the ultimate analysis, the districts are the final administrative units. There is tremendous dearth of research on the pattern of changes among the districts over the years with the states. Constitutional provision of states as the basic point of discussion is certainly responsible for this apathy to undertake district level study over all these years. Non-availability of comparable district level information is certainly a major barrier for the absence of experimental research on the districts, which, though, is the consequence of the former conjecture. It is also true that constitutional priority and emphasis on states might have provided negative incentive for both official statistical system and independent academic research on district as the starting point of analysis. We must not forget that even some richer states like Maharashtra and middle income states like West Bengal have made many remote districts the casualty for their prosperity around the metropolitan and big cities only.

Our task here not only sticks to districts as a whole, but separately for rural and urban areas of the districts. Time is now more than ripe to cross the border of the states, and put the districts on a common platform. There is very often a tendency to judge success or failure at a static point even when there is not much dearth in some basic information on inter-temporal evolution of performance of the districts. What we face today at the sub-state level must not have happened all on a sudden. Most economists try to dramatize their preconceived notions by condensing evolutionary phenomena through static models with nice properties across the states. The rising social instability and frequent failure of the states in more recent period in many regions of India to manage the social stability at the level of the districts have culminated over a reasonable period of time. The real task of the analyst is to test what has actually happened over time before passing any final comment. This gap in research has inspired us to organize the 'common districts' of India over the last two *Census years, 1991 and 2001*, in terms of 'common indicators', and try to find out possible answers to five widely debated queries:

1. To test inter-temporal transition of development across 'common districts' of India in terms of various social development indicators between 1991 and 2001 with the help of a test with Chi-square statistic on the basis of transition matrix from 1991 to 2001;
2. To judge the performance of the 'states' on the basis of district level information in terms of the same set of information;
3. To try to understand the relationship among various social development indices between rural and urban areas of the districts from 1991 to 2001;
4. To test whether district level divergence in social development indicators also conforms to the 'economic performance of the districts' in terms of *purchasing power, poverty and inequality* with the help of *NSSO 61st Round (2004-05)* data;
5. To trace state level performance from rise, fall and stagnancy of the districts in terms of some crucial social development indicators; and finally,
6. To identify the names of the best and worst districts at these two time points.

Prevailing data from Census of India help us derive three types of development indices namely *work participation index (WPI), human capital index (HCI) and health & housing index (HHI)*, which are used to get the *social development index (SDI)* for 417 common *rural* and 414 common *urban* districts. It is worth mentioning here that the indicators used for this study essentially represent infrastructure facilities across the districts. In a sense, therefore, this study is a test of district level convergence (or divergence) in India during the 10 year period from 1991 to 2001. When the district level data from the Census of 2011 will come to the public domain, it will help us test (1) the impact of a 'rising India' since 2000 on the lower geographical spaces at the district level away from the state capitals, (2) whether the 'district level divergence' established in this paper becomes much more intensified or not, and finally, (3) whether 'economic performance of the districts' on the basis of NSSO 66th Round (2010-11) data conform to the same on the basis of 'social development indicators'.

The statistical tests have yielded significant results to warrant doubtless that almost all the common districts have recorded some improvement in SDI, but districts from the backward states have failed to improve their rankings compared to the districts from the developed states. In other words, the better off districts in 1991 have been able to improve their social development at much faster rate till 2001 compared to the backward districts

Chart 1: Names of Top 10 Best Common Rural Districts in 1991 and 2001 in Social Development and Female Literacy

(Best to Worst Order)

Sr. No.	Distcode	Distname SDIR9	Distcode	Distname SDIR1	Distcode	Distname LRFR9	Distcode	Distname LRFR1
1	MH21	Sindhudurg	HP5	Kinnaur	**KE7**	**Kottayam**	**KE7**	**Kottayam**
2	MH18	Ratnagiri	KA13	Kodagu	***KE11***	***Pathanamthitta***	***KE11***	***Pathanamthitta***
3	KE12	Thrissur	***HP7***	***Lahul & Spiti***	**KE1**	**Alappuzha**	**KE1**	**Alappuzha**
4	***HP7***	***Lahul & Spiti***	HP9	Shimla	**KE8**	**Kozhikode**	**KE2**	**Ernakulam**
5	KE2	Ernakulam	KA9	Dakshina Kannada	**KE4**	**Kannur**	**KE6**	**Kollam**
6	KE1	Alappuzha	**HP3**	**Hamirpur**	MZ1	Aizawl	KE13	Trivundram
7	**HP3**	**Hamirpur**	HP6	Kullu	**KE2**	**Ernakulam**	**KE8**	**Kozhikode**
8	KE7	Kottayam	TN11	The Nilgiris	**KE12**	**Thrissur**	**KE4**	**Kannur**
9	KE11	Pathanamthitta	HP1	Bilaspur	**KE6**	**Kollam**	**KE12**	**Thrissur**
10	MZ1	Aizawl	UP23	Garhwal	KE9	Malappuram	KE3	Idukki

Chart 2: Names of Bottom 10 Worst Common Rural Districts in 1991 and 2001 in Social Development and Female Literacy

(Worst to Best Order)

Sr. No.	Distcode	Distname SDIR9	Distcode	Distname SDIR1	Distcode	Distname LRFR9	Distcode	Distname LRFR1
1	**BI31**	**Purba Champaran**	UP52	Rampur	**OR8**	**Koraput**	RJ4	Barmer
2	BI5	Bhojpur	**BI31**	**Purba Champaran**	**BI19**	**Kishanganj**	RJ15	Jaisalmer
3	**BI28**	**Pashchim Champaran**	**UP12**	**Budaun**	BI17	Katihar	RJ16	Jalor
4	UP31	Jalaun	**BI28**	**Pashchim Champaran**	AR3	East Kameng	RJ19	Jodhpur
5	**BI40**	**Sitamarhi**	**UP45**	**Moradabad**	BI33	Purnia	**MP20**	**Jhabua**
6	RJ15	Jaisalmer	**BI40**	**Sitamarhi**	***UP6***	***Bahraich***	**BI19**	**Kishanganj**
7	**UP45**	**Moradabad**	UP6	Bahraich	**MP20**	**Jhabua**	UP52	Rampur
8	**UP12**	**Budaun**	UP9	Bareilly	BI37	Sahibganj	***UP6***	***Bahraich***
9	UP25	Ghazipur	BI17	Katihar	NG3	Mon	UP12	Budaun
10	RJ11	Dhaulpur	BI21	Madhepura	BI1	Araria	**OR8**	**Koraput**

Chart 3: Names of Top 10 Best Common Urban Districts in 1991 and 2001 in Social Development and Female Literacy

(Best to worst order)

Sr. No.	Distcode	Distname SDIU9	Distcode	Distname SDIU1	Distcode	Distname LRFU9	Distcode	Distname LRFU1
1	MH21	Sindhudurg	KA13	Kodagu	***KE7***	***Kottayam***	MZ1	Aizawl
2	TR2	South Tripura	***TN11***	***The Nilgiris***	**KE11**	**Pathanamthitta**	MZ3	Lunglei
3	***TN11***	***The Nilgiris***	KA9	Dakshina Kannada	**KE2**	**Ernakulam**	***KE7***	***Kottayam***
4	KE2	Ernakulam	TN13	Tirunelveli	**KE1**	**Alappuzha**	**KE11**	**Pathanamthitta**
5	SK1	East Sikkim	TN1	Coimbatore	KE13	Trivundram	NG2	Mokokchung
6	**TN4**	**Kanniyakumari**	MG3	Jaintia Hills	**KE4**	**Kannur**	**KE12**	**Thrissur**
7	MG2	East Khasi Hills	SK4	West Sikkim	**KE12**	**Thrissur**	**KE2**	**Ernakulam**
8	KE12	Thrissur	HP9	Shimla	KE3	Idukki	**KE4**	**Kannur**
9	SK3	South Sikkim	MZ1	Aizawl	KE8	Kozhikode	MZ2	Chhimtuipui
10	MH18	Ratnagiri	**TN4**	**Kanniyakumari**	KE6	Kollam	**KE1**	**Alappuzha**

Chart 4: Names of Bottom 10 Worst Common Urban Districts in 1991 and 2001 in Social Development and Female Literacy

(Worst to best order)

Sr. No.	Distcode	Distname SDIU9	Distcode	Distname SDIU1	Distcode	Distname LRFU9	Distcode	Distname LRFU1
1	**BI42**	**Vaishali**	UP54	Shahjahanpur	RJ21	Nagaur	**UP12**	**Budaun**
2	UP21	Fatehpur	***UP12***	***Budaun***	***RJ16***	***Jalor***	**UP52**	**Rampur**
3	***UP12***	***Budaun***	UP52	Rampur	**UP12**	**Budaun**	***RJ16***	***Jalor***
4	**UP6**	**Bahraich**	UP45	Moradabad	**UP52**	**Rampur**	**BI19**	**Kishanganj**
5	UP16	Deoria	**BI13**	**Gopalganj**	**BI13**	**Gopalganj**	**MN2**	**Chandel**
6	UP55	Siddharthnagar	UP11	Bijnor	**BI19**	**Kishanganj**	**BI13**	**Gopalganj**
7	UP27	Gorakhpur	**UP48**	**Pilibhit**	RJ24	Sikar	UP45	Moradabad
8	UP58	Sultanpur	UP36	Kheri	BI21	Madhepura	UP54	Shahjahanpur
9	**UP48**	**Pilibhit**	**BI42**	**Vaishali**	**MN2**	**Chandel**	BI22	Madhubani
10	**BI13**	**Gopalganj**	**UP6**	**Bahraich**	RJ10	Churu	UP9	Bareilly

in 1991. And this finding is universal in India irrespective of rural versus urban divide. Therefore, it would not be exaggerated to conclude that there is a statistically significant trend of 'divergence' among Indian districts between 1991 and 2001. Since this period is almost synonymous with globalization, one may be prompted to conclude that the fruits of globalization have been harvested by the better off districts. Some sample results are posted below which report the best and worst 10 districts of India separately for rural and urban areas. The most interesting finding is that there is no district of West Bengal in any of the list. This certainly means that the districts of West Bengal have remained 'mediocre' in recent period. More complicated and detailed results would follow.

The main significance of the study is that what the Prime Minister of India has termed as "the gravest threat to India is her internal disturbances" can be traced as per district level performance. Therefore, as public policy analysts, we must disseminate the cause of the districts away from the state capitals in terms of infrastructure build up.

Investigating Seasonality Effects and Trading Strategies in Select IT Companies in India

Nabaghan Mallick[1] and Sathya Swaroop Debasish[2]

[1] Bhadrak Institute of Engineering & Technology, Bhadrak, Odissa
[2] Utkal University, Odissa
E-mail: n.mallickfinance@gmail.com; sathyaswaroop@yahoomail.com

ABSTRACT

The primary objective of the study is to investigate the existence of seasonality in stock price behavior in Indian stock market and more specifically in the IT sector. The period of the study is from 3rd November 1994 to 31st December 2010. For the purpose analysis, the study has employed daily price series that have been obtained from the official website of National Stock Exchange (NSE). The daily price series of selected seven IT companies were selected for this study, and used Kruskal Wallis for trading strategy, multiple regression technique to examine the significance of the regression coefficient for investigating day of week effects and week of the month effect. It is found that all the seven selected IT companies evidenced day of the week effect and mostly either on Monday, Tuesday or Wednesday. Only Patni and Wipro evidenced significant Thursday effect. Similarly, evidence on week of month effect mostly either on 1st week, 2nd week or 3rd week. Only Polaris and Wipro evidenced significant 4th week effect.

Keywords: Seasonality Effect, Trading Strategy

INTRODUCTION

Over the last hundred years, a vast number of the literature from both the practitioner and academic fields examined day-of-the-week effects or day seasonality on returns of various assets, such as stocks, debt securities, futures, foreign currencies and even commodities. The earliest research can be traced back to as early as the late 1920s. Calendar anomalies, relying on the assumption that a certain pattern of stock markets is formed on the basis of the past stock price, can be used to predict the future stock price. If the pattern is fixed, informed investors can utilize the pattern to earn a risk-free profit by trading the stocks. The study of seasonality implies that investors could employ the findings on anomalies to predict the future behavior of prices (Fama, 1965). Certainly, seasonal anomalies are in contradiction to any form of efficient market hypothesis (EMH), particularly the weak-form efficiency.

Capital market operations consist mainly of primary market operations and secondary market operations or stock market. The origin of stock market in India can be traced to the later part of the Eighteenth Century. The earliest security dealings were transactions in loan securities of the East India Company, the dominant institution of those days. Corporate shares came into the picture by 1830's and assumed significance with the enactment of the Companies Act in 1850. The introduction of limited liability marked the beginning of the era of modern joint stock enterprises. The American Civil War followed this in 1860-65. However, the bubble burst with the end of the Civil War and a disastrous slump followed which lasted for a long time and also resulted in complete ostracism of the broker community. The tremendous social pressure on the brokers led to their forming an informal association called, 'The Native Share and Stock Brokers' Association' (now known as the Bombay Stock Exchange) in 1887.

The Indian capital market is more than a century old. Its history goes back to 1875, when 22 brokers formed the Bombay Stock Exchange (BSE). Over the period, the Indian securities market has evolved continuously to become one of the most dynamic, modern, and efficient securities markets in Asia. Today, Indian market confirms to best international practices and standards both in terms of structure and in terms of operating efficiency. Indian securities markets are mainly governed by (a) The Company's Act1956, (b) the Securities Contracts (Regulation) Act 1956 (SCRA Act), and (c) the Securities and Exchange Board of India (SEBI) Act, 1992. The national stock exchange, or NSE, is a recent entrant in the stock exchange scene in India. It was incorporated in November 1992, at the behest of the Government of India. The shares of about 1,589 companies trade on this exchange. Its daily average turnover for the year 2009-10 is Rs. 28,476 crores. The total market capitalization of stocks trading in NSE is Rs. 67,45,724 crores, as on 31st March 2010. Regional exchanges also sponsor trading of some firms that are traded on national exchanges. This dual listing enables local brokerage firms to trade in shares of large firms without needing to purchase membership on the larger exchanges like BSE and NSE. Thus, for example, Infosys is listed on the Bangalore Stock Exchange apart from BSE and NSE. However, BSE and NSE are still the preferred exchanges for large traders.

OBJECTIVES OF STUDY

The primary objective of the study is to investigate the existence of seasonality in stock price behavior in Indian stock market. The study of seasonality is segregated into analyzing and measuring the day of the week effect in IT sector.

The specific objectives of the study are:

(a) To present a panoramic view of the Indian stock market.
(b) To present the prior studies on stock price seasonality, both in national and international market.
(c) To analyze the basic descriptive statistics like mean, median, standard deviation, kurtosis and skewness for daily return.
(d) To analyze the trading strategy of Indian stock market for buy with sale or hold.
(e) To examine the significance of regression coefficient for the daily effect using multivariate technique.

LITERATURE REVIEW

During the past five decades, much time and effort have been devoted in the field of finance to investigate the behaviour of certain speculative prices such as those of securities and commodity futures. Research efforts have been directed, in particular, to study price behaviour of common stocks or equity shares as they are popularly called in India with a view to understanding the underlying stochastic processes which determine the prices of these shares.

In an earlier study, Sharma and Kennedy (1977) found that the Indian markets obeyed the theory of random walk and concluded that markets were efficient. Ignatius (1998) examined seasonality in a BSE index and in the Standard and Poor's 500 stock indexes for the period 1979-1990. Pandey (2002) studied the presence of the seasonal or monthly effect in stock returns has been reported in several developed and emerging stock markets. This study investigates the existence of seasonality in the post-reform period. The study uses the monthly return data of the Bombay Stock Exchange's Sensitivity Index for the period from April 1991 to March 2002 for analysis. The results confirm the existence of seasonality in stock returns in India and the January effect. Sarma (2004) examined calendar effects during the post reform era in the Indian stock market. He investigated the BSE 30, the BSE 100, and the BSE 200 stock indexes to detect the day-of-the-week effect. Utilizing Kruskal-Wallis test statistics, the study concluded that the Indian stock market exhibited some seasonality in daily returns over the period January 1, 1996 to August 10, 2002. The major findings of the study are the Monday-Tuesday, Monday-Friday, and Wednesday-Friday sets have positive deviations for all the indices, The Monday-Friday set for all the indices has the highest positive deviation thereby indicating the presence of opportunity to make consistent abnormal returns through a trading strategy of buying on Mondays and selling on Fridays. Kumari and Mahendra (2006) studied the day of the week effect and other market anomalies in the Indian Stock Market over a period from 1979 to 1998 both in The Bombay Stock Exchange and in the National Stock Exchange. They found that the Monday returns were higher compared with the other days of the week but on the other hand the returns on Tuesday were negative. In the case of monthly returns they documented that the returns in April were significantly higher and different from the rest of the months. Tripathy (2010) investigated the expiration day and week effects for nifty futures by using statistical t-test, F-test and Kruskal-Wallis test for the period from November 2007 to November 2009. The study also analyzed the day of the week effect in Bearish phase and Bullish phase to see whether the day of the week effect was visible in these specific market phases or not. The study explains that the Day of the Week effect found to be absent in the Bullish as well as the Bearish phase. The study found that the trading volume for the NIFTY future index increased as the expiration date move towards nearer. It was highest around 10-15 days prior to expiration and decreased as the expiration approached.

Day of the Week Effect

The day of the week effect refers to the existence of a pattern on the part of stock returns, whereby these returns are linked to the particular day of the week. The last trading days of the week, particularly Friday, are characterized by the positive and substantially positive returns, while Monday, the first trading day of the week, differs from other days, even producing negative returns. The presence of such an effect would mean that equity returns are not independent of the day of the week, evidence against random walk theory.

Week of the Month Effect

Week of the month effect refers to the observation significantly deferent return on a particular week of every trading month, distinctively deferent from return on other week. A variation to month of the year effect, turn of the month effect in which the return on the last week of the month or first week of the successive month significantly deferent. The presents of such an effect would imply that abnormal returns can be generated by active trading on the weeks evidencing week of the month effect.

SAMPLE, SOURCE AND PERIOD OF THE STUDY

For the micro level study the researcher used a three stage approach of sample selection. In the first stage leading sector that contribution significance to the economy (in terms of GDP) were selected and it was purposed to use the leading companies under these sectors depending on availability of stock data and other criteria. In the second stage attempt was made to select nine banks based on the three criteria namely profit position, turn over and market capitalization. At the end of the second stage the total nine banks could be selected. In the third stage the researcher tried to obtained continuous data for the selected banks.

In this study we have taken seven selected companies from IT sector (I-Flex, Infosys, Patni, Polaris, Satyam, TCS and Wipro),

The period of the study is from 3rd November 1994 to 31st December 2010. For the purpose analysis, the study has employed daily price series that have been obtained from the official website of National Stock Exchange (NSE).

TOOLS OF ANALYSIS

It is found from the extensive review of prior studies that most of the earlier works on stock price behavior have used closing price for return generating procedure with an implied assumption of trading done at the closing price. The continuous compounded annual return is well accepted approach to measuring the daily returns. The natural log of daily relative mean index value is, thus the measure of daily used for this study. The log return is calculated based on the closing price.

The study has used basic descriptive statistics like mean and median for central tendency; standard deviation for measuring the dispersion; kurtosis for peakedness of the distribution and skewness to measure the symmetry of the return distribution. The hypothesis to be tested relates to equality of mean returns across all the five days and weeks.

Statistical Tools and Techniques Used

It is found from the extensive review of prior studies that most of the earlier works on stock price behavior have used closing price for return generating procedure with an implied assumption of trading done at the closing price. The continuous compounded annual return is well accepted approach to measuring the daily returns. The natural log of daily relative mean index value is, thus the measure of daily used for this study. The log return is calculated based on the closing price and is presented in equation 1.

$$R_t = \ln[\frac{C_t}{C_{t-1}}] \qquad ...(1)$$

where R_t = return on day 't'

C_t = Closing Price on day 't'

C_{t-1} = Closing on day '$t - 1$'

and ln = natural log.

The study has analyzed the returns on daily basis. In the first phase, we employ basic descriptive statistics like mean, median, standard deviation, Kurtosis and skewness. In the last phase, the study used multiple regression technique to examine the significance of the regression coefficient for investigating day of week effects.

Univeriate Analysis using Kruskal-Wallis Test

In the study **Kruskal–Wallis one-way analysis of variance** by ranks (named after William Kruskal and W. Allen Wallis) is a non-parametric method for testing equality of population medians among groups. It is identical to a one-way analysis of variance with the data replaced by their ranks. It is an extension of the Mann–Whitney U test to 3 or more groups. Since it is a non-parametric method, the Kruskal–Wallis test does not assume a normal population, unlike the analogous one-way analysis of variance. However, the test does assume an identically-shaped and scaled distribution for each group of the study period in between day of the week, week of the month and month of the year.

The hypothesis to be tested relates to equality of mean returns across all the five days and weeks. In other words, the null hypothesis is that mean returns across all the five days and weeks do not exhibit statistically significant differences. A nonparametric Kruskall-Wallis test (by computing *'H'* statistic) is applied in place of a conventionally used parametric one-way analysis of variance. In the seasonality literature, it appears that researchers tend to perform parametric tests (typically dummy variable regressions) on any data set without first checking the data's distributional properties which makes the testing results highly suspicious. It is undoubtedly true that non-parametric tests are less powerful than parametric tests when conditions for parametric tests are met. But, when the conditions do not hold, we must choose between a valid test with less power (i.e., a non-parametric test) and an invalid test with appealing (yet shaky) statistics (i.e., a parametric test). When the conditions are far from holding precisely, the choice is clear. The difficult case is when the conditions are closely or approximately met so that the higher testing power may justify the impreciseness. But, the challenge is to know how close is '*close.*' On balance, a non-parametric test is always in order, especially when in doubt. One obvious advantage of a nonparametric test is that it is independent of distributional assumptions. Another advantage is its immunity to outliers. In a rank-based non-parametric test, one of the disadvantages is loss of information. But, for a seasonality study, this is not a concern, because the focus is not on precise estimation of, say, daily returns. Therefore, it is felt that the Kruskall-Wallis test is an appropriate one for the data typified of non-normality, heteroscedastic variance like the security returns (Jason, 1996).

Notational expression of the hypothesis would be as under:

The accepted model for return is presented in equation 2

$$R_u = \mu + \iota_i + \varepsilon_{ij} \qquad \text{...(2)}$$

$i = 1, 2, ..., n$

$j = 1, 2, ..., 5$

where, μ is the overall daily or weekly mean, τj quantifies the day or week effect whose expected value is '0,' and is Eij mutually independent random variable. The null hypothesis for the given model would be that the population means are all equal.

H_0 : $\mu_1 = \mu_2 = \mu_3 = \mu_4 = \mu_5$ or
H_0 : $\tau_j = 0$ for j = 1, 2, …., 5 and
H_1 : $\mu_1 \neq \mu_2 \neq \mu_3 \neq \mu_4 \neq \mu_5$ or
H_1 : $\tau_j \neq 0$ for at least one value of j

The Kruskall-Wallis test requires the entire set of observations being ranked – higher the value, higher is the rank and vice-versa – then arranged into *nj* x 5 matrix where *nj* represents the rank of the return and columns represent the day-of-the-week or week of the month – Monday through Friday or 1st week through 5th week.

The formula for calculating the test statistic '*H*' is as under and provided in equation 3.

$$H = \left[\frac{12}{N(N+1)} x \sum_{j=1}^{5} \frac{R_j^2}{n_j} \right] - 3(N+1) \quad \text{... (3)}$$

where: *Rj* = sum of the ranks in the *j*th column, *nj* = number of cases in the *j*th column, *N* = sum of observations in all the columns.

To test whether the differences in the mean returns across the weekdays or weeks are statistically significant, we use the '*H*' statistic. The critical value of 'H' at 99 per cent confidence level and four degrees of freedom is 13.28.

The calculations compiled in chapter six present the deviations of actual from the expected average rank differences. A comparison of annual rates of return generated by a passive strategy of 'buy and hold' and various alternative active strategies as evidenced from Kruskal-Wallis analysis is presented.

Regression Analysis

Regression analysis is employed to further examine the day of week effect for the selected stocks. A regression analysis is a statistical method used to estimate the strength of a relationship between one or more dependent variable and one or more independent variables. It assumes that the relationship between the dependent and independent variables is linear; that these variables have equal variance (homoscedasticity); that there is no correlation between two or more of the independent variable (multicollinearity); and the data is normally distributed. Regression analysis can be simple involving one dependent variable and one independent variable, or multiple involving one dependent variable and two or more independent variable. Regression analysis was used by the researcher to gain a deeper understanding of the relationship between the log return of the closing price of one day with other day of the week, ist week with other week of the month, and one month with other month of the year. The regression analysis was to examine the significance of the seasonality of return for the stocks and indices.

Linear Regression

In linear regression, the model specification is that the dependent variable, y_i is a linear combination of the *parameters* (but need not be linear in the *independent variables*). For example, in simple linear regression for modeling n data points there is one independent variable: x_i, and other days parameters, β_0, β_1, β_2, β_3, β_4, ..., n (n for day, 5).

In order to test the day of the week effect, week of the month effect and month of the year effect on the stock return in the Indian selected companies and indices, The regression equation for day of the week is presented below in equation 4,

$$Rt = \infty + B_2D_{2t} + B_3D_{3t} + B_4D_{4t} + B_5D_{5t} + e_t \quad ...(4)$$

where R_t is daily returns, calculated using in above both equation D_{2t}, D_{3t}, ..., D_{5t} are dummy variables from Tuesday to Friday.

Descriptive Statistical Analysis

This chapter presents an analysis of the descriptive statistics namely mean, median, standard deviation, kurtosis and skewness for the selected companies for the daily return over the study period.

Analysis of Descriptive Statistics for Daily Return for IT Sector

Table 1 depicts the values of descriptive statistics for each of the week days for the selected seven companies in the IT sector. It is observed that relatively higher values of mean return (in consistent manner) is for Satyam in the range of –0.095 to 0.036, with the exception of Tuesday mean return with lower value of 0.00154. Only Polaris evidenced consistently positive mean return for each for the five week days with all day mean return 0.00021. Lower levels of mean return for the week days are observed for TCS in the range of –0.0025 to 0.00033 with all days mean of –0.0027. Further, it is found that very high level of mean return for some weekdays and lower levels for other week days is observed for Patni in the range of 0.035 to –0.0035 for Thursday to Friday, while lower values in range of levels of 0.0018 to 0.002 for Monday and Wednesday with all day mean of 0.00018. For Infosys, negative mean return is found for Friday with positive values for remaining weekdays and all day average return of 0.00292. In case of I-Flex, Satyam, Patni and Wipro there is evidence of inconsistently higher and lower values of mean return for weekdays with all day's average being at 0.0.0021, 0.02624, 0.00082 and –0.11331 respectively.

Table 1: Descriptive Statistics of Daily Return for Selected Companies in IT Sector

Name of Company	Parameter	Monday	Tuesday	Wednes-day	Thursday	Friday	All Days
I-Flex	Mean	0.00377	0.04936	0.00363	0.06104	–0.00165	0.0021
	Median	0.09453	0.03781	0.00967	0.09351	0.00141	0.0729
	Standard deviation	0.04113	0.03208	0.05024	0.03840	0.03721	0.04243
	Kurtosis	0.27052	0.68841	0.50452	1.09555	1.61185	3.21436
	Skewness	–0.01521	0.67962	0.07696	0.95485	–0.23194	0.01845
Infosys	Mean	0.00308	0.04046	0.00296	0.00292	–0.00489	0.00292
	Median	0.00671	0.00632	0.02098	0.00534	–0.00967	0.00183
	Standard deviation	0.04598	0.02141	0.05776	0.02281	0.04477	0.02538
	Kurtosis	0.44483	1.67627	1.81804	4.51152	2.83271	2.20648
	Skewness	0.15501	1.27561	0.07633	0.81067	–0.06396	0.58611
Patni	Mean	0.00183	–0.00018	0.00203	0.03508	–0.00352	0.00082
	Median	0.00672	0.00742	0.09451	0.00903	–0.00823	0.00942
	Standard deviation	0.02654	0.02240	0.03295	0.01720	0.02713	0.21273
	Kurtosis	1.77913	3.14896	3.65157	3.95244	1.52494	7.63077
	Skewness	0.92415	0.67089	1.04601	1.59921	0.69356	0.06015
Polaris	Mean	0.00074	0.03439	0.00047	0.00166	0.03981	0.00021
	Median	0.00521	0.00348	0.00167	–0.00764	0.00358	0.00124
	Standard deviation	0.21005	0.01901	0.03168	0.03261	0.03540	0.02604
	Kurtosis	7.33287	2.06663	14.73201	6.28889	35.18260	8.55858
	Skewness	0.03702	1.23650	0.57335	–0.65408	4.97291	0.78487
Satyam	Mean	0.00174	0.00154	0.00171	0.03605	–0.09512	0.02624
	Median	0.00129	0.00956	0.00089	0.00892	–0.00367	0.00863
	Standard deviation	0.02097	0.02515	0.02424	0.03105	0.02205	0.01979
	Kurtosis	0.96784	1.50032	1.30471	11.93544	2.07099	2.36733
	Skewness	–0.03734	–0.22463	–0.01702	2.85875	0.26806	0.94835
TCS	Mean	0.00033	0.00024	0.00025	–0.00196	–0.00257	–0.0027
	Median	0.00067	0.01276	0.00039	–0.00001	0.00653	0.00581
	Standard deviation	0.02104	0.02636	0.02848	0.03019	0.01927	0.02987
	Kurtosis	2.13601	2.80579	6.67192	3.52877	2.38805	8.20669
	Skewness	–0.03803	0.91629	0.72007	–0.2893	–0.02197	–1.2231
Wipro	Mean	0.03033	0.01039	0.02039	0.01041	0.00022	–0.11331
	Median	0.08732	0.00461	0.07901	–0.00123	0.00879	–0.00034
	Standard deviation	0.02593	2.71258	0.01831	2.71204	2.99671	0.01798
	Kurtosis	7.98644	–0.87587	7.72701	–0.87619	–1.09881	13.33486
	Skewness	2.38806	–0.00039	2.06871	–0.00071	–0.00904	0.92351

With regard to median, relatively higher values of median return for the weekdays are observed for Patni in the range of –0.0082 to 0.094, with the exception of Thursday median return of 0.00903. Lower levels of median return for the week days are observed for Polaris in the range of –0.0076 to 0.0052 with all day average median of 0.00124. Further, it is found that very high level of median return is observed for Wipro in the range of 0.087 to –0.0012 for Monday and Thursday, while lower values in range of levels of 0.0046 to 0.0087 for Tuesday and Friday with all day median of –0.00034. I-Flex is observed to have consistently positive median return for each of the five weekdays with all day median return 0.0729. For Patni, negative median return is found for Friday with positive values for remaining weekdays and all day median of 0.00942. In case of Infosys and Satyam, there is evidence of inconsistently higher and lower values of median return for weekdays with all day average being positive at 0.0018 and 0.0086, respectively. Both Polaris and TCS have lower levels of weekday returns with all day average median of 0.00124 and 0.00581, respectively. For I-Flex the all day median return is maximum with value 0.0729 and Wipro has all day median value minimum at –0.00034.

With regard to standard deviation of daily returns, higher values for the weekdays are observed for Wipro in the range of 0.018 to 2.99, with all day standard deviation of 0.01798. Lower levels of standard deviation for the week days are observed for TCS in the range of 0.019 to 0.028 with all day standard deviation of 0.02987. Further, it is found that very high standard deviation for some weekdays and lower levels for other week days is observed for I-Flex in the range of 0.032 to 0.050 for Tuesday to Wednesday, while for I-Flex, Infosys, Patni, Polaris, Satyam and TCS the standard deviation of returns is found consistent. Wipro evidenced inconsistently higher and lower values of standard deviation with all day value positive at 0.01798. Patni is found to have the minimum weekday standard deviation return for Thursday (0.0172), with all day standard deviation of 0.21273.

With regard to Kurtosis, relatively higher values of Kurtosis (in consistent manner) for the weekdays are observed for Polaris in the range of 2.06 to 35.18, with the all day Kurtosis of 8.55858. Lower range of kurtosis for the week days are observed for I-Flex in the range of 0.27 to 1.61 with all day average kurtosis of 3.21436. Further, it is found that very high range of kurtosis for some weekdays and lower levels for other week days is observed for Satyam in the range of 11.93 to 0.96 for Thursday and Monday, I-Flex is observed to have consistently positive kurtosis value for each of the five weekdays with all days average of 3.21436.

With regard to skewness of return series, higher values for the weekdays are observed for Polaris in the range of –0.65 to 4.97, with the all day skewness of 0.78487. Lower range of skewness for the week days are observed for I-Flex in the range of –0.23 to 0.95 with all day average skewness of 0.01845. The daily return series on Mondays and Fridays are negatively skewed for the selected IT companies. For Patni, skewness on all is positive, consistent but less skewed. Very high range of skewness for some weekdays and positive skewed is observed for Wipro in the range of –0.009 to 2.38 for Friday and Monday, with all day positive skewness of 0.92351. On basis of all day skewness, Satyam is more skewed with value of 0.94835 and TCS return is negatively skewed.

Analysis of Descriptive Statistics of Weekly Returns for IT Sector

Table 2 depicts the values of descriptive statistics for each of the weeks for the selected seven company in the IT sector. The statistical parameters studied are mean, median, Standard deviation, Kurtosis and Skewness. Relatively higher values of mean return (in consistent manner) for the weeks are observed for Polaris in the range of –0.0107 to 0.049, with the exception of 3rd week mean return of –0.0015. Only I-Flex and Satyam evidenced consistently positive mean return for each for the five weeks with all week average return of 0.0051 and 0.0324, respectively. Lower levels of mean return for the weeks are observed for Patni in the range of –0.0046 to 0.0038 with all week mean of 0.0554. Further, it is found that very high level of mean return for some weeks and lower levels for other weeks is observed for Infosys in the range of –0.0003 to 0.0335 for 1st week to 3rd week, with all week mean of 0.0579. For Wipro, negative mean return is found for 5th week with positive values for remaining weeks and all week average of 0.0705. In case of Infosys, Patni, Polaris, and TCS there is evidence of inconsistently higher and lower values of mean return for the weeks. I-Flex, Satyam and Wipro have lower levels positive return of week's returns with all week mean of 0.0051, 0.0324 and 0.0705, respectively while Polaris and TCS have lower levels negative return of week's returns with all week mean of –0.0041 and –0.0052, respectively . TCS is found to have the minimum weeks mean return for 2nd week (–0.0224).

With regard to median, it is observed that relatively higher values for the weeks are observed for I-Flex in the range of 0.0045 to 0.65, with the exception of 1st week median return with lower value of 0.0056. Three companies namely, I-Flex, Infosys, Patni and Satyam evidenced consistently positive median return for each for the five weeks. Lower levels of median return for the weeks are observed for Satyam in the range of 0.0001 to 0.017 with all week median of 0.0423. Further, it is found that very high level of median return for some weeks and lower levels for other weeks is observed for TCS in the range of –0.0097 to 0.0239 for all four weeks with all week median of 0.0093. For Polaris, negative median return is found for 1st week with positive values for remaining weeks and all week median return of 0.0765. In case of Wipro, there is evidence of inconsistently higher and lower values of median return for weeks with all week average being positive at 0.0012. I-Flex, Infosys, Patni, TCS and Wipro have lower levels of median returns with all week median of 0.0096, 0.0056, 0.0017, 0.0093 and 0.0012, respectively. TCS is found to have the minimum weeks median return for 4th week (–0.0097).

Table 2: Descriptive Statistics of Weekly Returns for Selected Companies in IT Sector

Name of Company	Parameter	1st Week	2nd Week	3rd Week	4th week	5th Week	All Weeks
I-Flex	Mean	0.0016	0.0287	0.0016	0.0023	0.0009	0.0051
	Median	0.0056	0.0045	0.0143	0.0056	0.6571	0.0096
	Standard deviation	0.0213	0.0381	0.0267	0.4306	0.0229	0.0441
	Kurtosis	1.3011	7.0306	3.2738	2.9471	2.3984	4.4284
	Skewness	0.5701	5.6306	–0.0197	0.0904	0.7723	0.0837
Infosys	Mean	–0.0003	0.0321	0.0335	0.0022	–0.0005	0.0579
	Median	0.0032	0.0056	0.0675	0.0063	0.0091	0.0056
	Standard deviation	0.0196	0.0267	0.0149	0.4302	0.0281	0.0375
	Kurtosis	0.1052	0.5112	2.8067	3.9551	0.7867	2.9446
	Skewness	0.0506	0.8645	1.3988	0.0842	0.2168	2.0702
Patni	Mean	–0.0012	0.0038	–0.0011	–0.0046	0.0021	0.0554
	Median	0.0028	0.0843	0.0075	0.0511	0.0098	0.0017
	Standard deviation	0.0279	1.3262	0.0530	0.0381	0.0376	0.0334
	Kurtosis	0.9865	19.3819	28.8095	4.3701	5.7373	1.9766
	Skewness	0.3246	–0.0071	0.4315	0.7915	6.1208	1.2714
Polaris	Mean	–0.0017	–0.0107	–0.0015	0.0496	–0.0037	–0.0041
	Median	–0.0056	0.0067	0.0097	0.0934	0.0765	0.0765
	Standard deviation	0.0376	0.0354	0.0402	0.0337	0.0281	1.3275
	Kurtosis	1.7394	3.9001	1.7057	3.6774	2.6113	1.4041
	Skewness	0.0368	–0.3665	0.0413	1.8336	0.0512	–0.0163
Satyam	Mean	0.0002	0.0012	0.0014	0.0011	0.0175	0.0324
	Median	0.0083	0.0723	0.0674	0.0008	0.0706	0.0423
	Standard deviation	2.9939	0.5404	0.0201	0.5421	0.0233	0.0235
	Kurtosis	–1.0995	4.7261	19.0906	3.6461	8.2099	3.3574
	Skewness	–0.0091	0.1987	0.9018	0.2271	2.4472	1.2202
TCS	Mean	0.0305	–0.0224	0.0305	–0.0220	–0.0011	–0.0052
	Median	0.0045	0.0035	0.0045	–0.0097	0.0239	0.0093
	Standard deviation	3.3233	2.3609	3.3184	2.3607	0.0167	0.0206
	Kurtosis	–1.0188	2.2978	–1.0189	2.2888	16.3963	2.2777
	Skewness	0.0082	–0.0142	0.0088	–0.0166	0.4409	0.0484
Wipro	Mean	0.0003	0.0194	0.0003	0.0139	–0.0006	0.0705
	Median	0.0045	0.2967	0.0041	0.0078	0.0086	0.0012
	Standard deviation	4.1636	0.0242	4.1592	0.0202	0.0195	4.2413
	Kurtosis	–1.3258	3.6184	–1.3254	6.6912	10.2891	–1.3471
	Skewness	–0.0171	1.7658	–0.0161	2.3093	–0.8565	–0.0002

With regard to standard deviation, it is observed that relatively higher values are for Wipro in the range of 4.16 to 0.019. Lower levels of standard deviation for the returns on the weeks are observed for Polaris in the range of 0.028 to 0.04 with all week standard deviation of 1.3275. I-Flex, Infosys and Polaris are observed to have consistently positive standard deviation for each of the five weeks with all week standard deviation of 0.0441, 0.0375. and 1.3275 respectively. Wipro has higher value of all week standard deviation with 4.24 and TCS have lower value of all week with 0.0206 and is found to have the minimum week standard deviation return for 5th week (0.0167). Infosys has lowest standard deviations value in 1st week with value 0.0196 and Wipro have highest standard deviations value in 3rd week of month with value of 4.1592.

With regard to Kurtosis, higher values for the weeks are observed for Patni in the range of 0.98 to 28.8, with the all week Kurtosis lower value of 1.9766, all week highly peaked(leptokurtic) except 1st week(0.9865). Lower range of kurtosis for the weeks are observed for Polaris in the range of 1.7 to 3.9 with all week kurtosis of 1.4041. Further, it is found that very high range of kurtosis for some weeks and lower levels for other weeks is observed for Satyam in the range of –1.09 to 19.09 for 1st week to 3rd week. Infosys is observed to have consistently positive kurtosis value for each of the five weeks with all week Kurtosis of 2.9446(normal). Kurtosis is found high in four weeks for Patni and Satyam, three weeks for Wipro, two week for I-Flex and Polaris and one week for TCS. In respect of all week kurtosis, I-Flex and Satyam are more peaked distribution (leptokurtic) with value of more then 3, Infosys having normal (mesokurtic) return distribution and other weeks more flat (platykutic) with the Kurtosis value less then 3.

With regard to skewness, it is observed that relatively higher values of skewness is for Patni in the range of –0.0071 to 6.12, with the all week skewness of 1.2714, 5th week highly skewed with value of 6.1208 followed by 4th week with value of 0.7915 and other weeks skewness inconsistent. Lower range of skewness for the weeks are observed for TCS in the range of –0.016 to 0.44 with all week skewness of 0.484. Further, it is found that the weekly return for Infosys has all positive but very less skewness for the weeks. Very high range of skewness for some weeks and positive skewness is observed for Wipro in the range of –0.85 to 2.309 for 5th week and 4th week, with all week negative skewness of –0.0002. With respect to all week skewness, Infosys is more skewed with value of 2.0702 and I-Flex, Patni, Satyam and TCS have relatively positive skewed return distribution while Polaris and Wipro evidence negative skewness.

The non-parametric test Kruskal-Wallis test for calculation of expected average rank and compares it with actual rank to find deviation for each pair of trading days and the paired combination of weeks. This is done for each of the selected companies and the four selected NSE indices. Such an analysis is performed for investigating the day of the week and the week of the month effect over the study period. Since the month-wise paired combinations are vary large in number, it was not feasible to present the findings for the month of the year effect.

Analysis of Kruskal-Wallis Test for Day of the Week Effect

In this section, we have calculated the expected Multiple Comparisons value and compared that with actual value to find the deviation for each of the ten pairs of trading days. Further, we have calculated Annual Returns for the active and passive strategies.

Table 3 presents the value of actual and expected multiple comparisons from Kruskal-Wallis test, along with the deviation for each pair trading day combination, with respect to the seven IT companies. It is observed that the deviation between actual and expected value is positive for all seven companies with respect to two combinations namely Monday-Wednesday, and Tuesday-Thursday. For the combination Monday-Wednesday, highest positive deviation of 44.16 is evidenced for I-Flex and lowest deviation 6.75 for Satyam. Similar observation is also found for the Tuesday-Thursday combination with highest positive deviation 52.75 for TCS and lowest positive deviation 16.33 for Patni.

This implies that with the respect to the seven IT companies positive higher return could be generated by following either of the activity trading strategy of Monday-Wednesday combination or Tuesday-Thursday combination, thus evidencing day of the week effect. Since the deviations are not positive across each of the seven companies for the other trading day combinations these pairs of combination are not considered for calculating the annual return as depicted in table 4.

Table 4 depicts the annual returns for each of the seven IT companies with respect the Monday-Wednesday, Tuesday-Thursday and buy-hold strategy. It is observed that I-Flex shows positive annual return for Monday-Wednesday combination (0.25%) and annualized return of 4.32% for the passive strategy of buy and hold over the study period.

Similarly in case of Infosys, TCS and Wipro the passive strategy of buy and hold generates annual return of 2.21%, 4.65% and 7.54%, respectively and also positive return of 0.41%, 0.27% and 0.57%, respectively for Monday-Wednesday combination. But the annual return for Tuesday-Thursday combination is negative at 0.32% for Satyam. On the other hand, both Patni and Satyam are observed to generate annual return of –1.21% and –5.63%, respectively for the passive strategy of buy and hold during the study period. Similar observation of negative return is also observed for the active strategy of Monday-Wednesday and Tuesday-Thursday, for the both Patni. The exception being the positive return of 0.54% for Monday-Wednesday with respect to Satyam.

On the whole, it is found that the active strategy of Monday-Wednesday and Tuesday-Thursday generates lesser return (less then 1% return) as compare to passive strategy of buy and hold over study period for the seven IT companies. Further, highest positive

Table 3: Actual and Expected Multiple Comparisons Value and the Deviations for the Pairs of Trading Days in IT Sector

Company	I-Flex			Infosys			Patni			Polaris			Satyam			TCS			Wipro		
Day	Actual	Exp.	Dev.	Actual	Exp.	Dev.	Actual	Exp.	Dev.	Actual	Exp.	Dev.	Actual	Exp.	Dev.	Actual	Exp.	Dev.	Actual	Exp.	Dev.
M-T	23.45	95.3	–71.85	84.56	95.54	–10.98	38.18	95.38	–57.2	139.74	96.34	43.4	56.99	96.88	–39.89	135.67	95.06	40.61	6.77	96.58	–89.81
M-W	140.56	96.4	**44.16**	130.45	96.45	**34**	137.16	96.39	**40.77**	125.55	95.37	**30.18**	103.09	96.34	**6.75**	137.58	95.16	**42.42**	107.43	96.49	**10.94**
M-TH	137.43	95.32	42.11	63.29	96.34	–33.05	128.45	95.33	33.12	50.67	95.74	–45.07	85.44	96.35	–10.91	39.56	95.38	–55.82	90.53	95.14	–4.61
M-F	104.56	95.36	9.2	93.54	96.33	–2.79	38.45	96.43	–57.98	84.83	96.23	–11.4	127.56	95.03	32.53	102.88	96.21	6.67	112.09	95.38	16.71
T-W	58.55	96.15	–37.6	20.45	95.31	–74.86	136.09	96.39	39.7	94.19	96.4	–2.21	108.09	95.45	12.64	45.06	96.35	–51.29	115.78	95.45	20.33
T-TH	134.56	96.38	**34.18**	115.48	95.17	**20.31**	111.59	95.26	**16.33**	124.09	95.3	**28.79**	132.67	95.38	**37.29**	147.78	95.03	**52.75**	128.56	96.26	**32.3**
T-F	56.55	96.1	–39.55	21.33	95.2	–73.87	71.45	95.39	–23.94	25.06	96.49	–71.43	48.79	96.03	–47.24	129.58	95.01	34.57	35.19	96.56	–61.37
W-TH	38.45	95.27	–56.82	108.4	96.09	12.31	30.98	96.45	–65.47	27.55	95.22	–67.67	10.56	96.3	–85.74	39.98	96.49	–56.51	98.56	96.43	2.13
W-F	65.45	95.32	–29.87	76.55	95.31	–18.76	88.03	95.23	–7.2	120.46	96.44	24.02	18.49	96.2	–77.71	76.45	95.64	–19.19	110.45	96.12	14.33
TH-F	100.9	96.11	4.79	73.96	95.05	–21.09	63.12	96.2	–33.08	36.11	96.45	–60.34	38.05	95.1	–57.05	72.45	95.1	–22.65	67.57	96.13	–28.56

Notes: M-W denotes the paired combination of Monday-Wednesday for which the actual and expected comparison values are calculated. Similarly for the other pairs of trading days.

Table 4: Annual Returns (in %) Generated by Paired Day Active Strategy and Passive Strategy in IT Sector

Company/Day	I-Flex	Infosys	Patni	Polaris	Satyam	TCS	Wipro
Mon-wed	0.25%	0.24%	–0.76%	0.41%	0.54%	0.27%	0.57%
Tue-Thurs	0.63%	0.34%	–0.27%	0.36%	–0.32%	0.63%	0.32%
Buy-Hold	4.32%	2.21%	–1.21%	1.32%	–5.63%	4.65%	7.54%

abnormal return is for Wipro and maximum negative return for Satyam, with respect to passive strategy.

Analysis of Kruskal-Wallis Test for Week of the Month Effect in IT Sector

Table 5 presents the values of actual and expected multiple comparison from the Kruskal-Wallis test, along with the deviation for each pair trading week combination, with respect to the selected seven IT companies. It is observed that the deviation between actual and expected value is positive for all seven IT companies with respect to two combinations namely 1st-2nd week and 1st-4th week. For the combination 1st-2nd week highest of positive deviation (43.48) is evidenced for Infosys and lowest deviation 2.09 for TCS. Similar observation is also found for the 1st-4th week combination with highest positive deviation of 40.04 for Wipro and lowest positive deviation of 2.67 for Polaris.

This implies that with the respect to the seven IT companies positive abnormal return could be generated by following either of the trading strategy of 1st-2nd week combination or 1st-4th week combination, thus evidencing week of the month effect. Since the deviations are not positive across each of the seven companies for the other trading week combinations. these pairs of combination are not considered for calculating the annual return as depicted in Table 6.

Consequently, the study has analyzed and calculated the annual return generated for 1st-2nd week and 1st-4th week combination along with passive strategy of buy-hold. Table 6 depicts the annual returns for each of the seven IT companies with respect the 1st-2nd week, 1st-4th week, and buy-hold strategy. It is observed that I-Flex shows positive annual return for 1st-2nd week combination (0.32%) and annualized return of 2.34% for the passive strategy of buying and holding over the study period.

Similarly in case of Infosys, the passive strategy of buy and hold generates annual return of 4.51% and also positive return of 0.44% for 1st-2nd combination. But the annual return for 1st-4th combination is negative at 0.78% for Polaris. On the other hand, Patni, Polaris and Satyam are observed to generate annual return of -1.24%, -0.45% and -7.25%, respectively for the passive strategy of buy and holding during the study period. Similar observation of negative return is also observed for the active strategy of 1st-2nd week and 1st-4th week, for the both Patni and Satyam. The exception being the positive return of 0.34% for 1st-2nd week with respect to Polaris. The study also observed that for I-Flex, Infosys, TCS and Wipro the active strategy for 1st-2nd week and 1st-4th week combination generate positive annualised return.

On the whole, it is observed that the active strategy of 1st-2nd week and 1st-4th week generates lesser abnormal return (less then 1% return) as compared to the passive strategy of buy and hold over study period for the seven IT companies. Further, highest positive abnormal return is for Wipro and maximum negative return for Satyam, with respect to passive strategy.

Table 5: Actual and Expected Multiple Comparisons Value and the Deviations for Pairs of Weeks in IT Sector

Company	I-Flex			Infosys			Patni			Polaris			Satyam			TCS			Wipro		
Week	Actual	Exp.	Dev.	Actual	Exp.	Dev.	Actual	Exp.	Dev.	Actual	Exp.	Dev.	Actual	Exp.	Dev.	Actual	Exp.	Dev.	Actual	Exp.	Dev.
1st -2nd	138.64	95.32	**43.32**	140.24	96.76	**43.48**	135.65	96.45	**39.2**	134.57	96.33	**38.24**	138.56	95.43	**34.13**	98.45	96.36	**2.09**	108.56	96.49	**12.07**
1st -3rd	30.56	95.29	-64.73	138.56	96.09	42.47	121.08	96.05	25.03	136.75	96.54	40.21	100.45	96.32	4.13	44.12	96.88	-52.76	138.45	96.43	42.02
1st -4th	112.54	95.4	**17.14**	133.76	95.35	**38.41**	130.54	95.88	**34.66**	98.55	95.88	**2.67**	125.46	95.36	**30.1**	134.36	96.77	**37.59**	135.34	95.3	**40.04**
1st -5th	28.45	96.1	-67.65	130.55	95.65	34.9	54.65	95.34	-40.69	45.09	95.32	-50.23	109.36	96.21	13.15	126.54	95.66	30.88	123.09	95.4	27.69
2nd-3rd	9.45	96.3	-86.85	118.09	96.34	21.75	88.65	96.67	-8.02	43.65	96.05	-52.4	125.64	95.12	30.52	127.45	95.78	31.67	90.45	96.02	-5.57
2nd-4th	111.45	96.43	15.02	67.45	96.09	-28.64	56.76	95.09	-38.33	56.05	95.23	-39.18	56.45	95.38	-38.93	34.45	96.08	-61.63	96.55	95.1	1.45
2nd-5th	124.04	95.23	28.81	76.3	95.32	-19.02	45.53	95.23	-49.7	18.45	95.3	-76.85	15.45	96.76	-81.31	6.66	96.56	-89.9	40.85	96.45	-55.6
3rd -4th	136.95	95.09	41.86	86.57	95.12	-8.55	10.67	96.33	-85.66	17.34	96.43	-79.09	30.47	96.4	-65.93	4.09	95.54	-91.45	36.06	96.2	-60.14
3rd -5th	67.53	95.2	-27.67	134.02	95.23	38.79	23.34	96.32	-72.98	125.47	95.67	29.8	13.48	96.03	-82.55	88.6	95.65	-7.05	43.33	95.42	-52.09
4th -5th	34.22	96.1	-61.88	98.34	96.55	1.79	33.23	95.13	-61.9	124.35	96.88	27.47	5.43	95.17	-89.74	67.59	95.18	-27.59	31.09	95.32	-64.23

Table 6: Annual Returns (in %) Generated by Paired Week Active Strategy and Passive Strategy in IT Sector

Company/Week	I-Flex	Infosys	Patni	Polaris	Satyam	TCS	Wipro
1st-2nd	0.32%	0.44%	–0.12%	0.34%	–0.68%	0.25%	0.87%
1st-4th	0.54%	0.74%	–0.25%	–0.78%	–0.08%	0.65%	0.22%
Buy-Hold	2.34%	4.51%	–1.24%	–0.45%	–7.25%	2.54%	4.65%

Analysis of Regression Results for Day of the Week Effect

In this section, we have used regression technique to analyze the findings of the day of the week effect. We have used four weekday dummies namely Tuesday dummy, Wednesday dummy, Thursday dummy and Friday dummy with the constant signifying the Monday effect. A significant value of a weekday dummy indicates presence of the day of the week effect for that weekday.

Table 7 shows the results of regression analysis regarding day of week effect for the selected IT companies. It is observed that for I-Flex, there is positive Tuesday effect (with B_2 co-efficient of 0.02506) found significant at 1%, while there is a significant (at 5% level) positive effect on Wednesday with the co-efficient (B_3) value of 0.00028. Further, the regression analysis failed to observe any significance for Monday, Thursday and Friday coefficients with regard to I-Flex.

For Infosys there is both positive Wednesday effect (B_3 coefficient value 0.00112) and Thursday effect (B_4 coefficient value 0.05206) found significant at 1%, while there is significant (at 5% level) positive effect on Tuesday with coefficient (B_2) value of 0.0654. Patni computers evidenced positive Monday effect (B_1 coefficient value 0.00078) found significant at 5% and negative Tuesday effect (B_2 coefficient value –0.0056) found significant at 1%, with no significance for Wednesday, Thursday and Friday coefficient.

Table 7: Regression Results of Day of Week Effect in IT Sector

Company	Constant	B_2	B_3	B_4	B_5	R^2	F-value
I-Flex	0.00008	0.02506*	0.00028**	0.00112	0.08523	0.68	7.33 (0.0014)
Infosys	0.00089	0.0654**	0.00112*	0.05206*	0.07412	0.88	2.88 (0.025)
Patni	0.00078**	–0.0056*	0.00336	–0.05603	–0.06589	0.58	5.56 (0.0017)
Polaris	–0.00075	–0.00985	–0.00852*	0.00001*	–0.03214	0.52	2.99 (0.0214)
Satyam	–0.00009	0.00203	0.00965**	0.00023	0.01111*	0.75	6.49 (0.0019)
TCS	0.00025	0.00503*	–0.00032*	–0.00045	0.06632	0.69	1.93 (0.112)
Wipro	–0.00085*	–0.00852	0.00011**	0.00111	–0.0334	0.59	2.47 (0.057)

Note: *, ** and *** denote significance at 1%, 5% and 10%, respectively; the values in parenthesis under F-value denote the p-value of the regression analysis.

In case of Polaris there is negative Wednesday effect (B_3 coefficient value –0.00852) found significant at 1%, and positive Thursday effect (with B_4 co-efficient value of 0.00001) significant at 1% level, without significant regression coefficients for other weekdays. For Satyam, there is positive Wednesday effect (with B_3 co-efficient of 0.00965) found significant at 5% and a significant (at 1% level) positive effect on Friday with the co-efficient (B_5) value of 0.01111. The study failed to observe any significance for Monday, Tuesday and Thursday coefficients with regard to Satyam. TCS showed positive Tuesday effect (with B_2 co-efficient of 0.00503) and negative Wednesday effect (with B_3 co-efficient value of –0.00032) both found significant at 1%. There was no significance for Monday, Thursday and Friday coefficients with regard to TCS. For Wipro there is negative Monday effect (with B_1 co-efficient of –0.00085) found significant at 1%, and significant (at 5% level) positive effect on Wednesday with the co-efficient (B_3) value of 0.00011. Further, the regression analysis failed to observe any significance for Tuesday, Thursday and Friday coefficients with regard to Wipro.

With respect to R^2 (coefficient of determination), the highest value of 0.88 is observed for Infosys and lowest value of 0.52 for Polaris. The R^2 values of the other companies are in the range of 0.52 to 0.88 which implies that the regression model is an appropriate one. Further, the F-value is relatively higher in the range of 1.93 to 7.33 with respect the selected IT Companies with I-Flex having highest F-value of 7.33 with P-value of 0.0014, followed by Satyam with F-value 6.49 and the corresponding P-value of 0.0019.

Regression Result Analysis for Week of the Month Effect in IT sector

Table 8 shows the regression results regarding week of month effect for the seven selected IT companies. It is observed that I-Flex, there is positive 1st week effect (with B_1 co-efficient of 0.0058) found significant at 1%, a significant (at 5 % level) positive effect on 3rd week with the co-efficient (B_3) value of 0.00258 but without any significance for 2nd week, 4th week and 5th week coefficients.

It is observed that for Infosys there is positive 2nd week effect (B_2 coefficient value 0.00111) found significance at 5% while negative 3rd week effect (B_3 coefficient value –0.00052) found significant at 1%. For Patni there is positive 1st week effect (B_1 coefficient value 0.0063) found significant at 5%, 3rd week effect (B_3 coefficient value 0.02222) found significant at 1%, and no any significance for 2nd week, 4th week and 5th week coefficient. Polaris showed positive 2nd week effect (B_2 coefficient value 0.00552) and negative 4th week effect (B_4 coefficient value –0.009) found significant at 5%, but without significance for 1st week, 3rd week and 5th week coefficient. For Satyam, there is negative 1st week effect (with B_1 co-efficient of –0.0065) found significant at 1%, and positive 3rd week effect (B_3 coefficient value 0.00111) found significant at 5%. Similarly TCS evidenced negative 2nd week effect (with B_2 co-efficient of –0.00057) found significant at 1% and

Table 8: Regression Results of Week of the Month Effect in IT Sector

Company	Constant	B_2	B_3	B_4	B_5	R^2	F-value
I-Flex	0.0058*	–0.00852	0.00258**	0.00112	–0.05096	0.71	2.88 (0.012)
Infosys	–0.0235	0.00111**	–0.00052*	–0.00226	0.00806	0.92	1.96 (0.092)
Patni	0.0063**	0.00052	0.02222*	0.08838	0.00001	0.68	5.53 (0.0027)
Polaris	0.0088	0.00552**	0.00006	–0.009**	–0.00008	0.79	2.65 (0.017)
Satyam	–0.0065*	0.75083	0.00111**	0.00008	0.01235	0.76	6.98 (0.0016)
TCS	0.0083	–0.00057*	–0.0152**	–0.08075	0.00069	0.59	3.99 (0.0018)
Wipro	–0.0074*	–0.00352	–0.00096	0.00852*	–0.08569	0.58	5.57 (0.0028)

3rd week effect (with B_3 co-efficient value of –0.0152) found significant at 5%. In case of Wipro there is negative 1st week effect (B_1 coefficient value –0.0074), positive 4th week effect(B_4 coefficient value 0.00852) both found significant at 1%, while the regression results fail to observe any significance for 2nd week, 3rd week and 5th week coefficient with regard to Wipro.

On the analysis of the values of R^2 (coefficient of determination), it is found that highest value of 0.92 is observed for Infosys and lowest value of 0.58 for Wipro, with values in the range of 0.58 to 0.92. A relatively high R^2 value is an indicator that which implies that the regression model is an appropriate one. Analysis of the last column of Table 8 show that the F-value found from the regression analysis is relatively higher in the range of 1.96 to 6.98 with Satyam having highest value of 6.98 (with P-value of 0.0016), followed by Wipro with F-value 5.57 and the corresponding P-value of 0.0028.

Major findings on Descriptive statistics of selected companies

The descriptive statistics techniques used for analysis of return for selected companies are mean, median, standard deviation, kurtosis and skewness. These statistics are calculated for each of the five trading days, over the study period covered from 3rd November 1994 to 31st December 2008.

With regard to average all day return, highest and lowest value is found for Satyam and Wipro, respectively. Similarly with regard to standard deviation for all day return, highest and lowest value is found for I-Flex and Wipro respectively. With respect to kurtosis for all day return, highest and lowest value is found for Wipro and Infosys respectively. Similarly with regard to skewnes for all day return, highest and lowest value is found for Polaris and Wipro respectively.

Major Findings of Descriptive Statistics for Weekly Return in Selected Companies

With regard to average all week return, highest and lowest value is found Wipro and TCS, respectively. Similarly with regard to standard deviation for all week return, highest and lowest value is found for Wipro and TCS, respectively. The kurtosis for all week return is highest and lowest for I-Flex and Wipro, respectively. Similarly with respect to skewnes for all week return, highest and lowest value is observed for Infosys and Polaris, respectively.

Major Findings on Kruskal-Wallis Analysis for Day of the Week Effect in IT Sector

Positive deviation between actual and expected values from the Kruskal-Wallis test is observed for all the seven IT companies with respect to two pairs of trading day namely Monday-Wednesday and Tuesday-Thursday with highest value of 44.16 (for I-Flex) and 52.75(for TCS), respectively. This indicates that abnormal return could be generated by following these pairs of trading days. On the whole, it was observed that the active strategy of buy and sell for Monday-Wednesday and Tuesday-Thursday combination generate relatively less return as compare to passive strategy of buy and hold during the study period. Further, the passive strategy generates highest positive return for the Wipro (7.54%) and lesser returns for Satyam (–5.63%).

Major Findings on Kruskal-Wallis Analysis for Week of the Month Effect for IT Sector

The study observed positive deviation between actual and expected values from the Kruskal-Wallis test for all the seven IT companies in respect of two pairs of trading week namely 1st week-2nd week and 1st week-4th week with highest value of 43.48(for Infosys) and 40.04(for Wipro), respectively. This implies that abnormal return could be generated by following these pairs of trading weeks. On the whole, it was observed that the active strategy of buy and sell for 1st week-2nd week and 1st week-4th week combination generate relatively less return as compared to passive strategy of buy and hold during the study period. Further, the passive strategy generates highest positive return for the Wipro (4.65%) and lowest returns for Satyam (–7.25%).

Major Findings of Regression Analysis for Day of the Week Effect

The study has analyzed the day of the week effect in the selected seven IT companies.

It is found that I-Flex has Tuesday effect and Wednesday effect significant at 1% and 5%, respectively. In case of Patni, the study finds Monday effect and Tuesday effect significant at 5% and 1%, respectively. Infosys is also observed to have significant Wednesday effect and Thursday effect both at 1%. For Satyam, the study finds Wednesday effect and Friday effect significant at 5% and 1% respectively. With respect to TCS, the study finds significant Tuesday effect and Wednesday effect, both at 1%. Wipro is also observed to have significant Monday effect and Wednesday effect at 1% and 5%, respectively. On the whole, there is an evidence of day of the week effect in the IT sector. Further, the value of R^2 (in the range of 0.52 to 0.88) is relatively higher which indicates that the deviation in the dependent variable is well explained by the independent variables (week day dummies). Moreover the F-value in the range of 1.93 to 7.33 is also relatively higher.

Major Findings on Regression Analysis for Week of the Month Effect in IT Sector

The study has analyzed the week of the month effect in the selected seven IT companies. It is found that I-Flex has 1st week effect and 3rd week effect significant at 1% and 5%, respectively. Further, Infosys has 2nd week effect and 3rd week effect significant at 5% and 1%, respectively. For Patni the study finds significant 1st week effect and 3rd week effect at 5% and 1%, respectively. Polaris is also observed to have significant 2nd week effect and 4th week effect, both significant at 5%. In case Satyam, the study finds 1st week effect and 3rd week effect significant at 1% and 5%, respectively. With respect to TCS, the study finds significant 2nd week effect and 3rd week effect at 1% and 5%, respectively. Wipro is also observed to have significant 1st week effect and 4th week effect, both significant at 1%. On the whole, there is an evidence of week of the month effect in the IT sector. Further, the value of R^2 (in the range of 0.58 to 0.92) is relatively higher which indicates that the deviation in the dependent variable is well explained by the independent variables (week dummies). Moreover, the F-value in the range of 1.96 to 6.98 is also relatively higher.

CONCLUSION

The study presented a comprehensive analysis of the stock price behavior, more specifically on the seasonality effect, in the Indian stock market. The seasonality effect is examined by a detailed analysis of day of the week effect and the period of study spans over fourteen year, i.e. from 1994 to 2008. The study found significant day of week effect for specific trading days. The multiple regression analysis also found evidence of day of week for the price series with regard to the selected banks. Further, the value of R^2

for the derived regression models for each of the selected companies relatively higher which indicates that the deviation in the dependent variable is well explained by the independent variables (day dummies). On the whole, the price series in the Indian stock market showed signs of return seasonality with respect to day of week.

REFERENCES

[1] Agathee, U.S. (2008), 'Day of the Week Effect: Evidence from the Stock Exchange of Mauritius (SEM)'. *International Research Journal of Finance and Economics*, 17, pp. 7-14.

[2] Alejandro, R.C. (2006), 'Day of the Week Effect on European Stock Markets', *International Research Journal of Finance and Economics,* Issue 2, pp. 53-70.

[3] Choudhary, K. and Choudhary, S. (2008), 'Day-of-the-Week Effect: Further Empirical Evidence', *Asia-Pacific Business Review*, Vol. 4, No. 3, pp. 67-74.

[4] Halil, K. and Hakan, B. (2001), 'The Day of the Week Effect on Stock Market Volatility', *Journal of Economics and Finance*, 25, pp. 181-193.

[5] Kumari, D. and Mahendra, R. (2006), 'Day-of-the-Week and Other Market Anomalies in the Indian Stock Market', *International Journal of Emerging Markets*, Vol. 1, No. 3, pp. 235-246.

[6] Pandey, I.M. (2002), 'Seasonality in the Malayasian Stock Market: 1992-2002', *Journal of Financial Management and Analysis*, 15(2), pp. 37-44.

[7] Nath, G.C. and Dalvi, M. (2004), 'Day-of-the-Week Effect and Market Efficiency-Evidence from Indian Equity Market using High Frequency Data of National Stock Exchange', Paper Presented at The Center for Analytical Finance, Indian School of Business, Hyderabad, December, pp. 19-21.

[8] Rahman, L. (2009), 'Stock Market Anomaly: Day of the Week Effect in Dhaka Stock Exchange', *International Journal of Business and Management,* Vol. 4, pp. 193-206.

[9] Sarma, S.N. (2004), 'Stock Market Seasonality in an Emerging Market', *Vikalpa*, Vol. 29, pp. 35-41.

[10] Sharma, J.L. and R.E. Kennedy (1977), 'A Comparative Analysis of Stock Price Behaviour on the Bombay, London and New York Stock Exchanges', *Journal of Financial and Quantitative Analysis* 12, pp. 391-413.

[11] Tripathy, N. (2010), 'Expiration and Week Effect: Empirical Evidence from the Indian Derivative Market', *Annual London Business Research Conference*, 12-14 July 2010, London, United Kingdom.

IT Applications Enhancing Supply Chain Management and Inventory Management Productivity Improvements in SMEs

Ashok G. Matani[1], Mahendra S. Tripathi[2] and Pallavi Matani[3]

[1] Govt. College of Engineering, Amravati
[2] Government Polytechnic, Amravati
[3] International Institute of Information Technology, Hyderabad
E-mail: ashokgm333@rediffmail.com; mahendrastripathi@yahoo.com; pallavi2012@gmail.com

ABSTRACT

Inventory is any asset held for future use or sale. These assets may be physical goods, used in operations and includes ram materials, parts, sub assemblies , supplier tools, equipments or maintenance and spare parts. In some service organizations, inventories are not physical goods which customers take with them, but provide capacity available for service customers, Inventories can also be intangibles, e.g. many organizations maintain inventories of intellectual assets and best practice knowledge bases. Managing inventory is one of the most important functions of operations management in both manufacturing and service organizations. Simply maintaining large stocks of inventories is costly and wasteful. Better information technology and applications of quantitative tools and techniques for inventory management have allowed dramatic reductions in inventories. In the United States, business organizations have reduced total inventory as a percentage of gross domestic product (GDP) from 8.3% to 3.8%. This increases net working capital and reduces cash flow requirements to run the business, resulting in improved operational and financial efficiency. Inventory reduction is a vital part of becoming a lean organization. Newer technologies such as wireless communication systems and radio frequency identification (RFID) chips are improving the efficiency and effectiveness of inventory management in supply chains. Better communications allows the company to schedule its production and supplier order more efficiently, thus, maintaining lower number of parts. This paper highlights the impact of efficient and effective SCM towards improved inventory management in SMEs towards productivity enhancement.

Keywords: Effective and Responsive Supply Chains, Logistics, Productivity, Inventory

INTRODUCTION

Fundamentally, supply chain management helps any firm get the right products to the right place at the right time, in the proper quantity and at an acceptable cost. The main objective of supply chain management is to manage this process efficiently by forecasting demand, controlling inventory, enhancing the network of business relationships a company has with customers, suppliers, distributors, and others and receiving feedback on the status of every link in the supply chain. To achieve this firms are today are turning to Internet technologies to web enabled supply chain processes, decision making, and information flows.

METHODOLOGY

Supply chain management is the management of all activities, which facilitate fulfillment of a customer order from a manufactured good to achieve satisfied customers at reasonable cost. This includes materials management as well as flow of information and money necessary to coordinate activities. The materials and logistics managers focus on activities within span of their purchasing, manufacturing and distribution processes. SCM can be executed effectively with clear understanding and segmenting the customers, listening and responding to market signals, using technology wisely.

- Managing information of physical goods and service
- Reduce inventory obsolescence

RESEARCH DESIGN

Various types of questionnaires have been supplied to different task groups namely industry, NGOs, educational institutions, government administrators and officials, and customers and their feedback is collected.

Sampling Technique and Sample Size

More than 100 food processing and allied industries operating in Vidarbha Region of Maharashtra State, having minimum annual turnover of Rs. 50 crores in the financial years 2008-09, 2009-10 and 2010-11 are contacted.

Tools for Data Collection

In addition to the above industries, different departments of Government of India and Maharashtra, various NGOs, and different manufacturers, distributors and customers, have been contacted for collecting the relevant required data. Moreover various reports published by industries, government departments; newspapers, journals, etc., are also considered. The data collected is being analyzed and different mathematical and statistical models are analyzed and tested for significance. Multiple regression analysis between various dependent and independent variables is being performed and multiple regression models developed.

FINDINGS

Supply Chain Solution Software is a streamlined system that provides logistics, global freight, financial services , mail services and consulting to enhance customer's business performance and improve their supply chains. Geographic Information Systems (GIS) and Global Positioning Systems(GPS) are used extensively in location, site selection, land use planning, environment science, transportation systems, trucking companies now track their tracks via GPS technology. In vehicle navigational system, vehicle location systems, emergency vehicle deployment and traffic management are using GIS and GPS for their value chains.

POLICY/MANAGERIAL IMPLICATIONS

- An organization will be able to increase perceived benefits while reducing price or cost
- An organization will be able to maximize value by designing procedures and systems that create and deliver the appropriate goods and services customers want to use
- Exploring pre and post production services and opportunities to increase revenue and provide new sources of income
- Value chain integration including improving internal processes for the client as well as external processes that tie together suppliers, manufacturers, distributors and customers.

CONCLUSIONS

Effective execution of the extended supply chain can lower costs, improve customer service performance and enhance asset productivity. Companies have used business intelligence to develop and share vendor scorecards, and customer service metrics and have provided customers, vendors and third party service providers with visibility into the status of orders, inventory, returns, delivery performance and other key operational parameters. The Vendor Scorecard is a very effective tool to both monitor and manage suppliers. Business intelligence systems can be used to optimize order quantities, pool suppliers and minimize materials inventory, thereby assisting in determination of optimal order quantities and set up in business systems to minimize costs. Business intelligence techniques used for inventory control include complicated cost-value equations and historical and demand forecasting.

REFERENCES

[1] Adam Everett E. and Ebert Ronald J. (2000). "Production and Operations Management: Concepts, Models and Behavior", Prentice Hall of India Pvt. Ltd., New Delhi.

[2] Burt David N., Dobler W. Donald and Starling Stephen L. (2005). "World Class Supply Management", 7th Edn., Tata McGraw Hill Publishing Co. Ltd., New Delhi.

[3] Burgess, R. (1998). "Avoiding Supply Chain Management Failures: Lessons from Business Process Recycling", *International Journal of Logistics Management*, 9(1), 15-23.

[4] Chary, S.N. (2003). "Production and Operations Management", Tata McGraw Hill Publishing Company Limited, New Delhi.

[5] Cobb, Chuch (2001). "Knowledge Management and Quality Systems", The 54th Annual Quality Congress Proceedings, American Society for Quality, 276-287.

[6] Croom, S.R. (2000). "The Impact of Web Based Procurement on the Management of Operating Resources Supply", *The Journal of Supply Chain Management*, 2, 4-13.

[7] Evans, J.R. and Collier, D.A. (2006). "Operations Management: An Integrated Goods and Services Approach", Thomson South Western, Australia.

[8] Jacobe, D.G. (2003). "Anatomy of a Supply Chain", *Logistics Today*, 44, 60-63.

[9] Kahl, S.J. (1999). "What's the Value of Supply Chain Software?" *Supply Chain Management Review*, 4, 12-18.

[10] Kulkarni, Sarika and Sharma, Ashok (2005). "Supply Chain Management", Tata McGraw Hill Publishing Company Limited, New Delhi.

[11] Krishnan, V.R. and Arora Pooja (2008). "Determinants of Transformational Leadership and Organizational Citizenship Behavior", *Asia Pacific Business Review Journal*, 4(1), 34-43.

[12] McGrath Michael E. and Hoole Richard W. (1992). "Manufacturing New Economies of Scale", *Harvard Business Review*, 33, 94-102.

[13] Mehdi Khosrow Pour (2007). "Innovations through Information Technology", *Proceedings of the 15th Information Resources Management Association International Conference*, USA, 3, 342-346.

[14] Pande Peter S., Neuman R.P., Caramagh R.R. (2006). The Six Sigma Way: Tata McGraw Hill Publishing Company Limited, New Delhi.

[15] Reddy, Ram and Reddy, Sabine (2003). Supply Chains to Virtual Integration, Tata McGraw Hill Publishing Company Limited, New Delhi.

Kottayam Port and Container Terminal: A Commercial Viability Study

Jacob George and P.S. James
Saintgits Institute of Management, Kottayam
E-mail: jacobkallikothu@gmail.com

ABSTRACT

This study evaluates the commercial viability of a new venture in Public Private Partnership (PPP) in the context of Logistics Infrastructure and links it to the need for the crucial stage of commercial feasibility study before the final decision to launch the project. A case study was conducted at Kottayam Port and Container Terminal Services Pvt Ltd (KPACT), between December 15th 2009 and January 31st, 2010, by the author to evaluate its commercial viability. By that time the Port was officially inaugurated, but had not started commercial operations. At the commencement of the project a market potential study based on secondary data had been done by the management. This study projected a demand of 500 Tonne Equivalent Units (TEU) per month (exports and imports) in the hinder land of Kottayam. This was the only commercial information available for the study. The author, independently, analyzed the commercial viability of the port using financial data and market research. KPACT, Kottayam, Kerala is an Inland Container Depot (ICD) in the Container Logistics Industry of India. It is a PPP with management by and 51% ownership of private partners. The ICD has started its commercial operations in 2011. KPACT is the first ICD in India using an inland waterway for its operation. The objective of the ICD is to provide infrastructure facilities for movement of custom cleared, stuffed export cargo containers from the hinder land districts of Kottayam, Idukki and Pathanamthitta to Kochi Port and import cargo from Kochi. The management has contributed highly innovated technical skills to the project. They constructed a 200 Tonne barge which is specially designed to go along the shallow water way and yet pass under the water lock there. They, for the first time in India, adopted the roll on- roll off system of container movement on trailers. They have also designed a modern Container Terminal by providing the facility of the Single Window System based on Electronic Data Interface connectivity and online tracking of goods and containers. But the management did not give commercial feasibility study the same importance as that of the technical feasibility study. The management has strategically planned to provide all port cargo and container handling facilities at minimum mark up while barge transportation along the water way will be the main revenue source. The break even analysis done during the study shows that at least two barges should be in operation each fully loaded for the ICD to break even at reasonable level. It, in turn, indicates the need for very intense and continuous marketing effort as the eventual market share has to be at least 80% of the total estimated market. In other words, the total market apparently is too small and the level of competition promises to be quite high. So the PPP's real challenge now turns out to be penetrating the market fast enough and deep enough to avoid default in bank loan repayment; marketing the concept of container transport among the local customers; popularizing transportation through water by barge as opposed to time-tested fast and reliable road transportation and making sure that the ICD consistently offer a more competitive rate for handling and transportation than the competitors, the Container Freight Stations in Kerala. The challenge promises to be quite uphill. This single case study brings out the fact that a PPP may well have to grapple with serious commercial issues after commissioning if the management focuses mainly only on technical problems during the project stage. So PPPs are well advised to do adequate commercial feasibility studies to anticipate management problems after commissioning.

Keywords: Kottayam Port and Container Terminal

OBJECTIVE OF THE STUDY

This study evaluates the commercial viability of a new venture in Public Private Partnership (PPP) in the context of Logistics Infrastructure and links it to the need for the crucial stage of commercial feasibility study before the final decision to launch the project.

METHODOLOGY

A study was conducted at Kottayam Port and Container Terminal Services Pvt Ltd (KPACT), between December 15th 2009 and January 31st, 2010, by the authors to evaluate its commercial viability. By that time the Port was officially inaugurated, but had not started commercial operations.

At the commencement of the project a market potential study based on secondary data had been done by the management. This study projected a demand of 500 Tonne Equivalent Units (TEU) per month (exports and imports) in the hinder land of Kottayam. This was the only commercial information available for the study. The authors, independently, analyzed the commercial viability of the port using financial data and market research.

ABOUT KPACT

KPACT, Kottayam, Kerala is an Inland Container Depot (ICD) in the Container

Logistics Industry of India. It is a Public Private Partnership (PPP) with management by and 51% ownership of private partners. It is a Design, Build, Finance and Operate (DBFO) Scheme.

KPACT is the first ICD in India using an inland waterway for its operation. The objective of the ICD is to provide infrastructure facilities for movement of custom cleared, stuffed export cargo containers from the hinder land districts of Kottayam, Idukki and Pathanamthitta to Kochi Port and import cargo from Kochi.

The first PPP Minor Port and ICD Project in Kerala, the Kottayam Port and Container Terminal, was inaugurated on 17th August 2009. This is also India's first port (notified under Indian Ports Act) and an Inland Container Depot (ICD) to utilise inland waterway with Customs notified area for Exports & Imports. The Kottayam Port and Container Terminal is a first of its kind project of Public Private Partnership under the ASIDE scheme of Government of India promoted by South Indian Chamber Of Commerce and Industry (SICCI) and KINFRA, a state government agency. The total outlay of the project is Rs. 9.56 crores.

Kottayam is connected to the Cochin Port by an inland waterway which is the National Waterway No. III. The project being developed at Nattakom on the banks of Kodur River connects to Vembanadu Lake and the National Waterway III. As per a survey conducted by the researchers, there are nearly 50 large exporters in the three districts of Kottayam, Idukki and Pathanamthitta who ship full containers. Every year nearly 11,000 fully loaded containers are transported to and fro from these districts to the Cochin Port and return by road. This project is to transport these containers in barges to Cochin Port through Inland Waterway. The total logistics cost can be reduced by up to Rs 4000/- from the present cost by the road transportation to Cochin port from Kottayam.

The management has contributed highly innovative technical skills to the project. They constructed a 200 Tonne barge which is specially designed to go along the shallow water way and yet pass under the water lock there. They, for the first time in India, adopted the roll on-roll off system of container movement on trailers. This is, instead of the lift on, lift off system using cranes. They have also designed a modern Container Terminal by providing the facility of the Single Window System based on Electronic Data Interface connectivity and online tracking of goods and containers. But the management did not give commercial feasibility study the same importance as that of the technical feasibility study.

LITERATURE REVIEW

I. Zhang (2005 A) talks of 5 critical success factors (CSFs) and several success sub factors (SSFs) for a PPP in Infrastructure sector. Those with significance index above 80 are listed below.

1. Economic viability
    - Long-term demand for the products/services offered by the project – 88
    - Sufficient profitability of the project to attract investors – 85.33
    - Long-term cash flow that is attractive to lenders – 84.55
2. Appropriate risk allocation via reliable contractual arrangements
    - Concession agreement – 86.67
3. Sound financial package
    - Sound financial analysis – 84.55
    - Appropriate toll/tariff levels and suitable adjustment formula – 83.18
    - Abilities to deal with fluctuations in interest/exchange rates – 80
4. Favourable investment environment
    - Stable political system – 81.33
    - Government support – 80.89
5. Reliable concessionaire consortium with strong technical strength (No SSR above 80)

II. Zhang (2005 B) identifies various barriers to PPPs, which are broadly classified into six categories:
    1. social, political, and legal risks;
    2. unfavourable economic and commercial conditions;
    3. inefficient public procurement framework;
    4. lack of mature financial engineering techniques;
    5. problems related to the public sector; and
    6. problems related to the private sector.

    Effective measures for removing these barriers and formulating an efficient PPP protocol have been identified and analyzed by drawing experience from worldwide practices and comparing and benchmarking the best practices. These measures are classified into nine areas:
    1. appropriate roles of governmental authorities;
    2. best value for money approach;
    3. effective management of adviser services;
    4. development of an appropriate PPP scheme;
    5. use of relational contracts;
    6. improvement of the procurement framework;
    7. suitable payment structure;
    8. appropriate terms for contract monitoring, termination, and step-in rights; and
    9. a workable transfer procedure.

III. Zhang (2006) indicates that best value should be the ultimate goal of various types of public private partnered infrastructure projects. This necessitates a Best Value Source Selection (BVSS) process, which must be well structured and sufficiently flexible to accommodate the general business requirements of the client, and the specific objectives, attributes, and conditions of the particular PPP project. The general requirements and specific objectives should be further defined in terms of BVCFs, against which alternative proposals are evaluated.

Twenty-one Best Value Contributing Factors (BVCFs) for PPPs in general have been identified in a systematic research approach. Descriptive comparison and rank agreement analysis show that there is no statistical difference in the ranking of these BVCFs between the academic and the industrial groups. The most important ten are stated below.

1. Transfer of risks related to construction, finance and operation
2. Reducing the size of public borrowing via off balance sheet financing
3. Benefits to local economy
4. Early project completion/ product or service delivery
5 .Acquisition of a fully completed and operational facility
6. Low project life cycle cost
7. Reduced public administrative costs
8. Reduced disputes and claims
9. Low tariffs/tolls
10. Long project life span

IV. Abdel Aziz (2007)'s study and analysis of the service-based PPP approaches in the United Kingdom and British Columbia, and the comparison of these approaches to a finance-based approach, highlighted a number of principles that would characterize the successful implementation of PPPs at the program level.

The principles included: (1) the importance of understanding the objectives of using private finance when selecting a PPP arrangement; (2) the implication of allocating project risks to the private sector; (3) the necessity of a broad and comprehensive PPP legal framework; (4) the need to assess the value for money when selecting a delivery system; (5) the importance of creating a PPP unit for policy development and/or implementation; (6) the necessity of maintaining the transparency in the selection process; (7) the importance of standardizing the procedures and contracts; and 8) the importance of using performance specifications. A PPP program could be characterized as successful based on the degree of achievement and understanding of these principles. In light of the identified principles, guidelines for successful implementation of PPPs were suggested.

The analysis of the guidelines suggests that successful implementation could be attained at the program level through: (1) enacting broad enabling legislation that is not limited to pilot/demonstration projects or to a specific government level; (2) selecting the delivery system ,traditional or PPP, that would provide the greatest benefits to the public or users; (3) allowing the use and selection of the financing approach that would achieve the best value and benefits to the public; (4) completing comprehensive analysis and articulating clearly the controversial issues such as the non complete clauses; 5) evaluating the various payment mechanisms and selecting the one that best achieves the government objectives; 6) creating PPP units particularly for policy development; and 7) protecting the employees who would be affected from the implementation of PPPs. It is suggested that government agencies looking at PPP implementation consider these principles and guidelines as strong criteria for a successful implementation of PPPs.

However none of them specifically considers payback period as an important parameter in the scheme. Payback period is admittedly not a very important parameter for the public partner who will be interested in the social benefit to the public at large. But for the private partner, it is critical to recover the capital investment within a reasonably short period. A second reason is that thinking in terms of payback period forces the investors, both public and private partners, to go for the right level of capital investment to make for the project to be commercially viable. This is done by linking capital investment to the annual stream of profits.

So, this article gives the payback period its due place in assessing the commercial viability of PPPs in Infrastructure Sector. And the effort, here, is to highlight the role of payback period analysis in bringing out probability of the success of the PPP.

ANALYSIS

The analysis consists of the direction that the ICD is taking and how midway corrections may be taken. The tariff of the ICD and fixing the price range of the barge transportation are enclosed (Annexure I). Reason for adopting Cost leadership strategy is as follows. The two main revenue sources are (1) Barge transportation, and (2) Road transportation. All other ICD related expenses like stuffing, handling, storage and documentation charges are kept to bare minimum to attract customers to the services of the ICD. Barge offers a cost structure of about Rs 5.88/km/TEU running cost way below Rs 12.6/km/TEU for road transportation. By encouraging barge transportation and ICD stuffing, high volume of transportation can be generated at reasonable rates leading to a profitable situation. Cost advantage is what the ICD offers to the customers.

The researchers did a break-even analysis based on the information given by the management (Annexure II A for one barge operation and Annexure II B for two barge operation). It is evident that a one-barge operation will lead to a long capital recovery period and/or reduced profits to the ICD. At full load, the profit margin is only Rs 2,90,850. Also it is not possible to enter into annual contracts with major shippers in various sectors without running into barge capacity issues. In Kottayam Region, major shippers in Foot ware, Media, Rubber Mats, Tyre Retreads and Tyre together, ship 562 TEUs (Exhibit 1). That is 60% of the market share.

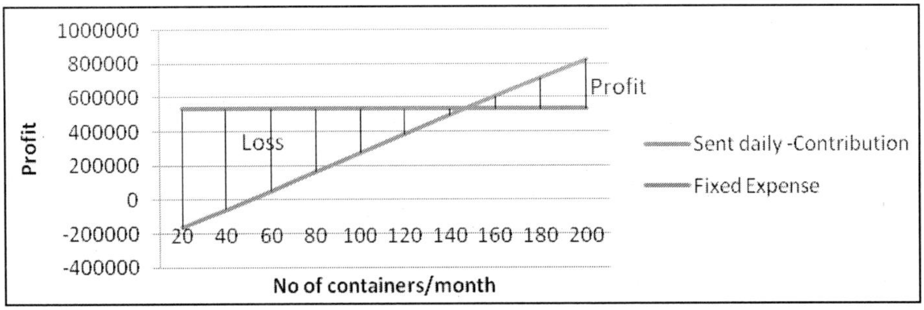

Exhibit 1: Break Even Analysis – One Barge Operation

When the payback period at full load was calculated, it was found to be 27.39 years (Annexure III A).

So one-barge operation is not recommended for the ICD.

For two barge operation, at full load, the profit margin is Rs 10,46,450. The ICD can recover cost quickly.

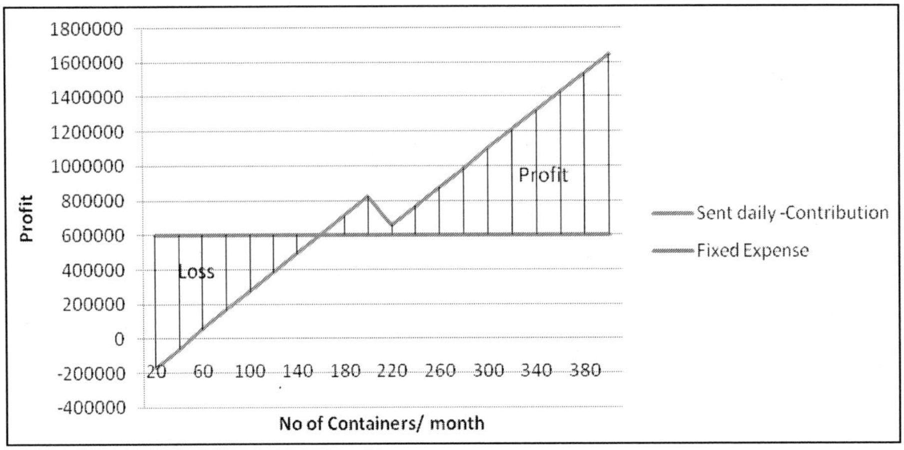

Exhibit 2: Break Even Analysis – Two Barge Operation

If the Port can come to an understanding based on an annual agreement with major customers, the business has a good chance for fast recovery of cost. But the port will have to go for a second barge to ensure timely dispatch of containers.

When the payback period at full load was calculated, it was found to be only 8.52 years (Annexure III B).

So two-barge operation is recommended strongly.

The researchers also did a comprehensive questionnaire (Annexure IV) based market survey of the potential Full Container load (FCL) customers of the port in the three districts of Kottayam, Pathanamthitta and Idukki towards the end of the period with the assistance of the students of his Institute. The total number of customers surveyed having regular full load shipments was 45. Altogether they exported 659 TEUs per month and imported 255 TEUs per month.

At the end of the survey, a detailed sector-wise analysis of the market (Exhibit 3) was done.

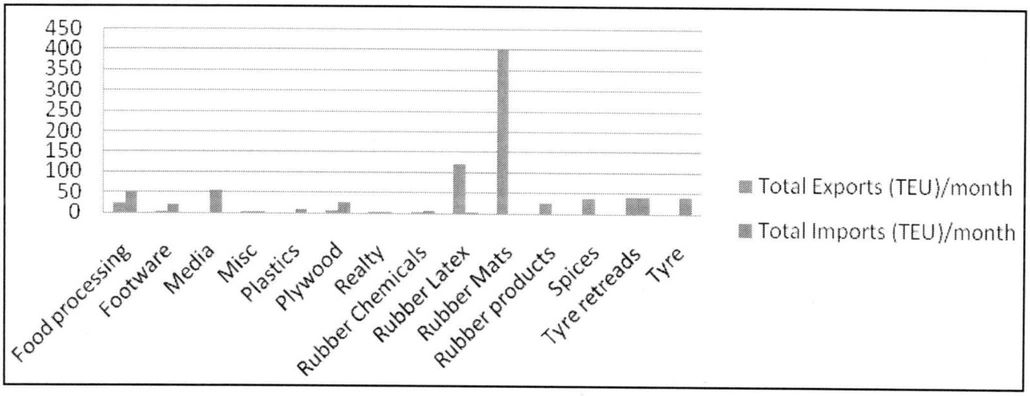

Exhibit 3: Sector-wise Exports and Imports from Kottayam Region

The dominant sectors are Food Processing (including cashew), Foot ware, Media, Rubber Latex, Rubber Mats, Spices, Tyre Retreads and Tyre.

More fragmented are Food processing, Ply woods, Rubber Products and Spices and the companies are spread all over the three districts. The ICD will have to provide truck and trailer services to bring in business.

Rubber Latex is an undependable market influenced by fluctuations in crude oil. In addition, they need flexi bag system for stuffing which the Port is not presently equipped with. But since it is about 10% of the total market it cannot be ignored in the long term.

Kollam is a market with its export of cashew nut. But it will take time to penetrate this market as the cost advantage has to be demonstrated to them with an operating ICD in full swing.

It is estimated that only about 50% of the market is Full Container Load (FCL) customers and the rest is Less Than Container (LCL) business mostly untapped and undeveloped. It is estimated that it will take at least 3 years to fully tap this set of customers based on the present pace of progress.

So the PPP's real challenge now turns out to be penetrating the market fast enough and deep enough to avoid default in bank loan repayment; marketing the concept of container transport among the local customers; popularizing transportation through water by barge as opposed to time-tested fast and reliable road transportation and making sure that the ICD consistently offer a more competitive rate for handling and transportation than the competitors, the Container Freight Stations in Kerala. The challenge promises to be quite uphill.

OVERALL STRATEGIC DIRECTION

A cost leadership strategy is recommended and barge transportation is to be promoted. (The ICD can provide road transportation also, but it is a costly alternative and normally to be avoided). It shall also be a good strategy to provide ICD facilities including stuffing, handling and transportation at minimum mark up to attract shippers and charge a reasonable rate for barge transportation. This obviously requires the ICD to go for volumes in transportation which is the normal way for a logistics sector enterprise.

SUGGESTED BUSINESS PLAN

1. Achieve 400 TEUs/month exports/imports within one year from the shippers of Kottayam region by
   (a) Making annual, volume-discounted, agreements with major customers in the sectors of Foot ware, Media, Rubber mats, Tyre and Tyre retreads (5 of who control 60% of the 914 TEU/month (estimated) market) at the earliest.
2. Gradually encourage cargo consolidation in the sectors of Spices, Food processing, Ply woods and Rubber products over the next three years by
   (a) Sending salesmen to all parts of the three districts to canvass potential shippers
   (b) Developing a trailer service in the region which is cost competitive
3. Aggressively market in Kollam district for the cashew kernel imports and cashew nut export by offering shippers of Cashew an cost competitive alternate route to NH 47 provided they transport containers to and from the port. And
4. Introduce flexi bag system for transporting rubber latex at the earliest and thus completely penetrate all the sectors in the market.

SUGGESTED CONTINGENCY PLAN

If negotiations with major customers do not result in long-term contracts, then keep operations at a low intensity and go for a single barge operation till business builds.

But, as can be seen, the annual agreement with major shippers is crucial to the long-term viability of the port.

CONCLUSION

The ICD is set for a bright future provided it sticks to the cost leadership strategy and base loading by big customers supported by annual contracts. It is advised not to lose focus on this by being differentiated that is, trying to be too many things to too many people.

Building one more barge, as one barge can transport only 200 containers in a month, is crucial to the long-term survival of the Port.

MAJOR FINDING

The management has strategically planned to provide all port cargo and container handling facilities at minimum mark up while barge transportation along the water way will be the main revenue source. The break even analysis done during the study shows that at least two barges should be in operation each fully loaded for the ICD to break even at reasonable level. The payback period also shows that the unrealistic payback period of 27 years can be reduced by around 70% if the ICD switches from one barge operation to two barge operation. It, in turn, indicates the need for very intense and continuous marketing effort as the eventual market share has to be at least 80% of the total estimated market. In other words, the total market apparently is too small and number of barges available is inadequate. The level of competition also promises to be quite high against existing road transportation as barges are much slower than trucks.

IMPLICATIONS

So the PPP's real challenge now turns out to be penetrating the market fast enough and deep enough to avoid default in bank loan repayment; marketing the concept of container transport as a safe and feasible one among the local customers; popularizing transportation through water by barge as opposed to time-tested fast and reliable road transportation and making sure that the ICD consistently offer a more competitive rate for handling and transportation than the competitors, the Container Freight Stations in Kerala. The challenge promises to be quite uphill.

This single study brings out the fact that a PPP may well have to grapple with serious commercial issues after commissioning if the management focuses mainly only on technical problems during the project stage. So PPPs are well advised to do adequate commercial feasibility studies to anticipate management problems after commissioning.

REFERENCES

[1] Abdel Aziz and Ahmed M. (2007), "Successful Delivery of Public-Private Partnerships for Infrastructure Development", *Journal of Construction Engineering and Management,* 133(12): 918-931.

[2] Zhang, Xueqing (2005), "Critical Success Factors for Public-Private Partnerships in Infrastructure Development", *Journal of Construction Engineering and Management,* 131(1): 3-14

[3] Zhang, Xueqing (2005), "Paving the Way for Public-Private Partnerships in Infrastructure Development", *Journal of Construction Engineering and Management,* 131(1): 71-80

[4] Zhang, Xueqing (2006), "Public Clients' Best Value Perspectives of Public Private Partnerships in Infrastructure Development", *Journal of Construction Engineering and Management,* 132(2): 107-114.

ANNEXURES

I. Tariff of the KPACT-ICD
II. KPACT – Breakeven Analysis
III. Payback Period Calculation
IV. Shippers' Questionnaire

Annexure I

Port and Container Terminal, Nattokom, Kottayam – 686 013
ICD Port code – IN KYM 6
Tariff

This rate will be applicable from 1st December 2009 till further revision

(All rates in Indian Rupees)

Tariff for Loaded Container Transportation

Kottayam Port and Container Terminal Services Pvt. Ltd Tariff For Warehousing and related services

(All rates in Indian Rupees.)

1.	Stuffing/De stuffing of Cargo	20′ Container	40′ Container
	(a) General cargo	3500	4600
	(b) LCL Cargo	1200	1600
2	Fork Lift hire Charges (optional)	600	900
3	Loading/Unloading	Rs 60- per ton	
4	Labor charges for examination	Rs 500	Rs 1000
5	Terminal charges for factory stuffed containers/factory de stuffing	Rs 500	Rs 1000

	Kottayam-Kochi	20′ Container	40′ Container
1	Via Road	Rs. 9500	Rs. 13500
2	Via Road	Rs. 7000	Rs. 11000

Ground Rent for Cargo		
(a)	Up to 15 days	Free
(b)	16th day onwards	Rs 100/sq mt. (minimum 5 sq mt. (No telescopic rates for longer storage)

Handling Charges			
1	Lift-on/Lift-off		
	(a) Empty container	250	350
	(b) Loaded container	500	700
2	Cleaning /Sweeping of containers	Rs. 50	Rs. 60
3	Washing of dry containers	Rs. 125	Rs. 250

Other Expenses		
1	Documentation Charges/Shipping Bill	50
2	ICD Overtime Charges (after/before normal working time)	100
3	Container Weighment Charges/20′ Container	150
4	Tally Charges/20′ Container	100
5	EDI Charges/Shipping Bill	70
6	Certificates	Actual expense

Annexure II (A)

KPACT – Breakeven Analysis – One Barge Operation

Volume	Barge – Daily Sent Contribution	Fixed Expenses
20	–166400	532750
40	–56400	532750
60	53600	532750
80	163600	532750
100	273600	532750
120	383600	532750
140	493600	532750
160	603600	532750
180	713600	532750
200	823600	532750

Assumptions

1. No of days barge is plying in a month = 20 (One trip/day)
2. Revenue/container= Rs 5500/-
3. Running exp of Barge to and fro = Rs 8820/- (Diesel) + Rs 5000/- (Labour) = Rs 13820/-
4. Maximum no of full containers transported per day = 10 (50 % of full capacity)

Fixed Expense (Estimated)	
Labour	43750
Salary	47500
Directors' Fees	30000
Electricity	18000
Diesel	10000
Telephone Charges	10000
Stationary	5000
Water	1000
Refreshments	1500
Crane and Fork Lift Rent	68000
Trailer Loan	48000
OD Interest	10000
Insurance	10000
Repairs and Maintenance	20000
Customs	20000
Cost Recovery	190000
Total Fixed Cost	532750

Annexure II (B)

KPACT – Breakeven Analysis – Two Barge Operation

Volume	Sent Daily – Contribution	Fixed Expense
20	–166400	600750
40	–56400	600750
60	53600	600750
80	163600	600750
100	273600	600750
120	383600	600750
140	493600	600750
160	603600	600750
180	713600	600750
200	823600	600750
220	657200	600750
240	767200	600750
260	877200	600750
280	987200	600750
300	1097200	600750

Volume	Sent Daily – Contribution	Fixed Expense
320	1207200	600750
340	1317200	600750
360	1427200	600750
380	1537200	600750
400	1647200	600750

Assumptions

1. No. of days barge is plying in a month = 20 (One trip/day)
2. Revenue/container = Rs 5500/-
3. Running exp of Barge to and fro = Rs 8820/- (Diesel) + Rs 5000/- (Labour) = Rs 13820/-
4. Maximum no of full containers transported per day per barge = 10 (50% of full capacity)
5. Cost of additional barge = Rs 114 lakhs depreciated over 25 years.

Fixed Expenses	
Labour	43750
Salary	47500
Directors' Fees	30000
Electricity	18000
Diesel	20000
Telephone Charges	10000
Stationary	5000
Water	1000
Refreshments	1500
Crane and Fork Lift Rent	68000
Trailer Loan	48000
OD Interest	10000
Insurance	10000
Repairs and Maintenance	40000
Customs	20000
Cost recovery	228000
Total Fixed Cost	600750

Annexure III (A)

One Barge Operation – Payback period Calculation

Total Investment = Rs 956 lakhs
Profit at full load per month = Contribution – Fixed expenses = Rs (823600 – 532750) = Rs 2, 90, 850

Payback period = Total Investments/Profit at full load per month = 95600000/290850 = 328.69 months = 27.39 years

Annexure III (B)

Two Barge Operation – Payback period Calculation

Total Investment = Rs 956 lakhs + Rs 114 lakhs for additional barge = Rs 1070 lakhs
Profit at full load per month = Contribution – Fixed expenses = Rs (1647200 – 600750) = Rs 10,46,450
Payback period = Total Investments/Profit at full load per month = 107000000/1046450 = 102.25 months = 8.52 years

ANNEXURE IV

KOTTAYAM PORT AND CONTAINER TERMINAL SERVICES PVT. LTD

KPACT

A Project Under Govt of India
Nattakom, Kottayam, Kerala - 686 013. Phone: 0481-2363955, 2363953
Fax: 0481-2362400 Email: kottayamport@gmail.com, Website: www.kottayamport.com

QUESTIONNAIRE

1. Name of the shipper ....

   Contact person ....

2. Contact no. .... E-mail: ....
3. What is the expected volume you export in a month?

Sl. No.	Type of Goods	Destination	20 ft	40 ft	LCL (in tones)
(a)					
(b)					
(c)					

4. What is the expected volume you import in a month?

Sl. No.	Type of Goods	Destination	20 ft	40 ft	LCL (in tones)
(a)					
(b)					
(c)					

5. Name of your CHA agent: ....
6. Name of your liner/shipping agent: ....
7. Do you have an export agent? Kindly give their contact details.

   ....

8. What type of stuffing you currently doing?
   [ ] Home (factory) stuffing [ ] CFS stuffing [ ] At Cochin airport
9. In January have you planned for any consignments?

	2nd Week		3rd Week		4th Week	
	20 ft	40 ft	20 ft	40 ft	20 ft	40 ft
Export						
Import						

10. Will you prefer Kottayam ICD for your next import/export? Yes / No

Managing Municipal Water Supply in India: Case Study of Delhi

Satpal Singh

National Institute of Urban Affairs, New Delhi
E-mail: satpal_sociologist@yahoo.co.in

ABSTRACT

Management of water supply has become a serious issue in India. The issue has drawn considerable attention because of Institutional debility and financial constraints that leads to mismanagement of water supply system. A wide range of changes in water sector has been observed in many parts of India. Changes in water sector include the handing over of some parts of the water management to the NGOs/RWAs/private operators for the water bill collection, water distribution through tankers and replacing old/leaking pipelines in water harvesting. In Delhi, the water supply is inadequate and is supplied unequally in many places of Delhi. Due to weak financial position, the Delhi Jal Board is dependent on the State Government for its operational expenses. The Board has been facing a number of constraints such as limited water resources, lack of technical manpower, low water pressure, widen demand-supply gap, poor cost recovery, inadequate infrastructure etc. As a result, the responsibility of water supply in Delhi is being increasingly shifted to the Residents Welfare Associations (RWAs) and Private Water Suppliers in the areas of collection water bill and distribution of water through tankers, etc. The present paper attempts to contribute to debate on water supply system in Delhi as well as its finances. It discusses the role private sector participation in managing water supply system. At last, the paper summarises the major findings of the study and attempts to suggest some measures for the improved water supply service in the city. This case study suggests the need for close monitoring and supervision on the functioning of private vendors in order to minimise the corruption in water management. It also suggests the need for reforms such as preparation of citizen report cards on a regular basis, continuous water supply system, training for water conservation techniques through IEC system to the local people, etc for the improved water supply system in the city.

Keywords: Municipal Water Supply, India

INTRODUCTION

Institutional responsibility for water management in urban areas has been divided between the state and the Centre as per the seventh schedule in the Indian Constitution. State Government generally plan, design and execute the water supply schemes through its different departments such as Public Health Engineering Department (PHED), State Water Board, etc. But, a wide range of changes in water sector has been observed in many parts of the country. Changes in water sector include the handing over of some parts of the management of water to the Private sector for water bill collection, water distribution through tankers and replacing old/leaking pipelines in water harvesting etc. Despite all these, the problem of water supply remains a big challenge before the institutions responsible for this service.

Provision of water supply has severe deficiencies with regard to population coverage as well as the service level. Studies on this subject reveal that only 50 percent of the urban population are directly connected to distribution networks and an additional 27 percent had access to public standpipes. Large metropolitan cities are becoming critical areas due to increasing water demand for domestic consumption, which often competes with other uses of fresh water (Nallathinga, Ramakrishna). There are large disparities in access and modes of access to water supply across states and cities. Statistics shows that Delhi has an average of 4 hours of water supply a day, Mumbai has 5 hours a day, Bangalore has 2.5 hours of water a day and Chennai has a meagre 1.5 hours of water a day. The study further shows that Chennai and Delhi are ranked as the worst performing metropolitan cities in terms of hours of water availability per day, while Mumbai is ranked as second worst performer and Kolkata fourth worst.

Regarding finances for water supply, most of ULBs are running short of funds in production and distribution of water on account of both technical inefficiencies and poor commercial practices. Water Tariff is generally low and do not recover operating and maintenance costs. Inappropriate pricing, lack of well designed tariffs and absence of metering all lead to wastage of water and make the water services delivery to the risk of poor maintenance due to inadequate recovery of financial costs (Nallathiga, Ramakrishna). The High Powered Expert Committee (HPEC) reveals that nearly 70 percent of water leakages are mainly from old pipes for consumer connection and due to malfunctioning of water meters. Importantly, subsidiaries on private taps are poorly targeted as more than 30 percent of the beneficiaries are poor because of low water tax, low tariff, fixed access charges, etc (India Infrastructure, May 2009). High level of non revenue water (NRW) is one of the major causes of poor finance which includes technical losses in the distribution network, errors in metering, unbilled water consumption etc.

Given this background, the present paper attempts to contribute to the debate on water supply system in Delhi. It also discusses the role of private sector participation in managing the water supply system. At last, the paper summarises the major findings of the study and attempts to suggest some measures for the improved water supply service in the city.

CASE STUDY OF DELHI

In the case study, the demographic and economic profile of the city are described as they have direct impact on the consumption and needs of the water supply service.

DEMOGRAPHIC AND ECONOMIC PROFILE

Delhi, being the National Capital of India, is the second fast growing metropolis in the country after Bangalore and is the third largest national metropolis after Kolkata and Mumbai. With regard to urbanisation, the city has highest urbanisation level amongst the country with the 93.18 percent of the total city's population and the density was highest in the country with 9340 persons per square kilometre as the census, 2001 (Table 1). It is estimated that the percentage of migration was 47.42 percent in 2007 whereas the natural growth of migration was 52.58 percent. In absolute terms, the natural increase in population was ₹ 2.21 lakh during the year 2007 while migration has been estimated at ₹ 2.45 lakh (*Economic Survey*, 2008-09). The large increase in population and its high concentration, along with the substantial growth in commercial, informal and small scale industrial sectors of the city's economy and proliferation of marginal informal settlements has substantial increased the demand for basic services of the city.

Table 1: Trend of Urbanisation in Delhi, 1951-2001

Census Year	Total Population	Urban Population		Annual Exponential Growth Rate	Decennial Growth Percentage
		Total	Percentage		
1951	1744072	1437134	82.40	7.3	106.58
1961	2658612	2359408	88.75	5.0	64.17
1971	4065698	3647023	89.68	4.4	54.57
1981	6220406	5768200	92.73	4.6	58.16
1991	9420644	8471625	89.93	3.8	46.87
2001	13850507	12905780	93.18	4.2	52.34

Source: Economic Survey of Delhi, 2008-2009 (page 31).

Delhi is also an important commercial capital in Asia. There has been a phenomenal growth of industries in Delhi and the character has steadily transformed from a historical capital to a commercial and industrial centre. A latest report prepared by the Directorate of Economics and Statistics of Delhi Government shows the sustained economic prosperity of the people and changing trend of various sectors. On the monthly basis, an average Delhiite earned ₹ 7995.25 in the year 2010-11 against the national average of ₹ 3000 as per the advance and quick estimates based on constant prices which reflects data factoring in inflation. While at the current prices, the per capita income of Delhi was ₹ 1.17 lakh that occupied third position after Goa and Chandigarh which had per capita income of ₹ 1.32 lakh and ₹ 1.20 lakh respectively. On the other hand, the occupational distribution of the city has shown that the construction sector has become one of the major contributors to the economic as its share was estimated to be around one-third of the total State Gross Domestic Product whereas the primary and secondary sectors have decreased their contribution. The contribution of the territory sector in the economy has also increased to 81.83 percent and 82.27 percent respectively during the year 2009-10 and 2010-11 (*The Times of India*, 21-05-2011).

WATER SUPPLY SYSTEM

The sources of water supply in Delhi are River Yamuna, Western Yamuna Canal, and the Upper Ganga Canal. Delhi Municipal Corporation (DMC) and Delhi Jal Board (DJB), a parastatal agency of Delhi Government, are responsible for the management of water supply in Delhi. Major portion of the water management looks after by the DJB in terms of planning, development and construction of water network while DMC has very limited responsibility for this service. The Board provides portable drinking water

Table 2: Statistics for Water Supply in Delhi

Description of Services	Number and Percentage
City Population (U.A.) (2001)	129,05,780
Availability of water (mgd)	783
Estimated water requirement (mgd)	1104
Access to piped water supply (in percent)	90
Number of private water tankers (as per revised budget estimate 2005-06)*	1100
Number of private tubewells (2001)*	2,00,000 (estimated)
Number of water standposts (Public Water Hydrants) (2001)*	11,533
Number of water connections (2009)	17,15,037
Frequency of water supply (in Hours)*	2-3
Water unaccounted for (in percent)	40-50
Demand-Supply Gap (mld)	almost 300

Source: Daga, Shivani, Centre for Civil Society, New Delhi.

Note: *Delhi City Development Plan, NCT of Delhi (Chapter 8, page 4).

not in the area of MCD's jurisdiction but also to the areas under control of the New Delhi Municipal Council (NDMC) and Delhi Cantonment Board (DCB). The provision of water supply is inadequate in Delhi in terms of quality and quantity because the Board does not have adequate funds, and institutional capacities to fulfil the water demand.

The statistics for water supply in Delhi are summarised in Table 2. It shows that the water availability of 783 mgd is inadequate when compared to the estimated requirement of 1104 mgd. Additional water requirement are estimated to be in the order of 220 mgd and 460 mgd by 2011 and 2021 respectively as per the appraisal report of Delhi City Development Plan. Data further show that as on 1.4.2009, about 17,15,037 lakh water meter connection was provided by the Board to its users which is below the standard (100 percent) suggested by the Ministry of Urban Development. The duration of water supply in Delhi is around 2-3 hours in a day that is also not upto the standard fixed in the Service Level Benchmark (SLB). Unequal distribution of water is an emerging issue in the city as the consumers receive 29 lpcd of water in Narela (lowest) compared to 509 lpcd in Cantonment area (highest). The Karol zone receives 337 lpcd.

The Service Level Benchmark for water supply in Delhi prepared by the Ministry of Urban Development, Government of India shows that except per capita water supply, others indicators such as coverage, non-water revenue, consumption metering, continuity, complaints redressal, collection efficiency are not upto the standard (Table 3).

Table 3: Service Level Benchmark for Water Supply in Delhi

Proposed Indicator	Benchmark	Status
Coverage (%)	100	71.5
Per Capita Supply (lpcd)	135	144
Non-Revenue Water (%)	20	52.4
Consumption metering (%)	100	55.3
Continuity (hours)	24	3
Complaints Redressal (%)	80	73.0
Quality of Water Supply	100	99.5
Cost Recovery (%)	100	41.4
Collection Efficiency (%)	90	86.3

Water quality is one of the important issues of the Delhi's water supply management. In order to improve the water quality, the DJB has opened a number of laboratories to check the quality of water both from the Water Treatment Plants as also from the distribution system. Delhi Jal Board gives assurance about the purity and effectives of chemicals (Alum/Poly-Aluminium Chloride) before these were actually used in the treatment process of water. However, the audit report of Delhi Government disclosed the fact that the number of water samples found unsatisfactory increased significantly from 0.73 percent in 2002-03 to 1.88 percent in 2006-07. In addition to this, out of 2090 unsatisfactory samples reported during 2006-07, no action reports were received in the Directorate in respect of 1874 (90 percent) unsatisfactory samples as of March 2007. This situation needs to be controlled.

Water Treatment Plants

As per the Delhi City Development Plan, there are eight water treatment plants in Delhi with the total installed capacity of 790 mgd to treat water inclusive of about 100 mgd of ground water abstraction. But these plants are underutilized and insufficient as there are short fall of 255 mgd at production point. To bridge the gap, the Board has taken various steps to enhance the water treatment capacity by constructing some more treatment plants. The Nangloi water treatment plant has been constructed with 40 mgd treatment capacity but it could function upto its full capacity due to non-supply of raw water through WJC system by the Haryana Government in spite of raw water supply available from Bhakra Vyas Management Board. Another treatment plant with 140 mgd capacity in Sonia Vihar has been constructed for the treatment of Ganga Water (stored in Tehri dam) through Upper Ganga Canal and drawn at Muradnagar. Simultaneously UP Jal Nigam has also started the work of laying of raw water conduit from Murad Nagar to Sonia Vihar. On completion and commissioning of these water treatment plants, the filtered water supply in Delhi will improve. The construction of another water treatment plant with 20 mgd capacity at Bawana is in the final stage of completion. With a view to rationalise the distribution of water, DJB has drawn up an elaborate plan for construction of Under Ground Reservoirs and Booster Pumping Stations (Official website of Delhi Jal Board).

Besides these initiatives, the Board has also set up nine water testing laboratories at treatment plants which examine and evaluate suitability of water to be supplied to public and control the water treatment process. In addition to this, the Board has also set up six modern zonal laboratories to check the water quality from Ranney Wells and Tube Wells in regard to Bacteriological and Chemical aspects in all parts of Delhi, namely, Central Laboratory water works at Wazirabad, testing laboratories set up at Okhla, Bhagirathi, Haiderpur, Greater Kailash, and Nangloi. Water testing charges are depending on the type of testing such as chemical charges, bacteriological examination and special tests like cyanide, chromium, etc. Apart, the Jal Board is also getting testes the drinking water from outside these agencies namely National Environmental Engineering Research Institute (NEERI) for ensuring its potability fortnightly for Eleven Physio-chemical parameters and two microbiological parameters. Health Department of Delhi Municipal Corporation, National Institute of Communicable Diseases (NICD) are also testing independently the drinking water being supplied by Delhi Jal Board to ascertain its potability.

Finances for Water Supply

The finances of DJB with regard to water supply are inadequate due to low cost recovery, defective meters, non-water revenue and inadequate recovery of financial costs. The reasons for low cost recovery include low water tariff, fixed access charges, etc. The report of NCT of Delhi shows that in case of defective meters, the DJB sustained a loss of ₹ 173.77 crore during 2003-07 to its failure to rectify meters timely. About 56 percent of the total water supplied in Delhi during the last five years did not fetch any revenue in loss of ₹ 1990.54 crore. The percentages of non-revenue water also increased from 53 percent in 2002-03 to 65 percent in 2006-07. A significant amount of ₹ 368 crore was in arrears for collection against outstanding bills. With regard to cost recovery of water supply, the service providers are not able to recover operations and maintenance costs and depend on the government for financial assistance.

Tariff for Water Use

The tariff for water use in Delhi is based on the principle of "use more pay more". This principle restricts the users to use water as per their requirements otherwise pay more charges for water. In this way, the tariff acts as a disincentive to consumer for excessive use of water or wastage of water. Special subsidy in the water charge has been allowed to the users of resettlement colonies where water charges are being recovered on assumed average of 10 Kl per connection per month. There is an exemption on the water use upto 6 Kl per connection in a month for all domestic consumers except service

Table 4: New Water Tariffs for the Different Category of Consumers, May 2010

Category/Monthly Consumption	Service Charge (₹)	Volumetric Charge (₹)
Domestic Consumers (Category-I)		
0 to 10	50	2
10 to 20	100	3
20 to 30	150	15
More than 30	200	25
Commercial/Industrial (Category-II)		
0 to 10	400	10
10 to 25	600	20
25 to 50	700	50
50 to 100	800	80
More than 100	900	100

Source: Official website of Delhi Government, www.delhi.gov.in

charge. In order to increase revenue, the board has revised water tariff in May 2010 with an increase of 10 percent every year. The Delhi Jal Board levy two types of user charges namely, service charge and volumetric water consumption charge. Both these charges are linked to the level of consumption. The water tariff for the government institutions/ offices is same as applicable to the commercial/industrial category with a provision of 15 percent rebate on total water bill amount of these units which provide certificate of adopting measures for water harvesting and/or recycling of waste water. The new water tariffs for the different category of consumers are illustrated in Table 4.

It is observed from the above Table that the Jal Board earns more revenue from the commercial, industrial and government institutions/offices as the water charges are very high as compared to residential units. Water charges as per water consumptions would be beneficial to the metered households but at the same time, it has a negative consequence for non-metered water consumers that are mostly located in low-income groups as they pay fixed amount for water on a monthly basis whether the consumption is low or high.

The story with regard to the cost recovery from water supply service is extremely poor, since the cost recovery is only 60 percent of the production cost of water and rest 40 percent is Non-Revenue Water. Not only this, there is a disparity in the cost of production and operations of water supply and water tariffs being charged. Only 35 percent of the cost of proper operation, maintenance and upkeep of the water supply and sewerage system are collected through water tariffs. The revenue generated from this service is hardly able to meet the cost of electricity bill and other requirement of chemicals like chlorine, etc. (www.rainwaterharvesting.org). High cost and low cost recovery both has put adverse impact on the efficiency of water supply system. It is imperative that the water tariff should be sustainable and able to meet the O&M cost and capital cost in full.

NEED FOR REFORMS

A review of the above financial position of the Delhi Jal Board shows that the current level of water supply suffers from various deficiencies which necessitate the need for reforms. These are discussed below:

Rainwater Harvesting

Recognising the need for improved water supply system, the Government of India provided comprehensive reforms agenda under the Jawaharlal Nehru National Urban Reform Mission (*Jn*NURM) in which Rainwater Harvesting reform in all types of buildings made an optional reform for all ULBs. It is an effective method of recharging ground water. In this regard, the Board has implemented the rainwater harvesting in its own buildings and structures. But there is need to take precaution that roof top rain water after the first 3 showers is drained out and only clear water runoff is allowed to the underground strata, else there is a danger of ground water pollution. Extensive training in the provision and monitoring is equally important (Delhi City Development Plan, 2006).

In addition to this, Delhi Government approved a scheme for "setting up of water mission and use of new technologies for conservation, harvesting and recycling of water" for implementing during Tenth Five Year Plan. Resident Welfare Associations (RWAs)/ Group Housing Societies are involved under the Bhagidari Scheme of the Delhi Government for implementing this reform. The report on the Government of NCT of Delhi (2008) has mentioned that the financial assistance is given under this scheme to RWAs/Group Housing Societies/Schools to a maximum of ₹ 50,000 or 50 percent of the cost of rain water harvesting system, whichever is less. The maximum limit was increased to ₹ 1 lakh with effect from 02 February 2007. The Jal Board has also provided the financial assistance of ₹ 51.19 lakh in 108 cases during February 2003 to March 2007. A periodical inspection of the Rainwater Harvesting system is recommended where the financial assistance has been granted to different beneficiaries/organizations.

PUBLIC-PRIVATE PARTNERSHIP

A wide range of changes in water sector in Delhi has been observed. The responsibility of water supply is being increasingly passed on to the Residents Welfare Associations (RWAs), and Private water suppliers in the areas of water bill collection and water distribution through tankers. The role of different actors is as discussed below:

Distribution of Water through Private Operators

To encounter the problem of water supply, a number of private operators have been involved in the distribution of water. They are mainly involved in the water distribution system to fulfil the water demand of the city without meeting the required quality standard. They generally rely heavily on the groundwater for their business. At present, there are more than 500 private water suppliers supplying untreated water through tankers. They supply water on behalf of the Delhi Jal Board to slums, unauthorised colonies, the colonies under Delhi Development Authority (DDA), and other places of Delhi in case of shortage of water, low pressure of adequate water, and due to repair works of supply lines. Not only this, they also supply water to individuals where the Jal Boards fails to supply adequate water. But they charges for water at their own discretion without assessing the affordability of the people. Due to this, mostly people prefer to buy water from the DJB's water tanker because they sell treated water, and safe to drink on free of cost. In case of shortage of water tankers, they hires tankers from the private vendors to fulfil the water demand specially in summer or during emergencies like breaking down of epidemics. With a view to tracking the movement of tankers, the Board uses the Global Positioning System (GPS) on departmental tankers through a service provider. Initially, the Jal Board installed GPS system on 24 tankers as part of a pilot project at the rate of '3861 per tanker per month for a period of three years on a service contract signed with the service provider in July 2005. However, there are serious problem of implementing the GPS system (Report on Government of NCT of Delhi, 2008). Besides, the private vendors sell the 'packaged water' known by various names such as 'bottled water' or 'mineral water' without any treatment. The manufacturers of 'packaged water' are making soaring profits from the existing water crunch in Delhi. The packaged water is also available in pouches, cups, bottles and bulky transparent jars, people buy the water not only because they are health conscious but also to stock drinking water in their houses. But at the same time, the quality of packaged water is a big question. There are a number of manufacturers who sells water directly from the tubewells, and borewells which needs to be purified. This is a very expensive procedure so most of the private vendors void the purification procedures. This has led to the fear of capture the water market by the 'water mafia'. Now a day, they are very active in Delhi. Apart from the private vendors, DJB also supplies packaged water under the brand name of 'Jal' which conforms to the standards laid down by BIS.

Involving Residents Welfare Associations (RWAs)

Although a large number of RWAs are emerging in the water management, their role is very limited largely in the areas of water bill payment and collection, distribution of water through tankers, provision of rainwater harvesting scheme, etc. Under the Bhagidari scheme, more than 100 RWAs are involved in the various activities of the water management. They have been supported not only by the Delhi Government but also by the private agencies and other civil societies. Their functioning has been restricted largely in the middle and posh colonies of Delhi. However, the Delhi government, the RWAs and the private sector are supporting the participatory governance through RWAs in a big way (Kundu, 2011).

WATER CONSERVATION

It is important to note that the shortage of water is mainly due to (i) leaking and broken pipes, and (ii) theft of water through illegal connections. The report of Delhi Government (2008) has mentioned that 56 percent of the total production of water did not generate any revenue due to theft, leakages and free supply. This led to revenue loss of ₹ 1990.54 crore during 2002-07. The level of non-revenue water in Delhi has increased from 53 percent to 65 percent during the same period.

To address these problems, the DJB has set up a separate leak detection and investigation (LDI) cell for detecting various leakages in the system. Leakages are detected through patrolling/surveying of trunk transmission mains and distribution networks by the Departmental staff of Leak Detection cell and various maintenance divisions (operating zones). The Board has also set up central control room to received complaints from the public regarding water leakages. As per the Economic Survey of Delhi of 2008-09, the Jal Board has replaced about 1200 km length of the old, damaged and leaking water mains just below the target of 1500 km replacement of old distribution lines fixed during the Tenth plan. Delay in repairing of leakages resulted in estimated loss of 84 million gallon of water valuing ₹ 21.79 lakh for the year 2006-07 since there were significant delays in 131 cases (18 percent) ranging upto 120 days or more in the same period. To minimise the number of leakages, proper feedback and monitoring mechanism is required.

CONCLUDING REMARKS AND WAY FORWARD

Concluding Remarks

The preceding discussion on water supply management in Delhi shows that the existing institutional arrangements for water supply suffers from various deficiencies like limited water resources and shortage of technical staff and infrastructure that need for support from the other stakeholders such as private vendors, RWAs, civic societies in the distribution of water. But due to certain shortcomings, the role of stakeholders is very limited and insufficient in reducing the water demand-supply gap in the city. With regard to private vendors, it is important that they supply poor quality of water and are charging very high amount for water without assessing the paying capacity of the people especially for middle and low income groups. The 'Water Mafia' is thriving and raking in huge mulla by exploiting the huge mismatch between demand and supply of potable water in many areas of the city. Close monitoring and supervision on the functioning of private vendors are needed to reduce the corruption level in the water management. Whereas, the RWAs are being supported not only by the Delhi Government but also by the private agencies and other civil societies. However, their functioning has been restricted largely in the middle and posh colonies of Delhi. They need to coordinate with the DJB to resolve their water problems.

On the other hand, the finances of the DJB are under severe strain. Main reason for this is the low cost recovery from water due to defective meters, non-water revenue because of high quantity of water leakages. Another reason is the large variation in the cost of production and operations of water supply and water tariff being charged. Only

35 percent of the cost of proper operation, maintenance and upkeep of the water supply and sewerage system are collected through water tariffs. In addition to this, the revenue generated from this service is hardly able to meet the cost of electricity of bill and other requirement of chemicals like chlorine, etc. The Jal Board is not able to recover operation and maintenance costs and are depended on the State Government for the financial assistance.

To overcome these problems, the DJB has undertaken various reforms to improve the service delivery level of water supply in the City such as rainwater harvesting, water conservation, involvement of private vendors and RWAs in the distribution of water, etc. But, there is need to take effective steps to implement these reforms in order to minimise the wastage of water through non water revenue, leakages, malpractices of water meters, defective meters, etc. For this, proper feedback and monitoring mechanism is also required.

Way-Forward

- A comprehensive policy on continuous water supply system (24/7 water) is required;
- Needs for improved standards for service connection and metering;
- A regular citizen report card is required for the accountability, transparency and monitoring of the different stakeholders involved in the management of water supply system;
- Need for effective participatory approach to improve the functioning of the RWAs;
- Water tariff should be revised at a regular interval;
- Defective water meters should be replaced in order to increased water revenue;
- People should be made aware and trained for the water conservation technique through IEC system.

REFERENCES

[1] Daga, Shivani, (unpublished) 'Private Supply of Water in Delhi', Market & Regulations, Centre for Civil Society, New Delhi.

[2] Economic Survey of Delhi (2008-09), National Capital of Delhi, Delhi Government, Delhi.

[3] *Economic Times* (2011), 'Delhi Leaves India Behind Earns More', article based on the report on Estimates of State Domestic Product, 2010-11 (Base Year 2004-05), Directorate of Economics and Statistics, Government of NCT of Delhi.

[4] India Infrastructure (2009), Volume 11, No. 10, May, India Infrastructure, New Delhi.

[5] Kundu, Debolina (2011), 'Elite Capture in Participatory Urban Governance', *Economic and Political Weekly*, Vol. XLVI, No. 10, March.

[6] Ministry of Urban Development (2011), 'The High Powered Expert Committee (HPEC) for Estimating the Investment Requirements for Urban Infrastructure Services', Report on Indian Urban Infrastructure and Services, Ministry of Urban Development, Government of India, New Delhi, March 2011.

[7] Ministry of Urban Development (2009), 'Handbook on Service Level Benchmarking', Ministry of Urban Development, Government of India, New Delhi.

[8] Nallathiga, Ramakrishna, 'Reforming Urban Water Supply Sector in India', Centre for Good Governance, Dr. MCR, HRD IAP Campus, Hyderabad.

[9] The NCT of Delhi (2006), 'City Water Supply System' (Chapter-8), Consultant: IL&FS Eco-smart Limited for the Department of Urban Development, Government of Delhi, New Delhi.

Websites

[1] www.delhijalboard.nic.in

[2] www.rainwaterharvesting.org

Measurement of Consumer Preference Levels with Reference to Consumer Behaviour: A Comparative Analysis of Banks in India

Richa Dixit
BCT Kumaon Engineering College, Dwarhat
E-mail: richadixit3@gmail.com

ABSTRACT

The research measures the consumer preference level with reference to his behavior. It determines how consumer behavior changes with reference to his preference level towards a particular product. Or we can also say the paper deals with special problem – Human Psychology which keeps changing. Study was conducted taking in view the banking sector in India during 2004 and 2009. 5 year trend with reference to consumer preference towards banks (Public and Private) were compared and analyzed. Survey method was used with questionnaire for data collection. Growth rate for past 5 year was also analyzed. Statistical tools were used for interpretation. The results shows that consumer preference level affects consumer behavior and can change it.

Keywords: Consumer Preference, Consumer Behavior

INTRODUCTION

Consumer preference is the way in which consumers in a free market choose to divide their total expenditure in purchasing goods and services. Using a limited number of assumptions, an individual's preferences can be built up into a utility. In psychology, preferences could be conceived of as an individual's attitude towards a set of objects, typically reflected in an explicit decision-making process (Lichtenstein & Slovic, 2006). Alternatively, one could interpret the term "preference" to mean evaluative judgment in the sense of liking or disliking an object (e.g., Scherer, 2005) which is the most typical definition employed in psychology. However, it does not mean that a preference is necessarily stable over time. Preference can be notably modified by decision-making processes, such as choices (Brehm, 1956; Sharot, De Martino, & Dolan, 2009), even in an unconscious way (see Coppin, Delplanque, Cayeux, Porcherot and Sander, 2010).

Reserve Bank of India (R.B.I) is called as the father of all banks in India. Banks are governed by the rules and regulations of RBI. India's rapid increase into globalization, high integration to the outer world, has increased the crises in the country. India's trade as proportion of GDP has shown a growth from 21.2% in 97-98 to 34.7% in 2007-08; in spite of Asian crises for the year 97-98.India has also tried to increase financial transactions with the outer world. Our expanded measure to globalization, i.e, the ratio of total external transactions (gross current A/c flows + gross capital flows) to GDP, this ratio is doubled from 46.8% in 97-98 to 117.4% in 2007-08. India's corporate sector has also shown an increase into external funding by last 5 years. Crises have affected the India's economy. Government along with RBI tries to overcome these crises. Disaster prevention, mitigation are important element contributing sustainable development policies. RBI is responsible for planning various banking policies, governing interest rates for borrowing and lending the money. R.B.I sets the C.R.R (cash reserve ratio), R.R (Repo Rate), Reverse Repo Rate (R.R.R), etc for lending transactions of the commercial banks in the country. Banks home loan lending rates depends on CRR, PLR (Prime lending rates), and R.R interest rates set up by the RBI. Loans are marked to PLR. More than 80% of current lending is subject to PLR.

MATERIAL AND METHODS

Primary information was collected using survey method. Questionnaire and interview was the tools used for collecting primary data from the banks RBI. Their employees were also contacted. Secondary data was collected using the websites, past information, brochures of the banks. Past 5 year data for 2004 and 2009-10 is analyzed. A comparative study was done analyzing their BPLR (Bench mark prime lending rates) & their home loan interest rates. Past trends in BPLR, CRR, Repo Rate was also compared and analyzed. Analysis was done using statistical tools like averages, mean, standard deviation and variance to find the variations and to make the comparison. % change compare to the previous year to the current year was also found. Total 30 major banks including private, public and foreign banks were contacted. Sample also includes RBI and the employees of the banks. Total sample size was approx. 90.

RESULTS AND DISCUSSIONS

Benchmark is usually a rate that is used as a yardstick to either evaluate performance or set other linked rates in market. Benchmark PLR is set by the bank, not by RBI.

CRR is the amount of funds that banks have to keep with RBI. If RBI decides to increase the percentage of this, the available amount with the banks comes down. RBI uses this methods (increase of CRR) to drain out the excessive money from the banks. R. R is the rate at which our banks borrow rupees from RBI. When the banks have any shortage of funds, they can borrow it from RBI. A reduction in Repo rate (R.R) will help banks to get money at cheaper rates. When RR increases, borrowing from RBI becomes more expensive. PLR (Prime Lending Rate) is the rate at which banks across a country lend the loan. R.R.R is the rate at which RBI borrows money from banks. Banks are always happy to lend money to RBI since their money is in safe hands with a good interest. An increase in RRR causes banks to transfer more funds to RBI due to these attractive interest rates. BPLR (Benchmark Prime Lending Rates) is the rate that commercial banks normally charges or expected to charge from their most credit worthy customers. It varies from bank to bank. But there is no uniformity in deciding the rates by the banks. Due to high competition, sometimes, bank lends money below their BPLR. For monitoring this, RBI, has form working group. To monitor and bring transparency in BPLR, the group has recommended a Base rate in place of BPLR. Base rate is the bare minimum rate below which banks will not be allowed to lend the money. Currently it is calculated as 8.55%.

TRENDS IN BPLR

The maximum and minimum spread lending rates around BPLR of public sector banks has remained broadly stable since march, 2004.Increase in BPLR also increase interest rates on home loans. While it increase in 2008-09 as shown in chart-2 below. Before 5 years, banks use to lend money at low rates@8.5% to 7.5%. Then again it was increased and now in the current year again it is been lowered down as earlier, may be due to high competition. BPLR ranges from 11%-16% from 2004 to 2009. BPLR of schedule commercial & public sector banks is less compare to foreign and private banks. As Public banks strictly follows the rules of RBI. BPLR for schedule commercial bank was 10.50% in 2004 & increased to 12.5% in 2009. BPLR for public sector banks was 10.5% in 2004 and increased to 13% in 2009. But private sector banks, BPLR for 2004 was 12% which increased to 16% in 2009. The BPLR for foreign banks was 12% in 2004 which increased to 15% in 2009.(refer to chart 1and 2 below).

The bank group-wise trends in the modal BPLR since March 2004 show three distinct phases. In the first phase between March 2004 and March 2006, the BPLRs of public sector banks and private sector banks remained almost steady and range bound, though the BPLRs of private sector banks were about 100 bps higher than those of public sector banks. BPLRs of foreign banks showed some variations, but converged to BPLR of public sector banks by March 2006. During March 2006 to June 2007, modal BPLRs of all three bank groups showed sharp upward movement in line with the general tightening

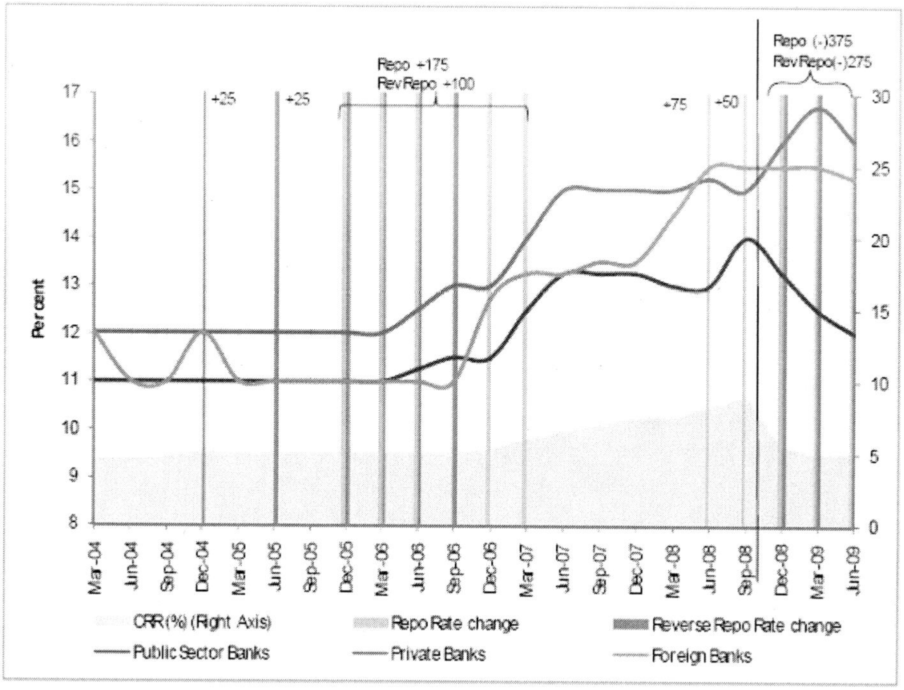

Source: RBI, "5 year trends in BPLR".

Chart 1: Bank Group-wise Model BPLR

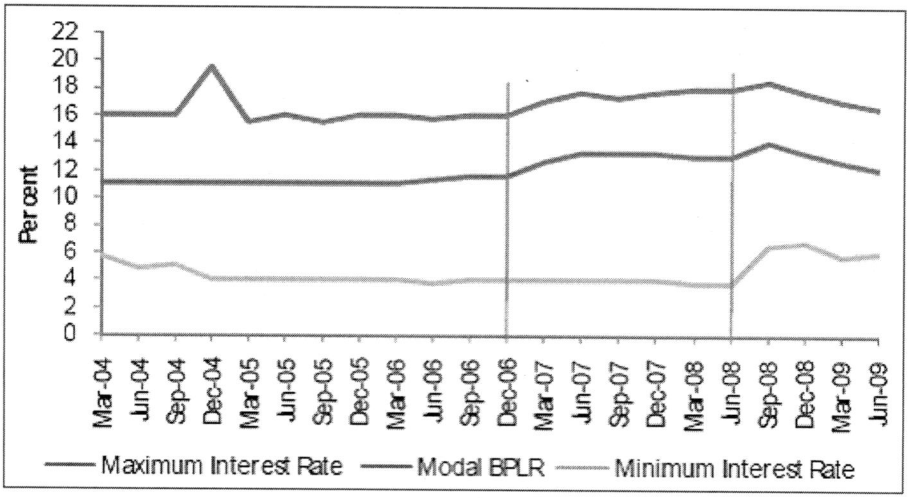

Source: RBI.

Chart 2: Maximum and Minimum Lending Rates of Public Sector Banks

of monetary conditions. Even in this phase, modal BPLRs of private sector banks remained at around 100 bps higher than those of public sector bank. Modal BPLRs of foreign banks remained close to those of public sector banks. In the next phase from June 2007 to September 2008, the divergence in the modal BPLRs of public sector banks and private sector banks widened somewhat; modal BPLRs of foreign banks converged to the modal BPLR of private sector banks. However, since September 2008, modal BPLRs of private and public sector banks have diverged significantly. The modal BPLRs of public sector banks have shown a significant decline since September 2008, while those of private banks' after showing an upward movement till March 2009, and have exhibited a downward movement (Chart 1).

TREND IN REPO RATE

RBI cut Repo rate and reverse Repo rate to encourage banks to provide high credits/ loans. This helps the bank to lend more loans in the country. Home loan rates of banks are closely related to the Repo rate set by RBI. Inflation may cause change in Repo rate as well. In 2003, R.R was around 7%, and then home loans rates were 9.75%. In 2004, R.R came down to 6%, banks lending rates also came down to 7.5%. In 2005, again R.R increased to 7.75% with the increase of home loan rates to 10.5%. In July, 2008, R.R increased to 8.5%, rates climbed to 11.5%.By the end of the year, RR went down to 6.5% home loan rates stayed to 11.5%. In 2009 RR came down to 5.5%, now again banks wanted to cut their rates. Now either the RR will rise or home loan rates may fall.

RESULTS

The results indicate that consumer behaviour gets change according to his preference level. Consumer preference level towards public sector banks were measured high compare to private sector banks. It was found that due to high rates and less security of investments, consumer behaviour changes and he prefers more the public or government banks products. The analysis brings out the results that there are high variations in interest rates and BPLR of banks in India. There is lack of uniformity in the system while deciding the BPLR. On an average, PLR of RBI has shown an increase in year 2010 than 2004. During 2004, PLR of RBI, varies from 10.25% to 11% while in 2010, it is 11-12% approx. 1% increase. Where as, BPLR of schedule commercial banks & Public sector banks on an average, varies from 12.25% to 11.98% for the year 2009-10. While in case of Private and foreign banks, average rates vary from 13.93% to 14.87% for the year 2009-10 (refer to the Table 1 and 2). The study finds that there are high variations in the rates in 2010 at 2.24% compare to year 2009 at only 0.70 % in case of public sector banks.

Table 1: A Comparative Analysis of Average Interest Rates among Major Public Sector Banks of India for 2004 and 2009

Sl. No.	Name of the Banks	2004 % (Fixed)	2009 % (Fixed)	% Change	2004 % (Floating)	2009 % (Floating)	% Change
1	SBI	9.5	11.75	–24	8.50	10.36	–22
2	Bank of India	8.88	9	–1	8.00	13.99	–75
3	PNB	9.08	10.60	–17	8.12	9.87	–22
4	SBBJ	10	11.75	–18	7.91	10.17	–29
5	Canara	8.75	12	–37	8.08	10.13	–25
6	Central Bank of India	9	10.63	–18	8.50	10.13	–19
7	United Bank of India	9.5	11.52	–21	9.25	10.25	–11
8	Syndicate Bank	8.42	12.50	–49	7.66	9.73	–27
9	Union Bank	8.17	8.5	–4	8.08	9.41	–17
10	Vijaya Bank	8.08	11.13	–38	7.75	10	–29
11	Indian Overseas	9.28	11	–19	8.03	9.79	–22
12	OBC	8.92	11.13	–25	8.41	10.21	–21
13	Dena Bank	9.08	11.13	–23	7.50	10.69	–43
14	UCO bank	7.25	12.44	–72	8.41	10.10	–20
15	Allahabad Bank	11	11.10	–91	7.75	9.72	–25
Mean		8.99	11.08	–23	8.13	10.30	–27
Variance		2.18	2.34		0.58	2.00	

But in case of private sector or foreign banks, it was just opposite. There are more variations in BPLR and home loan interest rates as mentioned in the Table 3 and 4. There is high impact of RBI on baking sector. When RBI has increased rates from 2004-09, the banks have also increase their rates. The study also finds that variation among the private sector and foreign banks is more compare to the public or government banks. Considering the average of their variance including all the rates, it comes out to be –37% increases in private or foreign banks rates compare to the public sector banks. It implies that due to high competitions, private or foreign banks may lend the loan at very low rates in starting of the disbursement process. Sometime they lend money below BPLR. It doesn't imply that their rates are really low. As the variations in their rates is quite high. They may do it as a marketing strategy to sell and market their home loan

Table 2: A Comparative Analysis of Average Interest Rates among Major Private Sector Banks of India for 2004 and 2009

Sl. No.	Name of the Banks	2004 % (Fixed)	2009 % (Fixed)	% Change	2004 % (Floating)	2009 % (Floating)	% Change
1	Axis (UTI)	9.75	12.5	–28	7.5	10.5	–40
2	HDFC	7.61	12.5	–64	7.58	10.5	–39
3	ICICI	8.5	13.75	–62	7.5	11.25	–50
4	IDBI	8	12.63	–58	7.5	10.75	–43
5	Centurion Bk	7.5	15.75	–110	7.5	13.75	–83
6	Bank of Rajasthan	8.5	12.60	–48	8	11.60	–45
7	Indusind Bank	8.38	11.75	–40	8.12	10.63	–31
8	Citi Bank	7.25	9.75	–35	8.25	9	–9
9	Standard Chartered	8.25	13.50	–64	7.88	12.50	–59
10	J & K	12	11.01	8	12	10.81	10
11	ABN Ambro	7.75	12.75	–65	7.25	11.75	–62
12	HSBC	9.33	8.49	9	9.33	10.75	–15
13	Kotak Mahindra	9.5	8.5	11	7	8.49	–21
14	Deutsche Bank	8	11.25	–41	8	11.25	–41
15	Federal Bank	11	10.45	5	11.75	9.45	20
Mean		8.75	11.81	–35	7.84	10.87	–39
Variance		1.68	3.86		2.31	1.84	

product. There processing charges may also vary time to time. If we analyze their rates in long run, there is high variations compare to public/government banks which ultimate raises the total loan amount of the customer in long run. Thus the customer should be very careful while borrowing the loan from the banks. The study proves that there are high variations among the rates in private sector as compare to public sector banks. Therefore we have seen how consumer preferences changes towards the banking products with respect to public and private sector banks. This is the reason, in spite of high growth in private sector, consumer prefers public sector banks product more. This gives them a feeling of security of their investment.

Analysis of tables and their mean states that consumer prefernce level is more towards public banks in India compare to private banks.

Table 3: A comparative Analysis of BPLR among Major Public Sector Banks of India for 2009 and 2010 (Current Study)

Sl. No.	Names of Banks	BPLR % (2009)	BPLR % (2010)	% Change
1	SBI	12.25	11.75	4
2	Bank of India	12.50	12	4
3	PNB	12	11	8
4	SBBJ	12.75	12.25	4
5	Canara	13.25	12	9
6	Central Bank of India	12.5	12	4
7	United Bank of India	12.25	12	2
8	Syndicate Bank	12.50	12	4
9	Union Bank	12	11.75	2
10	Vijaya Bank	12.75	12.25	4
11	Indian Overseas	12.50	12	4
12	OBC	11	12	–9
13	Dena Bank	12.75	12.50	2
14	UCO bank	13	12.25	6
15	Allahabad Bank	9.75	12	–23
Mean		12.25	11.98	2
Variance		0.698	2.24	

Table 4: A Comparative Analysis of BPLR among Major Private Sector Banks of India for 2009 and 2010 (Current Study)

Sl. No.	Names of Banks	BPLR % (2009)	BPLR % (2010)	% Change
1	Axis (UTI)	12.25	16.75	–14
2	HDFC	12.50	15.75	–21
3	ICICI	12	14.75	3
4	IDBI	12.75	12.75	6
5	Centurion Bk	13.25	15.75	–21
6	Bank of Rajasthan	12.5	15	0
7	Indusind Bank	12.25	17	–2
8	Citi Bank	12.5	15	–9
9	Standard Chartered	12	15.50	–9
10	J & K	12.75	12.75	0

Sl. No.	Names of Banks	BPLR % (2009)	BPLR % (2010)	% Change
11	ABN Ambro	12.75	13.50	–6
12	HSBC	12.25	16	–31
13	Kotak Mahindra	15.5	15.50	0
14	Deutsche Bank	12.25	12.75	12.25
15	Federal Bank	14.25	14.25	14.25
Mean		13.93	14.87	13.93
Variance		2.14	1.83	

REFERENCES

[1] www.rbi.org.in

[2] "Housing Finance mechanism in India", www. Scribd.com

[3] Duvvuri Subbarao, Governor (2009), "Impact of the global financial crises on India: Collateral damage and response" seminar on global economic crises and challenges for the Asian economy in changing world at Tokyo.

[4] National housing bank annual report (2004-05).

[5] All banks as mentioned here were contacted.

[6] www.planningcommision.com

[7] Richa Dixit, Ashutosh Dixit (2010), "Impact of RBI on major banks housing schemes in India: A comparative Study of Home Loans & variations in their BPLR", published in the Proceedings on Disaster Mitigation in Housing in India, by Centre of Excellence in Disaster Mitigation & Management, Indian Institute of Technology (IIT) – Roorkee, Vol. 2, pp. 263-270.

[8] Preeta vyas,(2005), "Measuring consumer preferences for sales promotion schemes through conjoint design in FMCG sector" IIM-Ahemdabad, India.

Micro Finance: "A Road Ahead for Development"

Anu Sharma and Prakash Kumar Choudhary

Gurgaon College of Engineering, Gurgaon
E-mail: anu_24sharma@yahoo.co.in; prakash1820@gmail.com

ABSTRACT

Micro Finance is a tool for poverty alleviation and improving socio-economic conditions of the poor. Micro financing is a new method to meet the credit requirement in rural areas. Since the bank borrowing requires collateral and the deprived class does not have any type of such collaterals, the success of Bangladesh Grameena Bank which was started by Prof. Muhammed Yunus, in 1976 attracted the attention of Indian policy makers towards the micro finance and micro credit. Micro Finance institutions other than banks are engaged in the provision of financial services to the poor. The study is aimed at analyzing the impact of micro credit on socio economic empowerment of women. The whole study is based on State Bank Institute of Rural Development (SBIRD) Hyderabad. State Bank of India pioneered the ushering in of a new wave of prosperity in the villages and urban slums through SHG Bank Linkage. In order to make very good understanding various schemes and products of the bank relating to SHG-Bank Linkage was introduced and top management desired to analyze the cost factors associated with serving these groups and the socio- economic impact on life style of individual members participating in the SHG movement. The purpose is to find out the fine tune about various products and schemes of the bank relating to SHG bank linkage and also to take strategic business decision for successful implementation and long term sustainability.

Keywords: Microfinance, SHG-Bank Linkage Program, Rural Finance, SBI

INTRODUCTION

Micro finance is a tool for poverty alleviation and improving socio-economic conditions to the poor. Micro Finance is a new method to meet the credit requirement in rural area. Since the bank borrowing requires collateral and the deprived class does not have any type of such collaterals, the success of Bangladesh Grameen Bank which was started by Prof. Muhammed Yunus, in 1976 attracted the attention of Indian policy makers towards the micro finance and micro credit. Micro Finance institutions other than banks are engaged in the provision of financial services to the poor. In the recent period, considerable emphasis has been placed on promotion of micro credit enterprises in view of perceived inadequacies of existing agencies in providing productive credit to those with little or no previous access to formal credit facilities. Micro finance programme through SHG has been effective in making positive social change to the group members. Micro Finance is a programme for the poor and by the poor to mobilize the savings and use them to meet the financing needs.

"My father always wished I was a boy. SHG proved how fortunate he is, to have a girl."
– Narrates a women in SBI bank's advertisement

CONCEPT OF SHG

A Small helping group (SHG) is a registered or unregistered voluntary association of poor people of 15 to 20, from the same socio-economic background, improving primarily in saving and credit activities. A SHG is formed democratically without any political affiliations. It can be all women-group, all men-group or even a mixed group. However, over 90 percent of these groups have only women members. The SHGs are also popularly called DWACRA Groups (Development of Women & Children in rural areas).

"A lot of directed lending is indeed wastefully and hugely in efficient. But microfinance is a form of directed lending that greatly improves efficiency. This is hard- nosed economics, not the bleeding- heart variety."
– Swaminathan S Anklesaria Aiyar, Consulting Editor, *Economic Times* in 2004.

State Bank of India brought a new wave of prosperity in the villages and urban slums through SHG-Bank linkage. Through the ambitious target of credit linking 12 lac SHGs by March 2009, the bank has enabled thousands of villages to become totally money lender-free. The micro credit programme is a part of Bank's continuing journey towards women empowerment providing dignity, self- esteem and economic independence to the women community in the country. Products like SHG credit card, SHG gold card and Sahayog Niwas- a housing loan product for SHGs are all tools in this direction. In order to make very good understanding various schemes and products to the bank relating to SHG-Bank linkage was introduced and top management desired to analyze the cost factors associated with serving these groups and the socio-economic impact on life style of individual members participating in the SHG movement. The purpose is to find out the fine tune about various products and schemes of the bank relating to SHG bank linkage and also to take strategic business decision for successful implementation and long term sustainability.

"SBI in India, with 13,000 branches, is reaching down by acquiring the portfolios of dozens of microfinance institution."

– Elizabeth Littlefield, CEO CGAP and Director, *World Bank* in 2005

OBJECTIVES

The study aimed at gauging the "actual impact of the SHG-Bank linkage programme on the socio-economic status of the target group and its members.

As per the directions of the Micro Credit & Financial inclusion department at corporate centre, the following points were taken as the parameters of the study:

- To examine the extent of involvement of women in SHG's.
- To study the performance of Micro Financing in rural areas.
- To analysis the impact of micro credit on socio economic empowerment of women.
- To calculate the changes in saving and borrowing pattern.
- To know the status of the end-use of funds.
- To assess the impact on economic and social status of the members.
- To find out the impact on living conditions of the member households.
- To find out the need and level of capacity building of SHG members.
- To know the level of satisfaction of the end-users of SHG loan.
- To know the relevance of SHGs beyond credit delivery.
- To improve the literacy among the entire member by introducing communication skills, creating self confidence and developing decision making power, etc.

REVIEW OF LITERATURE

A study of Seibel & Parhusip (1990) based on the premise mention that rural micro-entrepreneurs are unable to organize themselves; they need subsidized credit for increasing their income and are too poor to save. While, Yaron, Benjamin & Piprek (1997) have traced this traditional approach in rural finance leaning leaning heavily towards direct interventions to Keynesian influence. Under this approach, in addition to the assumptions listed above, the key problem areas, absence of modern technology in agriculture, low savings capacity in rural areas and prevalence of moneylenders.

Ryne (2001) observe that these interventions demonstrated techniques for lending to the poor with better outreach and cost recovery. Despite the contextual differences, the unifying thread of these early innovations lay in their certain common principles like reliance on character or peer pressure rather than collateral as loan security, leveraging social capital, positive incentives for repayment and interest rates that approached or covered cost. The design features of the programme emphasize that these do not have envisage any subsidy support from the government in the matter of credit and charges market related interest rates based on the premise that sub- market interest rates could spell doom; distort the use and direction of credit (Kropp &Suran, 2002).

Harper (2002) has also given illustrations of commercial banks being active in promotion of microfinance. If the commercial banks and RRBs do adopt some of the methods of microfinance institutions, there may be a possibility of the Indonesian experience being repeated in India.

State Bank of India (SBI) is the largest commercial bank in India. The Sakoli agricultural development branch of SBI in Bhandara district, Maharashtra was in deep trouble in mid 1990s as the branch could not recover the loans disbursed to the farmers in 15 villages. The farmers were unable to repay the loans due to the failure of crops. SBI decided to close the branch. The branch manager visited these villages and persuaded a few of the villagers to form Self Help Groups (SHGs) by explaining them the benefits of SHGs and the process of saving certain amount of money every month. After a lot of persuasion, the reluctant villagers formed an SHG. After the SHG was formed, the villagers, who in 1995 were finding it difficult to save even Rs 5 a month, were individually saving Rs. 500 per month by 2005. In a span of a decade, the 15 villages, with a predominant farming community, had changed for the better. The SHGs had borrowed Rs. 5,00,000 to buy tractors.

According to Chandan Jamdage, the manager from SBI who started the microfinance initiative in these villages, "When a SHG comes together, they save small sums on a regular basis. The process gradually builds financial discipline. They also learn to handle resources of a size beyond their individual capacities. The SHG members begin to appreciate that resources are limited and have a cost. Once the groups shows mature financial behavior, the bank feels confident about giving them loans." Linking banks and SHGs has become one of the largest and fastest growing microfinance programs in India. In March 2005, microfinance reached 1.43 million SHGs with 21 million members, making a difference to the lives of over 100 million poor people in the country. SBI was the largest player in the microfinance sector in India and financed more than 300,000 SHGs as of March 2005.

With more than 9000 branches, and more than 4,000 branches of its associated banks, SBI catered to the needs of agriculturists and landless laborers through 6,600 semi-urban and rural branches. SBI had setup 974 branches exclusively for development of agriculture through credit deployment. The Prime Minister of India, Manmohan Singh remarked that SBI needed to play a major role and guide all the other banks in increasing the market for rural credit. At the bicentennial celebrations of SBI in June 2005, he said "You (SBI) have to leverage your strengths, develop new capabilities, and show initiative to venture into uncharted territories so that you continue to be in the vanguard of India's growth in this century..."

The origin of SBI dates back to the early 19th century, when the Bank of Calcutta was established in Calcutta (present day Kolkata in the state of West Bengal) in June 1806 under the aegis of the British-run, Government of Bengal. Three years after its inception, the bank was renamed Bank of Bengal on receiving its charter. It was a unique banking institution as it was the first joint-stock bank in British India. Next came the Bank of Bombay in April 1840 followed by the Bank of Madras in July 1843. By 1876, the three presidency banks, together with their branches, agencies and sub-agencies, covered major inland trade centers in India. Bank of Bengal had 18 branches while the other two had 15 branches each. Initially, the business of these banks was restricted to discounting bills of exchange or other negotiable private securities, keeping cash accounts and receiving deposits and issuing and circulating cash note The last quarter of the 19th century witnessed rapid commercialization in India owing to the expansion of the railway network to cover all the major geographic regions of the country. The three presidency banks were both beneficiaries and promoters of this commercialization process as they became involved in the financing of practically every trading, manufacturing and mining activity in the Indian subcontinent. The three presidency banks were amalgamated in January 1921 to form the Imperial Bank of India. The new bank performed the triple role of a commercial bank, a banker's bank and a banker to the government... SBI has been actively involved in the microfinance sector as it serves both the social and commercial objectives of the bank. It was the largest player in the microfinance sector in India in terms of loans disbursed to SHGs. SBI has been actively involved in the microfinance sector as it serves both the social and commercial objectives of the bank. It was the largest player in the microfinance sector in India in terms of loans disbursed to SHGs.

METHODOLOGY

The study aimed at gauging the actual impact of SHG- Bank Linkage programmed on the socio-economic status of the target group and its members. The study also explored all the factors, based on field research in 4 circles of SBI Bank, presenting a reality check of what is happening out there. It includes:

Methods

The main methods adopted for the study were:

- Interview with individual SHG members and Group leaders at their premises
- Interaction with the Branch Managers, Field Officers and MRT leaders.
- Scanning of latest literature, study reports, research reports and other published works on SHG-Bank linkage was used as a tool to gain better insights.

Materials

The following materials were made use of to collect data and information required for this project work:

(a) A structured survey format prepared for the group and another one for the group member.
(b) The following techniques were followed while designing the questionnaire and during the interviews.
  (i) **Pre-post technique** (comparing before and after situations ie. in respect of changes in saving and borrowing pattern, impact on living conditions, etc.)
  (ii) **Control sampling technique** (comparing with and without situations, i.e. in respect of end use of funds, satisfaction level of users, etc.)

  The views and ideas which emerged during the interaction with the SHG members were also used to evaluate other points.
(c) Articles in newspapers, websites of various research/developmental institutions, study reports published by researchers.

Sample Size

It was decided to conduct the study in **four Circles**, viz., Hyderabad, Bhubaneswar, Mumbai and Bhopal. As of March 2008, the SHG linkage in these Circles was as under:

A total of **738 members** (6 districts, 5 branches in each district, 5 SHGs in each branch and on an average 5 members in each SHG) constituted the final sample, from which the data was collected and analyzed for the purpose of study. It is understood that this was one of the biggest sample in a study relating to SHG.

RESULT AND DISCUSSION

The sample data collected has been analyzed using various statistical methods and techniques. The information culled out from the data has been brought out hereunder:

Composition of Sample

1. The actual data in respect of distribution by caste is provided below:

Circle	OC	BC	OBC	SC	ST	Minorities	Total
Hyderabad	161	136	0	60	7	11	375
Mumbai	20	9	33	22	36	5	125
Bhubaneswar	61	4	30	19	0	6	120
Bhopal	62	8	42	6	0	0	118
Total	304	157	105	107	43	22	738

Source: SBIRD, Hyderabad.

2. The Same data when converted to percentage, the following pattern emerges.

Circle	OC	BC	OBC	SC	ST	Minorities	Total
Hyderabad	43%	36%	0%	16%	2%	3%	100%
Mumbai	16%	7%	26%	18%	29%	4%	100%
Bhubaneswar	51%	3%	25%	16%	0%	5%	100%
Bhopal	53%	7%	35%	5%	0%	0%	100%
Total	41%	21%	14%	15%	6%	3%	100%

Source: SBIRD, Hyderabad.

3. Composition of Sample by Age

Circle	19-25 Years	26-35 Years	36-50 Years	Above 50 years	Total
Hyderabad	7%	44%	43%	6%	100%
Mumbai	2%	38%	46%	14%	100%
Bhubaneswar	8%	42%	43%	7%	100%
Bhopal	8%	42%	48%	2%	100%
Total	7%	42%	44%	7%	100%

Source: SBIRD, Hyderabad.

Across all Circles studied, it is amply clear that majority of the members are from the age group of 26 – 50 years. The reason for the stability of the SHG movement can also be gauged from the above table, which throws up the following facts of life.

- Many of the members get married before 25 years and they will try to put their family in a safe net in subsequent years.
- Life between 26 and 50 years is the prime life for any person.
- They plan properly for their future life including stability for their children.
- Their mental maturity also helps in strengthening of the group.

(a) Changes in Savings and Borrowing Pattern

From the data gathered across SHGs in four circles, the economical management available as on the survey data is as under:

Circle	Minimum Thrift (Amt in Rs.)	Maximum Thrift (Amt in Rs.)
Hyderabad	150	15000
Mumbai	1000	5000
Bhubaneswar	600	10700
Bhopal	600	10000

Source: SBIRD, Hyderabad.

Interestingly, the average thrift amount in respect of three Circles viz., Hyderabad, Bhubaneswar & Bhopal is almost at the same level of Rs. 3500 plus. Considering that the SHGs taken as sample were at least 5 years old, the minimum thrift of Rs. 150-600 indicated that the members have utilized the savings money for consumption. Our interactions with the members have revealed that at many places, the members were sharing the thrift amount after one year or so and using it for either consumption or repayment of earlier loans. This could probably weaken the strength of the SHG in difficult times, an aspect that has to be taken care of by the branches while sanctioning fresh loans.

(b) End Use of Funds

The data utilization of loan amount for various purposes is collated as under:

Circle	Consumption Purpose	Productive Purpose	Both Purpose	Total
Hyderabad	21%	67%	12%	100%
Mumbai	22%	76%	2%	100%
Bhubaneswar	13%	69%	18%	100%
Bhopal	8%	75%	17%	100%
Total	18%	70%	12%	100%

Source: SBIRD, Hyderabad.

It is premised while collating the data that wherever the loan is utilized for the purpose of investing in existing business/existing agriculture production, paying the fees for children's higher education, etc., it should be treated that the loan was utilized for productive purpose. As per the information shared by the members during our interactions, the share of loan utilized for productive purposes was coming to 70% which showed a healthy trend. But, the worrying challenge was how to ensure that they were really investing the money for the said purpose. Had it not been used for the claimed purposes, once the loan amount goes up in subsequent doses, it would become difficult for the members to repay the loan from the income generated from that activity or otherwise.

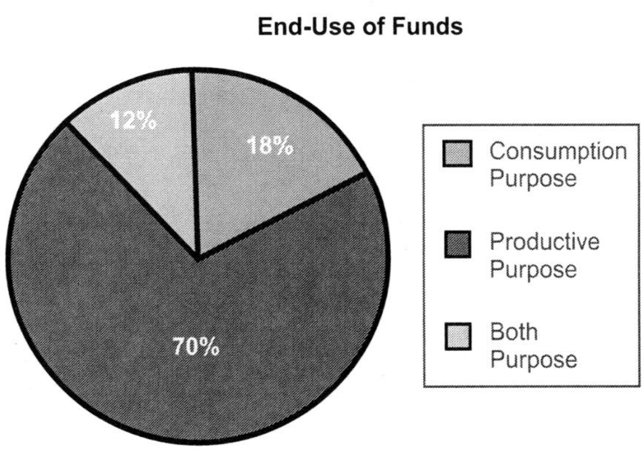

(c) Impact on Economic and Social Status of the Members

The asset holding pattern of the group members on individual basis, before and after, SHG-Bank linkage was collected through questionnaire and the position indicated as under: Data in respect of assets in the form of house, consumer durables, livestock, other productive assets (other than landholdings) were collected and tabulated as under:

Assets Holding (Pre-SHG)

Circle	Minimum Assets (Amt in Rs.)	Maximum Assets (Amt in Rs.)
Hyderabad	0	440000
Mumbai	0	300000
Bhubaneswar	22000	300000
Bhopal	25000	180000

Source: SBIRD, Hyderabad.

Assets Holding (Post-SHG)

Circle	Minimum Assets (Amt in Rs.)	Maximum Assets (Amt in Rs.)
Hyderabad	0	780000
Mumbai	0	543000
Bhubaneswar	28000	300000
Bhopal	28000	200000

Source: SBIRD, Hyderabad.

The information shared by the members, showed an improved situation as regards the assets held by the members after SHG-Bank linkage. One can, therefore, safely conclude that the economic status of the members improved after the SHG-Bank linkage, which is a welcome sign for the bankers and the society at large.

Distribution of Sample by Landholding

Circle	Landless	Marginal Farmer	Small Farmer	Others	Total
Hyderabad	66%	29%	5%	0%	100%
Mumbai	48%	2%	32%	18%	100%
Bhubaneswar	7%	3%	48%	42%	100%
Bhopal	4%	6%	61%	29%	100%
Total	44%	16%	25%	15%	100%

Source: SBIRD, Hyderabad.

It is observed that majority of members in Hyderabad (66%) & Mumbai (48%) Circles were landless laborers. In Bhubaneswar & Bhopal Circles, many members were from the families of Small Farmers and Others. However, there were some apparent inhibitions while sharing this information by the members as some of them were not interested to share the family landholdings or even the landholdings in the name of husbands. In Bhubaneswar & Bhopal Circles, it was noticed that even though there was land in the name of the family members, it was mostly unproductive land or only mono-cropped land. Obviously, the information gathered could not be interpreted in right perspective to draw conclusions.

The consumption pattern (consumption here includes expenses incurred for food, clothing, education, health & festivals in a year by all the family members) before and after linkage was as under:

Consumption Pattern (Pre-SHG)

Circle	Minimum Consumption (Amt in Rs.)	Maximum Consumption (Amt in Rs.)
Hyderabad	3000	65000
Mumbai	3000	35000
Bhubaneswar	5000	90000
Bhopal	18000	85000

Source: SBIRD, Hyderabad.

Consumption Pattern (Post-SHG)

Circle	Minimum Consumption (Amt in Rs.)	Maximum Consumption (Amt in Rs.)
Hyderabad	5000	98000
Mumbai	3500	45000
Bhubaneswar	6000	100000
Bhopal	18000	95000

Source: SBIRD, Hyderabad.

The improvement in consumption pattern itself could be further solidifying the efforts of bankers through SHG-Bank linkage. This could be treated as a measure in improvement in the life-style of the members.

Impact on Other Economic Factors

Furnished below are the responses to the questions on various other parameters, which indicated that there was noteworthy improvement/knowledge gained after the linkage.

Parameter/Circle →	Hyderabad	Mumbai	Bhubaneswar	Bhopal
Access to institutional credit	100%	100%	90%	98%
Decreased dependence on money lenders	83%	92%	80%	91%
Knowledge of importance of economic activities	76%	37%	64%	76%

Source: SBIRD, Hyderabad.

The members have expressed more satisfaction about the access to bank credit due to the linkage. It also helped in decreasing the dependence on money lenders to a greater extent. In this process, (except in Mumbai Circle) they have also acquired knowledge about importance of various economic activities.

(d) Impact on Living Conditions

The responses to the questions on relevant parameters are tabulated below. The position indicated that there is remarkable improvement/knowledge gained after the linkage.

Parameter/Circle→	Hyderabad	Mumbai	Bhubaneswar	Bhopal
Improvement in communication levels (talking freely, without fear)	100%	100%	65%	68%
Improvement in Self- Confidence	100%	100%	65%	70%
Improvement in decision making	100%	100%	60%	61%
Knowledge in family planning methods	100%	100%	41%	56%
Vaccination for children	100%	100%	37%	52%
Improvement in Sanitation	100%	100%	36%	46%
Protesting social evils (Like addiction to liquor, domestic violence)	100%	100%	45%	56%
Sending children to school	100%	100%	68%	71%

Source: SBIRD, Hyderabad.

There is perceptible improvement in communication skills, self-confidence and decision-making of the members after joining the SHGs. They have gained better awareness about family planning methods, importance of vaccination to children, sanitation, importance of sending children to schools etc. Protesting social evils has become an important development in the SHG movement, which has since been making a clear dent in removing the social evils from the society. Thus, there is an overall improvement in the situation, both economically as well as socially, for the members after joining the SHGs.

(e) Need and Level of Capacity Building

Data has also been gathered about the literacy level among group members and the trainings they received for various activities.

Literacy Level among the Sample

Circle	Illiterate	Can Sign	Primary Education	Secondary Education	Higher Education	Total
Hyderabad	12%	24%	42%	19%	3%	100%
Mumbai	32%	14%	18%	30%	6%	100%
Bhubaneswar	9%	14%	26%	41%	10%	100%
Bhopal	3%	17%	36%	33%	11%	100%
Total	13%	20%	34%	27%	6%	100%

Source: SBIRD, Hyderabad.

Nearly 20% of the sample population comprising of people who were able to sign have admitted that they have learned signing only after joining in the Group. Thus, credit goes to the SHG movement and the Branch Managers/Operating functionaries who guided the members to learn at least how to sign. What's more, nearly 33% members were above Primary education level. This gave them the required strength to manage their group as well as its accounts. It is observed that in cases where the group was maintaining proper books of accounts, it was basically thanks to the members who were well-educated.

Distribution of Sample by Training Received

Circle	Training Received	Training not Received	Total
Hyderabad	5%	95%	100%
Mumbai	9%	91%	100%
Bhubaneswar	23%	77%	100%
Bhopal	27%	73%	100%
Total	12%	88%	100%

Source: SBIRD, Hyderabad.

It is a sad part to know that the training imparted by Government Departments / NGOs for taking up gainful productive activities, was at a low of overall 12% in the total sample and only 5% in Hyderabad Circle. While Hyderabad Circle (State of Andhra Pradesh) was well ahead in SHG movement and the Government was also providing loans at low interest rate, the training for SHG members was precious little. This could result in the SHG members not being able to take up gainful productive activities even with high doses of loan amounts. This may increase the default percentage in the long run as the members may not be able to generate enough income to ensure repayment at the right time. This aspect needs to be taken care of while financing higher loans to the groups.

(f) Whether the Groups are Satisfied with SHG-Bank Linkage?

Circle	Satisfaction Level with Bank Linkage
Hyderabad	100%
Mumbai	100%
Bhubaneswar	95%
Bhopal	98%

Source: SBIRD, Hyderabad.

CONCLUSION

In India, great no. of people lives in rural areas in which the need for development is growing in order to achieve economic empowerment. This is possible through SHG movement and in the Andhra Pradesh more than 1.5 Lakhs of SHG, but the majority of them is involved in small scale activities and in the same time they have no access to technological development. It is high time for the government to consider the matter seriously and make some marketing plans to promote the SHG's product to the greatest extent.

The Indian economy presently is at crossroads; on one hand, the optimists are talking of India reaching the top 5 economies of the world by 2050 and on the other is the presence of 260 million poor forming 26% (1999-2000) of the total population languishing in abject poverty. The enormity of the task can be gauged from the latter numbers and if India is to stand tall among the comity of developed nations, there is no denying the fact that poverty alleviation & reduction of income inequalities has to be among the top priorities. In the above backdrop, the impressive gains made by SHG Bank linkage programme providing the rural population with financial services offer a ray of hope. However, the empirical evidence suggests that increasingly the deficiencies of earlier schemes are seeping into this programme as well. This needs to be taken care at least from now onwards. Simple number game may lead to self-deceit and bad results in the coming days.

REFERENCES

[1] Akanji, O.O. (2001), "Microfinance as a Strategy for Poverty Reduction". *Economic and Financial Review*, 39(4): 111-134.

[2] Arjun Y. Pangannavar, 2009. Rural development: women self groups. Southern economist. Vol. 47. February.

[3] Bouman, F.J.A. and O. Hospes (1994), "Financial Landscape Reconstructed" in Bouman, F.J.A. and O. Hospes (eds.) Financial Landscape Reconstructed. The fine art of mapping development. Boulder: Westview.

[4] C. Jayanti, 2001. Empowering women. *Yojana*, vol. 25, June.

[5] Chakravarty, S., 2005. Credit policy. *Yojana*, vol. 49, June.

[6] Credit Guidelines for Self-Help Groups – A tool for credit rating" published by Tamilnadu Corporation for Development of Women Ltd., Nov 2000.

[7] Diagne, A. and Zeller, M. (2001), Access to Credit and its Impact on welfare in Malawi, International Food Policy Research Institute: Washington DC. Research Report 116.

[8] Deubel, T.F. 2006. Banking on culture, micro credit as incentive for cultural conservation in Mali. *In Microfinance Perils and Prospects*, (Fernando, J.L.ed.): 133-153.

[9] Dichter, T.2006. Hype and Hope: The worrisome state of Micro credit movement, The South African Institute of International Affairs (www.saiia.org.za/).

[10] Gangaih C. and Naidu C.V., 2006. Impact of self help groups on income and employment. *Kurukshetra*, vol. 54, March, pp. 10-13.

[11] Gurumoorthy, T.R., 2000. Self help groups empower rural women. *Kurukshetra*, vol. 48, February, pp. 12-14.

[12] Kropp, E.W. and Suran, B.S., 2002. Linking banks and SHGs in India: an assessment, NABARD, Mumbai.

[13] K. Srinivasa Rao, 2008. Micro finance to the poor: a tool for poverty alleviation and women empowerment. *The Management Accountant*, vol. 2, February.

[14] Micro credit Summit Campaign.2005. State of the micro credit summit campaign report 2005, Washington, DC.

[15] P.J. Christabell, 2007. Women empowerment through capacity building – the role of micro finance. Finance India, September.

[16] Remenyi, J., 2000. Is there a state of the art in microfinance? in microfinance and poverty alleviation case studies from Asia & the Pacific (Remenyi, J. & Quinones, B.Ed.) Londen: Pinter.

[17] Rutledge, Oxon as quoted in Buckley, G. 1997. Microfinance in Africa: Is it either the problem or solution? *World Development* 25(7): 1081-93.

[18] Sudersana Reddy G. and Panduranga V. Patti, 2008. Role of micro finance in rural development. *Gitam Journal of Management*, vol. 7, January, pp. 173-186.

[19] Vasant Desai, 2005. Rural development. Himalaya Publishing House, Mumbai.

[20] Yunus Mohammad, 2004. Grameen Bank – Micro credit and millennium development goals. Economic and Political weekly, vol. 39, March.

PFI in Gujarat Ports Success Factors and Bottlenecks

Ashwani Kumar Pradhan
K.J. Somaiya Institute of Management Studies and Research
E-mail: akpradhan@simsr.somaiya.edu

ABSTRACT

Public Private Partnership (PPP) and Private Finance Initiative (PFI) have been accepted as an essential method for the development of physical infrastructure in India. It has not however delivered adequate results so far. Many successful PPP initiatives were taken in U.K. Research projects have been carried out in U.K. and subsequently in Hong Kong (China) and Australia to identify the relative importance of 18 critical factors for success of PPP in these countries. There has been a phenomenal development of port capacity in Gujarat State. This development, which is mainly in the intermediate ports of the State sector, has been mainly due to the policy initiatives taken by the State Government. The reasons can be summarized in terms of the critical success factors which have been found most important in the re search papers: efficient risk allocation, output based specifications, private management skill, private sector technical innovation, optimal use of assets, long term nature of contracts and risk transfer. These success factors have been qualitatively analyzed below to show how they have helped in l in ensuring that adequate PFI has been forthcoming in Gujarat, and has resulted in stepping up port traffic from 17.15 million tons (MT) to 295 MT in 2009-10. Gujarat ports can successfully serve the hinterland of Western India including Gujarat and Northern India and provide economic advantage to industry and make our exports very competitive in the international market. There are however some bottlenecks which have to be removed for a faster growth and consequent benefits to industry and economy in the hinterland. These include lack of adequate rail freight capacity for container traffic as well as a traditional mindset among industry players and their logistics managers who prefer J.N.P.T. to Gujarat container port terminals. This results in higher costs and congestion at J.N.P.T. and NSICT has forcibly enforced move count restrictions on all carriers operating there. If more exim traffic could be made to flow through Gujarat ports, not only will it reduce congestion at Nhava Sheva but also reduce logistics costs and add to India's competitive edge in the international markets.

Keywords: PFI, Gujarat Ports

A strong growth in India's trade reflected buoyancy in the overall GDP growth in the last decade. Fuelled by increasing globalization and liberalization of trade policies, there has been a surge in India's global trade in FY11 is expected to be USD500bn a ~6 fold-increase in the last 10 years. This increase in trade volumes is largely driven through the maritime route as India is fortunate to be surrounded by sea on three sides. Ports handle ~95% of the volume and ~70% of the value of India's cargo. Since 1982, port traffic in India has grown at a factor of 1.5x of India's real GDP growth. Post-liberalization, traffic growth picked up from sub-7% levels, to ~9.7% levels in the last decade. Thus for India to achieve 8% GDP growth, it is imperative that port traffic has to grow at 11-12%. The maritime agenda released by the Ministry of Shipping in January 2011 forecasts total port traffic in India to grow at 10% CAGR from FY11-20.

India has 13 Major Ports (with the addition of Port Blair now) and ~200 Minor (or non-major) Ports. This definition is driven by regulatory set-up and not the size of the ports. Major Ports are those ports defined so by the Central Government and are typically managed by a Port Trust. In contrast Minor ports are typically handled by the State Governments. Of the ~200 non major ports, only ~60 are active and handle traffic as per the Ministry of Shipping.

Pre-liberalization, traffic at Major Ports grew at 7% CAGR, while Minor Ports registered a 5.4% CAGR. The trend has been reversed since then, with growth in Minor Ports (17.7% CAGR) outstripping the 7.1% CAGR registered by Major Ports. The trend is expected to continue with an expected 11.4% growth in non major port traffic and a 9.3% growth in major port traffic over FY11-20 according to the Maritime Agenda released by the Ministry of Shipping. Container cargo and coal are expected to drive the growth in Minor Ports over FY10-17. Container traffic in minor ports is expected to grow at 38% CAGR, followed by coal (32%).

Gujarat is one of India's principal maritime states with a natural coastline of about 1600 km, which accounts for ~25% of India's total coastline (excluding the coastlines of Andaman and Nicobar Islands, and Lakshadweep group of Islands). Gujarat accounts for ~75% of the non major port traffic in India. There are 40 non-major ports which are under the jurisdiction of Gujarat Maritime Board (GMB). Out of 40 non-major ports, traffic is handled through 17 non-major ports. Gujarat's non major ports have experienced a traffic growth of 12.6% CAGR in FY02-10. The remaining 23 non-major ports are used for fishing activities and have traffic only of small volume. The leading non-major (GMB) ports in Gujarat include Pipavav Port, Mundra Port, and Essar Port at Hazira, Sikka, Magdalla and Dahej. GMB ports handled a total of 231mn tones of cargo in FY11, up 12% YoY. Several major international ports/shipping liners have equity stake in the Minor Ports in Gujarat such as Dubai Ports, AP Moeller etc. How is it that a single state has been able to carve out such a large market share in the ports segment from amongst all other states which are also blessed with a natural sea front?

To get a better perspective on this it is important to understand the success factors for ports and understand in detail how Gujarat stacks up against each of the parameters. Port development in Gujarat has been possible mainly due to opening up of this sector to private finance initiative (PFI) through Public Private Partnership (PPP).

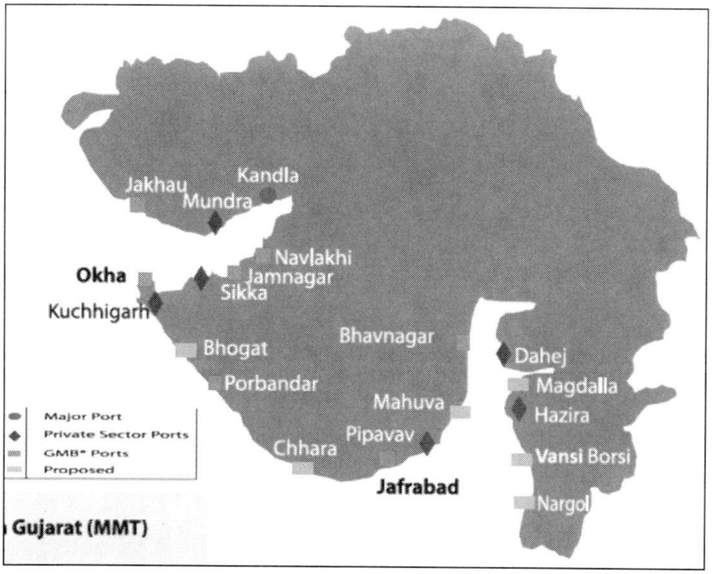

Fig. 1: Ports in Gujarat

Many successful PPP initiatives were taken in U.K. Research projects have been carried out in U.K. and subsequently in Hong Kong (China) and Australia to identify the relative importance of 18 critical factors for success of PPP in these countries. (Chan et al., 2008). These are not however specific to port development.

I have made an attempt to analyse specific success factors for the phenomenal growth of ports and port throughput in Gujarat. The findings enumerated below are based on analysis of PPP projects in India, particularly in the port sector and my interactions with four of the largest private port developers in India:

SUPPORT FROM STATE GOVERNMENT FOR CREATING THE RIGHT ENVIRONMENT

Government of Gujarat took one radical step that changed the scenario of the port sector in Gujarat. This was the formation of the Gujarat Maritime Board (GMB) in 1982 as the first autonomous State Board of Gujarat to develop, facilitate, administer and regulate the Gujarat's non major ports. (Shah, V.P., 2011). PORTS in India used to be inefficient State monopolies. Gujarat also was the pioneer in encouraging public private partnership in the port sector and developed the concept of port liberalization utilizing the same to become India's fastest-growing maritime state. GMB experimented with different forms of privatization models to promote private participation in Gujarat ports leading to enhancement of the capacity of the ports at the same time making them revenue generators for the state. These were as under:

Captive Jetty Model

This model was conceptualized in the mid 1980s and allowed the port based industries to develop their own jetty to cater to their import-export requirements. The industry was given a concession in wharfage rates to be set off against the cost of construction of the jetty. In view of this proactive step of the Government, many private sector companies developed their captive jetty facilities in Magdalla, Hazira, Mul-Dwarka, Jamnagar, Sikka and Dahej. With the rolling out of the captive jetty model, the traffic increased by over 6 times in the early 1990s from the mid 1980s. Today a total of 24 captive jetties/SPMs dot the coastline of Gujarat.

Privatization under the Build Own Operate and Transfer (BOT) Model

As a part of short-term development strategy, existing port facilities were offered to private companies to develop through private investment under the private jetty model developed by Build-Operate-Transfer mode. The aim was to handle cargo through mechanized handling system and to increase the efficiency of operations. The private jetties are granted permission for a lease period varying from 5 to 25 years depending on the quantum of investment. Presently there are 12 operational private jetties at different locations in the state and there are various future proposals for further development.

Port Policy set out in 1995

The State rolled out Port Policy in the year 1995 after liberalization of economic policies of Government of India. This policy spelled out an explicit strategy of port-led development, including the proposal for creation of 10 completely new, world-class ports, with dominant private-sector participation. The policy was intended to: (1) remove the hurdles in developing green-field ports on PPP (Public Private Partnership) model; (2) select new sites of ports which were close to industries and had adequate rail and road connectivity; (3) develop ports with draft of more than 15 meters to accommodate large modern ships; (4) identify sites with adequate land to support infrastructure (Shah, 2011). The type of cargo breakup of major ports in India was studied and the policy was framed in such a way that such cargo could be catered to at Gujarat ports.

EFFICIENT RISK ALLOCATION BETWEEN THE GOVERNMENT AND PRIVATE PARTNER

Port projects involve high investment and technical problems during construction, and have a long gestation period. Hence the private partner is taking a high risk, but will have commensurately high returns if the project is successful. Therefore risks have to be allocated to the party best able to bear them. In that context, the port policy, the model concession agreement and the Gujarat Infrastructure Development Board (GIDB) Act were very helpful in providing assurance to the investors. The concession agreements between the GMB (licensor) and private partner (licensee) were designed paying heed to the following risk factors:

- *Land Acquisition* – The State Government allocated adequate land for the projects or took up the acquisition of required land. The private partner thus did not have to worry about this matter.
- *Market Risk* – The private party had to take this risk as it was better capable of making an assessment of market conditions and long term demand and supply situation and would have decided to invest funds only if it found the risk worth taking.
- *Financing Risk* – While financing risk was borne by the port developer (licensee) and the lenders, certain safeguards were provided to mitigate risks.
- *Political Force Majeure* – A change in law or Government policy which would adversely impact the private partner's costs, revenues or obligations. However the Concession Agreements provided safeguards for the private developer. These were typically either in the form of suspension of his obligations during the tenor of the Force Majeure event or the flexibility for extension of concession period or relaxation of certain concession conditions for the duration of the relevant Force Majeure period.
- *Capital Protection in the Event of Termination* – In the event of a prolonged political force majeure event, the licensee can terminate the agreement. The licensor (GMB) is obliged to purchase the Immovable contracted assets and Essential Moveable Contracted Assets for a consideration equivalent to the higher of (i) the depreciated replacement cost of assets or (ii) the debt obligations and a recompense of the equity invested with a nominal return

  It may be mentioned that no disputes regarding obligations have arisen so far between the GMB and the major port developers. This has been a very positive factor for the growth of ports in Gujarat.
- *Output Based Specifications* – GMB has followed the policy of flexibility on output parameters: The GMB while defining the broad contours of the ports, left detailed specifications to the developers. No minimum output was specified in any of the

concession agreements (unlike the first agreement between JNPT and the NSICT). This has been listed as a positive factor by the operators and has not impacted the increasing throughput at all the ports.

NATURAL MARINE ADVANTAGES

Gujarat sought to exploit its natural maritime advantages. The state's deeply indented shores provide 1,600 kilometers of coast, the most of any state. Almost all India's coastline is hit by seasonal monsoon, necessitating the construction of costly breakwaters (jetties without breakwaters have to stop loading in the monsoon months). The Gulf of Kachchh in Gujarat is the only coastal area in India that is monsoon-free, and so ports and jetties located there can function all year without breakwaters. The Gulf of Kutch also has the deepest water in India: a natural draft of 17 meters without dredging is available at ports like Mundra and Positra, deep enough to accommodate the biggest container ships and large bulk carriers. Very large crude carriers of up to 400,000 tons can anchor at SPMs in deep waters many kilometers from the shore and unload their cargo through pipelines. No other part of India's long coastline can accommodate such large vessels. (Shah, 2011)

Proximity to Hinterland for Cargo and Major International Shipping Routes

The most critical aspect which drives the success of any port is the location. Gujarat's ports are located in close proximity to the land-locked hinterland of North India and its ports can cater to about 1/3rd of Indian industrial states such as Rajasthan, part of Uttar Pradesh, Delhi, Punjab, Haryana, Jammu & Kashmir and Himachal Pradesh, over and above catering to its own industrial centers. Overseas cargo servicing this hinterland accounts for ~88% of the non major port traffic in Gujarat. Further, Gujarat ports enjoy a significant distance advantage over the ports in Mumbai and JNPT which are in any case reeling under hhigh capacity utilization and lower efficiency. (Sengupta, 2011) In addition Gujarat is itself a highly industrialized state and also generates its own cargo. For e.g., the 4000 MW Ultra Mega Power Project being set up in Mundra by Tata Power is expected to generate about 14 mt of coal which will provide captive cargo for Mundra Port. The state accounts for 22% of the country's exports, has the country's largest gas based single location sponge iron plant, the largest denim producer and has Asia's largest grass root refinery near Jamnagar which imports its crude through a Single Point Mooring (SPM) in the Gulf of Kachchh where crude is transported by VLCCs. Gujarat also has the country's only LNG import terminals at Hazira and Dahej. In the recently held Vibrant Gujarat Investors Summit, the state received 1415 letters of Intent for investment of about Rs.65000 crores and 1577 letters of permission for setting up 100% Export Oriented Units having proposed investment of Rs 8000 crores. Thus in addition to being the gateway for cargo originating in the Northern and Central hinterland, Gujarat itself contributes significantly to the traffic being handled by its ports.

The distance between the major container depots in North India and the ports of Gujarat is lower as compared to JNPT, Nhava Sheva and Gateway Terminals the three major container terminals in India. Accordingly the freight charges for moving container cargo from major North India container depots to Gujarat ports are cheaper than to Mumbai ports (Sengupta, I., 2011).

Originating Station	Destination Station	Charges (Rs)
Dadri, Greater Noida	JNPT/NSICT/GTIL	19800
Dadri, Greater Noida	MUMBAI PORT	19800
Dadri, Greater Noida	MUNDRA PORT	16700
Dadri, Greater Noida	PIPAVAV PORT	16950
Jaipur	JNPT/NSICT/GTIL	16500
Jaipur	MUMBAI PORT	16500
Jaipur	MUNDRA PORT	13700
Jaipur	PIPAVAV PORT	12900
Ludhiana	JNPT/NSICT/GTIL	22900
Ludhiana	MUMBAI PORT	22900
Ludhiana	MUNDRA PORT	18900
Ludhiana	PIPAVAV PORT	18900

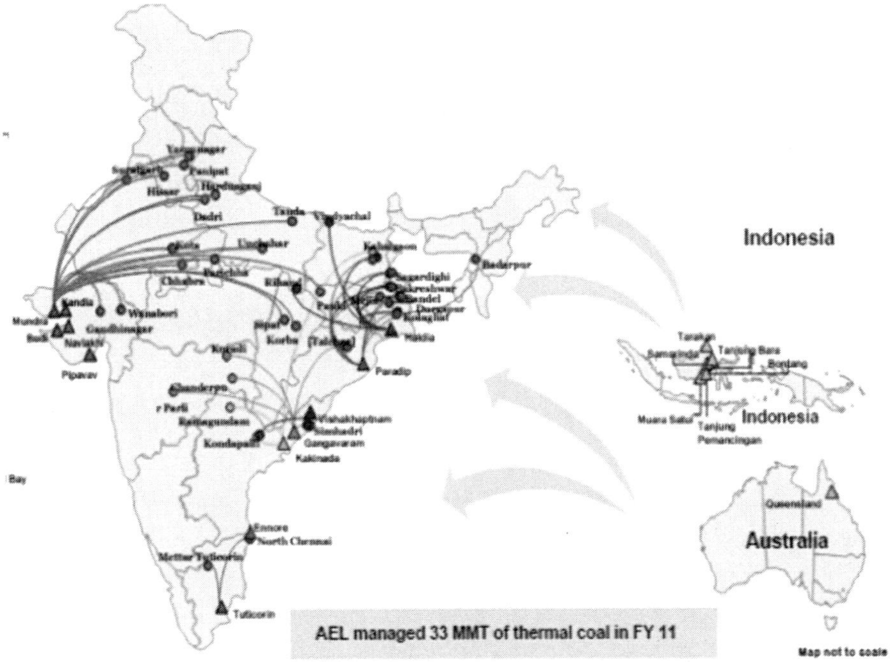

Fig. 2: Connectivity of Gujarat Ports

Accordingly the ports in Gujarat enjoy a distinct distance advantage over the other major ports in the West Coast. The bottleneck is availability of rail container services to Gujarat ports. Concor is now concentrating on providing new services and has introduced direct services to Mundra and Pipavav from Moradabad and Kanpur. (Business Line, August3, 2011)

The map (Fig. 2) shows also the connectivity ports in Gujarat enjoy with the Northern hinterland and the coal markets in East Asia.

Further Gujarat is also extremely well connected to major international shipping routes (e.g. crude from the Middle East, coal from Indonesia and Australia and container cargo from Salalah, Rotterdam, etc.). The ports in Gujarat are located close to the mainline ports like Mumbai and JNPT and hence are a natural port of call for international ships stopping on their way to Mumbai.

Ports	America Far East Route	Europe Asia Route
Mumbai	888	1656
JNPT	898	1666
Kandla	1390	1566
Mundra	1340	1516
Pipavav	1088	1616

Well Developed Road and Rail Connectivity

Another most important aspect for the success of the ports is its connectivity. Connectivity with national network of railways and roads is a very important factor for over all development of Port sector. In India, the railways are a monopoly of the central government. Despite many decades of planning, the railways have been unable to meet the needs of even these major ports, and so have lacked both the finances and motivation to help develop the minor ports run by state governments. This aspect was taken very seriously by Government of Gujarat and steps have been taken to implement the same for the 4 ports developed on the PPP model – Mundra, Hazira, Dahej and Pipavav. Steps are being taken to provide rail connectivity to two remaining ports of Dahej & Hazira. Bharuch Rail Company Ltd. has been formed to provide connectivity to Dahej.

The state government, private port players, and the railways all participate in these SPVs. This arrangement has overcome the usual financial and managerial constraints: the railways are happy to collaborate in ventures that require limited funds from them but generate substantial additional revenue. Through SPVs, broad-gauge links have been built between the new ports at Mundra and Pipavav and the Delhi- Mumbai rail artery, thus providing national connectivity to the minor ports. To meet India's burgeoning traffic needs, the railways now plan to build a new, Dedicated Freight Corridor (DFC).

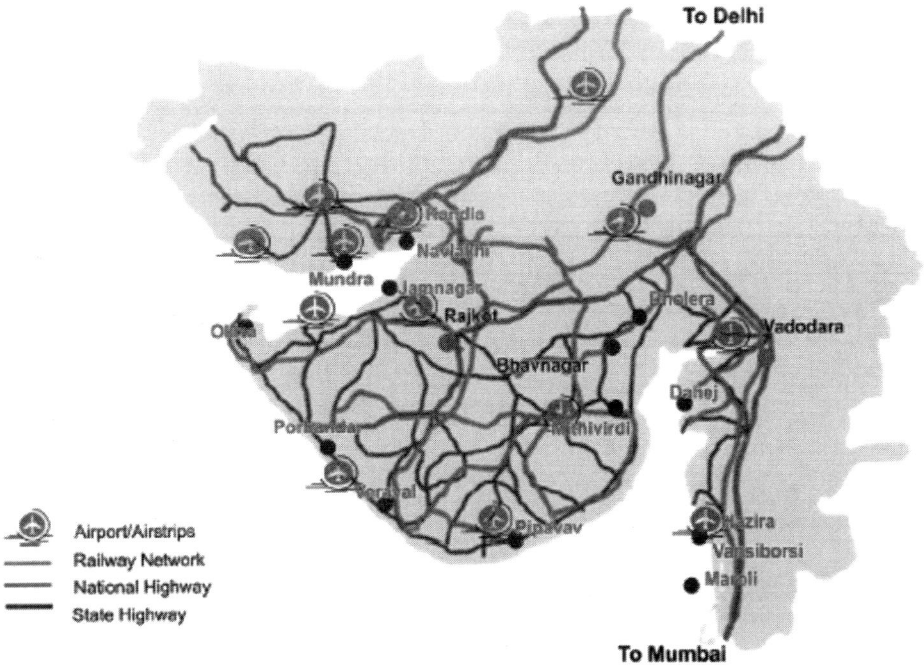

Fig. 3: Rail, Road and Air Connectivity of Gujarat Ports

Gujarat is getting ready to link its ports to this new rail corridor. By doing so, it hopes to get the lion's share of hinterland traffic. It can also hope to add at least 10 percent in value to hinterland cargo through consolidation, packaging, and processing. The rail, road and air connectivity from Gujarat ports is as in Fig. 3.

DELHI MUMBAI INDUSTRIAL CORRIDOR (DMIC) AND WESTERN DEDICATED FREIGHT CORRIDOR (DFC)

If the rail freight corridor is built in a manner that the Gujarat ports such as Mundra, Kandla, Pipavav, Bedi, Porbandar, and Dholera, among others, are connected through short feeder routes, the economic viability of the corridor as well as the minor ports would increase. (Business Line, January 6, 2006).

Also, in view of developments of different investment/industrial regions in the Gujarat state and taking account the movement of freight along the DFC & to Gujarat ports, GMB in consultation with Gujarat Infrastructure Development Board (GIDB) has prepared infrastructure Master plan for strengthening the rail and road connectivity to DMIC/DFC. Thus, providing connectivity to ports is one of the top priorities of GMB and it is focusing on providing seamless opportunities for multi-modal transportation.

According to M.D. Gujarat Infrastructure Development Board, "Gujarat Government is working on a logistics policy, inclusive of ports, roads, railways and air systems. Since the policy framework is in its early stages, all stakeholders, including those from the industry, will be consulted before chalking it out, he added. There is a need to create linkages between various standalone infrastructural projects such as ports, and make them accessible through creation of a more nodal system" (*Business Line*, June 30, 2010).

Availability of Adequate Area for Developing Support Infrastructure and Industries

In order for ports to develop to their full potential it is extremely important for them to have adequate area for support infrastructure. Also once a port is set up there is potential to develop related industries in close proximity of the port. The Gujarat Government has fully utilized the central government's policy for Special Economic Zones (SEZs). In fact with over 33 SEZs being approved in the state, Gujarat has become the SEZ capital of India. To ensure cargo for its port-led strategy, the state aims to create industrial parks linked to port industries. An excellent example of this is Mundra which is developing a 32000 acre SEZ next to the port. It is modeled on the mega SEZs which are set up in China which have world-class infrastructure like captive power supply, water supply and ports in close proximity. Also under the SEZ policy announced by the central government in February 2006, companies setting up factories in SEZs will have a total tax holiday for five years, 50 percent tax exemption for the next five years, and exemption for reinvested profits for five years more. They will also have the system of a single point clearance for all industrial approvals and greater flexibility in labour laws. Further, as Mundra is set up in a semi-arid area like Kutch, there is adequate land available around the port for development and given the low population density around there are minimal issues for displacement and resettlement.

Proactive Investment Climate and Infrastructure Development

Gujarat has also historically fostered extremely positive climate for industrialization and the entrepreneurs have had the ability for risk taking. There are three large corporates who have driven the development of the minor ports in the Gujarat – these are Adani (Mundra, Hazira and Dahej); Essar Ports (Hazira, Vadinar and Salaya) and Gujarat Pipavav Ports (Pipavav). Collectively these ports have a capacity of over 200 mtpa and in FY11 handled a cargo of over 100 mtpa. In addition the largest major port in the country i.e. Kandla which handled total cargo of 80 mmt in FY10 is also located in Gujarat. These entrepreneurs have all invested significantly in these ports to build state of the art cargo handling facilities, have developed significant captive cargo around the port and have tied up with large international ports/liners like DP World (Adani), Maersk (Pipavav) and Port of Antwerp (Essar) to develop world class facilities which provide them a significant competitive advantage for the future. A brief snapshot of these ports is given below:

Parameter	Mundra Port	Essar Ports	Gujarat Pipavav
Locations	Gujarat (Mundra, Dahej, Hazira), Goa (Mormugao), Australia (Abbott Point)	Gujarat (Hazira, Vadinar, Salaya), Orissa (Paradip)	Gujarat (Pipavav)
Capacity (MMTPA)	115	88	14
Cargo Handled (MMTPA)	50	40	9
Type of Cargo Handled	Container, Coal, Bulk, LNG	POL, Coal, Iron Ore, Steel, other dry bulk	Container, Coal, Fertilizer, Other Bulk
Anchor Clients	Adani Enterprises, IOCL	Essar Oil, Essar Steel, Essar Power	Maersk, Safmarine
Draft (m)	17.5	20 (Vadinar), 14 (Hazira)	14.5

Further, these port developers have all made significant investments in the form of debt and equity to set up their projects at world class scale. Hazira LNG port was financed almost entirely through equity. Dahej LNG port had strong support from the promoter public sector oil companies. Mundra and Pipavav ports also had the backing of strong promoter companies. Domestic financial institutions and Banks like IDFC, IL&FS, IIFCL, ICICI Bank and State Bank of India have all actively supported port financing.

In another bold initiative, Gujarat Government has decided to permit other landlocked States in India to have their own ports on its 1600 km. long coastline. It is actively following it up with Andhra Pradesh, Assam, Haryana, Himachal Pradesh, Jharkhand, Madhya Pradesh, Orissa, Punjab and Rajasthan and some other States. (Business Line, September, 11, 2010.)

Capacity Bottlenecks at Major Ports

In FY06, under the National Maritime Development Programme, the Department of Shipping identified projects in the ports sector that needed investments for upgradation and enhancement of capacity, efficiency and competitiveness. Capacity at major ports was to be hiked from 508mmt in FY08 to 1002mmt by FY12E. Implying 19% CAGR additions in capacity. However given the restrictive regulations for Major Ports (in terms of pricing, firing labour force etc) there are significant delays in the envisaged addition. Only 120mt of additional capacity has been added till FY10 implying a CAGR of 11%. This has led to a shift in the capacity addition targets. As per the Maritime Agenda 2010-2020 released by the Ministry of Shipping in Jan 2011, it is proposed to increase the capacity to 741mtpa by FY12E (26% lower than original targets). Containers continue to be the focus area: As per the NMDP and Committee on Infrastructure, container capacity was envisaged to be increased from 62mtpa in FY06 to 223 by FY12E, implying a 24% CAGR in additions. However even with the revised targets, execution has fallen short of the target, with capacity increasing to ~121mtpa by FY10 (18% CAGR). Accordingly all major ports are suffering from significant capacity constraint which has impacted cargo turnaround times. Capacity additions at other Minor ports has also fallen short and only ~110mtpa capacity has been added at minor ports all over India over FY07-10, implying a 14% CAGR, well short of the 20% CAGR envisaged in the earlier proposal.

The high levels of capacity utilization at major ports are depicted below (Fig. 4).

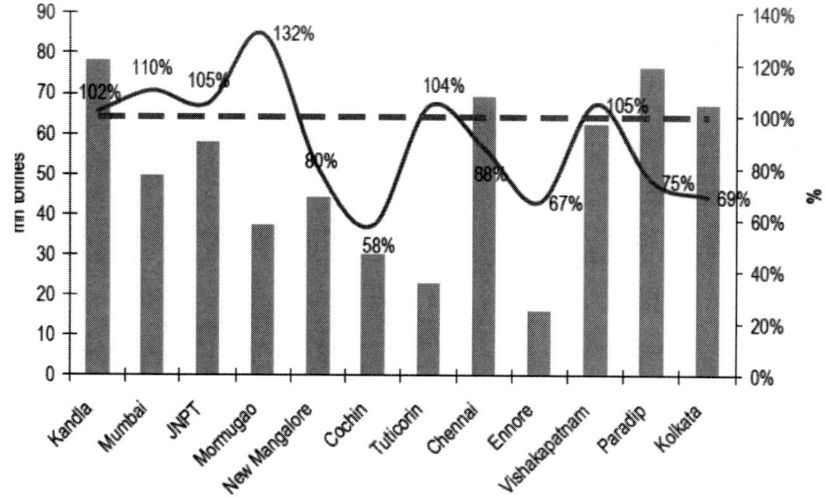

Fig. 4: Capacity Utilization at Major Ports

Gujarat spells a different story. Capacity at minor ports in Gujarat has increased from 182 in FY07 to 244 in FY10, exceeding the planned target of 238 by FY12. Further, all minor ports are in investment mode and propose to take the capacity to 404mtpa by FY14E. Thus the cargo handling times and ship turnaround times will be much more efficient

Shift in Cargo from Container Ports Needs to Ramp Up

Today on the West Coast of India, we have three container gateway ports namely Nhava, Mundra and Pipavav that are fighting for their piece of pie of the North West India's EXIM trade. While almost 68% of India's total EXIM trade move through the above the three gateway ports, Nhava is the clear leader with a 48% share and the balance 20% is shared between Mundra and Pipavav. Despite all the infrastructure advantages at Mundra and Pipavav, and the capacity constraints, slow cargo turnaround time and logistical cost disadvantage of Nhava Sheva and JNPT, the shift in cargo to Mundra and Pipavav still needs to accelerate. If one goes by the number of rail trips that Concor and the private rail operators have operated between the NCR and Ludhiana to Nhava and Mundra/Pipavav as this is a fair indicator on the flow of traffic, you will observe that 84% of the cargo from and to the NCR moves via Nhava and 68% of the cargo from and to Ludhiana moves via Nhava. To push more cargo through the logical gateways of Mundra and Pipavav, the service providers namely the shipping lines, rail operators and the port will have to come forward. Shipping lines need to offer more services; rail operators need to offer more departures and the port needs to offer incentives to encourage more and more shippers to shift to ports like Mundra and Pipavav (Sengupta, I., 2011).

CONCLUSION

Gujarat has pioneered the concept of port liberalization in India and used this to become the country's fastest-growing state. It has shown vision in converting Minor Ports into some of the biggest ports in the country. The state has broken new ground with different forms of privatization. It has devised SPVs to build rail links between new ports and the country's main rail system. The state's private ports have greatly improved its ability to take advantage of the central government's scheme for Special Economic Zones. Thus the ports form a gateway not just to cargo but also to overall economic development around their location (Swaminathan S.A. Aiyar, 2008).

The impact of the proactive and investor friendly measures of the Gujarat Maritime Board is demonstrated in the form of increased traffic at Gujarat ports (Fig. 5).

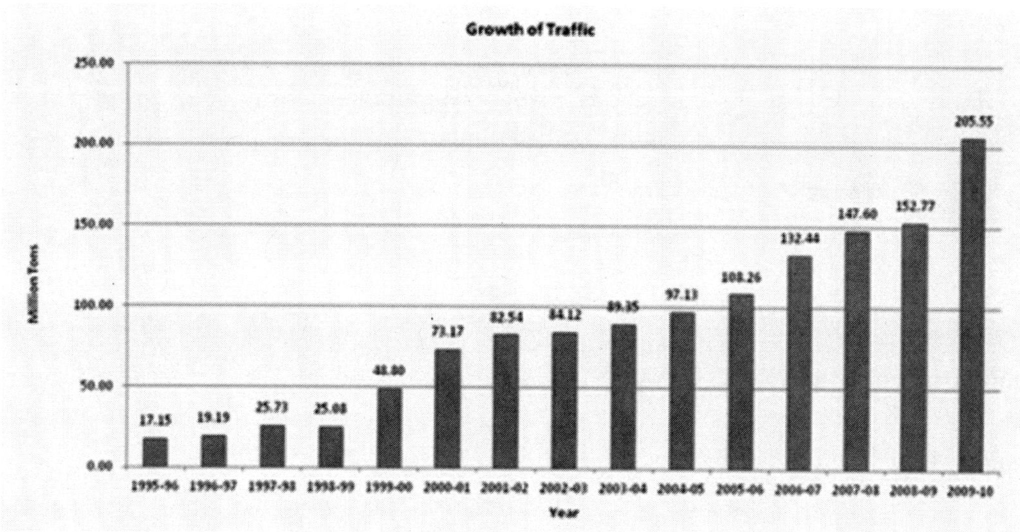

Fig. 5: Growth of Traffic at GMB Ports

During FY 2011, GMB ports handled a cargo of 231 mmt. Gujarat Ports currently account for nearly 25% of the national cargo and about 75% of the cargo handled by the all non-major ports of the country.

Gujarat currently boasts of the highest number of operational ports for handling varieties of commercial cargo. The overall port capacity of GMB ports has registered growth of 110.37% i.e. from 135 million metric tonnes per annum (MMTPA) in 2001-02 to 284 MMTPA in 2010-11. As a result of the new capacity augmentation projects in the pipeline, the capacity of the GMB ports is expected to double by the year 2015. This growth is also expected to continue to be buoyant going forward as the minor ports in Gujarat are largely handling cargo commodities like coal, petroleum and oil products and containers all of which are cargo commodities for the future and which are expected to show high growth rates going forward. The government expects container traffic and coal traffic at the minor ports to grow at CAGR of over 30% in the next 5 years. Petroleum imports are expected to grow at over 15% in the future and petro product exports are expected to be a sizeable portion of India's exports (16%) by 2014.

Going forward the GMB plans to double the cargo being handled out of Gujarat ports. The GMB is looking to interlink the 45 ports of the state using the Integrated Port Management System, wherein the data regarding cargo handled, arrival and departure of the ships will be updated daily.

ACKNOWLEDGEMENTS

I thank Shri S. Srikant, Research Scholar for his help in research for this paper.

I acknowledge the help and information provided to me by Shri C.N.Patel of the Gujarat Maritime Board. I also thank the executives of Mundra Port, Pipavav Port, Hazira LNG Port and Dahej Petronet LNG port for their responses.

REFERENCES

[1] *Business Line*, January 6, 2006; June 30, 2010; August 3, 2011; September 11, 2011.

[2] Chan, Albert P.C. et al., Measures that Enhance the Achievement of Value for Money in Public Private Partnership (PPP) Projects; Building Abroad, Montreal, October, 2008.

[3] Sengupta, Indrajit, Gujarat Ports – A Logical Gateway; GMB e-musings, 2011.

[4] Shah, V.P., "Journey from Start to Stars"; GMB e-musings, 2011.

[5] Swaminathan S. Anklesaria Aiyar, "The Benefits of Port Liberalization", Centre for Global Prosperity and Liberty, *Development Policy Analysis*, December 2008.

Promoting Clean Energy in India: Renewable Energy Certificates and PAT

Vineet Kumar Sarawagi
Adhunik Power and Natural Resources Limited
E-mail: vksarawagi@hotmail.com

ABSTRACT

Different types of Market based Mechanism are developed by the government to make improvements in energy efficiency in energy-intensive large industries. Mandate for Renewable Purchase Obligation (RPO) to Distribution Licensee, Captive Power Plants (CPPs) and Open Access Customers was given in Januray '10. Whereafter approximately every state has given certain percentage as a minimum RPO for each obligatory entity for next financial years. Similarly, Bureau of Energy Efficiency (BEE) have given a mandate for Designated Consumers (DCs) to reduce their energy consumption by certain percentage which can also be further traded if achieved, as Energy Saving Certificates (ESCerts) on energy exchanges. There are other regulations and norms which are also coming in the market, like NAMA, etc. Since these regulations are at very nascent stage, needs lot of modifications and changes. Maximum of the State Designated Agencies (SDA) don't understand their role till now and in the same fashion, PAT is hardly understood by Energy Auditors. All these are making the power market very complex and thus increasing the scope of work by consultants and Energy Exchanges. Seeing all these development very soon we are going to have 3rd Energy Exchange in the market.

To Promote Clean Energy, Feed-in Tariff (FIT) and Clean Development Mechanism (CDM) were the only concepts prevailing in the market before the concepts of tradable renewable certificates. But one can go for CDM and REC/ESCs together but can not go for FIT with RECs. In the same time regulators are also thinking to link the Indian Renewable/Energy Certificate market with different types of schemes available in the market for promoting Clean Energy. All these practices always give a hope for new renewable generation but at the same time increase the hurdles for existing power generators, basically CPPs.

Keywords: Renewable Purchase Obligation (RPO), Renewable Energy Certificate (REC), Perform, Achieve & Trade (PAT), Clean Development Mechanism (CDM), Captive Power Plants (CPP)

INTRODUCTION

The National Mission on Enhanced Energy Efficiency (NMEEE) is expected to enable about INR 75,000 Cr. worth of transactions in energy efficiency and will help in saving about 5% of our annual energy consumption by 2015, and nearly 100 MT of CO_2 every year. The most innovative and challenging new initiative to be introduced under the Mission is the "Perform, Achieve and Trade" (PAT) mechanism which would assign energy efficiency improvement targets to the country's most energy-intensive industrial units, with the provision of allowing them to retain any energy-efficiency improvements in excess of their target in the form of Energy Savings Certificates (ESCerts). Units will also be allowed to use purchased ESCerts to meet their targets. Other Mission initiatives include expanded use of the carbon market to help achieve market transformation towards more energy-efficient equipment and appliances (MTEE-Market Transformation of Energy Efficiency), and the creation of two funds, i.e. the Partial Risk Guaranty Facility[1] and Venture Capital Fund[2] (FEEED – Framework for Energy Efficient Economic Development). Another major goal of the Mission is the promotion of Energy Service Company (ESCO) based to upgrade energy efficiency in buildings, municipalities and agricultural pumpsets by energy-efficiency investments, to be paid over several years from the resulting energy savings (EEFP-Energy Efficiency Financing Platform).

Similarly, the Concept of Tradable Renewable Energy Certificates/Credits (TREC) arose in 1990s during CPUC's (California Public Utilities Commission) electricity restructuring programme. Like the rest of the world, California's energy market was also dominated by regulated and integrated utilities. These utilities were generally required to maintain "public purpose" programs, environmentalists and renewable energy advocates feared that a competitive electricity market would increase investment risk in renewable energy sources. To address this problem, the commission ultimately adopted a concept called a "renewable portfolio standard," which bound retail electricity suppliers to purchase RECs (Renewable Energy Credits) equivalent to a certain percentage of their total annual energy sales. The Renewables Obligation can be very effective support mechanism for renewable. It is expected to create a market that offers one of the highest levels of support for renewable electricity, with-out causing high costs to the end consumers. The objective of these obligatory systems is to create long-term stable playing field along with creating reasonable conditions for existing plants. The system also wants to stimulate technology development and cost efficiency, promoting new investments.

---

[1] Partial Risk Guaranty Facility will provide back-to-back guarantees to banks for loans to energy-efficiency projects so as to reduce the perceived risks of these projects

[2] Venture Capital Fund would support investment in the manufacturing of energy-efficient products and provision of energy-efficiency services.

RENEWABLE PURCHASE OBLIGATION

Under Renewable Purchase Obligation (RPO), minimum quantum of electricity should be procured by all the Obligated Entities from Renewable Sources of electricity[3] expressed as percentage of their total annual procurement of Electrical Energy on yearly basis. The minimum quantity of electricity to be purchased is defined in terms of different percentage given by different state electricity regulatory commissions in notifications. The percentage vary from 16%(Nagaland) to 0.75%(Meghalaya) for Financial Year 2011-12. Different percentage is given by different states for different types of power. Orissa gives separate percentage for Solar, Non-Solar and Co-generation whereas Rajasthan gives separate percentage for Solar, Bio-mass, Wind only and in the same time states like Bihar give only a single percentage of power to be procured. But maximum of the states gives two types of percentage, i.e. for Solar and Non-Solar. Different state Agencies are appointed by the commission of respective states as a nodal agency for RPO. The notification by honorable CERC was given on 14th Januray'10, still there are some states which have not come with the final regulation (Chhattisgarh, Manipur, Mizoram, etc.) on RPO and some of them have not finalized the nodal agency for the state till now. State Nodal Agency for the country is National Load Dispatch Centre.

If the entities are unable to purchase the RE power, they will have to purchase Renewable Energy Certificate from Energy Exchanges.[4] Thus, a market exists for RECs because energy supply companies are required to redeem certificates equal to their obligation under the RPO program. The concept of Renewable Energy Certificate (REC) seeks to address the mismatch between availability of RE sources and the requirement of obligated entities to meet their renewable purchase obligation. It is also expected to encourage the RE capacity addition in States where there is potential for RE generation as REC framework seeks to create a national level market for such generators to recover their cost. Any generating company already having Power Purchase Agreement (PPA) for sale of renewable energy at a preferential tariff[5] are not eligible for participating in the

---

[3] Renewable energy sources means renewable sources such as small hydro, wind, solar including its integration with combined cycle, biomass, bio fuel cogeneration, urban or municipal waste and such other sources as recognized or approved by Ministry of New and Renewable Energy (MNRE)

[4] There are two energy exchange in, a) Indian Energy Exchange (IEX), and b) Power Exchange of India (PXIL). Very soon we can be having 3rd energy exchange, namely Power Exchange of India.

[5] Preferential Tariff means the tariff fixed by the Appropriate Commission for sale of energy, from a generating station using renewable energy sources, to a distribution licensee. This system have historically been the driving force behind renewable energy development in the EU, as witnessed by the success of the current German and Spanish systems, and the previous

REC scheme. In case of pre-mature termination of the agreement, they will be eligible for participating in the REC scheme for a period of three years from the date of termination of such agreement or till the scheduled date of expiry of PPA whichever is earlier.

There are two categories of these certificates, both with a maximum validity of one year:

1. **Solar Certificates:** issued to eligible entities for generation of electricity based on solar as renewable energy source. These are to be sold to the obligated entities to enable them to meet their renewable purchase obligation for solar,
2. **Non-solar Certificates:** issued to eligible entities for generation of electricity based on renewable energy sources other than solar. These are to be sold to the obligated entities to enable them to meet their obligation for purchase from renewable energy sources other than solar

These certificates are traded on last Wednesday of every month between 1300-1500 hrs, and the market is cleared by 1700 hrs. Buyers have to pay on the same day and the seller receives on the next day. Banking of the Certificates is not facilitated by the exchanges. Many of the states mandates obligated entities to deposit certificates purchased from the power exchange with the State Electricity Regulatory Commission within 15 days of the purchase.

DETERMINATION OF FORBEARANCE AND FLOOR PRICE OF REC

Forbearance price for REC is a maximum price and not the guaranteed price whereas Floor Price is a minimum guaranteed price for REC. The same are notified by CERC separately for Solar and Non-Solar RECs. The Forbearance price has been derived based on the highest difference between cost of generation of RE technologies/RE tariff[6] and the average power purchase cost (APPC)[7] of 2009-10 for the respective states. The same

---

success of the Danish policy (as well as even earlier experience in the state of California). As generation costs differ across renew-able energy technologies, the tariff is usually different by technology and is provided for a specified period of time. The price may also decline over time, tracking expected renewable energy cost reductions. This is supposed to financial barriers and costs.

[6] Costs of Generation/RE Tariff for different technologies for FY 2009-10 have been assumed as per the CERC RE Tariff Regulations 2009, for the sake of uniformity for calculations of forbearance and floor price.

[7] APPC: The APPC for a state represents the weighted average pooled power purchase by distribution licensees (without transmission charges) in the state during the last financial year (2009-10).

is to be revised for FY 12-13, draft notification seeking comments on the same is already given by Central Electricity Regulatory Commission (CERC) on its website. The floor price has been determined keeping in view the basic minimum requirements for ensuring the viability of RE projects set up to meet the RE targets. This viability requirement covers loan repayment & interest charges, O&M[8] expenses and fuel expenses in case of Biomass and Cogeneration. Current Applicable Forbearance and Floor Price is given in Exhibit 1.

Exhibit 1: Forbearance and Floor Price

	Non Solar REC (Rs./MWh)	Solar REC (Rs./MWh)
Forbearance Price	3,900	17,000
Floor Price	1,500	12,000

Source: CERC Suo Motu Petition No. 99/2010; dt: 1st June 2010.

Indian REC market have seen 5 trading sessions[9] till now, with 1st trading session as a mock trading session. From the exhibit: 2, it can be seen that non-solar REC have traded at forbearance as well as floor price in just 4 trading sessions, whereas because of lack of Solar REC, there was no trading in the same and thus no price discovery of solar RECs. The Price Discovery Mechanism for REC is Closed Double-sided Auction.[10]

Exhibit 2: REC Traded on Energy Exchange

Auction Date	REC Type	Buy Bid (No. of certificates)		Sell Bid (No. of certificates)		MCP (Rs./Certificate)	
		PXIL	IEX	PXIL	IEX	PXIL	IEX
29/6/2011	Solar	0	–	0	–	0	–
	Non Solar	10000	72,002	3183	21,331	1500	1,505
25/5/2011	Solar	0	30,001	0	–	0	–
	Non Solar	4500	70,377	5322	150	1500	1,500
27/4/2011	Solar	0	–	0	–	0	–
	Non Solar	0	260	565	4,046	0	1,500
30/3/2011	Solar	3025	–	0	–	0	–
	Non Solar	324	14,002	274	15,143	2225	3,900

Source: Indian Energy Exchange (IEX) and Power Exchange of India (PXIL).

8 O&M: Operation & Maintenance.

9 Till 1st July 2011.

10 The buyers place orders by specifying their priority. High priority buy orders are considered first and the matching proceeds in that order from high to low priority buy orders. The settlement price is the average of the buyer's and seller's price. The order matching proceeds by matching price, then volume and then, if need be use pro-rata/time priority basis.

Procedure for Application of Issuance of Renewable Energy Certificates is well defined by CERC and Exchanges, the same can be understood better with the pictorial presentation in the Exhibit 3.

Exhibit 3: Procedure for Application of Issuance of Renewable Energy Certificates

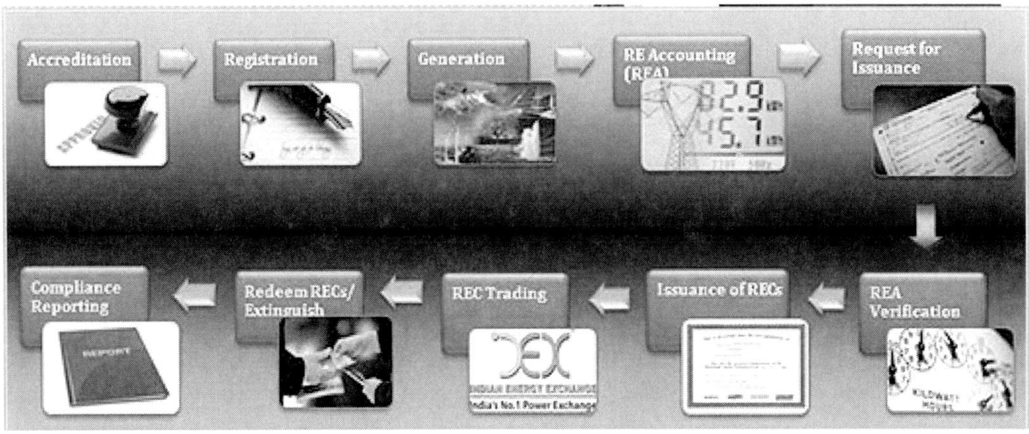

Source: Indian Energy Exchange.

Features of RPO regulation by different states

Obligatory Entity (entities liable for RPO)

1. Distribution Licensee(s) of the state
2. Any other person consuming electricity (a) generated from conventional Captive Generating Plant[11] for his own use and or (b) procured from conventional generation through open access[12] and third party sale.

Captive Power Plants (CPP) comes under the purview of the regulation depends on its size and the state. Some states say that the minimum capacity of CPP eligible for RPO is 5MW (Bihar, Gujarat, Jharkhand, Karnataka, Maharashtra, Orissa, etc.), whereas some says it to be 1MW (Chhattisgarh, Himachal Pradesh, Rajasthan, J&K, Manipur,

[11] Captive generating plant means a power plant set up by any person to generate electricity primarily for his own use and includes a power plant set up by any co-operative society or association of persons for generating electricity primarily for use of members of such cooperative society or association.

[12] Open Access means the non-discriminatory provision for the use of transmission lines or distribution system or associated facilities with such lines or system by any licensee or consumer or a person engaged in generation in accordance with the regulations specified by the Appropriate Commission.

Mizoram, Nagaland, Uttar Pradesh, etc.) and in the same time some does not give any minimum capacity of CPPs (Uttarakhand, Meghalaya, etc.).

Effect of Default (in case of non-fulfillment of RPO)

1. The respective state electricity regulatory commission may direct the obligated entity to deposit into a separate fund, to be created and maintained by such obligated entity, such amount as the Commission may determine on the basis of the shortfall in units of RPO and the forbearance price decided by the Central Commission, Provided that the fund so created shall be utilized, as may be directed by the Commission, for purchase of the certificates (Applicable for all states).
2. Obligatory entities may also be liable for penalty as may be decided by the Commission under section 142 of the Electricity Act 2003(which ask penalty maximum to the tune of 1.00 Lacs)(Different for different states),
3. The obligated entities may be in breach of its license condition if it fails to deposit the amount directed by the Commission within 15 days of the communication of such direction (Different for different states).

Banking of Power

Few states like Uttarakhand & Madhya Pradesh, also provide the facility of banking of un-used Power. Uttarakhand asks 12.5% whereas MP asks 2% out of the total power banked with them. Uttarakhand will return the power only during the period other than

Exhibit 4: Status of Accreditation and Registration of RE Projects (as on 30 April 2011)

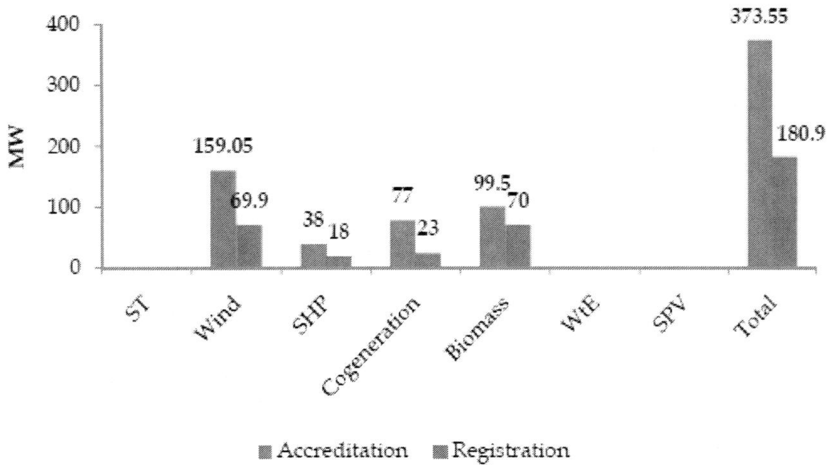

Source: Carbon Bazar 2011

17:00 hrs. to 22:00 Hrs , whereas MP may return from 15th July to 15th October from 2300 hours to 2400 hours and 0000 hours to 1700 hours only.

Some state commissions (Manipur, Mizoram, etc.) also *caps the maximum tariff for renewable energy*, depending on the case to case basis. In some states(Himachal Pradesh, J&K, Meghalaya, Uttarakhand, etc.), it is mandatory for obligatory entities to submit necessary details regarding total consumption of electricity and power purchase from Renewable Energy sources for fulfillment of RPO on yearly basis to the State Agency, whereas in some states (Jharkhand, Orissa, etc.), the notification on the same does not talk anything about collection of data. *Overriding Effect to the notification on RPO* is also provided by some states (Himachal Pradesh, Manipur, Mizoram, Nagaland, etc.).

Because of lack of Renewable Power in the market (only 180.9 MW RE Projects registered by April '11), commission allow obligatory entities to approach the respective state electricity regulatory commissions for carry forward of compliance requirement to the next year. Status of Accreditation and Registration of RE Projects (as on 30 April 2011) can also be seen in the Exhibit 4.

REC ACROSS THE WORLD

United Kingdom

The Regulation comes into effect in UK by April'02. REC in India is known as ROC (Renewable Obligation Certificate) in United Kingdom, regulated and controlled by OFGEM (Office of the Gas and Electricity Markets). One ROC is issued for each megawatt-hour (MWh) of eligible renewable output and no. of ROC generated depends upon the types of technologies used, i.e. multiplier effect.[13] Some technologies get more, whereas some get less. For instance, offshore wind installations receive 2 ROCs per MWh, onshore wind installations receive 1 ROC per MWh and sewage gas-fired plants receive half a ROC per MWh. The penalty revenue is to be recycled back to certificate holders.

Generating stations are accredited by OFGEM as being capable of generating electricity from eligible renewable sources. OFGEM issues and maintain ROCs. It also calculates the annual buy-out price, receives and disburse fund. It publishes an annual report on the operation of and compliance with the requirements of the Orders.

[13] Multiplier effect: Generation Units are given RECs on case to case basis, depending on the type and size of energy generated for each 1 MWh generated. This give generation of 'PHANTOM' RECs, which are actually not involved in renewable electricity generation, but may be used to meet energy retailer's Renewable Energy Target (RET) liabilities. There are many variables which impact the no. of Phantom RECs, i.e. place, timing and type of installation, life of plant, etc.

Australia

Australia was one of the first countries to introduce an obligation system. In April 2001 the Mandatory Renewable Energy Target (MRET) was introduced as an instrument to increase the contribution of renewable sources to Australia's electricity demand. The MRET is aimed at reducing both greenhouse gas emissions and developing the renewable energy industry. The MRET is backed by a system of Target Renewable Energy Credits (TRECs), comprising of Large-scale Renewable Energy Target (LRET) and Small-scale Renewable Energy Scheme (SRES). Phantom RECs exists and are created by small generation units of wind, solar and hydro electricity systems.

United States of America

First state based Renewable Portfolio Standard (RPS)[14] was introduced in Iowa in 1983, the number of US states with RPS programs has risen substantially. Till date there are more than 30 states with mandatory RPS programs, of which about approx. 5 states have voluntary goals. Most of these requirements take the form of a "renewable portfolio standard" (RPS) or "alternative energy portfolio standard" (AEPS) which requires a certain percentage of a utility's power plant capacity or generation to come from renewable or alternative energy sources by a given date. The standards range from modest to ambitious, and qualifying energy sources vary. Some states also include "carve-outs" (requirements that a certain percentage of the portfolio be generated from a specific energy source, such

Exhibit 5: RPS Target of Different States of America

State	Year Enacted	Date Revised	Governor Partisanship*	Legislature Control*	Preliminary Target	Final Target	Who's Covered	Credit Trading
Arizona	2001	2006	Rep	Split	0.2% by 2001	15% by 2025	Utility	No
California	2002	2005	Dem	Dem	13% by 2003	33% by 2020	Investor Owned Utility Municipal Utility	Yes
Colorado	2004		Rep	Rep	3% by 2007	10% by 2015	Utility Investor Owned Utility Rural Electric Cooperative	Yes
Connecticut	1999	2003	Rep	Dem	4% by 2004	10% by 2010	Utility	Yes
Delaware	2005		Dem	Split	1% by 2007	10% by 2019	Retail Electricity Supplier	Yes
District of Columbia	2005			Dem	4% by 2007	11% by 2022	Utility	Yes
Hawaii	2004		Rep	Dem	7% by 2003	20% by 2020	Utility	No
Illinois†	2005		Dem	Dem	2% by 2007'	8% by 2013	Utility	No
Iowa	1991		Rep	Dem	none	105 MW	Utility	No
Maine	1999		Ind	Dem	none	30% by 2000	Utility	Yes
Maryland	2004		Rep	Dem	3.5% by 2006	7.5% by 2019	Electricity Supplier	Yes
Massachusetts	1997		Rep	Dem	1% new by 2003	4% new by 2009	Utility	Yes
Minnesota	1997		Rep	Dem	1,125 MW by 2010	1,250 MW by 2013	Xcel only	No
Montana	2005		Dem	Split**	5% by 2008	15% by 2015	Utility	Yes
Nevada	1997	2005	Rep	Split	6% by 2005	20% by 2015	Investor Owned Utility	Yes
New Jersey	2001	2004	Rep	Rep	6.5% by 2008	20% by 2020	Utility	Yes
New Mexico	2002	2004	Rep	Dem	5% by 2006	10% by 2011	Investor Owned Utility	Yes
New York	2004		Rep	Split	none	25% by 2013	Investor Owned Utility	Yes
Pennsylvania	2004		Dem	Rep	1.5% by 2007	18% by 2020	Utility	Yes
Rhode Island	2004		Rep	Dem	3% by 2007	16% by 2020	Electric Retailers	Yes
Texas	1999	2005	Rep	Rep	2,280 MW by 2007	5,880 MW by 2015	Retail Supplier	Yes
Vermont	2005		Rep	Dem	none	load growth by 2012	Retail Electricity Supplier	Yes
Wisconsin	1999	2006	Rep	Rep	none	10% by 2015	Utility	Yes

Source: PEW Centre: Global Climate Centre.

as solar power) or other incentives to encourage the development of particular resources. RPS Target of some of the states is given in Exhibit 5.

Japan

Initially feed-in-tariff system was proposed in Japan, but in later phase of time Renewable Portfolio Standard (RPS) approach was approved in April'03. The RPS placed an obligation with the electricity suppliers to supply 1.4% of total electricity consumption from renewable sources by 2010. But, the design of the Japanese RPS system does not provide the necessary incentives for creating new renewable energy capacity. The certificate market is less transparent in Japan, which creates uncertainties among potential investors.

PERFORM, ACHIEVE AND TRADE (PAT) MECHANISM[15]

In order to further accelerate as well as incentivize energy efficiency, the Perform Achieve and Trade (PAT) mechanism is being designed. The PAT scheme is involved in

Exhibit 6: Tentative Milestones for PAT

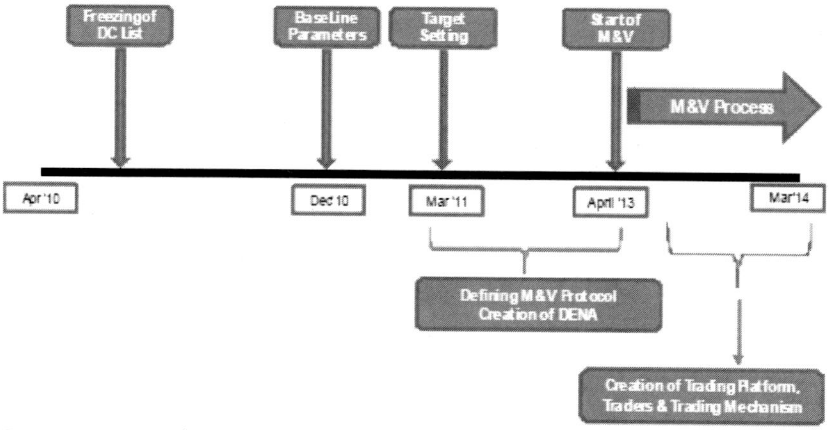

Source: Bureau of Energy Efficiency.

---

[14] Renewable Portfolio Standards (RPS) or Alternative Energy Portfolio Standard (AEPS) are state policies mandating a state to generate a percent of its electricity from renewable sources. Each state has a choice of how to fulfill this mandate using a combination of renewable energy sources, including wind, solar, biomass, geothermal, or other renewable sources. Some RPSs will specify the technology mix, while others leave it up to the market. For example, Arizona has greater solar resources than Oregon, and North Dakota has greater wind resources than Georgia.

[15] Source: Beaurau of Energy Efficiency, India.

order to incentivize industry to achieve better energy efficiency improvements than their specified Specific Energy Consumption (SEC) improvement target in a cost-effective manner. Tentative Milestones for PAT is shown in Exhibit 6. The Designated Consumers[16] will have the choice to reduce energy consumption either through implementation of energy efficiency measures or through purchase of Energy Saving Certificates (ESCerts).[17] The additional certified energy savings can be traded with other designated consumers who could use these certificates to comply with their SEC reduction targets.

The Energy Savings Certificates (ESCerts) will be issued by Energy Efficiency Services Ltd. (EESL) and traded on special trading platforms to be created in the two power exchanges (IEX and PXIL). The Ministry of Power (MoP) has notified industrial units and other establishments consuming energy more than the threshold in 9 industrial sectors (namely Thermal Power Plants, Fertilizer, Cement, Pulp and Paper, Textiles, Chlor-

Exhibit 7: Different Sectors and Sub-Sectors along with the Range of SECs and No. of DCs

	Sectors	Sub-Sector	Range of SEC	Product to Calculate SEC	No. of Probable DCs
1	**Power plant**	Coal, Gas, Oil	2300 – 3400 kcal / kwh	Electricity	146
2	**Fertilizer**	Natural Gas, Naptha	5.86 – 9.11 Gcal/T of Urea	Urea	23
3	**Cement**	Dry, Wet	665 – 900 Kcal/Kg of Clinker (Thermal) 66 – 127 KWH/ T (Elect)	Cement	83
4	**Integrated Steel**	Integrated, Sponge Iron	6.15 – 8.18 Gcal / tcs	Crude Steel	101
5	**Sponge Iron**		4.4 – 7.6 Gcal / T (Thermal) 72 – 135 KWH/T (Elect)	Sponge Iron	
6	**Aluminum (Smelter)** **Aluminium (Refinery)**	Refinery, Smelter	15875 – 17083 KWH/T 3.28 – 4.12 MKcal / T of Alumina	Molten Aluminium/ Alumina	11
7	**Pulp & Paper**	Wood, Agro, RCF	25.3 – 121 GJ/T	Paper/Pulp	51
8	**Textile**	Spinning, Processing, Composite, Fiber yarn	3000 – 16100 Kcal/kg (Thermal) 0.25 – 10 KWH/Kg (Elect)	Fabric/yarn	128
9	**Chlor-Alkali**	Membrane cell, Mercury	2300 – 2600 kwh/ T of caustic soda	Caustic Soda	20

Source: Bureau of Energy Efficiency.

[16] Those who would have the obligations to fulfil the annual energy savings targets and the total compliance targets.

[17] ESCerts are issued When energy efficiency improvements surpass targets with 1 MTOE (Metric Tonne of Oil Equivalent) or 1kgOE improvement above target (=1 ESCert). Banking of ESCerts allowed during each cycle – 1st cycle ESCerts to 2nd cycle and 2nd cycle ESCerts to 3rd cycle.

Alkali, Iron & Steel, Aluminum and Railways) in March, 2007 as 563 DCs (refer to Exhibits 7).

As per the studies, the wide bandwidth of specific energy consumption (SEC) within an industrial sector is indicative of the large energy-savings potential in the sector. The wide bandwidth is also a reflection of the differences in the energy-saving possibilities amongst plants because of their varying vintage, production capacity, raw material quality, and product-mix. These SEC improvement targets are based on the trend of energy consumption and energy-savings potential of the plants. Each DC is mandated to reduce its SEC by a fixed percentage, based on its current SEC (or baseline SEC) in 1st PAT Cycle (FY 11-12 to FY 13-14). The Market Design of PAT is shown in Exhibit 8.

Exhibit 8: Market Design for PAT

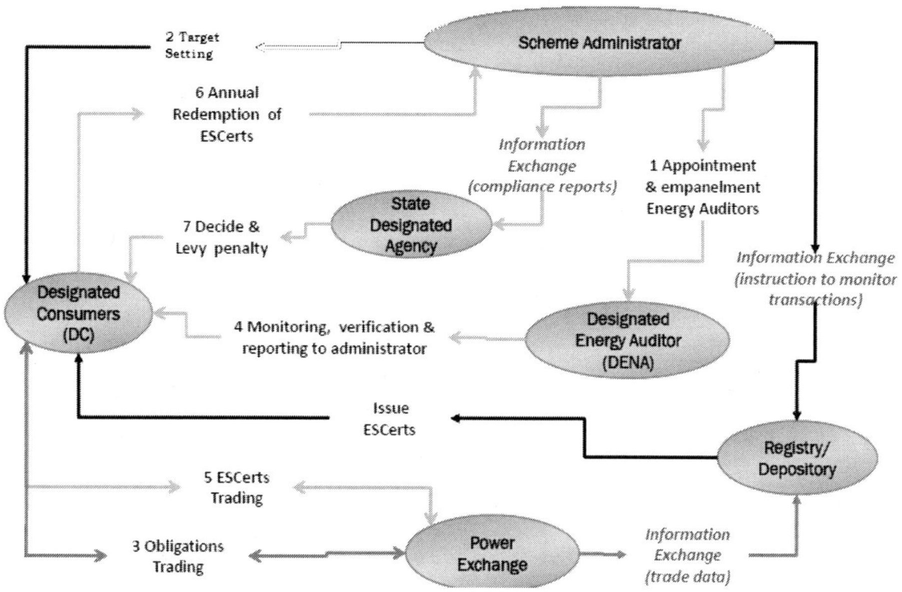

Source: Carbon Bazar 2011.

SUGGESTIONS AND RECOMMENDATIONS

RPO regulations are still not finalized by some of the states and many have not finalized the nodal State Agency for the implementation of the same. The Concept being new to the market needs special training to the concerned officials and the industry person is required. These teething problems may well be solved over time when the actors become more familiar with the system and market forces bring about a more stable equilibrium. Penalty for failure to meet the RPO should be more practical and effective. Since, the fund is to be managed by the entity itself and also have the flexibility to carry forward the obligation; it does not seem that effective. Banking and borrowing of the certificates can also be implemented in different and more effective ways.

The objective of providing greater support to renewable energy can be achieved through some modifications in the proposed regulations because poor policy design can be a big reason for failure in meeting targets. This can be done by using a *Multiplier-based mechanism* for different sources, wherein different number of tradable REC can be generated from different sources of energy. The same exists in Italy and in UK. It can have a pre-specified schedule of declining multipliers, this can also provide with a benchmark for cost reductions to be achieved. Validity of tradable RECs can be extended from one year, as it extends to 2years in Italy, 5 years in Belgium(Flanders) and unlimited validity in Poland, Denmark and Netherlands. Penalty for failure to meet the RPO should be more practical. Failure to pay buyout price due to insolvency or other reasons can be addressed through a *Mutualization Mechanism*[18] as in the case of the UK.

SCOPE OF FURTHER STUDY

Internationalization (integration of schemes in the country with similar types of schemes outside) is possible, even desirable, but requires that several conditions be met, and many details ironed out. Many more issues (like Banking of Power, Multiplier Mechanism, Penalty provisions, Validity, etc.) which are not still not answered properly can be further worked out. Some financial model can also be worked out for movement of trading price of RECs.

Lot more work can be done on PAT and its viability, the concept still very new to the industry, a lot can happen over PAT. NAMMA is another new concept in the area of Clean Energy.

REFERENCES

[1] Berry, D. (2002). 'The Market for Tradable Renewable Energy Credits', Ecological Economics, 42, pp. 369–79.

[18] Mutualisation is the mechanism introduced in England & Wales and Scotland to ensure investor confidence in the RO is maintained. It is triggered only when supplier insolvency results in a large enough shortfall in the buyout fund (calculated by Ofgem) which is equivalent to or larger than the trigger. Ofgem will notify the other suppliers of the shortfall and requests that suppliers make a payment to the buyout fund proportionate to their share of the Obligation. The buyout fund is then re-distributed in the usual way to suppliers in line with the proportion of ROCs they presented. The payments are staggered quarterly and recycled immediately to minimise the burden on consumers and suppliers. A cap exists on the size of the shortfall that can be recovered, to protect against the fund causing smaller suppliers to go into insolvency.

[2] *Bureau of Energy Efficiency*, India.

[3] Central Electricity Authority.

[4] COAG review of specific Renewable Energy Target (RET) issues(2009); Alternative Technology Association Environment, Victoria.

[5] Electricity Act 2003.

[6] Energy Conservation Act, 2001.

[7] Indian Energy Exchange.

[8] Michael Gillenwater, "Redefining RECs—Part 1: Untangling Attributes and Offsets", 36. Energy Policy 2109-2110 (2008); Ed Holt and Lori Bird, *National Renewable Energy Laboratory, Emerging Markets for Renewable Energy Certificates: Opportunities and Challenges* 7 (January 2005).

[9] National Load Dispatch Centre.

[10] Nielsen, L.T. Jeppesen (2003). 'Tradable Green Certificates in Selected European Countries—Overview and Assessment', Energy Policy, 31(1), pp. 3–14.

[11] Office of the Gas and Electricity Markets (OFGEM), United Kingdom.

[12] Pew Center on Global Climate Change, United States of America.

[13] Power Exchange of India.

[14] Renewable Energy: Changes to the Renewables Obligation (Scotland) Order 2010: Statutory Consultation.

[15] Renewable Energy in India: Progress, Vision and Strategy; paper by Ministry of New and Renewable Energy, Government of India.

[16] Roadmap for Implementation of Renewable Energy Certificate Mechanism for India: Guidelines and Operating Rules for Exchange Platform(s) (2010) submitted to "Renewable Energy and Energy Efficiency Partnership (REEEP)" by Indian Renewable Energy Development Agency Ltd. and ABPS Infrastructure Advisory Private Limited on July 2010.

[17] Report on Development of Conceptual Framework For Renewable Energy Certificate Mechanism for India (2009); Submitted to Ministry of New and Renewable Energy (Government of India), by ABPS Infrastructure Advisory Private Limited on June 2009.

[18] Singh, A. (2009). 'A Market for Renewable Energy Credits in the Indian Power Sector', *Renewable and Sustainable Energy Reviews*, 13, pp. 643–52.

[19] S.K. Soonee, S.K., Garg, M. and Prakash, S., Renewable Energy Certificate Mechanism in India.

[20] State Electricity regulatory Commissions.

[21] Wikipedia.

Protection of Intellectual Property in Indian Small and Medium Sized Enterprises

Arvind Kumar[1] and Ashish Ransom[2]

[1] Dr. Ram Manohar Lohia National Law University, Lucknow

[2] Indian Law Society, Pune

E-mail: arvind.ransom@gmail.com

ABSTRACT

SME's i.e Small and medium enterprises are the backbone of developing economies. SMEs represent over 90% of enterprises in these economies. The driving force behind these SMEs is the large number of innovations which has led to the growth of the national economy through employment creation, productive investments and value-added exports. Since this growth is innovation based therefore intellectual property rights (hereinafter referred to as IPRs) have assumed an unprecedented significance. In the knowledge-based society of our times IPRs have a profound influence on the social, economic and technological progress .New products, brands and creative designs appear almost daily on the market that are the result of continuous innovation and creativity in SMEs. Thus In order to improve the business environment and encourage innovation in this sector it is necessary to provide robust policy framework and formidable legal protection to the IPRs of SMEs especially against unauthorized exploitation. Little groundwork exists on the use of IP protection by businesses, especially in respect of SMEs, in fast developing countries such as India. Evidence indicates that SMEs in India do not use formal IP protection as a competitive strategy, and adapt to the threat of imitation by using informal methods such as trade secrets, maintaining product quality, and constant innovation. My paper advocates promoting IP as a tool for enhancing SME competitiveness. It requires an integrated approach involving awareness creation on the benefits of IP and ensuring effective enforcement of IP rights together with promotion of other competitive strategies. My paper also lays emphasis on the strong need for more research into the nature and characteristics at the enterprise level and how best to adapt formal IP registration systems so that SMEs can be encouraged to register their technological innovations and derive benefits from them. The impending question is does India have a policy for securing intellectual property of its SME sector from unauthorized exploitation?

Keywords: SMEs, Unauthorized Exploitation, IPR Protection, Policies

INTRODUCTION

Intellectual property (IP) is a method for legally protecting the knowledge or intellectual activity. The system of Intellectual Property (IP) rights creates a mechanism to resolve the "Appropriability" problem, by creating property rights over knowledge. At the SMEs level, IP has been a significant source of comparative advantage of business enterprises and a major driver of their competitive strategies. Looking from the perspective of developing nations like India where SMEs represent over 90% of enterprises, IP protection cannot overlooked anymore. SMEs are often the driving force behind a large number of innovations and contribute to the growth of the national economy through employment creation, productive investments and value added exports. However, various ad hoc surveys and studies indicate that, despite the importance of SMEs for the vitality of the economy and the potential offered by the IP system for enhancing the competitiveness of SMEs, most of them do not use or do not get the best out of their use of the IP system. Their innovative and creative capacity is not always fully exploited as many are not aware of the intellectual property system nor the protection it can provide for their inventions, brands, and designs. To date there have been very few systematic research and publications on the nature and characteristics of IP creation as well as on the relationships between IPR systems and instruments and the IP-driven growth and competitiveness of business firms.

Even if for a second, we forgot competition oriented arguments and adopt a larger social perspective as set forth in the Millennium Development Goals by the world leaders in 2000 for reducing poverty and hunger, improving health and education, we find that our capacity to achieve these objectives would be seriously compromised if adequate protection to IPRs is not provided. The impasses and the collapse of the WTO Ministerial Meeting over consensus on access to essential (but patented) drugs in the context of paragraph 6 of the Doha Declaration on the Agreement on Trade-Related Aspects of Intellectual Property Rights (TRIPS Agreement) and Public Health brought home closer the intimate relationship between (IPRs) and achievement of these objectives.

Therefore if we leave, a good invention or creation unprotected, it may not only be lost to larger competitors that are in a better position to commercialize the product but we also put ourselves several steps backward in our fight against hunger and poverty. To help SMEs more fully utilize their IP assets in their business activities, India will have to establish a comprehensive policy framework to assist entrepreneurs, SME-support institutions in increasing awareness and use of the IP system among SMEs.

DEFINITIONS: MICRO, SMALL AND MEDIUM ENTERPRISES IN INDIA

There exists several definitions of the term small and medium enterprises (SMEs), varying from country to country and varying between the sources reporting SME statistics. The commonly used criteria at the international level to define SMEs are the number of employees, total net assets, sales and investment level.

The European Union makes a general distinction between self-employment, micro, small and medium sized businesses based on the following criteria:

NUMBER OF EMPLOYEES

Table 1

0	Self Employed
2-9	Micro Business
10-49	Small Business
50-249	Medium-sized business

Source: Effective Policies for Small Business: A Guide for the Policy Review Process and Strategic Plans for Micro, Small and Medium Enterprise Development (2004), UNIDO and OECD.

In the Indian context, micro, small and medium enterprises as per the MSME Development Act, 2006 are defined based on their investment in plant and machinery (for manufacturing enterprise) and on equipments for enterprises providing or rendering services. According to the Micro, Small and Medium Enterprises (MSME) Development Act of 2006, (India) a micro enterprise is where the investment in plant and machinery does not exceed twenty five lakh rupees. A medium enterprise is where the investment in plant and machinery is more than five crore rupees but does not exceed ten crore rupees. A small enterprise is where the investment in plant and machinery is more than twenty five lakh rupees but does not exceed five crore rupees.

In the case of the enterprises engaged in providing or rendering of services, as

(a) a micro enterprise is where the investment in equipment does not exceed ten lakh rupees.
(b) a small enterprise is where the investment in equipment is more than ten lakh rupees but does not exceed two crore rupees.
(c) a medium enterprise is where the investment in equipment is more than two crore rupees but does not exceed five crore rupees.

According to the Ministry of Micro, Small and Medium Enterprises, recent ceilings on investment for enterprises to be classified as micro, small and medium enterprises are as in Table 2.

But irrespective of the definitional differences, there exists operational similarities among the enterprises in this sector. The contribution of micro, small and medium

Table 2

Classification	Manufacturing Enterprises*	Service Enterprises**
Micro	Rs 2.5 million/Rs 25 lakh	Rs 1million/Rs 10 lakh
Small	Rs 50 million/Rs 5 crore	Rs 20 million/Rs 2 crore
Medium	Rs 100 million/Rs 10 crore	Rs 50 million/Rs 5 crore

* Investment limit in Plant & Machinery.
** Investment limit in equipments.

enterprises (MSME) sector to manufacturing output, employment and exports of the country is quite significant. According to estimates, in terms of value, the sector accounts for about 45 per cent of the manufacturing output and 40 percent of the total exports of India. The MSME sector employs about 42 million persons in over 13 million units throughout the country. There are more than 6000 products, ranging from traditional to high-tech items, which are being manufactured by the Indian MSMEs.

Graph 1 shows that the SME sector observed better growth rates vis-à-vis the overall industrial sector in India.

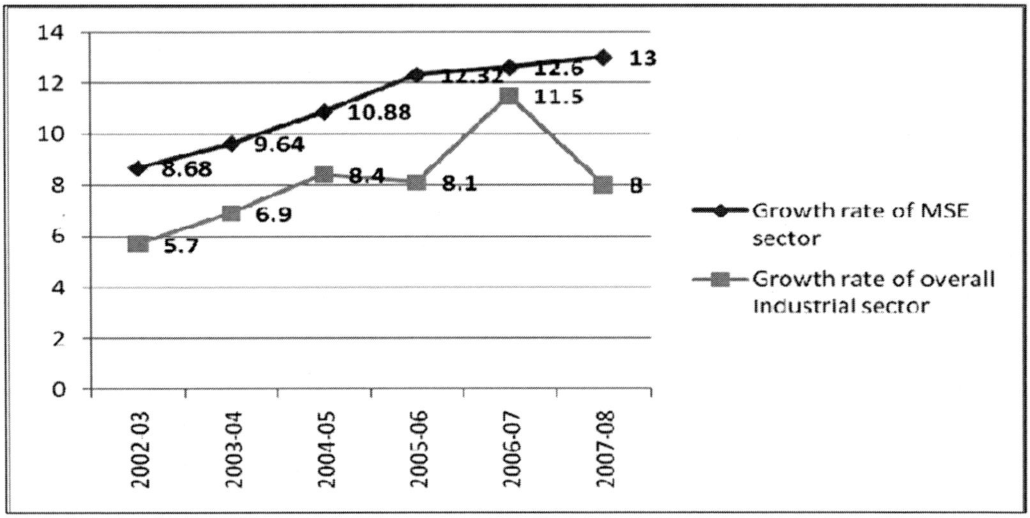

Source: Annuaal Report 2008-2009. Ministry of Micro, Small and Medium Enterprises. www.msme.gov.in

Graph 1: Comparison of the Growth Rates in Micro and Small Enterprises and the Overall Industrial Sector

From Graph 2 it can be witnessed that the contribution of the SME sector to the gross domestic product (GDP) has increased from 5.86% in 1999-2000 to 5.94% in 2006-07.

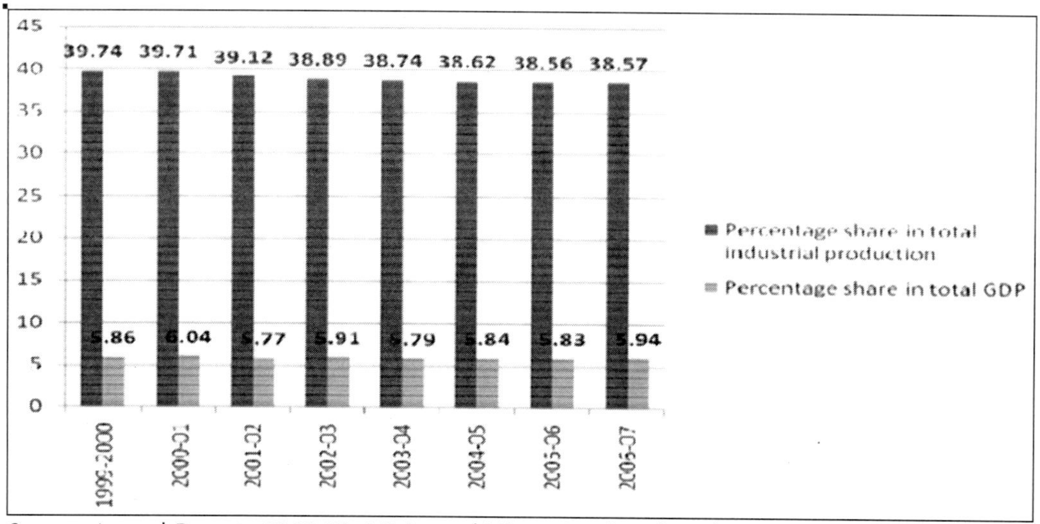

Source: Annual Report , 2008-09, Ministry of Micro, Small and Medium.

Graph 2: Contribution of SME (%) at 1999-2000 Prices in Total Industrial Production and GDP

SMEs: THE REAL ENGINES OF GROWTH

Small and Medium Enterprises (SMEs) play a significant role in the economic growth of the country owing to their contribution to production, exports and employment. The sector contributes 8 per cent to the country's GDP, 45 per cent to the manufactured output and 40 per cent to the country's exports. It provides employment to 60 million people through 28.5 million enterprises.

Significantly, the SME sector has maintained a higher growth rate vis-à-vis the overall industrial sector during the past decade. According to a survey, exports from these enterprises have been on the rise, despite increased cost of raw materials, sluggish global demand and stiff international competition. Today, the sector produces a wide range of products, from simple consumer goods to high-precision, sophisticated finished products. It has emerged as a major supplier of mass consumption goods as well as a producer of electronic and electrical equipment and drugs and pharmaceuticals.

SMEs constitute over 90 per cent of total enterprises in most of the economies and are credited with generating high rates of employment and account for a major share of industrial production and exports. In India too, SMEs play a pivotal role in the overall industrial economy of the country. With its agility and dynamism, the sector has shown admirable innovativeness and adaptability to survive the recent economic downturn and recession.

Apart from providing the support to the large industries, SMEs have played an important role in the development of States in terms of the employment generation. More than 55 per cent of these enterprises are located in six major States of the country, namely, Uttar Pradesh, Maharashtra, Tamil Nadu, West Bengal, Andhra Pradesh and Karnataka.

The SME sector has slowly come into the limelight, with increased focus from the government and other government institutions, corporate bodies and banks. Policy based changes; investments into the sector; globalisation and India's robust economic growth have opened up several latent business opportunities for this sector.

A recent study by Grant Thornton International Business Report (IBR), 2011 reveals that businesses in India are considerably optimistic about their economic prospects for 2011.

Optimism amongst Indian business owners (84 per cent) remains well ahead of the global average of 24 per cent and double the Asia Pacific average of 33 per cent. Confidence levels over economic performance are higher for India this year with 93 per cent of Indian business owners optimistic about the country's economy for 2011.

India also enjoys favourable demographics. The working-age population is likely to witness a significant growth this year leading to an increase in employment optimism levels to 77 per cent in 2011 as compared to 47 per cent in 2010.

The survey also reveals that 93 per cent of Indian business owners expected increased in revenues in 2010 and about 25 per cent are positive about exports as compared to the global average of 22 per cent.

With all these developments, there is a huge potential for SMEs to enter the international markets and create an upsurge in the employment opportunities for India. It also provides an opportunity for the sector to go international and market its 'Made in India' brand in order to explore more opportunities and enhance possibilities globally.

SIGNIFICANCE OF INTELLECTUAL PROPERTY FOR SMALL AND MEDIUM ENTERPRISES (SMEs)

SMEs form the backbone of the Indian manufacturing sector and have become entrepreneurial engine of economic growth in India. It is estimated that about 70% of the employment growth comes from the SMEs in the Asian region and they account for almost 90% of industrial units in India and 40% of value addition in the manufacturing sector.

Intellectual Property and Other Assets in the Business

The assets in the business may be largely divided into two classes: tangible assets i.e. physical assets - including buildings, machinery, financial assets & infrastructure and intangible assets - ranging from Intellectual capital (IC) like creativity, innovation and know-how to ideas, brands, and designs. There is no doubt that the physical assets play very important role in any company to determine the competitiveness in the business arena but the intangible assets may play a bigger role and describe the potential value in the business. There are numerous examples in the industry as IBM, Aricent, Denso etc., where the data shows that the business value increases overnight as a result of acquisition of important patents in key technologies.

In order to acquire the IP rights SMEs may have following categories of intangible assets:

- Patents and utility models for Innovative products and processes;
- Copyright and others related rights for cultural, artistic, literary works as well as for computer software;
- Trademarks for distinctive signs;
- Industrial Design rights for creative designs, including textile designs;
- Topographies of integrated circuits for microchips;
- Geographical Indication for goods of a given quality or reputation attributable to the geographical origin; and
- Trade secrets for the business secrets for commercial purpose.

Intellectual Property and Market Value of the Business

There is always a demand of legally protected products/services in the business arena provided that the SMEs always take care of the protection, management and enforcement of the products/services. Than definitely IP becomes a valuable business asset.

- IP rights may engender the revenue in the business through the licensing, sale, assignment or cross licensing.
- A potential patent/IP rights may open doors to a number of financing opportunities like: Private Investors, Venture Capitalists (VCs) or specialized banks towards SMEs and enhance their worth. At that time it becomes very important for the SMEs to have IP ownership to convince them for the commercialization of legally protected product / service in their business.
- IP assets may have great potential to raise the value of the business through M&A, Joint Venture (JV) and Collaboration Schemes.

OPPORTUNITIES OFFERED BY INTELLECTUAL PROPERTY TO SMEs

IP affects SMEs in almost every aspect of business development and competitive strategy from product development to product design, from service delivery to marketing, and from raising financial resources to exporting or expanding businesses abroad through licensing or franchising. IP offers many opportunities for SMEs:

Enhancement of Market Value and the Competitiveness of SMEs

The value of IP is often not adequately appreciated and its potential for providing opportunities for future profit is widely underestimated by SMEs. However, when IP is legally protected and there is demand for the IP-protected products and/or services in the marketplace, IP can become a valuable business asset.

- IP may generate an income for SME through the licensing, sale, or commercialization of the IP-protected products or services that may significantly improve an enterprise's market share or raise its profit margins.
- IP rights enhance the value or worth of SME in the eyes of investors and financing institutions.
- In the event of a sale, merger or acquisition, IP assets may significantly raise the value of enterprise, and at times may be the primary or only true assets of value.

The strategic utilization of IP assets can, therefore, substantially enhance the competitiveness of SMEs. SMEs should make sure that they are ready to face the challenge and take measures to exploit their IP and protect it wherever possible.

IP as a Business Assets

An enterprise's assets may be broadly divided into two categories: physical assets - including buildings, machinery, financial assets and infrastructure - and intangible assets ranging from human capital and know-how to ideas, brands, designs and other intangible fruits of a company's creative and innovative capacity. Traditionally, physical assets have been responsible for the bulk of the value of a company, and were considered to be largely responsible for determining the competitiveness of an enterprise in the market place. Increasingly, and largely as a result of the information technologies revolution and the growth of the service economy, companies are realizing that intangible assets are often becoming more valuable than their physical assets. In short, large warehouses and factories are increasingly being replaced by powerful software and innovative ideas as the main source of income for a large and growing proportion of enterprises worldwide. And even in sectors where traditional production techniques remain dominant, continuous innovation and endless creativity are becoming the keys to greater competitiveness in fiercely competitive markets, be it domestic or international.

IP as an Investment

Making the right investments is crucial for enhancing the market value of SMEs. Investing in equipment, property, product development, marketing and research can strongly enhance company's financial situation by expanding its asset base and increasing future productivity. Acquiring intellectual property may have a similar effect. Markets will value company on the basis of its assets, its current business operations and expectations of future profits. There are numerous examples of SMEs that have seen their market value increase overnight as a result of their acquisition of important patents in key technologies. Similarly, a good trademark with a good reputation among consumers may also enhance company's current value and may decisively contribute to making company's products and services more attractive to consumers. Investment in developing a good IP portfolio is, therefore, much more than a defensive act against potential competitors.

The Value of IP Assets

A crucial point about legal protection of intellectual property is that it turns intangible assets into exclusive property rights, albeit for a limited period of time. It enables SMEs to claim ownership over its intangible assets and exploit them to their maximum potential. In short, IP protection makes intangible assets "a bit more tangible" by turning them into valuable exclusive assets that can often be traded in the market place.

Increasingly, investors, stock market brokers and financial advisors are becoming aware of this reality and have begun to value IP assets highly. Enterprises worldwide are also more and more acknowledging the value of their IP assets, and, on occasions, have included them in their balance sheets. Many enterprises, including SMEs, have begun to undertake regular technology and IP audits. In a number of cases, enterprises have realized that their IP assets are in fact worth more than their physical assets. This is often the case for companies operating in knowledge-intensive and highly innovative sectors, or companies with a well-known brand name.

NEED OF UMBRELLA PROTECTION

There are certain problems, typical of developing countries, in IP financing. The whole exercise is to create and own an IPR at this juncture of their development is an arduous task. The whole journey from inventing, to obtain a patent, then to get venture capital to exploit the patent, build a business around it, grow it larger and then go public is riddled with problems. Once the product is developed or IP is at the stage of exploitation, the issue of financing of IP arises, i.e., securitization, licensing/franchising etc. In IP financing, the risk of infringement litigation is not uncommon when two companies are dealing in the same stream of technology. Small companies are usually not in a position to pursue infringement litigation. Financing companies have to take into account these risks while financing IP as security. Similarly, for management of IPR, a good support system is required, including legal, technical, financial and administrative functions. Let us discuss the policy areas where SMEs need prioritized protection:

Securitization of Intellectual Property Assets

Financial constraints and lack of infrastructure are hurdles creating and maintaining IP in developing countries like India. Capacity building for innovation is a very significant requirement in IP infrastructure. The industries in India need to appreciate that a good portfolio makes good business sense. The basic premise of financing intellectual property is – how to convert a creative idea into a financial asset.

Financial assets are the possession of an entity, which are held for purposes of producing revenues. Intellectual property rights (IPRs), like other financial assets, be they manufacturing plants, bonds, or goodwill, cost capital to produce or acquire, and are owned for purposes of generating a cash return. Many companies treat proprietary IPRs as patents, copyrights and trademarks as a discrete asset. In recent years, there has been a growing awareness that IP assets can be monetized. IP can be sold, licensed, used as collateral or security for debt finance, or it can provide an additional or alternative basis for seeking equity from private investors, venture capitalists, specialized banks and sometimes even from regular banks. IP assets may help a company to obtain business finance from investors/lenders.

The investor/lender, in undertaking an appraisal of the request for equity assistance or loan, will assess whether the new or innovative product or service offered by a company is protected by a patent, a trademark, an industrial design, or copyright or related rights. Such protection is often a good indicator of the potential of a company for doing well in the marketplace. IP ownership is thus important to convince investors/lenders of the market opportunities open to the enterprise for the commercialization of the product or service in question. For securitization, proper valuation of IP is very crucial. Valuation of IP is also important to secure loans or finances for business. So far, the valuation of IP has remained highly subjective for both lenders and borrowers and is generally not understood by most people. There still dearth of established norms for satisfactory evaluation on which uniform policy or guidance needs to be issued.

Significance of IP Infrastructure in Capacity Building for Innovation in SMEs

Before one may think of financing of IP, there has to be IP worthy of protection and leveraging. Most of the companies in developing countries do not possess enough of that. Increasingly, it is being realized that the real innovation bottleneck is not the supply of new knowledge, but external factors surrounding the process, including lack of necessary infrastructure.

It has often been highlighted that in developing countries, a great gap exists between IPR and economic development policies, leading to low financial support for IPR institutions at all levels. IPR is not been mainstreamed in the national development policies nor into donor assistance programmes. India needs to prepare a national policy process that generates a national action plan with priorities. Since India is rich in traditional knowledge (TK), genetic resources and folklore, capacity building in IPR policymaking/ administration should cover developing countries' desire to establish protection and benefit-sharing arrangements for TK, folklore and biodiversity.

Policy-makers must carefully consider which type of protection is appropriate for each innovation whose needs are being served, and how to weigh expected costs and benefits. The development of indigenous technological capacity is a key determinant to decide these issues. Capacity building in the technical field is very crucial to India. Bearing in mind the limited resources provided for IP technical assistance today, its effectiveness, its inclusiveness in terms of stakeholders, and its openness in addressing both strengths and weaknesses of current programmes, exploring ways to improve them are essential. Surprisingly though, very limited independent analytical work has been undertaken in this area and the literature is scare.

At the national level, key factors that need to be addressed in innovation capacity building are technology and information infrastructures, legal framework, business support services, human resources and financial infrastructure. The help of international agencies can be taken to build this infrastructure. Commercialization of innovation into new processes and products that can benefit the economy requires infrastructure such as universal standards, policy and guidelines, venture capital, skilled labour, organized alliances and networks. Equal emphasis needs to be given to the provision of these infrastructures to ensure that world-class research and its commercialization can take place.

Building Information Infrastructure

Automated information systems are key requirements for efficient administration of IPR and an important indicator of institutional capacity. Although some larger, higher income developing countries have fully automated systems for searching and application processing to grant IPR, a large number of countries still have manual, paper-based systems. This not only hinders efficient processing of applications, but also greatly complicates collection of important statistical and management information.

Legal Framework

The legal awareness about IP rights is very low in developing countries and because of that most of inventors/innovators do not take advantage of the laws. The industry has yet to learn defensive as well as aggressive management of their IPRs, by protecting their own rights while at the same time not to infringe others' in order to avoid any infringement suits. India faces arduous institutional challenges in implementing IP protection. The challenges include formulating appropriate legislation, administering IPRs in line with international obligations, and enforcing and regulating IPR in a pro-competitive manner appropriate to national levels of development. Most of these countries lack an effective implementation of IP laws.

Judicial delays are the order of the day, which means that cases can take years to see resolution and payment of damages on IPR violations. A specific enforcement mechanism may lead to an effective implementation of these rights. In Chennai, where there is a separate Deputy Police Commissioner who deals with copyright infringement, the industry has reported a steep decline in film and music piracy. This success could be repeated in other sectors provided government and industry cooperate in dedicating sufficient resources to strictly enforce IPRs.

Business Support Services

Another important plank of innovation facilitators is that of business support services through appropriate government agency or professional association that forges and maintains a link between the inventors/innovators, research organizations and SMEs with respect to sourcing of technologies, knowhow, equipment, workshops and test laboratories for quality assurance, and formulation of demand-driven research projects, and ready commercialization of inventions. In India, an extensive system of broad public consultation has evolved over the years, which includes public workshops on issues such as protection of biodiversity and traditional knowledge, use of compulsory licensing, and the need of high level expertise in the academic, business and legal communities. But the government should vigorously go ahead with policy on industrial location and incentives for the development of sub-sectoral clusters of SMEs. Such clusters would share facilities, with common pool of information network on markets, venture capital, databases, etc. Sustaining regional innovation clusters requires continuous interaction between research centers, universities and local business leaders in order to sustain cluster growth and the development of new knowledge-based industries. A prime example of such clusters and initiatives is the National Innovation Foundation (NIF). The Department of Science and Technology and the Government of India constituted the NIF with an aim to recognize and support the creative potential of innovators at the grassroots and harness their creativity to help make India self-reliant and a leader in sustainable technologies. Further, in this regard the Government of India through various ministries should set up nodal agencies that provide entrepreneurial assistance, investor facilitation, processing of all applications which require government approval, assisting entrepreneurs and investors in setting up projects and in monitoring the implementation of projects.

CONCLUSION AND FEW SUGGESTIONS

In an increasingly international marketplace, many companies are finding that prosperity is best achieved from specialization, as opposed to diversification. Thus protection for intellectual property rights of the SMEs become all the more important. Counterfeiting and piracy harms commerce and the public well being, and undermines confidence in the quality of brand name products, resulting in billions of dollars of lost revenue, investment, future sales, and growth opportunities. It also harms legitimate businesses and workers who play pivotal roles in creating, manufacturing, distributing, and selling genuine products. In addition, because infringing products are often substandard in quality, they can harm consumers in a myriad of ways. Consumers are vulnerable to harm when infringing products penetrate the process between the manufacture and sale of goods - known as business supply chains.

Protecting supply chains from counterfeit and pirated goods requires close public-private sector collaboration. Both must work in concert to identify infringing goods and prevent them from entering the marketplace and international channels of commerce. In this interplay, SMEs should actively endeavor to ensure the security of their production and distribution chains. Indeed, close cooperation is required between government and enterprises for effectively securing protecting consumers and right holders.

It is also important to make the public aware that the manufacture and the trafficking of counterfeit and pirated products, including the importation and exportation of such products, is illegal and may result in severe civil and/or criminal penalties. To this end, the following measures should be taken:

- Undertaking campaigns to inform importers and exporters of the severity of penalties associated with the unlawful trafficking or distribution of counterfeit and pirated goods.
- Undertaking broad educational campaigns that address the harm counterfeiters cause to society and the economy.
- Developing educational programs for consumers and retailers on identifying and avoiding counterfeit and pirated products.

But the onus is not on the government alone, SMEs must keep in mind the following measures to get best out of their IP rights:

- Registering IP assets at the earliest in order to take full advantage of IP rights while undertaking advertising and other promotional activities.
- Checking carefully to make sure that SME does not infringe the IP rights of others. In this respect, it is advisable to conduct trademarks and patent searches before commercializing products and services which may conflict with the IP rights protected by other persons or enterprises.
- Use, or make reference to, IP rights in advertisements and other promotional activities in order to make customers and potential customers aware of the IP protection of products and services.

- Monitoring the market and be ready to contact an IP lawyer or an official enforcement authority wherever infringement of IP rights is detected.

REFERENCES

[1] Altenburg, Tilman, (1999). "Linkages and spill-overs between transnational corporations and small and medium-sized enterprises in developing countries opportunities and policies", *German Development Institute,* Berlin.

[2] Chen, Edward K.Y, (1997). "The total factor productivity debate", *Asian-Pacific Economic Literature*, Vol. 11, No.1, May.

[3] CIPR, (2002). Integrating Intellectual Property Rights and Development. Report submitted to the Secretary of State for International Development, United Kingdom (London, CIPR).

[4] Harvie, Charles and Boon-Chye Lee, (2002). "East Asian SMEs: Contemporary issues and developments – An overview" in Charles Harvie and Boon-Chye Lee (eds.), *The Role of SMEs in National Economies in East Asia* (Cheltenham, Edward Elgar).

[5] Kitchenside, Gary, (2002). "Best Practices in Using IP to Promote SMEs and Start-ups", paper presented at the WIPO Asian Regional Workshop on the Use of Information Technology and Management of Intellectual property Rights by Small and medium-sized Enterprises, Bangkok, Thailand, 25-27 February.

[6] Kitchenside, Gary, (2002). "Case Studies – The successful use of trademarks, petty patent/utility models and industrial design in enhancing competitiveness of SMEs", paper presented at the WIPO Asian Regional Workshop on the Use of Information Technology and Management of Intellectual property Rights by Small and medium-sized Enterprises, Bangkok, Thailand, 25-27 February.

[7] Lam, N. V., (1999). "The 2000s – A decade of SMEs in ASEAN?" in Foundation for International Human Resource Development, SMEs toward Year 2000 through Greater Mekong Subregion Cooperation (Bangkok, FIHRD).

[8] Lee, Yuke Chin, (2002). "Industrial information for SMEs: Types, availability, form, source, access, and cost demonstration", paper presented at the WIPO Asian Regional Workshop on the Use of Information Technology and Management of Intellectual property Rights by Small and Medium-sized Enterprises", Bangkok, Thailand, 25-27 February.

[9] Momaya, Kirankumar, (2001). "International Competitiveness: Evaluation and Enhancement", *Hindustan Publishing Corporation*, New Delhi.

[10] Mulcahy, Richard, (2003). "New ideas, new firms? Intellectual property and SMEs

in the United Kingdom", paper presented at the WIPO Seminar on Intellectual property and Small Businesses, Baku, Azerbijan, 4-5 June.

[11] Tangkitvanich, Somkiat, (2002). "SME development in Thailand's automotive industry", paper presented at the ASEAN Roundtable 2002 on Entrepreneurship and SMEs in Southeast Asia's Economic Development, Singapore, 7-8 November.

[12] Tuteja, S.K., (2002). "Role of SME support institutions in promoting effective intellectual property management, acquiring protection, commercializing inventions and marketing Brands", paper presented at the WIPO Asian Regional Workshop on the Use of Information Technology and Management of Intellectual property Rights by Small and medium-sized Enterprises", Bangkok, Thailand, 25-27 February.

[13] Wattanapruttipaisan, Thitapha, (2002). "SMEs subcontracting as bridgehead to competitiveness: Framework for an assessment of supply-side capabilities and demand-side requirements", *Asia-Pacific Development Journal*, Vol. 9, No. 1, June, pp. 65-87.

[14] Wattanapruttipaisan, Thitapha, (2002), "Promoting SME development: Some issues and suggestions for policy consideration" in UNESCAP, *Bulletin on Asia-Pacific Perspectives* 2002/03, United Nations publication, Sales No. E.02.II.F.69.

[15] WIPO, (2001). *WIPO Intellectual Property Handbook: Policy, Law and Use* (Geneva, WIPO).

[16] Yoshihara, Kinio, (1988). "The Rise of Ersatz Capitalism in South-East Asia" (London, Oxford University Press).

[17] Young, A., (1994). "Lessons from the East Asian NICs: A contrarian view", *European Economic Review*, No. 38, May.

[18] Young, A., (1995). "The tyranny of numbers: Confronting the statistical realities of the East Asian growth experience", *Quarterly Journal of Economics*, Vol. 110, No. 3, August.

Public-Private Partnership (PPP) Model – A Study of Infrastructure Projects in India

Leena Painter[1] and Jai Parkash[2]

[1] DRP & RBP Commerce College, Surat
[2] Sri Aurobindo College of Commerce & Management, Ludhiana
E-mail: leena3174@gmail.com; jaiparkash1983@gmail.com

ABSTRACT

With a surprising growth rate of around 9% the Indian Economy is now falling short of vital support systems, like road transportation and highways, railway tracks, bridges, airports, electricity, water supply, waste management etc. To cope up with this growth, there has to be a massive and rapid increase in infrastructure involving investment of millions of dollars. The concept of Public-Private Partnership (PPP) model has emerged as an instrument to attract private investment in the infrastructure sector. This was necessary on the part of the government as PPP will help increase the volume of investment and the level of operational efficiency in provision of infrastructural facilities throughout the country. Like many other developing economies, Indian government is seen dependent on the PPP model for solving their Socio-economic problems and for providing improved delivery of infrastructural services. Consequently both central and state governments are now encouraging private participation including foreign investment and foreign loans for growth and development of the infrastructure. This paper tries to evaluate the contributory role of PPP model in the infrastructural development of India. The findings suggest that through PPP model significant improvement can be seen in the infrastructure of India in the past few years, but this development is uneven. PPP's have been successful in India but majorly in sectors like Telecommunication, Roads and Highways, Ports and Urban Infrastructure. Less attention is given to sectors like Water supply, Health, Housing, Waste Management, etc. Also it is found that project distribution between different states of India is uneven. Therefore it is suggested that reason must be found out for this uneven sectoral distribution of PPP projects and innovations must be done to stimulate private investments in improving infrastructural facilities in sectors of less attention.

INTRODUCTION AND CONTEXT OF THE STUDY

Rapid industrial & economic growth coupled with increasing population has put more pressure on existing physical as well as social infrastructure. India require improved infrastructural services in terms of quantity and quality to support the pace rapid socio-economic development. There is a huge gap of demand & supply of physical infrastructural services such as roads, seaports, airports, power, urban infrastructure, etc., as well as social infrastructure services like Education, Health & Family Welfare, Tourism & Culture, Urban Infrastructure-Urban Public Transport, Urban Drinking Water & Waste, Solid Waste Management, etc. This has also been a stumbling block on India's competitiveness on international economics front. Studies carried on by the international agencies like World Bank, Asian Development Bank and other multilateral agencies have time and again reiterated the strong linkages between infrastructure investments, economic growth, and reduction of poverty.

In order to provide world class infrastructure the resources available with the Central & State government are not enough. The Central & State Governments are realizing the impeding impact of infrastructure on sustaining economic growth and thus are striving for the development of infrastructure in their respective State. Resources at the disposal of the Governments alone cannot ensure this. And therefore need of resources from the private sector are needed to be diverted.

11th Five-Year Plan (2007–12) of the Government of India had development of infrastructure as its main theme. The Plan estimates that investments to the tune of $492 billion are needed during the five-year period in the roads, railways, ports, power, and water sectors. This means almost doubling infrastructure spending from its current 5 percent of GDP. Of this, the private sector would need to contribute a little over 30 percent – or some $160 billion – about *four* times more than it has done in the past five years. (World Bank report, 2009)

Keeping in view the need of huge investment required for infrastructure development and the limited available resources of the Government, public-private partnership is considered to be the option to tap the financial resources from the private sector. The Government spending on infrastructure development needs to be increased over the period of time also the private participation need to spread out considerably to address the huge resource demand. PPPs are encouraged essentially because of mutually beneficial relationship between public and private sector in terms of risk, returns and skills. The public sector has the prime objectives of citizens' support and overall socio-economic development while the private sector can bring in financial resources, operational & managerial efficiencies, world- class technologies and commercial risk sharing.

CONCEPTUAL FRAMEWORK OF PUBLIC-PRIVATE PARTNERSHIP

Public-Private Partnership (PPP) is a funding model in form of a long term agreement between government agencies and a private partner for providing a qualitative infrastructure good or service. They are targeted towards financing, designing, implementing, and operating infrastructure facilities and services. Under a PPP approach public sector expertise are complimented by the strength of the private sector such as technical knowledge, greater awareness of commercial and managerial principles, ability to mobilize additional investment, innovation, better risk management practices, and knowledge of operating good business models with high level of efficiency. (Ghosh et. al ; 2011)

Public Private Partnership being a generic term, there are various definitions of PPP. As per a research report of World Bank (2007), Public-Private Partnership is defined as 'an agreement between a government and a private firm under which a private firm delivers as asset, a service, or both , in return for payment contingent to some extend on the long term quality or other characteristics of outputs delivered'. The Indian definition of PPP states that Public-Private Partnership Project means a project based on contract or concession agreement, between a Government or statutory entity on the one side, and a private sector company on the other side, for delivering an infrastructure service on payment of user charges.

Benefits from PPP model flow to both public and the private partner and so there are enormous opportunities in India for upliftment of economy especially in infrastructure and service sectors through such models. Therefore PPPs have become central features to modernize public services and infrastructure in many countries around the world. One of the reasons for the success of the PPP model is that it provides the better of two worlds. While private sector efficiencies provide the competitive edge which is the sine qua non of any business venture, partnership with the government ensures continuity, stability and most importantly credibility, which is any business' greatest asset.

Vickram Cuttaree of The World Bank, Europe & Central Asia Region, 2008, reported on case studies conducted by him of PPP projects in various countries like UK, Chile, Mexico, Australia, Europe, Central Asia etc. As per him 'Most PPP failures can be attributed to inadequate or non-existent feasibility studies, including unrealistic traffic forecasts and undefined public contribution of funds'. Common reasons for failure put forth by him are:

- Poor legal framework and enforcement,
- Weak institutional capacity and PPP strategy
- Unrealistic revenue and cost estimations
- Lack of thorough financial and economic analysis
- Inappropriate sharing of risks
- Lack of competitive procurement
- Public resistance (willingness to pay not assessed)

Key success factors put forth by him include:

- Careful planning of PPP project

- Solid revenue and cost estimate
- User willingness to pay and communication plan
- Extensive feasibility study with use of PPP experts
- Compliance with contractual agreement.
- Appropriate Legal and Regulatory Framework
- Strong Institutions with appropriate resources
- Competitive and transparent procurement
- Mitigation and flexibility in managing macro-risks

LITERATURE REVIEW

A number of research studies have been undertaken in the past on various aspects of infrastructure and its effects on development {Barry (1994), Bond Gary (1994), Chandavarkar (1994), Jamal-ud-din (1994), Kohli (1994 and 1995), CMIE (1995), CII (1995), Jha (1995), GOI (1996) and Nayak (1999)}. Some studies are devoted to estimation of productivity of infrastructure investments while others are attempts to find a nexus between growth and investments on infrastructure. (Nayak P,1999). Also various studies are conducted the World Bank, Asian Development Bank and other funding agencies.

RESEARCH PROBLEM AND OBJECTIVE

In India despite wide adoption, PPPs have time and again faced serious criticism. There had been problematic PPPs which have raised concern about role of private sector in the public sector. This paper tries to evaluate the contributory role and performance of public-private tie-ups in India.

METHOD AND SOURCE OF DATA COLLECTION

Various World Bank Reports, Asian Development Bank Reports and data from PPP database were downloaded. This secondary data was studied and analyzed for the said study. Also a comparative study of PPP data, with regards to state-wise figures and sector-wise figures, available on www.pppdatabaseindia.com for the year 2005 and 2009 was compared.

PPP PROJECTS IN INDIA

Government of India has been showing keen interest to expand the use of PPP in infrastructure sector, both physical and social. Physical infrastructures like Roads/ Highways, Telecom, Energy, etc were on top priority. In recent years social infrastructure sector like health and education, urban development, water management etc are added to the list. Number of states are exploring PPP model for service delivery improvement in their respective states. The government has established a Viability Gap Fund to support PPPs. Also a Project Development Fund is established to finance PPP project preparation expenses. Policies and guidelines have been framed at both Central and state level to facilitate PPPs in the infrastructure sector. To facilitate PPP many states have stated establishing PPP cells and enabling of legislation and have set up agencies to facilitate it.

As per the World Bank report, (2008) India's PPP program was one of the largest in middle and low income countries with commitment of over $10.5 billion during 2006-07. Sector wise PPP investment during 1990-2007: Telecom – 45%; Energy – 35%; Transport – 20%.

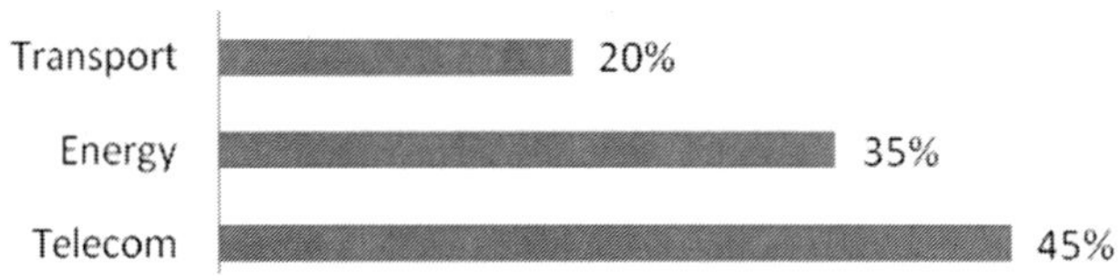

Source: World Bank Report,2008

Fig. 1: Sectorwise Investment PPP Investment during 1990-2007

World Bank has provided the India Infrastructure Finance Company Limited (IIFCL) with an International Bank for Reconstruction and Development (IBRD) line of credit (LOC) of $1.195 billion for on-lending to eligible infrastructure sub-projects. IIFCL is a wholly government-owned financial institution that was established in 2006 to catalyze long-term private financing for PPP projects in infrastructure, and to foster innovations in the sector. Over the life of the Bank project (2009-2015), IIFCL's support is expected to bring at least 150 new PPPs to financial closure, with a four-fold increase in the amount of private capital available. World Bank financing will support a sub-set of this pipeline of projects, mainly in the roads, power and ports sectors (World Bank Report, 2009).

As per report of Asian Development Bank (2010), a key indicator of the success of the Initiative can be seen from the PPP projects pipeline being developed across each of the states and the sectors across the country. With support from Initiative-supported PPP Cells and facilities in most cases, a large pipeline of projects has emerged across the states. A project pipeline of over 900 projects has been developed across selected states is shown in Fig. 2.

The Public Private Partnership Appraisal Committee (PPPAC) in India has been adding value by shortening the approval process within the government, reducing the transaction costs and acting as a central focal point for identifying and disseminating best practices in rolling out PPPs across sectors and ministries of the government.

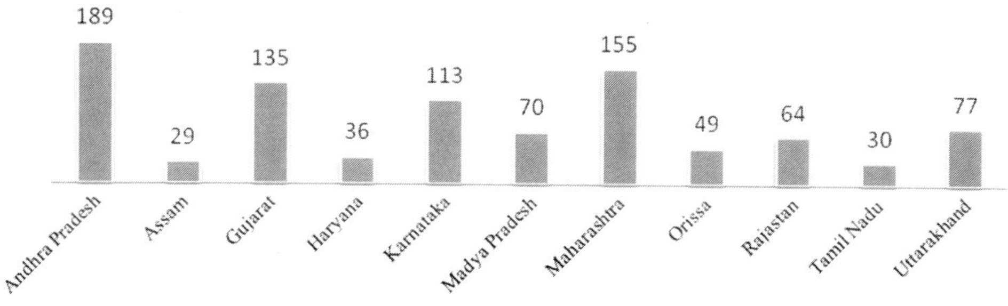

Source: www.adb.org

Fig. 2: Project Pipeline Across Selected States in Number

The Thirtieth PPPAC meeting, chaired by Finance Secretary, met on January 6, 2010 and granted approval to 4 projects of Ministry of Shipping. These projects are in 3 States. The estimated project cost of the approved projects is Rs. 4120.29 crore. Since its constitution in January 2006, PPPAC has granted approval to 141 projects, with an estimated project cost of Rs.148,807.56 crores. These include National Highways (hundred and twenty-two projects), Ports (fifteen projects), Airports (two projects), Tourism Infrastructure (one project) and Railways (one project). (www.caclubindia.com)

There were number of projects which could be successfully completed. As per the report of Asian Bank over 200 projects have achieved financial closure in the last 2 years alone with total estimated project cost of US$18 billion. Projects that have achieved financial closure in the year 2008-2010 are shown in the following figure.

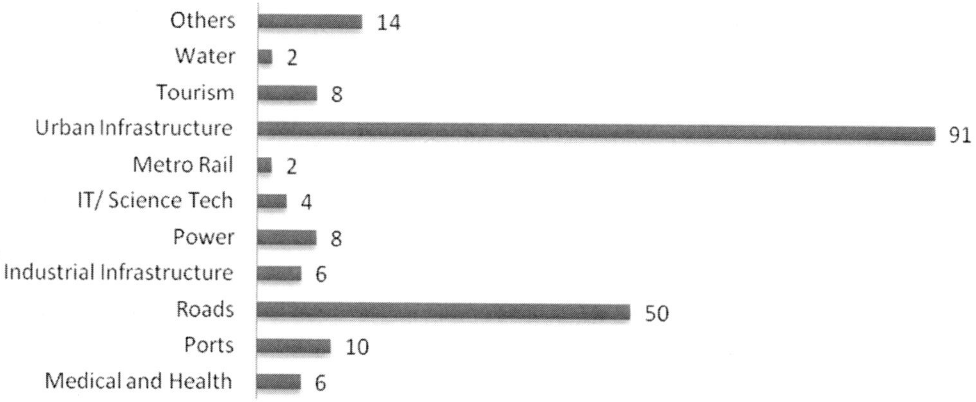

Source: www.adb.org

Fig. 3: No. of Projects that Achieved Financial Closure in 2008-2010

India saw a series of far reaching policy changes in the infrastructure sector in the past decade. Acceptance, development and use of PPPs in the infrastructure sector has now more than 10 years of precedence in India, majority of projects coming in line in the past few years. It has achieved significant success in Telecommunication & Transport sub sectors in the initial years. Later a steep increase trend was seen in the transport PPPs. But that pace of development seems to have dissolute in the recent years. The reasons may be many varying from political, administrative, and or the residual a mix of

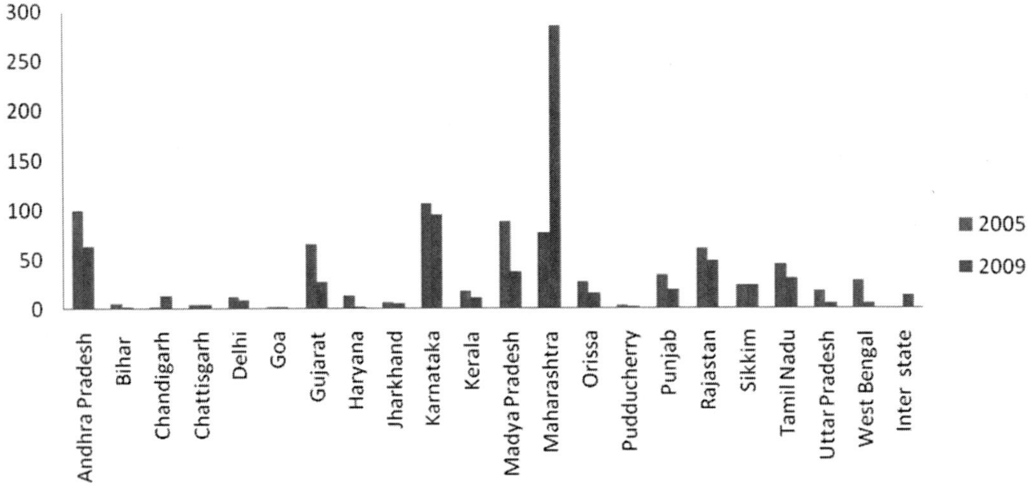

Source: Compiled from data available on www.pppindiadatabase.com

Fig. 4: Comparison of State-wise PPPs for 2005 and 2009 in Number

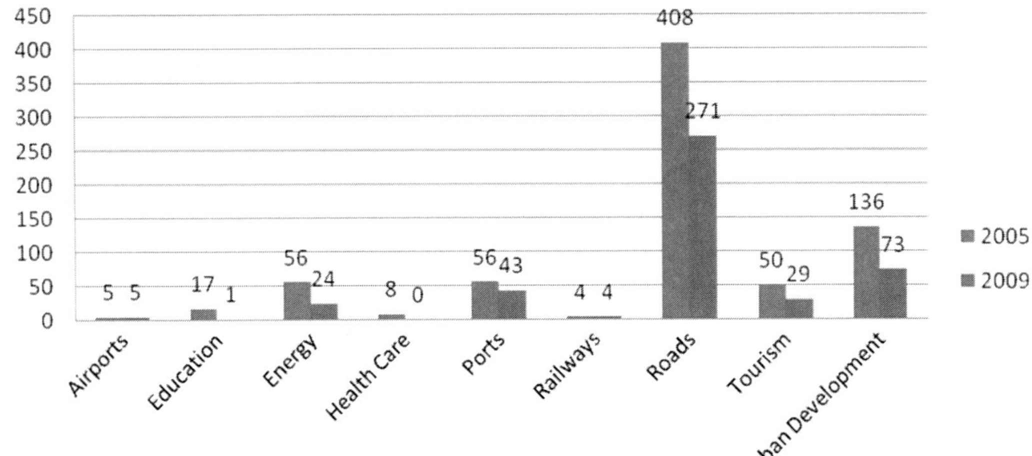

Source: Compiled from data available on www.pppindiadatabase.com

Fig. 5: Comparison of Sector-wise PPPs for 2005 and 2009 in Number

experience and learning. To study these changes in the infrastructure sector a comparative study of PPP projects, state-wise and sector-wise is presented below.

Figure 4 shows state-wise comparison of PPP projects on record for the year 2005 and2009. [based on Table 1 in Annexure I] Andra Pradesh, Maharashtra, Madya Pradesh, Karnataka, Gujarat and Rajastan are the states where PPPs are widely accepted for infrastructural development. But it is observed that except Maharashtra all other states have declined in approval of new PPP projects.

Figures 5 show comparison of sector-wise distribution of PPPs for 2005 & 2009 in number. [Based on Table 2 in Annexure I]Sectors like Roads/highways, Ports and Urban development have bagged maximum PPP projects. Service sector infrastructure areas like Education, Health care have negligible allotment in both the years. Also when we compare the figures of both the years we find a decrease in the number of projects in all the sectors.

FINDINGS AND SUGGESTIONS

Very few states are successful in attracting private participation towards the development of their state. This will lead to imbalanced development of the infrastructure facilities across India. Reasons for this imbalance allotment must be found out and states with lesser infrastructure facilities must be concentrated on by the Central as well as the respective state government. Also reasons for the decline in number of projects over the years must be found out.

The outcome of sectoral imbalance can be seen by Indian telecom industry providing cost-effective services globally where as semi-urban and rural India is still deprived of electricity supply. National Highways Authority of India (NHAI) has VII phased highway development program including construction of expressways and four-laning and six-laning of major highways connecting various major parts of the country, but provision of safe drinking water in rural, semi-urban or even some parts of urban area is still a challenge. Crucial sectors like education and health care are still deprived of major developmental projects.

Infrastructure of rural India is in a gloomy state with huge potential for large investments in both hard and soft infrastructure: roads and communication, drinking water and sanitation, education, health, and agriculture. Investments in rural areas in sectors like wasteland management; rainwater management, crop residue management, storage and distribution of agricultural produce, energy efficiency in household and farm sectors, afforestation and reforestation will have long term positive impacts on poverty reduction and livelihoods. But sadly this area is still out of the purview of PPP.

The present study is based on the analysis of various PPP projects across different sectors and also their distribution across various Indian states is studied, which bring out the essentials of general policy framework of PPP in infrastructure development. However, each sector of physical & social infrastructure has its own relevance & importance and considering the complexities involved, it is felt that a separate research for each sector needs to be carried out for formulation of sector specific policies & guidelines for the PPP projects.

In the early years of this decade, India saw a series of far reaching policy changes in the infrastructure sphere. That momentum seems to have dissipated in the past few years, due to a variety of reasons, mostly political, some administrative, and the residual a mix of learning and stasis. Also since the onset of the global financial crisis in late 2008, long-term financing to sustain the development of infrastructure has become difficult to obtain.

CONCLUSION

It is clearly seen from the study that PPPs in India have proved positive in the infrastructural development of India. There is wide participation of Private sector in developments of sectors like Roads/ highways, Telecom, Urban Development etc. Still there is a urging need to accelerate the pace of investments through PPP in the key infrastructure areas. Therefore a large part of proposed investment in infrastructure will have to come from the private sector. The participation of private investment in the infrastructure sector will depend on the central and state policy decision. Quantum and quality of investments will depend on dynamic policy making followed by well thought out implementation strategy. Government need to take some concrete steps in order to attract large investment, it will needs to showcase successful public private projects, expedite processing to facilitate PPP projects at all levels, build capacities on human resource front & standardize the documents, introduce realistic user charges, involve community and ensure that there is a level playing field for all the stakeholders.

REFERENCES

[1] Chandavarkar, A. (1994): *Infrastructure Finance: Issues, Institutions and Policies*, World Bank, Washington DC.

[2] Ghosh Arindam & Gope Asit, *Public-Private Partnership Projects: A Tool for Economic Enrichment*, The Management Accountant, Vol. 46, Issue 3, March 2011, Pgs184-189.

[3] Hedley Smyth & Andrew Edkins, *Relationship management in the management of PFI/PPP projects in the UK*, International Journal of Project Management, Volume 25, Issue 3, April 2007, Pages 232-240.

[4] Kohli, H. (1995): *Infrastructure Development in Asia and Pacific: Toward A New Public-Private Partnership,* World Bank, Washington DC.

[5] Nayak, P. (1999): "Infrastructure: Its Development and Impact on Agriculture in North-East India", Journal of Assam University, Vol. IV, No. 1, pp. 59-65.

[6] PPP policy gaps to be filled in core push, *Economic Times,* March 29,2011.

[7] 25 categories to qualify as infrastructure *Business Standard*, March 12,2011.

[8] http://www.worldbank.org.in

[9] http://www.adb.org/India/PPP/projects.asp

[10] http://www.pppindiadatabase.com

[11] http://www.pppinindia.com

[12] http://www.ppi.worldbank.org

[13] http://www.caclubindia.com/news/pppac.asp

ANNEXURE I

Table 1: Comparison of State-wise PPPs in 2005 and 2009 in Number

State	2005	2009
Andhra Pradesh	99	63
Bihar	6	2
Chandigarh	2	14
Chattisgarh	4	4
Delhi	12	9
Goa	2	2
Gujarat	65	27
Haryana	14	2
Jharkhand	7	6
Karnataka	106	95
Kerala	18	11
Madya Pradesh	88	37
Maharashtra	77	285
Orissa	27	16
Pudducherry	3	2
Punjab	34	19
Rajastan	61	49
Sikkim	24	24
Tamil Nadu	45	30
Uttar Pradesh	18	5
West Bengal	28	5
Inter state	0	13
Total	**740**	**450**

Table 2: Comparison of Sector-wise PPPs in 2005 and 2009 in Number

Sector	2005	2009
Airports	5	5
Education	17	1
Energy	56	24
Health Care	8	0
Ports	56	43
Railways	4	4
Roads	408	271
Tourism	50	29
Urban Development	136	73
Total	**740**	**450**

Public-Private Partnership Model as a Development Engine for Andhra Pradesh, India

Sudha Vepa and Swati Mathur
Osmania University, Hyderabad
E-mail: sudhavepa@gmail.com; swaticmathur@gmail.com

ABSTRACT

The success of the on-going Eleventh Five Year Plan (2007-2012) for India proposed in 2006 critically depends on the development of infrastructure which in turn depends on the success of Public Private Partnerships (PPP) projects in infrastructure in India. The Public Private Partnership (PPP) Model has emerged as one of the favoured method for development of infrastructure in India, especially in infrastructure, health, and education as the government is moving from its role of traditional way of provider of services to facilitator and regulator of services. Many states in India have adopted the PPP mode for developing infrastructure and Andhra Pradesh (A.P) is one of the pioneering and leading states for PPP projects. A.P. is the fourth largest state in India having an estimated population of 80 million and in the last five years has recorded an average GSDP of 9.14%, higher than the annual average growth of GDP (All India) which is 8.49% only.[1] A survey by the World Bank and Confederation of Indian Industries in 2008 has found AP to have the third best investment climate after Maharashtra and Gujarat. Sound Infrastructure support is required to support this economic growth and A.P. is extensively using PPP model as an engine for development of infrastructure when compared to the rest of India. Against this backdrop, this paper makes a comparative study / analysis of the PPP projects in A.P. with the rest of India. It highlights the initiatives taken by the Government of A.P. for encouraging PPP projects and other factors that may have resulted in not only the State's economic growth in terms of Gross domestic State product (GSDP) and development in infrastructure but making it a favourite destination for PPPs. The paper also conducts a sector-wise analysis of the PPPs in Andhra Pradesh to identify the sectors that have used the model more than the others. It also highlights the problems that resulted from the adoption of PPP model as a growth engine by the A.P. Government. The

[1] World Bank, "Andhra Pradesh: Agenda for Economic Reforms", Report no. 15901-IN, World Bank, Washington, DC, USA.

study is exploratory and makes use of empirical data that has been collected from published information of the concerned Departments of the Government of A.P, nodal agencies and the private partners involved. The paper concludes with a positive note that PPP is a tool for infrastructure development and A.P will lead the way for all of India to develop its infrastructure at an equally swift pace.

Keywords: Infrastructure, Public Private Partnerships (PPPs), Andhra Pradesh (A.P.), Gross State Domestic Product (GSDP)

INTRODUCTION

The economic development and growth of a country is directly related to a well-developed infrastructure. World Development report 1994 published by the World bank under the title "Infrastructure for Development" mentions that "The adequacy of infrastructure helps to determine one country's success and another's failure- in diversifying production, expanding trade, coping with population growth, reducing poverty, or improving environmental conditions". Quality infrastructure is the vital link for sustained and balanced economic development and essential determinant in growth of the all states. The Eleventh Five Year Plan (2007-2012) for India proposed in 2006, foresees a total investment in physical infrastructure (electricity, railways, roads, ports, airports, irrigation, urban and rural water supply and sanitation) to be about Rs. 20,56,150 crores. The investment strategy of the Government of India primarily relies on promoting investment through a combination of public investment and private participation through Public private partnerships (PPPs). The success of the on-going Eleventh Five Year Plan critically depends on the development of infrastructure which in turn depends on the success of Public Private Partnerships (PPP) projects in infrastructure in India.

Many states in India have adopted the PPP mode for developing infrastructure and Andhra Pradesh is one of the pioneering and leading state for PPP projects. The first PPP project was initiated in 1996 between the AP government and L&T for the development of IT Park called "HITEC city" in Hyderabad. It is the first successful and sustainable project through the PPP model putting Hyderabad in the global information technology map and today there are 99 projects in A.P costing around 67,999 crores implemented through PPP mode.

ANDHRA PRADESH STATE PROFILE

Andhra Pradesh is the fourth largest state in the country which has been agriculturally prosperous and now has also emerged as the key state for IT, pharmaceuticals and biotechnology. Over 70 of the 500 top global corporations are present here. It is the first state to have a comprehensive ITES/BPO Policy and also offers a wide range of fiscal and policy incentives for businesses under the Investment Promotion policy 2010-2015. (www.ibef.org). The state is a key player in the country's power sector with the highest hydel power generation and with its proactive policies ensures a good investment climate for investors contributing to a GSPD of US $85.8 billion in 2009-10. The Government of A.P. (GoAP) has taken proactive measures towards PPP approach to facilitate infrastructure for sustainable economic development. The strategy paper on infrastructure by government of A.P. envisages that infrastructure is one of the 17 growth engines identified that will create the highest economic impact in short term. There is a multiple and complex linkage between infrastructure and economic growth, as infrastructure affect production and consumption directly and production and consumption affect the GSDP of the state. Dr V.K.R.V Rao a noted economist says "the link between infrastructure and economic development is not a once for all affair. It is a continuous process and the progress in development has to be preceded, accompanied and followed by progress in infrastructure, if we are to fulfil our declared objectives of generating a self-accelerating process of economic development". The study conducted by Majumder (2004) on infrastructure and regional development in India concluded that there exists a substantial and significant association between levels of development and levels of infrastructure. From the last decade, the government of A.P. is using PPP model extensively for

Table 1: Year-wise GSDP and PPP Projects in A.P.

Year	GSDP at Current Prices 2006-07 (Rs. in cr)	No. of PPP Projects Initiated in A.P.	Cumulative No. of PPP Projects in A.P.	Total Project Cost (Rs. in cr)	Cumulative Project Cost in (Rs. in cr)
Before 1999-2000		3	3	1,246	1,246
1999-00	1,28,797	7	10	6,695	7,941
2000-01	1,44,723	5	15	2,830	10,771
2001-02	4,56,711	14	29	2,291	13,062
2002-03	1,67,096	6	35	2552	15,614
2003-04	1,90,017	2	37	2755	18,369
2004-05	2,11,802	1	38	5,450	23,819
2005-06	2,39,683	6	44	3,919	27,738
2006-07(R)	2,77,286	7	51	3,355	31,093
2007-08(P)	3,26,547	14	65	3,909	35,002
2008-09(Q)	3,77,346	8	73	6,480	41,482
2009-10(A)	4,06,641	14	89	7,678	49,160
2010-11*	Not compiled	15	103	18,739	67,899

Note: R – Revised, P – Provisional, Q – Quick and A – Advanced Estimates.
Source: Compiled from Directorate of Economics & Statistics, A.P. & www.ppp.ap.gov.in

accelerating infrastructural development and there is a positive growth trend in GSDP and number of PPP projects initiated for development of infrastructure in A.P. in Table 1. In the year 1999-2000 the GSDP of A.P. was only Rs 1,28,797 crores which more than tripled to Rs 4,06,641 crores in the year 2009-10 by which A.P. contributes to 8.2% of the nation's GDP (Table 2 & 3). At the same time the PPP projects initiated in A.P also increased drastically from 7 projects in the year 1999 to 99 projects in the year 2010. Trend analysis represented in Graph 3 shows that there is an increasing growth trend in initiating PPP projects for the infrastructural development in A.P which is indirectly facilitating and sustaining the growth of GSDP in the state. Cumulative growth is considered as there is a variation in the number of PPP projects initiated every year and the year in which PPP projects for ports, airport have been initiated show high project costs when compared to other years.

It can be seen from the above Table 2 that the A.P ranks second after Karnataka for undertaking 99 projects through PPP mode and ranks first with reference to investment in PPP projects by investing Rs 67,999 crores for infrastructural development. The state is contributing 8.2% to the nation's GDP and shows an average GSDP growth rate of 12.3% when compared to 11.8% of all the states. States like Karnataka, Maharashtra, Madhya Pradesh, Punjab and Rajasthan are using the PPP model extensively for facilitating infrastructure and also contributed significantly to nation's Gross Domestic Product (GDP) while the north eastern states like Arunachal Pradesh, Mizoram, Nagaland, Manipur, Tripura have not used PPP model at all for development of infrastructure. They also show a marginal contribution to the GDP as seen in Table 2.

The Government of Andhra Pradesh has taken many initiatives to promote PPP projects for development of social and physical infrastructure in the state which have

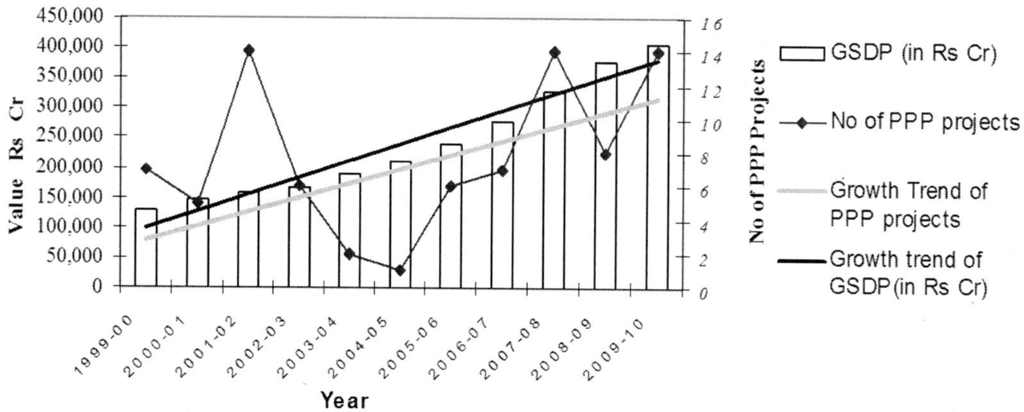

Source: Compiled from Directorate of Economics & Statistics, A.P. & www.ppp.ap.gov.in

Graph 1: Growth Trend of GSDP and PPP projects in A.P.

Table 2: State-wise Distribution of PPP Projects in India and GSDP

Sl. No.	States	No. of PPP Projects/(% of Total Projects in India) (www.pppindia database.com)		Rank	Total PPP Project Costs/(% of Total PPP Project Cost in India) (www.pppindiadat abase.com) Rs. (Cr)		Rank	GSDP as a % of GDP (CMIE as of 2007-08, Current Prices)	Avg. GSPD Growth Rate (%) 2000-01 to 2007-08, Current Prices (CMIE)
1	Andhra Pradesh	99	(13.4%)	2	67,999	(18.4%)	1	8.2	12.3
2	Arunachal Pradesh	0	(0%)	25	0	(0%)	29	0.1	11.7
3	Assam	4	(.54%)	18	391	(0.1%)	23	1.8	10
4	Bihar	6	(.81%)	17	2,095	(0.6%)	17	2.9	10.4
5	Chhattisgarh	4	(.54%)	19	838	(0.2%)	20	2	17.4
6	Delhi	12	(1.62%)	15	11,316	(3.1%)	11	3.6	13.3
7	Goa	2	(0.27%)	22	250	(0.1%)	24	0.44	14.3
8	Gujarat	65	(8.78%)	5	39,668	(10.7%)	4	7.8	15.6
9	Haryana	14	(1.89%)	14	11,163	(3.0%)	12	3.9	14.9
10	Himachal Pradesh	1	(0.14%)	24	475	(0.1%)	22	0.6	7.4
11	Jammu and Kashmir	3	(0.41%)	20	6,320	(1.7%)	15	0.8	9.6
12	Jharkhand	9	(1.2%)	16	1,704	(0.5%)	18	1.8	11.6
13	Karnataka	106	(14.3%)	1	44,664	(12.1%)	2	6	11.9
14	Kerala	18	(2.43%)	12	17,225	(4.7%)	7	4.2	12.5
15	Madhya Pradesh	88	(12%)	3	6,938	(1.9%)	13	3.6	8.8
16	Maharashtra	77	(10.4%)	4	44,136	(11.9%)	3	15	12.9
17	Manipur	0	(0%)	26	0	(0.0%)	28	0.15	9.4
18	Meghalaya	2	(0.27%)	23	762	(0.2%)	21	0.2	11.5
19	Mizoram	0	(0%)	27	0	(0.0%)	27	0.1	9.6
20	Nagaland	0	(0%)	28	0	(0.0%)	26	0.2	9.9
21	Orissa	27	(3.65%)	10	13,348	(3.6%)	9	3	15.5
22	Punjab	34	(4.6%)	8	3,653	(1.0%)	16	3.7	9.9
23	Rajasthan	61	(8.24%)	6	15,027	(4.1%)	8	4.5	11.5
24	Sikkim	24	(3.24%)	11	13,111	(3.5%)	10	0.06	12.4
25	Tamil Nadu	45	(6.08%)	7	18,626	(5.0%)	6	7.7	11
26	Tripura	0	(0%)	29	0	(0.0%)	25	0.3	10.2
27	Uttar Pradesh	18	(1.08%)	13	26,596	(7.2%)	5	8.7	9.6
28	Uttarakhand	3	(0.4%)	21	1,275	(0.3%)	19	0.9	13.7
29	West Bengal	28	(3.8%)	9	6,487	(1.8%)	14	7.8	11.5

Table 3: Sector-wise Report of Infrastructure PPP Projects in India vs. Andhra Pradesh

Sl. No.	Sector	No. of PPP Projects in India		No. of PPP Projects in Andhra Pradesh		% Share of No. of PPP Projects in A.P. with Whole of India	% Share of PPP Projects in A.P. with Whole of India Based on Total Costs
		No. of Projects	Project Cost (Rs in cr)	No. of Projects	Project Cost (Rs. in cr)		
1	Roads and Highways	408	176,418	41	18,041	10	10
2	Ports	56	70,494	7	21,560	13	31
3	Airports	5	19,111	1	2,478	20	13
4	Railways	4	1601	0	0	0	0
5	Power	56	67,248	4	19,080	7	28
6	Urban Infrastructure	136	27,717	13	3,812	10	14
7	Health care	8	1,743	3	1,049	38	60
8	Tourism	50	4,487	24	1,176	48	26
9	Education	17	1,850	6	803	35	43
	Total	740	3,70,399	99	67,999	13	18.4

Source: Compiled from www.pppindiadatabase.com

turned out to be positive and have enabled the state to keep in pace with the target of Eleventh Five Year Plan.

1. A.P is the first state to enact the "Infrastructure Development Enabling Act" (IDEA) which came into effect from August 2001.This act provides guidelines for process for selection of developers, addresses issue of project delivery process, risk sharing, dispute resolution and collection of user charges. It applies to all infrastructure projects implemented in the state.
2. An AP state PPP cell was created in April 2007 under the Department of Finance, Government of Andhra Pradesh as per the MOU signed by the Department of Economic affairs, Ministry of Finance, Government of India for mainstreaming PPP projects at state level. It is a nodal agency for processing all PPP projects in the state. The PPP cell has created a repository of all information relating to PPP's in state, including best practices, guidelines, schemes, and shelf of projects which can be undertaken through PPP route. The cell coordinates with all the government departments and Ministries of state at all stages of Project development and also interacts with PPP cell at central level for proving assistance through Viability Gap Funding. The PPP cell has signed a Memorandum of Understanding (MOU) between Asian Development Bank (ADB), Department of Economic Affairs (DEA) and the State Government to provide advisory technical assistance under ADB Technical Assistance Project.

3. Infrastructure Corporation of Andhra Pradesh (INCAP) was set up in May 2005 as a public limited company under the Department of Infrastructure and Investment, Government of A.P to identify, conceptualize, promote, advice and to create Special Purpose Vehicles (SPV) that will provide impetus to infrastructural projects on PPP mode in the state. Some of the major projects undertaken by INCAP are Development of Krishna Godavari Gas Network in energy sector, Outer Ring Road Project for Hyderabad, Development of Inland Water Ways, all new Airports, development of District Central Library at Visakhapatnam etc. It is designated the role of a developer, advisor, financier and manger to render a full range services from in every phase of project development from inception to completion.
4. Andhra Pradesh Industrial Infrastructure Corporation (APIIC) incorporated in 1973 provides industrial infrastructure through development of industrial areas. It has developed more than 300 industrial parks, food processing zones and Special Economic Zones (SEZs).The first successful PPP project was HITEC City project in 1996 with 89% equity by L&T and 11% by APIIC in shape of land . The Corporation is a principle facilitator in developing mega projects like Visakha Industrial water supply, Gangavaram port, Hyderabad International Convention centre, Pahamlylaram Financial District Hardware Park, etc. The corporation is a nodal agency for government sponsored growth centres, export promotion, industrial parks and integrated infrastructure development centres.
5. "Infrastructure & Investment department" has been created by the GoAP to achieve the development and growth objectives of the State through creation of adequate and 'state-of-the-art' infrastructure facilities in the State. The Department is responsible for facilitation and monitoring of the Project from conceptualization to the last stage in project delivery. For this purpose the department utilizes the services of Andhra Pradesh Invest, Andhra Pradesh Infrastructure Authority (APIA) for facilitating Public Private Partnership (PPP) Projects in infrastructure and INCAP for execution and monitoring of infrastructure projects implemented by it, and also the technical support staff such as Engineering Departments of the respective line departments.
6. AP Urban Finance and Infrastructure Development Corporation (APUFIDC) is a nodal agency for improving urban infrastructure, monitoring reforms in Urban Local Bodies(ULBs) of A.P. under Jawaharlal Nehru Urban Renewal Mission (JNNURM) and provides financial assistance by way of loans and advances, technical or any other assistance and guidance to the Urban Local Bodies, Municipal Corporations, and Urban Development Authorities. JNNURM in A.P has 95ULBs under it and has received sanction for 268 projects costing 12,528 crores out of which 27 infrastructure projects costing Rs 1,143 cr are completed which is a big step in improving the quality of life for citizens in urban A.P.

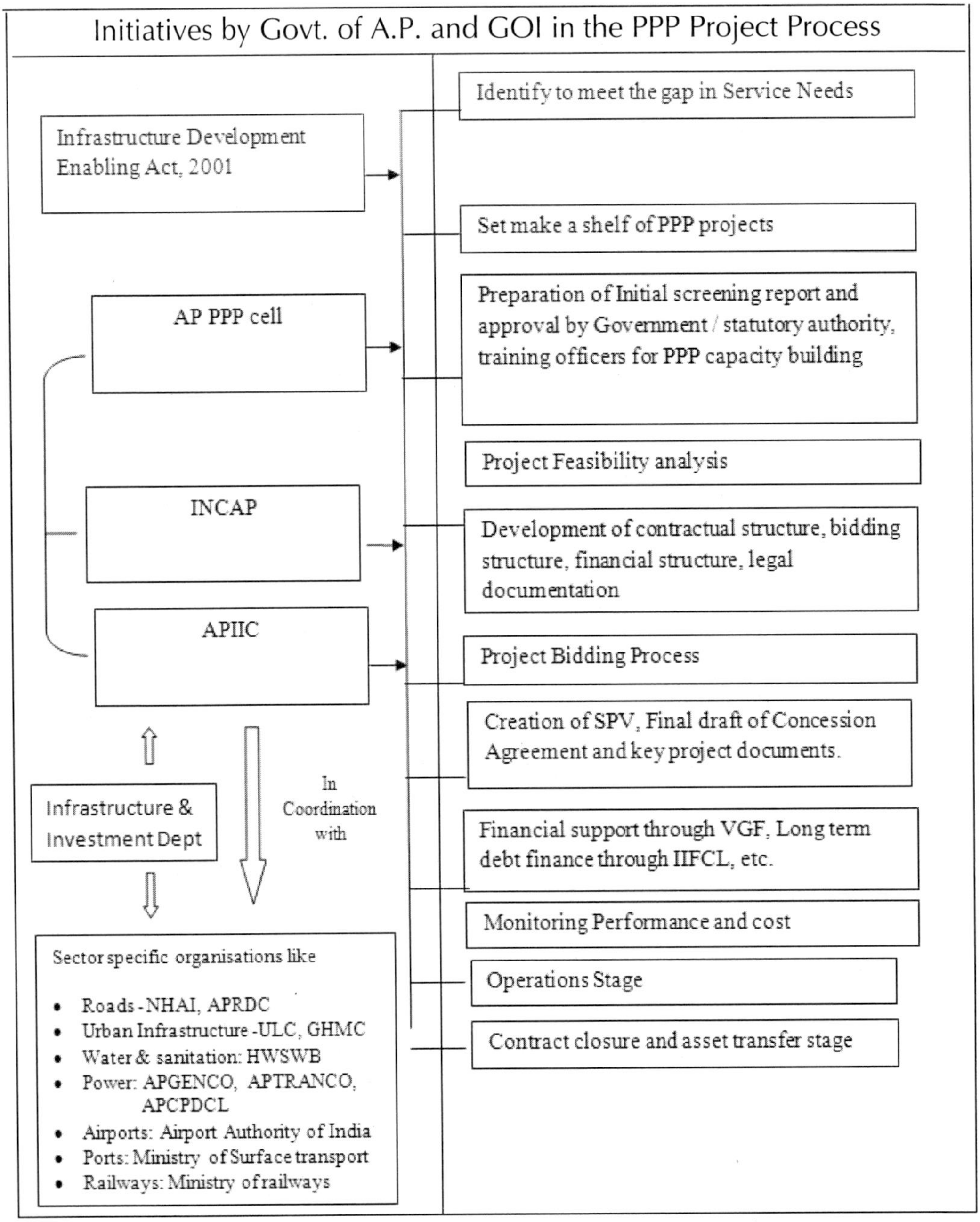

The above chart shows the various steps involved in a PPP process from initiation to implementation and contract closure with the support provided by the nodal agencies like AP PPP cell, APIIC and INCAP, at every step in coordination with the sector specific organisations in all sectors. The PPP cell provides financial and technical support and provides a shelf for projects in various sectors to be undertaken through PPP mode, while INCAP, APIIC coordinate the entire PPP process and help in creating the "Special Purpose Vehicle" (SPV). The entire process of PPP contract is under the guidelines provided by "A.P. Infrastructure Development Enabling Act" (A.P. IDEA). The Infrastructure & Investment Department acts as an intermediary and facilitates implementation of PPP Projects and hands over the project after execution to the respective departments for operation and maintenance. E.g. all port projects in A.P. were implemented by this department, Rajiv Gandhi International Airport project was implemented by Infrastructure and Investment department and later handed over to AAI. (www.ppp.ap.gov.in). APUFIDC monitors ULB's of A.P. for promoting projects for developing urban infrastructure.

MAJOR PPP PROJECTS COMPLETED IN THE STATE

- "Hitech City" is the first major successful PPP project in the State developed in 1996 by Larsen & Toubro (L&T) with 89% equity and APIIC with 11%. The project provides state of the art facilities with a dedicated power supply. More than 100 MNCs are operating from the project. The project provides employment generation to more than 65,000 persons.
- Rajiv Gandhi International Airport, Hyderabad was the first Greenfield Airport in India on PPP model (Build Operate Own transfer mode) initiated in the year 2000 with a consortium formed by owned by GMR infrastructure (63%), Airport Authority of India (13%), Malaysian Airports (11%) and Government of A.P. (13%) with a project cost of Rs 2478 crores. It operations commenced in 2008 and shares 4% of gross revenue annually to GOI and caters up to 12 million passengers per annum.
- Gangavaram Port is the green field sea port established near Visakhapatnam with a project cost of Rs 2000 crores on a Build Own Operate Transfer (BOOT) mode and commenced the operation from August 2008. Its world class multipurpose port to handle ships up to 2,00,000 DWT. It's the deepest port in India with a depth of 21 meters. The port has handled the largest coal vessel to call at Indian ports. Krishnapatnam Port is developed near Nellore on Built Operate Share and Transfer basis (BOST) with a project cost of Rs 1350 crores and commenced the operation from March 2009.
- Visakapatnam Industrial Water Supply Project (VIWSP) is the second successful water sector PPP project in India after Tirupur Integrated Water supply which was started in the year 2003 and opened for operation in December 2004. The project was developed by APIIC and IL&FS.

- Hyderabad International Convention Centre & an Integrated Township project consists of an integrated township, 18-hole international golf course, a convention centre with 6000 seating capacity and a business hotel. The convention center and business hotel commenced operation from 2006. The project is jointly promoted by APIIC Ltd (26%) and EMAAR Properties (76%). Besides equity return, APIIC receives 2% and 3% respectively of Gross Annual Revenue as lease rentals.

The other upcoming important PPP projects under various stages of development in the State are the Hyderbad Metro Rail Project at Hyderabad, part of Outer Ring Road project, Major Bridge across River Godavari at Rajamundry, Development of Greenfield airports at Nellore, Ongole, Tadepalligudem, Kurnool, Kothagudem, Ramagundam and Nizamabad. The support extended by the State Government and the GOI has attracted many private developers to partner with State Government in developing PPP projects in A.P. The major Private players involved in infrastructure projects in A.P. are L&T infrastructure Ltd, GMR Infratech, IVRCL Infrastructure & projects Ltd, Sadbhav Engineering, Ramky Infrastrcutures Ltd, IL&FS, NCC infra, etc.

Chart showing Major PPP projects Milestones and Initiatives by Government of A.P.

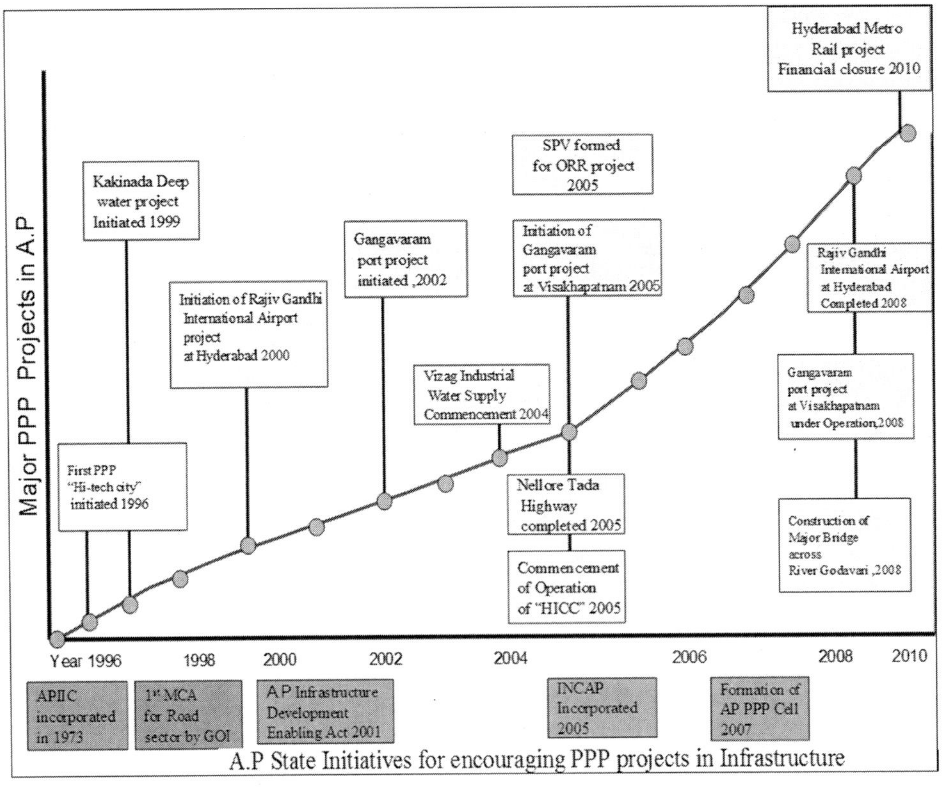

SECTORORAL DISTRIBUTION OF PPP PROJECTS IN A.P.

Table 3 below shows the sectoral distribution of the total projects and the investment made in each sector through PPP in India and in A.P. and it is evident that the pattern of distribution of projects in A.P is similar to the whole of India with some sectors using the model more than the others. A.P. is contributing to 18 percent of the total project investment undertaken on PPP mode in India by investing 67,999 crores and 13 per cent to number of projects undertaken having 99 projects under PPP mode. A.P. is dominating in health care, tourism and education sectors showing that other states in India need to concentrate more in these sectors.

Table 3: Sector-wise Report of Infrastructure PPP Projects in India vs. Andhra Pradesh

Sl. No.	Sector	No. of PPP Projects in India		No. of PPP Projects in Andhra Pradesh		% Share of No. of PPP Projects in A.P. with Whole of India	% Share of PPP Projects in A.P. with Whole of India Based on Total Costs
		No. of Projects	Project Cost (Rs in cr)	No. of Projects	Project Cost (Rs. in cr)		
1	Roads and Highways	408	176,418	41	18,041	10	10
2	Ports	56	70,494	7	21,560	13	31
3	Airports	5	19,111	1	2,478	20	13
4	Railways	4	1601	0	0	0	0
5	Power	56	67,248	4	19,080	7	28
6	Urban Infrastructure	136	27,717	13	3,812	10	14
7	Health care	8	1,743	3	1,049	38	60
8	Tourism	50	4,487	24	1,176	48	26
9	Education	17	1,850	6	803	35	43
	Total	740	3,70,399	99	67,999	13	18.4

Source: Compiled from www.pppindiadatabase.com

In A.P. the road sector has been leading with number of projects on PPP mode having 45 projects costing 18,041 crores because of the average size of the projects whereas the port sector is leading in investment made having 7 projects costing 21,560 crores due to much larger size of the projects. Power sector has 4 projects costing 19,080 crores followed by 13 projects in urban infrastructure costing 2,478 crores, 24 projects in tourism costing 1,176 crores and 6 projects in education costing 803 crores showcasing a need for railways, urban infrastructure, health care and education sectors to concentrate more.

ISSUES INVOLVED IN USING PPP FOR DEVELOPMENT IN A.P.

An analysis of investment in infrastructure through PPP mode on all India basis shows that the share of A.P is still low except in some sectors like roads, ports, tourism and education (Table 3).

1. Though A. P has developed a cross -sectoral enabling legislation and dedicated agencies for promoting PPP but there is insufficient skilled staff who could harness and publicize the potential of business opportunity for PPP's in different sectors and look into the structuring of individual customised PPP's contracts.
2. Very small projects in urban infrastructure are developed through PPP mode having and 13 projects costing 3,112 crores. There is a need to undertake complex PPP projects and the Urban local Bodies (ULB's) in A.P. do not have desired legal framework, policies and procedures to make them more flexible and respond to the needs and priorities for initiation of PPP clientele in sectors like solid waste management, health and education.
3. In urban infrastructure, potential use of PPP's in water and sanitation still remain untapped though there is a huge service delivery gap with only 65% of the population having access to tapped water and only 33% having access to sewerage (Chary S., ASCI). The main reason is public resistance to pay higher user charges backed by political support. The other issues are organizational capacities, legal framework, processes and institutions involved and lack of experienced private developers in this sector. Education and Health sector also have the same issues.
4. Delay in the approval process, unfavourable legal and regulatory environment causing slow progress in PPP development (ADB report 2006). Roads being the most dominant sector in PPP, the projects are delayed due to land acquisition and environmental clearances by the government and handing it over to the private developer. The part of the Outer Ring Road Project was to be completed by 2010 but was delayed to land acquisition problem.
5. Unstable political climate is one a major concern for private stakeholders to take up long term complex projects.

CONCLUSION

Differences in projects and their institutional environment make each project unique in certain ways and this needs to be considered when structuring a PPP agreement and critical success factors need to be identified for refining new PPP contracts. There is also a need for full documentation of completed projects, best practices, documenting successful and failure projects in form of case studies to facilitate sharing of experiences. The PPP cell needs to strengthen further and act as a "one-stop" for investors and a nodal point for facilitating and coordinating among different ministries, tiers of government and private stake holders to encourage more private developers to participate in the PPP projects. The nodal agencies should have very clear delineation and balance project roles, responsibilities, and risks among the PPP partners to commensurate with their potential returns based on the infrastructure sectors. Regional workshops conducted by Asian development bank in A.P. have highlighted awareness and capacity issues in the different departments to handle PPP projects. Asian Development Bank (ADB) evaluation study (2009) on PPP in infrastructure development suggested that the respective costs and benefits associated with traditional public sector procurement and the use of PPP modalities have to be clearly established through public comparator analysis and value for money analysis so that the users are not heavily burdened to pay. It also mentioned that support for PPP project development will be crucial for success of future programs.

The study concludes that though there are some issues to be addressed, still A.P. is one of the leading state for promoting PPP projects in infrastructure. With its proactive policies and improving infrastructure, it has ensured a good investment climate to the investors there by creating a positive growth trend in GSDP of A.P. PPP has proved an effective method for infrastructural development in A.P and an effective model on which other states in India can develop their infrastructure an equally swift pace.

REFERENCES

[1] Aziz, A.M.A. (2007). "Successful delivery of public-private partnerships for infrastructure development", *Journal of Construction Engineering and Management*, pp. 133, 918.

[2] Chary, Srinivas, "Public Private Partnerships in Urban Infrastructure ad Service Delivery", PPT prepared for training program for IAS officers, ASCI, Hyderabad, 8th August 2010.

[3] Economic Survey of India 2005-2006, pp. 132-153.

[4] Garvin, M.J. and Bosso, D. (2008). "Assessing the Effectiveness of Infrastructure Public—Private Partnership Programs and Projects", *Public Works Management & Policy*, 13(2), 162.

[5] Kumaraswamy, M.M. and Zhang, X.Q. (2001). "Governmental role in BOT-led infrastructure development", *International Journal of Project Management*, 19(4), pp. 195-205.

[6] Kaur Gunjeet, L. Lakshmanan (2010). "Infrastructure financing – Global pattern and the Indian experience", Dept. of Economic Analysis & Policy, SS(DEAP): 4/2010 available at www. Infrastructure Financing- Global Pattern and the Indian Experience-RBI.Pdf

[7] Garmendia, Estache, Shafik, "Infrastructure services in developing countries: Access, Quality, Costs and Policy reform", World Bank Policy Research Working Paper 3468, December 2004.

[8] Kumar Birendra, "Innovative instruments needed to spruce up infrastructure financing", available at http://www.financialexpress.com/old/fe/daily/20000101/

[9] Kumar, Rajiv, Palit, Amitendu and Singh, Karan (2007). "Sustainability of Economic Growth in India", CIGI Working Paper No 25. Available at SSRN: http:// ssrn.com/abstract=990082

[10] Li, B., Akintoye, A., Edwards, P. J. and Hardcastle, C. (2005b). Critical success factors for PPP/PFI projects in the UK construction industry, *Construction Management and Economics* 23: 459–471. doi:10.1080/01446190500041537

[11] Li, J.H. and Li, Q.M. (2007). Financial risk assessment of Chinese PPP projects in urban rail transit: Case study of the 4th Beijing Metro Line, *Construction Economy* (10): 23–26.

[12] Mor, Nachiket and Sehrawat, Sanjeev (2006). "Sources of Infrastructure Finance", IFMR Working Paper Series, October 2006.

[13] Prudhomme, R., *Infrastructure and Development*, Washington DC, Paper prepared for the ABCDE (Annual Bank Conference on Development Economics), May 3-5, 2004.

[14] World Development Report 1994, *Infrastructure for Development*, Oxford University Press, New York, p. 2.

[15] World Bank Report (2006). "India: Building Capacities for Public Private Partnerships", South Asia Region, Energy and Infrastructure Unit and Finance and Private Sector development Unit, Washington DC.

[16] World Bank, "Andhra Pradesh: Agenda for Economic Reforms", Report no. 15901-IN, World Bank, Washington, DC, USA.

Websites Used

[1] http://adb.org/documents/reports/consultants/39659-ind-tacr.pdf

[2] http://www.aponline.gov.in/apportal/index.asp

[3] http://www.aprdc.in

[4] http://www.apidc.org/

[5] http://www.apind.gov.in/apstatebrochure.pdf

[6] http://www. businessweek.com /magazine/content/07_12/b4026001.htm

[7] http://www.ercap.org/
[8] http://www.india.gov.in/
[9] http://www.infrastructure.gov.in/
[10] http://www.ibef.org/
[11] http://www.incap.co.in
[12] http://www. indiainfrastructure.com
[13] http://morth.nic.in
[14] http://www.moneycontrol.com/competition/ivrclinfrastructural projects/comparison/IVR
[15] http://www.nhai.org
[16] http://www.ppp.ap.gov.in
[17] http://www.pppindia.com
[18] http://www.pppindiadatabase.com/
[19] http://www.planningcommission.nic.in/aboutus/speech/spemsa/msa009.doc
[20] http://www.pppinindia.com/pdf/state_ppp_initiatieves_compendium.pdf
[21] http://psiru.org/reports/2008-11
[22] http://www.worldbank.org/ppi
[23] http://unpan1.un.org/ intradoc/groups/public/documents/

Risk Rating of Infrastructure Projects by Indian Banks: A Conceptual Framework

Vikas Srivastava
National Institute of Bank Management, Pune
E-mail: vikass@nibmindia.org

ABSTRACT

The gross credit to infrastructure sector from the commercial banks in India has grown 59% year on year in 2011. Indian bankers are on a learning curve as far as financing of infrastructure projects is concerned. For that matter, the project promoters, policy makers and regulators are not better off. Most of this new investment is structured as project financing which differs from traditional corporate finance, both in structure as well as financing mechanism. The lack of understanding of project finance and the contractual structure involved lowers the confidence level of lenders, which in turn may be contributing to impeding the growth of infrastructure. Most of these projects are rated as BBB or lower by the banks internal rating models thereby increasing the cost of the funds for the project developers. This lacuna requires a fresh look at the way projects are being appraised and rated by the bankers. It is apparent that the standard appraisal and rating formats employed in traditional corporate financing – primarily based on the strength of the promoter, financial viability and the security safeguards – is not able to capture the entire complexities involved in financing infrastructure projects. The present research therefore lays down a conceptual framework for project assessment and risk measurement, which the Indian banking industry can use while determining the viability and bankability of projects.

INTRODUCTION

Infrastructure is an umbrella term for the manifold activities referred to as "social overhead capital" by economists like Paul Rosenstein-Rodan, Ragan Nurkse and Albert Hirschman. The India Infrastructure Report, 1996, defined infrastructure as: "*the physical framework of facilities through which goods and services are provided to the public.*" Infrastructure's linkage to the economy is multiple and complex because it directly affects production and consumption, creates negative and positive spill-over effects (externalities) and involves large flow of expenditure. The Reserve Bank of India (RBI) in its Circular dated November 30, 2007 (DBOD No. BP.BC.52/21.04.048/2007-08), defined Infrastructure as: "Developing or developing and operating or developing, operating and maintaining an infrastructure facility in Energy, Logistics and Transportation, Telecom, Urban and Industrial Infrastructure, Agro Processing, Construction for storage of Agro Products, Schools and Hospitals, Pipelines for Oil, Petroleum and Gas, Water and Sanitation." This definition includes both physical and social infrastructure services.

INVESTMENT REQUIREMENTS IN INFRASTRUCTURE SECTOR

The eleventh five year plan envisages stepping up of the gross capital formation in infrastructure from 5% of GDP in 2006-07 to 9% of GDP by end of the plan period in 2011-12, which could be critical for achieving 9% growth. It has estimated an investment requirement of Rs 20,56,151 crores (Table 1) in infrastructure, around 30% of which is expected to be financed by the private sector.

Table 1: Infrastructure Investment in the Eleventh Five Year Plan

Sectors	Rs. Crores	Sectoral Share
Electricity (including NCE)	666, 525	32.4%
Roads and Bridges	314,152	15.3%
Telecom	258,439	12.6%
Railways (incl. MRTS)	261,808	12.7%
Irrigation (incl. water shed)	253,301	12.3%
Water supply and sanitation	143,730	7.0%
Ports	87,995	4.3%
Airports	30,968	1.5%
Storage	22,378	1.1%
Gas	16855	0.8%
Total	20,56,151	100%

In the light of budgetary constraints and constraints faced by fund providers to infrastructure both Equity (Sources: Domestic Developers, Infrastructure focused companies, equipment and operations/maintenance suppliers, Export credit agencies, Multilateral agencies, private equity and infrastructure funds etc) and Debt (Sources: Bank loans, Capital market bonds, international banks, pension and Insurance funds, external commercial borrowings etc), the financing gap is quite huge. It has been pointed out that the debt financing gap can be as high as Rs 1,62,496 crores (Table 2). Government has recognized private sector as a means of meeting the financing requirements for infrastructure development. The conditions for participation of private sector are, in most cases, different from those of the traditional financiers.

Table 2: Likely Sources of Debt and Gap

Item	Total XI th Plan (Rs. Crores)
Domestic Bank Credit	423, 691
Non Bank Finance Companies	224,171
Pension/Insurance Companies	55,414
External Commercial Borrowings	122,263
Likely Total Debt Resources	825, 539
Estimated Requirements of Debt	988, 035
Gap between Requirements and Likely Debt Resources	162,496

Source: Eleventh Five Year Plan document, Planning commission.

In the light of heavy requirements of funds, managerial constraints in the public sector, technology making it feasible to unbundle infrastructure development and financing, globalization and presence of international financial markets which present greater risk sharing and new instruments to fund infrastructure, the Government has identified that the way forward to develop infrastructure is through Public Private Partnerships (PPP).

PPP's refer to the long-term, contractual partnerships between the public and private sector agencies, specifically targeted towards financing, designing, implementing, and operating infrastructure facilities and services that were traditionally provided by the public sector. These collaborative ventures are built around the expertise and capacity of the project partners based on a contractual agreement which ensures appropriate and mutually agreed allocation of resources, risks and returns. During the last ten years, infrastructure was being developed through increasing investments by the private sector on a commercial basis under the "private ownership and operation" approach. Under this option, the private entity not only operates the infrastructure, but also owns the allied assets. The various approaches can assume any of the following arrangements, the most important among them being: Build Operate Transfer (BOT); Build Own Operate (BOO); Build Own Operate Transfer (BOOT); Build Operate Lease Transfer (BOLT), Management Contract (MC) and Service Contract (MC).

Due to the necessity of private sector participation, the need for incurring heavy institutional debt and in order to provide conducive environment for infrastructure funding and sustaining the growth momentum, the Reserve Bank has put in place several mechanisms to steer the fund flow from banking sector towards infrastructure and accordingly issued specific guidelines from time to time.

IDENTIFICATION OF PROBLEM

The banking sector has been showing a CAGR of almost 30% year on year growth in lending to infrastructure and infrastructure has almost a 33% share in industrial credit by banks. The deployment of gross bank credit to Infrastructure stands at Rs 3,52,360 crores. (Handbook of Statistics on Indian Economy, RBI)

This leads to an unhealthy asset liability mismatch. In addition, the combination of high capital costs and low operating costs of infrastructure projects implies that initial financing costs constitute a very large proportion of the total cost. Infrastructure project financing entails a complex and varied mix of financial and contractual arrangements between multiple parties. Apart from this, regulatory uncertainty increases the risk profile of infrastructure projects.

This requires a fresh look at the way projects are being funded either by Traditional on Balance sheet funding or by Project Financing and the advantages and disadvantages thereof.

Indian banks and project developers generally follow project finance technique which is based on "no recourse or partial recourse" method, whereby the security structure involves a large number of contracts and agreements rather than tangible collaterals. Also for appraisal, the issues involved in each sector are significantly different from sector to sector, except for promoter evaluation, so each project and sector is unique. Each sub-sector of the infrastructure is inherently unique in terms of its administrative and organizational structure, the regulatory framework governing its operations, the level of technology, and the degree of commercialization. It can be inferred that if banks are using the same credit rating model across sectors, it will lead to inappropriate assessment of risk rating and inappropriate pricing decision.

For project appraisal, the issues involved in each sector are significantly different, and, the existing rating models used by banks to measure various elements of risk are not able to capture the sector-specific issues and the effect of legal and contractual framework. Some factors in rating model are qualitative and leave scope for managerial discretion, and, therefore, a unique loan pricing cannot be arrived at. Therefore, it is suggested that for infrastructure project appraisal, as each project and each sector are unique for rating, probability distribution method for measurement of risk may be used. Accordingly, critical risk factors for each sector may be identified. This will lead to a unique rating for the project, and, if this is higher than hurdle-risk rating, the project may be financed by the bank. A project appraisal framework is also suggested which will directly correspond to risk measurement. In this section a heuristic or judgmental rating framework is suggested for measurement of risk which corresponds to project appraisal as well.

LITERATURE REVIEW

Lending institutions take four types of major credit decisions: (i) Sanction or extension of existing credit limits, (ii) Liquidation, (iii) Foreclosure and (iv) Renegotiation. In all these decisions, the central task is to anticipate failure or success of a borrowing entity, because the prospect of recovery of the loan is itself tied to the business fortunes of the borrower. In taking these decisions, banks and financial institutions carry out an extended credit appraisal exercise using both qualitative and quantitative information about the borrowing firm and its business environment. Finally, when all factors are weighed, the actual decision is made on the basis of judgment. Most bankers maintain that the loan granting is a judgmental call. Currently, there is evidence of an increasing interest among lenders in the analytical or quantitative tools that can help them take lending decisions more professionally. The use of quantitative or analytical methods provides demonstrative evidence of exercise of diligence in sanctioning loans. Need for such evidence is felt acutely by executives haunted by anxiety of staff accountability. Banks hope to crank up their lending functions – now showing signs of paralysis – back to life, by using reliable analytical tools. For a summary of the ideas of this school of management thought, Roy Rowan's *The Intuitive Manager* is referred to.

The quantitative support systems based on discriminant analysis are finding popular use in credit decisions. Multiple Discriminant Models are a result of empirical studies which aim at identifying attributes of business firms that can predict their failure or success. In other words, these models skim and scan over the borrowing entity and identify surface characteristics, on the basis of which they attempt to forecast how firms will fare. A summary of discriminant analysis made in the last three decades is available in a paper by V. Nirmala and others (1995). A scrutiny of past research shows that these models were developed specifically for banks and were employed only for credit decision making of larger magnitudes. The authors differentiated their approaches by choosing different sample sizes and population group of firms, applying different definitions of failures and non-failures (bankruptcy, loan default, etc.). There are basically two main discriminant methods – Univariate and Multivariate.

Project finance lending is often viewed more risky than corporate finance lending. The premise for this view is that the ability of a single asset to generate cash is less certain than a corporation's ability to generate cash from a presumably diversified base of assets, customers and revenue streams. Furthermore, Greenfield projects are viewed as equivalent to start ups with no operating history and significant construction risks (Dymond, 2003). The best quantitative data on project finance default and recovery rates come from the recent response to the Basel Committee's proposed new risk for project financing (Esty, 2002). Four leading project finance banks provided loan data to Standard and Poor's Risk solutions to analyse the historical probability of default (PD) and Loss Given Default (LGD) for their aggregate loan set Combined. These banks represent 24 per cent of the global project finance market. The results of the study are striking. The 10-year cumulative default probability for project finance loan was calculated to be 7.5 per cent – a rate equivalent to BBB+, rated as corporate unsecured loans.

Recovery rates are even more striking: the mean LGD was 25per cent and the median was 100 per cent. In other words, once a project finance transaction has defaulted, the average outcome for the lenders is a recovery rate of 75per cent of the exposure, and the most frequent outcome is a 100 per cent recovery of loan value. These recovery rates exceed recovery rates for secured and unsecured corporate loans with equivalent default probabilities. Most of these data are publicly unavailable.

There may be numerous causes of default in the case of a infrastructure loans which may fall into the following categories: Failure to complete construction, Poor technical operating performance of the asset, Non-payment by the off-taker or other contractual counterparty delinquency, Decline in market price of output and so on. Optimization of the infrastructure asset may be a solution (Patten, Hahn, 2003).

However, in the infrastructure finance, little work is done as far as measurement of credit risk is concerned. In the global context, Development of Basel II Conforming Model was developed by Jorg Orgeldinger (*Basel II and Project Finance*, Winter 2006). Standards and Poor's use a framework of analysis that extends well beyond traditional approach of rating projects in the power sector (Standard and Poor's, 2001). Fitch applies project finance ratings to different types of projects including telecommunications, power projects, toll-roads, mines and pipelines. He divided the risk into several components: sponsors, pre-completion, operation, off-take, structural, etc.(Fitch, 2001). The World Bank has developed the software – INFRISK – for the rating of project risk (Dailami *et al.*, 2002).

However, in the Indian context, except for some articles, not much research work has been done particularly with regard to measurement of risk. However, there is enough literature available on the need for investment in infrastructure.

RATIONALE FOR PROPOSED RATING FRAMEWORK

If credit can be defined as "nothing but the expectation of a sum of money within some limited time", then credit risk is "the chance that expectation will not be met".

The definition of default employed in Basel II, is based on two sets of conditions: first that "the bank must consider that the obligor is unlikely to pay in full" and second that "the obligor's past due is more than 90 days on any material credit obligation." The former is a subjective condition and the latter is an objective condition where the number of days past due that triggers default is 90 days and the minimum past due threshold amount is the level of materiality fixed by the bank. In the case of infrastructure projects, number of days past declared commencement of operations date that triggers a default is two years. Now it is extended to two plus two years in the case of legal default and two plus one year in case of issues beyond the control of sponsor.

Depending on the credit risk that a particular project faces, the bank has to make provision for capital against it. *Expected Credit Risk Loss (EL)* is intended to make provision for reserve requirements against doubtful accounts, calculation of PLR (default premium), pricing credit-risky instruments (bonds and exotic options), and for calculation of risk adjusted profitability (e.g. RAROC).The bank can also suffer far more than the expected losses, say, during economic downturns. These losses are called *Unexpected Losses (UL)* or uncertain losses. Strong capital base is required to absorb the unexpected losses (UL) as and when they arise.

Figure 1 indicates that capital base should keep on increasing in tandem with the increase in the amount of risk.

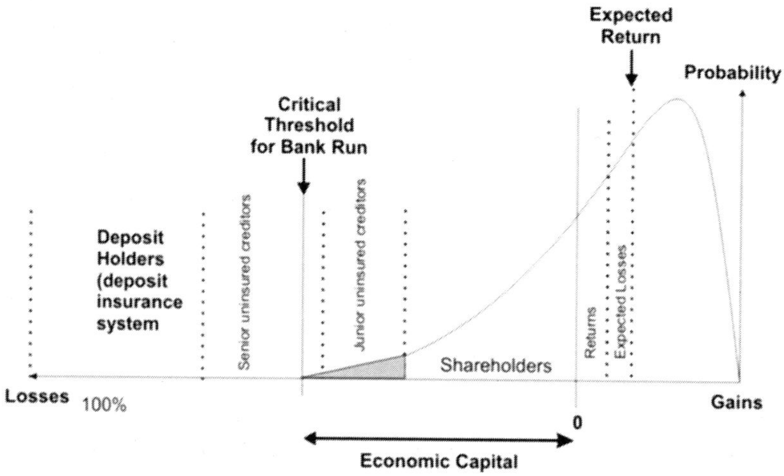

Fig. 1: Risk Return Framework for Bank Capital

Credit ratings represent a 'considered opinion' of the inherent credit quality of a company and/or credit instrument and act as a summary of diverse risk factors to indicate the default probability of the borrower. The capital provisioning has to be done in direct relation to the overall risk rating of the credit portfolio. With the advent of Basel II, the capital requirements have increased manifold as shown in the Table 3.

The percentage change in capital requirements is the maximum in the case of project loans. Moreover, bankers being conditioned by decades of security-backed lending practices, the rates applied by them to infrastructure loans would be higher on account of their incomplete understanding of legal and contractual structure of project financing. This would in turn require higher capital provisioning (for these loans) which would increase the pricing, thereby making it costly for project developers. In the final analysis it will have a direct impact on the viability of many of the projects.

As Indian commercial banks start appreciating the need for a structured credit risk management framework, it is imperative for them to incorporate some mechanism that

Table 3: Impact of Basel II on Banking Industry Capital

Asset Class	Percentage of Total Capital under Capital Requirements	Percentage Change in Required Capital by Asset Class	Change in Capital as Percentage of Current Total Capital Required for All Assets
Corporate	61	22	14
Sovereign	1	238	3
Inter bank	8	49	4
Retail	24	(28)	(7)
Securitization	1	108	1
Equity	3	(17)	0
Project Finance	2	22	0
Total	100%		
Total Increase in capital			**14%**

Source: 'Results of the Second Quantitative Study', Basel Committee on Banking Supervision, November 5, 2001, p. 5.

will comprehensively and objectively capture and evaluate realistically the credit worthiness of infrastructure project developers in the perspective of changing scenario.

CONCEPTUAL BACKGROUND FOR PROPOSED RATING FRAMEWORK

Heuristic Models

Heuristic models being judgmental, these help in problem solving, which in turn lead to learning and discovery. These methods in most cases employ experimentation and trial and error techniques. A heuristic method is especially used to rapidly come to a solution that is reasonably close to the best possible answer, or 'optimal solution'. Heuristics are "rules of thumb", educated guesses, intuitive judgments or simply *common sense.* In more precise terms, heuristics stand for strategies using readily accessible, though loosely applicable, information to control *problem solving* in human beings and machines. There are four essential categories for heuristic models:

1. Classic rating questionnaire
2. Qualitative systems
3. Expert systems
4. Fuzzy Logic systems

While heuristic or judgmental credit assessment models rely on subjective experience of credit experts, statistical models attempt to verify hypothesis using statistical procedures on an empirical database.

Statistical Models

For credit assessment procedures, this involves formulating hypothesis concerning potential credit worthiness criteria. The hypothesis may consist of statements as to whether higher or lower values can be expected on an average for solvent borrowers compared to insolvent borrowers. As the solvency status of each borrower is known from the empirical data set, this hypothesis can be verified or rejected. The categories of statistical models which were identified in literature review are : Discriminant Analysis, Regression Analysis, Artificial Neural Network, Causal Model, Option Pricing Model and Cash Flow Simulation Model.

The goodness of fit of any statistical model thus depends heavily on the quality of empirical data set used in its development. The first data set should be large and relevant. As data is limited in case of infrastructure projects, as most of the projects have not reached the termination or completion date for concession agreement, statistical models were not used.

Minimum Qualifying Criteria for a Rating System

A rating system must meet the following criteria:

- *Target value Probability of Deault (PD)*: It must be possible to represent the rating result as a default probability.
- *Completeness:* The rating result should take into account all available information relevant to credit worthiness.
- *Less subjectivity:* The rating results should be reproduced by various subjects, i.e. using the same information; different analysts should come to the same rating scale.
- *Acceptance*: In the eyes of the user the rating model should assess the borrower's credit worthiness accurately.
- *Consistency:* The rating model must not contradict the accepted theories and models.

SUGGESTED RATING FRAMEWORK

It is suggested that the credit rating officer at the branch/corporate credit department initiate the rating exercise. It is imperative that the industry rating be obtained from the economic cell, which should also specify critical contracts and regulations for a particular sector as well as sector-specific benchmarks so as to avoid perpetuating the errors. The credit officer must then input the data on company's financial, management, business and payment records in the rating model. The rating should then be forwarded to the risk management department.

The suggested framework can be used for this purpose. The process of credit risk measurement of this model can be explained by breaking down the process into the following four steps:

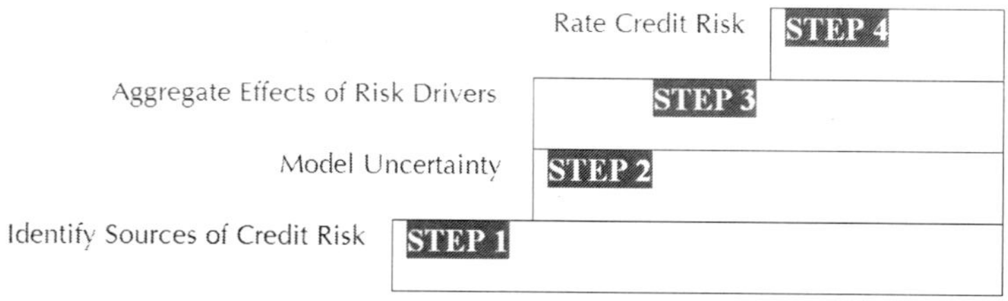

IDENTIFYING SOURCES OF RISK

When a loan proposal is analysed for profitability, the risk factors are identified as above. The above-mentioned factors are the sources of uncertainty and they are termed as "Risk Drivers".

For the purpose of systematic analysis, all the possible risk factors have been identified for the two sectors, that is road and power, in this research. This identification, definition and classification of the risk drivers are termed as Formation of the Risk Matrix. This is explained in detail in Figure 2.

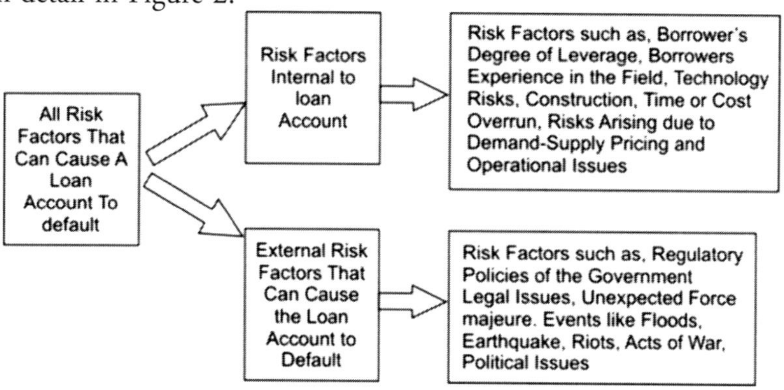

Fig. 2: Formation of Risk Matrix-identification and Classification of Risk Drivers

IDENTIFICATION OF RISKS

The risks, which can have an impact on the credit quality of the project, are termed as "risk drivers". Through descriptive research and survey method, risks are identified. It can be said that the 'Sources of Risk' give birth to the 'Risk Drivers' which disrupt the cash flow of the project. Risk drivers can lead to default which can be classified into four distinct areas as follows:

Table 4: Levels of Risk Drivers

Sr. No.	Risk Driver	Description
1.	**Project Level Risks** (a) Contractual (including Construction, operations, supply and offtake contracts) and Management Foundation (b) Technology, Construction and Operations (c) Competitive and Demand risk (d) Legal Structure (e) Financial Strength	Project level risks are the risks intrinsic to the project's business and the industry in which it operates
2.	**Force Majeure – Political risk**	Political risk arises out of government's intervention in the project operations like expropriation, regulatory controls, etc.
3.	**Force Majeure – Non-Political Risk**	Floods and earthquakes, civil disturbances, strikes, catastrophic mechanical failures, etc., which can disrupt a project's cash flow
4.	**Regulatory Risk**	Regulatory risk arises due to legal systems, lack of corporate governance, etc.
5.	**Market Risk**	Demand Risk, Forex Risk, Interest Rate Risk, Political Risk, Demand Risk, etc.

RISK MANAGEMENT AND MITIGATION THROUGH ALLOCATION

The risk management strategy should be effective (should command optimal behavior from deal participants) and efficient (reduce the cost of funding). So one must allocate risk to a party that controls the risk or has the greatest impact on its outcome (effectiveness). For example construction risk can be allocated to EPC contractor through a fixed price turnkey contract along with profit sharing (equity participation) to induce optimal behavior

Also, when possible and cost effective to do so, one must write a detailed contract specifying actions quality and performance. Contracts work best when risks are predictable, verifiable and contracts enforceable. However, when not all risks are predictable, verifiable or enforceable, sponsors have to depend on indirect allocation through residual risk bearing through residual profit sharing (equity). Also risks should be allocated to a party that can bear it at the least cost. (Efficiency). In case of dealing with the Government , one must write a contract with the Government and when negotiation, contracting and other transaction costs make complete contracting unfeasible, we can use residual risk and return to realign incentives and induce optimal behaviour.

Exchange rate and Interest rate risks can be marketable risks as there are derivative instruments like currency swaps, interest rate swaps etc to hedge them. And lastly as a banker one should remember that to the extent possible, debt should bear more downside risks and equity should bear more upside risks (symmetric risks).

So in a nutshell, after the identification of the risks, default risk has to be reduced by credit enhancements like guarantees, insurance, etc., so that the project's credit risk gets reduced. Various agreements like those of financing, construction, sales or off-take, suppliers and insurance are used.

MODELING FOR UNCERTAINTY

Credit Risk Modeling is the process of representing the effect of various risk drivers, which give rise to uncertainty in the credit worthiness of a loan proposal. Uncertainty lies in the borrower's cash flow that could be used for servicing the loan but could undergo deviations from the expected or projected cash flows due to the effect of risk drivers.

The effect of risk drivers can be represented using Probability Distributions. These are useful tools in depicting how the risk drivers cause the projected cash flows that have to be used for servicing the loan to deviate from projections. Let us consider a risk driver like demand for toll-road or traffic. In this example, due to competition, the demand for the toll-road is not up to the projected level. Say, the projected toll revenue is Rs. 20 lakhs for the first year. Due to the element of uncertainty caused by competition, there is a 25 per cent possibility that revenue will be only 90 per cent of the projection, i.e. Rs. 18 lakhs; there is a 15 per cent possibility that sales will be only Rs. 17 million (85%) and so on. Now with the help of above data, we plot the deviation from expectation (Impact of Risk Driver) along the X-axis and the likelihood of the deviation along the Y-axis to get a smooth continuous curve that is the Probability Distribution. This Probability Distribution is the model for uncertainty caused by this risk driver.

AGGREGATING THE EFFECT OF RISK DRIVERS

This credit risk measurement framework proposes the measurement of risk factors contributing to credit risk by analyzing them along three dimensions (Dailami, Mansoor *et al.*, 1999):

- *Dimension 1*: The Effect Dimension (impact of a risk factor)
- *Dimension 2*: The Uncertainty Dimension (likelihood of the risk factor happening)
- *Dimension 3*: The Risk Concentration Dimension

Credit risk will be calculated as the products of Effect, Uncertainty and Risk Concentration.

Dimension 1: The Effect Dimension (Impact of Risk Driver)

The impact of the risk driver is the extent of the deviation that the risk driver can cause on the cash flows, for instance, market risk, where the toll collections by the borrower are not upto expectations. Now, the extent of deviations in projected cash flows due to the happening of the risk driver has to be determined. For this purpose deviations can be classified as follows:

(a) Unacceptable level of Deviation (above 75% deviation)
(b) Very High level of Deviation (50%–75% deviation)
(c) High level of Deviation (25%–50% deviation)
(d) Marginal level of Deviation (10%–25% deviation)
(e) Low level of Deviation (less than 10% deviation)

Historical precedents, if not available, experts' opinions, are used for determining the most likely extent of deviation possible. Now, using the estimates of the most likely extent of deviation and percentage chance that the deviation will not cross the most likely deviation, a probability distribution is plotted.

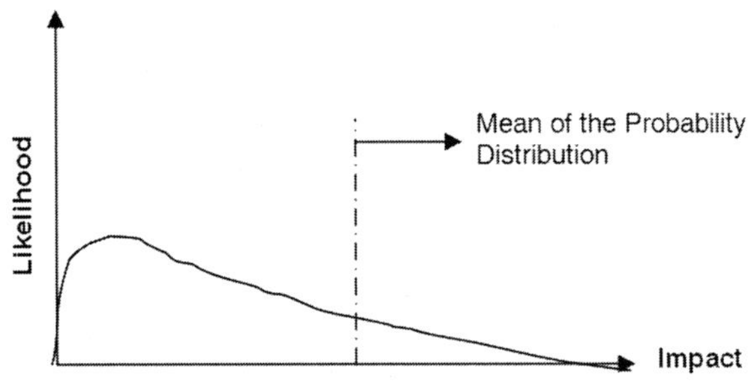

Fig. 3: Probability Distribution Curve

The mean of the probability distribution gives the effect of dimension or impact of the risk driver. Thus, for each of the risk factors, the corresponding probability distribution and the impact are identified. This dimension is considered as fixed for all loans given to a particular sector, since within the same sector the impact of risk drivers is almost similar. So, for instance all the infrastructure loans in the road sector will be assessed using the same set of values for this dimension effect.

Dimension 2: Uncertainty Dimension (Likelihood of Risk Driver Happening)

The likelihood of a particular risk factor happening varies for each of the loan proposals according to its inherent characteristics. The banker, based on the Risk Defining Score card given in the Table 2, can assign the likelihood score.

Table 4: Defining Risk Score

Risk Level	Score
Almost Certain Risk Factor	5, 4.5 or 4
Quite Likely Risk Factor	3.5, 3, or 2.5
Possible Risk Factor	2, 1.5 or 1
Highly Unlikely Risk Factor	0.5 or 0

Importance of Risk Mitigants

The Risk Mitigants which are used for reducing the risk level due to each of the risk drivers are taken care of as follows:

Table 5: Risk Mitigation Score

Risk Mitigation	Score
High Level of Mitigation	–5, –4.5 or –4
Medium Level Mitigation	–4, –3.5, –2.5 or –2
Low Level of Mitigation	–1.5, –1, –.5 or 0

Net Likelihood Score = Risk Level Score + Risk Mitigation Score

Dimension 3: Risk Concentration Dimension

Dimensions 1 and 2 can help to prioritize identified risks by estimating probability and impacts, exposing the most significant risks; but this deals with risks one at a time and does not consider possible patterns of risk exposure, and also does not provide an overall understanding of the risk faced by the loan proposal as a whole. This task of aggregating the effects of all risk drivers is performed by the third dimension. The measure of this dimension is the relative importance or concentration of each risk driver among all possible risk drivers.

The process of finding the magnitude of this dimension is similar to the methodology followed in the case of Dimension 1. The difference is, Dimension 3 is found out only at an *Aggregate level* for the risk drivers. Probability distributions can be used to model the effect of the risk driver (this process is similar to that followed for measuring Dimension 1). While the mean of the probability distribution gives the impact of the risk driver, the risk concentration is obtained in two steps.

Step 1

Area of the probability distribution under high level of deviation to unacceptable level of deviation (above 25 per cent deviation level) gives the importance of the risk driver. For example, for a risk driver like traffic (Risk Driver 1), the following steps are taken as explained.

This probability distribution represents Risk Driver 1 in two dimensions (likelihood-impact). For determining Dimension 3 (risk concentration) the area under the distribution for unacceptable levels of impact is found out. In this case, the unacceptable levels of impact is considered as any deviation above 25 per cent.

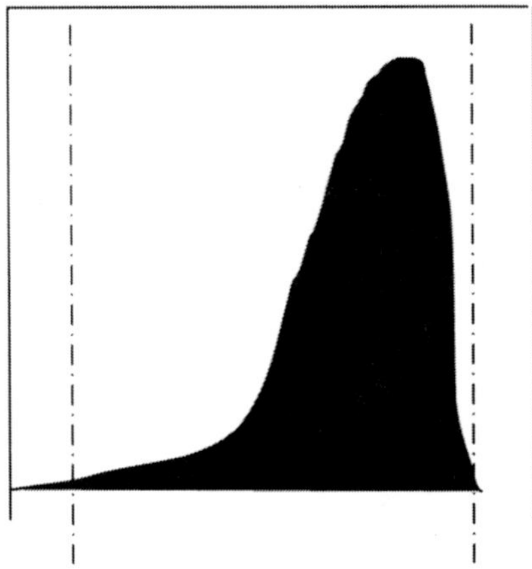

Fig. 4: Area of Distribution

For Risk Driver 1, the area falling under unacceptable levels of impact which is represented by dotted lines is 100 per cent of the total area.

Step 2

Relative Weights: After finding the area under the unacceptable region of impact for all possible Risk Drivers, the researcher will sum the values of area for all risk drivers to get the total area. Then, it is proposed to find the percentage area of unacceptable impact out of the total area for each risk driver. This will give the Relative weights. This percentage value gives the risk concentration of each risk driver. An example of risk concentration derived for a loan product is given in Fig. 5.

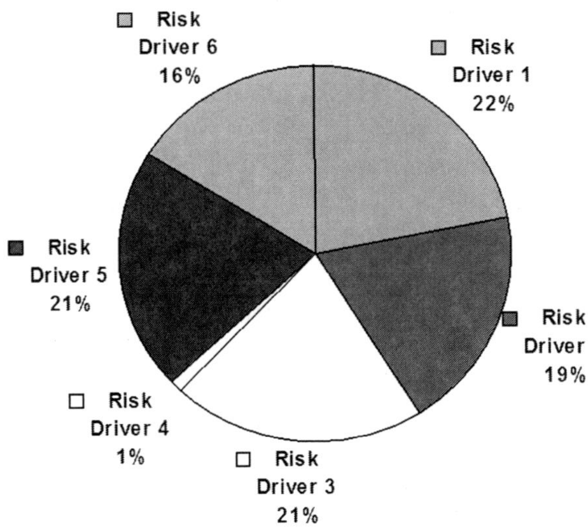

Fig. 5: Risk Concentration

Aggregating the effect of risk drivers to get a risk score: The Credit Risk Score for each Risk Driver is obtained using the following formula

Credit Risk Score = Impact * Likelihood

Then for obtaining the aggregate credit risk score due to all risk drivers, the credit risk scores for each risk driver should be multiplied by the corresponding Dimension 3 value and all the resultant scores are then added together to get the *Aggregate Credit Risk Score*.

CREDIT RISK RATING

The Credit Risk score obtained in the previous step is put into one of the rating classes for the purpose of decision making and pricing. The rating classification is given in Table 6.

Table 6: Credit Risk Rating

RR-9 Unacceptably High Risk Risk Score>=XX%	**RR-8** Extremely High Risk Risk Score >=XX% and below XX%	**RR-7** Very Very High Risk Risk Score >=XX% and below XX%
RR-6 Very High Risk Risk Score >=XX% and below XX%	**RR-5** Very High Risk Risk Score >=XX% and below XX%	**RR-4** High Risk Risk Score >=XX% and below XX%
RR-3 Moderate Risk Risk Score >=XX% and below XX%	**RR-2** Low Risk Risk Score >=XX% and below XX%	**RR-1** Very Low Risk Risk Score >=XX% and below XX%

Note: Here RR stand for Risk Rating.

Higher the Credit Risk Score, greater is the risk involved. While assessing a loan proposal, it should be ensured that the risk rating for each of the individual risk drivers is below the *Hurdle Risk Rating*.

For this model to function well, a proposed appraisal sheet for infrastructure is also suggested.

SUGGESTED APPRAISAL FORMAT

It is evident from the research that stand-alone models of assessment and risk measurement may lead to a faulty pricing decision, as poor rating attracts a higher default premium. The rating exercise may not be comprehensive on account of variables, which are unique to the sector concerned. It is evident from the conceptual framework discussed above that, if the appraising officer can give the likelihood and impact scores along with risk mitigants score, a better rating exercise can be undertaken for the project which will keep its dynamic nature intact. Raw scores can then be modeled by the credit (risk) department to arrive at the risk rating of the project.

Corresponding to this an appraisal format is suggested. This appraisal format uses all the eight factors used in the survey and the most important sub-variables as identified in statistical research. It is suggested; however, that benchmarks need to be changed from sector to sector so as to retain the dynamic content of the model and advice should be given to the appraising officer simultaneously. It is expected that this model will straightway lead to calculation or measurement of the risk since credit officers can simultaneously give scores on likelihood, impact and mitigants as suggested in the risk model above. The format is given in Table 7.

Table 7: Suggested Appraisal Format

Risks	Risk Factors	Likelihood	Impact	Possible Mitigants
Project Construction Risk	Project Completion Risk: Completion within Schedule and Budgeted Cost			
	Strength of EPC Contractor			
	Land Acquisition and Required Regulatory Clearances			
	Lenders Independent Engineer's Reports			
	Quality of Workmanship			
	Environmental Compliance			
Technology Risks	LIE Report on Technology			
	Risks with New/Unproven Technology			
	Technology Support for Construction			
	Testing and Commissioning Risks			
	Availability of Utilities – Power, Water, etc.			
Market Risks	Market Capacity and Long Term Demand Supply			
	Cyclicality/Recessionary Trends in Demand			
	Competition from New Entrants			
	Contractual Agreement with Buyer			
	Price Risk: Volatility, Product Price Depreciation			
	Charges Economical for Off-taker			
	Bids Servicing Costs			
Legal Risks	Collateral and Security Strongly Enforceable			
	Structure of Arbitration Mechanism, Dispute Redressal			
	Trustee and Intercreditor Issues			

Financial Strength	Project Debt: Equity			
	Project DSCR			
	Reasonableness of Capital Costs			
	TOL/TNW			
	Stability of Cash Flows			
	Foreign Exchange Risk			
	Internal Rate of Return			
Manage-ment Quality	Transparency in Shareholders Agreement			
	Management: Track Record & Competence, Succession Issues			
	Financial Prudence: Strict Control on Cash Flows			
	Strict Control on More Borrowings, Equity Infusion			
	Accounting Quality: Revenue Recognition, Depreciation Policies, etc.			
Force Majeure Risks	Risks Due to Acts/Policies of the Government			
	Insurance Coverage			
	Risks Arising Due to External Factors Like WTO, Global Economic Changes, etc.			
	Claims Arising Due to Operating Accidents			
	Risk of Disruption Due to Labour Trouble, Force Majeure Events, etc.			
Operat-ing Risks	Pricing of Operations and Management Contract			
	Track Record of O&M Contractor			
	Defining Events of Default			
	Input Linkages			
	Termination/Quick Replacement in Case of Suboptimal Performance			

This assessment model directly corresponds to credit rating mechanism discussed above. It is suggested that this model should retain its dynamic nature with respect to sectoral issues and banks may be advised to choose benchmarks carefully for each sector. However measurement of risk becomes fairly easy with this model.

CONCLUSION

Validation of Suggested Appraisal Format

The term validation is defined in the minimum requirements of the IRB approach of Basel II as under:

> "The institution shall have a regular cycle of model validation that includes monitoring of model performance and stability; review of model relationships and testing of model outputs against outcomes."
>
> (Basle II, 2001)

There are two methods of validation – Qualitative and Quantitative. These two methods of validation complement each other. A rating procedure should only be applied in practice if it receives a positive assessment in the qualitative area. A positive assessment only in the quantitative validation is not sufficient. In this study on account of lack of quality of data, quantitative validation was not undertaken.

However before adoption by Scheduled Commercial banks, the model needs further validation on a larger number of accounts and over a greater time period. This will lead to refinement of the proposed model.

However, it is expected that the research and its findings particularly with reference to qualitative and critical risk factors will help the bankers when they move to Foundation IRB and Advanced IRB approaches.

REFERENCES

[1] Altman, E.I. (1968), "Financial Ratios, Discriminant Analysis and the Prediction of Corporate Bankruptcy", *The Journal of Finance*, September, pp. 589- 609.

[2] Balu, K. (2002), *Infrastructure Financing by Indian Banks and Financial Institutions,* Indian Institute of Bankers, Mumbai.

[3] Basel Committee on Banking Supervision (2001), Internal Rating-Based Approach to Specialized Lending.

[4] Beenhakker, H.L. (1997), *Risk Management in Project Finance and Implementation*, Quorum Books, Westport, CT.

[5] Chen, A.H.J., Kensinger, W. and Martin, J.D. (1989), *Project Financing as a Means of Preserving Financial Flexibility*, University of Texas.

[6] Dailami, Mansoor *et al.* (1999), *INFRISK: A Computer Simulated Approach to Risk Management,* World Bank, Washington DC

[7] Esty, B. and Sesia Jr. A. (2005), *An Overview of Project Finance: 2004 Update*, Harvard Business School, Case # 205-65.

[8] Flyvbjerg, B.N. Bruzelius and Rothengatter, W. (2003), *Megaprojects and Risk: An Anatomy of Ambition*, Cambridge University Press, Port Chester, New York.

[9] Mohan Rakesh (1996), *The India Infrastructure Report.*

[10] Orgeldinger, John (2006), "The Development of Basel II Confirming Model", *Journal of Structured Finance*, Winter.

[11] Project Finance Recovery Study (2002), Standard & Poor's Risk Solution, March, p. 5.

[12] Standard and Poor's (1999), Infrastructure Finance: Project Finance.

Project Finance Software

- *INFRISK*: Risk Management Simulation Software, The World Bank Institute, Software to assist in the measuring and managing of project risks.
- *CRISIL RAM:* For rating projects.

Rural Empowerment through Self Help Groups (SHGs): A Study of West Bengal

Bikram Singh[1], Debasish Sarkar[2], Manish Ur Rahman[2] and Sajal Kumar Maiti[3]

[1] University of Calcutta, Kolkata
[2] Goenka College of Commerce and Business Administration, Kolkata
[3] Hooghly Mohsin College, Hooghly
E-mail: bsbikramsingh@gmail.com; sarkar_debasish@hotmail.com; manish.ur.rahman@gmail.com; maitisajal@rediffmail.com

ABSTRACT

A major cause of poverty among rural people is lack of access for both individuals and communities to productive assets and financial resources. This is caused by the fact that the formal credit institutions that function smoothly in the developed urban areas cannot cater to the credit needs of rural poor due to lack of information about the borrowers, lack of proper collateral among the poor people (which are acceptable to the formal financial institutions), apart from enforcement-related problems in case of default. The failure of formal lending institutions and the apparent success of Bangladesh's Grameen Bank in reaching the rural poor have recently inspired numerous non-governmental organizations (NGOs) and governments of less-developed countries to establish group-lending schemes to deliver credit at low cost and reasonable interest rates to small-scale rural entrepreneurs (Coleman ,1999). India is no exception to this. From 1st April, 1999, the Government of India (GOI) initiated a programme called Swarnjayanti Gram Swarojgar Yojana (SGSY) which is a self-employment programme under the Ministry of Rural Development, GOI, that aims at providing assistance to the BPL 'Below the Poverty Line' rural poor for establishing micro-enterprises through bank credit and government subsidy to acquire an income-generating asset. A theoretical study (Ghatak and Guinnane, 1999) has shown that in closed communities, where group members are known to each other, group lending promotes screening, monitoring, state verification and enforcement of repayment. In closed village communities, in the group-formation stage, the member could choose safer partners that reduce their effective cost of borrowing and improve rate of repayments of loans to avoid the social sanction of his/her peer group (Basely and Coate, 1995). Experiences of Grameen Bank in Bangladesh have shown that availability of collateral free tiny loans for income generating activities for poor have a significant impact on the lives of poor families. A study by the National Bank for Agriculture and Rural Development (NABARD), covering

560 SHG member households from 223 SHGs across 11 states, has shown many positive results regarding the impact of participation of rural poor in the SHGs (NABARD, 2002). The present study attempts to assess: (i) the role of SHGs in rural empowerment in West Bengal (ii) the degree of success in rural empowerment achieved by SHGs in West Bengal. The territorial jurisdiction of the study is West Bengal. The study covers all the districts of West Bengal. Period of study is 2000-2010. The study is a desk study based on secondary data. The sources are the reports of the Ministry of Self-Help and Self-Employment, Government of West Bengal, NABARD, SIDC, SIDBI, SUDA, etc. Finally data have been analyzed with the help of descriptive statistics. There were a number of traditional and informal ways of providing credit before the emergence of the SHGs. All of those paid very little attention to the question of both empowerment and sustainability. Along with this, there was a casual approach towards the accountability of the credits leading to adverse impact on both repayment as well as further outreach. The interesting finding of this study is that SHGs have started playing a significant role in rural empowerment in West Bengal and most of the effective SHGs happen to be female groups, indicating a high potential for rural women empowerment in West Bengal. SHGs are treated as a successful tool in poverty alleviation across the developing nations. Findings of the present study may be relevant to the policy makers in India to evaluate how far the SHGs have become effective and what further steps need to be taken to enhance their performance.

Keywords: SHGs, Rural Empowerment

INTRODUCTION

A major cause of poverty among rural people is lack of access for both individuals and communities to productive assets and financial resources. This is caused by the fact that the formal credit institutions that function smoothly in the developed urban areas cannot cater to the credit needs of rural poor due to lack of information about the borrowers, lack of proper collateral among the poor people (which are acceptable to the formal financial institutions), apart from enforcement-related problems in case of default. The failure of formal lending institutions and the apparent success of Bangladesh's Grameen Bank in reaching the rural poor have recently inspired numerous non-governmental organizations (NGOs) and governments of less-developed countries to establish group-lending schemes to deliver credit at low cost and reasonable interest rates to small-scale rural entrepreneurs (*Coleman* ,1999). India is no exception to this. From 1st April, 1999, the Government of India (GOI) initiated a programme called *Swarnjayanti Gram Swarojgar Yojana* (SGSY) which is a self-employment programme under the Ministry of Rural Development, GOI, that aims at providing assistance to the BPL 'Below the Poverty Line' rural poor for establishing micro-enterprises through bank credit and government subsidy to acquire an income-generating asset.

A BRIEF REVIEW OF LITERATURE

A theoretical study (*Ghatak* and *Guinnane*, 1999) has shown that in closed communities, where group members are known to each other, group lending promotes screening, monitoring, state verification and enforcement of repayment. In closed village communities, in the group-formation stage, the member could choose safer partners that reduce their effective cost of borrowing and improve rate of repayments of loans to avoid the social sanction of his/her peer group (*Basely* and *Coate*, 1995). Experiences of Grameen Bank in Bangladesh have shown that availability of collateral free tiny loans for income generating activities for poor have a significant impact on the lives of poor families. A study by the National Bank for Agriculture and Rural Development (NABARD), covering 560 SHG member households from 223 SHGs across 11 states, has shown many positive results regarding the impact of participation of rural poor in the SHGs (*NABARD*, 2002).

OBJECTIVES OF THE STUDY

The present study attempts to assess:

(i) the role of SHGs in rural empowerment in West Bengal
(ii) the degree of success in rural empowerment achieved by SHGs in West Bengal.

METHODOLOGY

The territorial jurisdiction of the study is West Bengal. The study covers all the districts of West Bengal. Period of study is 2000-2010. The study is a desk study based on secondary data. The sources are the reports of the Ministry of Self-Help and Self-Employment, Government of West Bengal, NABARD, SIDC, SIDBI, SUDA, etc. Finally data have been analyzed with the help of descriptive statistics.

BRIEF FINDINGS

There were a number of traditional and informal ways of providing credit before the emergence of the SHGs. All of those paid very little attention to the question of both empowerment and sustainability. Along with this, there was a casual approach towards the accountability of the credits leading to adverse impact on both repayment as well as further outreach. The interesting finding of this study is that SHGs have started playing a significant role in rural empowerment in West Bengal and most of the effective SHGs happen to be female groups, indicating a high potential for rural women empowerment in West Bengal.

POLICY IMPLICATION

SHGs are treated as a successful tool in poverty alleviation across the developing nations. Findings of the present study may be relevant to the policy makers in India to evaluate how far the SHGs have become effective and what further steps need to be taken to enhance their performance.

REFERENCES

[1] Besley, T. and Coate, S. (1995), Group Lending Repayment Incentives and Social Collateral, *Journal of Development Economics*, 46, pp. 1-18.

[2] Coleman B.E. (1999), The Impact of Group Lending in Northeast Thailand, *Journal of Development Economics*, 60, pp. 105-141.

[3] Dasgupta, R. (2001), Working and Impact of Rural Self-Help Groups and Other Forms of Micro Financing: An Informal Journey Through Self-Help Groups, *Indian Journal of Agricultural Economics*, 56(3), pp. 370-386.

[4] Ghatak, M. (1999), Group Lending Local Information and Peer Selection, *Journal of Development Economics,* 60, pp. 27-45.

[5] Ghatak , M. and Guinnane, T.W. (1999), Economics of Lending with Joint Liability: Theory and Practice, *Journal of Development Economics,* 60, pp. 195-228.

[6] Maheshwari, S. R. (1995), *Rural Development in India,* Sage Publications India Private Ltd., New Delhi.

[7] NABARD (2002), Ten Years of SHG-Bank Linkage: 1992-2002, NABARD

[8] Pitt, M.M. and Khandekar, S.R. (1998), The Impact of Group Based Credit Programmes on Poor Households in Bangladesh: Does the Gender Participants Matter?, *Journal of Political Economy*, 106, pp. 958-996.

Social Performance of Micro Finance Institutions – A Study

T. Chandrabai[1], K. Venkata Janardhan Rao[2] and Suresh Kandulapati[1]

[1] Padmasri Dr. B.V. Raju Institute of Technology, Vishnupur, Narsapur, Medak
[2] Kakatiya University, Warangal
E-mail: chandrabai10@gmail.com; janardhan_kv@yahoo.co.in; suresh.k@bvrit.ac.in

ABSTRACT

A major crisis broke out for microfinance institutions (MFIs) operating in the state of Andhra Pradesh after a complaint lodged by some of the borrowers of MFIs against their alleged "usurious interest rate" and "forced loan recovery" practices. For this, Andhra Pradesh government has passed an ordinance to protect the poor from exploitation by the MFIs. In these circumstances it is imperative for the micro finance institutions to aim at sustainable growth by rendering diversified and transparent services to their clients. The social value of microfinance relates to the way financial services improve the lives of poor and excluded clients and their families, and widen the range of opportunities for communities. Social responsibility requires an adaptation of the corporate culture to the MFIs socio-economic and ethical context, an adequate human resource policy, credit guarantees adapted to the local conditions, and balanced relationships between staff and clients. The main objective of this study is to analyze the quality and appropriateness of services provided by the MFIs after the crisis in Medak district. A structured questionnaire is used for collecting the data from convenient sample size of 250 clients (from rural areas of Medak district). Statistical techniques are used to test the data. The results are based on the client's satisfaction and their economical development, based on quality of the services provided by MFIs. Implication: If the social performance is poor it leads to unsustainable economic development.

Keywords: Social Performance, Micro Finance Institutions, Services, Sustainable Growth

INTRODUCTION

In a state of crisis it is imperative for the micro finance institutions to aim at the sustainable growth by rendering diversified and transparent services to their clients. This can be achieved not only by financial performance but also with the social performance of micro finance institutions. Social performance is the effective translation of an institution's social mission into practice. The social value of microfinance relates to the way financial services improve the lives of poor, excluded clients, their families, and widen the range of opportunities for communities. An MFI which sets itself a social mission will find lines of direction for its activity. The SPI-CERISE tool is founded upon four major dimensions of social performance-outreach, adaptation of services, client benefits and social responsibility.

SIGNIFICANCE OF THE STUDY

Microfinance is considered as a tool for socio-economic development. It is one way of fighting poverty in rural areas where the poorest people live. It puts credit, savings, insurance and other basic services within the reach of poor people. Through micro finance institutions the poor people can obtain small loans; thus, there is an urgent need for microfinance institutions to improve their ability to reach the poorest families and to satisfy their growing demand for a range of financial services. This includes the safe and flexible savings services that poor people need and value. This study helps to identify the quality of services (both financial and social) needed to be provided by the MFIs for attaining sustainable growth in a state of crisis. We can also identify the clients' satisfaction and their economic development.

OBJECTIVES OF THE STUDY

- The main objective of this study is to analyze the services provided by the MFIs in Medak district.
- To compare the services provided by the micro finance institutions before and after the crisis.
- To find the clients' expectations after crisis in Medak district.

SOURCES OF DATA COLLECTION

Data is collected from both primary and secondary sources. The primary data is collected by administering a structured questionnaire, with interview from the clients. Secondary data sources are also used to collect the data for this study which include books, journals and websites. The collected data is analyzed by using statistical techniques such as mean, weighted average and Analysis of Variance.

SAMPLE SIZE

By using convenient sampling technique a sample size of 250 is taken from five mandals (each 50) in Medak district.

METHODOLOGY

There are four major dimensions for measuring social performance, viz., outreach, adaptation of services, client benefits and social responsibility. Here, we selected the dimensions – adaptation of services and client benefits. We divided these, further, into range of services, quality of services, transparency and social capital of clients. Likert five-point scale from "strongly disagree" to "strongly agree" is also employed for the study.

HYPOTHESES

H_1: There is no significant difference between the range of services and client expectations
H_2: There is no significant difference between quality of services and client expectations
H_3: There is no significant difference between transparency and client expectations
H_4: There is no significant difference between social capital and client expectations
H_5: There is no significant difference between MFIs services in Medak District

Range of Services – Abbreviations

- It is convenient to take the loans from MFIs-RS1
- Providing insurance products-RS2
- Solving clients' complaints-RS3

Quality of Services– Abbreviations

- Less waiting time to collect the loan-QS1
- MFIs are providing better services than banks and money lenders-QS2
- Enquiry about drop out clients-QS3
- Using good communication and relations with clients-QS4

Transparency – Abbreviations

- MFIs charging reasonable interest rates-T1
- Clients receive written statements on their loan transactions-T2

Social Capital of Clients – Abbreviations

- MFI loans satisfied client's needs-SC1

- Prospered economically through the loans and services of microfinance institutions-SC2.

HYPOTHESES TESTING

Table 1: Clients Responses on MFIs Services

Range of Services				
Parameter	RS1	RS2	RS3	
	4.34	5.00	2.98	
Quality of Services				
Parameter	QS1	QS2	QS3	QS4
	4.64	2.58	4.28	3.50
Transparency				
Parameter	T1	T2		
	2.18	4.90		
Social Capital of Clients				
Parameter	SC1	SC2		
	2.14	3.18		
Client Expectations				
Expecting more services	3.34			
Expecting less interest rates	3.42			

Source: Primary Data.

From Table 1:

H_1: For $v_1 = 1$, $v_2 = 4$, $F_{0.05}$ (range of services, expected services) = 7.71 and it is less than calculated value 9.31. Hence, the hypothesis is rejected.

H_2: For $v_1 = 1$, $v_2 = 4$, $F_{0.05}$ (quality of services, expected services) = 7.71 and it is greater than calculated value 0.967. Hence, the hypothesis is accepted.

H_3: For $v_1 = 1$, $v_2 = 4$, $F_{0.05}$ (transparency, expected services) = 7.71 and it is greater than calculated value 0.563. Hence, the hypothesis is accepted.

H_4: For $v_1 = 1$, $v_2 = 4$, $F_{0.05}$ (social capital, expected services) = 7.71 and it is greater than calculated value 6.03. Hence, the hypothesis is accepted.

H_5: For $v_1 = 4$, $v_2 = 4$, $F_{0.05}$ (actual services, expected services) = 6.39 and it is greater than calculated values. Hence, the hypothesis is accepted.

FINDINGS

- Most of the people from the sample are illiterate and self help groups. MFIs providing loans to the people below poverty line, illiterate women and men, farmers, casual laborers and landless tenants.

- It is found that they are getting different types of loans from micro finance institutions, and the loan processing time is less and easy. The maximum distance that a client will travel to receive a loan is very less, generally at their homes.
- From the sample the percentage of male people selected is 30%, the percentage of female people is 70%, the percentage of literate is 29% and the number of illiterate is 71%.
- The income level of sample up to Rs. 50,000 per annum is 25%, Rs. 50,000 to Rs. 1,00,000 per annum is 59%, Rs. 1,00,000 to Rs. 2,00,000 per annum is 16%.
- Some clients took loan from a single institution, and majority of the clients took from more than one institution before the crisis. After crisis the institutions are not using flexible loan procedure. The clients are restricted to take loan from more than one institution.
- It is observed that the loan processing charges were exorbitant before the crisis. Now there is no such charge for loan processing. Prior to crisis they were charged certain amount for the services. After the crisis they barred all services except loan linked insurance affordable at zero service charges.
- Post crisis only 60% of the clients are attending the weekly meetings. MFIs rarely conducted socio-economic studies to assess the situation of their clients.
- They are charging the interest rates ranging from 22% to 24%, after crisis.
- Prior to crisis MFIs prompted the clients to save certain amount. But after the crisis the MFIs are not insisting the savings from clients.
- After crisis MFIs are allowing flexible repayment procedure. But before the crisis they applied irresponsible collection practices.
- The loan procedure is transparent through the staff discussions about the interest rates, services provided and repayment procedure. They provided the written slips on the payments made by the clients.
- From Tables 2, 3, and 4 we can find the post crisis interest rates, Services provided by the MFIs before and after crisis and income level of the clients respectively.

Table 2: Post Crisis Details of Interest Rates Charging by MFIs (in %)

Institution	Weekly	Monthly	Seasonal
SKS	22.22	–	–
Spandana	22	21	20
Basix	24	22	21
L&T	–	22	–
Share	22	–	–
Sharada	22	–	–
Banks	8	–	–

Table 3: Services Provided by the MFIs Before and After Crisis

Sr. No.	Parameter	Before the Crisis	After the Crisis
1.	Emergency loans	100% provided with some processing charges	After repayment of existing loans
2.	Services	– Agriculture and business development – Insurance – Mobile finance – Training	Insurance & Training
3.	Service charges	Charged based on the service	No charges
4.	Interest rate	Client opinion is that it is high interest rate	Ranging from 22-24% but more than banks
5.	Attending for meetings	100%	60%
6.	Savings	MFIs prompted the clients to save certain amount.	No savings
7.	Repayment of loan	Not flexible	Flexible
8.	Irresponsible collection practices	MFIs used	Not using now

Source: Primary Data.

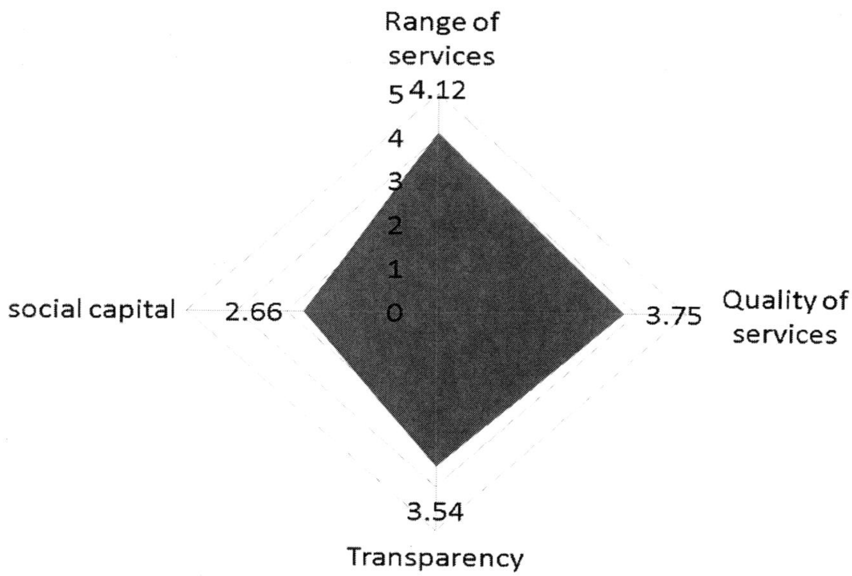

Graph 1: MFI with Main Focus on Range of Services

Table 4: Income Level of Clients Per Annum (in %)

Area	Up to 50,000	50,000–1,00,000	1,00,000–2,00,000
Narsapur	25	57	18
Hathnura	33	54	13
Shivampet	16	69	15
Jinnaram	25	60	15
Thoofran	27	54	19

Source: Primary Data.

DISCUSSIONS

There is no significant difference between the quality of services, transparency, social capital and client expectations because the majority of the clients are from rural areas and not well educated. Their major expectations are low interest rates, more services like awareness, business development programmes and more loan amount.

CONCLUSION

Microfinance is considered as a tool for socio-economic development. The social value of microfinance relates to the way financial services improve the lives of poor. MFIs have to play major role in socio-economic development. In a state of crisis it is imperative for the micro finance institutions to aim at the sustainable growth by rendering diversified and transparent services to their clients.

The study observed that the range of services is meeting their expectations. It is observed that, post crisis; there is a change in interest rates, service charges and adapted flexible repayment procedure for the clients. Still, clients are expecting less interest rates and more upgraded services.

SUGGESTIONS

MFIs can provide services through more qualified staff, so that they are able to supervise and educate the clients effectively.

MFIs can upgrade their services to achieve sustainable growth.

REFERENCES

[1] SPI-Final Report: Towards measuring social performance of micro-finance institutions: A proposal (Manfred Zeller, Cecile Lapenu and Martin Greeley).

[2] Assessing and managing social performance in microfinance by IFAD (International Fund for Agricultural Development) document developed in 2008.

[3] Vetrivel S.C. & Chandra Kumarmangalam S. (2010). *Role of Microfinance institutions in rural development International.* Journal of Information Technology and Knowledge Management, Volume 2, No. 2, pp. 435-441.

Websites

[1] www.cgap.org/gm/document-1.9.47613/FN65_Rev.pdf.

[2] www.microfinancegateway.org

[3] http://indiamicrofinance.com

[4] www.cgap.org

Telecom Growth Trajectory in India

Hiranmoy Roy, Sunil Kumar, Arvind K. Jain and R. Jayaraj
University of Petroleum and Energy Studies (UPES), Dehradun
E-mail: hroy_au@yahoo.com

ABSTRACT

Today, India's telephone network is one of the largest communication network in the world which containues to grow at blisteing pace. The Indian Telecommunications network with over 621.28 million connections is the third largest in the world and the second largest among the emerging econimies of Asia. This paper is designed to analyse the growth of telecom in India. The paper is scattered in to different sections including history of telecom in India, methodology, survey of literature, India as a major player, modern growth story of telecom in India, teledensity, mobile technology growth, present scenario, internet usage, and consumer behaviour with resppect to the mobile telephony leading to force the companies adopting the concept of number portability, making the aspect true that "Consumer is the King".

Keywords: Telecom Sector, Growth Trajectory, Teledensity, Mobile Telephony, Number Portability

TELECOM GROWTH TRAJECTORY IN INDIA

During 1880's, there were only two telephone companies namely The Oriental Telephone Company Ltd. and The Anglo-Indian Telephone Company Ltd. They approached the Government of India to establish telephone exchanges. The proposal was declined on the grounds that the establishment of telephones was a Government monopoly and that the Government would not allow others to undertake the work. But within few years, the Government changed its earlier decision and a license was given to the Oriental Telephone Company Limited of England for opening telephone exchanges at Kolkata, Mumbai, Chennai (Madras) and Ahmadabad. January 28, 1882, is a Red Letter Day in the history of telephone in India. On this day Major E. Baring, Member of the Governor General of India's Council declared opening of the Telephone Exchange in Kolkata, Chennai and Mumbai.

The telephone exchange at Kolkata named as "Central Exchange" was opened at 7,

Council House Street. The Central Telephone Exchange had 93 numbers of subscribers. Bombay also witnessed the opening of Telephone Exchange in the same year. For the past decade or so, telecommunication activities have gained momentum in India. Efforts have been made from both governmental and non-governmental platforms to enhance the telecom infrastructure in the country. The idea is to help modern telecommunication technology penetrate India's socio-culturally diverse society, and to transform it into a nation of technology aware people.

METHODOLOGY AND DATA SOURCE

This paper is based on the study of existing works on telecom sector and analysis of secondary data. The secondary data were collected from different Government reports. Time series data is analyzed to see the levels of growth of telecom sector in different time periods. This paper is basically investigative in nature. Different literatures available on telecom (these reports are published mainly by Department of Telecommunications, Govt. of India) are surveyed to analyze the growth of telecom in India. The secondary data were collected from different sources as mentioned in the paper. Tabular analysis of data is made to study the telecom sector in India and its growth.

LITERATURE REVIEW

We have reviewed following literature relating to telecom sector study.

Manas Bhattacharya – (Vision 2020)

The basic purpose of this paper is to construct a vision of Indian telecom sector for the year 2020. Development being a continuous process, the choice of the year 2020 is just an arbitrary division of time, a pre-defined time horizon to take stock of what is likely to be achieved. The present paper isolates the agents of change based on international experiences and also in India in this development continuum. The agents of change, as observed from international perspective, have been broadly categorized as economic structure, competition policy and technology. Economic reforms and liberalization have driven telecom sector through several transmission channels.The paper is divided into six sections. Section 1 gives a brief account of the era of competition that was witnessed in Indian telecom sector and the results achieved. Analysis of the results, particularly comparison with other major countries opened avenues for further discussions on economic structure, synergy between telecom and IT, competition policy and technology. Logical extension of the arguments, as they developed, extended to a vision for 2020 in each of the sections of the paper.

Rekha Jain (1999)

This paper addresses the issue that tariff rebalancing and interconnection regulation plays a critical role in reforming the telecom sector in India, characterized by rapid technological changes and monopoly service provision by the incumbent. Due to rapid advances in technology, the prices of long distance communication have fallen more dramatically and incomparably more than that of the wire line local access. Further, the competition among the long distance segment has resulted in a sharp decline in prices, almost bringing them near to costs. However, the decline One of the most crucial and debated issues in interconnection regulation. Therefore, the charging regime has to be efficient, fair and unambiguous to protect the interests of all the telecom players. TRAI began tariff balancing as early as in 1999, and the exercise has gone through

National Telecom Policy (NTP) 1994 and 1999

Indian telecom sector has undergone major transformations through significant policy changes. The reforms began in 1980s with opening up of telecom equipment manufacturing for private sector. Historically, the telecom network in India was owned and managed by the Government considering it to be a natural monopoly and strategic service, best under state's control. However, in 1990's, the examples of telecom revolution in many other countries, which resulted in better quality of service and lower tariffs replicated in India and led the Indian policy makers to initiate a change process and thus finally resulting in opening up of telecom services for the private sector.

Annual Report (2006-07)

Today's, India's Telephone network is one of the largest communication networks in the world which continues to grow at a blistering pace. The Indian Telecommunications network with more than 621.28 million connections is the third largest in the world and third largest among the emerging economies of Asia. Today, it is the fastest growing market in the world. The telecommunication sector has been continuing to register significant success during the recent years and has emerged as one of the key sectors responsible for India's Resurgent Economic Growth. The sector which was growing at the rate of 20 percent up to the year 2002-03, has moved to a higher growth path of an average rate of more than 40 percent. This rapid growth has been possible due to various proactive and positive decisions of the Govt., liberal policies and contribution of both private and public sector.

Broad band Policy (2004)

Recognising the potential of huge Broadband service in growth of GDP and enhancement in quality of life through societal applications including tele-education, tele-medicine, e-governance, entertainment as well as employment generation by way of high speed access to information and web-based communication, Government have also taken a policy to accelerate the growth of Broadband services.

Demand for Broadband is primarily driven by Internet and personal computer penetration. It is a fact that the current level of Internet and Broadband access in the country is low as compared to many Asian countries. Penetration of Broadband, Internet and Personal Computer (PC) in the country was 0.02%, 0.4% and 0.8% respectively at the end of December, 2003. Currently, high speed Internet access is available at various speeds from 64 kilobits per second (kbps) onwards and presently an always-on high speed Internet access at 128 kbps is considered as 'Broadband'.

New Telecom Policy (1999)

The Government of India recognized that provision of world class telecommunications infrastructure and information is the key to rapid economic and social development of the country. It is critical not only for the development of the Information Technology industry, but also has widespread ramifications on the entire economy of the country. It is also anticipated that a major part of the GDP of the country would be contributed by this sector. Accordingly, it is of vital importance to the country that there be a comprehensive and forward looking telecommunications policy which creates an enabling environment for development of this industry.

Annual Report (2008-09)

This is the 12th Annual Report of TRAI. Till date TRAI is regulating telecom sector in India and it took number of initiative for the development of initiatives for the development this sector in terms of growth of subscriber's base, growth of telecom network, emphasis on protecting the interest of the consumer's and monitoring quality of telecom services are being highlighted in this report. This report consists of three parts relating to these above three aspects.

INDIA, EMERGING AS A MAJOR PLAYER

In 1975, the Department of Telecom (DoT) was separated from P&T. DoT was responsible for telecom services in entire country until 1985 when Mahanagar Telephone Nigam Limited (MTNL) was carved out of DoT to run the telecom services of Delhi and Mumbai. In 1990s the telecom sector was opened up by the Government for private investment as a part of new economic policy. Therefore, it was necessary to separate the Government's policy wing from its operations wing. The Government of India corporatised the operations wing of DoT on October 01, 2000 and named it as Bharat Sanchar Nigam Limited (BSNL). Many private operators, such as Reliance India Mobile, Tata Telecom, Vodafone, BPL, Bharti, Idea etc., successfully entered the high potential Indian telecom market.(DoT 2006-07)

The Indian government was composed of many factions (parties) which had different ideologies. Some of them were willing to throw open the market to foreign players and others wanted the government to regulate infrastructure and restrict the involvement of foreign players. Due to this political background it was very difficult to bring about liberalization in telecommunications.

Liberalization started in 1981 when Prime Minister Indira Gandhi signed contracts with Alcatel CIT of France to merge with the state owned Telecom Company (ITI), in an effort to set up 5,000,000 lines per year. But soon the policy was let down because of opposition from leaders of the opposite political party. She invited Sam Pitroda a US based NRI to set up a Center for Development of Telematics (C-DOT), however the plan failed due to political reasons. During this period, after the assassination of Indira Gandhi, under the leadership of Rajiv Gandhi, many public sector organizations were set up like the Department of Telecommunications (DoT), VSNL and MTNL. Many technological developments took place in this regime but still foreign players were not allowed to participate in the telecommunications business.

The demand for telephones was ever increasing. It was during this period that the P.N Rao led government introduced the national telecommunications policy [NTP] in 1994 which brought changes in the following areas: ownership, service and regulation of telecommunications infrastructure. They were also successful in establishing joint ventures between state owned telecom companies and international players. But still complete ownership of facilities was restricted only to the government owned organizations. Foreign firms were eligible to 49% of the total stake. The multi-nationals were just involved in technology transfer, and not policy making.

During this period, the World Bank and ITU had advised the Indian Government to liberalize long distance services in order to release the monopoly of the state owned DoT and VSNL; and to enable competition in the long distance carrier business which would help reduce tariff's and better the economy of the country. The Rao run government instead liberalized the local services, taking the opposite political parties into confidence and assuring foreign involvement in the long distance business after 5 years. The country was divided into 20 telecommunication circles for basic telephony and 18 circles for mobile services. These circles were divided into category A, B and C depending on the value of the revenue in each circle. The government threw open the bids to one private company per circle along with government owned DoT per circle. For cellular service, two service providers were allowed per circle and a 15 years license was given to each provider. During all these improvements, the government did face oppositions from ITI, DoT, MTNL, VSNL and other labor unions, but they managed to keep away from all the hurdles.

After 1995 the government set up TRAI (Telecom Regulatory Authority of India) which reduced the interference of Government in deciding tariffs and policy making in the telecom sector. The DoT opposed this. The political powers changed in 1999 and the new government under the leadership of A.B Vajpayee was more pro-reforms and introduced better liberalization policies. They split DoT in two- one policy maker and the other service provider (DTS) which was later renamed as BSNL. The proposal of raising the stake of foreign investors from 49% to 74% was rejected by the opposite political party and leftist thinkers. Domestic business groups wanted the government to privatize VSNL. Finally in April 2002, the government decided to cut its stake of 53% to 26% in VSNL and to throw it open for sale to private enterprises. TATA finally took 25% stake in VSNL.

This was a gateway to many foreign investors to get entry into the Indian Telecom Markets. After March 2000, the government became more liberal in making policies and issuing licenses to private operators. The government further reduced license fees for cellular service providers and increased the allowable stake to 74% for foreign companies. Because of all these factors, the service fees finally reduced and the call costs were cut greatly enabling every common middle class family in India to afford a cell.

MODERN GROWTH

A large population, low telephony penetration levels, and rise in consumer income and spend owing to strong economic growth have contributed to making India the fastest-growing telecom market in the world. The first and largest operator is the state-owned incumbent BSNL which is also the 7th largest telecom company in world in terms of number of subscribers. BSNL was created by corporatization of the erstwhile DTS (Department of Telecommunication Services), a government unit responsible for provision of telephony services. Subsequently, after the telecommunication policy was revised to allow private operators, companies such as Bharti Telecom, Tata Indicom, Vodafone, MTNL, and BSNL have entered the space major operators in India.

However, rural India still lacks strong infrastructure. Today, india's telephone network is one of the largest communication network in the world which containues to grow at blisteing pace. The indian Telecommunications network with over 621.28 million connections is the third largest in the world and the second largest among the emerging econimics of Asia (TRAI).

Today, it is the fastest growing market in the world. The telecommunication sector continued to register significant success during the year and has emerging as one of the key sectors responsible for indian's resurgent economic growth. The sector, which was growing in the ange of 20 to 25 percent uo to the year 2002-2003, has moved to a higher growth path of an average rate of more than 40 percent. This rapid growth has been possible due to various proactive and positive decisions of the Government and contribution of both the public and the private sector.

The total number of telephones in the country crossed the 621.28 million mark at the end of March, 2010. The overall tele-density has increased to 52.74% in March 2010. In the wireless segment, 36.96 million subscribers have been added in March, 2010 while 8.11 million subscribers were added in December 2007. The total wireless subscribers (GSM, CDMA & WLL (F)) base is 584.32 million now. The wire line segment subscriber base stood at 36.96 million with a decline of 2.64 March, 2010.

The table below shows the growth process in telecom coverage over the last two decades.

Year	Direct Exchange Lines	Year Over Year	Teledensity
1987-88	3800.80		0.48
1988-89	4166.50	9.62	0.51
1989-90	4589.50	10.15	0.55
1990-91	5074.50	10.57	0.60
1991-92	5809.90	14.49	0.67
1992-93	6796.70	16.98	0.77
1993-94	8025.60	18.08	0.89
1994-95	9795.30	22.05	1.07
1995-96	11978.40	22.29	1.28
1996-97	14542.60	21.41	1.53
1997-98	17801.70	22.41	1.85
1998-99	21601.50	21.35	2.20
1999-00	26,652.50	23.38	2.69
2000-01	32,695.50	22.67	3.18
2001-02	38433.50	17.55	3.67
2003-04	41,492.30	7.96	3.88
2004-05	42,820.20	3.20	3.93
2005-06	NA	NA	NA
2006-07	NA	NA	NA
2008-09	42,900.72	–2.64	4.78

Note: NA – Not available.
Source: TRAI consultation papers.

From the above table we can see that there has been a decline in the growth rate of fixed service which to a large extent has been due to the remarkable growth in the mobile service growth. This growth to a certain extent is phenomenal as the service introduced since 1996. Since March 2003 the growth rate in mobile service has been a robust 160%.

Effective Teledensity Estimated on the Basis of Service Area as on 31-03-201*

Service Area	Rural	Urban	Total Density
Assam	18.47	96.54	29.99
Bihar	14.65	127.96	30.07
Delhi			127.49
Gujarat	33.52	95.82	58.46
Haryana	39.37	100.63	59.7
Himachal Pradesh	52.53	298.15	79.35
J&K	26.93	113.19	49.91
Karnataka	24.08	142.62	67.81
Kerala	44.65	84.18	80.36
Madhya Pradesh	15.41	90.76	35.28
Maharashtra	32.41	108.00	67.24
North East	25.36	100.11	43.22
Orissa	20.61	133.25	39.3
Punjab	42.20	124.01	75.44
Rajasthan	31.42	120.89	52.76
T. N.	38.44	122.65	83.73
U.P. (East)	18.24	104.68	37.37
W.B.	24.29	119.73	52.74

* Population data/projections are available state-wise only.
Source: TRAI consultation papers.

Thus from the given statistical data we can come to a conclusion that there has been robust growth in the telecom network both for fixed and cellular which is one of the positive indicators towards economic development.

TELE-DENSITY GROWTH – PRE-REFORM POST PERFORMANCE AND TARGETS

In the year 1948, the tele-density was 0.02. Later 1998, the tele-density rose to 1.94. It shows the performance of Pre and Post privatization in India.

- In the pre-reform the growth was generally driven by the public sector monopoly showing nothing but a marginal growth.
- Reform process started in NTP 1994

Tele-density Growth in Post-reform Period

Year	1998	1999	2000	2001	2002	2003	2004	2005	2006	2007	2008	2009	2010 (up to July)
Tele-density	1.94	2.33	2.86	3.58	4.28	5.11	7.02	9.11	13.5	18.5	22.5	47.88	52.74

Source: TRAI consultation papers.

- TRAI was formed in 1997
- First tariff order issued in 1998 and hence policy was effective from 1998
- NTP 99 pushed the reforms further

The growth rate of 2005-10 and growth rate of 2004-05 is greater than growth rate of 50 years that is 1948-1950. The growth started in 1998-2003 period. It further intensified during 2003-05. Growth was mobile driven and privatization played a key role in it.

GROWTH OF MOBILE TECHNOLOGY

There were 584.32 million telephone connections by the end of March, 2010.The figure further raised to 590,198,359 connections (GSM) and 26,675,111 CDMA Connections of RTL by May 2011. This is almost more then six times of 98 million connections as on March 2005. The number of wiresless subscribers has surpassed the number of fixed line subscribers. The overall teledensity increased from 8.95 percent as on March 2005 to more then 42.61 percent as on March, 2010. The number of internet and broadband subscribers increased from 69 lakh and 13 lakh respectively, as on March 31, 2006 to 86 lakh and 20 lakh respectively as on December 31, 2006. Further, 710 cities have been provided with broadband connectivity by the public sector undertakings (Choudhury 2005) raising the number of Broad Band users reached to 4.15 million mark by May 2008.

India registered fastest growth in the Mobile Telecommunication in the world. In the year 2009, China was on the top of the chart in case of Subscriber Base with 747 million User, next to India with 525 million Subscriber Base followed by Indonesia, Philippines, Thailand, Malaysia, Australia and Singapore.

In a global Scenario, it shall be worth mentioning in the study that in YOY Addition of Subscribers, India leads the chart with 53 Million Customer, followed by China and respective other countries. The study also reviled various other aspects of the Telecommunication related to Wireless Penetration that is highest in Singapore followed by Australia, keeping India in the Last position. As far as Average minutes of usage per subscriber per month are concern China leads the chart followed by Singapore, keeping India on the third Position. In terms of Revenue Australia Stands first while India Stands

Second Last. The call charges a remains equal in Australia and Philippines followed by Malaysia, Singapore and other countries. The Call charges in India Stands Minimum in the global spectrum.

In 1947 Bell Labs introduced the idea of Cellular Communication with Police Cars thus giving rise to the basic concept of mobile telephony. AT&T took charge and proposed to allocate a large number of radio-spectrum frequencies so as to widespread of mobile telephony services shall become 4. In the year 1968 AT&T and Bell Labs proposed a cellular system of many small, low powered, broadcast towers each covering a 'cell', a few miles in radius and collectively covering a large area. And thus year 1991 marked the beginning of commercial cellular services based on GSM Standards in Finland.

Telecommunication Sector in India got liberalized in the year 1992 allowing private sector to participate. Year 1993 marked the beginning of foreign investment to the tune of Rs 20.6 million in the sector. Government started providing license to cellular operators in 1994 to operate in metros in duopoly mode. The number of operators henceforth started increasing and Kolkata in August 1995 became the first metro to have a cellular network.

In the initial 5-6 years the average monthly subscribers additions were around 0.05 to 0.1 million only and the total mobile subscribers base in December 2002 stood at 10.5 millions. However, with the proactive initiatives taken by regulator and licensor, the monthly mobile subscriber additions increased to around 49.15% per year during 2009-10. Further In comparison to April 2011 and May 2011 the all India Subscriber Base in case of GSM increased by 9533357 Subscribers.

Mobile telephony followed the New Telecom Policy 1994; still growth was tardy in the early years because of the high price of handsets as well as the high tariff structure. To look into the emerging issues Government of India established Telecom Regulatory Authority of India [TRAI]. The alarming situation got aroused in the year 1999 when FDI inflow into telecom sector falls by almost 90% to Rs.2126.7 million, initiating the need of tariff rebalancing exercise. Government of India on March 1999 announced fresh National Telecom Policy, still in the year 2000 FDI investment dropped down to Rs 918 million forcing further to amend TRAI Act to the Government.

The industry heralded several pro consumer initiatives. Mobile subscriber additions started picking up. The number of mobile phones added throughout the country in 2003 was 16 million, followed by 22 million in 2004, 32 million in 2005 and 65 million in 2006. In the year 2009, the number was 525.09 million and 584.32 million in March, 2010 making the country Second to China in terms of Subscriber Base.

As far as the use of technology is concern, India, opted for the use of both the GSM (global system for mobile communications) and CDMA (code-division multiple access) technologies in the mobile sector. Besides the landlines and mobile phones, some of the companies also provide the Wire Less in Local Loop [WLL] services. The mobile tariffs in India have also become lowest in the world. A new mobile connection can be activated with a monthly commitment of US$5 only. In April-June, 2010 alone 38.6 million handsets were sold in India.[1] The data reveals the real potential for growth of the Indian mobile market.

MOBILE TELEDENSITY

The high rate of growth combined with slow down of the fixed services has meant in the increase in the proportion of fixed to cellular services. From the low of 2.33% in 1997 the growth has increased to 98% in September 2004. The number of mobile phones surpassed the number of fixed subscribers at the end of 2005. The rising trend of mobile is well continued during 2009-10, further followed in 2011.

Year	All India	Mobile Teledensity	Year Over Year Growth
1996-97	339.03	0.04	
1997-98	882.32	0.09	160.25
1998-99	1195.45	0.12	35.49
1999-00	1884.31	0.19	57.62
2000-01	3583.70	0.35	90.19
2001-02	6577.36	0.62	81.86
2002-03	12981.88	1.21	99.19
2003-04	33200.60	3.09	159.60
2004-05	42970.00	3.94	NA
2005-06	NA	NA	NA
2006-07	NA	NA	NA
2008-09	52500.16	44.72	42.27
2009-10 (up to July)	54800.28	49.60	58.17

Note: NA – Not available.
Source: TRAI consultation papers.

PRESENT SCENARIO

In the fixed line arena, BSNL and MTNL are the incumbents in their respective areas of operation and continue to enjoy the dominant service provider status in the domain of fixed line services. For example BSNL controls 27.83% of fixed line share in

[1] *Business Standard,* October 8th, 2010.

the country. On the other hand, in the mobile telephony space, Airtel controls 35.88% subscriber base followed by Reliance with 40.94%, BSNL with 33.17%, Vodafone with 46.66% subscriber base (as per June 2005 data).

Telephone Exchanges out of their 35,000 Exchanges. Keeping in mind the viability of providing services in rural areas, an attractive solution appears to be one which offers multiple service facility at low costs. A rural network based on the extensive optical fiber network, using Internet Protocol and offering a variety of services and the availability of open platforms for service development, viz., the Next Generation Network, appears to be an attractive (DoT 2006-07).

Table showing Position of Telecom in India till the end of March, 2010.

Wireline and Wireless Connction

	Dec. 2009	**March 2010**	**% Change Over March 2009**
Subscriber's Base (in million)			
(i) Wireline	37.06	36.96	–2.64
(ii) Wireless	525.09	584.32	49.15
Total	562.19	621.28	44.58
Rural	174.53	200.81	64.13
Urban	387.63	420.47	36.73
Traffic (Minutes Use/Sub/Month)			
Wireless Full Mobility			
(i) GSM	411	410	–15.20%
(ii) CDMA	318	307	–14.00%
Tele-density			
(i) Wireline Tele-density	3.16	3.14	–4.06%
(ii) Wireless Tele-density	44.72	49.6	47.14%
Total Tele-density	47.88	52.74	42.61%
Rural Tele-density	21.16	24.29	62.61%
Urban Tele-density	110.96	119.73	33.87%

Source: TRAI Performance Report, March 2010.

The Market Share of each Operator as on May 2011 across India in case of GSM and CDMA is as under:

Group Company-wise % Market Share – May 2011

Sl. No.	Name of Company	Total Sub Figures	% Market Share
1	Bharti Airtel	167,065,289	28.31%
2	Vodafone Essar	139,426,769	23.62%
3	IDEA	93,754,764	15.89%
4	BSNL	87,618,769	14.85%
5	Aircel	57,061,824	9.67%
6	Uninor	25,386,287	4.30%
7	Videocon	7,054,198	1.20%
8	MTNL	5,234,574	0.89%
9	Loop Mobile	3,130,643	0.53%
10	Stel	3,165,944	0.54%
11	Etisalat	1,299,298	0.22%
12	All India	590,198,359	100.00%
	Total RTL (as of April 2011)	26,675,111	

Source: www.coai.com

As far as optimization of cost is concern optic-fibre network can be easily converted to Next Generation network and then used for delivering multiple services at a very effective and affordable cost. The total revenue in the telecom service sector is Rs. 40265.12 crores in 2010 as against Rs. 39,756.64 crore in 2009, registering a growth of 1.28%. The total investment in the telecom services sector reached Rs. 200,660 crore in the financial year 2010. Telecommunication has revolutionized the growth of Information Technology and established as fastest growing Industry in India. Internet subscriber base has risen to 6.94 million in 2005-2006 and 81,000,000 in the year 2010.

Internet Usage and Population Statistics

Year	User	Population	% Pen	Usage Source
1998	1,400,000	1,094,870.677	0.1	ITU
1999	2,800,000	1,094,870.677	0.3	ITU
2000	5,500,000	1,094,870.677	0.5	ITU
2001	7,000,000	1,094,870.677	0.7	ITU
2002	16,500,000	1,094,870.677	1.6	ITU
2003	22,500,000	1,094,870.677	2.1	ITU
2004	39,200,000	1,094,870.677	3.6	C.I.Almanac
2005	50,600,000	1,112,225,812	4.5	C.I.Almanac
2006	40,000,000	1,112,225,812	3.6	IAMAI
2007	42,000,000	1,29,667,528	3.7	IWS
2009	81,000,000	1,156,897,766	7.0%	ITU
2010	81,000,000	1,173,108,018	6.9%	ITU

Source: www.InternetWorldStats.com

Under the Bharat Nirman Programme, the Government of India identified 66,822 revenue villages in the country, which have not yet been provided with a Village Public Telephone (VPT), and required to be connected. However doubts have been raised about what it would mean for the poor in the country.

In recent past digital divide and rural communication has become a key thrust area for the government and the industry. The demand of rural India now being meet by the cellular operators thus bridging the divide between the connected and the unconnected.

The wireless industry has more than 95% of the telephone subscribers in the country, i.e of the 806.13 million subscribers as of 31st January 2011, the industry contributed more than 771.18 million. The wireless subscription in urban areas increased from 501.30 million in December 2010 to 512.26 million at the end of January 2011, whereas rural subscription increased from 250.89 million to 258.93 million showing positive growth trend of 3.20% as compared to urban subscription of 2.19%.

At present more than 70% of the total of 2589.93 million rural subscribers are connected to the cellular mobile services.

CONSUMER IS THE KING

Till recent days, Indian Tele-communication Industry has seen sea changes and faced lots of up's and downs but the fact cannot be negated that Telecommunication has become an essential element of an individual's life. When, in case mobile phone stops ringing even for a while, it seems life without breadth. To some of us even it seems life becoming meaningless. The mobile to the extent has become synonymous to oneself, Still the fact cannot be ignored that 'Consumer is the King', evident from the fact that the mobile operators fighting to grab the market share, giving loads of schemes and value added services to the customers, making the mobile telephony more than just required for communicating across through voice.

Bringing 3G technology in picture, mobile operators started committing the customer's next generation experience in Telecommunication taking the expectations of the customers further to next higher level.

While in the beginning only two operators were allowed to operate in each telecom circle, duopoly under a fixed license fee regime for 10 years in the year 1994. As the number of circle went on increasing with the increase in consumer base multiple operators started operating in the given circle that lead to mobile war among the operators, highlighting their superiority over others to the customers further made the customer more demanding for better offers and services from operators. But in the process the customer were facing the problem that every time they go with new operator their mobile number gets changed. Hence some of the customers though wanted to opt for better offers and services either have to keep the multiple numbers or have to continue with the same operators without having any choice.

As the pressure build up from the customers, and to break the monopoly of the operators and offer more flexibility to the customer, making the environment more competitive for the operators TRAI asked the operators to bring in the concept of 'Mobile Number Portability – MNP' in India, where customer can remain with its mobile number still opting to switch from one operator to other and avail the choice of service required by him.

In the midst of complex environment, 10 to 12 operators, operating in 22 circles having over 700 million subscriber base MNP was launched in January 2011. Commendable efforts put together by the players in the Industry made such a complex thing happen for the public, the convenience of changing their service providers without having to change their mobile numbers. Hence forth with MNP in place subscriber got the 'FREEDOM OF CHOICE' to switch between mobile operators.

Within couple of months of introduction of MNP the preference of the operator by the consumer started reflecting. The consumer preferred GSM players over other, although the number was not very significant and only 5 million subscribers that remains less than 1% of the total subscriber base opted for the change.

Table Showing Early Trends of Consumer Preference of GSM Service over CDMA & Consumer Shift Across Various Mobile Operators.

MNP-Trend: Number of Port

Sl. No.	Operator	Total Subscriber in Million	Subscriber Ported In	% Subs Ported In	Subs Ported Out	% Subs Ported Out	Net Addition	% Net Addition
1	Vodafone	127.36	488250	0.38	295489	0.23	192761	0.15
2	Idea	84.29	391191	0.46	240402	0.29	150789	0.18
3	Airtel	155.8	530615	0.34	382400	0.25	148251	0.1
4	Aircel	51.83	162664	0.31	117822	0.23	44842	0.09
5	Uninor	20.31	31019	0.15	24689	0.12	6330	0.03
6	Videocon	6.01	5404	0.09	11633	0.19	–6229	–0.10
7	MTNL	5.43	3793	0.07	14851	0.27	–11052	–0.20
8	TTSL	86.05	197404	0.23	236793	0.28	–39389	–0.05
9	BSNL	88.82	107724	0.12	257817	0.29	–150093	–0.17
10	Reliance	128.87	44753	0.03	351170	0.27	–306417	–0.24

Source: DoT & TRAI (for subscriber data as of 31st January 2011).

Although the available initial data revealed the preference of GSM Service over CDMA by the consumers but still the larger Picture is awaited, and it cannot be ignored that MNP has given the tool in the hands of the customer to choose and demand best service and operator. The fact still shall remain true that 'CUSTOMER IS THE KING' and cannot be ignored. The intense competitive environment shall define Survival of the Fittest in the days to follow.

CONCLUSION

The revealed preference of the subscribers in favour of wireless telephone is continuing unabated. The mobile server which was popularly associated with tycoons has been transformed into mass consumption services. This is confirmed from the rising share of mobile phones (CMPs and WLL) whice has increased from 71.69 percent as on March 31, 2006 to meore than 79 percent (1054.25 lakh CMPs and 441.73 lakh WLL), as on December 31, 2006 and more than 95% of the telephone subscribers in the country are with wireless Industry.

The share of mobile phones has thus surpassed the share of landlines and this trend is likely to continue. Though the Public Sector Units entered late in the mobile sector, BSNL has provided an impressive 69.45 million phones as on March, 2010.

It is difficult to ascertain fully the employment potential of the telecom sector but the enormity of the opportunities can be gauged from the fact that there were 4.59 million Public Call Offices in March, 2010 up from 2.3 million in December 2004.

The value added services (VAS) market within the mobile industry in India has the potential to grow from $500 million in 2006 to a whopping $10 billion by 2009.

The private sector has continued its dynamism and enterpreneurial spirit to play a significant role in the growth of telecom sector. The share of private sector in the total telephones has increased from 57 percent as on March 31, 2006 to 87.24% as on March, 2010. Of the 584.32 million phones provided during 2009-10, major share, i.e. 509.78 million (above 87 percent) was provided by the private sector.

Until recently, only the PSU's BSNL and MTNL were allowed to provide Basic Phone Service through copper wires in India. MTNL is operating in Delhi and Mumbai only and all other parts are covered by BSNL. However private operators have now entered the fray, although their focus is largely on the cellular business which is growing rapidly.

The boost in Indian Telecom market has also given rise to illegal setups and practices. Following the directives issued by the Minister of Communications & IT, Govt. of India, and the Department of Telecom has set up Vigilance Telecom Monitoring (VTM) Cells at Delhi, Mumbai, Chennai, Hyderabad and other important locations to vigorously detect the illegal Telecom setups in the country. VTM cells continuously monitor the operators to check the grey market calls and also ensure that the license conditions are fully complied

REFERENCES

[1] Government of India (2006-07), "Annual Report Department of Telecommunications", Ministry of Communication and IT.

[2] Government of India (2008-09), "Annual Report Department of Telecommunications" Ministry of Communications and IT.

[3] Choudhury, Ashish (2005), Growth of Telecom in India, Nokia, India.

[4] TRAI, Consultation Papers.

[5] National Telecom Policy, Department of Tele Communication.

[6] Govt. of India (2004), Broadband Policy, Department of Telecommunications, www.dot.gov.in

[7] Borko Furht, Mohammad Ilyas (2003), Wireless Internet Handbook, CRC Press: USA.

[8] Malhotra K, Gardner S, Rees D. (2005), Evaluation of GPRS Enabled Secure Remote Patient Monitoring System, ASMTA, and Riga, Latvia.

[9] Hovenga E., Kidd M., Cesnik B. (1996), Healthcare Informatics: An Overview. Churchill Livingstone, New York.

[10] Harnett B. (2006), Telemedicine Systems and Telecommunications. J Telemed Telecare.

[11] Win K.T., Susilo W. (2006), Information Security and Privacy of Health Data, *International Journal of Healthcare Technology and Management*, 7: 492-505.

[12] Wootton R., Craig J. (1999), Introduction to Telemedicine, Royal Society of Medicine Press, London.

[13] Darkens A.W., Cary M.A. (2000.), Telemedicine and Telehealth: Principles, Policies, Performance, and Pitfalls, Free Association Books, London.

[14] Benson T., Neame R. (1994), Healthcare Computing: A Guide to Health Information Management and Systems Longman, Harlow.

[15] Norris A.C. (2002), Essentials of Telemedicine and Telecare, John Wiley, UK.

[16] Gold W.R., Manning T., Street Jr R. (1997), Health Promotion and Interactive Technology: Theoretical Applications and Future Directions. Lawrence Erlbaum Associates.

[17] Herscovici & Christodoulou (2002), Wireless Telemedicine Systems Overview Telemedicine, IEEE Antenna's and Propagation Magazine, 44.

[18] Heuser S. (2006), 'Telehealth Systems Slowly Gaining: Devices help CcurbVisits to Hospital, The Boston Globe.

[19] Seaton B, Tsoukatos T. (2004), A New Way of Aaccessin Clinical Information on the Move. *The British Journal of Healthcare Computing & Information Management*, 21: 27-28.

[20] Pederson C.D. (2002), Electronic Communications & Internet Opportunities in the Danish Health Services, *The British Journal of Healthcare Computing & Information Management*, 19, 22-25.

[21] Lauter K. (2004), The Advantages of Elliptic Curve Cryptography for Wireless Security, *IEEE Wireless Communications*, 62-67.

[22] Malhotra K., Gardner S., Patz R. (2007), Implementation of Elliptic-Curve Cryptography on Mobile Healthcare Devices, *IEEE International Conference on Networking, Sensing and Control*, London, United Kingdom. April 15-17.

[23] Malhotra K., Gardner S. (2006), Evaluating Security Issues in Mobile Internet Healthcare Systems, *PGNET2006*, Liverpool John Moores University, Liverpool.

[24] Subramanian, Dilip (2004), 'Impact of Deregulation on a Public Sector Firm, Case Study of ITI', *Economic and Political Weekly*, Vol. XXXIX, No. 49, pp. 5233-5245.

[25] Economic Research Unit (2002), Indian Telecommunication Statistics, Department of Telecommunications, Government of India. New Delhi.

[26] Broad Band Policy (2004), Department of Telecommunications, Ministry of Communication and IT, Government of India.

[27] Government of India (1999), New Telecom Policy, Department of Telecommunications, Ministry of Communication and IT.

[28] Jain, Rekha and Trilochan Sastry (1999), 'Assessment of Socioeconomic Impact of Rural Telecom Services: Implications for Policy', *Workshop on Telecom Policy Initiatives: The Road Ahead.*

[29] Manas Bhattacharya (Vision 2020), Department of Telecommunications, Ministry of Communication and IT, Government of India.

Tweaking a Drunken Horse to Dance: SHG-Bank Linkages in SGSY with Respect to Khurda District of Orissa

Pravash R. Mohapatra
PJCMT, Bhubaneswar

ABSTRACT

Self employment programme has been a priority area in India right from the beginning. As a result of which numerous self-employment programmes were experimented, modified, consolidated and integrated into Swarnajayanti Gram Swarojgar Yojana (SGSY) and implemented in April 1999. SGSY is a mechanism through which physical and financial resources are mobilised in rural areas and public resources are transferred to identified groups of poor who are willing to constitute a small informal group (SHG) from the same socioeconomic status to evade chronic case of socio-economic crisis and vulnerability of one kind or the other. The approach of SGSY rests on the basic premise that there is a tremendous potential within the poor to help themselves and this potential can be harnessed by organising them into groups with a given amount of physical, financial and human resources. The Micro-finance programmes envisage increasing outreach of small financial services through Self-Help Groups (SHGs) in general and women groups in particular. Micro-finance has to be utilised in such a way that it benefits the SHGs to improve the quality of life of their members and if properly implemented would lead to the increment in income by enhancing members' productivity and ensuring timely repayments and adequate peer or social monitoring. Thus, considered as the DNA or the basic building blocks of rural development, and their performance determine the health of the developmental programme. The microfinance component of the programme is referred to as a small-scale financial intermediation inclusive of savings, credit, insurance, business services and technical support. Since the inception, SGSY has made rapid progress over time covering more than 31 lakh Self-Help Groups (SHGs). However, only 22 per cent of the SHGs were provided with bank finance for undertaking income generating activities including micro enterprises. This shortcoming has been attributed to failure of public intervention to enhance the credit absorption capacity of SHGs as well as to the failures of credit delivery systems to reach the poor. Since most of the SHGs were engaged in low technology and less productive traditional activities of primary sector, the income gains to SHGs were very less. In this paper Khurda District, home to the capital city of Orissa is taken as a sample for the study, to analyse the impact of SHG-Bank linkage. Empirical analysis are done on secondary as well as primary data by using statistical tools like least square method and multiple regression to know the impact of banks or the MFIs (micro finance institutions) on the SHGs. In addition to the practice of unscientific "Strategic Management Process" bottlenecks in the shape of political intervention, myopic implementers coupled with natural calamity of all kind spirals down the growth curve of Orissa. Factors like arrangement of loans, subsidies, education level, social class, landed property etc are taken for the study with the member of SHG. Continuing with the same momentum, the said programme may cause more harm than good to the rural poor, what could otherwise be their lifetime opportunity to become an entrepreneur.

Keywords: SGSY, SHGs, MFIs

INTRODUCTION

Growth is a natural process but development required deliberate intervention. Self employment programme being the key to development for the people living below the line of poverty, has been the priority area of Govt. of India right from the first five year plan. As a result of which numerous self-employment programmes were experimented, modified, consolidated and integrated into Swarnajayanti Gram Swarojgar Yojana (SGSY) and implemented in April 1999. SGSY is a mechanism through which physical and financial resources are mobilized in rural areas and public resources are transferred to identified groups of poor who are willing to constitute a small informal group (SHG) from the same socioeconomic status to evade chronic case of socio-economic crisis and vulnerability of one kind or the other. Being a holistic programme of self-employment, SGSY tries to bring in all the components needed for successful implementation of micro-enterprises like formation of a self-help groups, provision of timely and adequate credit, training, technology and marketing. The microfinance component of the programme is referred to as a small-scale financial intermediation inclusive of savings, credit, insurance, business services and technical support. The objective of SGSY is to bring the assisted poor families (*Swarozgaris*) above the poverty line by ensuring an appreciable level of income sustainable over a period of time. This objective is proposed to be achieved by organising the rural poor into SHGs through the process of social mobilization, training, capacity building and provision of income-generating assets. This process aims at building the poor's self-confidence through community action, collective decision-making, prioritization of their needs and resources so as to improve their collective bargaining power and empower them socially and economically. Two important components attract the rural poor to come under the SGSY schemes are credit and subsidy. For the successful implementation of both, banks need to play a vital role. Hence is the importance of the linkage.

Financing these rural poor, after forming a group has been an integral part to create micro level entrepreneur for this self employment programme (SGSY). Arranging the economic inputs like land, labour and capital etc., to set up a business venture is a mammoth task for people, who essentially starve to fulfill the basic needs. Arrangement of capital is the most crucial part of the process. Increase in income may help them crossing the poverty line. Impact studies on the implementation of various grass-root level self-employment ventures have not been able to resolve the issues relating to the successful and sustainable income impact of such programmes on the intended beneficiaries. To address the problem of financial accessibility to the poor, the government, often sets ambitious targets through nationalization of banks and extension of directed credit, provides subsidies and launches welfare schemes like loan waivers. The picture has changed recently after the realization and success of SHGs in the form of sustainability and loan repayment. The SHG members are getting priority over an individual to set up micro level enterprises and to obtain loan and other inputs. Many governments of developing and under-developed nations treat SHGs as the panacea of the problem of credit inaccessibility in rural areas and advocate extension of credit through SHG-Bank route to the poor.[1] In line with the "BOP" bottoms of pyramid strategy, new mantras revolves around the believe that :-poor are bankable, lending to the poor is sustainable & profitable, the success story that SHGs have recorded all over, made it to the fact that the programme is not only highly replicable but the solidarity groups formed for the channelisation of credit become vehicles for a variety of desirable developments and it act as a roadmap for the poor to come out of poverty trap, as shown in the Exhibit 1.

Exhibit 1: The SHG Concept

The approach of SGSY rests on the basic premise that there is a tremendous potential within the poor to help themselves and this potential can be harnessed by organizing them into groups with a given amount of physical, financial and human resources. The Micro-finance programmes envisage increasing outreach of small financial services through Self-Help Groups (SHGs) in general and women groups in particular. Micro-finance has to be utilized in such a way that it benefits the SHGs to improve the quality of life of their members and if properly implemented would lead to the increment in income by enhancing members' productivity and ensuring timely repayments. Thus considered as the DNA or the basic building blocks of rural development, and their performance determine the health of the developmental programme.

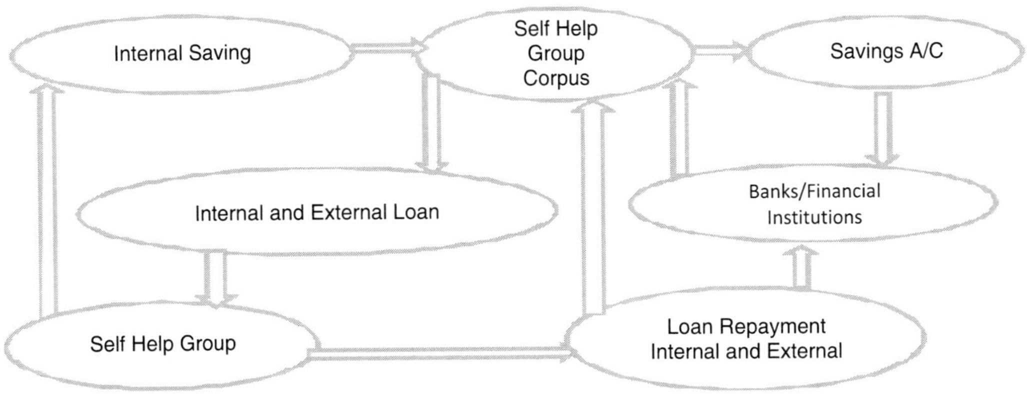

Exhibit 2: SHG-Bank Linkage Model

A group (Exhibit 2) of people after forming an SHG to the bank to get their SHG linked with credit. Here, the urge to get linked is spontaneous. Since there is hardly any facilitation involved in forming or nurturing the group in a particular social set-up, the formal financing institutions are always skeptical about the creditworthiness of the group borrowers. The reluctance to render credit services to the SHGs is high and credit supply is not free from unnecessary hassles like excessive documentation, legal formalities and insistence on collaterals. Once the banks feel that the necessary banking habits have been instilled in the group members through their internal loaning and saving activities, they are no longer reluctant to link the SHGs with credit facilities.

District Khurda, home to the capital city of Orissa (39.9% people are BPL: Census 2001) financial and physical performance of the SGSY scheme in Khurda district are shown in the Table 1 since SGSY is operational till the financial year 2006-07.

The performance of SGSY scheme in Khurda district is exhibited in the Table 1. Financial data (Col: 3 & Col: 4) are given in Rs. in lakhs. The percentage of achievement of the financial performance are given in Col:5. Similarly the physical aspect of the scheme

Table 1: The SGSY Performance of Khurda-DRDA: At-a-Glance

Financial and Physical Performance of SGSY – Khurda during the Year 1999-2000 to 2006-2007 (Rs. in lakhs)							
Year	**Sl. No.**	**Financial**			**Physical**		
		Total Funds Available	**Expendi-ture**	**% of Exp.**	**Target**	**Achieve-ment**	**% of Achievement**
1	**2**	**3**	**4**	**5**	**6**	**7**	**8**
1999-00	1	572.18	326.99	57	3654	2997	82
2000-01	2	583.27	332.37	57	4531	2685	59
2001-02	3	349.24	333.9	96	3765	3713	99
2002-03	4	249.02	218.75	88	1843	2212	120
2003-04	5	216.3	245.36	113.4	2211	2433	110
2004-05	6	236.2	346.18	147	1735	2343	135
2005-06	7	130.51	209.35	160	1735	1869	108
2006-07	8	188.54	219.69	117	1974	1994	101
Total		2525.26	2232.59	88.41	21448	20246	105
Mean		315.65	279.07	88.41	2681	2530	105

Source: DRDA Khurda.

are given in the (Col: 6 & Col: 7) in number of Swarozagaries made during the time period (Col:1). Percentage of the physical aspect is given in Col: 8. the sum of the total is given and the mean value is also given below. The percentage shown in the total of both financial as well as in the physical performance are taken over the funds availability and the target respectively. Four times out of eight years in financial performances and five times in as many years the physical performance (in percentage) have crossed cent per cent mark, shown in the achievement. Looking at the mean value, 105 per cent are achieved by spending only 88.41 per cent funds. This says that the result of 100 per cent of funds spent could have resulted in a better performance. Only 2530 number of Swarozogaries are taking the advantage of the scheme in Khurda district annually. Going by the 39.9 per cent of BPL population of Orissa (As per the 2001 census), 738150 (Approx) number of people in the district are BPL. 2530 number of beneficiaries per year is just 0.342 per cent of the BPL bracket availing the benefit under SGSY.

To examine the trend and to study the pattern of financial performance further trend Analysis of Funds availability for SGSY Khurda are made by using the Method of Least Squire.

$Y = A + B X$, $A = \Sigma Y / n$, "n" is the number of years. Here the value of A= 315.65
$B = \Sigma X Y / X^2$ Here the value of B is –31.67

Eight years of data are analyzed in the Table 2. Since the series is of even number, hence the mid value is calculated and the sum of squire of X, which is 168, is taken.

Table 2: LS Analysis of SGSY on Funds Availability in Khurda (Rs. in lakhs)

Year	X	X^2	XY	Trend
1999-2000	–7	49	–4005.26	537.34
2000-01	–5	25	–2916.35	474
2001-02	–3	9	–1047.72	410.66
2002-03	–1	1	–249.02	347.32
2003-04	1	1	216.3	283.98
2004-05	3	9	708.6	220.64
2005-06	5	25	652.55	157.3
2006-07	7	49	1319.78	93.96

Source: DRDA Khurda.

From the trend analysis it is clear that the funds availability for SGSY in Khurda has reduced over the years. What should have been the other way round. Means instead of showing a growth trend, the values are in descending order. The negative trend here indicating that the pace of the implementation also has come down, since it is having a direct link to the availability of funds.

In addition to it the trend analysis of annual expenditure on SGSY scheme of Khurda District is calculated bellow in Table 3.

Table 3: Least Square Analysis of SGSY on Expenditure in Khurda (Rs. in lakhs)

Year	X	X * X	XY	Trend
1999-2000	–7	49	–2288.93	-51.05
2000-01	–5	25	–1661.85	43.27
2001-02	–3	9	–1001.7	137.59
2002-03	–1	1	–218.75	231.91
2003-04	1	1	245.36	326.23
2004-05	3	9	1038.54	420.55
2005-06	5	25	1046.75	514.87
2006-07	7	49	10764.81	609.19

Source: DRDA Khurda.

Trend Analysis of Expenditure for SGSY in Khurda Dstrict. $Y = A + B X$, $A = \Sigma Y / n$, n is the number of years. A= 279.07, $B = \Sigma X Y / X^2$. Here the value of B is 47.16.

Since the series is of even number, hence the mid value is calculated and the sum of squire of X, which is 168 is calculated. By analyzing the value of Y it is clear that the expenditure trend is on a growth path.

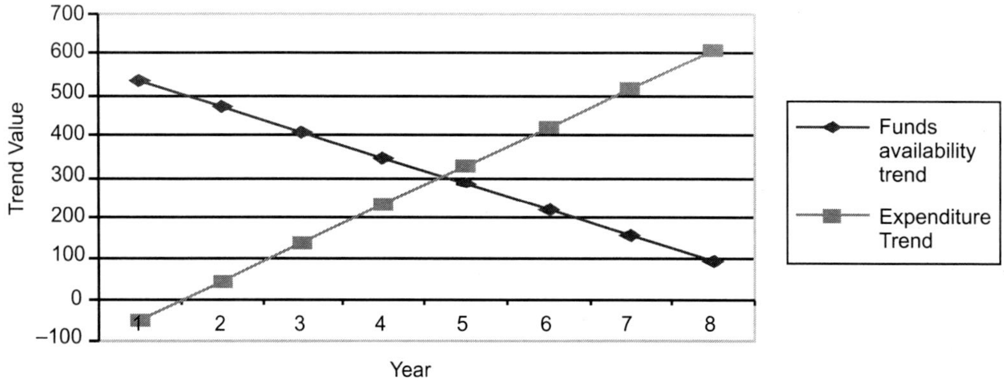

Graph 1: Financial Trend Analysis of SGSY Khurda (Rs. In lakhs)

In the Graph 1, the X-axis represent the year from 1999-2000 to 2006-2007 and the Y-axis is the trend value. The blue line is the availability of funds and the violet line represent the expenditure trend. The available funds as it is clear from the above diagram, is not having a growth pattern where as the growth is visible in the expenditure pattern. The direction of both the line are opposite, instead of the other way round. That shows huge gap in planning, and implementation. SGSY is the umbrella scheme, taking care of not only self employment but sustainability as well. Any mistake either in planning and implementation will not only affect one Swarozagary but a group (SHG) and their families, hence all kind of precautionary measures should be taken. As visible from the graph that it is heading towards a disaster, since the gap is growing between both the trend after each passing year. The bigger worry is, It is likely to reach on a point of no return and will be beyond the point of repair. This may dent the behavioral aspect of the scheme and cause more difficulty for the implementers. In order to examine root cause of such negligible outcome a primary survey was made.

The field study is conducted in two sample Blocks of Khurda district, to get an answer to the questions like: The role of capital in setting up a micro enterprises such as, the availability of capital, the mode of availability, the bottlenecks remains in the procedure for availing it, the repayment methods, interest charged etc. It highlights the nature and functions of the intervention in getting the rural poor covered under SGSY. It is a well known fact that improvement in the living condition of the rural poor is a multidimensional problem and innumerable factors (variables) impact development. Hence in the data analysis, multiple regression model has been used to examine not only the availability of capital but how are they obtaining it. Appropriate selection of economic activities and proper linkage for financial inflow would pave the way for the success of this programme.

METHODOLOGY FOR SAMPLE SELECTION, DATA COLLECTION AND ANALYSIS

Data used in this analysis was collected from the primary sources based on the field survey conducted during October 2008–June 2009. The study covered Balianta and Banpur blocks, in the district of Khurda. Two Panchyats each of the two blocks were identified, the former one being nearer to Bhubaneswar, the capital city of Orissa and the later one is the farthest from the capital in the district. The (gram panchyats) GPs were

Table 4: Distribution of Sample Beneficiaries Across Balianta and Banpur (Nos. of Beneficiaries)

Sl. No.	Blocks	Name of GPs	Number of Beneficiaries		Complete Response Received
1	Balianta	Budhipada	SHG	10 X 4	40
			Individuals	15	15
			G.P Total		**55**
		Balakati	SHG	14 X 4	56
			Individuals	14	14
			G.P Total		**70**
		Block Total			125
		Sub Total (Rejected 3)			**122**
2	Banpur	Sunakhala	SHG	16 X 4	64
			Individuals	10	10
			G.P Total		**74**
		Balugaon	SHG	15 X 4	60
			Individuals	26	26
			G.P Total		**86**
		Block Total			160
		Sub Total (Rejected 6)			**154**
Total		2 Blocks	4 GPs	(@ 4 X 55) SHGs	285 Respondents
				65 Individuals	
		Total Valid Respondents			**276**

Rejection (data–questionnaire) 9 in numbers.
Source: Survey Data.

selected through purposive sampling to ensure that these GPs would adequately represent the Khurda district with respect to socio-economic conditions of the State. Out of the four panchyats, a total of three villages were chosen from each panchyat for the field survey by using convenience sampling. The selection of villages was done carefully so that these would properly represent the implementation of the SGSY programme in the blocks as well as in the districts. Individual members and leaders within the SHGs and individuals were the final sampling units. The SHGs constituted before 2005 are considered as matured groups and same is the case for individual beneficiaries. Four beneficiaries (two leaders and two members) each were selected randomly as beneficiary respondents in each SHGs. The schedules for beneficiaries were administered on each of them. A total of 285 beneficiary respondents were covered in this study. However, missing data in some of the schedules (nine in numbers) restricted the number of respondents to 276. The distribution of sample of individuals and member of SHGs were considered for the survey.

The beneficiaries samples profile is detailed in Table 4, it is evident that from both the GPs taken under Balianta Block, a total of 40 and 56 numbers of beneficiaries are chosen as members of 10 and 14 numbers of SHGs respectively. In addition to it 15 numbers of samples are individual beneficiaries of Budhipada GP and 14 are from Balakati GP. The total numbers of beneficiaries taken from the Balianta Block are 122. Similarly from the Banpur Block the beneficiaries surveyed are 64 in numbers, from 16 SHGs of Sunakhala GP and 60 numbers are from 15 SHGs of Balugaon G.P respectivelly. In addition to it 10 and 26 sample are individual beneficiaries from Sunakhala and Balugaon G.P are also taken as samples respectively.

Table 5: Statistical Characteristics (Mean) of Sample Beneficiaries

Variables		Total Beneficiary Availed SGSY Benefits	Total Sample Beneficiary Joined before 2005	Total Sample Beneficiary Joined after 2005
		Mean		
		N = 276	N = 139	N = 137
1	**2**	**3**	**4**	**5**
1	Average Size of Land Possessed (Acre)	1.685	1.70	1.67
2	Average Amount of Individual Loan (Rs.)	7025.5	9454	4597
3	Average rate of interest charged per Month (%)	2.49	2.47	2.51
4	Average rate of interest charged by Banks per month (%)	0.68	0.68	0.67
5	Average rate of interest charged by Money-lenders per month (%)	4.4	5.24	3.56

Source: Survey Data.

Table 5 reveals that the average land holding of the beneficiaries was only 1.685 acres. An average amount of individual loan was as high as Rs. 7,025. The figures relating to the average interest charged to members of the SHGs by various credit suppliers indicates that the bank interest rate per month is the lowest (i.e, 0.68 per cent) followed by SHGs (2.49 per cent) and the rural money lenders (4.4 per cent). This clearly shows that other things being equal, the interest cost of the credit extended to the rural people have reduced significantly the advantage to the rural borrowers.

From Table 6, it is seen that the maximum respondents' (54.05 per cent) daily per capita income was upto Rs. 50 which was well below the poverty line income (Rs. 67.75 per day) as set by the Ministry of Rural Development for designating BPL people in their five yearly BPL censuses. In Baliantta and Banpur, (0.82 + 39.34 = 40.16) and (20.96 + 61.29 = 82.25) per cent of the total respondents of the respective Blocks earn a daily income in the range of Rs. 0–50. It hints out that the older beneficiaries are not having a sizeable income growth. They are running out of steam in the middle of the road to development and the cause may be inadequate financial inflow for the smooth operation of their unit.

Table 6: Distribution of Respondents by Maturity and Per Capita Daily Income Class (Nos. of Beneficiaries)

Income Class (Rs./Day)	Maturity Status of Beneficiaries								
	Balianta N = 122			Banpur N = 154			Total N = 276		
	New	Old	Sub Total	New	Old	Sub Total	New	Old	Grand Total
1	2	3	4	5	6	7	8	9	10
0 – 25	0 (0.00)	1 (100.00)	**1 (0.82)**	19 (61.29)	12 (38.71)	**31 (20.13)**	19 (59.37)	13 (40.63)	**32 (14.32)**
26 – 50	25 (52.09)	23 (47.91)	**48 (39.34)**	52 (54.74)	43 (45.26)	**95 (61.04)**	77 (53.84)	66 (46.16)	**143 (54.05)**
51– 99	16 (44.44)	20 (55.56)	**36 (29.50)**	14 (56.00)	11 (44.00)	**25 (16.91)**	30 (49.18)	31 (50.82)	**61 (20.81)**
100-149	8 (26.67)	22 (73.33)	**30 (24.59)**	1 (33.34)	2 (66.66)	**3 (1.94)**	9 (27.27)	24 (72.73)	**33 (8.91)**
150 and Above	2 (28.58)	5 (71.42)	**7 (5.73)**	0 (0.00)	0 (00.00)	**0 (0.00)**	2 (28.57)	5 (71.43)	**7 (1.89)**
Total	51 (41.80)	71 (58.19)	**122 (100.00**	86 (55.84)	68 (44.16)	**154 (100.00)**	137 (49.63)	139 (50.37)	**276 (100.00)**

Notes: Figures in the parentheses for columns no. 2,3,5,6,8 and 9 are row-wise percentages to total and for columns no. 4, 7 and 10 are column-wise percentage to total.
Source: Survey Data.

From the Table 7 it is evident that more beneficiaries have invested in the relatively bigger unit (42.76 per cent). It is may be easier to pursue for the officials to go for a bigger unit, taking viability into consideration. (More investment leads to more return)

Table 7: Percentage of Beneficiaries Investment Made (Rs. '000)

Balianta and Banpur (N = 276)				
0 -10	**11 – 25**	**26 – 50**	**51 & above**	**Total**
1	**2**	**3**	**4**	**5**
31 (24.60)	23 (18.25)	14 (11.11)	58 (46.04)	126 (45.65)
11 (13.58)	20 (24.69)	16 (19.76)	34 (41.97)	81 (29.35)
4 (9.09)	12 (27.27)	11 (25.00)	17 (38.64)	44 (15.94)
1 (4.34)	5 (21.73)	8 (34.78)	9 (39.15)	23 (8.33)
0 (0.00)	1 (50.00)	1 (50.00)	0 (0.00)	2 (0.72)
47 (17.02)	**61 (22.10)**	**50 (18.12)**	**118 (42.76)**	**276 (100)**

Notes: 1. Figures in the parentheses for columns no. 1,2, 3, 4 and 5 are row-wise percentages to total.

2. Investment is not taken as a veriable in the estimation of relationship with income.

Source: Survey Data.

Table 8: Total Sample of Balianta and Banpur by Average Income and Asset Value

Sl. No.	Variables	Balianta and Banpur	Taken SGSY Benefit before 2005	Taken SGSY Benefit after 2005
		N = 276	N = 139	N = 137
1	**2**	**3**	**4**	**5**
PRE INVOLVEMENT IN SGSY				
1	Average Income of the Respondent Family income (Rs.)	30.05	29.5	30.6
2	Adjusted Family Income (Rs.)	5.9	5.8	6.0
3	Average Value of Asset Possessed (Rs.)	21731.7	21470.6	21990.3
4	Adjusted Value of Assets Possessed (Rs.)	4261.1	4209.9	4311.8
POST INVOLVEMENT IN SGSY				
5	Average Income of the Respondent Family (Rs.)	46.4	46.3	46.6
6	Adjusted Family Income (Rs.)	7.4	7.3	7.4
7	Average Value of Asset Possessed (Rs.)	39975.6	47549.0	32475.7
8	Adjusted Value of Asset Possessed (Rs.)	6345.3	7547.5	5154.9

Note: The income and asset values are deflated taking into consideration the CPI-IW price index for 2001- 02 (5.1) and 2006-07 (6.3) with a base of 1986-87 prices.

Source: Survey Data.

or it may be relatively safe to monitor a relatively bigger unit than that of a smaller one. How ever many beneficiaries have discontinued the enterprises owning to some difficulty. Some of them have resumed the activities after the intervention by either the officials of the banks, motivated by NGOs or pursued by Govt. officials. In some cases the continuity has been distorted more than once.

Table 8 reveals that there has been an increase in the respondents' income and assets during the pre and post involvement in SGSY period. In the pre SGSY stage the average income was Rs. 30.05 where as in the post SGSY it goes up to Rs. 46.04. Similarly average value of assets possessed are Rs. 21731.7 in pre SGSY period and the value for the same in the post SGSY period is Rs. 39975.6.

However, a review of the incremental income in Balianta and Banpur taking into consideration the duration of existence of the programme indicate that, the annual growth of income was more for the new beneficiaries. Which may be interpreted as the longer you stay within the SGSY bracket, you will end up in paying more.

Table 9 reveals that, in Balianta as many as 48.18 per cent of respondents did not add any value to their total asset during the intervening period. It is important to mention here that as many as 72.06 per cent of respondents in Balakati G.P and a total of 48.18

Table 9: Respondent Beneficiaries' Asset Position
(Nos. of Beneficiaries)

Sl. No.	Panchyat/Block	Change of Asset between Pre and Post SGSY-Intervention Period		
		Change of Asset		Total
		Positive	No Change	
1	**2**	**3**	**4**	**5**
1	Budhipada	40 (74.07)	14 (25.93)	54 (100)
2	Balakati	19 (27.94)	49 (72.06)	68 (100)
Balianta N = 122		59 (48.37)	63 (51.63)	122 (100)
3	Sunakhala	37 (52.12)	34 (47.88)	71 (100)
4	Balugaon	47 (56.63)	36 (43.37)	83 (100)
Banpur N = 154		84 (54.55)	70 (45.45)	154 (100)
Total N = 276		**143 (51.82)**	**133 (48.18)**	276 (100)

Notes: Figures in the parentheses for columns no. 3, 4 and 5 are row-wise percentages to total.
Source: Survey Data

per cent did not experience any increment in their asset value. However the positive impact of the SGSY intervention was recorded among 51.82 per cent of the respondent.

Similarly Table 10 reveals that 15.95 per cent of beneficiaries experience no change in their income during the pre and post-SHG periods. However, there were 83.9 per cent who experienced a positive change in their income. It is also evident from the table that as high as 21.43 per cent beneficiaries in Banpur did not experience a change in their income.

Table 10: Respondent Beneficiaries' Income Position (Nos. of Beneficiaries)

Sl. No.	Panchyat/Block	Change of Income Pre and Post SGSY-Intervention Period		
		Change of Income		Total
		Positive	No Change	
1	2	3	4	5
1	Budhipada	51 (94.50)	3 (5.50)	54 (100)
2	Balakati	60 (88.23)	8 (11.77)	68 (100)
Balianta N = 122		111 (90.98)	11 (9.02)	122 (100)
3	Sunakhala	55 (77.47)	16 (22.53)	71 (100)
4	Balugaon	66 (79.52)	17 (20.48)	83 (100)
Banpur N = 154		121 (78.57)	33 (21.43)	154 (100)
Total N = 276		**232 (84.05)**	**44 (15.95)**	**276 (100)**

Notes: Figures in the parentheses for columns no. 3, 4 and 5 are row-wise percentages to total.
Source: Survey Data.

ECONOMETRIC MODEL

An econometric of multiple regression approach has been used. The dependent variable measures whether there has been an increase in income or not with respect to other independent variables. The multiple regression of income change is calculated with other independent variables; believe to play a dominant role in the growth of income. It is also possible that apart from these independent variables taken for the coefficient, other factors may also have a role to play in the income growth. More over the factors impacted poverty or income growth for one individual to another may vary. All these issues may lead to distortion in reaching to conclusion. To establish a relationship of the impact of independent variables on income (the dependent variable) the multiple regression model is tested.

$$Y = a + b_2X_2 + b_3X_3 + b_4X_4 + b_5X_5$$

Y is the dependent variable and X_2, X_3, X_4, X_5 are independent variables. While a, and the regression coefficients b_2, b_3, b_4, b_5 are constants.

RESULTS AND ANALYSIS

Table 11 represents the parameter estimates of the multiple regression of the dependent variable (Yin) on a selection of 7 explanatory independent variables as detailed above. The correlation was made on the total dataset consisting 276 observations (beneficiary members covered under SGSY). The beneficiaries are drawn from a rural setup like Balianta and Banpur blocks. Since more than one factor (variables) may have an impact on poverty in a rural set up.

Table 11: Coefficients

Explanatory Variables	Regression Coefficient B	Standard Error	T
(Constant)	60.733	7.338	8.277*
Asset	0.502	0.208	2.407**
Maturity	3.610	0.588	6.141*
Interest	–2.776	0.808	–3.436*
Investment	6.292	2.156	2.918*
Loan taken	–0.662	0.382	–1.734

"a" is the dependent variable: Income.
* Significant at 1% level of significance.
** Significant at 5% level of significance.

As the tables given above, the landed property and asset holding of the beneficiary members' may be treated as a proxy to factors of production like land and capital. These variables have shown significant, strong and positive coefficients indicating that ownerships of more and more assets and land properties are more likely to experience an increase in income. This significant finding is contradictory to the basic objective of SGSY that envisages increment of income of the landless, disadvantaged and deprived people those are living below the government designated poverty line. Insufficient capital asset perpetuates the poverty of the poor. This finding indicates that the creamy layer of the SGSY beneficiaries (having a sizable property and other capital asset) would garner benefits under the programme. Further, this also shows that more under-privileged, deprived and disadvantaged member would end up loosing more from the facility provided through this self-employment venture under SGSY. Negative yet significant correlation with interest charged vs. income shows that banks can play a crucial role not only in controlling interest but can save the poor from loan sharks.

Tenure of association with SGSY has a strong, positive and significant relationship with the dependent variable. This variable is a proxy that represents experience in implementing self-employment initiatives under SGSY. This means that other things being equal, an older SHG member will be more enterprising and more prone to use innovative skills and technology so as to maximize profits from his/her economic unit and after walking on the road of development learn the way to maintain good relation with the banks. It was expected that the investment made in SHGs towards implementation of self-employment ventures would step up the expenses on productive economic activities thereby giving rise to income of the beneficiary entrepreneurs via enhancement of productive capacity. The variable associated with loan taken by the group have a negative and statistically insignificant relationship with the dependent variable.

Reason for this may have been due to the following:

(a) There may have been a huge transaction cost like processing cost, costs incurred on visits of beneficiaries to the banks, interest costs, etc. On an average the interest rate charged at the group level was 2.49 per cent per month (or 29.88 per cent per annum). The sharp increase in the cost of the loan-able funds with the SHGs and individuals may have handicapped the beneficiaries to register an increase in their income.
(b) The ingestible fund may have been invested in a less productive and less profitable ventures like agriculture and livestock activities. 66.45 per cent of the total respondents involved in either agriculture or livestock, it is quite possible that the return on these occupational activities had not been sufficient to register an impact on the dependent variable. These activities are also influenced by seasonality factor, resulting in change in the income status. This may lead to lowering of the ROI (return on investment) and the interest rate of repayment (EMI) remains constant.
(c) Keeping in view the marginal propensity to consume of the rural poor, the money meant for investment in economic units might have been diverted towards meeting beneficiaries' emergency needs having no or negligent productive capacities.

CONCLUDING REMARKS

This analysis depended on the field data to examine some of the selected income effect of rural poor those are living below a particular benchmarked poverty line income and have been persuaded to take the benefit under SGSY for removing bottlenecks in the generation of income and employment in rural areas. The study indicated that the investment made by the Government have a negligible income impact on asset-less rural poor and indicated that under-privileged, deprived and disadvantaged members would in every possibility end up losing more from the facility provided through this self-employment venture under SGSY. The year of association with SGSY and assets of the beneficiaries found to be significantly impacting the income. However, the insignificant and negative relationship between the loan taken under the programme and the dependent variable indicated the possible presence of high transaction costs, improper utilization of ingestible resources and/or respondents' high marginal propensity to consumption over savings. However banks and MFIs can play a vital role to accelerate the objectives of this programme.

REFERENCES

[1] Government of India (2003), 'Guidelines: Swarnjayanti Gram Swarozgar Yojana', Ministry of Rural Development, New Delhi.

[2] Government of India, 'Annual Report' (several years), Ministry of Rural Development.

[3] Guha, S. and Gupta, G. (2005), 'Micro-Credit for Income Generation: The Role of Rosca', *Economic and Political Weekly*, 40: 4, 1470-1473.

[4] Gujarati, D.N. (2004), 'Basic Econometrics', 4th Edition, Tata McGraw Hill, New Delhi.

[5] Hall, R. (2001), 'Organisations – Structures, Processes and Outcomes', 7th Edition, Pearson Education Asia.

[6] Hartarska, V. (2005), 'Governance and Performance of Microfinance Institutions in Central and Eastern Europe and the Newly Independent States', *World Development*, 33: 10, 1627-1643.

[7] Keynes, J.M. (1936), 'The General Theory of Employment, Interest and Money', Macmillan Cambridge University Press, New York.

[8] Hossain, S. and Ming-Yu, Cheng (2002), 'Bangladesh: Building for a Better Future?', *International Journal of Social Economics*, 29: 10, 813-821.

[9] Kothari C.R. (2004), Research Methodology 'Methods and Techniques', New Age International Publication, New Delhi.

[10] Ackoff, Russell L. (1961), 'The Design of Social Research', University of Chicago Press, Chicago.

[11] Anderson, T.W. (1958), 'An Introduction to Multivariate Analysis', John Wiley & Sons. New York.

[12] Edwards, Allen. L. (1957), 'Techniques of Attitude Scale Construction', New York, Appleton – Century-Crofts.

[13] Ferber, R. and Verdoorn, P.J. (1962), 'Research Methides in Economics and Business', New York: The Macmillan Company.

[14] Ghosh, B.N. (1982), Scientific Methods and Social Research, New Delhi: Sterling Publishers Pvt. Ltd.

[15] Tripathy, K.K. and Jain, Sudhir, 'Micro-finance & Self-employment Activities towards Income Generation and Poverty Alleviation in Rural Areas under SGSY'.

Use of Fly Ash Reinforced with Jute Geotextiles as a Pavement Subgrade

H.P. Singh
NERIST, Itanagar
E-mail: singh.harendra121@gmail.com

ABSTRACT

Thermal power plants or similar plants which use pulverized coal as a fuel have been producing million tons of fly ash annually. Conventional disposal of this large quantity of fly ash which gets easily air-borne and thus constitutes a serious pollution- hazard to the community is a very expensive operation. These materials are very loose, fine, non-plastic and of low unit weight. Their utilization in civil engineering and other works is a challenging task. Keeping this in view a study was conducted to strengthen the fly ash obtained from Satyam Steel Factory situated at Banderdewa, Arunachal Pradesh, India, by using Jute Geotextile as reinforcement. In this study specimens of fly ash compacted to its maximum dry density at the optimum moisture content were prepared without and with Jute Geotextile in the CBR mould. Jute Geotextile sheets equal to the plan dimensions of CBR mould were placed in five different combinations of 1 layer, 2 layers, 3 layers, 4 layers and 5 layers at different locations (i.e. at different embedment ratio, z/d) in the CBR mould and corresponding to each combination of Jute Geotextile, the CBR (California Bearing Ratio) value was determined in the geotechnical engineering laboratory. Tests result indicates that on inclusion of Jute Geotextile in the fly ash sample, the CBR value of fly ash increases. It was also observed that when the number of Jute Geotextile layer is increased from 1 layer to 2 layers, the CBR value of fly ash further increases and this increase is maximum corresponding to fly ash reinforced with 4 layers of Jute Geotextile. Thus there is a significant increase in CBR value of fly ash reinforced with Jute Geotextle sheet and this will reduce the thickness of pavement subgrade.

Keywords: CBR Value, Shear Strength, Fly Ash, Jute Geotextile, Embedment Ratio

INTRODUCTION

With the boom in population and industrial growth, the need for power has increased many folds. Nearly 70% of India's total installed power generation capacity is thermal, of which 90% is coal based generation, with diesel, wind, gas and steam making up the rest. Thermal power generation through coal combustion produces minute particles of ash commonly known as fly ash that causes serious environmental problems. The potential areas where fly ash can be utilized in large scale are structural fill, light weight aggregate, road construction, land reclamation, soil stabilization, mine filling, etc. The use of fly ash in these areas can solve the problem of its disposal to a great extent. Toth et al. (1978) studied the use of fly ash as a structural fill and found that the physical behavior of fly ash is similar to that of silt and the structural fill made with fly ash could perform better than the fill madewith natural materials. Leonards and Balley (1982) successfully used the untreated pulverized coal ash, with more cementing qualities as a material for structural fill to support thefoundation of a new precipitator for a power generating station in Indianapolis, U.S.A. Sridharan et al. (1997) investigated the geotechnical characterization of various ash ponds in India and reported that fly ashes, in general posses low unit weight, good frictional properties, low compressibility and they are well suited for their use as a structural fill. If these materials are strengthened by using the ground improvement techniques, they can be utilized as a foundation material for buildings, roads subgrade, embankments, etc. The concept of soil reinforcing with tension resisting elements has been widely accepted in engineering practice. Reinforcing elements in the form of rods, sheets, strips, membranes, fibers, etc., are typical traditional soil improvement techniques (Saran, 2010). Aggarwal and Sharma (2010) studied the application of Jute fiber in the improvement of subgrade characteristics. From this study it was concluded that jutefiber reinforcement reduces the maximum dry density andincreases the optimum moisture content of the subgradesoil. The CBR value of the subgrade soil increased up to 250% with the inclusion of bitumen coated jute fiber. Bera et al. (2008) conducted a series of unconfined compressive strength tests on unreinforced fly ash as well as fly ash reinforced with jute geotextile and found that inclusion of jute geotextiles within the specimen as reinforcement enhances the peak value of unconfined compressive strength. This progress is more effective with a higher number of jute geotextiles reinforcement layers. But it is effective up to four layers of reinforcement and beyond that it is marginal. Choudhary and Verma (2005) studied the behavior of Fly ash Sub grades reinforced with geogrid sheet and jute geotextile. It was observed that fly ash can be effectively utilized in the construction of pavement after suitably reinforcing it with geotextiles. In case of single layer of reinforcement, its location within the specimen has marked influence on the extent of improvement in CBR and for optimum benefits the embedment ratio should be kept equal to 1.0. The CBR value of reinforced fly ash increases with increasing number of reinforcing layers and it is significant for four numbers of reinforcing layers placed within the specimen at equal vertical spacing. It was also observed that Jute geotextiles can be gainfully exploited in situations like road embankments in rural areas. Tolia et al. (2000) studied the application of jute geotextiles in highway engineering. From the field experiments carried out at various places it was observed that the jute geotextiles play an effective role in various applications in highway engineering. The jute geotextiles can be more effective, eco-friendly and economical if used judiciously and jointly with other measures. The jute geotextiles in their present form are suitable for separation, filtration, drainage and reinforcement functions. Juyal et al. (2003) studied the application of natural geotextiles for minespoils and landslides rehabilitation in the Himalayan region. It was found that in the area treated with geotextile, there was goodestablishment of vegetation within a period of about 3 years as compared to control. The soil erosion was checked drastically. Ministry Of Railways (2007) made a case study about the Use of Geo-Jute for Turfing on the Approach Banks of Bridge No. 50 on River Gandak for Restoration of Chhitauni–Bagaha Rail Link Project in Varanasi Division of North Eastern Railway. After inspection, it was observed that turfing is well grown-up on slopes of both sides of rail and road embankment. No erosion or slip/breaches of the slope/bank was observed. The slope is well maintained. No formation problems have been reported so far in the bank. It was concluded that in this project, the Geo-jute has fulfilled its objectives.

In this paper the experimental results pertaining to the influence of Jute Geotextile sheets on the CBR value and shear strength parameters (c and ϕ) of locally available fly ash has been presented.

EXPERIMENTAL PROGRAMME

Materials Used

The fly ash used in this investigation was procured in moist state from the Satyam Steel Factory, Banderdewa, Itanagar, Arunachal Pradesh whose various index properties and maximum dry density at optimum moisture content were determined in the geotechnical engineering laboratory of NERIST.

Table 1: Physical Properties of Fly Ash

Sl. No.	Properties		Value
1	Specific Gravity		2.48
2	Liquid Limit		NP
3	Plastic Limit		NP
4	Maximum Dry Density (kN/m^3)		12.88
5	Optimum Moisture Content (%)		31
6	Grain Size Distribution	% Gravel Size (>4.75mm)	0
		% Sand Size (0.075mm-4.75mm)	21
		% Silt Size (0.002mm-0.075mm)	71
		% Clay Size (<0.002mm)	8

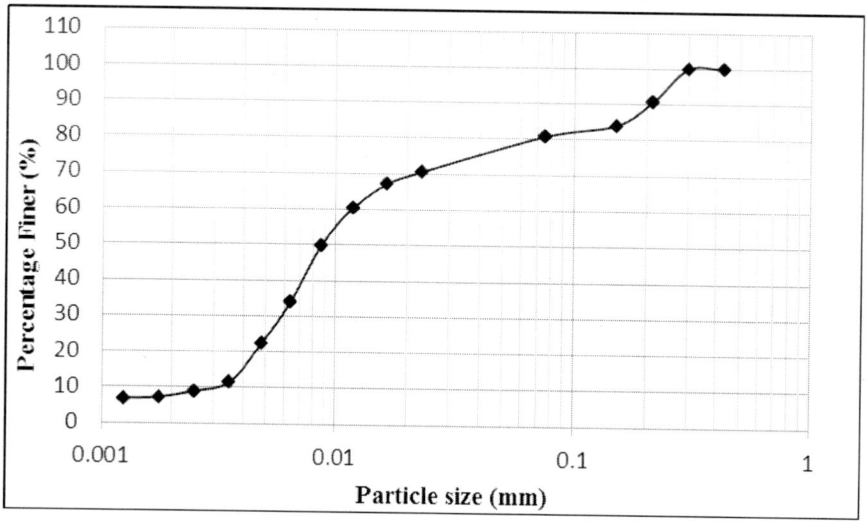

Fig. 1: Particle Size Distribution Curve of Fly Ash

The grain size distribution curve of fly ash is shown in Fig. 1 and the index and other properties of fly ash are given in Table 1. The reinforcing element considered in the present investigation is the natural Jute Geotextile sheet (woven type) having area of aperture 4 mm^2 and wall thickness 1.5 mm. The view of Jute Geotextile sheet is shown in Fig. 2.

Fig. 2: A View of Jute Geotextile Sheet Used in the Present Study

VARIABLES OF STUDY

Two series of experiments were performed on specimens of fly ash compacted to their maximum dry density at the corresponding optimum moisture content (OMC). In the first series (series-I), a single layer of reinforcement cut in the form of disc equal to plan dimension of CBR mould (147 mm f), was placed horizontally at varying depths (z) form the top of the compacted fly ash specimen. The embedment ratio, (i.e. z/d, where d is the diameter of plunger) for the reinforcing element was varied as 0.50, 0.75, 1.0 1.25 and 1.5 respectively. In the second series (Series-II), varying number of reinforcing discs at equal vertical spacing was placed within the test specimen. The number of reinforcing discs (N) was varied from N = 1 to N = 5. In addition some quick tests on triaxial test set up were also conducted to determine the shear strength parameters (c and ϕ) of reinforced fly ash. The CBR value and the shear strength parameters (c and ϕ) of unreinforced fly ash were also determined for comparison of the test results.

SAMPLE PREPARATION AND TESTING

The desired amount of oven dried (100-105°C) fly ash was taken and mixed thoroughly with water at its OMC. The fly ash was then compacted to its Proctor density into the mould using standard procedure up to the required height for placing the reinforcing element. The reinforcing element was then placed horizontally inside the mould over which the remaining fly ash was compacted to Proctor density as per IS: 2720, Part VII (1974) and the top surface of the specimen was made level. After the compaction of the specimen, a filter paper and a perforated metallic disc were placed over the specimen and the whole mould assembly was then transferred to a tank containing water for soaking of the sample. After 4 days (i.e. 96 hours) of soaking, the mould assembly was taken out and the top surface of sample was exposed to air for half an hour to dry up. When the top surface of specimen became in dry state then it was brought to a motorized loading frame for testing. The CBR value of the test sample was determined as per the standard procedure laid down in IS: 2720, Part XVI (1965). A strain rate of 1.20 mm/min was used for all the tests and all the specimens were tested in a similar manner. The samples for triaxial tests were prepared at maximum dry density corresponding to optimum moisture content of fly ash in a split mould. The reinforcing element (Jute Geotextile sheets) was placed at desired locations (at equal vertical spacing) in the split mould during the preparation of samples. The triaxial compression tests were conducted and shear strength parameters (c and ϕ) of fly ash and fly ash reinforced with Jute Geotextile sheets were determined as per the standard procedure.

RESULTS AND DISCUSSION

The test results of series-1 and series-2 tests are presented in Tables 2 and 3 respectively. With the result of triaxial tests, the modified failure envelopes were drawn for unreinforced fly ash and fly ash reinforced with 1 layer and 4 layers of geotextile sheets which are shown in Fig. 3. The values of shear strength parameters (c and ϕ) of fly ash and reinforced fly ash were computed from the plots of Fig. 3 and are presented in Table 4.

Result of Tests Series-I

In series-I tests, the depth of embedment (z) of the reinforcing element was varied from 0.25d to 2.0 d in order to ascertain the influence of the location of the reinforcing layer on the load- displacement response. It is observed from Table 2 that, in general,

Table 2: Results of Series-I Tests

Embedment Ratio (z/d)	**CBR Values (%)**	**Strength Ratio** $\frac{(CBR)_{Reinforced}}{(CBR)_{Unreinforced}}$
Unreinforced	0.766	–
0.25	0.875	1.142
0.50	0.924	1.206
0.75	1.045	1.360
1.00	1.143	1.492
1.25	1.116	1.456
1.50	1.094	1.428
1.75	1.082	1.412
2.00	1.070	1.396

Table 3: Results of Series-II Tests

Number of Reinforcing Layers	**Embedment Ratio (z/d)**	**CBR Value (%)**	**Strength Ratio** $\frac{(CBR)_{Reinforced}}{(CBR)_{Unreinforced}}$
0	0	0.766	–
1	0.25	0.875	1.14
2	0.25, 0.50	2.298	3.00
3	0.25, 0.50,0.75	2.457	3.24
4	0.25, 0.50, 0.75, 1.00	3.940	5.14
5	0.25, 0.50, 0.75, 1.00, 1.25	3.904	5.09

Table 4: Shear Strength Parameters of Reinforced Fly Ash

Number of Reinforcing Layers	**Cohesion (c) kN/m^2**	**Angle of Shearing Friction (ϕ) (Degree)**	**Percentage Increase in (c)**	**Percentage Increase in (ϕ)**
0	34	28	–	–
1	52	30	53	07
4	91	42	167	50

there is a marked influence due to the presence of reinforcement within the fly ash on its CBR characteristics

and the CBR value is observed to be higher in all cases of reinforced fly ash specimens compared to that of an unreinforced specimen. Further, it is observed that the extent of improvement in the CBR value depends on the embedment ratio (z/d), i.e. the relative position of the reinforcing layer within the specimen and there is an optimum depth of

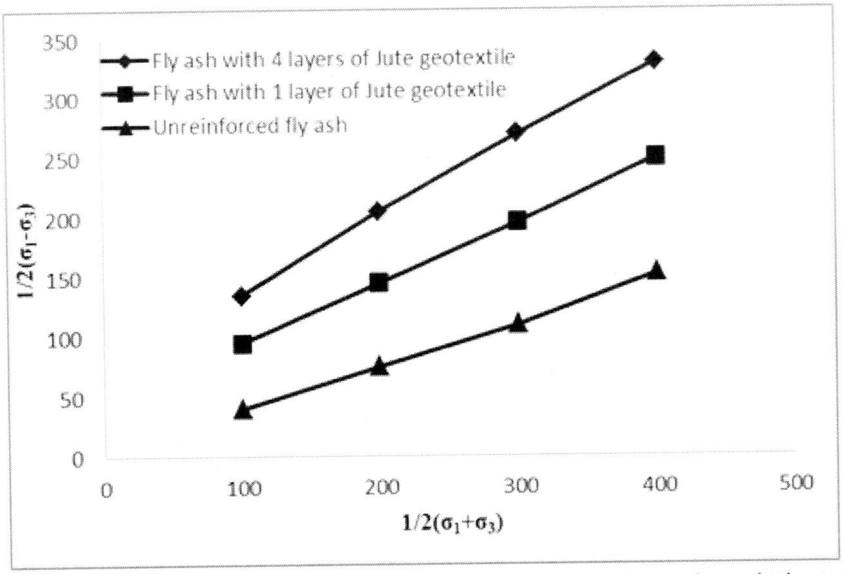

Fig. 3: Modified Failure Envelopes of Unreinforced and Reinforced Fly Ash

embedment (z = d) for which the strength ratio is observed to be maximum. It is because of the improved redistribution of load provided by the reinforcement when placed at this depth.

At lesser depth of embedment (z < d), although there is a marginal increase in CBR value, it is not significant because of the fact that when reinforcement is placed at shallow depth, the effect of reinforcement layer is greatly reduced due to smaller overburden and the soil mass above the reinforcement is not enough to generate appreciable frictional resistance. Further, it is observed that deeper depth of embedment (z > d) also do not lead to any significant improvement in the CBR value. This is due to the fact that the frictional resistance developed in the reinforcement when placed at deeper depths is lower because the vertical stress intensity getting decreased at deeper depths resulting in a decrease in the CBR value.

Result of Tests Series-II

In series-II tests varying number of reinforcing discs (N) at equal vertical spacing were placed within the specimen and CBR tests were conducted on each of these specimens in order to ascertain the influence of the varying number of reinforcing layers on the load-displacement response. The number of reinforcing layers was varied from N = 1 to N = 5 and the embedment depth for the successive layers from the top was kept as 0.25 d, 0.5 d, 0.75d 1.0 d and 1.25 d, respectively. From Table 3 it is observed that CBR value in case of multilayer of reinforcement is much higher as compared to that obtained in case of series-1 tests. Further, the CBR value increases with increasing the number of layers of geotextile sheets. The increase in CBR value is marginal when the number of reinforcing layers is less. When the number of reinforcing layers is increased to N = 4, there is a significant increase in the CBR value. In fact when reinforcing layers are placed within the fly ash specimens, it behaves as a composite material and the restraining force exerted by reinforcement transfers to the fly ash and reorientation of the minor principal strain occurs in the vicinity of the reinforcement. As a consequence, a part of the reinforcement zone where relatively large reinforcement force has developed, behaves like a rigid mass and transfers a major part of the load into a deeper zone resulting in an increased penetration resistance thereby increasing the CBR value in this situation.

The variation of CBR value of fly ash with the number of Jute geotextile layers has been presented in the Fig. 4. It is observed from the Fig. 4 that the optimum number of Jute geotextile layers is 4 for which there is maximum improvement in CBR value of fly ash.

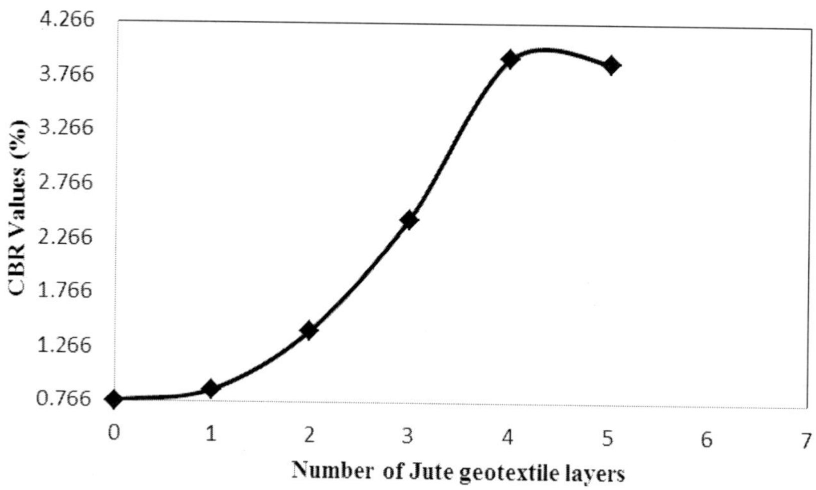

Fig. 4: Variation of CBR with Number of Geotextile Layers

Result of Triaxial Tests

The result of triaxial tests is shown in Table 4. It is observed from Table 4 that when Jute geotextile layers are added to the fly ash its shear strength parameter (c and ϕ) increases. It is further observed that when the number of Jute geotextile layers is increases these parameters are further increases and this increase is maximum at 4 number of Jute geotextile layers.

This is due to the fact that addition of Jute geotextile layer makes the fly ash a composite material whose strength and stiffness is more than that of fly ash alone.

CONCLUSIONS

The CBR value of Fly ash increases when the fly ash is reinforced with Jute Geotextile. In case of single layer of Jute Geotextile, the location of reinforcement within the fly ash specimen has marked influence on the extent of improvement in CBR and for optimum benefits; the embedment ratio should be kept equal to 1.0. The CBR value of fly ash increases with the increase in number of Jute Geotextile and this increase is significant when the fly ash is reinforced with 4 numbers of Jute Geotextile at equal vertical spacing.

Hence fly ash can be utilized in the construction of pavement after suitably reinforcing with Jute Geotextile.

ACKNOWLEDGEMENT

Author is thankful to the Head of Department of Civil Engineering, North Eastern Regional Institute of Science and Technology, Itanagar, India for providing laboratory facilities and assistance for conducting the tests. The help and support extended by Mr Omo Yachang and Sri Rameshwer Bora Laboratory Assistant in carrying out the experiments is gratefully acknowledged.

REFERENCES

[1] Aggarwal, P. and Sharma, B. (2010), "Application of Jute Fibre in the Improvement of Subgrade Characteristics".

[2] Bera, A.K., Ghosh, S. and Ghosh, A. (2008). "Unconfined Compressive Strength Properties of Fine Grained Soils Reinforced with Jute Geotextiles", *National Seminar on Geotechnique in Present Development Scenario*, Kolkata, September, 14-19.

[3] Boddu, S. (2002). "Behavior of Eccentrically and Obliquely Loaded Footing on Reinforced Fly Ash", *M.Tech.Thesis;* IIT Roorkee, Roorkee.

[4] Choudhary, A.K. and Verma, B.P. (2005). "Behavior of Reinforced Fly Ash Subgrade", *Journal of Institution of Engineers (I);* 86, 19-21.

[5] IS: 2720, Part VII (1974). "Determination of Moisture Content – Dry Density Relation using Light Compaction", *Bureau of Indian Standards;* New Delhi.

[6] IS: 2720, Part XVI (1965). "Laboratory Determination of CBR", *Bureau of Indian Standards,* New Delhi.

[7] Juyal, G.P., Katiyar, V.S., Sastry, G., Singh, G., Joshie, P. and Arya, R.K. (1991). "Geojute for Rehabilitation of Steep Minespoil Areas". Bulletin No. T-26/D-19, CSWCRTI, Dehradun.

[8] Kaushik, N.P and Ramaswami, G. (2000). "Performance of Compacted Ash Test Fills", *Fly Ash Disposal Beyond 2000 AD*; Norosa Publishing House, New Delhi.

[9] Leonards, G.A. and Bally, B. (1982). "Pulverized Coal Ash as Structural Fill", *ASCE Journal of Geotechnical Engineering Division*, 108(4), 517-531.

[10] Ministry of Railways (2007). "Guidelines for Application of Jute Geo-Textile in Railway Embankments and Hill Slopes", No. RDSO/2007/GE: G-0008, 2007.

[11] Saran, S. (2010). "Reinforced Soil and its Engineering Applications", *I.K. International Publishing House Pvt. Ltd.,* New Delhi.

[12] Sridharan, A., Pandian, N.S. and Rajshekher, C. (1997). "Geotechnical Characterization of Pond Ash", *Proc. of the Symposium on Fly Ash Utilization;* IISc, Banglore, 43-58.

[13] Tolia D.S., Yadav O.P., Bhagwan J., Sharma N.K., Singh K. and Rao S.R. (1997). "Application of Jute Geotextiles in Highway Engineering", Geotechnical Engineering Division, Central Road Research Institute, New Delhi.

[14] Toth, P.S., Chan, H.T. and Cragg, C.B. (1978). "Coal Ash as Structural Fill with Special Reference to Ontario Experience", *Canadian Geotechnical Journal*, 25, 694-704.

Author Index